David D. Braunstein

Best wishes

E. Braunstein 2/25/89

NATIONS AT RISK

THE IMPACT OF THE COMPUTER REVOLUTION

EDWARD YOURDON

YOURDON PRESS

1501 BROADWAY, NEW YORK, N.Y. 10036
15/17 RIDGEMOUNT ST., LONDON WD1E 7BH, ENGLAND

Printed in the United States of America

Library of Congress Cataloging-in-Publication Data

Yourdon, Edward.
  Nations at risk.

  Bibliography: p.
  Includes index.
  1. Computers and civilization. I. Title.
QA76.9.C66Y68 1986   303.4'834   85-22618
          ISBN 0-917072-04-9

10   9   8   7   6   5   4   3   2   1

For Toni,
who deserves this book
more than all the rest.

ACKNOWLEDGMENTS

Many people contributed ideas and suggestions during the three years that I gathered material and began writing early drafts of this book. Students in seminars that I conducted in London, Amsterdam, Toronto, Copenhagen, Sydney, Melbourne, and throughout the United States challenged my assumptions, questioned my predictions, and added their own obervations of the trends in this fast-moving field of computers. While I continue to worry that the average "computer professional" doesn't spend enough time thinking about the ramifications of computers in today's world, I was greatly encouraged to see that there are at least *some* computer programmers, systems analysts, and engineers who are devoting a great deal of thought—as well as time, energy, and money—to see that society understands the opportunities, as well as the dangers and risks, associated with the computer-based Information Age.

Closer to home, I received advice and encouragement from all of my colleagues and friends at YOURDON inc. as I struggled to turn a mass of material into a readable manuscript. Thanks are due to Gerry Madigan, Carol Crowell, Teresa Ridley, Dan Mausner, Charles Decker, Alisa Wessof, Kayla Serrano, Alex Gersznowicz, Bob Spurgeon, Paul Radding, Trond Frantzen, and Herb Morrow. Outside the YOURDON community, I also collected ideas and advice from Larry Saper, Gardner Dunnan, and Christopher Pidgeon; my thanks to them. Ruthless and sharp-eyed, this hardy band ferreted out errors of substance and style, spotted typographical errors, and chided me for gross misuse of the English language. They all deserve a great deal of credit for whatever positive impact the book may make; any errors that remain are, of course, my responsibility.

My family also deserves heartfelt thanks for their help and encouragement. My mother provided some family Civil War letters that fit perfectly in a chapter on the impact of computers on social communications; my extended family of sisters, half-sisters, parents, and step-parents helped follow the project through from beginning to end. And my children—Jenny, Jamie, and David—gave me the perspective of a new generation that already knows more about computers than the "veterans" of my generation. Jamie and David also contributed some computer art for one of the chapters, and were disappointed only that they couldn't do their work in color.

Last, but far from least, my wife Toni—who continues to be my business partner and best friend—gave me the love and support without which I could never have finished the book. And then, as a finishing touch, she copyedited the entire manuscript and corrected all of the errors that all my other friends found. More than that, one cannot ask.

Edward Yourdon
New York, November 1985

CONTENTS

PREFACE

It was ordained at the beginning of the world that certain signs should prefigure certain events.

Marcus Tullius Cicero (106-43 B.C.)
De Divinatione I

In the year of our Lord 1983, on the 26th day of April, a remarkable document appeared from the President's Commission on Excellence in Education. It was entitled *A Nation At Risk*. It described in graphic terms the deplorable state of the U.S. education system. It warned of the resulting threat to the economy and to the nation's way of life. It made a number of specific recommendations, one of which was a new emphasis on computer literacy for our children. It received considerable media attention when first published, but the situation has not changed substantially. Not yet. We still have a major national problem. I believe that every American citizen has a moral obligation to read the report in its entirety. Indeed, I could plausibly argue that every American parent has a legal responsibility to read it, to the extent that the law holds parents responsible for the safekeeping of their children.[1] Every day wasted increases the peril for children who will be reaching adulthood as we enter the 21st century.

This book was inspired by *A Nation At Risk*. Its title suggests an attempt to enlarge upon the scope of that formative work of some eighteen scholars and educators. If the United States is a nation at risk, then so are many others. Truly, all nations are at risk now because of the onrush of technological developments. The balance of power among nations will not only be determined by how well we master technology today, but also how effectively we pass it on to our children. If you believe, as I do, that our children are our greatest asset, then you must also believe that the investment we

---

[1] The report is available from the Superintendent of Documents, U.S. Government Printing Office, Washington, D.C. 20402, for $4.50. If you can't afford it, send me a letter; if I'm in a good mood, I'll probably send you one free.

1

make in their future will determine whether our country—or some other country—will survive as a major power over the next twenty years.

But children are not the only subject of this book: I write primarily about computers and how they affect our children and our country. Several thousand books have been written about computers over the past two decades (some 2,400 new titles on computers were published in 1984 alone), and one might reasonably expect that every possible point of view has been expressed. Perhaps so. But I have been able to find, thus far, only one or two books that touch upon my principal area of concern: that precisely *because of the existence of computer technology,* the country is at risk. I write as an American citizen, and I will document my case with American statistics. However, my travels through Western Europe, Australia, Canada, and portions of Asia and South America have convinced me that the same is true of most "advanced" countries and most Third World countries, too.

This is a rather bold statement; it will provoke a variety of reactions. But before you close the pages and consign this book to the back shelf of your library, let me hasten to reassure you that I will not argue that every child must have a computer in his bedroom. I will not argue that every adult should learn BASIC. (On the contrary, I will argue in Chapter 29 that BASIC is a dangerous disease that can cause permanent brain damage to children or adults.) I will not argue that every man, woman, and child on earth will soon become a computer programmer. Nor will I argue that computerized robots will take over the earth.

But I will argue that almost every manufactured product and every service-oriented business in most countries now relies on computers as a vital component. The military establishment has long since referred to this phenomenon as "embedded computer systems," now an apt phrase for almost every artifact of society. Many writers over the past decade—from Daniel Bell to Alvin Toffler to John Naisbitt—have eloquently pointed out that we have moved from the Agricultural Revolution (Toffler's "first wave") through the Industrial Revolution (the "second wave") to the third-wave computer-based Information Revolution (Bell's "postindustrial society").

Yet we have barely begun to understand the full impact of this new state of affairs. Many of us work in companies roughly analogous to buggy whip manufacturing companies at the beginning of the age of the automobile. Far worse, we are training our children to manufacture buggy whips, even though their world will have progressed from horse-drawn carriages to automobiles to interplanetary space travel by the time they grow up. Moreover, we have only begun to glimpse the Dark Side of the Force of computing. While we have seen a small sampling of computer crime, and while we read about (or perhaps have experienced directly) the occasional loss of jobs caused by robots or automation, we know almost nothing about other, more subtle, dangers: government-sponsored invasion of privacy; psychic stress on the part of children who (contrary to TV commercials) sometimes find computers difficult and alienating; grossly incorrect business decisions caused by personal computers in the hands of naive laymen; and a host of other problems that I will document throughout the book.

The purpose of this book is to survey the impact of the computer revolution in broad terms, and to see—in more direct, detailed terms than has been done before—how this revolution puts our nation at greater and greater risk each day. Today's computer technology, coupled with the frenetic pace of technological development, has put the United States in a race for economic survival with a dozen other countries around the world. We can still win that race, but only by recognizing where we have already fallen behind and what we must do to catch up. We have less than ten years to win the race, probably less than five. I believe that the struggle for computer-based economic supremacy will have been decided by the early 1990s. This book points the way, or at least one way, to win. But it is up to you and the other 235 million citizens of the United States to decide whether you really want to win badly enough to marshal the necessary resources and energies. For the sake of our children, I hope so.

CONTEXT

Item: By 1990, 60 percent of all jobs in the United States will require familiarity with computers. By the year 2000, 80 percent of all jobs will require computer literacy. But children in poor school districts are receiving four times less access to computers than children in affluent school districts, and boys outnumber girls in summer computer camps by a factor of three to one.

Item: In the late 1940s, experts predicted that the world would only require twelve computers. Today, there are more computers on earth than people. In 1972, Hewlett-Packard almost decided not to build electronic calculators because it didn't think anyone would buy them when slide rules cost only $20. As late as 1977, the president of Digital Equipment Corporation (the second largest computer company, after IBM) remarked that he couldn't see any use for a computer in the home.

Item: The computer industry is now larger than both the steel industry and the auto industry. It represented 8 percent of the American gross national product (GNP) in 1985; by 1990, it will represent 15 percent of the GNP. If the trend continues, every man, woman, and child in the world will work for a computer company by the early part of the next century.

Item: By 1986, every American citizen over the age of five will have access to a general-purpose programmable computer. Every child born in the 1980s will have written 10,000 lines of computer code by the time he or she graduates from high school; this is the equivalent of two years of full-time work on the part of an adult programmer.

5

Item: Nearly 75 percent of the "knowledge workers" in large American companies have access to word processing equipment already; however, eight out of ten such workers still rely on a secretary to write and revise their documents. The market for clerical word processing systems is already 60 percent saturated; the market for manager-level office automation is only 20 percent saturated.

Item: By the end of 1983, approximately 18 percent of American organizations had some form of electronic mail (E-mail); the number of E-mail messages and subscribers is expected to grow by at least 50 percent each year, reaching the level of 9 billion messages per year by 1990. However, there are only 225,000 subscribers to commercial E-mail services (which facilitate intercompany communications), compared to some 500,000 telex machines and 470,000 facsimile transmission machines. The combined revenues of commercial electronic communications services (telex, fax, and E-mail) is only about $1.5 billion per year, compared to more than $24 billion annual revenues for the U.S. Post Office, despite the fact that approximately 75 percent of all business-to-business communication is generated by the sender's computer and ultimately processed by the receiver's computer.

Item: By 1986, some 250,000 automatic teller machines (ATMs) and 3 million personal computers will be generating roughly 5 percent of the 95 million payments processed by the banks each day. By the end of the 1990s, banks as we now know them will disappear; money will be recognized as *information in motion*, and its movement will be managed by its owners rather than banks.

Item: In 1985, as many as 2 million American workers were using personal computers to perform part or all of their work out of the office. By the early 1990s, twelve to fifteen percent of the working population will work in this fashion; the resulting savings in oil for transportation will probably eliminate entirely the need for imported oil.

Item: The personal computers of today are approximately 100,000 times faster, cheaper, and smaller than the early experimental computers built during World War II. If automobile technology had improved as much during the past fifty years, we would be able to drive across the United States for less than a nickel. But there is more to come: the computers of 1999 will be between 1,000 and 10,000 times more powerful than today's machines.

Why does this matter? And, in general, why do computers matter? Why do we care about the future direction of the computer field?

The reason is very simple: computers now represent such a pervasive force in our lives that there is no realistic way to avoid them. True, there are a few Stone Age primitives in remote jungles who can afford to ignore computers. And there are a few die-hard Luddites who will persist in living out their lives without the benefit of computers. But most of us already find that our day-to-day lives are affected by (and controlled by) computers of all shapes and sizes. Anyone living in today's industrialized society cannot escape the presence of computers; more important, anyone who has the slightest interest in the forces that will shape his or her life over the next ten to twenty years cannot afford to be ignorant of the trends in the computer field.

Most of us are affected by computers in one or more of the following ways: as users of computer systems; as producers of computer systems; as investors in computer technology; or simply as citizens who are affected by computer systems (or by the companies and government agencies who use computer systems).

Today, virtually everyone is a user of computer systems. Computers are in our cars, in our electric toasters, in our coffee makers, and in almost every other device that we come into contact with. Computers produce our paychecks and our bank statements. They tell the government whether we are paying our taxes, and whether the taxes we have paid are within reasonable limits for the demographic group to which we belong. Unfortunately, the average person has little or no direct control over the way computers produce his paychecks or his bank statements. Nor does he have any influence over the manner in which computers tell the government about the taxes he has paid.

A "user," as computer technicians use the term, is someone who has an active involvement with a computer system. A user is someone who has some power to decide whether he wants to use a particular computer system or a product (or service) that contains a particular computer system. He may decide to buy a Brand X coffee machine instead of a Brand Y coffee machine because the programming instructions built into the Brand X machine are easier to understand. He may choose to do business with Bank A instead of Bank B because Bank A's automated teller machine (clearly a computer-controlled device) has more features than Bank B's, or because Bank B insists that he use the automated teller machine while Bank A gives him the choice of communicating with a human. In a business environment, a user is someone who decides whether to (a) ask the company's in-house data processing department to build a "management information system" for him, or (b) use the services of an outside consulting firm to get the job done more quickly, or (c) do the job himself on an inexpensive personal computer . . . *if* he understands the choices and the tradeoffs.

And therein lies an important point. The most successful managers, business people, government leaders, and citizens during the next twenty years will be those who know not only how to use a computer but also what to use it for, and what alternative choices exist. That means, of course, having a reasonable idea of what computers are, and what they can do. And it also means having a good idea of what computers will be able to do next year, five years from now, and twenty years from now. Look at it this way: If someone had told you in the early 1970s, with absolute certainty, that within ten years you could buy a portable computer for less than $3,000 that had the power of a multimillion dollar mainframe computer, wouldn't that have given you several ideas that would have made you rich, or famous, or powerful (or all three)?

There are potentially more users than "producers" of computer systems, but producers nevertheless play a pivotal role in the future development of computer technology. A producer, in the context of this book, is someone directly involved in, or responsible for, the development of computer hardware and/or software systems. Anyone who works for IBM or Apple, for Microsoft or Lotus, or for any of 8,000 other hardware/software companies in the United States, is a producer of computer systems. So are an enormous number of producers who work in "ordinary" companies—e.g., the people who work in the computer departments (sometimes known as MIS or EDP or ADP departments) developing computer systems that many thousands of users throughout their organization will use.

Producers have an obvious need to think about the future of the computer field. This is particularly true because continuing research and development in the computer field will steadily reduce the cost (and/or increase the performance) of computers by ten to fifteen percent each year for the foreseeable future. Hence, commercial uses of computers which are just barely practicable today will be 10 percent more practicable next year . . . and 10 percent more practicable the year after . . . and ultimately ten times more practicable than they are today.[1] A user's first reaction to this improving technology generally is to continue doing the same old things that he was doing before—but just a little faster and a little cheaper. So it may well be the producer of computer systems who will need the insight and the imagination to suggest entirely new ways of doing business (or entirely new businesses) that could be profitably pursued. In Chapter 33, I will examine the issue of "visualizing" entirely new computer-based products and services and offer some suggestions to facilitate the process in American companies and government agencies.

The term "investor" usually conjures up images of Wall Street moguls who make and break empires. Recently, it has also been associated with the term "venture capitalist," which is generally understood to mean anyone who can invest millions of dollars in computer companies and/or other high-tech, razzle-dazzle companies. But investors are also the thousands of individuals, like you and me, with modest portfolios of a few thousand dollars— individuals who invested their money a decade ago in such blue-chip companies as General Motors, Exxon, and AT&T, and who now wonder if they should be investing their money in Apple and Tandem and Lotus Development Corporation.

Investors always dream of being the first to discover a hot new company, or even better, the hot new company in a hot new industry. Anyone who has ever looked at the Dow Jones industrial

---

[1] There will also be quantum jumps in technology, which will lead to "instantaneous" improvements of 100 percent or even 1,000 percent.

average must harbor a secret wish that he had invested in IBM or Xerox in the 1950s. Anyone even vaguely associated with the computer field must wish that he had been able to buy some insider stock at DEC or Apple or Data General. But today, many of these computer companies are considered old and staid, and are under attack from younger, smaller companies with audacious plans for products that will leapfrog them into the Fortune 500 in the 1990s.[2] If you are an investor, where should you be looking? Which companies should you invest in? To answer these questions, of course, you must have some idea of where the computer industry is going over the next ten to twenty years.

Finally, there are citizens—the great mass of 235 million Americans, a number that will grow to 300 million or more by the end of this century. As noted earlier, every American over the age of five will have access to a general-purpose programmable computer[3] by 1986. By 1990, it is likely that every citizen over the age of two will be interacting with his or her own computer; and by the end of this century, we may well find that computers are implanted into babies at birth—either (optimistically) to monitor such vital functions as heartbeat, or (pessimistically) to link every citizen into a nationwide computer network more insidious than George Orwell could possibly have imagined when he wrote 1984.

Citizens are not necessarily users or producers or investors, though there is obviously a great deal of overlap. But citizens do vote, and they will find it increasingly important to know how computers can, and should, be used by governmental authorities, schools, churches, and other social institutions to improve their lives. In fact, it is more important for citizens to be aware of

---

[2] An example: Apple Computer Company was founded in 1976 by two bright young men in their early twenties; by 1983, the company made the Fortune 500 list. (And by 1985, both founders had left the company.)

[3] I distinguish here between "general purpose programmable computer" (such as an Apple II or IBM PC or Commodore 64) and a "special purpose" or "embedded" computer that might be used to control your coffeepot or your dishwasher. By 1985, the average American home had forty electric motors, almost all of which are "invisible"; similarly, the average American home already had two to three invisible embedded computers, and that number will grow to equal the number of electric motors by the end of the century. However, general-purpose computers are those that can be used creatively, consciously, and for different tasks at different times, depending on the mood of the user.

computer trends than it is for users, producers, and investors because it takes citizens longer to organize an effective lobby to persuade their government to take action in any area. If you read in your newspaper this morning that someone has invented a computer which enables the IRS to communicate, via brainwaves, with your innermost thoughts about tax evasion, you can be reasonably sure that a dozen new companies will be incorporated by lunchtime to make a profit from this new technology. It is also likely that there will be a dozen petitions, a dozen citizen protests, and a dozen lawsuits filed by such organizations as the American Civil Liberties Union. But the issue will still be under debate ten years from now. The trick is to get a glimpse of the likely technological developments before they occur, so that the appropriate legal/social/political groundwork can be laid early enough to be effective. It also helps to see what uses governments and other social institutions are making of today's computer technology. This gives us a clue to their likely uses of future technology. (I will discuss this at length in subsequent chapters of the book.)

Computers are not the first technological invention to have made a major impact on our lives. Many of the previous comments could have been made about the television, radio, airplane, automobile, steam engine, telephone, and telegraph. And the social, economic, and governmental ramifications of these inventions were widely discussed . . . with approximately the same level of naiveté with which many people discuss computers today. There is much to learn from the early reactions to other technological innovations, lessons that we should apply to the continuing introduction of computer technology.

However, keep two things about computers in mind. First, while the underlying technology of the automobile, telephone, television, etc., has improved gradually over a period of decades, the technological improvements in the computer field have occurred, and continue to occur, *ten times as fast*. Computer people love to point out that if the automotive industry had shown the same degree of improvement as the computer industry, we would be able to purchase an automobile today for less than $100, and we would be able to drive it across the United States on a spoonful of gasoline. Automobile enthusiasts may argue that this will someday happen

—but the point is that automobiles have been part of our society for almost a century, and such order-of-magnitude improvements haven't happened yet. Computers, on the other hand, have been in existence for roughly forty years, and five order-of-magnitude improvements have been made, with several more (i.e., a factor of 1,000 or more) promised for the 1990s.

Second, remember that computers make use of many other technologies that have already been developed. Computers by themselves are a powerful force; combined with telephones, they take on an added dimension of power; combined with television, they take on yet another dimension of power. Just as monosodium glutamate (MSG) brings out the flavor of other foods, computers tend to "bring out" dozens of other technologies, ranging from biology to music, from telecommunications to astrology.

As you can see, I am concerned in this book with such questions as "Where are we going?" in the computer field, and "What are the consequences of current trends?" But ultimately I am concerned with more fundamental questions: "What are the important questions?" "What are the important trends that we should be anticipating?"

Since the computer phenomenon is indeed so large and pervasive today, it is difficult to know where to begin. What should be explored first? I have chosen the following major categories, and the rest of the book will examine them in detail:

- **The use of computers in society**. How are computers being used in the home today? What is the future of the "electronic cottage"? How are computers being used by children? In what other ways is the computer invading the household?

- **The use of computers by government**. What influence do national governments have on computer technology and the computer industry? Can we expect these influences to continue? How is the government involved in the issue of privacy and confidentiality of personal data?

- **The use of computers in business**. How are computers being used in business-oriented situations today? What impact are personal computers having? What will be the impact of artificial intelligence on the business arena?

- **The computer industry.** How big is the computer industry? How fast is it growing? Which parts are growing most quickly? What can we expect in the future?

- **Computer software.** What is the state of the art in computer software today? What is being done about the current shortage of computer programmers and systems analysts? What new technologies are being developed, and what can we expect during the next ten to twenty years?

- **Computer hardware.** What is the state of the art today? Why does it matter if computer hardware continues to get cheaper and faster? What technological developments can we expect over the next ten to twenty years?

These and other questions concern me, and should concern you. I want you to read each of the following chapters on the assumption that one or more of these issues will affect you immediately, directly, and personally. Even if you can escape the onslaught of computer technology described in the following pages, your children won't. Read the material for their sake, if not for your own.

I realize that some people are more interested in some aspects of computers than others, and I have organized the sections of material accordingly. All of us are citizens and should therefore be concerned with social issues and with all aspects of the government's use of computers; hence, these two sections of material come first. Anyone who works in a business environment should be concerned about the impact of computers on his company's competitive position, regardless of whether he works in the company's data processing department. And almost everyone should be aware of the importance of the computer industry—by the early 1990s, it will be the largest industry on earth. Fewer people will be concerned with issues of computer software and hardware, so I have saved this material for last. However, you can read the chapters in any order that you find convenient; I have cross-referenced material that appears in more than one chapter, but each chapter basically stands on its own.

As you read, I want you to keep one thing uppermost in mind: I am not writing this as an "expert," nor should you be reading the material as a "student." The computer field is still new, even after forty years. There are far, far too many things that the "professionals" simply don't know. There are many aspects of the computer revolution that should be determined not by experts, but by lay people . . . by people like you and your family, by your neighbors, and by the people you work with.

There is only one thing that can prevent you from participating in the major decisions that will be made during the next five to ten years regarding the use of computers in society: abdication.[4] Ironically, many computer professionals are already abdicating any role that they might play in these great decisions, even though they are generally aware of many of the technological developments described in this book. But for everyone else—the user, the investor, and the average citizen—abdication is usually caused by utter ignorance of computers.

There is no excuse for ignorance, no matter how little you know or care about computers. If you do feel ignorant now, this book should provide the beginning of an education. If not, it will certainly provide you with a list of references: books, magazine articles, and other sources of information. If nothing else, it will provide you with dozens of questions to pursue on your own.

CONCLUSION: WHAT SHOULD YOU DO NOW?

Now that you have read this chapter, the most important thing you can do is make your own assessment of the likely impact of computers on your life over the next five to ten years. You know far better than I do, of course, whether you are primarily an investor, a producer of computer systems, a user of computer systems, or simply a citizen. And you are obviously in a far better position to

---

[4] The same problem exists in many other areas, ranging from arms control to world hunger. For example, even though *A Nation At Risk* (to which I referred in the Preface, and from which I will present some specific statistics in Chapter 2) is a powerful, compelling document, very few people have read it. When I spoke about this report to an audience of 200 computer professionals at the 1985 Regional Conference of the Data Processing Management Association, only 2 percent had read the report. I had the distinct impression that fewer than 10 percent had even heard of it.

determine specifically how you can take advantage of the growing presence of computers.

Of course, you might argue that you don't have specific answers to such a question, and that you bought this book precisely for that reason. Fair enough. You might wish to return to this page after you have finished Chapter 39. On the other hand, it's hard to imagine that anyone in the United States, Canada, England, or any other industrial nation has been entirely oblivious to the presence of computers over the past few years. You must have some idea of the effect that computers now have, and will come to have in the future, over your life.

As you contemplate this issue, keep in mind the "technology transfer" phenomenon and the "order of magnitude" aspect of computer technology. Even if computers never got any faster or cheaper than they are today, they would still provide enormous opportunities for you and your children—because not that many people are using them. Only 24 percent of small businesses with fewer than twenty people have a computer; only 36 percent of small businesses with twenty to ninety-nine employees have a computer. Only 10 percent of white-collar workers have their own computer workstation, and a considerably smaller fraction of middle and top managers have direct access to a computer. Only about 2 percent of American households have a home computer, and only 20 percent of those computers are equipped with a modem that permits the computer to be linked, via phone line, to other computers and information services. And while well over 90 percent of all American schools have a computer, this belies the very low ratio of computers to children: in 1985, there were approximately 1,275,000 computers for 56 million students, or an average of 1 computer per 44 students.

Within five to ten years, all of these numbers will have changed dramatically. Computers will have permeated every nook and cranny of society. But for now, and for the next few years, there is a "window of opportunity." Question: *What are you going to do about it?* This is an important question to consider, and I think you should try to answer it even before you have gone on to the rest of this book. Scribble your answer in the margin now, and then come back to review it when you have finished Chapter 39.

In addition to the technology transfer issue, you must keep in mind that almost every aspect of computer technology will improve by one to three orders of magnitude —i.e., a factor of 10 to a factor of 1,000—in the next five to ten years. So you should be asking yourself now, "How will I be affected when computers are ten times faster and ten times cheaper and ten times smaller? What plans can I start making now to take advantage of this? What advantage will my competitors have if they begin using such computer technology and I don't?" Chapter 36 explores these questions further and suggests a number of interesting applications for more powerful computers. However, you should be able to generate some initial thoughts in this area now.

You should consider these questions as if the only person who cares about the answer is you, as if the only person who is going to do anything is you—because, in the United States, that is the way it is likely to be. You should be aware that in several other countries (Japan, France, and Russia, for example) questions like these are being discussed at the federal government level, and centralized national plans are being developed. Whether you think this is good or bad, the reality is that the U.S. government is not developing any plans for making its citizens more effective and competitive with computer technology, aside from exhorting its citizens, in reports like *A Nation At Risk*, to invest more time and money to make children computer literate. But as an adult, you're on your own.

So are the adult citizens (and children) of many other countries. But many of these countries—especially the smaller ones—have a keener sense of the global competition for jobs and markets, and perhaps a more prescient view of the future. In any case, you can be sure that there are many, many businessmen, investors, and developers of computer systems in other countries—countries ranging from Australia and Brazil to Yugoslavia and Zaire—who are asking themselves how they can prosper and even dominate their industry by being the first to massively exploit current technology, and the first to harness the tenfold increase in power of the new computers of the 1990s.

PART

I

COMPUTERS AND SOCIETY

2

COMPUTERS AND CHILDREN

The question I ask myself is, "Suppose the computer is only a violin." That would be a shame, because while experts can use a violin to make you weep, it is not a universal instrument like, say, the pencil. It's very difficult to learn to play the violin, in fact, it takes about the same amount of time and effort as learning to be a really good computer-program designer.

Alan Kay
Chief Scientist, Atari [1]

Children. They are the bane of our existence; they are the light of our lives. They can be incredibly creative, and they have an intuitive grasp of some intellectual concepts that adults can't even articulate; and yet they can be maddeningly slow to learn other things—ranging from table manners to simple arithmetic—that we take for granted. They comfort us when our own problems seem too much for us to bear; they drive us mad with their own petty complaints and their incessant questions. They question our motives, our techniques, our ethics, our music, our clothes, our values, our intelligence, our sense of fair play, and our basic understanding of what the world is all about; yet they forgive us when we fail, and they love us even when we are short-tempered and curt and downright cruel to them. With them, we often feel hobbled and held back; without them, we are nothing. Nature has given them to us not only to perpetuate the race, but to improve it. They are our hope for the future.

Today's children are fundamentally different from those of a hundred years ago; they are different from us thirty or forty years ago. It is not just that they are an inch taller than the average child of the 19th century, or that their life expectancy is twenty years greater. No, the difference is something more profound, and it has to do with *information*. A child born in 1982 can look forward to graduating from high school in the year 2000 having spent 12,000 hours in a classroom, having watched 17,000 hours of TV, having observed 600,000 TV commercials, and 20,000 TV murders. Today's child will also have written 10,000 lines of computer code (roughly the equivalent of two years' full-time work for today's experienced, adult computer programmer).[2]

Today's child, as we well know, is growing up in a world of gadgets that did not exist when his parents were born; he is accustomed to product obsolescence, technology obsolescence, and even information obsolescence. Half of the inventions, patents, and generally useful knowledge in his life will have occurred during the most recent ten years of his life. As anthropologist Margaret Mead points out, "Everyone born before World War II is an immigrant in time."

Margaret Mead also points out that children and adolescents today are the first generation of a "prefigurative" culture; adults thirty to fifty years old make up the first and only generation of a "cofigurative" culture; and all generations before that were members of a "postfigurative" culture. In a postfigurative culture, children learned virtually everything from their parents, because their parents had already experienced everything the child was likely to experience: things didn't change from one generation to the next. In the cofigurative generation that was born during World War II and grew up in the 1950s and 1960s, things were beginning to change so rapidly that parent and child had to learn together about the impact of television, atomic bombs, polio vaccine, and other wonders of the time. But now things have progressed to the prefigurative culture: the current generation of parents is saddled with experiences, skills, and painfully acquired knowledge that often turn out to be nothing more than extra baggage, slowing them down to the point where they can't keep up with their children. Computers are just one example of this phenomenon—but an example that adult teachers and parents see quite vividly.

Before we abandon hope and simply turn today's children loose, we should remember that a few things do remain constant; not everything we have learned is irrelevant. Learning about learning, for example, is something that we know about, and it is something that we can teach our children if we can be imaginative enough and open-minded enough to realize that what we learned about will probably have little or no bearing on what our children learn about. It is far more important for us to examine (or try to remember) why we learned certain things. Was there a point to learning Latin? Was there a reason for learning penmanship, or was it simply an outgrowth of the clumsy writing tools we had, coupled with an archaic fascination with calligraphy? Children are exceptionally good at spotting the difference between learning for the sake of learning, and learning for the sake of social (or religious) ritual; brute force may be sufficient to make them "learn" certain obsolete skills, but we risk their trust in us when we attempt it.

This is particularly true when it comes to computers, a subject that the teachers themselves don't understand very well. If the computer is a tool, then what other tools does it replace? Does it make the library virtually obsolete? Yes! Does it make the pencil obsolete? Yes! Should it make us abolish courses in penmanship? Yes! Does it make the study of mathematics obsolete? No! The computer is a tool that renders such primitive tools as the quill pen, the pencil, and the library largely obsolete;[1] but it does not eliminate the need for studying language, mathematics, art, science, reading, or other fundamental skills.

With this in mind, let us examine the impact of computers on children, and the impact of children on computers. Our concerns are the following:

- Computers in the schools.

- The effect of socioeconomic disparity on computer literacy.

- The issue of gender bias and sex equity and computers.

- The issue of "technostress," a term coined by Craig Brod.[3]

[1] To illustrate how insidious this problem can be, think back to your own high school days: What was the library used for? In most cases, it was the location for "study hall": a "quiet" place where students were kept in captivity during periods when they had no other classes scheduled. They weren't allowed out of school, and they weren't allowed in the cafeteria, and they had to be kept quiet to avoid disturbing other students. The library was a perfect choice; in addition to observing strict silence, there was even some minor possibility that students would find a book to read. But it was a minor possibility indeed.

COMPUTERS IN THE SCHOOLS

By now, it is surely not news that computers are invading the classroom. They are multiplying like cancer cells: there were just under 500,000 computers in American schools in 1983; there were 1,275,000 by 1985; and the number is expected to reach 4,872,000 by 1990.[4]

Obviously, this trend can't continue for too many years, or there will be more computers than schoolchildren.[2] However, we have a long way to go before we overpopulate the classroom with computers: in 1984, there were approximately 56 million schoolchildren in the United States. So even if the number of computers did double each year,[3] it would be 1994 or 1995 before total saturation occurred. On the grand scale of world history, that's not a long time—but it's long enough for almost an entire generation of children to be involved in the transition process. As a result, parents of this generation will have to take personal responsibility for the computer literacy training of their children.[4]

Of course, computers have long been a fixture in American universities. In schools like MIT, Stanford, and Carnegie-Mellon, students were able to gain some limited access to computers as early as 1959-61. By the mid-1980s, computer terminals and personal computers are as ubiquitous as telephones; a few engineering universities now require all new freshmen to bring their own personal computers to school with them.

Indeed, computers have become so common in universities that the liberal arts colleges have begun to contemplate the new issues raised by the pervasive influence of computers. As historian Joseph Ellis writes,

---

[2] Not that that's such a bad idea. Perhaps every school child needs two computers, one at home and one personally reserved for him at school. Maybe he needs a third one to carry with him as he walks from home to school. . . .

[3] This is doubtful, because computer purchases already have a noticeable effect on school budgets. Continued advances in computer technology, which we will discuss in Chapter 37, will reduce the cost of computer equipment by roughly 10 to 15 percent each year—or (more to the liking of the computer manufacturing companies) provide 10 to 15 percent more power for the same price.

[4] This theme is pursued in more detail in one of my recent books, *Coming of Age in Computerland* (Prentice-Hall, 1985).

. . . the liberal arts colleges have a special responsibility to raise dicey questions about the limitations of computers and the new social priorities shaped by information technology. . . . A computer literate graduate should not only possess the requisite technical skills but should also have encountered and thought about the following kinds of questions. Do computers encourage centralization and bureaucracy at the expense of human idiosyncrasy? Why are nearly all "hackers" male? Is it true, as J. David Bolter argues in *Turing's Man*, that the computer era will mitigate against emotional intensity, making a Michelangelo less likely (a clear loss) as well as a Hitler (a clear gain)? How serious are the threats to privacy and individual freedom conjured up by the traditional opponents of the new technology?[5]

Meanwhile, most of the activity, debate, and chaos occurs in the elementary and high schools. Much has been written about the use of computers in these schools.[6,7,8] The relevant areas to explore are these:

- How are computers being used in the schools?

- What are their advantages?

- What are their disadvantages?

- What do the teachers think of all of this?

- What do other professional educators think?

- What are the likely trends over the next five years?

In the mid-1980s, the answer to "How are computers being used?" varies widely from country to country, from state to state, from city to city, from school to school, and even from classroom to classroom. The situation is extremely fluid and depends on such factors as the available budget for computers and who controls it—the school board, the high school principal, the math teacher, or a city/state regulatory agency. In countries like France and Russia, many of the decisions about the use of computers in schools are made at the national level. In the United States, the level of decision making ranges from the federal level (for research grants and subsidies) to the state level (which may set some educational standards) to the level of the individual school (which may be attempting its own innovative efforts in a financially destitute or educationally conservative state, e.g., the Lamplighter School in Dallas, which pioneered much of the computer literacy training in Logo for children).

It also depends on where the people in charge of computer literacy decide to invest day-to-day operational control (e.g., in the math department, the science department, a newly formed computer liaison department, etc.). In some cases, even day-to-day issues are set by regulatory policy outside the school itself; for example, New York City public school regulations in 1985 even dictated the number of and exact placement of electrical power outlets in the city-subsidized "computer laboratories."

The use of computers in the schools also depends on the availability of help and guidance from neighboring universities and private industry. Various high-technology cities—Boston, Stanford, Dallas, Austin, Princeton, and other "silicon valleys"—provide a nucleus of talented consultants, parents, and industry-sponsored educational activities. And universities with a strong interest in computer-related research—MIT, Harvard, Berkeley, NYU, Purdue, Carnegie-Mellon, UCLA, Brown, Rutgers, and many others—are also a tremendous resource for the local schools. But a rural school hundreds of miles away from the nearest university or high-tech firm can obviously suffer, as can a school in the midst of a geographical region that still bases its economy on agriculture, mining, fishing, or some other moribund industry.

The availability of worthwhile software is also important. This changes on a daily basis, and is also a matter of geography and local funding policies. For example, schools in Minnesota have access to software through a statewide educational consortium called MECCA that schools in New York either don't have access to or don't know about.[5] An encouraging development in this area is the

[5] By contrast, in May 1985 I visited one of the public high schools in New York City that specializes in science and mathematics, so that I could see how they were using computers. The school had two computer laboratories, one filled with IBM PCs, and the other filled with Apple II computers. When I expressed my surprise to the computer teacher that the Apple II lab had no word processing programs, his immediate answer was, "The NYC School Board didn't provide any such software." When I suggested that the teacher himself might buy a copy of a simple word processing package called Bank Street Writer for $39.95, he looked at

creation of the Educational Products Information Exchange Institute (EPIE) in Water Mill, N.Y.; it provides a comprehensive listing (both in book form and on-line) of available educational software.

Perhaps the most important factor in determining how computers will be used in the schools is the ability of individual teachers to deal with a new technology, which they don't always trust, and which frequently terrifies them. I have great respect and sympathy for these teachers: already overworked and underpaid in most cases, they are now asked, for the first time in their lives, to deal with something that the children clearly adapt to more quickly than they do. Parents will generally admit that it's something that they themselves can't accomplish—just as they have trouble dealing with discipline, sex education, morality, and a number of other social skills. Computers are one more thing foisted upon the teachers. Some can handle it with the same skill, dedication, and creativity that they apply to everything else they do; some are simply overwhelmed.

With this background, let me summarize the typical uses of computers in American schools:

- **Video games**. Believe it or not, some schools haven't figured out what else to do with computers and feel that video games will at least make the children feel comfortable with machines. But there is more to this than meets the eye: I will discuss the relevance and importance of video games and other computer-based games in Chapter 5.

- **"Drill and practice" computer-based education programs**. Programs of this kind exist for spelling, mathematics, science, and a variety of other topics. In most cases, the student can choose a level of difficulty; a few of the more sophisticated "computer-assisted instruction" programs will automatically determine, based on the student's success with initial questions, whether to

---

me as if I were from another planet. I considered donating my own copy of the program, but decided that city policy probably also forbade the use of any program not on the official list. In any case, the students in that laboratory were learning BASIC and some other useful things—but they weren't learning word processing. For shame!

skip ahead to more advanced topics, or whether to fall back to remedial topics. Such software exists at several grade levels, though it does not appear that there is an educationally integrated set of programs that would, say, help teach French at every level from kindergarten through 12th grade. It is also important to note that most of the straightforward drill and practice programs are based on a reward system, and often pit the student against the computer in some kind of contest—e.g., the student may find that he is on a race course, racing a car of his choice against a car driven by the computer; the speed with which he is able to supply correct answers determines whether his car stays ahead of the computer's car. Alternatively, the student may find that he is defending a spaceship against invading aliens; answering computer-supplied questions correctly gives the student the opportunity to shoot down those awful aliens. We will return to this point below when we discuss the issue of gender bias in computer education. Though drill and practice programs have come under heavy criticism recently, we should consider the alternative: many human teachers are hardly any better! And we should review some sobering statistics from the study that motivated this book, *A Nation At Risk*.

> International comparisons of student achievement, completed a decade ago, reveal that on nineteen academic tests American students were never first or second and, in comparison with other industrialized nations, were last seven times.
>
> Some 23 million American adults are functionally illiterate by the simplest tests of everyday reading, writing and comprehension.
>
> About 13 percent of all seventeen-year-olds in the United States can be considered functionally illiterate. Functional illiteracy among minority youths may run as high as 40 percent.
>
> Many seventeen-year-olds do not possess the "higher order" intellectual skills we should expect of them. Nearly 40 percent cannot draw inferences from written material; only one-fifth can write a persuasive essay; and only one-third can solve a mathematics problem requiring several steps.[9]

- **Learning how to program.** Logo is currently the most popular programming language for elementary school students; BASIC rears its ugly head in the middle school (4th grade through 8th grade) and high schools throughout the land. In a relatively small number of high schools, students can learn PASCAL, which might enable them to pass an "advanced placement" test to receive credit for a year's college work. I will discuss the virtues of Logo, BASIC, PASCAL, and other programming languages in Chapter 29. For now, all you need to know is that learning a computer programming language is somewhat akin to studying the theory of internal combustion engines in a driver education course. Or, as Professor Judah Schwartz of the Center for Educational Technology points out,

> My personal view is that computing makes very little sense as a subject in elementary grades. It's usually justified in the same way that the teaching of Latin was justified for hundreds of years; namely, that it's supposed to help you think more clearly. [10]

Thus, the well-intentioned effort that schools are investing in Logo programming courses may be largely wasted. If you are a parent, there is probably not much you can do about this. But don't compound the problem by forcing your child to learn a programming language at home.

Computer simulation games. These programs allow the student to recreate various historical events, such as the Lewis and Clark expedition, or the Revolutionary War, or the corporate acquisition of company X by company Y, or the economy of 18th-century England. By changing various parameters, the student can explore alternative scenarios in a manner that is often more lifelike and interesting than would otherwise be the case. It encourages the student to explore "what-if" scenarios that are rarely, if ever, presented in textbooks: What if Britain had entered the American Civil War on the side of the Confederacy? What if the atomic bomb hadn't worked in 1945? What if the United States had not made the Louisiana Purchase? What if Hitler had attempted the invasion of England two months earlier? What would have happened if Stalingrad had fallen in 1940?

Word processing. At an age where the student is expected to write school reports—anywhere from 3rd to 8th grade, depending on the school system—computers can be a powerful tool for producing higher-quality material than can be produced with pencil and paper. Because the task of physically producing the document is so much easier, the student can concentrate on content and can learn the virtues of revision and rewriting. This becomes controversial fairly quickly, though. The availability of spelling-checkers raises the question of whether students need to memorize the spelling of words, just as the advent of cheap calculators ten years ago raised the issue of whether young students needed to continue learning long division by hand, and whether college mathematics majors needed to continue learning, as I did, how to calculate the sine of an arbitrary number when it could be calculated by punching one or two keys on a calculator.

- **Mathematics**. High school students can make good use of computers to help learn about graphs and charts, to see algebraic equations played out in front of them, etc. Elementary school students can use a variety of innovative education programs distributed by companies like Sunburst Software to learn division, multiplication, and basic number skills.

- **Music**. A computer can help a child compose music, creating the equivalent of sheet music on the display screen. And the music can be played on the computer's speaker, or through an external synthesizer.

- **Art**. Children can use computers to create charts, graphs, and other stylized drawing,. For example, diagrams such as Figure 4.1 (on page 71), and Figures 20.2, 20.4, and 24.1 were drawn by my Apple Macintosh as I wrote this book. And children of all ages can compose "creative" pictures: my eight-year-old son, Jamie, created an interesting representation of a computer with an hour's work; my five-year-old, David, prefers more abstract pictures.

The Advantages of Computers in Schools

I frankly doubt whether many educators or parents ask this question carefully before they succumb to the onslaught of computers.

THE COMPUTER!

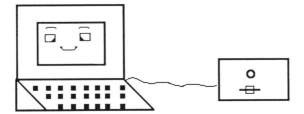

Jamie's picture

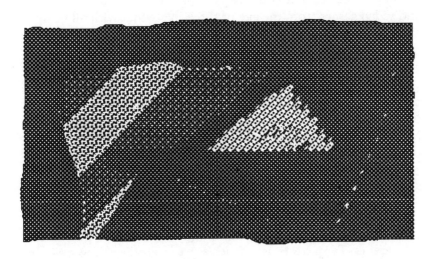

David's picture

It is simply an article of faith that every child must know something about computers in order to survive in life—and those who learn about it early will be at an advantage over those who don't.

The motivation for this is based on the statistics presented at the beginning of Chapter 1: by 1990, 60 percent of all jobs in the United States will require computer literacy, and by the year 2000, 80 percent of all jobs will require computer literacy. Assuming that this is true, it is obviously important to teach computer literacy to children as one of their fundamental skills.

There is indeed growing evidence that this prediction will come true. More and more administrative people are expected to learn how to use word processing machines, data entry terminals, order entry terminals, airline reservation terminals, etc. More and more often, citizens in all walks of life are expected to interact with computer-controlled cash machines, coffeepots, dishwashers, and even automobiles. And our children play with computerized toys and video games from the age of three. Note that with all of these examples, the ability to write computer programs in a language like BASIC is not the issue; the issue is to interact with and work with a computer to get a job done.

Schools teach—or should teach—a variation on the idea that the computer is a tool that can be used to accomplish a number of intellectual tasks more quickly, more easily, and more effectively. More importantly, the sophistication of one's tools affects the way one acts in a society and, some would argue, the tools affect the way one thinks. Craig Brod makes this point very forcefully in his excellent book, *Technostress.*

> Tools have always set in motion great changes within human societies. Tools create us as much as we create them. The spear, for example, did much more than extend a hunter's reach; it changed the hunter's gait and use of his arms. It encouraged better eye-hand coordination; it led to social organizations for tracking, killing, and retrieving larger prey. It widened the gap between the unskilled hunter and the skilled hunter and made pooling of information more important as hunting excursions became more complex. There were other, less obvious effects: changes in the diets of hunting societies led to sharing of food and the formation of new social relationships. The

value of craftsmanship increased. People began to plan ahead, storing weapons for reuse. All of these new tool-related demands, in turn, spurred greater development of the brain. Brain complexity led to new tools, and new tools made yet more complex brains advantageous to the survival of the species.[11]

A computer can be used as a tool for writing and, properly used, a computer can help the writer organize and revise his thoughts, polish them and correct them until he has a respectable document. The computer can be an effective tool for organizing lists (or files) of information, so that selected subsets can be retrieved on demand; this makes it possible for the student to gather research data and look for correlations and patterns. The graphics capability of most modern personal computers makes it possible to present those correlations and patterns in pie charts, bar charts, or a number of other effective visual ways.

There are other advantages, too: electronic mail (so that homework assignments can be sent electronically to the teacher instead of turning in scraps of paper) and research access to public databases (so that the student can abandon the library and retrieve information about selected subjects from massive databases maintained on mainframe computers thousands of miles away). Many of the applications for society, government, and business that we will see in the next several chapters apply equally to students and adults alike.

The Disadvantages of Computers in Schools

Fortunately, neither educators nor parents have fallen prey to the strident TV commercials produced (primarily) by the manufacturers of personal computers. At least, not completely. There are some doubts—doubts that are well articulated—about the usefulness, or even the relevance, of computers in the schools. One of the most eloquent expressions of concern about the overemphasis on computers was made in 1984 by Derek Bok, president of Harvard University:

Finally, the educational benefits of technology also remain in dispute. There is still little proof that new devices yield lasting improvement in learning. Many studies purport to find such gains. But most of them can be explained on the grounds that students using computers were temporarily motivated by the sheer novelty of the machines or that more effort and better teaching went into the computerized courses than were devoted to the conventional courses with which they were compared. Thus, the learning improvements that early investigators reported from computer-assisted instruction shrank to virtually nothing when the same teacher taught both the experimental and the conventional classes with comparable amounts of preparation. Similarly, the gains achieved in computer experiments lasting less than four weeks dropped by more than two-thirds when the experiments continued beyond eight weeks and the novelty of the new technology began to wear off.[12]

Basically, the problems and the disadvantages are these:

- Computers are often introduced into schools with no planning. Even the best of tools or educational concepts can fail if rushed into the classroom with no preparation.[6]

- Many teachers are untrained. They simply don't know what to do with the machines once they arrive. Because of limited access to computers, limited budgets for teacher training, and other demands on their time, many teachers may never be trained. This problem is not unique to the United States. In France, for example, where 200,000 computers will be installed by the end of 1985, the schoolteachers' union has complained that the computers will undermine the authority and prestige of the teachers. While the teachers are paid a special bonus for basic training during the summer vacation, they nevertheless fear they will make a poor showing beside their pupils.[14]

---

[6] If it is any consolation, the situation is even worse in Russia. The Politburo decreed early in 1985 that the September 1985 school term was the target date for introducing a new course in the school curriculum aimed at improving computer literacy among secondary school students. Every school is required to have such a course, and it is estimated that 50,000 computer classrooms will be set up as a result. But, as British reporter Nick Anning points out, "the decision at such relatively short notice has highlighted the shortfall in properly qualified teaching staff and the lack of the necessary bulk production of Soviet micros for school use."[13] We will examine more aspects of computers in Russia in Chapter 12.

- Much of the available educational software is poorly docu-mented, uncreative, overly expensive, and unrelated to any-thing else in the standard educational curriculum. There are exceptions to this, of course, but there are not yet any standards by which educational software can be judged.

- Local school districts sometimes budget money to purchase computer hardware, but not software . . . or they may have forgotten about maintenance of the computer equipment.

- Drill and practice programs have dubious educational value. As Seymour Papert points out in *Mindstorms*:

    In many schools today, the phrase "computer-aided instruction" means making the computer teach the child. One might say the computer is being used to program the child. In my vision, the child programs the computer and, in doing so, both acquires a sense of mastery over a piece of the most modern and powerful technology and establishes an intimate contact with some of the deepest ideas from science, from mathematics, and from the art of intellectual model building. [15]

- Schools suffer terribly from the rapid obsolescence of com-puters. Because of limited budgets, it's very difficult for them to throw away old machines. But because many of the older machines are fairly fragile, they have succumbed to the years of tender ministrations on the part of students: disk drives are broken, keyboards don't work, etc.

- Economic disparities between rich and poor prevent everyone from gaining equal access to computer facilities. This problem is discussed in more detail below.

- "Gender bias," both in a conscious and unconscious form, prevents many girls from enjoying access to computers that boys take for granted. This is discussed in more detail below.

- There is often a complete lack of understanding or agreement about the purpose of introducing computers into the schools. That is, neither the school board nor the teachers nor the parents have decided (or even discussed) whether computers are being introduced so that all students can learn to write computer programs, or so that they can get a taste of computer literacy, or so that they can experience the computer as a tool in all of their educational activities—or perhaps something else altogether.

- Most computers in schools cannot communicate with one another; hence, children have no opportunity to experience such things as electronic mail. Worse, most computers have no modem (the device that allows a computer to connect to telephone lines), so they cannot access outside public utility systems or databases.

- Because of limited access to computers, many teachers have been forced to devise educational programs in which each student uses the computer only five minutes a day, or perhaps one hour per week. A study of California schools[16], for example, showed that half of the elementary schools with a computer reported that the students spent less than fifteen minutes per day, on average, using the computer.[7] I remember a similar situation in my high school driver-education class, and it was extremely frustrating during those long periods of time when someone else was doing the driving, but at least I didn't need to think of the automobile as an essential tool for my other school courses. If one believes that the computer is a tool to be used several hours a day for all subjects—as a pencil is today—then teachers are faced with the problem of trying to teach penmanship, mathematics, and a host of other subjects where the entire class shares one pencil, and each student has access to the prized writing instrument for only five minutes a day.

ECONOMIC EQUITY ISSUES

The issue here is very simple: Poor children in poor school districts have considerably less access to computers than affluent children in

---

[7] The same study showed that of roughly 22,000 sixth graders in the California schools, 78 percent had never used a computer in school.

affluent school districts. One study conducted by the National Science Foundation showed that children in the 12,000 poorest school districts had four times less access to computers than chidren in the 12,000 most affluent school districts in the country. A television report on the same subject indicated that in Philadelphia, public school students had only one computer for every 425 students, while private schools in the same city had one computer for every 20 students.[17] Overall, 70 percent of the wealthier schools have computers, while 60 percent of the poorer schools do not. Still another survey showed that 89 percent of the schools with more than 1,000 students have PCs, while only 52 percent of those with under 200 students have PCs.[18]

This phenomenon is nothing new. The same statistics could probably be found for the number of microscopes or electronic equipment or football uniforms or many other pieces of equipment—indeed, even such basic things as textbooks—that we expect our schoolchildren to have. Computers, of course, have a lot more visibility today, and because of the importance of computers in the job market, the economic disparity raises more concern than does the disparity in specialized equipment that only a small number of students may need. (Not that this should eliminate our concern for the lack of microscopes and other scientific equipment in the poor school districts.)

Assuming that computers continue to generate the same degree of interest over the next several years, we can expect that the schools will be completely saturated sometime within the 1990s. But there could well be a period of ten to fifteen years during which the disparity between rich children and poor children is widened even further because of this issue of computers. Some legislation is currently pending to provide equal computer access, but it is not likely to have much of an impact. It is more likely to ensure, as is the case in the Soviet Union,[8] that every school has at least one computer—a single computer to be shared among hundreds of students.

Inevitably, private industry will be involved in deciding how much "remedial training" is required to provide basic computer

---

[8] As we will see in Chapter 12, the Soviet Union will probably not have one computer per school until 1990. In this respect, they are ten years behind the United States, and falling farther behind each day.

literacy for today's high school graduates. If a company can hire an adequate number of people who can read, write, and use a computer, then it will probably have little interest in the welfare children who, when they leave school, can neither read nor write nor compute. If, on the other hand, a company is unable to find a sufficient number of school-trained people, it may have to do the training itself. And, of course, the government will continue to move in its Byzantine fashion, and will eventually include computer literacy training with whatever other remedial training programs it offers.

But the "bottom line" is inescapable: For the next ten to fifteen years, the official organs of society charged with educating our children will be unable to keep up with the exploding computer revolution. The only realistic solution is an individual one: only the individual parent can prevent a child in a poor school district from being put at a further disadvantage. Parents must take it upon themselves to buy a home computer and appropriate software and textbooks to introduce computers to their child. This won't be easy—among other things, parents have the same kind of fear and trepidation about the new technology that teachers have!

This is not completely an issue of economics, even though we are talking about poor children in poor school districts. It is possible to buy a small, inexpensive computer for under a hundred dollars, and it can be hooked into the existing home TV system. A hundred dollars sounds like a lot of money, but it sure isn't any more than a TV costs! When 98 percent of the U.S. population already has a TV in the home, there is a strong implication that even the poorer segments of the population can find enough money when and if they want to. If a welfare family can afford a TV, then it can also afford a home computer. Such a statement will raise the hackles of some readers, but I think it is a position that needs to be considered. No matter how strongly one feels that such problems should be solved by a centralized government authority (a philosophical position whose virtue I don't intend to argue here), the reality is that it won't happen until the middle of the 1990s. Even if the entire defense budget of the United States were cancelled next year and devoted instead to computer literacy programs for our children, it would take five to ten years to figure out how to spend and physically distribute the money—and, as I have indicated already, we don't yet know how best to apply computer technology to the educational needs of our children.

For now, like it or not, parents must take personal responsibility. Parents may make mistakes —as they do with every other aspect of child-rearing!—but so will the teachers. And at least parents have the virtue of caring for their children. We can't guarantee this of all parents and all children, but the odds are better, in most cases, than they are with overworked, underpaid teachers who rarely affect more than a year of a child's education.

If economics turn out to be the key issue for a family, there are alternatives. In many urban parts of the country, public libraries have already stocked personal computers for overnight lending. And then there are the YMCAs and the churches and the Boy Scouts and the Police Athletic Leagues and a dozen other organizations that do their best to reach out and help children. No doubt there are some children in the wilderness of Appalachia or deep within the bowels of the innermost urban slums who are doomed never to see a computer . . . but they probably come from the same minuscule portion of our society that lives without access to telephone, television and radio. For everyone else, the message is very simple: there will be no short-term salvation from the schools or the government, and there is no excuse for parents not to shoulder this task on their own.

THE PROBLEM OF GENDER BIAS

Gender bias is a phenomenon that we have seen in other fields of engineering during this century, and in the field of science for the last several hundred years. It is based on the premise that only men can be (or should be) involved in engineering/science professions, and that women cannot (or should not) be so involved. Sometimes the bias is blatant; more often (especially since it violates many laws in this country and abroad), it is subtle. It is all the more tragic when we see evidence of such bias from leaders whom we would otherwise regard as role models for ourselves and our children.

This point struck me recently when I visited my alma mater,

MIT, for a college reunion. Engraved on the wall of one of the main buildings—a wall that I walked past every day of my undergraduate life—was a quotation from one of the early presidents of the Institute:

> I see proceeding from our technology of the future a vast army of vigorous young men, able to play their part manfully and effectively anywhere in the world.

Richard Cockburn MacLaurin,
MIT President, 1909-1920

I'm sure Mr. MacLaurin was a very nice man, and that he meant no harm by his remark. But what about all of the women whose existence he effectively denied?

Unfortunately, the problem continues today with computers. I say "unfortunately" because it is more than an issue of keeping women out of the field of computer science—that would be bad enough! But as I have already pointed out, computer literacy will be essential for 60 to 80 percent of the jobs in the United States during the lifetime of our children. To deny girls/women an aggressively equal opportunity to join in the computer revolution is to doom them to lower-class status.

Naturally, most educators and most parents would vigorously deny that this is happening. Unfortunately, early statistics on the use of computers suggest otherwise. A 1982 survey of 5,300 students at summer computer camps, conducted by Stanford University, indicated that the boys outnumbered the girls by a ratio of three to one. Only 27 percent of the students in the elementary programming classes were girls; only 14 percent of the students in advanced classes were girls.[19] Similar disparities have been observed by a number of teachers throughout the country.

Note that there may be a significant difference between computer literacy classes in "normal" schools and computer literacy classes in summer camp. In a normal classroom environment, computer literacy may be a required subject (though this is by no means universal); a summer computer camp, on the other hand, is always a voluntary proposition. Informal evidence suggests that parents initiate the idea of computer camp with their sons (for whom science, engineering, computers, and auto mechanics are considered part of the formula for success in later life); girls, on the other hand, have to ask for the privilege. This phenomenon can even be seen in middle-class private schools, where the parents generally know that both sons and daughters will end up in white-collar jobs. A recent survey of my sons' school indicated that boys and girls had approximately the same number of home computers through fifth grade, after which boys had twice as many home computers as girls.

Gender bias takes on a number of other, more subtle, forms, too. Consider the ceremony that often takes place when the first computer is brought into the classroom. The teacher (who may be of either sex) often picks out a boy, and says to the class, "Freddie, why don't you carry the computer up here and show us all how it works?" The unspoken messages that the class hears are these: (1) computers are heavy, and only strong males can deal with them, and (2) computers are complicated, and only boys can show us how they work.

As we have already observed, many of the drill and practice educational programs are based on the concept of rewarding a student by allowing him (or her) to destroy aliens, shoot down airplanes, blow up villages, race his car faster than the computer's car . . . or other things that tend to excite young boys, but not always young girls. Imagine how the boys would react if their education programs required them to manipulate rabbits and Barbie Dolls![9]

Also, many schools have after-school computer clubs for middle-school children, ranging in age from eight to twelve. For boys, this is a time for "wolf-pack" behavior: they swoop down upon the computer, pushing everyone else aside (including girls less than seven feet tall), and then proceed to play their latest, most violent video games. An adventurous girl may show up at the first meeting of such a club, but will generally not return.

---

[9] It has been argued that the game of Pac-Man appeals to both sexes because it does not require the player to manipulate guns or rockets. On the other hand, it requires the neuter-looking Pac-Man to follow a mazelike path, gobbling "energy pellets," which enable it to cannibalize smaller Pac-Men—until it is eventually overcome by hungrier blobs. Violence is still present in the game . . .

We have little or no evidence to indicate whether boys are "better" at computer programming than girls; if other scientific disciplines are any guide at all, we should expect no significant differences. On the other hand, some early experiments suggest that boys and girls go about the process of computer programming differently: girls are more interested in the process of programming, while boys are more interested in results.[10] As researcher Karla Pretl found while watching young boys and girls working on Logo projects,

> Most of the boys sought immediate closure on one program and moved on to another. The girls, in distinct contrast, fussed with their programs, perfecting them by adding more details.[20]

Indeed, nobody should think that boys and girls approach computer programming or any other intellectual task in the same way; there may well be some problems for which girls are more likely to derive elegant solutions, and others where boys will find a more brute-force "short-cut" solution. My only concern is that boys and girls alike be given equal access, equal encouragement, and equal education in the use of a tool that will play such an important role in their adult lives.

THE PROBLEM OF TECHNOSTRESS

One last issue to worry about with children is the danger of their being overwhelmed by the pressures of high-technology life and high-technology education. This is an important issue, because most TV commercials and magazine ads show nothing but smiling children and smiling teachers, all having the time of their lives as they play their video games or write their Logo programs. We all know that teachers and parents are nervous about computers, but it never occurs to us that some children may be just as overwhelmed or bored or frightened of computers as their parents.

[10] A colleague at MCC (Microelectronics Computer Corporation) noticed a similar phenomenon when teaching soccer to boys and girls: the girls tended to play well in midfield and were interested in issues of strategy and tactics. They weren't as interested, though, in scoring goals, which was all that the boys cared about.

Researchers are only now beginning to study the issue; the work of Craig Brod[21] and Sherry Turkle[22] stands in stark contrast to the optimistic writings of Seymour Papert[23], who sees Logo as the salvation for almost everything that could possibly ail children. Brod points out that some children use video games and computer programming as a way of escaping the pressures of their "real world" life; Turkle points out that children approach computers quite differently at different developmental stages in their lives. More importantly, she points out that the computer becomes a reflection of our own personality—especially for children—and as such, it becomes a "second self" whose psychological implications are only beginning to be understood.

Brod's interview with a sixteen-year-old boy, David, provides compelling evidence of the technostress that can be caused by computers:

> After a day of programming, generally I'm pretty grumpy. I save what I have on disk, or if it's really going bad, I will just turn it off and get rid of the whole thing, the steps that frustrated me. And then I'm reasonably free of it. The biggest problem with relating to my family is that they get demanding. They want me to talk with them, especially my mother. But I don't want to do that. I'm tired. I'm edgy. I just want to be left alone.[24]

Most of us are not psychotherapists or child psychologists; we have to make the best of our amateur abilities as we raise our children. I strongly urge you to read Brod's book and Turkle's book to hear points of view quite different from the cheerful, upbeat TV commercials that bombard your psyche every day. If you don't have time to read the books, keep these points in mind:

- **Not all children like computers or are "good" at computers.** Sometimes this may be the result of gender bias problems discussed above; sometimes it may simply be a sign that they prefer baseball or music over computers; and sometimes it may indicate that they lack necessary typing skills. In any case, don't take it for granted that your child knows more than you do about computers, or that he/she will learn more quickly.

- **Don't use the computer as a surrogate parent**. Just as you use discretion in your choice of TV programs, so you should use discretion in the choice of computer games and programs you let your child use. Just as you would be concerned if your child sat catatonic in front of the television for sixteen hours, so you should be concerned if your child sits glued to the computer for sixteen hours.

- **Watch for gender bias issues**. If you have a son, you may not have to deal with it (though fairness requires that you at least point out to him what's going on). If you have a daughter, make sure that you volunteer the same degree of computer access that you would volunteer for a son; make sure that she isn't experiencing discrimination in school; make sure that she understands that computer literacy is important regardless of her sex or her intended future profession.

CONCLUSION: WHAT SHOULD YOU DO?

If you have no children, you don't have to do anything about the suggestions made in this chapter. If your children are grown and gone, it's probably too late to do anything about their computer literacy training. If they are under five, you can probably delay making any decision for a few years. In fact, until your children begin doing serious schoolwork, you might feel that computers are much more of a luxury than a necessity.

But if you have a child in the middle years of schooling or in high school, you should play an active role in his computer literacy training. Specifically:

1. **Determine whether your child needs his or her own computer.** If the child is not yet in high school, and if he has ample access to computers at school (or if he has access to your computer at home), and if he has not asked for his own computer, then you can put away your pocketbook. If he is in high school, you should definitely get one; if he does not have adequate access to computers in school, you should seriously consider getting one for him. And if he asks for one (for any reason other than video games) you should definitely get him one.

2. **Decide what computer your child needs.** There is no single "right" answer for this, any more than there is a single "right" school or "right" teacher. Your choice will almost certainly be affected by your budget. It may also be affected by your interest in using the same computer for business purposes. Also, one can make a good argument for getting your child the same type of computer he or she is using at school. Aside from these considerations, I suggest that you avoid the cheap $200 computers made by Atari, Radio Shack, or Commodore; you and your child will quickly outgrow it. If you want a computer that will be most useful for your own business activities as well as your child's education, get an IBM PC. If you want a computer with the broadest range of educational software, get an Apple II. If your child is primarily interested in word processing or graphics, get an Apple Macintosh.

3. **Take an active part in the school's computer literacy program.** As I suggested above, this means that you have to visit his school and find out what it is doing, what its philosophy of computer training is (if it has one), how well trained its teachers are, etc. But more than this, you can express your views to your child's teacher and the school administration. You can attend PTA meetings to voice your feelings. And if you have any computer-related experience (even if only by virtue of having acquired a home computer last week), you can offer to lend your assistance to the teachers; in every case that I have seen, they have been grateful for the help. Show them educational software they can't buy on their own; bring your home computer to your child's classroom if his class doesn't have one (or if yours is better); give the teacher advice on printers, modems, and devices the teacher may not know well; offer to teach an evening programming course for teachers, or a Saturday course for children. This is one of the very, very few areas where the American educational system is not in control, and where you will be welcomed with open arms if you offer your help. You won't have this chance a few years from now.

4.   **Decide with your child what software to buy.** Chances are you won't get away without buying at least one video game. Let him pick it out; let him see how much it costs so that he can compare it with his allowance, and with the cost of whatever other toys you provide. If your child is relatively young (third grade or younger), word processing won't be of any interest; buy a word processing program only if you plan to use it yourself. Do buy Logo, though. This is probably the language your child is learning in school, and you can both explore it together. Look for at least one other program you can use together, such as the Sargon III Chess program. Also, get at least one graphics program (MacPaint or MacDraw for the Macintosh, Mousepaint for the Apple II, or PC Draw for the IBM PC). Consult your friends and your children's friends.

5.   **Encourage your child's interest in computers, but don't force computers on him.** Remind him about the computer if it has lain dormant for several weeks. Point out opportunities where his homework would be more easily completed on the computer.

6.   **Keep up with your child.** Keep in mind that if you don't do this for your child, nobody will; but other parents will and already are making this extra investment in their children. We have seen numerous incidents during the past decade (and indeed, since this country was formed) of parents pushing their children to educational superiority. Whether this is good or bad is beyond the scope of this book. I merely observe that computer skills are joining the list of academic subjects that Vietnamese-American, Chinese-American, and Japanese-American parents (and other nationalities, too) are pushing their children to master. The major advantage that we have in the United States is the larger number of computers in the classroom, as well as access to a much wider, cheaper range of home computer hardware and software than is found in any other country. This is a major advantage.

Keep in mind that it is not just a matter of educational superiority. You may not care if your child's computer literacy skills get him into Harvard, MIT, or Stanford. But you should care whether he can get a job when he grows up; and you should want him to be equipped with the skills that will allow him to participate successfully in society. As an analogy, consider how you would have felt as a parent in the 1950s if your child's school did not have a driver's education course; you would have taught your child to drive by yourself. So, in the 1980s, you must teach your child how to use computers if the school cannot do it—*even though you may not know how to use computers yourself.*

References for Chapter 2

1. "A Serious Player," *Technology Illustrated*, October 1983, pages 67-70.

2. Rochester, Jack B., and John Gantz, *The Naked Computer*, New York: William Morrow and Company, 1983.

3. Brod, Craig, *Technostress*, Reading, Mass.: Addison-Wesley, 1984.

4. Parker, Suzy, "Trailing Computer Race," *USA Today*, September 5, 1985.

5. Ellis, Joseph J., "The Computer Revolution and the Liberal Arts Curriculum," *Mount Holyoke Alumnae Quarterly*, Summer 1985.

6. Bramble, William J., and Emanuel J. Mason, with Paul Berg, *Computers in Schools*, New York: McGraw-Hill, 1985.

7. Coburn, Peter, et al., *Practical Guide to Computers in Education*, Reading, Mass.: Addison-Wesley, 1982.

8. Papert, Seymour, *Mindstorms*, New York: Basic Books, 1980.

9. *A Nation At Risk. The Imperative for Educational Reform*, Washington, D.C.: U.S. Government Printing Office, The National Commission on Excellence in Education, April 1983.

10. Brady, Holly, and Melinda Levine, "Is Computer Education Off Track," (interview), *Classroom Computer Learning*, February 1985.

11. Brod, *op. cit.*, page 13.

12. Bok, Derek, *The President's Report 1983-84*, Harvard University, page 3.

13. Anning, Nick, "USSR starts dp for schools," *Computing*, September 5, 1985.

14. Gee, Jack, "French Teachers Fear the Micro," *Computer Weekly*, September 12, 1985.

15. Papert, *op. cit.*, page 5.

16. *Student Achievement Results in California Schools*, 1981-82 Annual Report, Sacramento, Calif.: California State Department of Education.

17. *NBC Nightly News*, February 4, 1983.

18. Williams, Dennis A., "A Status Report on Computers in Schools," *Personal Computing*, September 1985.

19. Miura, Irene, and Robert D. Hess, "Sex Difference in Computer Access, Interest and Usage," Stanford University, presented at the *91st Convention of the American Psychological Association*, August 1983.

20.   Frank, Shirley, "Are Girls Better At Computer Details, Too?", *Equal Play Magazine*, Spring-Fall 1983, pages 11-14.

21.   Brod, *op. cit.*

22.   Turkle, Sherry, *The Second Self*, New York: Simon and Schuster, 1984.

23.   Papert, *op. cit.*

24.   Brod, *op. cit.*

3

THE ELECTRONIC COTTAGE

Watching masses of peasants scything a field three hundred years ago, only a madman would have dreamed that the time would soon come when the fields would be depopulated, when people would crowd into urban factories to earn their daily bread. And only a madman would have been right. Today it takes an act of courage to suggest that our biggest factories and office towers may, within our lifetimes, stand half empty, reduced to use as ghostly warehouses or converted into living space. Yet this is precisely what the new mode of production makes possible: a return to cottage industry on a new, higher, electronic basis, and with it a new emphasis on the home as the center of society.

Alvin Toffler
The Third Wave

The computer is beginning to have an important influence on the way we work. For the past 250 years, since the Industrial Revolution began, a growing percentage of the adult population in the United States has considered it normal to spend their waking hours in centralized factories or offices, carrying out their tasks under the watchful eyes of a supervisor. But for a growing number of workers in the United States, this is no longer true; these people work at home. Or, as I am doing this very moment, they work in airplanes while the pilot awaits permission to taxi down the runway.

They do their work, of course, on computers. Mine happens to be an Epson PX-8 "Geneva" computer, a machine popular (in 1985) with writers and traveling businesspeople. When I return home at the end of a three-day business trip, I will have accomplished three days' work, the results of which will be stored on one or more small tape cassettes like the ones used on portable dictation machines. My work (this chapter and the next two of this book) will then be "uploaded" onto an IBM PC, and then "downloaded" into the Apple Macintosh that I am using to prepare the manuscript. Without this marvelous technology, I would have spent those hours on the airplane staring out the window or reading a spy thriller. I miss reading the spy thrillers, but I am more than compensated by the knowledge that I no longer have to spend so much time working in a "classical" office.

To understand this new form of working, which is also known as telecommuting, we must examine several key issues:

- Who are the people who participate in the electronic cottage industry?

- Why are they attracted to it? What are the benefits?

- Why do employers find it attractive?

- What are the problems and disadvantages?

- Will the trend continue?

THE PARTICIPANTS
IN THE COTTAGE INDUSTRY

As I pointed out in the Preface, the United States (like most other Western countries) has moved out of the Industrial Revolution and is well into the Information Revolution. We work with words, with ideas, with paper, or with information transmitted from one computer to another computer. When we examine the computer industry in Chapter 23, we will see that the computer industry itself represented about 8 percent of the GNP in 1985; but the information processing industry—which includes the people whose job is to produce, transmit, disseminate, digest, analyze, and consume information—accounted for 60 to 80 percent of the GNP. Because computers are so heavily involved in this information processing business, a large number of white-collar workers are becoming familiar with computers. Indeed, 50 percent of white-collar workers will have their own personal computers, or will have direct access to a mainframe computer by 1990.

All of this lays the foundation for the electronic cottage. Modern businesses depend on information processing; even small businesses carry out their information processing on computers today. The information itself is stored on a computer disk and can be accessed by anyone who has (a) a computer, or a computer terminal, and (b) a telecommunications link to the central computer that houses the organization's data and that acts as a switching station, permitting access to other individuals.

And since personal computers are now so small, so cheap, and so portable, there is no longer any need to carry out the information processing in a centralized office. The computer I am using right now weighs less than five pounds. It is battery-powered and runs for eight hours without recharging. It fits comfortably into my briefcase, and it has a telephone hookup (a modem) that makes it possible for me to connect to my office computer (or any other computer) from any telephone in the world.[1] The entire machine costs less than a thousand dollars. If I had been willing to spend around $2,500, I could have purchased a far more powerful machine (the Hewlett-Packard Portable, or the Data General One, or the Kaypro 2000) that also has built in spreadsheet facilities, IBM-compatible software, a larger screen, and more memory. But I'll wait two years, and by then that technology will have dropped in price considerably. . . .

Admittedly, I am somewhat of a computer fanatic—but so are more and more people. A recent survey in the July 1985 issue of *Creative Computing* indicated that over a third of the readers who had a personal computer had more than one. Personal computers are spreading like mushrooms after a rainstorm.

With this proliferation of personal computers, a new category of worker is beginning to appear: the cottage industry worker. He or she fits into one of the following categories:

---

[1] I exaggerate slightly. I actually had to buy a second modem to use the telecommunication linkup from London, and I've never considered it in Brazil. Australia was O.K. but expensive, and Canada (Halifax, to be precise) was O.K. but primitive: the operator had to consult another human operator to find the long-distance toll rate from Halifax to New York City.

- A freelance person who works on a fee basis for clients.

- A "moonlighter" who works at a normal job during the day, but who spends his evenings writing novels, writing computer programs, copyediting books, etc.

- An entrepreneur who, perhaps with his or her spouse, has decided to leave the safe, comfortable, boring office life to start a new company.

- A normal employee who works on a salaried basis for a normal company, but who is not required to spend five days per week in the office.

There are examples of each of these categories in many different professions in the United States. The freelance contractor might be a computer programmer, or a technical writer, or a copyeditor, or a typist (usually known today as a word processor), or a market research consultant, a lawyer, etc. He bills his client on an hourly basis, or a daily basis, or at the end of a project. He may visit his client at the beginning of a project or during occasional periods requiring face-to-face discussions, but much of the work is done at home, or on an airplane, or wherever it is convenient. And much of the communication with his client (including the billing) takes place via a computer-to-computer linkup.

The moonlighter operates in much the same way, but his work is usually a sideline intended to augment his normal salary. Since the extracurricular work is done typically in the evenings and weekends, it is all the more desirable to do it at home; the availability of computers in the home and at the client's office makes all of this much more efficient than ever before.

The entrepreneur is the same kind of person that has been starting businesses in America for the past 200 years: someone driven by greed, ego, or a dozen other reasons to build a business of his own. He may be the freelancer whose business has grown so large that he finds it necessary to hire additional help; he may be the moonlighter who finds that he can get enough work to support him, and that the normal job is no longer necessary. Or she may be someone who drops out of the normal office environment. The computer may be the basis for the new business (e.g., for a software company or a software consulting firm), or it may be a crucial tool for the business (e.g., a computer-aided design system for an architectural company, or a tax-preparation software package for an accounting firm), or it may simply be a general-purpose business machine that does all the things for the small company that a mainframe does for a larger company. This last point is important. The fact that powerful personal computer systems cost only a few thousand dollars has made it easier to start a small company and succeed than ever before because the entrepreneur can automate his accounting procedures, automate his inventory control, explore business alternatives with spreadsheet packages, and generally make much smarter decisions than an entrepreneur (who typically has no business experience) was able to do ten years ago.[2]

The last category is the least obvious, but the most important in the long run: the normal employee who continues working for the same employer (for the same weekly salary), but who finds it desirable and practical to spend a portion of his working time outside the office. Such employees are not usually identified as a separate category of worker, but they are definitely participants in the cottage industry revolution.

All of these are important categories, and they may become more important in the future—depending largely, I think, on how quickly large business organizations react to this phenomenon. If a large business allows its employees to function as freelancers, or moonlighters, or entrepreneurs (or, to use a currently popular term, "intrapreneurs") in the manner described above, then it will be able to keep its employees and prosper. But if it does not, then large business organizations will stagnate, and there will be a fundamental industrial shift toward small companies and self-employed people.

Thus, it will be important to watch the actions of Big Business over the next five to ten years to see whether they acknowledge the

---

[2] However, as we will see in Chapter 17, small companies are not yet using PCs as aggressively as large companies. Only 23.9 percent of companies with one to nineteen employees are using PCs, while 85.4 percent of companies with more than 1,000 employees are using PCs.

presence of the electronic cottage. Later in this chapter, I will discuss some of the advantages that Big Business can enjoy with this new mode of work; but first let's explore why employees think so highly of it.

ADVANTAGES OF
THE ELECTRONIC COTTAGE

For the worker, the advantages of the electronic cottage industry are numerous. They include the following:

- The opportunity to make more money.

- Better working conditions.

- Better computer support.

- More flexible working hours . . . and days . . . and weeks.

- Fewer interruptions.

- More opportunity to satisfy both personal and professional careers.

- Less time wasted on travel to and from the office.

- Tax advantages.

Let's deal with each of these in turn. The opportunity to make more money is obviously something that is attractive to many workers. But how can this be? Quite simply, freelancers and moonlighters and entrepreneurs are often able to charge higher fees for their services than each could as a normal employee. This may be because the large organization finds it difficult or impolitic to recognize the worker's superior talent and reward him appropriately. Or it may be because the worker is willing to work long hours if he is paid for each hour, while the large organization either (a) expects those long hours without any additional compensation, or (b) doesn't have enough work to require long hours. The large organization and the freelancer/moonlighter/entrepreneur also understand—even if only implicitly—the tradeoff between risk and reward. The large organization offers stability (or at least it claims to); it offers a pension plan; it offers insurance benefits and a variety of other nonsalary (and often untaxed) forms of compensation; in return, it tends to pay a lower salary. The individual working on his own often doesn't need or want those benefits, especially if he or she is young and single, and entirely uninterested in the subject of insurance and pensions.

In some cases, the freelancer/moonlighter/entrepreneur is simply taking advantage of the supply-and-demand relationships in the marketplace. In the computer industry, for example, there is currently an acute shortage (which we will discuss in more detail in Chapter 28) of experienced, talented computer programmers and systems analysts; consequently, there is often an opportunity for an employee to quit his salaried job and return to work in the same office the next morning as a consultant—having perhaps doubled his compensation in the process.

Of course, not everyone needs or wants more compensation. (I know that sounds un-American, but it's true.) In some cases, an older, experienced worker finds that his children have grown and that he no longer needs the same high level of income; nor does he need the same level of stress. Perhaps he would rather work a little less and spend more time pursuing hobbies. Or there may be the rare case where a worker has made a fortune in some unrelated area—real estate, horse racing, the stock market, drug smuggling, or a lucky draw at the lottery—and he doesn't need to work at all.

But this doesn't apply to most people. The reason for the lack of interest in more income is based on something else: high taxes. Many professional workers are part of a two-income family. Both husband and wife work, and their combined income is sufficient for two cars, three TV sets, and a variety of other expensive toys (including, of course, the personal computer). They don't really need a 10 percent increase in their income, especially when they realize that the city, county, state, and federal government will take 90 percent of it away. What's the point of working harder for that raise?

This brings up the interesting possibility of a tradeoff between time and money, a tradeoff which Big Business typically does not offer its employees today, but which is fairly easy to manage as a freelancer or moonlighter or entrepreneur. Look at it this way: suppose your boss called you in at the end of the year and said to you, "Gwendolyn (or Marvin), you've done a terrific job for us this past year. We're going to give you the maximum possible raise, which is 10 percent. Alternatively, you can work 10 percent fewer days."

Given such a choice, what fool would take the money? Ten percent fewer working days is five weeks of additional vacation per year—and it's tax free. (At least it is in 1985: the government hasn't gotten around to taxing people for their vacation time. Maybe they will now. Maybe I shouldn't be pointing this out.) Ten percent more money, even for a family making a combined income of $100,000 per year, works out to $3,000 to $4,000 after taxes, and that's only an extra $60 per week. For a young clerical person making $15,000 per year and trying to maintain a social life while paying the rent, $60 may be significant—it may mean spending an extra night per week at the disco. But for a successful professional couple in their thirties or forties, it's nowhere nearly as significant as the opportunity to escape the office for an extra five weeks. For a resident of New York City, it means being able to get out of New York City (which no New Yorker will publicly admit wanting to do, but which every New Yorker desperately wishes to do from mid-July until after Labor Day when pollution and humidity once again return to bearable levels).

Your boss probably never gave you an offer like the one above. But if you were a cottage industry worker, it would come with the territory. When you finish a project for a client, you can decide whether or not to take a week off before taking on the next project. This oversimplifies the situation, of course, but it is nonetheless true that a cottage industry worker has much more control over his time and his income, or at least the tradeoff between the two, than does a normal salaried employee.

And there are tax advantages that generally compensate for the loss of insurance and pensions that the big companies offer. Having a legitimate office in one's home makes it possible to deduct a variety of expenses; the IRS is instantly suspicious of such deductions, but they are allowable for the cottage industry worker. Indeed, even the personal computer becomes a legitimate business deduction! And the cottage industry worker generally has a lot more flexibility when it comes to setting up his own pension plan and insurance benefits than does a normal salaried employee. There is no reason, of course, why Big Business couldn't offer this flexibility, but it usually doesn't . . . at least not in 1985.

Aside from the financial advantages, the other major benefit enjoyed by the cottage industry worker is quality of life. Again, I will admit that I oversimplify the situation sometimes. Some Big Business companies have wonderful office facilities and a variety of employee benefits that actually make the "womb to tomb" employment prospect very attractive; and it is true that many cottage industry workers have to put up with less than pleasant working conditions while they try to get themselves established.

Nevertheless, it is difficult to imagine that any white-collar worker's office-at-home could be less pleasant than the vast majority of office environments that I have visited around the United States. Muzak blares through loudspeakers; the noise level of typewriters and people and telephones makes normal conversation nearly impossible, or conversely, the office has the noise level of a morgue, and one is afraid to speak above a whisper. Desks look as if they were inherited from the Civil War; office supplies are nonexistent, or are doled out by Keepers of the Paper Clips as if they were national treasures. Decent food is nowhere to be found, and the Coke machine never works. Anyone caught even thinking of having a beer at lunch, or sneaking a look at the latest *Playboy/Playgirl*, is summarily dismissed. And for this we spend two hours a day shlepping through traffic jams? Any manager who thinks that such thoughts and opinions are not zipping through the brain cells of his workers every day should have his own brain cells examined. Thirty years of Muzak may have turned his brain cells into mush.

A cottage industry worker can choose his own furniture; he can choose whether or not to have a beer at lunch, and he can read whatever magazine he wants to during his coffee break. He presumably lives in a house that pleases him, more or less, and he presumably chose the furniture that he uses for his work. He chooses his own art, or lack of it, and he can decide whether to listen to Muzak, Beethoven, the Beatles, Madonna, or nothing at all.

Assuming that he has sufficient willpower, he can also refuse to answer the phone or the doorbell, and thus achieve freedom from interruptions—unless there are other members of the family roaming around. Most American houses and apartments are pretty quiet places, at least from 8:00 A.M. until 4:00 P.M., when the kids get home from school.

In addition to all of this, there's a good chance that the personal computer at home is better than the computer support in the office environment. This will gradually change over the next five years, but today many office workers use "dumb" terminals connected to a centralized mainframe computer that is desperately trying to deal with hundreds of other such terminals simultaneously. The result is often an annoyingly slow response time: when one hits the "enter" key on the keyboard (a nearly universal signal to the computer, meaning "Hey, I've told you something and I'm waiting for an answer!") Ten or fifteen seconds may go by before the computer responds. Meanwhile, the worker has begun daydreaming about how nice it would be at home where the powerful personal computer, having nobody else to serve, responds instantly. Again I oversimplify: there are times when the worker needs the immense computational power of the mainframe (though that can be had by making the personal computer act as if it were a mere dumb terminal, and connecting via telephone lines to the mainframe in the office); and there are more and more "smart" terminals and personal computers appearing in the office environment.

WHY THE EMPLOYER
LIKES THE COTTAGE INDUSTRY

It's not just the workers who enjoy this new mode of working; enlightened employers are also realizing a number of benefits:

- **Access to skilled workers who might not otherwise be available**, such as physically handicapped people, or mothers with young children. Employers are especially appreciative of this when they have lost a full-bodied, full-time worker because of pregnancy, an accident, or because the spouse moves away. With telecommuting (or "homeworking" as the British call it), it is possible to continue employing someone even if he/she lives hundreds of miles away.

- **A reduced demand for scarce, expensive office space.** Office space is a major expense for many organizations in high-cost urban areas; rents of $50 to $60 per square foot are not unusual. For other companies, office space is a "fixed" resource that cannot be expanded: they have what they have, and any increase in staff has to fit into the existing space. Since a major premise of the cottage industry is that they prefer their own cottage to the corporate office, the problem can be minimized.

- **An opportunity to make short-term commitments for staff use**, rather than lifetime obligations to a normal employee. Hiring a full-time employee may mean budget preparations for pensions, insurance, and other benefits; a cottage industry person can be hired for a one-month period, with no strings attached. In many companies, it is not the hiring of the full-time person that causes the problems; it is the difficulty of firing them when they are no longer needed, or when they are deemed incompetent. This will no doubt be considered a union-busting statement by some readers, but one cannot ignore the benefit that employers see in this aspect of the cottage industry.

- **Higher productivity and more motivation** on the part of the worker, for all of the reasons discussed earlier. A pilot study comparing the productivity of cottage industry workers for a clerical position in a company—data entry, order entry, insurance claim processing, etc.—showed productivity gains of 15 to 20 percent or more. Recent experiments by Control Data, Blue Cross/Blue Shield, and Electronic Services Unlimited showed productivity increases ranging from 35 percent to 50 percent.[1]

- **Reduced costs associated with reduced cost of travel.** If the worker has to drive to the office, or use expensive public transportation, someone has to pay—and it is usually the employer, who must offer high enough wages to offset the worker's transportation costs. If the cottage industry worker stays at home, nobody pays for any transportation. The offsetting cost is that of the telephone line and electrical power that connect the worker's PC to the rest of the world.

- **More efficient use of staff resources during periods of bad weather**, when a large portion of the day would normally be consumed with the misery of getting to and from the office. Commuting takes up two to three hours per day even in normal weather for many urban and suburban residents; it can take four to six hours in bad weather. Cottage industry workers invest that time in more productive ways—either working or relaxing with their children who have been kept home from school.

PROBLEMS WITH THE COTTAGE INDUSTRY

It would be unrealistic to stop at this point without pointing out that there are problems and disadvantages to the new mode of work that I have outlined. But when people talk about the problems, it is often with the perspective that it is an all-or-nothing proposition. Thus, prospective cottage industry workers say, "Oh my God . . . do you mean I'll never be able to go into an office and see real adults again? I'm going to be stuck at home forever?" And managers will say, "Do you really think that I would trust Harry or Wilma to sit at home and work unsupervised day after day?"

The answer to all of this is: it makes sense for some people and not for others. It makes sense sometimes, depending on the nature of the work we're doing (i.e., when we need to be able to concentrate, and/or when we don't require interactions with others), and it doesn't make sense other times. A manager might trust one of his people to spend one afternoon a month working at home on a computer, but he might trust another worker to work at home four days a week, with one day in the office to participate in staff meetings.

Two different surveys provide an interesting illustration of the different attitudes toward the electronic cottage. A study by McClintock[2] pointed out that male telecommuters outnumber females by two to one, and that women are three times more likely than men to work in nonprofessional telecommuter jobs; it also pointed out that most telecommuters spend more time with their families, and enjoy working at home because they can set their own hours. A different study by Honeywell Technalysis[3] indicated that 56 percent of the knowledge workers in large corporations would continue going into the office every day even if they had telecommunications technology available, while 36 percent preferred the option of working half-time at home and half-time in the office, and only 7 percent preferred working full-time at home. The Honeywell survey went on to point out that younger workers preferred telecommuting more than older workers, and that female workers were substantially more willing to work at home than male workers; higher-paid employees (those earning over $55,000 per year) expressed a higher preference for work in the office than lower-paid people.

So, with this in mind, let me summarize some of the problems that have been encountered, which will justifiably slow down the spread of the cottage industry:

- Managers are often worried that they won't be able to supervise their workers effectively if they aren't within sight.

- There is a concern that freelancers, moonlighters, and entrepreneurs may not have the same degree of loyalty and understanding of the organization's needs as a full-time employee.

- In some types of work, security considerations make the manager reluctant to allow his people to work at home with confidential data. The manager also worries about the risks involved with allowing remote telephone access to his mainframe computer.

- Some workers don't like their homes or their family, and prefer to be as far away from them as possible.

- Other workers get lonely, and complain that they need the informal interchange of ideas with co-workers.

- Still others find that they gain weight rapidly because of frequent trips to the refrigerator.

- Some find that they lack the discipline to work if the boss isn't physically present. Others find that they lack the discipline to stop working because the work day is no longer so well defined and because the distinction between office and home blurs.

- There are insurance considerations that neither the worker nor the employer/client thinks about in many cases. If the worker's computer catches on fire while he is doing client work on his computer at home, who is liable for the damages? If part or all of the computer equipment is provided by the client and it gets stolen (or breaks), who is liable?

- Union problems: unions object to the idea of clerical people working at home, fearing that employers will exploit them.[4] This kind of union concern began several years ago when other industries (especially the garment and textile industries) began offering homeworking options to their workers, but it has escalated recently with the proliferation of data entry and word processing cottage industry work.

- Similarly, there are sometimes tax problems. If the freelancer has only one client, and that client used to be the worker's normal employer, the IRS will consider the new relationship to be a sham; it will insist that the employer withhold taxes from the freelancer just as it does for all other employees.

- Over and above everything else, people intuitively feel that such a major cultural change will bring trauma and unforeseen problems. Most of us are very used to the office environment—older people more than younger workers—but from childhood we have seen TV shows and movies that have prepared our young psyches for life in the office. Nobody has prepared us for life in the cottage.

Many of these problems are legitimate, and they may preclude the use of a cottage industry approach for some people, some companies, and even some industries. But many of the problems are just excuses. For example, the manager who complains that he won't be able to effectively supervise his worker if the worker is not physically present is making quite a confession: he is effectively saying that the only thing he can manage is the worker's physical presence (along with what researcher Charles McClintock at Carnegie Mellon University calls "social cues"—neat appearance, proper dress, good manners, etc.).[5]

And the manager who worries about the lack of loyalty of the freelancer is generally making excuses. Freelancers can be just as loyal as anyone else; frequently more so, since they are in business for themselves, and they are often more sympathetic to such client problems as cash flow than are employees. The loyalty of full-time employees runs the gamut from downright betrayal to mortgaging a house for the sake of the company.

Security issues are a legitimate concern for some industries, especially given the rather primitive level of computer security today. I expect this problem to be solved technologically within the next five years for all but the most sensitive military applications, but whether or not one wants to trust the good intentions of people working at home is another matter altogether. Once again, security problems can occur with full-time employees working under close scrutiny in the office. Indeed, most of the classic computer crimes over the past ten years have been exactly of this sort. There are precious few incidents in the real world caused by "hackers" like the young hero in the movie *War Games*.

THE TRENDS

In 1985, estimates of the number of people working with computers in an environment outside the office range from 100,000[6] to 2 million[7]. Nobody is quite sure, because it's not the sort of thing that many people have looked at closely yet. But even if the larger figure is accurate, it represents only 2 percent of the working population of the United States.

However, a trend in motion tends to stay in motion until something explicitly stops it. Personal computer hardware and software will continue to improve, as we will see in later chapters of this book, thus making it more and more practicable to work at home. Telecommunication technology will also improve, making it more and more economical to communicate with a distant office mainframe. I have not seen any optimistic reports suggesting that our problems of traffic congestion and mass transit failures will get any better over the next ten years, so the problems of commuting to work are likely to stay bad and get worse. I must admit that there is a growing awareness of the importance of good office design and ergonomically designed office furniture; maybe the bleak picture I painted above of the typical American office will be less valid in ten years.

Meanwhile, the cost of energy remains a short-term mystery. The price of oil goes up and down as the moods of OPEC ministers go up and down. It is possible that the cost of transportation will decrease over the next five to ten years, but it's just as possible that the price of oil will increase dramatically. At this point, the energy consumption of a personal computer and appropriate telecommunication facilities is approximately twenty-nine times cheaper than the cost of driving to and from work, and approximately eleven times cheaper than normal mass transit (whatever that is; we don't have any such thing where I live in New York City), according to a classic study by Jack Nilles of workers in Los Angeles.[8]

The significance of this savings should not be underestimated. If 12 to 15 percent of the American workers who presently commute to work could be transformed into telecommuters, we would entirely eliminate the need for imported oil in the United States, according to Alvin Toffler.[9] A study in *Transportation Quarterly* in 1982 forecast that if half of all U.S. office workers worked in neighborhood office centers by 1990 (which is an overly optimistic forecast, in my opinion), 238,000 barrels of oil per day would be saved.

All of this leads to a consensus among several people observing the situation: by the early 1990s, between 10 percent and 20 percent of the work force will be spending part or all of their time working at home on their own computers somewhere outside the traditional office environment.

This poses both an opportunity and a potential crisis for Big Business. I firmly believe that young workers will, over the next five to ten years, gradually come to expect a cottage industry work-style to be as much a right as the other benefits they expect from a company. Indeed, as discussed above, having one's own personal computer at home is probably much more important than a company-paid life insurance plan or retirement fund: it ranks right up there with stock options. So a company that refuses to consider this new kind of work arrangement runs an increasing risk that the more talented young workers will shrug their shoulders and go to work for a more enlightened company across the street.

Alvin Toffler summarizes the potential long-term impact of the electronic cottage most eloquently:

> The leap to a new production system in both manufacturing and the white-collar sector, and the possible breakthrough to the electronic cottage, promise to change all the existing terms of debate, making obsolete most of the issues over which men and women today argue, struggle, and sometimes die.
>
> We cannot know if, in fact, the electronic cottage will become the norm of the future. Nevertheless, it is worth recognizing that if as few as 10 to 20 percent of the work force as presently defined were to make this historic transfer over the next 20 to 30 years, our entire economy, our cities, our ecology, our family structure, our values, and even our politics would be altered almost beyond our recognition.
>
> It is a possibility—a plausibility, perhaps—to be pondered.

Alvin Toffler
The Third Wave

CONCLUSION

After reading through this chapter, you may be wondering what its relevance is in your life. To answer this, you must answer three related questions about your working environment:

- How much of my work could I practicably consider doing out of the office, away from the people I normally see on a day-to-day basis?

- How much of my work do I want to do out of the office?

- Do the computer facilities exist in my company for this kind of work, or could they readily be acquired?

After considering these questions, you may decide that telecommuting is not for you. Your job may require that you be physically present. You may find the thought of isolated work at home unappealing; or you may find that your company's mainframe computer does not facilitate remote communication with personal computers.

Beware of falling into the all-or-nothing trap. Make sure you consider the questions above in a part-time context. For example, "Would it make sense for me to work at home one day a week?" or "What are the tradeoffs of working at home Tuesday and Thursday afternoons when the children get out of school early?"

If you find that the idea of some homeworking does make sense, then the next step is to see whether your boss will allow it. (If you are a manager yourself, you should consider this same issue on behalf of your subordinates.) No doubt some problems and questions will arise—e.g., the issues of staff coordination, insurance, and security mentioned earlier in the chapter—and you must examine these questions calmly and rationally with your manager. If your manager has serious reservations, suggest experimenting with telecommuting on a trial basis in a limited way.

If the idea of telecommuting strongly appeals to you, but your boss (and/or the entire organization) is dead set against it, perhaps the time has come to seriously examine your employment situation. Perhaps you should change jobs. Perhaps you should change your employment status to that of contractor, in which case you can negotiate (or dictate) different working conditions. Or perhaps you should wait a year and try again.

However, do not make the mistake of assuming that this is all a fad.

References for Chapter 3

1. "It's Rush Hour for Telecommuting," *Business Week*, January 23, 1984.

2. Lang, Sylvia, "Computers Interface Job, Home," *USA Today*, June 3, 1985.

3. "There's No Place Like Home?" Survey sponsored by Honeywell Technalysis, October 1984.

4. "Homeworking Trend Raises Union Fears," *Computing*, September 5, 1985.

5. Lang, *op. cit.*

6. Olson, Margrethe H., "Remote Office Work: Changing Work Patterns in Space and Time," *Communications of the ACM*, March 1983.

7. Lang, *op. cit.*

8. Eder, Peter F., "Telecommuters: The Stay-at-Home Work Force of the Future," *The Futurist*, June 1983.

9. Toffler, Alvin, *The Third Wave*, New York: William Morrow and Company, 1980; Bantam Books, 1981.

4

THE NETWORK NATION

Some day we will build up a world telephone system making necessary to all peoples the use of a common language, or common understanding of languages, which will join all of the peoples of the earth into one brotherhood . . . When by the aid of science and philosophy and religion, man has prepared himself to receive the message, we can all believe there will be heard throughout the earth, a great voice coming out of the ether, which will proclaim, "Peace on earth, good will toward men."

General John Carty
Chief Engineer, AT&T, 1907 [1]

It is hard to imagine how different the lives of our great-grandparents must have been from the lives we lead today. So much of it is different, of course—the nature of work, the life span, the lower infant mortality rate, the level of affluence, the technology of transportation—that it is almost like comparing the cultures of two different planets. But there is one aspect that is particularly important: the technology of communication.

As little as 150 years ago, person-to-person communication basically took place in one of two forms: direct, face-to-face conversation or handwritten letters. The art of letters was cultivated by those who had the time, money, and education; men and women often spent several hours—over the course of several days or weeks —composing and refining their thoughts and observations of some event that had touched their lives, and which they wanted to communicate to someone far away ("far" meaning, in many cases, only 100 miles distant, but in other cases across the country or on the other side of an ocean). But how would those words be understood by someone receiving them several weeks later—someone who no longer had access to the immediacy of the event, someone for whom the smell and the sound and the thousand subtle nuances had to be conveyed by the scratchings of a quill pen on pages of parchment? Imagine, for example, how a young lady named Emily, living in the wilderness territory of Wisconsin, must have felt in 1861 when she received the following letter from her fiance, my great-great-grandfather Daniel Webster Prentice, who was an eighteen-year-old medical intern in Washington, D.C.:

Washington D.C. July 22, 1861

Dearest Emily,

I received your letter yesterday at the same time I posted one for you, and so waited till this evening to write again. Thank you for the beautiful rose bud that you gathered for me, on the 4th of July, to be sure! I shall take good care of it, though it does not go into <u>our</u> collection but into my drawer. Neither have I collected any flowers since the last you sent,—have been but seldom in the country and then had no way to carry them. You say I must describe "home scenes" to you,—I don't know how—never attempted it, and you are so hard to please that I am afraid to attempt until you tell me how—describe a "home scene" next time you write and I will try. I do not think you were very goodnatured to tell me that "everything else" I have written was uninteresting "of course," after I have written about twenty letters! If you meant to scold me, it is all lost because you did not say what you were scolding me for, and I do not feel conscious of deserving it—perhaps it was something in that letter that "required no answer." If it was, I don't remember it.

Please write me <u>good natured</u> letters—I need them now and will try to deserve them. You are not teasing me when you (say you) do not expect to be home in six times three months—you would not be so cruel as to say it without you had a reason for it—though I can see none. Ma says positively you <u>shall</u> come home in the fall—she only wishes she had never let you go;—and though the Dr. keeps his own counsel, Ma says she <u>knows</u> he will not consent to let you stay.

So, you see, my dear, not being wanted at home will be no excuse for staying away and I shall still anticipate seeing you in three months. I only fear one thing and that is your "folks" moving away.

You know the war is not far off and there is a possibility of Congress being moved. There was a terrible, <u>terrible</u> battle in Virginia yesterday about twenty five miles from here, the greatest battle ever fought in this country,—the lowest estimate of those killed is five thousand of the federal troops, the highest ten thousand, so that the truth is probably between the numbers.

The place is called "Bull's Run" about three miles this side Manassas Junction, and is mostly strongly fortified with entrenchments and masked batteries. The place furnished water to the Confederate Army and Gen. McDowell thought if he could get possession, they would be forced to retire from the Junction. The slaughter was awful, the number killed on both sides seems to be about the same judging from the reports from those engaged.

The wounded, dying and dead have been coming into the city all day today and those escaped come staggering almost dead with fatigue, some barefooted, without coats, guns, knapsacks and cartridge boxes —everything thrown away in their haste to get away.

In spite of the rain, the avenue has been crowded today with people seeking news—groups on almost every corner with a soldier in the midst telling of the battle. The second R.I. Regiment was almost cut to pieces and of the N.Y. Five Zouaves only three hundred are yet accounted for, they charged a battery in the woods and when nearly up to it, the masked battery in the woods just at their side, opened upon them and mowed them down like grass.

Of a Connecticut regiment only <u>four</u> men are accounted for, a Captain and three privates. The Captain thought he alone of the whole Regiment was left until he met the men.

What I tell you is what I have heard from the soldiers engaged in the battle. The 69th and 79th N.Y. Reg'ts suffered severely as in fact did every regiment engaged. The Confederates had the best arms of every kind and knew how to use them too. I heard an Ohio officer say that he saw them fire upon a regiment advancing upon a battery and the men fell like leaves—he never saw such an awful sight in his life. The road was strewn with baggage, wagons, horses and men, spades, picks, knapsacks, canteens and muskets lying around in every direction. . . .

. . . You asked me to picture home scenes, but you had little idea, dearest, that you would hear such news from so near home. But, for all, the city is as quiet as can be expected under the circumstances, the weather has cleared off and the tired soldiers are asleep almost at every corner "down town". There was much fear expressed yesterday evening that Beauregard was coming into the city, and some talk of militia being ordered out, but I have not heard anything of it yet—they would be of no use, since they are not drilled, only be in the way of other troops. If it had been Davis' intention to take the city, he would have had it by this morning, while our troops were all exhausted. As I said before, the rain has stopped so we did not get wet going to Georgetown today.—I didn't deserve the scolding you gave me for taking Charley out in the rain—he went on business for Pa and I went to oblige him.

So my dear, you may apologize and thank me for not scolding you for writing such a <u>cross</u> letter—perhaps I should but for other more important matters which I would have let you read in the papers, if you had not said once you had rather 'hear them from me rather than a stranger', though everything else is "uninteresting." . . . [1]

Words like these carry the sound of battle and the cries of the dying across the void of a hundred years—but what could it have meant to a young woman a thousand miles away in 1861? There was no immediacy. There was no way for her to say, "Wait a minute—tell me that part again. I didn't understand it." There were no pictures to reinforce the words. Most of all, there was no interaction. The communication took place in one direction at a time.

Even when physical proximity allowed for two-way conversation, society generally had fairly strict standards for civilized people to follow. A chance encounter on the street might permit one level of conversation, but not others; planned encounters—e.g., a luncheon date—required several exchanges of notes, delivered back and forth by messenger boys over a period of several days, to determine a convenient time and date for two ladies or gentlemen to meet. Under certain well-prescribed conditions—e.g., during the Christmas season—there were certain hours of the day when a family was expected to receive visitors, presumably of the proper class and social level. But unexpected visits were a tenuous affair: a visitor presented a calling card to the butler or maid, whereupon he might or might not find that the master or mistress of the house was officially at home and in a mood to receive him.

What a different social culture we have developed since then! Now, when the telephone rings, we all jump like Pavlovian dogs! No matter how indisposed, no matter how certain we might be that the caller is the last person on earth we want to talk to, it takes an

---

[1] The letter goes on like this for several more pages . . . And there were several other letters indicating that Emily made Webster's life quite miserable until she finally returned from Wisconsin and married him in 1865. Years later, Webster became one of the very first in Washington, D.C., to acquire a telephone, helping to usher in a new era of communications.

enormous effort of will to avoid responding to that strident ring. Even with an answering machine—one of the greatest inventions of the past decade!—it is only the most steel-willed individual who can resist listening in to see whether the phone really should have been answered.[2]

The telephone is, of course, only one of the forms of communication we depend on today; there are also television (in all its myriad forms), telex, radio, and the movie. All of these media permit rapid, almost instantaneous, dissemination of information from one part of the world to one or more far-distant parts of the world. The scale of this information transfer is often awesome—as illustrated by the "Live Aid" concert of July 13, 1985, in which simultaneous concerts in Philadelphia and London were beamed by sixteen satellite systems to nearly 2 billion people in an effort to raise relief funds for a starving population in Africa.

Indeed, the "Live Aid" concert was a shining example of one positive aspect of modern information technology: it permitted a more horizontal transfer of information between members at each level of an organization (or society), rather than the vertical transfer so often found in an authoritarian organization. The vertical approach is often characterized by such terms as chain of command, the implication being that information is transferred (and filtered in a variety of conscious and unconscious ways) to successively higher and higher levels of authority, with each level of authority deciding whether or not to retransmit the information (perhaps in some modified form) to other levels beneath it. Thus, in Figure 4.1, subordinate A passes information to manager X (which may be true information, or perhaps the information that A wants X to have, or the information that A thinks X wishes to hear); X then decides whether to pass this information back down to subordinates B and C. This scheme—regardless of whether one thinks it

---

[2] It is interesting to note that most business organizations have retained more of the formality of old-style communications. Most managers have a buffer of one or two levels of secretaries who will announce whether or not he is "away from his desk," or "gone for the day," or "in a meeting," or some other euphemism which the caller clearly understands as a polite—and perfectly acceptable—form of saying, "He's here, and you know he's here, but he really doesn't want to talk to you now. I will take a note so that he will be officially informed of your call, and he'll get back to you later."

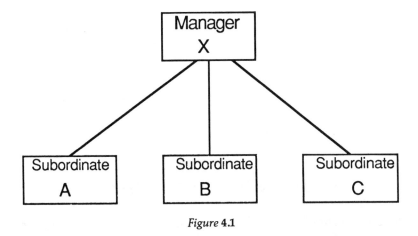

Figure 4.1

good or bad—depends on the ability of X to control the information once he gets his hands on it; it assumes that A, B, and C are unable to communicate directly with one another, either because they lack the technology, or because they have been forbidden (with a sufficiently impressive show of authority) to communicate directly with one another.

The "Live Aid" concert was the antithesis of this kind of vertical information transfer. More important, it achieved something that the vertical system has not yet in the history of the human race ever achieved: information transfer to half of the human race on an instantaneous basis. No government organized the "Live Aid" concert; no politician spoke, nor did the head of any major organized religion. Yet half of the human race watched a live, uncensored event, and was able to draw its own conclusions about a major problem of world hunger. The worldwide contribution of $65 million within forty-eight hours is one tangible measure of the impact it had. The fact that so many people shared in a human event is something more intangible, something that we do not yet know how to measure, but which history will surely record as significant.

Obviously, information technology can also have disastrous consequences if misused. It cannot be entirely neutral so long as the cameras and the broadcast circuits and microphones are under the control of human beings. Live TV coverage of a minor disturbance can create the impression of a major riot; early TV interviews with election voters can create the impression of a landslide victory for one candidate long before the polling booths are closed. With both these examples, we see another important effect of modern information technology: feedback. The act of observing a phenomenon, no matter how neutral the observer tries to be, may change the phenomenon by inciting otherwise torpid citizens to escalate a minor disturbance into a major riot, or by causing undecided voters to throw their votes in with the "apparent" victor of an election.[3]

THE EFFECT OF COMPUTERS

While the technology of telephone, television, movie camera, and radio are indeed impressive, there is one thing none of them does effectively: interactive communication between large numbers of people. Television is basically a one-way communication device: we sit, glassy-eyed and slack-jawed, and watch whatever gets beamed onto the screen. We have the freedom to change the channel or even turn off the set, but that hardly qualifies as interactive communication. Some live interview shows allow viewers to phone in their comments or questions, but the information transfer is controlled in the vertical fashion we discussed earlier: if the TV host doesn't like your question, he doesn't repeat it for the rest of the viewing audience.

Similarly, the telephone permits instantaneous, interactive conversation, but only between two people. Conference calls involving three or four people can be accomplished, though often only with the assistance of a telephone company operator. And a conference call involving a hundred people, or a thousand people, is out of the question.

All of this is changing with the widespread distribution of computers. To be fair to earlier technologies, it is the combination of the

---

[3] In the field of physics, this phenomenon is often referred to as the Heisenberg Uncertainty Principle. One cannot, according to this principle, simultaneously determine the mass and velocity of a nuclear particle: the act of observing either mass or velocity causes the other to change. Because of the instantaneous nature of modern information technology, and the feedback it generates, we now have the same principle: we cannot "observe" a social phenomenon without changing it.

computer and the telephone and (at least in countries like the United Kingdom and France) television that creates a fundamentally new form of information transfer: instantaneous, interactive communication among an arbitrarily large number of people. This is accomplished through such devices as electronic mail, electronic bulletin boards, teleconferencing, and public information utilities.

Only on occasion is the communication actually on-line, instantaneous, and interactive—but the possibility is there. Consider the possibilities when I use my personal computer, while I am writing these words, to dial a popular information utility known as The Source.[4] It is 12:04 A.M. on a Sunday morning, but I can see that there are fifteen other late-night computer adventurers who have also dialed the same computer system. I have no idea who they are, or what they are doing (they might be checking the stock market, or retrieving a list of the best Mexican restaurants in Austin, Texas, or any one of a thousand other services available from The Source), nor do I have any idea of where in North America they reside. But if I wanted to, I could send a message simultaneously to each of them;[5] indeed, I could send a message to any of roughly 100,000 subscribers to The Source.[6] We are all connected to one another; we all have the same umbilical cord.

THE FUTURE OF THE NETWORK NATION

Though television seems to us quite advanced today (because we remember its more primitive past), the combination of television, telecommunications, and computers is not at all advanced—not

---

[4] Actually, it required using my IBM PC to communicate since I am typing this manuscript on an Apple Macintosh computer, which is (currently) unable to do more than one thing at a time. With a more sophisticated computer, I could—on the same computer—type a manuscript with one hand, and communicate with The Source by typing with the other hand. If I could type with my toes, I could carry on four conversations simultaneously; and if I had the kind of "voice recognition" technology that we will discuss in Chapter 37, I could thoroughly confuse myself by trying to do five things at once.

[5] One application of this idea is that of ongoing, multiuser computer games, which I will discuss in Chapter 5.

[6] If I had chosen another popular utility, Compuserve, I would have had access to 250,000 people; in the case of the Dow Jones system, another 100,000 people. MCI Mail claims an almost equal number of subscribers; even my bank allows me to communicate electronically to other banking customers, though I have never felt the urge to do so.

yet. Developments over the next five to ten years will link all of these technologies together; the effect upon our methods of social interaction will be profound. Computer scientists like me have only the vaguest idea of the sociological ramifications of the technology we are introducing. Telecommunications specialists have a perspective based on 100 years of "classical" telephone technology, which makes them very much like army generals, always figuring out how to better fight the last war. And the television moguls have their own perspective, too; it seems based on entertainment and drama more than anything else. How all of these technologies will come together is something that none of us can predict accurately.

One thing that seems fairly certain—based on early experiences with electronic mail, public utility systems like Compuserve, and myriad electronic bulletin boards—is that there will be hundreds, possibly thousands, of small affinity groups springing up around the country. Groups of individuals who have never met one another, and probably don't know each other's true names and addresses, will communicate via telephone/computer linkups to discuss common problems, interests, or strategies for lobbying the government on some issue. Occasionally, we will see massive affinity groups coming together spontaneously; the "Live Aid" concert was only the beginning.

Where this will lead in the long run is a matter of some speculation, great debate, and an almost mystical view of new "levels of consciousness" for the human race. Psychologist Peter Russel puts it this way in *The Global Brain*:

> I would like you to come with me on a great adventure, an exploration of humanity's potential as seen through the eyes of the planet, and to share with me a vision of our evolutionary future. The journey will take us beyond this place and time, allowing us to stand back and behold humanity afresh, to consider new ways of seeing ourselves in relation to the whole evolutionary process.
>
> We shall see that something miraculous may be taking place on this planet, on this blue pearl of ours. Humanity could be on the threshold of an evolutionary leap, a leap that could occur in a flash of evolutionary time, a leap such as occurs only once in a billion years. The changes leading to this leap are taking place before our eyes—or rather behind them, within our own minds.[2]

This view, and British chemist James Lovelock's "Gaia Hypothesis" [3], provide some interesting ways of thinking of life fifty to one hundred years from now. Briefly stated, the Gaia Hypothesis suggests that the entire range of living matter on Earth, from viruses to whales, from massive redwood trees to lichen on the North Slope, plus the oceans and the air and the land surfaces, all appear to be part of a giant ecosystem able to regulate the temperature and the composition of the air, seas, and soil so as to ensure the survival of life. The notion of an ecosystem is not at all new; the notion that it is alive as an integrated whole is more radical and thought provoking. The notion that humanity, in the aggregate, might be the living brain of this massive system, is even more thought provoking. But if such a concept is to make sense, the brain "cells" need to communicate; electronic mail, videotext, and the combination of telephone, television, and computers may be the catalyst that actually causes this disparate mass of brain cells to come together and function as a single entity.

Whether the Gaia Hypothesis turns out to be anything more than a hypothesis is clearly beyond the scope of this book—and probably beyond the scope of our lifetimes. In the meantime, the kind of global communication that we can look forward to in the next five to ten years will still be a radical change for all of us.

CONCLUSION

If this chapter has had any impact on you, then my advice is very simple: join the network. Don't miss out on it; you can still join the 21st century before it arrives.

Actually, there are several different networks you can join. I recommend Compuserve and The Source because they are relatively cheap; they provide a wide, exotic range of information services; and you will immediately become part of an electronic community of 100,000 to 250,000 people. As an alternative, join the E-mail (electronic mail) network in your company. You will suddenly find yourself part of a community that carries on a nonstop communication twenty-four hours per day, seven days per week.

The second thing you must do, if this chapter has had any impact on you, is read any (or preferably all) of the books on the reference list. Russel's *The Global Brain* and Lovelock's *Gaia* will give you a perspective on humanity that you probably have never had.

References for Chapter 4

1.   Pool, Ithiel de Sola, *The Social Impact of the Telephone*, Cambridge, Mass.: MIT Press, 1977.

2.   Russel, Peter, *The Global Brain*, Los Angeles: J.P. Tarcher, Inc., 1983.

3.   Lovelock, James, *Gaia: A New Look at Life on Earth*, New York: Oxford University Press, 1979.

5

COMPUTER GAMES

Games are the most important thing ever invented, because they detach us from the current reality and allow us to create fantasies that we can partially control. This is important. It's very difficult to imagine humans without games being really human.

Alan Kay
Chief Scientist, Atari [1]

Where would we be without games? And where would the computer industry be without games? For that matter, where would any high-technology industry be without the allure of entertainment and game-playing as an enticement? Television, telephone, and automobile technology serve mankind well in a number of serious ways—but a quick look at the marketing strategy or TV commercials used to sell any products in these industries illustrates the importance of entertainment. And this is not the result of modern-day Madison Avenue advertising gurus; listen to the comments of E. J. Hall, vice president of the American Telephone and Telegraph Company in 1890:

More wonderful still is a scheme which we now have on foot, which looks to providing music on tap at certain times every day, especially at meal times. The scheme is to have a fine band perform the choicest music, gather up the sound waves, and distribute them to any number of subscribers. Thus a family, club or hotel may be regaled with the choicest airs from their favorite operas while enjoying the evening meal, and the effect will be as real and enjoyable as though the performance were actually present in the apartment. [2]

Remember that this was being presented as an application of the telephone, not the radio.

While it is true that modern computers were first introduced for reasons quite other than entertainment,[1] it is almost certainly true that you, as a consumer, would never have become interested in personal computers (or this book, probably) were it not for the influence of the entertainment industry. Before personal computers hit the marketplace, there were video games. Beginning with the primitive game of "Pong," invented by Atari founder Nolan Bushnell in 1972, we have witnessed the growth of a multibillion-dollar industry whose products have names like "Frogger," "Zork," "Adventure," "Pac-Man," and "Donkey Kong." In 1982, Americans spent $5 billion in quarters playing such games in machines around the country, and the sale of game machines reached $3.5 billion in 1983 before beginning its decline.[3]

This chapter is not about the video game industry per se, nor am I concerned about the machines that still populate the pizza parlors and shopping arcades around the country. However, I think that the gut reaction of parents (negative) and children (positive) to computer-controlled games should be an indication that there are powerful forces at work. Just as entertainment (and social games) provided much of the marketing "pizzazz" for earlier technologies, video games have certainly been a powerful force in the introduction of personal computers during the 1982-85 time frame. And it is not over yet. Radically improved computer hardware and software will make possible a level of game technology that we can barely imagine today. On the assumption that some part of the entertainment industry will foist it upon the public over the next several years, we should have some idea of what is coming and how it will affect us.

THE FASCINATION
WITH COMPUTER GAMES

Let's begin by asking why children (and some adults) are so fascinated by the computer games that we see in arcade parlors, on

---

[1] That is, unless you consider war to be a game. As we will see in Chapter 11, the major force behind the development of modern American computers was the Department of War during World War II.

Apple II and Commodore 64 computers at home, and occasionally on the mainframe display terminal in the office. Psychotherapist Craig Brod provides three reasons:

> First, players can improve their skills noticeably over a short period of time. Second, like a science fiction novel, a video game provides an alternate world in which to operate; mistakes can always be corrected, even if this calls for another quarter. Third, the games themselves adapt to the player: game speed, response time, and level of difficulty often change automatically according to how the player is faring. [4]

Brod also points out that, given a choice between playing physical sports and video games, many children prefer video games: there is no physical danger, no risk of broken arms or bruised knees. Many would argue that physical bumps and bruises are an experience that children should have. However, I think we should consider substituting video violence for physical violence for adults who need some release for their aggressions. I will return to this point below.

Video games also have a property that educators first began to notice with educational TV shows such as "Sesame Street": a rapid change of pace, so that the child only has to concentrate on a single topic for a short period of time. This stands in stark contrast to the numbingly slow pace of activity in the typical classroom. Similarly, the computer-controlled video game usually allows the action to proceed at a pace far faster—and more satisfying—than can be found in the typical sandlot baseball game, where every moment of action is surrounded by several moments of wasted time, arguments, searches for lost balls, etc.

THE BENEFITS OF COMPUTER GAMES

For reasons discussed below, many parents and educators worry about the harmful effects of computer games. Indeed, there are dangers and problems—but this does not mean that we should throw the baby out with the bath water. The fact that so many children perceive the games to be fun means that if we can include some real benefits in the game-playing process, children will accept it without resisting.[2]

Certainly, one of the largest potential benefits of computer games is that of a learning tool, as Sandra and Winston Long point out:

> . . . the games are based on the same principles—challenge, fantasy and curiosity—that motivate learning. The games provide active involvement, the option of quitting when the task goes beyond the learner's ability level, short periods of intense activity, flexible time schedules for learning, and a controllable environment. All of these are powerful factors in learning.
>
> The chance for mastery is another powerful learning component that is inherent in video games. Society has allowed young people few areas in which they can be masters. In video gaming, practice does produce mastery, the quest for which is another strong internal motivator.[5]

While nobody would argue that video games improve large motor skills of a child, it could be argued that they help develop eye, hand, and brain coordination. And they help teach the child a number of things about planning and strategy, about creative thinking, and the need to search for solutions by testing hypotheses. It teaches them about competition, about the joy of winning, and the pain of losing.

And the computer games certainly teach children something about computers. Even if they learn nothing else, they become familiar with the mechanical skills of communicating with a computer: if the game runs on their home computer, they learn how to manipulate the keyboard, how to insert a floppy disk into the computer, and how to respond to a number of otherwise incomprehensible error messages from the computer. They learn that it doesn't always work correctly and that it breaks—in short, that it is no more infallible or omnipotent than any of the other

---

[2] I worry sometimes that this sounds too Orwellian; perhaps I am showing some of my instincts as a normal parent. Very few parents can deny that they spend a significant amount of time and energy looking for innocent ways of presenting otherwise unpalatable things (food, medicine, social lessons, warm clothing, etc., etc.) in a form that makes them look like fun.

household gadgets with which they come in daily contact.[3] Even if nothing else good comes of the experience, the act of playing video games should make the computer a more familiar device when it is presented to them in other contexts.

THE DANGERS OF COMPUTER GAMES

It seems that much effort has been invested in studying all of the things that are wrong with computer games. Rather than repeat at length what every parent seems to know instinctively, I will summarize the more obvious dangers and problems:

- **Computer games can be expensive.** Even at 25 cents per game, the costs can mount rapidly; some studies have found children spending as much as $100 per month on video arcades. A video game that runs on a home computer typically costs $30 to $40, and some are much more expensive. An adequate library of computer games is thus likely to set you back several hundred dollars. I think I have invested a far larger sum of money in "action figures" (otherwise known as "dolls") and "transformers" for my two sons, but each individual toy is much less expensive than a typical computer game.

- **The cost of video games can lead to computer piracy.** If Mom and Dad won't spend $39.95 for "Donkey Kong," how is the child going to get it? Simple: make a copy of an original floppy disk purchased by a friend. This problem is obviously not restricted to computer games, but it helps foster an attitude that might lead to more serious computer "hacking" and computer crime later on. Parents are often oblivious to or tolerant of such behavior,[4] and sometimes even encourage it on the theory that "the games ought not to be so expensive."

[3] Contrast this casual acceptance of the machine with the reaction of a typical adult who is almost afraid to touch the keyboard for fear that something will break. Even veteran computer programmers wince when they see their children pounding chubby little fists on the keyboard of a personal computer; when *they* first started using computers, anything other than the lightest touch *would* break the keyboard, which would put the entire multimillion dollar machine out of action.

[4] Indeed, the child often gets the idea for all of this by watching his parents make copies of their favorite TV program on their video cassette recorder. It is understandably difficult for a child to distinguish between the copying of a TV program—something which used to be illegal, but which the TV industry finally had to admit was unstoppable—and the copying of a floppy disk.

- **Computer games can become addictive.** While many people scoff at this idea, parents will tell you of their children sitting mesmerized for hours as they play the same game over and over again. When video arcade parlors first began appearing, children throughout the United States began skipping school or work to spend hours playing the games. As an overall social phenomenon, this seems to have faded—but for individuals, it can still be an intense phenomenon.

- **Video game parlors often attract drugs and crime.** A child who plays his computer games at home has some control over his physical environment; so does the parent. But many of the newer and "sexier" computer games exist only on the arcade machines found in the pizza shops and shopping malls.[5] Anything that attracts a group of adolescents is also likely to attract some undesirable people and/or behavior; depending on the locale and the circumstances, it may be drugs, alcohol, kids from bad parts of town, etc. Whether or not this can be blamed on computer games *per se* is highly debatable; the fact that computer games are associated with this kind of social problem is a fact of life. Various small towns across America have passed ordinances outlawing video machines from pizza parlors. Twenty years ago, they outlawed pinball machines. Presumably, juke boxes were received with the same degree of enthusiasm by our grandparents' generation.

- **Computer games are sometimes used as surrogate parents.** The bored babysitter, the single parent, or anyone else who finds it

[5] The reason for this difference between the home games and the arcade games has to do with hardware technology: the video arcade machines use high-resolution display screens that provide a considerably sharper, clearer image (often two to four times sharper than the child's home computer). And the video machine often uses two or three different computers to control different aspects of the game (e.g., one computer to deal with the joystick or other input devices controlled by the player, another machine to deal with the ever-changing display screen, yet another computer to deal with the logic of the game itself, etc.). Finally, the arcade machine is likely to have a reasonably sophisticated voice synthesizer that can pronounce a variety of messages in a voice that would make Darth Vader proud; the child's home computer typically has no voice output at all.

difficult to entertain a demanding young child is sorely tempted to use television as a surrogate for direct human supervision. Now we are finding the same thing with computer games; they are (in my opinion) no worse and no better than television in this respect. Some television programs are probably far more educational than anything that I as a parent could provide; other programs would probably warp my child's personality far more than if I spent the entire hour yelling at him. Similarly, some of the more creative, educational computer games can be an intellectually enriching way for the child to spend an hour when his parent or babysitter is unwilling or unable to participate; other games will reinforce the child's growing detachment from the human race.

THE FUTURE OF COMPUTER GAMES

The generation of computer games that appeared on the market in 1982 and 1983 was dramatically more sophisticated than the pathetic game of "Pong" that Nolan Bushnell introduced to the world in 1972. Nobody would be willing to spend hours playing Bushnell's primitive version of Ping-Pong after experiencing such quasi-3D games as "Zaxxon." But it is important to remember that people played "Pong" fanatically for quite a long time until something better came along.

Similarly, it's fair to say that the wolf-packs of people playing "Pac-Man" and "Donkey Kong" have disappeared. In fact, a recent survey by *Consumer Reports* showed that the number of home computers used for games dropped from 69 percent in 1983 to 55 percent in 1985, while the number of home computers used for word processing rose from 59 percent to 85 percent in the same period.[6] But children and adults are still playing, and they will continue playing until new generations of computer games come along. It is a virtual certainty that such new games will come; this is a natural consequence of the improved computer hardware technology and computer software technology that will gradually appear over the next five to ten years. As we will see in Chapters 34 through 38, it is likely that computer hardware in the year 1999 will be approximately 1,000 to 10,000 times more powerful than the computers we are using today. The same advanced computer technology that will first be used in weapon systems and business computer systems will eventually find its way into computer games. Indeed, we began this chapter by suggesting that games may be the first commercial market for such advanced hardware.

Here are the kinds of things that we can expect:

- **Radically improved computer graphics**. Many computer games currently use very crude graphics: the icons that represent humans and aliens and spaceships are more crude than the stick figures drawn by a five-year-old child. Movies such as *The Last Starfighter*, which was introduced to the public in 1984, give some indication of the kind of sophisticated computer-generated graphics that are possible. That movie required an hour of computer time on one of the world's largest, most powerful supercomputers to create the images of space battles; within five to ten years, the same technology will be available in home computers. Among other things, this will include vividly real 3-D graphics.

- **Laser disk technology**. The graphics described above will be improved simply because more dots (or "pixels") per square inch will be shown on the screen, thus allowing higher resolution; also, more powerful computers will be able to change the composition of the pictures more quickly. But there is another approach to improved graphics: laser disk technology, in which the computer can, at microsecond speeds, selectively retrieve frames of pictures that have the kind of resolution that we expect from high-quality television sets. Early versions of laser-disk computer games began appearing in video arcades in late 1984, but they were expensive and sluggishly slow. Look for order-of-magnitude improvements in this area in the near future.

- **Dramatically improved voice output, and other sensory outputs**. At the present time, the visual dimension of computer games is barely adequate, and the audio dimension is pathetic; the dimensions of smell, taste, and touch are lacking altogether. To provide these additional sensory inputs, we may have to put the game player in an enclosed compartment (primitive versions of which already exist for the games that simulate the activities of a jet pilot or race car driver). Alternatively, we might consider attaching computer-controlled electrodes to the game player, so that appropriate signals could be fed directly to his brain. By the mid-1990s, it will certainly be technologically possible and economically feasible to surgically implant a microchip in the human hand (or nose, or elbow, or some other innocuous part of the human body) to serve as a sensory interface to other external computer systems. The possibilities seem rather ghoulish today, but will probably be accepted as commonplace by our children's children.

- **Dramatically smarter games.** Today, many computer games already exceed the ability of human players. After all, if the game depends on speed and eye-brain coordination, a human is hardly a match for even today's computers. But when the deciding factor is skillful strategy or intuition, current computers cannot necessarily win. Computers, for example, still lose to the top world-class chess players. Significantly more powerful computer hardware will give the game-playing machines more of an opportunity to "dumbly" examine moves and countermoves, strategies and counterstrategies *ad nauseam* until they find a winning move. And significantly smarter machines, using artificial intelligence technology discussed in Chapter 21, will lead to even more skillful gameplaying machines.

- **Ongoing, continuous, multiplayer games.** At the present time, a game called "Megawars" is played on an ongoing basis on the Compuserve information utility system: at any moment, between a dozen and a hundred people all over North America are engaged in a form of "Space Invaders" against one another. Each player joins one of two teams, and then cruises through the make-believe galaxy, looking for teammates with whom he can join forces to hunt for enemies. Successful "kills" eventually lead to promotions, and players eventually find themselves commanding larger, more powerful ships and fleets. The game is crude; there are no graphics, and the commands for manipulating the ships, firing at enemies, etc., are difficult to learn. But it is a beginning, and I firmly believe it is the forerunner of nationwide—indeed, even international—contests that will eventually replace the rowdy, boisterous, destructive sports contests we watch on television today. In Roman times, spectators came to the stadium to watch Christians devoured by lions; today, fans in several countries come to equally large stadiums to watch opposing soccer (football) teams mangle each other, after which the spectators mangle one another. Given the alternative of a computer game with a reasonable simulation of vision, sound, smell, and even physical pain, we may find that tomorrow's spectators stay in their living room but derive more pleasure than ever by venting their aggression upon other players a continent away. It will be a strange world, to be sure—but if entertainment continues to have the same influence on technology that it has in the past, it is a world we are likely to witness during our lifetime.

- **A wider selection of educational games.** Already many of the major publishers of software games are indicating the appropriate age range for child-oriented computer games. While many are still pure adventure games, there is and will continue to be more and more available software that actually teaches the child something useful.

References for Chapter 5

1. "A Serious Player," *Technology Illustrated*, October 1983.

2. Pool, Ithiel de Sola, *The Social Impact of the Telephone*, Cambridge, Mass.: MIT Press, 1977, page 44.

3. "Video Games Enter Technology Time Warp," *High Technology*, June 1983.

4. Brod, Craig, *Technostress*, Reading, Mass.: Addison-Wesley, 1984, page 142.

5.   Long, Sandra and Winston Long, "Rethinking Video Games," *The Futurist*, December 1984.

6.   "The Best Liked Software," *Consumer Reports*, September 1985.

6

COMPUTERIZED HOME CONTROL

> The poorest man may in his cottage bid defiance to all the forces of the Crown. It may be frail—its roof may shake—the wind may blow through it—the storm may enter—the rain may enter—but the King of England cannot enter—all his force dares not cross the threshold of the ruined tenement!
>
> William Pitt
> *Speech on the Excise Bill*

We in America no longer fear that our homes will be attacked by the king of England, but we still feel as passionately about our modest hovels as did the earl of Chatham when he made his impassioned speech to the House of Lords 200 years ago. Whether it is a one-bedroom apartment in Houston, an old farm in Vermont, a split-level ranch home in Omaha, or a brownstone in Brooklyn Heights, our home is indeed our castle. The computer offers us new ways to protect it and enhance it.

The "smart" home is still several years away for most consumers, but experimental versions can already be seen in various parts of the country. As with personal robots, which we will discuss in Chapter 9, the smart home is still largely the province of the tinkerer and hobbyist; but we can be reasonably certain that many novel features will gradually find their way into standard homes of the 1990s. This chapter provides a glimpse of such a home.

The primary uses for computers in the home are these:

- Energy conservation.

- Sentry duty.

- Maintenance of comfort in the home.

- Inventory control.

- Generalized process control.

We will explore each of these in turn.

ENERGY CONSERVATION

The average home consumes and also wastes a tremendous amount of energy. Energy is required to heat the house in winter and cool it in the summer; energy is also required to cook the meals (with gas-powered ovens, as well as electric-powered microwave ovens and toasters), wash the laundry and dishes, "compact" the trash, and a variety of other household chores. And then there are the discretionary uses of electricity for lighting, television, video cassette recorder (VCR), phonograph, home computer (we mustn't forget that one!), hair dryers, alarm clocks, sewing machines, and a dozen other instruments.

The home of the 1980s is estimated to have forty electric motors [1], and one or two televisions. The home of the 1990s will be considerably more complex; one writer suggests that we will have homes with twenty television monitors, thirteen personal computers, a host of control, communications, and security systems, all connected through a local area communications network.[2] Whatever the number turns out to be, it is obvious that the home of the future will consume a significant amount of energy.

I am ignoring at this point the very likely possibility that the appliances of the future will be intrinsically more energy-efficient. Even with such improvements, there is likely to be continued interest in making the most effective possible use of whatever energy is required throughout the home. The computer can provide assistance in the following ways:

- **Scheduled usage of appliances for off-peak periods when energy rates are lower.** The laundry can be scheduled automatically for the middle of the night, as can similar background chores. In

Chapter 9, we will discuss the possibility of special-purpose home robots that could be assigned the mindless task of vacuuming or mowing the lawn; these tasks could also be done during a period when electric rates are lower.[1] At the present time, this seems a fairly simple matter: if electric rates vary at all, it is usually for large blocks of time, such as the period between midnight and 7 A.M. But in the future, with each house able to dynamically alter its use of energy, it's quite possible that the electric rates could vary from moment to moment.

- **Automatically turning off idle appliances**. The most obvious example of this is home lighting: many of us, reared in an age of cheap electricity, still have the habit of leaving lights on when we leave a room. There is no reason why a computer couldn't sense the absence of people in the room and simply switch off the lights. This is an aspect of process control, which is discussed in more detail below.

- **More efficient operation of some appliances**. During the early energy crisis of 1973-74, we began to appreciate that an automobile driven at 55 mph consumes much less energy than an automobile driven at 70 mph; it may take longer to make the same journey, but we save energy. The same is true with many other appliances: we make inefficient use of the energy resource simply because we are in a hurry. However, if the appliance use could be monitored by a computer, in our absence, then it could be used over a longer period of time with less energy consumption. Many examples come to mind: cooking certain meals, vacuuming the house, laundry, and possibly some aspects of heating and cooling.

- **Harnessing external sources of power**. Most of us are accustomed to the idea of energy on demand: when we turn on a switch, we expect electricity or gas or oil to flow at whatever rate we desire. But other sources of energy may be available:

[1] One obvious reaction to this idea is, "I don't want to be kept awake all night long by a vacuum cleaner or lawn mower." But if the lawn mower were only an inch wide, it would make virtually no noise; a one-inch-wide vacuum cleaner might be a little noisier, but a small one would be quiet enough that it might be able to clean the rooms far away from the bedrooms without waking anyone.

geothermal energy from deep within the earth; energy from wind and water; thermal energy from the sun; and electrical energy from the sun provided by photovoltaic converters. Aside from the cost involved, there is also the issue of transient behavior: winds change direction; clouds block the sun; spring floods and summer droughts can affect the flow of water; etc. Once again, we can imagine the usefulness of a computer that can keep a microsecond-by-microsecond watch on the shifting sources of energy, and balance those outside sources with conventional sources.

COMPUTERIZED SENTRY DUTY

A source of great concern to many Americans today is the pervasive specter of crime. Whatever the current statistics may be, it is obvious that many of us worry about burglary, assault, rape, and even murder. Protection on the streets and in the office is an issue that is beyond the scope of this book; but computer-assisted protection of our homes is something that is rapidly becoming more and more practical.

Most of us depend on the simplest forms of physical security for our homes: locks. If one lock is good, two locks are better. We use Medeco locks, Fichet locks, and others that our parents never heard of; we use police locks, dead-bolts, bars, and anything else that we can think of to prevent the rascals from breaking down our doors. We put grates over our windows; we worry about intruders coming in through skylights and down our chimneys.

We use other forms of security, too, though most are fairly primitive. Apartment dwellers depend on doormen; members of a suburban community may have a private, roving guard patrol. Some of us depend on dogs, cats, snakes, or even birds to warn us of an intruder. And we depend on our neighbors and the local police, with a certain amount of trepidation, to watch over things when we're gone.

In addition to all of this—technology that has been with us for thousands of years—we are gradually beginning to depend on mechanical gadgets. We have mechanical timers that turn our lights on and off (as well as televisions, phonographs, and other appliances) in a pattern that we hope a burglar will interpret as real. And we have burglar alarms ranging in price from a few hundred dollars to tens of thousands of dollars; one security industry consultant estimates that one in eleven households in the United States now has some form of security system.[3] Most of these gadgets are electronic detectors without any significant "intelligence"—e.g., electronic devices that can detect sound waves or body heat or pressure (the weight of the human foot on a floor) or the disruption of an electrical signal or electromagnetic field. The only thing that is at all interesting about these devices is that they are getting cheaper, more sensitive, and small enough that the intruder may not notice them until it is too late.

The introduction of computers offers us two advantages: intelligence, and communication with the outside world. An intelligent home sentry can maintain a schedule of the departures and expected arrivals of household members; it can combine this with existing electronic devices to better determine whether somebody entering the house is expected or not. Additional information about household members and their guests could also be recorded: body weight, height, and anything else that electronic sensors could use to distinguish one person from another.[2] An intelligent computer, armed with a voice synthesizer and voice recognition equipment, could conceivably function as an intelligent sentry: "Hark! Who goes there? What is the password of the day? What is your mother's maiden name, and what is your Social Security number?" Obviously, none of this is guaranteed to prevent criminal entry into the house, but it improves the odds.

Once an intrusion is detected, a computer could contact the outside world for help. Some dumb electronic systems already do this, but most are capable of calling only a single number, and playing a single prerecorded message.[3] At the very least, a com-

---

[2] Along the way, we would also be able to distinguish between humans and smaller animals—but that opens the way for criminal-controlled dogs and cats, etc.

[3] To illustrate the consequences of this, consider the plight of one homeowner who installed a fire-detection system that would automatically call the fire department if a fire broke out. He left it installed for several years, during which time the fire department changed its phone number. When the inevitable fire finally did break out, the fire-detection system dutifully dialed the old number and broadcast its message to an automated system within the telephone company that was simpy trying to tell all callers that the phone number had been changed!

puterized system should be able to (a) determine whether to call the police, the FBI, or the fire department, (b) continue calling until the phone is answered, and (c) announce the time and circumstances of the intrusion. It might then allow the police to indicate (by touching the appropriate button on their touch-tone telephone, or their own computer system, if the home sentry is appropriately connected) several appropriate responses: tear gas, klieg lights, John Philip Sousa marches at 100 decibels, or whatever would make the intruder stop in his tracks and head quickly in the other direction.

There are some costs associated with this technology, over and above the money needed to buy the equipment. A computerized sentry system that hooks into the local police department invites a degree of government surveillance that many will find distasteful. And a sophisticated computer system designed to detect and repel intruders may lead to a decline in the traditional forms of security: people may stop using their locks. This opens up a host of problems; after all, there is no guarantee that the housebreakers of the future will be technologically naive. Indeed, they may be far more sophisticated than the average homeowner.

COMPUTERIZED COMFORT CONTROL

One thing that we expect from our homes is comfort: home is a refuge from the noise and the dirt and the pollution of the outside world. We expect it to be well heated or comfortably cooled, depending on the season; we expect the lighting to be sufficient, but not glaring; we expect to hear Muzak, or white noise, or Madonna, or silence, depending on our mood. Such pleasures of the senses are available to us today by manually manipulating switches and knobs, or (in the case of temperature) simple electromechanical devices that respond in some predetermined fashion.

Here again there are obvious opportunities for intelligent home control devices. As suggested above, a computer could turn out the lights when it detects that everyone has left a room; the opposite—turning on the lights when someone enters the room—is more important in terms of comfort. And since different people prefer different air temperatures, why not entrust the computer to set the temperature depending on who is in the room? Why not arrange the musical program depending on who is in the room and what mood they're in?[4]

Since we know that computers are good at communicating, we should build them into our home control system, too. It should be possible to call the home computer from the office (or the airport, or the golf course, or anywhere else) and instruct it to (a) begin cooking a predetermined meal, (b) begin recording a TV show whose existence we've just become aware of,[5] (c) preset the music selection, temperature, and lighting for our arrival, and (d) draw a hot or cool bath to be ready when we come in the door.

COMPUTERIZED INVENTORY CONTROL

The housekeeper of a large family will often tell you that the most difficult task in running the household is keeping track of supplies. Have we run out of toilet paper? Do we need more milk? How many gallons of ice cream should we buy for this weekend's teenage pajama party? Weekly shopping lists can be drawn up as in days of old, but things do change rapidly in today's household—as do the prices of groceries and supplies in the store: if there is a terrific sale on toilet paper, and there's plenty of room in the basement, why not buy a year's supply?

Large businesses carry out this kind of computerized inventory control as a normal part of their operation. Why shouldn't we apply it to the household, too? Of course, businesses generally maintain strict control over the flow of goods into and out of the warehouse; a human is generally required to type a message into the computer when things are taken out of the warehouse and when new shipments arrive. We could hardly expect this of the typical family.

---

[4] I'm obviously ignoring the problem of multiple, incompatible people in the same room. I'll leave that problem of diplomacy for some future author.

[5] This assumes that television remains as "dumb" as it is today, which we should not count on. It's more likely that we'll be able to call up any program we want, whenever we want it, and that we'll be able to selectively record or view any program based on such selection criteria as subject matter, personality, keyword, etc. Thus, I might program my VCR to automatically record any program that mentioned Egypt, or that includes Clint Eastwood, or that mentions the phrase "peanut butter."

However, most grocery store items carry computer-readable "bar codes" that are used to speed things up at the cash register. This technology could easily be extended to handle inventory control in the home. We might have to outfit our refrigerators and closets with bar-code readers, but the concept is certainly straightforward.

Indeed, we might take another lesson from modern businesses. If our home computer detects that we are running low on toilet paper, why not place the order directly with the computer system in the grocery store? Payment could be made, of course, by having the necessary monies debited from our personal bank account into the store's account. We will discuss this kind of banking application of computers in Chapter 7.

COMPUTERIZED PROCESS CONTROL

The term "process control" is used in many industries to describe mechanical or computerized equipment that controls the smooth functioning of an assembly line, chemical plant, or manufacturing process. As indicated above, a home computer system could be connected to a fire-detection system and could call the appropriate authorities if a fire broke out; this is one obvious kind of process control in the home.

Many other examples come to mind. Some involve safety for the inhabitants or major problems for the home itself. A computer could easily monitor the home for chemical or gas fumes, excessive levels of carbon monoxide, subfreezing temperatures that would burst water pipes, etc. Computers could be used to monitor the home for moisture and leaks through the walls and roof; for dry rot; and presumably even for termites. At the moment, this kind of monitoring would be expensive—but primarily because it would be added onto (or inserted into) the house as an afterthought. If it were built into the house from the beginning, the cost could be modest indeed.

For the suburban home, similar possibilities exist for lawn and garden care. Computers could monitor the soil for moisture content as well as important chemical nutrients; deficiencies could be corrected by having the computer automatically turn on a water sprinkler, with appropriate chemical nutrients (or organically pure nutrients, depending on the homeowner's preference) mixed in with the water. Hedges and plants could be monitored for invasions of Japanese beetles, grasshoppers, and other pests; neighboring dogs and cats and even children could be kept at bay with appropriate computer monitors.

SOURCES OF INFORMATION

The computerized home of the future is not here yet, and you should not expect your neighborhood real estate agent to have one for you in the immediate future. Though the technology for the kind of home control described in this chapter is available today, there are three problems with it: it is too expensive for most people to bother with; it does not come with the house, but must be added on; and the various components, if they do exist, are separate and do not communicate well with one another.

As we will see throughout this book, the cost of computer hardware will continue to drop steadily for the remainder of this decade, so the home control devices that depend on computers *per se* will soon become cheap enough for everyone to afford. Those components that depend on electromechanical devices—on motors and flywheels and pulleys—may or may not get cheaper as time goes on.

Far more important than the cost of the components is the issue of built-in versus add-on. If the home computer applications described in this chapter were built into a typical suburban development house or a typical high-rise apartment building, they would probably add less than 2 percent to the overall cost; that kind of increment can easily be hidden or disguised by the builder. Probably the most important built-in component is the communications network that will carry signals from room to room, from component to component. The homeowner may insist on his own brand of central home computer, and he will certainly have his own individual appliances, but he will not wish to install his own wiring throughout the house. Once there is a common communication network that all appliances and devices can hook into, it becomes much easier to provide integrated control—so that we don't end up with a dozen computers issuing conflicting demands to various parts of the house!

All of this is of interest to three or four separate industries and professions. For ongoing information about the state of the art in home control, you can consult:

- Professional computer and engineering societies, such as the IEEE (Institute of Electrical and Electronic Engineers) and ACM (Association for Computing Machinery).

- Various hobbyist magazines, such as *Popular Mechanics*, *Popular Electronics*, *High Technology*, and the magazines devoted to individual home computers. Don't bother looking at *House and Garden* for this kind of information.

- Utility companies that are truly interested in energy conservation. Check with your local electric or gas company to see if they have any model homes or research projects.

- The building industry. Large construction companies and architecture firms are already designing smart office buildings to satisfy the needs of businesses, and to deal with the large-scale energy savings that can be achieved in fifty-story office buildings. This technology will be transferred to fifty-story apartment buildings as soon as it becomes evident that the consumer market actually wants that intelligence, and eventually to single-unit homes.

- The architecture and city planning departments of some universities. While the construction industry may not be ready to build smart homes yet, some universities have been thinking about the issues for several years; they will be happy to share many of their current ideas with you.

References for Chapter 6

1. Rochester, Jack B., and John Gantz, *The Naked Computer*, New York: William Morrow and Company, 1983.

2. Jurgen, Ronald K., and Tekla S. Perry, "The High Tech Home," *IEEE Spectrum*, May 1985.

3. Horgan, John, "Electronic Watchdogs," *IEEE Spectrum*, May 1985.

7

COMPUTERIZED BANKING

A power has risen up in the government greater than the people themselves, consisting of many and various and powerful interests, combined into one mass, and held together by the cohesive power of the vast surplus in the banks.

John C. Calhoun
Speech, May 27, 1836

The time is 10:00 on a Sunday evening. The weekend is just about over; the children are asleep, the dishes are washed, the Sunday newspaper read and piled in heaps in the corner. It's time for a little banking . . . which, as in most households, consists primarily of paying more bills than one expected, shuffling some money from the savings account into the checking account to cover the shortfall, or possibly moving a little money from checking into savings if there was an unexpected surplus.

Banking used to be a Saturday morning chore, and it took almost the entire morning. Fortunately, nobody in the family minded (except me), because my two young sons had a morning's mind-numbing TV cartoons to watch, my wife had errands and shopping to do, and my teenage daughter preferred sleeping until lunchtime. Saturday morning also gave me the opportunity to run to the post office for additional stamps with which to mail my checks, and even the opportunity to visit the bank in person if necessary. Not anymore: I don't write checks and I don't use stamps. I use my home computer for my banking.

Actually, visiting the bank is something that I haven't done for almost five years—ever since the first automated teller machine (or

ATM, as I will call them throughout this chapter) was installed outside our neighborhood branch office in 1980. I find banks to be noisy places with long lines and surly bank tellers who clearly regard my presence as an interruption of their siesta. They speak Serbo-Croatian or Urdu, if they speak at all. And their speech usually consists of telling me to get in another line—or to get approval from the branch manager, a harried individual who always looks as if he wishes he were anywhere else but here. To which I have always mentally responded, "Me, too!"

The age of electronic banking is upon us. Nobody but a masochist visits the inside of a bank anymore; and by the end of the 1980s, nobody in his right mind will even stand in line to deal with an ATM. By the end of the 1990s, banks as we now know them will have disappeared from the face of the earth. The "cohesive power of the vast surplus in the banks" that John Calhoun worried about 150 years ago will have dissipated into the hands of hundreds of millions of individuals, and into business organizations that will take care of their own financial transactions.

CONSUMER ADVANTAGES
OF ELECTRONIC BANKING

The advantages of electronic banking for the consumer are fairly obvious; the largest single advantage is convenience. Instead of being forced to deal with "banker's hours" of 9:00 A.M. to 3:00 P.M. (with occasional extended hours and a brief few hours on Saturday morning), it is now possible to conduct most banking business twenty-four hours per day, seven days per week.

Thus, in New York City, it is not uncommon to see a dozen people queued up waiting to get cash from an ATM at midnight on Saturday night, or at 7:30 A.M. on Monday morning, or at any other odd hour of the day or night. Much of this would not be necessary if all of society worked on a cashless basis, but we are several years away from that. Even if the technology were available, there are still many shops and services that insist on cash for a number of old-fashioned and new-fashioned reasons. Small cash transactions can't be traced, and are not taxed as easily; this alone will delay a total conversion to the cashless society. Thus, we will need ATMs for another decade or more—but ATMs certainly represent an improvement over waiting in line inside a bank.

Home computer banking systems extend this convenience one step further. Though they don't dispense cash, they do allow one to conduct a number of simple banking transactions from the convenience of home twenty-four hours per day, seven days per week. From my home computer, which at this moment is 102 miles away from my neighborhood branch office, I can do any of the following:

- Check the balance of my checking account and savings account.

- Determine how much interest has been credited to my account.

- Find out what checks have cleared today, or for any period during the past sixty days.

- Determine the amount owed on my MasterCard and VISA credit cards.

- Review my credit card activity for the past sixty days.

- Pay a bill to anyone in the United States, and tell the bank when I want the bill paid. (This takes between two days and five days.)

- Set up a schedule of recurring payments to one or more people (or stores, or companies) so that the payment will be made periodically with no further instructions from me.

- Cancel or modify such recurring payment instructions.

- Apply for a bank mortgage or credit card.

- Send a message to appropriate officials in the bank with questions or comments about their service.

There is another advantage to this kind of home banking, one that the ATM machines provide on a more limited basis: float. It is to my advantage to keep as much money in my savings account (or other interest-bearing accounts) for as long as possible, and to pay bills (or withdraw cash) at the last possible moment. If I pay my bills by writing checks and mailing them through (shudder!) the

U.S. Post Office, I can only guess as to the amount of time that the check will be in transit; and if I can only withdraw cash during banking hours, then I am forced to take cash out of the bank even though I might not need it for several days.

All of this disappears with ATMs and home banking systems. Well, not quite: there is always a little float. Most banks that provide home banking services advise their customers that there will be a period of two days to five days before an electronic transfer between your account and the payee's account actually takes effect.[1] Question: who gets the interest during those two to five days? And even with ATM machines, it's likely that you will withdraw cash a little earlier than you really need it. But at least the trend is in the right direction.

ADVANTAGES FOR THE BANKS

The advantages of ATMs and home banking are even greater for the banks themselves. After all, you didn't think they were doing it for the consumers, did you?[2] The motivation for the banks is the following:

- It lets them shift some of their business to "off hours" without the cost of human service.

[1] If the payee is a merchant known to the bank (e.g., the phone company), the transfer takes two days; otherwise it takes five days. In all home banking systems I know of, the transfer is accomplished by having the bank's computer produce a check—i.e., a piece of paper like the normal checks we write—and then depositing the check or mailing it. But if payer and payee have accounts at the same bank, the transfer should take place immediately and electronically. It is only a matter of time before banks actually operate this way.

[2] Actually, there is one sense in which banks are installing ATMs and home banking for the benefit of the consumers even if they see no short-term economic advantage: simply to forestall competition from the bank across the street. As banks become increasingly deregulated, they find it possible to offer more and more widely diversified services—from life insurance to discount stock brokerage services to IRA accounts. Banks are clearly in the service sector of the economy, and they are beginning to realize that they are in the information processing business—i.e., the information is a service that they can provide their customers. To the extent that they are judged by the marketplace on their ability to provide that service, they must provide it just to maintain market share. An alternative is to specialize—e.g., to abandon the retail banking market (the business of providing banking services for individual customers like you and me) and focus instead on high-volume corporate banking where personal, humanized service may remain an important factor.

- It shifts some of the transaction processing workload from their personnel to the customers themselves.

- It allows them to move some of their services to off-bank premises.

- It begins the long, slow process of eliminating paper, or hard-copy records of financial transactions.

All of this is important because of one factor common to all banks: volume. A hundred years ago, there was time for a bank teller to record deposits and withdrawals with quill pen and ledger card, and even enough time for him to say a pleasant, "Good morning!" to the customer. No longer: some 95 million checks are processed each day in the United States, which comes to a total of 35 billion each year.[1] Checks written on scraps of paper account for 90 percent of the dollar value of all payments in the United States today.

The banks began dealing with this problem nearly seventy-five years ago with Electronic Accounting Machines (EAM), the fore-runners of modern computers made by the forerunners of modern computer companies, NCR, Burroughs, and IBM. In the 1950s and 1960s, the banks began installing modern computer systems, and their automation efforts continue today. Electronic Fund Transfer (EFT) systems, corporate cash management systems, and a variety of major applications are in various stages of completion in banks around the country. An even more massive effort is beginning in some of the more aggressive banks: "information models," or "enterprise models," that allow them to make sense of the incredible amount of disparate, unrelated data they currently maintain on computer disks, magnetic tape, punched cards, and scraps of paper.[3]

ATM machines and computerized home banking are just one aspect of this drive toward automation. According to Ulric Weil, some 80,000 ATM machines existed in 1983, and the banking industry expects to have approximately 250,000 installed by 1986[2]; some 46 ATM machines per day are being installed across the country.

---

[3] We will discuss information models in Chapter 18. It is not just the banks who are dealing with this problem of massive, unintegrated computer files. Most large business organizations are in the same position. So is the government, thank goodness!

The economics of ATM machines are rather interesting: they require approximately 5,500 transactions per month to break even (i.e., to cost less than an equivalent human bank teller); assuming that the ATM is available twenty-four hours per day to the consumer marketplace, that works out to one transaction every eight minutes, around the clock. The average ATM transaction requires about two minutes (based on my own personal experience), which means that the ATM machines must be used to approximately 25 percent of capacity for them to cover their cost.

Measuring all of this in simple, present-day economic costs is misleading, though. First (and most important), we have to assume that the alternative human cost of bank clerks will continue to increase inexorably over the years, while the cost of ATM hardware/software technology will presumably continue to decline. This becomes even more important when we consider the cost of providing human bank teller service during off hours—e.g., at 3:00 A.M. on a Saturday night.

There are other economic advantages associated with the off-hour service: it gives the banks the opportunity to spread out their processing costs. If all deposits, withdrawals, transfers, and other bank transactions take place between 9:00 A.M. and 3:00 P.M., then it follows that a considerable amount of work has to be done during those hours. Some of it is done by the human tellers who enter the transactions into their banking terminals, but much of it is also done by the huge back-office mainframe computers that record the transactions, check them for accuracy, update the files, compute new customer bank balances, etc. If it all has to be squeezed into a six-hour "window," the bank may be forced to buy more computer equipment, hire more computer staff, etc. If, on the other hand, it can be spread more evenly throughout a twenty-four-hour period, then a smaller computer may suffice.[4]

---

[4] The issue is actually far more complex, though my basic point is valid. If more bank transactions have to be processed in a shorter amount of time, it becomes more and more difficult to calculate the amount of computer power required to handle the transactions with an acceptable response time (in the same way that it is more difficult for the phone company to provide adequate service on Christmas and Thanksgiving than it is at 3:00 A.M. on a random Wednesday night). The extra load on the computers increases the chance of hardware and software failures, for reasons that we will discuss in Chapter 27; and the consequences of a failure are much worse if 10,000 people are simultaneously entering computers than if 10 people are trying to get cash out of their ATM machine at 3:00 in the morning. On

There are other motivations for the shift to ATMs and personal banking. First, it gets the customer involved in data entry, a trick that the phone company learned long ago when it installed direct-dial service. Now the customer can enter the details of his bank withdrawal or deposit—and while the computer must obviously check for accuracy, the time-consuming part has been shifted from a bank employee to the customer. Also, the work is carried out in a small workspace, often out on the street, so the bank can begin moving out of the expensive, cavernous offices it can no longer afford. It can install ATMs in shopping centers and other locations where it would be entirely uneconomical to rent space for its own people. Better yet, it can rely on the customer to use his own home or apartment to house the personal computer that talks to the bank computer.

Home banking accomplishes another shift, too: the burden for purchasing the equipment is shifted from the bank to the consumer. At the present time, it's not quite that simple: the banks usually provide telecommunication facilities so that the customer only has to make a local phone call to connect his computer to the bank's mainframe. And many banks are offering discounts for modems that are required to hook the home computer into a telephone line. Since many consumers would have no other reason to purchase a modem, the bank is subsidizing the purchase in order to lure the customer onto their system.

But the long-term economics surely favor the banks. If an ATM breaks down, it is the bank that must fix it (and the customers, standing in line, blame the bank). If the consumer's personal computer breaks down, he has nobody to blame but himself or the computer manufacturer (but surely not the bank); and he pays for the repair or replacement himself.

---

the other hand, banks have historically counted on a large chunk of idle time between 3:00 P.M. and the following morning, during which time they could carry out all of their computer processing and produce enormous printed reports that could be distributed to all of the branch offices in time for the opening of business. If the bank is open all night long, then much of that idle computer time disappears, which is part of a paradigm shift for the banks: instead of operating in batch mode, with periodic computer printouts summarizing the state of affairs as of yesterday afternoon at 3:00, they must now operate in a real-time, on-line mode, with computer display terminals providing up-to-the-second information on the status of any customer's account. This is not an easy shift to bring about.

DANGERS OF ELECTRONIC BANKING

As with almost all other applications of computers, there are dangers and problems with ATM machines and electronic home banking. Let me summarize each, and then discuss them in detail:

- Potential invasion of privacy.

- Potential for misuse of collected information.

- Possibility of new forms of crime and errors.

- Perceived loss of security associated with cancelled checks and sales receipts.

- Possibility of lost or stolen bank cards.

- Loss of "float."

- Perception that the home banking system is too expensive and too time consuming for what it does.

Invasion of privacy is an obvious area of concern: we usually worry about the government invading our privacy,[5] but the banks are obviously part of this concern. Most American citizens would prefer not to have the details of their financial transactions broadcast to the general public, or even to the government; it should be noted that Europeans and citizens in various other countries feel even more strongly about this than we do!

Since banks have been computerized for a long time already, one must ask a rather obvious question: in what way do ATM machines and home banking systems increase the risk of invasion of privacy? Increased crime is something different; but additional loss of privacy? There is only one additional aspect that I can think of: banks (and all the people and agencies and companies to whom the banks give their records) will now know not only how much money we withdrew from the bank, but also when. Consider this interesting illustration:

---

[5] The subject of privacy and the government is discussed in Chapter 14.

A bank somewhere in America knows which of its customers paid a streetwalker last night. The bank knows because of its computer. The bank in question has a 24-hour automated teller machine . . . Alarmed to discover a flurry of withdrawals between midnight and 2:30 A.M., the bank president put an investigator on the trail. He discovered that the bank was in the neighborhood of a "red light" district and that customers were stopping for cash en route! [3]

Aside from this, the banks already know how much money we deposit, how much we withdraw, and to whom we send our money. If we gradually begin to change all of our financial transactions to credit cards, debit cards, and other devices discussed in the next section, then the banks (and thus the government) will have successfully invaded our privacy on a more substantive basis. But for now, ATMs and home banking systems do not represent an additional invasion of privacy; nor is there much of an opportunity for additional misuse of the information so gleaned, other than the kind of example shown above.

New forms of crime and error, on the other hand, are certainly possible. Loss or theft of the bank cards used with ATM machines are one obvious threat; misuse of the home banking system by family members, friends, or casual visitors is another obvious example. Attempts by hackers to break into a home banking system and plunder the accounts of random individuals is, of course, the kind of dramatic crime we see on television shows, but it is not likely to occur very often, if at all. It is much more likely that someone inside the system—e.g., a bank clerk or computer operator or systems analyst—will discover a new loophole in the system that enables him to siphon off large amounts of money. If crimes occur outside the bank, they are likely to take a more traditional form. There have already been reports of criminals holding bank customers at gunpoint in off-hours ATM service areas,[6] and one could imagine a burglar of the future breaking into a house and

---

[6] Many of the ATMs are on the street, entirely unprotected; this makes the bank customer an obvious and easy prey as soon as he has withdrawn cash. Others are in a locked anteroom of the bank itself, and the customer's bank card is required to unlock the door. But bank customers are notoriously careless, and will often hold the door open for the next person trying to rush in the door.

shouting at his frightened victims: "Quick! Your bank password or your life!" In effect, then, the ATMs and home banking systems offer slightly new scenarios for carrying out the same kinds of crimes that have taken place for hundreds of years.[7]

The loss of "paper" records   bothers many people dealing with ATMs and home computer systems. Bank customers (including me) also worry sometimes about depositing large sums of money into an ATM machine without the reassurance that a human bank teller has received it in his hands. This is an understandable problem, because computers do break down and it's hard to argue with them. The banks are keenly aware of this; most have hot-line telephones strategically placed next to the ATM machines, as well as twenty-four-hour phone numbers for home banking customers to use. Just as it required a long time for people to get used to paper currency in place of their gold coins (a transition that some have not yet gone through), so it will require several years for people to get used to the fact that their deposits and withdrawals exist only as electronic blips somewhere on a computer. I still have every check I have written since I first opened a checking account in 1964; it is obviously difficult for me to throw all those musty old pieces of paper away. No doubt my children won't have that problem.

Reliability problems, service problems, loss of bank cards, and a host of other issues will also delay the widespread introduction of ATMs and home banking systems to some extent. But as the level of human service in the banks gets worse and worse (a phenomenon that I suppose is not completely inevitable, but which certainly is a trend in New York City), ATMs and home banking systems will seem a more and more pleasant—and effective—alternative.

"Float"   is another area of concern for consumers; ultimately, the banks will have to relinquish much of this source of profit. They have already begun moving in this direction: they allow me to keep

---

[7] As an example of how easy such crimes can be, consider the clever criminal who hung an "Out of Order" sign on the night deposit box of a bank years ago; he then proceeded to stand next to the deposit box, wearing a guard's uniform and holding a large canvas sack. All through the evening, customers came to the bank, read the sign, and proceeded to put their deposits into the "guard's" sack. Shortly after midnight, the guard wandered away, never to be seen again.

my money in an interest-bearing account until the payee (the person to whom I write my check) actually cashes it. This means that the float becomes his problem, not mine. However, if both of us look carefully at our bank statements, we're likely to find that either his bank or my bank actually had the use of the money overnight, or even a few days. Ultimately, the owner of the money wants to reduce the float to zero, and wants to control—to the microsecond!—when the transfer of funds will take place.

Banks, on the other hand, have counted on float for centuries as a way of financing their operation.[8] There will always be a little bit of float, but as the consumer marketplace gets smarter, and as it acquires more powerful technology, float will gradually disappear. There is nothing terribly wrong with this: it simply means that the banks will have to charge explicitly for whatever services they render, rather than making the money without anyone knowing about it (or without anyone being able to do anything about it).

There is one final problem that confronts the home banking user: it's not always clear that his banking needs demand such a high-technology solution; to some, it seems like using a sledgehammer to crack a walnut. For the consumer who (a) never had a home computer, (b) has no desire to get one, (c) writes only a dozen checks a month, and (d) always knows his current bank balance, home banking may be a waste of time. Even a computer fanatic like me was "turned off" when home banking first appeared in New York City in 1983. The service was expensive ($10 per month, regardless of whether it was used or not) and slow; response time from the bank's computer was so sluggish that it seemed to take ten minutes to pay a bill. And then there was the float of five days that was never mentioned in the TV commercials, but well documented

---

[8] I should emphasize here that I am not talking about the massive float represented by the "fractional reserve system" upon which the entire banking system is based: we all know that if everyone showed up at the bank's front door to withdraw his money, every bank in the country would have to shut its doors. It is interesting to note, though, that ATM machines and home banking systems (and, more important, the corporate counterparts which sit in the controllers' offices in large companies around the country) could exacerbate this phenomenon enormously. Nobody has to physically visit the bank any more to withdraw his money—all he has to do is type a command on his computer terminal. The possibilities are staggering, but I'll leave that to some novelist to pursue; all I am concerned with here is the float associated with money in transit from payer to payee.

in the fine print of the user manual. So I discontinued the service and switched to another bank's home system in early 1985. Now I'm happy.

FUTURE TRENDS

The future of ATMs and computerized home banking is one of significant growth for the next decade. The motivating factors for the consumer, as well as for the banks, are long-term factors. Thus, industry experts foresee the following kind of growth:

- A rise in electronic payments from 2 billion in 1981 to approximately 16 billion in 1986.

- An increase in the number of home banking terminals (or personal computers) from 500,000 in 1983 to 3 million by the end of 1985.

The continued increase in ATM machines is largely under the control of the banks; as long as they see the economics working in their favor, they will presumably continue installing new machines. The growth of home banking, though, depends on the consumers' willingness to install home computers. Few, if any, will buy a home computer exclusively for the purpose of home banking;[9] thus, to the extent that projections of home banking use are predicated on home computer sales, there may be some nasty surprises in the future.[10] Many, many market forecasts that involve widespread consumer acceptance of a computerized product have turned out to be wrong in the past few years. But the banks, as is their wont, take the long-term view: as one New York banker recently said, "We'll

---

[9] On the other hand, the availability of convenient home banking may be enough for the consumer to take the personal computer out of the closet, or to take it out of his children's room. Recognizing this, the banks have concentrated on modems as the thing to subsidize. Even if the consumer bought a computer and then abandoned it or gave it to his child, he probably didn't buy a modem—because it never occurred to him that his computer might communicate with some other computer.

[10] However, there is an alternative medium for providing home banking services: cable TV. Chapter 8 discusses the subject of videotext, which eliminates the need for home computers and modems.

be happy if 10 to 12 percent of our retail banking business is done on a home computer by the early 1990s." That kind of conservative view of the future is likely to come true.

Along with ATMs and home banking, we will see a proliferation of new forms of credit cards. Among them will be:

- Interbank cards that allow ATM transactions across state lines, and from one bank to another.

- Debit cards.

- Smart cards.

The interbank cards already exist in a primitive form: MasterCard and Visa are the two best-known examples. These credit cards allow, as we all know, purchases at hundreds of thousands of retail outlets around the world. But they are not debit cards: payment for the purchase does not come out of our bank account at the instant of purchase, but rather at some point after a statement is sent. The time delay—our old friend float—offers opportunities for some, and costs for others (primarily the consumer).[11] It also leads to inefficient processing of the transaction as it goes from the retailer to the retailer's bank, to the interbank clearing house, to the consumer's bank, to the consumer, and then from the consumer's checking account back to the bank. Most of the intermediate steps are computerized and presumably fairly inexpensive. However, the initial step of writing up the purchase on a credit card slip and then going through a credit authorization process, and the final step

---

[11] Consider the cash-flow aspect of the typical credit card purchase: I may have $100 in my bank account at the instant that I make a $100 purchase on my credit card, but that fact is not recognized by anyone. If my bank balance is in an interest-bearing account, it earns between 5 percent and 8 percent annually (as of July 1985); the interest may or may not be compounded daily. Meanwhile, my purchase has to go through several stages of processing before I finally see it on my monthly statement; since it is a current purchase, I typically have 28 to 31 days to pay for it before I start incurring interest. Thus far, it would appear that I am ahead of the game, because I can continue earning interest on the money in my bank account until the credit card payment is due. However, neither the banks nor the retailers are fools, and they have built this cost (or opportunity loss, depending on how you want to view it) into their price. If I don't get around to paying the credit card bill on time, then the credit card company (or the bank with which it is associated) immediately begins treating it as a loan, with interest rates ranging from 18 to 21 percent, depending on the usury laws in various states. At this point, the banks are obviously ahead of the game!

where the consumer writes the check, puts it into the (shudder!) U.S. Postal System, to be received by the bank and eventually processed by the bank's computer is more or less manual and therefore much more expensive.

And while the interbank cards will allow me to purchase a plane ticket or pay for a restaurant meal in any civilized part of the world, they do not allow me to go to an ATM machine anywhere in the world to withdraw cash. I can go into a bank almost anywhere in the world, and use my New York City credit cards to get cash, but I can't do it in the middle of the night. Obviously, there is a market for this kind of service, and the banks are beginning to respond. There are now a few credit cards that can be used in ATM machines in multiple states of the United States, and similar services are beginning to be offered throughout the countries of Western Europe; a number of telephones in airports now allow long-distance calls to be made by credit card.

American Express also has a service (which has actually been in existence for several years) that allows a customer to use his American Express card to receive traveler's checks at several different machines around the country. But since traveler's checks are an obsolete form of paper money whose float tends to be considerably longer (to the benefit of American Express, but not the customer), this service has not had much impact.

The next logical step for retail outlets is the interstate—indeed, international—debit card. A debit card is like a credit card, except that it can be used to instantaneously debit the customer's bank account and credit the retailer's account. If the retailer enters the details of the transaction through an appropriately intelligent cash register, then the bank-to-bank, account-to-account transfers should be accomplished entirely automatically. Among other things, this should lead to lower service charges rendered to the retailer (charges which are inevitably passed on to the customer); instead of the current level of 4 to 5 percent that the banks charge retailers for use of credit cards, we might see charges of 1 to 2 percent. And control over the float would end up where it belongs: in the hands of the one who owns the money.

There are two problems with debit cards: costly computer processing, and problems of security. The current generation of debit cards is not smart—they are simply pieces of plastic with some numbers embossed on them. Hence anyone can steal them, and even if the customer were required to furnish a password, it would have the disadvantage of being verbally transmitted from customer to retail clerk for each transaction. And the very definition of a debit card implies instantaneous processing of the transaction by the retailer, the retailer's bank, and the customer's bank—each of whom could be separated from one another by hundreds of miles.[12] This means that the transaction must be sent via telephone lines (and/or satellite) from one computer to another and then back to the retailer. This demand for instantaneous processing can become quite expensive in terms of computer time and communications costs.

All of this will lead to smart cards by the end of this decade. A typical smart card will have its own built-in computer (embedded directly within the plastic card), together with enough built-in memory to maintain (a) identification information about the card's owner, (b) security information that can be used to verify the card-user's authenticity without having to refer to a remote mainframe computer, (c) historical data about transactions that have been processed since the last time the card was recharged, and (d) information about the monetary credit that the card currently contains. The customer would refill the credit in much the way he takes his postage machine to the post office to be refilled; credit would then be depleted as he made purchases, until the card would eventually be empty.

Such a smart card would permit local processing of transactions—i.e., the information would be transferred directly from the card to the retailer's smart cash register, which would then upload its collection of credits thus accumulated directly to the bank on a daily basis.

The security mechanism built into the card could be almost arbitrarily complex. The card could require the user to enter his Social Security number, his birthdate, his parents' birthdates, or any other such information. It could be set to self-destruct after three erroneous attempts to provide the information, or it could

---

[12] In most cases, we would expect the customer and the retailer to be in the same physical location. But this is no longer true for many purchases: the customer places his order over the phone, or by mail, to a retail store in a different geographical location, furnishing to the retailer a credit card number to which the purchase should be charged.

"pretend" to permit the transaction, but instead send warning signals to the retailer's machine.

Many organizations besides banks are interested in the smart cards for related purposes: the Social Security Administration, various state motor vehicle bureaus, the Defense Department, the Passport Office, etc. Current laser technology permits about 1,200,000 "bits" of information to be recorded on a single plastic card—about 30,000 words of text. This is sufficient to record voluminous information about the owner's military record and medical history, details of traffic violations, information about food stamp and welfare eligibility, Social Security payments, and a host of other bureaucratic details. Future technology will permit more sophisticated security mechanisms: storage of digital data representing the user's voiceprint, fingerprint, or the pattern made by the capillaries in the retina.[4] At the present time, the hardware technology for these smart cards has not quite dropped in cost to the point where the banks will distribute one to every customer: the unit cost for each card is in the $3 to $4 range. However, it is quite likely that prices will drop, and that this kind of card will eventually replace the credit cards we have come to depend on for the past twenty years.

There is one final development to watch for in the area of electronic banking: the gradual disappearance of the banks themselves. As John Calhoun pointed out in 1836, banks were (and still are) powerful because they are the repository of the "vast surplus" of profits accumulated by individuals and business. But for the most part, the banks themselves are not the owners of great wealth. Indeed, articles published throughout the mid-1980s argue that many leading banks actually have a negative net worth, if their loans to underdeveloped countries are valued accurately.

Banks were also crucially important 150 years ago because they were the central mechanism for distributing money between buyer and seller, and we could trust their well-guarded vaults for safeguarding money in the interim period between transfers. It made sense to pay a fee to a banker to protect our money and to distribute it properly according to our instructions. But now money is a much more ephemeral concept. It is no longer a bag of salt, or an ounce of gold, or even a green piece of paper; it is, for the vast majority of our financial transactions, simply information in motion. And, sad to say, we don't really need the banks to handle that for us much longer. The binary ones and zeroes needed to represent any conceivable amount of money can be recorded on a sliver of magnetic tape small enough that I can hide it and protect it just as effectively as a bank; and my personal smart card can distribute the money from my employer to me, and from me to the retailer, just as effectively as a bank can.

This probably won't affect consumers for some time; not everyone trusts technology enough to withdraw his money from banks yet.[13] But large corporations are quickly getting to the point where they will conduct many of their financial transactions directly: if companies X and Y do business with each other—where each is a customer of the other at different times—why should they bother with the overhead of a bank to settle their accounts? Even if it is only a one-way relationship—i.e., where X is a customer of Y, but Y is not a customer of X—an intercompany credit and debit system is technologically possible already. The gradual emergence of barter networks signals the beginning of this trend; various forms of government regulation and legislation may slow it down, but even the government cannot prevent the inevitable.

This does not mean that all banks will go bankrupt. First of all, technology trends of the kind discussed in this chapter are gradual. Even if the technology were free, it would take twenty years or more for people to get used to the idea of managing their money directly. Meanwhile, smart banks will recognize that their true value in the market no longer has anything to do with physical security of gold nuggets, but rather with financial service. On a short-term basis, they can provide this service by offering technology that the customer would otherwise not understand or not be able to afford. In the medium term, the bank can serve as a communications network that allows all of the individual and corporate smart cards to talk to one another over "secure" channels.

In the long run, the banks should offer—for a fee—the one thing that they own exclusively: knowledge. In dynamic, turbulent times, how can the individual best manage his financial assets? Since his assets can be moved from place to place instantaneously

---

[13] Of course, there are those who don't trust banks either. Such people have buried their Krugerrands in their garden.

by pushing a button, he doesn't need help making the transfer; he needs information that will help him decide on the best transfer. This is the kind of service that stock brokerage companies, life insurance companies, and a number of other related industries are beginning to focus on. It is, in my opinion, the only possible salvation for companies that have, for so many hundreds of years, made money by sitting on other people's money and profiting from the float.

References for Chapter 7

1. Weil, Ulric, *Information Systems in the Eighties*, Englewood Cliffs, N.J.: Prentice-Hall, 1982.
2. *Ibid.*
3. *Chicago Tribune*, August 12, 1976, Section 3, page 1.
4. Latamore, G. Berton, "Putting Intelligence in Your Wallet," *High Technology*, June 1983.

VIDEOTEXT

Inside the flat a fruity voice was reading out a list of figures which had something to do with the production of pig iron. The voice came from an oblong metal plaque like a dulled mirror which formed part of the surface of the right-hand wall. Winston turned a switch and the voice sank somewhat, though the words were still distinguishable. The instrument (the telescreen, it was called) could be dimmed, but there was no way of shutting it off completely. . . The telescreen received and transmitted simultaneously. Any sound that Winston made, above the level of a very low whisper, would be picked up by it; moreover, so long as he remained within the field of vision which the metal plaque commanded, he could be seen as well as heard. . . You had to live—did live, from habit that became instinct—in the assumption that every sound you made was overheard, and, except in darkness, every movement scrutinized.

George Orwell
1984

Welcome to the world of videotext. It hasn't turned out exactly as George Orwell planned: it's better in some respects, and probably worse in others. But it's here, and it's becoming part of our world. Indeed, in France and England, it's already a much more significant part of day-to-day life than it is in the United States.

Videotext (also spelled "videotex" by many writers) means different things to different people. One writer defines it in the following way:

Videotex, or Viewdata as it is less frequently known, allows a subscriber interactive use of large amounts of information. Rather than simply *selecting* from the 100 or so pages that the teletext service broadcasts, the videotex user can process thousands of pages of data, contribute to an existing data base, and conceivably communicate this action to other subscribers, thereby multiplying the connections exponentially. More concretely, videotex supporters see the service opening the way to new forms of learning, shopping, banking, communicating, and indeed, working. [1]

Videotext is a term used more in England than here; Americans do sometimes use videotext, [2] but they also use "electronic retailing," [3] "information utilities," [4] "computerized services in the home," [5] and whatever else strikes their fancy. In its most general use, videotext means any kind of interaction between remote users, who may communicate through their TV computer terminal or personal computer, and a central computer that provides information and services.

We have already discussed several specific applications of what the British include in their videotext definition:

- In Chapter 2, I pointed out that one of the educational benefits of computers for children is the ability to access large databases of research material, thus rendering the school library virtually obsolete. Unfortunately, most school computer systems don't yet have the modem hardware that allows a computer to be hooked to a telephone line.

- In Chapter 3, I discussed the cottage industry phenomenon that allows people to carry out part or all of their work at home.

- In Chapter 4, I outlined the broader social ramifications of a country—and a world—that gradually finds itself communicating instantaneously and interactively with a new medium that enhances the telephone and the television.

- In Chapter 5, I observed that one of the future forms of computer games will be multiuser games that operate twenty-four hours a day. One of the American videotext companies, Compuserve, already offers such a game.

- In Chapter 7, I discussed the growing trend toward banking at home, using a home computer.

There is one significant difference between the interactive applications in the previous several chapters, and the applications envisioned by many videotext proponents: the nature of the communication medium. In previous chapters, I assumed that the user communicated via a personal computer, connected to other computers via a modem connection to the telephone line. There is a significant problem with this assumption: not very many people have home computers (between 1 and 2 percent of the American population, depending on whose estimates you believe), and according to a recent study by the Yankee Group,[6] only 20 percent of home computer owners have a modem.[1]

An alternative is the communications medium that nearly everyone has: television. As I observed in Chapter 2, nearly 98 percent of the households in America have a television set; other industrial nations are rapidly approaching the same level of saturation. Of course, some households have poor TV reception, but cable TV and direct satellite transmission facilities are spreading rapidly. In 1968, only 5 percent of U.S. households had cable TV; by 1982, the figure had climbed to 19 percent , and by 1990 it is estimated that 50 percent of all households will have cable TV.[8] This kind of high-quality, multichannel, communications medium permits a variety of interactive videotext applications.

There have been equally rosy forecasts about the rapid proliferation of home computers; many of these have turned out to be overly optimistic. But there is a difference with videotext: American homes already have a television, and they already have a variety of other reasons for wanting cable TV or satellite reception. They want their sports programs, their soap operas, and their favorite evening comedy shows. If they pay for this, the videotext facility can be dragged along with it for almost no additional cost.

---

[1] Modems come in various shapes and sizes, and permit communications at different speeds for different costs. A simple modem costs about $100, and will transmit data across a telephone line at speeds of 300 "baud," or roughly thirty characters (five average-length English words) per second. A higher-quality modem will transmit at 1,200 baud or 2,400 baud, but may cost $500 to $800. Home computer modems are beginning to come on the market at speeds of 10,000 baud[7] at a cost of $2,000, but none of the popular videotext utilities in 1985 supported speeds above 1,200 baud. Meanwhile, big corporations transmit their data from one location to another at speeds ranging from 19,200 baud to 50,000 baud.

Actually, there is one cost: the communications device that allows the user to interact with the videotext service through the television set.[2] In the simplest case, this might be a keyboard, which could be bought separately for less than $100. (Indeed, videotext companies might provide it free, just as home banking services offer large subsidies to consumers today for the purchase of a modem.) More elaborate TV systems in the late 1980s and early 1990s will undoubtedly have a combination of voice output, voice recognition, and some keyboard input.

What kind of services will we look for on our videotext system of the 1990s—aside from electronic mail, electronic banking, and interactive games that we have already discussed? There are three broad categories of videotext service:

- Information services.

- Shopping services.

- Education at home.

All of these, as you can see, are variations on a common theme. But they appeal to different segments of the marketplace, and they will be provided by different vendors. We will examine each in turn.

INFORMATION SERVICES

This type of videotext service is already offered on a wide scale in the United States, though it is primarily available through home computers, connected via telephone lines. Examples of such services are the following:

[2] We are also assuming a certain amount of computerized intelligence in the TV set itself, but the television industry is pursuing that already. They want higher-resolution TV monitors; they want the ability to have "split screens" so that the viewer can watch two different shows simultaneously; they want to provide an English television program, with Spanish dubbing from another channel; etc. The basic television set of the late 1980s and early 1990s will have considerably more power than today's top-of-the-line home computer, and it will be equipped to hook into a variety of other electronic household gadgets.

- Dow-Jones provides a wide variety of financial information on publicly held companies, as well as general news events. Information on stock trading activity, as well as financial data provided by the companies to the Securities and Exchange Commission, is available. This puts information previously accessible only to major brokerage firms into the hands of individuals.

- The Official Airline Guide (OAG) has an on-line system that can be accessed directly, or through other cooperative services (such as Dow-Jones or MCI Mail). It provides up-to-date information on virtually all plane flights, with current prices between cities throughout North America. Since airline fares have been deregulated, this service has proved to be a boon to the traveler.

- The Source, one of the country's "general" utility systems, has an on-line version of the *Mobil Hotel and Restaurant Guide*. Subscribers can retrieve a list of four-star hotels in Houston, Mexican restaurants in Detroit, and Cajun restaurants in Hoboken. Similar services can be found on Compuserve, the country's other major general information utility.

- Lockheed's "Dialog" system provides access to nearly 400 independent databases, compiled by government agencies, professional societies, and private organizations. Records can be retrieved based on keywords and other criteria (e.g., "Give me a list of all articles published on electronic mail in *Business Week* between January and March, 1985").

Altogether, there are nearly 450 commercially marketed databases in the United States; at least 50 of them are suitable for home use, and perhaps more when one considers the wide range of research that high school and college students might wish to carry out.

In addition, there is a market for "general" news on demand—though it is not yet clear how much people are willing to pay for it. How much is it worth to get an up-to-the-minute report on the weather in County Cork, Ireland? Maybe your niece is having a birthday party there today, and you're worried that it will rain; you can't get that information by dialing a local phone number today, unless you happen to live in County Cork. How much is it worth to be able to find out the president's travel itinerary for next week (assuming that the secret service is willing to publish such information), or the agenda before the House of Representatives this afternoon? The obvious provider of this kind of information is the kind of organization already in that business: newspapers, televisions, and radio stations. All of them are introducing experimental pilot projects around the country to test the economic viability of such a service.

Finally, there is the commercial version of electronic mail. In the cottage industry discussed in Chapter 3, the worker generally communicates with his employer or his client through a corporate computer system; all that is required is the home computer, the modem, and the telephone number of the company's mainframe computer system. But there are also commercial services that allow electronic mail—either in pure electronic form, or in "voice mail" form, or in "hard copy" form—between a subscriber and anyone else in the world. Well, not quite: if the recipient is not a subscriber, then he can't receive the message via voice mail (a digitally recorded rendition of the sender's message—i.e., something like the telephone answering systems, on a larger scale), nor can he receive mail electronically. But organizations like MCI Mail, Western Union's "Easy Link," GTE-Telenet's "Telemail," and ITT's "Dialcom" make it possible to send a telex, or a normal letter to anyone else, regardless of whether the recipient is a subscriber or not.

MCI Mail is, in my opinion, the forerunner of many services to come. The service is available from a local phone number virtually anywhere in North America; it involves a negligible annual subscription fee, and offers delivery services ranging from four-hour courier delivery anywhere in the country, to overnight mail via the (shudder) U.S. Post Office. MCI Mail will record your letterhead (or multiple letterheads) and signature (or various different signatures) on its computer system, so that they can be reproduced by a laser printer. You can store your mailing list on their system, so that you can send personalized form letters to friends or clients, and the cost is surprisingly modest.[3]

ELECTRONIC SHOPPING

Another obvious application for videotext is computerized shopping—either from a local store, or from a remote outlet that has either a wider variety, better prices, or some other way of attracting consumers. Compuserve, which already boasts some 250,000 subscribers, has one such service; one can shop for the best price on cameras, televisions, and other appliances, and then order by computer, using a credit card. More recent services, such as CompuSave,[9] plan to connect the concept of videotext to the "sexy" technology of videodisk; while this shopping service won't be available in individual homes, it can be provided in shopping centers and other convenient outlets.

Why would anyone be interested in electronic shopping? There are only two reasons: convenience and price. If you are buying a brand-name commodity item (e.g., a Nikon camera or a Panasonic television), then price is probably the most important factor. If you are far away from a convenient shopping outlet, price may be less important than the convenience of being able to order over a terminal or telephone. In both cases, of course, you have to assume that you are dealing with a reputable supplier who will live up to the terms of the sale (e.g., he'll ship via United Parcel Service (UPS) if he says that he will) and who will provide adequate service and support.

Note that you would not be inclined to use computerized shopping for something like fresh vegetables or a pound of hamburger—unless the supplier was the grocery store that you normally visit in person, and you were reasonably sure that he knew you personally (even though your order is being transmitted electronically), and that he wouldn't send you wilted lettuce or spoiled meat. With that kind of service, there would be many rainy

---

[3] I will discuss the use of electronic mail by business organizations in more detail in Chapter 19. There are currently about 225,000 subscribers to commercial E-mail services, and that is expected to increase to more than three million by 1987. By 1990, these subscribers will be transmitting nine billion messages per year to one another.

winter days and nights when I would happily order my groceries from a computer terminal or a TV screen rather than venturing out into the storm. Of course, my neighborhood grocery stores don't yet have videotext shopping, but the technology is available today, and it's only a matter of time before some enterprising high-tech grocer sees a market opportunity in an industry where it's almost impossible to achieve product differentiation.

ELECTRONIC EDUCATION

There's a very special kind of information that some consumers would like to get: the information normally associated with education. For many college students, education is as much a social process as it is an intellectual process—and I would not look forward very much to the prospect of my children living at home for another four years while they got their college degrees through a terminal. Both children and parents need a bit of relief from one another by the time the child is seventeen or eighteen.

The prime candidates for electronic education, in my opinion, are adults. Most of us who finished college twenty years ago can scarcely remember anything we learned—which is just as well, because most of the facts that were drummed into our heads are obsolete or irrelevant today. The underlying principles and philosophies probably weren't taught at all, or they were glossed over—or, in fairness to all those college professors who tried so hard, we students simply didn't grasp the principles in our desperate attempts to memorize the facts.

If the information explosion continues, most of us will need to be reeducated every ten years. For many of us, this is a philosophical suggestion that can be ignored; for some, it is a vital economic necessity. People trained in a variety of mechanical or agricultural skills twenty years ago are finding today that their jobs have disappeared altogether, or that the jobs have migrated to some other country where someone is willing to do higher-quality work for a fraction of the salary.

Many of us grew up in the days when correspondence courses addressed this need: "You can keep your job during the day, while you work a few hours in the evening learning to be a famous artist!

A staff of experts will review every bit of work you send us! Yes, indeed!" Many of these schools were—and still are—quite legitimate, but even in the best case, they suffer greatly from the lack of interaction between teacher and student, and between various students all struggling with the same material at the same time. A mixture of television, workbooks, interactive computer-assisted instruction, electronic mail communication with a real teacher, and occasional live meetings with other students is probably the ideal combination.

The technology for all of this is here today; we see pieces of it in such things as the public-service educational programs offered as a joint venture of television and local universities. And we now have a prototype of the real university of the future: the Electronic University, founded by Ron Gordon.[10] Gordon was president of Atari before it was acquired by Warner Communication Systems, so he is no stranger to computers. He began his "TeleLearning" program in late 1983, and by November 1984, he had over 1,500 students enrolled. The Electronic University is working together with some 2,000—that's two thousand—participating schools that will grant college credits to students who complete a course and pass a proctored final exam.

Economic motivation is, of course, a strong force for adults. And as futurist Harold Shane points out, jobs and economies are likely to continue changing for the foreseeable future. He prescribes a "seamless curriculum," which provides an educational model for students ranging in age from one to seventy. It provides for "drop-ins" and "drop-outs," and it makes extensive use of a paracurriculum, which is defined as "out-of-school experiences that help to strengthen the intellectual ability, general background, and coping power of the child or youth."[11] I would add to this only that adults need as much help in coping with today's world as do children!

The Future

Videotext is here today; it will grow, and it will prosper. I make this rather optimistic, almost rash, projection based on one observation: videotext (especially as conceived by the British and French) is closely allied with that universal source of banal entertainment, the television. If videotext depended entirely on being useful, and if it depended entirely on home computers and modems (as so many American videotext services do today), then its growth would be more erratic and probably much slower. Indeed, until American videotext services do switch over to the cable TV medium, they are likely to find that the rosy forecasts produced by the market research departments are nothing more than hot air.

Like the television, the automobile, and the telephone, videotext is a concept that will creep into our homes under the guise of amusement and entertainment. We will then gradually recognize it as a useful, if not essential, service. Then we shall have to return our attention to the words of Mr. Orwell at the beginning of the chapter because as Joseph Goebbels pointed out in Nazi Germany, he who controls the media controls the people's minds. I will return to this unpleasant subject in the next section of the book.

References for Chapter 8

1.   Mosco, Vincent, *Pushbutton Fantasies: Critical Perspectives on Videotex and Information Technology*, Norwood, N.J.: Ablex Publishing Corp, 1982.

2.   Hirsch, Phil, "First U.S. Videotex Service Up," *Computerworld*, November 14, 1983.

3.   Harris, Marilyn A., "Electronic Retailing Goes to the Supermarket," *Business Week*, March 25, 1985.

4.   Block, Robert S., "A Global Information Utility," *The Futurist*, December 1984.

5.   Mayer, Martin, "Coming Fast: Services Through the TV Set," *Fortune*, November 14, 1983.

6.   Edersheim, Peggy, "Increasing Computer Linkups Spur Fast Growth for Modems," *The Wall Street Journal*, September 6, 1985.

7.   "10,000-BPS Modem Breakthrough," *Infoworld*, July 22, 1985.

8.   Weil, Ulric, *Information Systems in the Eighties*, Englewood Cliffs, N.J.: Prentice-Hall, 1982.

9.   "Electronic Retailing" *op. cit.*

10.   "A School Without Walls," *PC Magazine*, April 16, 1985.

11.   Shane, Harold, *The Educational Significance of the Future*; Foundation Monograph Series, Phi Beta Kappa, 1973.

9

PERSONAL ROBOTS

Rule 1: A robot must never hurt a human or through its action allow one to come to harm.

Rule 2: Robots must obey human orders, unless they conflict with Rule 1.

Rule 3: Robots must never hurt themselves, unless doing so conflicts with Rules 1 and 2.

Isaac Asimov
I, Robot

A discussion of computers and society would be incomplete without a mention of the anthropomorphic form of computers: the robot. The subject has fascinated people since the early 1920s; indeed, the term came into general usage based on Karel Capek's reference to "Rossum's Universal Robots" in *R.U.R.* in 1920. One could argue that Mary Shelley's *Frankenstein* was an even earlier conception of a personal robot (though not a very friendly one), and that the Biblical "Golem" came even earlier.

Today, most of the discussion about robots is concerned with industrial robots: machines that can take the place of human workers on the assembly line, in the mines, and in a variety of physically unpleasant or dangerous occupations. A few million such robots have been built, and they are becoming more and more common in automobile companies and other high-production assembly line industries. The general public has also become accustomed to hearing about robots used for bomb disposal duties, underwater salvage activities, and other exotic tasks.

126

Though industrial robots are indeed an important application of computers, my discussion of them in this book will be relatively brief. My primary reason for this (much to the annoyance of robot specialists, I'm sure) is that they have already become irrelevant. As we will see throughout this book—especially in Chapters 23 to 26—a growing segment of the American economy is concerned not with the production of things but rather with the production of information. To the extent that the American economy depends heavily on the production of cars and planes and widgets, it is of some interest to discuss whether they will be manufactured by humans or robots. But when we see in Chapter 23 that the computer industry is already equal in size to the Big Three automobile manufacturers and twice the size of the steel industry, the subject of robots becomes less significant. The business of information processing consumes somewhere between 60 percent and 80 percent of the GNP of the entire country, so it is even less interesting to talk about mechanical machines that manufacture things.

Industrial robots attracted such attention in the 1930s through the 1970s largely because of the gloomy prospect of mass unemployment as machines took over the jobs of men and women—a subject that had already been debated a century earlier, as steam engines took over manual labor. Valid as that argument may have been in past decades, it is now largely irrelevant, since the major source of employment now is not in the manufacturing area anyway. Obviously, each job lost to a robot may be a personal disaster; but the experiences of the late 1970s and early 1980s suggest that American manufacturing jobs lost to human workers in Japan, Singapore, and other Third World countries are a far larger problem to worry about. As a recent article in *The Futurist* pointed out,

> The threat to unemployment is vastly overrated. The number of robots is growing at less than 35% per year, and there is little historical evidence to suggest that robots have ever caused a net increase in unemployment. The Japanese, for example, have more robots than all other countries put together, and they have the highest productivity growth rate in all industrial nations. Yet the unemployment rate in Japan is less than 3%.
>
> It is also wrong to assume that a human job is lost for every robot installed. The new technologies of robotics and computer-integrated

manufacturing will create entirely new industries, employing millions of people (and robots, too) in jobs that don't exist today. Robots will make possible new methods of manufacturing, construction, tunneling and deep drilling. They will be used for undersea mining, manufacturing in space, and farming of the oceans, all of which would otherwise be impossible or impractical. . .

Of course, there will be many new human jobs created just in the industries that manufacture, sell, install and maintain robots. A recent study done for the state of Michigan predicts that by 1990 the number of jobs created in the robot-manufacturing industries alone will be between 35% and 75% of the number of jobs lost in the robot-using industries. And if the increased productivity resulting from more efficient production technology makes American products more competitive on the world market, the net effect on employment will be overwhelmingly positive in almost all sectors of the economy.[1]

There is another reason for bringing our discussion of industrial robots to a rather abrupt end at this point. The real future of such robots in a manufacturing environment depends on substantial improvements in vision, voice recognition, tactile sensors, and a variety of skills that fall into the broad area of "artificial intelligence." Significant progress is being made in this area, and we will discuss some examples and applications of artificial intelligence in Chapter 21; however, there is still a long way to go. Capek's initial vision of a robot in *R.U.R.* was that of a machine so intelligent that it eventually revolted against its human masters and took control. This theme continued through the next several decades, until the 1960s, when people finally understood that computers were not yet in any position to threaten human intelligence. Movie viewers were entertained by the vision of HAL in the movie *2001*, and it has been used as a metaphor since 1968. But hardly anyone takes it seriously, even today. Some of the more optimistic artificial intelligence enthusiasts may argue that the "real" HAL will appear by the end of the 1990s, but as one critic recently commented about the artificial intelligence community (paraphrasing Winston Churchill), "Never has so little been produced by so many promising so much."

Unfortunately that statement also sums up the current state of affairs with personal robots. There are some enthusiasts, such as Arthur Harkins, the director of the graduate program on futures research at the University of Minnesota, who predict that by the year 2000, we will be using robots as sex partners. Mr. Harkins stated:

> The great bulk of human relationships are formulated on ritualistic actions—having breakfast at a certain time, keeping the house in a certain way, or performing sex in a certain manner. The technology of the year 2000 will support robots performing many of these functions —especially for the lonely, imprisoned, deformed or badly scarred. The Japanese have already developed all kinds of mechanical substitutes for human sexual organs, which are implanted into a robot and can be embellished with heat and other types of humanlike characteristics.[2]

But it would take quite an optimist to recommend abstinence until the day that robot sex partners arrive!

Most experts today agree that the personal robot industry is roughly in the same position as the personal computer industry in 1975: the products are crude, expensive, and not very functional. The people who bought personal computers in 1975 were hobbyists and tinkerers, people who understood enough of the inner workings of machines that they could assemble them from individual components and fix them when they broke. We are in roughly the same position in 1985 with personal robots.

Among the more popular personal robots today is the "Hero-1" robot from Heathkit. It looks like the R2D2 robot in the movie *Star Wars*; it costs $1,200 disassembled (in which case the consumer should be prepared for seventy to eighty hours of assembly time), or $2,500 assembled. It can be connected to a personal computer, such as an Apple II, and programmed to carry out various tasks. It uses sonar to detect sound, and has a variety of built-in spoken phrases such as, "No, I don't do windows," and "Stop, thief!"

One enterprising hobbyist programmed his Hero-1 to detect the presence of his three cats, at which point it would say, "I'll get you, ha, ha." Another tinkerer carefully programmed his robot and left it in a closet before inviting guests to his home for a cocktail party. When the guests opened the closet to hang up their coats, the robot scooted out, squeaking, "Thank you, thank you! I've been trapped by that ogre for weeks without food!"

All of this is amusing, but not terribly practical; as a result, the personal robot industry is languishing. About half a dozen small companies have each sold between a few dozen and several thousand personal robots ranging in price from $500 to $8,000. Heath Company is apparently the most successful, having sold some 8,000 Hero machines in the past two years; overall, though, the personal robot industry generated sales of only $25 to 50 million in 1984.[3]

There is some hope for the future, but it assumes one or more of the following scenarios:

- Very simple-minded, specialized, single-purpose computers that can carry out one household task efficiently. For example, a small household robot might do nothing but mow the lawn; it might be only a few inches wide, and it might take all day to finish the job, but it could be useful at that task. Similarly, there might be a market for a small robot that did nothing but roam a house or apartment all day long, chasing cockroaches and vacuuming small dustballs.

- A modest improvement in artificial intelligence, combined with a modest degree of vision, voice output, voice recognition, smell, and intelligent motion. A robot thus equipped might make a useful sentry, roving endlessly about the house (or an office or factory) looking for intruders, stray cats, chemical fumes, or the outbreak of fire. Such a semi-intelligent robot could also serve as a very limited servant, or companion, for bedridden invalids or handicapped people. Indeed, it could prove handy as a memory aid for children, senile senior citizens, and all of us other forgetful people who can never remember where we put our favorite tool or toy or magazine.

- A continued advance in hardware technology that will bring the cost of such personal robots down to the level where people can afford them. The kind of intelligence described above probably can't be built at all in 1985; if it could be built, the resulting robot would probably cost $100,000 or more. Even a $1,200 disassembled Hero-1 is too expensive for a consumer marketplace. The personal robot industry won't take off (in the way that the personal computer industry took off) until the cost of the technology is 10 to 100 times cheaper than today.

- There is something else to remember: the jobs that we currently think robots could do might be done in some other way by the time robot hardware is sophisticated enough and cheap enough. As consultant Nelson Winkless points out, "I don't think (a robot is) ever going to do windows, I really don't. I think by the time we teach them to do windows, windows won't get dirty. Teflon windows or something, I don't know. . . "[4]

Because of all this, it is probably a good idea to ignore the subject of personal robots for another few years—unless you're an adventurer, an eccentric, and/or a tinkerer. If you do purchase a personal robot with the idea of making it do something useful, be prepared for the kind of mayhem experienced by a restaurant owner in Edinburgh:

EDINBURGH (Reuter)—A robot dressed in a black hat and bow tie appeared in court Tuesday after running amok in a restaurant where it was employed to serve wine.

Within its first hour on the job, the second-hand robot became uncontrollable, knocking over furniture, frightening customers and spilling a glass of wine, the court was told.

The following day, the robot, exhibited Tuesday in the court, was still incapable of controlling the wine glasses, testimony said. Eventually its head fell into a customer's lap.

The London supplier of the robot is suing an Edinburgh firm, which made the final sale to the restaurant for the purchase price of $6,100.

But the Edinburgh firm maintains that it cannot bill the restaurant until the robot is in proper working order. [5]

References for Chapter 9

1. Albus, James S., "Robots and the Economy," *The Futurist*, December 1984.
2. Rochester, Jack B. and John Gantz, *The Naked Computer*, New York: William Morrow and Company, 1983.
3. "R2D2 May Be a Wiz, but Robots for Home Use Still Can't Do Much," *The Wall Street Journal*, April 25, 1985.
4. Gorney, Cynthia, "Robotic Pets: Not Yet R2D2," *Washington Post*, September 9, 1985.
5. "Wine Robot Loses Head," *Halifax Gazette*, June 26, 1985.

10
PREDICTIONS I

It is our less conscious thoughts and our less conscious actions
which mainly mold our lives and the lives of those who spring
from us.

Samuel Butler
The Way of All Flesh, 1903

For the past nine chapters, we have seen an overview of the impact
of computers on various aspects of society during the next five to
ten years. The current state of affairs is fairly close to what I have
shown; of that I am certain. As for the future, each of us must look
into his own crystal ball; mine is as cloudy as yours. I have a clear
view of the future of computer technology, but that very clarity
distorts my view of the impact of future computer technology on
society. You and I and our neighbors and our children are all part of
society. Each of us plays a role in determining—either by doing
something or by doing nothing at all—whether computers will be
used as I have suggested.

In this chapter, I will summarize the key, "bottom-line" results
that I see in each of the areas covered by Chapters 2 through 9. Then
I will discuss some meta-consequences of the future impact of
computers on society. Finally, I will return to the perspective
suggested in Chapter 1: What are the strategic implications of these
futuristic scenarios for the user of computer systems? What are the
implications for the producer (or manufacturer) of computer systems? What about the investor? And, of course, what about the
citizen?

SUMMARY OF FUTURE TRENDS FOR PART I

Chapter 2 discussed the impact of computers on children. The fundamental message of this chapter is that by the mid-1990s, every child in this country will be substantially more computer literate than the average professional computer programmer today. But along the way, there will be a very painful transition period, during which time some children will learn much more about computers, more quickly, than others. This is due to economic factors, gender bias factors, and general confusion within the schools.

It is reminiscent of the transition period during which earlier technologies gradually saturated the population—e.g., the telephone, automobile, and television. I vividly remember my high school years as a period when the lucky one-third of the student population had a television at home, and the unlucky two-thirds did not. I was in the unlucky majority, not because my family couldn't afford one, but rather because they thought the device was evil and would warp my mind. Among the many consequences of this situation was my teachers' recognition that they could not require us to watch an educational television program as a homework assignment, since they couldn't guarantee that all students had access to a TV set; they could merely suggest to the fortunate minority that they take advantage of the privilege. Today, teachers take it for granted that children have a television, probably in their own bedroom, and assign television programs as homework without a second thought.

We will see a similar phenomenon with computers. During the next five to ten years, those children with access to computers and the wherewithal to use computers as an effective tool will reap social benefits, educational benefits, and (ultimately) remunerative benefits. It is up to you as a parent to help ensure that your child is part of the lucky minority.

Chapter 3 presented a view of the future work environment. There is no question that the electronic cottage will spread far beyond the 2,000,000 people who currently enjoy it; the only questions are how prevalent the phenomenon will be, and how soon. Again, there will be a transition period during which the new technology (and the associated social culture) gradually spreads.

This will create two classes of people who will find that they have less and less in common with one another. Today, there are still manufacturing towns where everyone works at the same company, where everyone travels together to work the 8:00 A.M. shift. Even in a large city, workers share the common experience of the bus or the subway as they ride to their different jobs. But how can I communicate today with someone who doesn't know what electronic mail is all about? How can I explain my method of working to someone who assumes that if I'm at home, I'm on vacation? [1]

I personally do not believe that the cottage industry will involve more than 20 to 25 percent of the work force by the middle of the next decade, but that estimate could be wrong. In any case, even 20 percent—even 15 percent—will have far-reaching consequences above and beyond the worker-employer issues I discussed in Chapter 3. It will affect transportation patterns, energy costs, the price of office real estate, the nature of marriages and families, the population distribution between urban centers and suburbia, and so on. Since the government has shown that it is generally unable to plan even for the things it knows will happen—e.g., acid rain, nuclear arms proliferation, the budget deficit, etc.—it seems unreasonable to ask it to take on the planning for this issue. But at some level—if only the personal level—we all need to start planning for this new world. You can start planning tomorrow; ask your boss what he thinks of the idea of your working at home one day a week with your personal computer. If he gives you a blank look, you should consider updating your resume and looking for a more forward-thinking employer.

Chapter 4 emphasized the larger issues of communication via computer and telephone/computer/television combinations. If you don't use electronic mail, perhaps this chapter didn't have any

---

[1] In case you think this puts me on the defensive, let me emphasize that it's just the opposite: people who work in an electronic cottage not only know that they are better off, they soon begin to feel smug and superior about it. They find themselves increasingly frustrated that they can't send messages to their neighbors in the middle of the night, via MCI Mail or Telenet, and they gradually begin to think of those neighbors as second-class troglodytes—just as the early owners of telephones and automobiles probably thought of their less fortunate, less enlightened neighbors.

impact on you. And you may think that we already live in a "network nation" of instantaneous communication; after all, the whole world is on display for you on the 7:00 P.M. national TV news, and the commentators show no mercy about breaking into your favorite TV show whenever they think there is special news that merits your attention.

But such a view is amazingly superficial . . . whenever they think you should be allowed to see some news, they break into your TV show. But what about when you think the news is important? And how much coverage do you really think each news event gets on the 7:00 P.M. national news? A minute? Two minutes? Who decides what makes it onto the news and what doesn't? Surely not you . . . and you . . . and you. The information transfer, spontaneous as it may seem, is not under your control, not instantaneous—or real time—(unless those in control want it to be instantaneous), and not interactive (you can talk back to your TV, but it doesn't hear you).

The difference between this world, which we all know, and the world of on-line, real-time, interactive, worldwide, horizontal information transfer is like the difference between communicating in the days of Julius Caesar—whose messengers required a month to carry a message to the extremities of the Roman Empire, and from whose extremities they often never returned—and today's world of telephone and television. Suppose you had asked Julius Caesar, or perhaps one of his messengers, what impact the television and telephone would have on their lives. Could they have begun to imagine that it would lead to something like the "Live Aid" concert?

Chapter 5 discussed the future of computer games. You may not feel that computer games, or video games, are important today, or that they have any socially redeeming features. Nevertheless, it is important to realize that computer games will continue to become more sophisticated, and that they will serve as market research for serious applications of new technology. This will be particularly true as computer scientists work with forms of input-output to replace the keyboard—e.g., voice input, and communication via brain waves or electrodes implanted into the body.

Chapter 6 suggested that computers could play multiple roles in the typical household. The technology discussed throughout that chapter is largely available today; however, it is expensive, and the components were not designed to work with one another. Moreover, current homes are not designed with computers in mind. Hence the cabling (to connect several different computer-controlled devices) would have to be put in throughout the house, which would make a mess of the walls. You should be able to find computerized homes of the sort described in the May 1985 *IEEE Spectrum* by the end of this decade, but the twenty- to forty-year life of the typical home means that the technology won't be widespread until well into the next century.

Chapter 7 predicted that banks will disappear by the end of the century. It's hard to imagine that such large, powerful organizations could succumb to such an ignominious fate, but remember what happened to the dinosaurs! Besides, the banks aren't so big and strong as they may appear: any newspaper will tell you what a tenuous position most of them are in. They might end up being nationalized, or the Federal Reserve might change the rules of the game to get them out of their current crisis with worthless Third World loans—but that really wasn't the point of Chapter 7. Its main point was that banks are still based today on the concept of a large fortress keeping outlaw gunslingers from walking away with nuggets of gold. We are beginning to realize that money is an artifact, an arbitrary but useful way of providing a standard measure of the value of goods and services. As such, it represents nothing more than information. Buying and selling tangible goods and services thus involves moving that information from one place to another—from one computer disk record to another. We don't need banks to do that for us; we can do it ourselves.

Chapter 8 discussed videotext as one specific form of the network nation discussed in Chapter 4. Videotext has already made quite an impact in England and France, where the government subsidizes the technology and even provides free videotext terminals to hundreds of thousands of consumers. In America, the government is (thankfully) playing a passive role. However, rosy market forecasts of rapid videotext growth in America have thus far proved to be optimistic: the average consumer has not yet been convinced that electronic shopping and other similar services are worth paying for. I am convinced that there is a threshold above which these services will grow dramatically. The threshold within an individual household takes the form of (a) a family that already has several other reasons for using a personal computer, and finds that videotext represents a small, incremental cost for a useful service, such as electronic shopping, or (b) a free videotext terminal with several services that have immediate, tangible value. For society as a whole, we will have reached a threshold when entire cities have the service, or when it becomes as common and familiar as, say, the home video cassette recorder. This should certainly occur during the early to mid-1990s.

Finally, in Chapter 9, we discussed personal robots. I think there are many useful applications for special-purpose home robots, but we are several years away from seeing them at prices anyone will seriously consider. Your children will tell you when it is time to buy one. When they are cheaper than a cat or a dog or a pet gerbil, you should give your live pet to the ASPCA and get an electronic pet.

META-CONSEQUENCES OF THE SOCIAL IMPACT OF COMPUTERS

In addition to specific predictions and forecasts, there are some global issues that transcend all of them individually. It's interesting, for example, to see that many specific applications of computers in society depend on society's "view"—i.e., the perception of the average man in the street, the average housewife, the average teacher, the average school student—of the usefulness or importance of computers. Technological developments are fairly predictable; predictions about social trends are more like predictions about the weather: better done in retrospect. As Winston Churchill said in Cairo in 1943,

> I always avoid prophesying beforehand, because it is much better policy to prophesy after the event has already taken place.

Thus, to the extent that any of the predictions in the past several chapters depend on the consumer marketplace deciding that it wants or needs some new computerized gadget or service, remember: the marketplace will do what it wants, when it wants, not when IBM says so, and not when this book says so.

On the other hand, keep in mind another implication made in several of the previous chapters: new computer applications will be dragged along, free, with other related technologies. As the television industry and the telephone industry build faster, smarter televisions and telephones that do the same job they are doing today with extra capacity, it will cost nothing to give the consumer an additional feature or service that he might not have bought on his own.[2] This will be a natural consequence of cable TV, satellite TV transmission, and videotext. It will also happen as existing dumb appliances (like the vacuum cleaner, the lawn mower, and the microwave oven) gradually acquire more and more computerized intelligence for the same price. It might be very difficult to convince someone to buy a personal robot today—but if the standard vacuum cleaner in 1992 looks the same as today's model, costs less than today's model, operates in today's dumb mode, and also is capable of asking, in seventeen different languages, which room you would like vacuumed today, chances are that people will shrug their shoulders and use the new feature.

Another meta-consequence is that existing corporations will look radically different ten years from now. General Motors, for example, is undergoing a radical shift already: in 1984 and 1985, it acquired EDS (a billion-dollar computer software and consulting firm) and Hughes Aerospace. By the year 2000, it intends to derive at least 25 percent of its revenues from nonautomobile products and services. IBM, to cite another example, is clearly a different kind of company from the Tabulating Machine Company from whence it originated; by 1992, more than half of IBM's revenues will come from nonhardware items. And consider Coleco: it was originally

---

[2] Of course, this is easier to control for companies that have a near monopoly on the market, or such a dominant position that they feel they have to match the functionality of the leader's product. In a more fragmented industry—where there are thousands of companies and none has any significant market share—the newer technology might be incorporated into better products at the same price, or the same products (in terms of functionality) at a cheaper price. Some customers might opt for increased functionality; others might opt for price reduction.

the Connecticut Leather Company in the 19th century; then it became famous for its Coleco video games and computers in the early 1980s; then it caused mass riots in shopping centers in 1984 because of its popular Cabbage Patch doll. What kind of company will it be in 1995?

CONCLUSION: WHAT SHOULD YOU DO?

What does all of this mean for investors, producers, citizens, and users of computer systems tomorrow? Everyone will have a different reaction, of course, but I feel that all four groups should see the following implications of the continuing impact of computers upon society:

1. **Teach your children well.** In millennia past, farmers knew that their livelihood depended on the number of strong children they could breed, for it was the physical strength of their children that would keep them well fed in their waning years. So it is today, too—but instead of physical strength, we will be looking for intellectual strength, for an ability to dance with technology as it hops and skips across the globe. Just as our ancestors made sure that their horses and their children were well fed before they allowed themselves a meal, so we must ensure that our children are well fed intellectually on the stuff of computers. You'd better check out your school and see what they're doing; you'd better read *Mindstorms*, and *Technostress*, and *The Second Self*, and the other references at the end of Chapter 3. You'd better devote as much time and energy to their word processing lessons and their computer literacy lessons as you devote to their violin lessons and their art lessons. There are a lot of unemployed musicians and artists today; why add one more to the list?

2. **Be aware that computers are a fundamentally different communications medium.** If you are beginning to use electronic mail for the first time, remember that it's not the same as the telephone: the receiver can't hear your vocal intonations. A manager who uses electronic mail to send criticisms to his

subordinate is likely to find that it backfires; the subordinate—with one or two commands on the keyboard—can send that message to everyone else on his level (remember the horizontal information transfer concept) to say, "Look what that idiot said about me." If you are not using electronic mail or videotext or electronic banking, be aware that there are now several hundred thousand people in the country who—metaphorically speaking—have something above and beyond the five senses of sight, sound, touch, taste, and smell that you have. It might as well be telepathy; whatever it is, you don't have it, and it puts you at a disadvantage that grows larger with each passing day.

3.   **Look for new markets, products, and services that you can offer to society.** For example, consider starting a business to provide an on-line, up-to-the-minute database (information service) on educational computer games, so that a parent can dial up Compuserve or The Source to get a thorough product review of good math education programs for left-handed eight-year-old children. Consider starting an electronic butler service bureau that will allow urban apartment residents to dial your computer (from their home computer, or from their office computer) and request shopping, cleaning, valet, or other services to be performed. Consider developing a software product that will allow intelligent inventory control for the groceries that a family buys—a program that will keep track of patterns of food usage, storage capacity, price patterns, and budget constraints to make optimum use of the family food budget over several months.

4.   **Take advantage of the prefigurative culture.** It is very likely that the real money-making businesses and services will not be anything as mundane as the ideas in the paragraph above. They will be far more novel, and they will be invented by children who are not as mentally constrained about computer technology as you and I are. As communications consultant Colin Cherry points out:

Inventions themselves are not revolutions; neither are they the cause of revolutions. Their powers for change lie in the hands of those who have the imagination and insight to see that the new invention has offered them new liberties of action, that old constraints have been removed, that their political will, or their sheer greed are no longer frustrated, and that they can act in new ways. New social behavior patterns and new social institutions are created which in turn become the commonplace experience of future generations.

Such realization does not come easily, quickly, or even "naturally," for the invention can first be seen by society only in terms of the liberties of action it currently possesses. We say that society is "not ready" meaning that it is bound by its present customs and habits to think only in terms of its existing institutions. Realization of new liberties, and creation of new institutions, means social change, new thought and new feelings. The invention alters society, and eventually is used in ways that were at first quite unthinkable.[1]

My interpretation of this statement is very simple-minded: the new ideas for uses of computers are not going to come from our generation, but rather from our children's generation. However, that is no reason for us not to enjoy and even profit from this turn of events. We can help our children, we can encourage them, we can finance their efforts, we can applaud their successes, and profit from their creativity.

Or we can ignore what they are doing and watch history pass us by. We can stifle their creativity, and watch other nations, one by one, accomplish what we could not.

Reference for Chapter 10

1. Pool, Ithiel de Sola, *The Social Impact of the Telephone*, Cambridge, Mass.: MIT Press, 1979, p. 112.

COMPUTERS AND GOVERNMENT

11
TRADITIONAL GOVERNMENT INFLUENCE

Worthless.

Sir George Biddell Airy, K.C.B., M.A., LL.D., D.C.L., F.R.S., F.R.A.S.
(Astronomer Royal of Great Britain),
estimating for the Chancellor of the Exchequer the potential value of the
"analytical engine" invented by Charles Babbage. September 15, 1842

Government. Hardly anyone has a positive reaction to that word any more. Even those who feel that governments have a useful and important role usually agree that they are so large, so sluggish, and so out of step with the times that even their best efforts lead to counterproductive results.

When the word government is combined with the word computer, the reaction is almost universally negative. No doubt there is someone somewhere in the United States who can cite an incident where the government has actually done something useful and constructive with computers—but most of us would argue just the opposite. Computers are the excuse that the government uses when it is late sending its tax refunds (as millions of taxpayers discovered in the spring of 1985), or when it can't find someone's Social Security payment. Computers seem to be the final excuse needed by millions of bureaucrats to turn their brains permanently into the off position, so that they can stare vacantly when you ask them a simple question. "I can't help you with that, sir," the bureaucrat will intone listlessly. "It's the computer that decided that you owe $235,874,239.23 in back property taxes. I had nothing to do with it."

Still others find computers to be a frightening tool in the hands of an all-knowing, all-seeing, all-curious government. Computers allow the government to keep track of our lives, our actions, our spending patterns, our medical records, and our political preferences. Or do they? Exactly what does the government do with computers? And what will they be doing in the future?

These questions are the subject of Chapters 11 through 15. Though we are obviously interested first and foremost in our own government's use of computers, we should also review briefly the governmental activities in a number of other countries. Government attitudes toward computers in England and France contrast sharply with that of the U.S. government; the governments of several Third World countries are also beginning to play a role that we should be aware of. And such countries as Russia are also interesting examples of how centralized governments sometimes face major dilemmas when they try to introduce modern computer technology.

We begin in this chapter by reviewing the general domain of interest in computer technology on the part of governments. Then, in Chapter 12, we will examine current governmental activities in several representative countries. Chapter 13 explores the governmental regulations that are becoming more and more common in the mid-1980s. Chapter 14 examines the issue of personal privacy in a computerized age. And Chapter 15 provides some overall predictions about the future relationship of computers and government.

Broadly speaking, governments have traditionally been interested in computers for three different (but related) reasons:

- Record-keeping activities.

- Military interests.

- Economic interests.

RECORD-KEEPING ACTIVITIES

Since the first village chief took control of his tribe in Stone Age times, there has been an undying interest in keeping track of things: counting, filing, organizing, listing, computing, and reporting on every conceivable aspect of the lives of the individuals, as well as the well-being of the collective unit. This must have been a difficult task for the village chief, but he no doubt learned quickly to make use of human computers who could remember facts and figures for years. Tribal elders, historians, priests, and even witch doctors played this role admirably.

With the invention of writing and the gradual use of papyrus and parchment, things became easier: it was no longer necessary to rely on human memory, which was limited in terms of capacity and longevity. As long as there was an ample supply of papyrus, and as long as the ink didn't fade and the papyrus didn't crumble into dust, governments could amass as much data as they wanted. How early must it have been when the first bureaucrat discovered that information is power?

The traditions of the Egyptians, the Sumerians, the Chinese, and the Greeks have been passed down from generation to generation: governments around the world—at the national level, and at the village level—still find pleasure in amassing data for data's sake. Oblivious of the high-technology world around them, most still use quill pens and papyrus to record the details of births, deaths, property taxes, school enrollments, and all of the other records of day-to-day life in the tribe.

What does this record keeping involve? It varies from village to village and from country to country, but we can almost always find the following:

- **Data capture.** In many cases, a government clerk has to write down (or "capture") information regardless of whether he or the citizen involved perceives any value in the process: it's "the way things are done." In some cases, it's the law. The Constitution of the United States, for example, mandates that the citizens of the country will be counted at least once every ten years, so that representation in the House of Representatives can be reapportioned. That data-capture activity might be considered useful, since it determines how many representatives the state of Wyoming will be allowed to send to Washington,[1] but the data capture involved in recording many other tidbits of information

---

[1] It also turns out to be a dangerous activity, as we will see in Chapter 14. The government doesn't just keep a tally of individuals any more; it asks several hundred additional questions during the decennial census, and the law requires us to answer the questions.

has dubious value at best. Unfortunately, governmental policy sometimes outlives the legislators who invent it. It was not until the middle of the 20th century that the British Parliament repealed the law requiring a British sailor to stand watch on the cliffs of Dover, gazing out over the English Channel for Napoleon's invasion.

- **Data transformation.** This is a fancy way of saying that the information provided by the citizen to his government is often used to create new data. One simple example of this involves computations: When we tell the government how much money we earned, or how much property we own, or how many children we have, then the government tells us—based on a mathematical calculation—how much money it wants us to pay. Another simple example is the creation of a new record based on information provided: if we tell the government about the birth of a child, it will generate a new record. The child's record will be linked to that of his parents within the governmental data storage system, and it will also have an independent life of its own.

- **Data analysis.** This, of course, is something that computers are very good at doing—but governments were doing it long before computers came along. How many taxpayers do we have in the country? How many tons of potatoes did the State of Idaho produce last year? How many billions of dollars in revenue can we raise if we impose a tax on bubble gum? What is the correlation between the legal drinking age and the number of automobile accidents? There are an endless number of such questions that government officials want to ask; and they learned long ago that by asking the right question in the right way, they could receive the answers they wanted to hear, and justify the actions they had already taken. Consequently, smart data analysts learned early on to figure out what the required answer was, and then search for the appropriate data to justify that answer. This is more difficult if the data analysis is done automatically by an apolitical computer—especially if the computer is capable of the associated data capture by itself, without any human intermediary to filter the input. This is currently causing quite a dilemma in Russia, as we will see in Chapter 12.

- **Data retrieval.** For a variety of reasons, good and bad, governments have always wanted the power to burrow into the piles of data they accumulate in order to retrieve one or more interesting items of information. "Let me see the record on Taxpayer Jones," is a command that has been issued during every government regime since mankind first agreed to huddle together and pay a common tithe for the privilege of being governed. "Let me see the records of all those scoundrels in the village of Moribundia," is a command that has also been heard from more than one high-level bureaucrat. It may not be easy to find that record (or collection of records) if there are millions of taxpayers and thousands of Joneses, particularly if the records consist of stone tablets or papyrus scrolls that fill entire buildings. From very early days, government "information engineers" devised clever ways of indexing and cross-referencing and cataloging, so that the required information could be retrieved quickly.

MILITARY INTERESTS

Everything that the government wants to do in the general sense, it also wants to do in the special sense of military activities. The military organization of any country is like a vast business, or a small government, depending on how one wants to look at it; indeed, the terms business, government, and military are almost interchangeable from an information processing point of view.

Military organizations are concerned with issues of data capture, data transformation, data analysis, and data retrieval. But since they tend to have more of a sense of urgency than, say, the village council of Lower Slobovia, they put a premium on efficiency and effectiveness (but generally not economy). They want their data captured reliably; they want their data analyzed accurately; they want their data retrieval demands to be answered quickly. In olden days, this meant that the military had more clerks, and perhaps brighter clerks, than the village elders could afford (or were willing to tolerate). Today, it means that the military tends to have larger, faster, more powerful computer hardware, and they invest more money than their commercial counterparts in dealing with the "software crisis" that we will discuss in Chapter 27.

It is useful to distinguish between weapons systems and logistics systems within military organizations, although the boundary between the two is getting fuzzier all the time. Weapons systems are concerned with guidance of, or control of, or proper operation of, weapons: bombs, planes, ships, torpedoes, missiles, tanks, and whatever other instruments of destruction the military is hatching in the research and development (R&D) labs. Until recently, weapons were carried, shot, dropped, or thrown by human hands: the required calculations had to do with distance and trajectory. At what angle should the cannon be aimed? How much gunpowder should be used to lob a ten-pound shell across the moat to smash down the castle wall?

In more modern times, the calculations have involved at least two moving bodies: the missile/bullet/bomb and the target. Even more complex is the three-body problem involving a moving target, a moving object from which the weapon is to be fired (a ship, plane, tank, etc.), and the missile. Indeed, it was the demand for such calculations that ultimately led to the development of the modern computer: antiaircraft batteries in World War II needed to know where to aim their salvos in order to shoot down incoming enemy aircraft, a calculation that could have been done manually, but not by the average fire controller. Even a trained mathematician would not have finished his antiaircraft calculations until the day after the enemy plane had dropped its bombs and returned home.

Today's weapons systems involve the same mathematics and same fundamental military issues, but the level of sophistication has increased enormously, and the speed with which everything happens is almost beyond comprehension. In fact, it *is* beyond comprehension. There is serious doubt among computer scientists, physicists, and engineers as to whether the "Star Wars" program proposed by the U.S. Defense Department can ever be built successfully.[2]

---

[2] Many of the technical issues in this debate involve lasers, aerodynamics, nuclear defense technology, and a wide range of topics beyond the scope of this book. However, there is also concern that the computer software, which will drive the entire system, may also be so complex that it will never work. See "The Star Wars Defense Won't Compute," by Jonathan Jacky in the June 1985 *Atlantic Monthly* for an interesting discussion of this problem. Turn to Chapter 27 for a discussion of an even broader range of computer software problems.

In addition to weapons systems, the military organization has soldiers to feed and clothe; supplies and munitions and vehicles to keep track of; retirement pay and pension plans, hospital insurance; and all of the other "bureaucratic" data-gathering, data-analysis and data-retrieval problems that other business organizations and other government agencies have. Indeed, many of the "logistical" computer systems currently operating within military organizations look surprisingly like the systems in a bank, or an insurance company, or the Department of Health and Human Services.

ECONOMIC INTERESTS

In addition to its own natural interest in computers, governments around the world are beginning to realize that computers are an industry of significance. We have all seen the interest that national governments take in such industries as steel, automobiles, textiles, fishing, and mining. Now it is being applied to computers.

There are two reasons for this: economic well-being of a politically large (or important) group of citizens, and perceived importance of the industry to the well-being of the country. This can be illustrated with a counterexample: the shoe industry. The United States once had a thriving shoe industry, but it has largely disappeared during the past twenty years. Does anyone care? Presumably those who were employed by shoe companies care, and those who owned the shoe companies cared; but there weren't enough of them to create an effective lobby. Is anyone worried about the strategic importance of shoes? Not that I've heard of! Obviously, the prospect of being cut off from our supply of shoes and being forced to walk around barefoot is not very attractive—but I doubt that it would take more than two weeks for a local shoe industry to rise from the ashes and flourish again. Meanwhile, most of us have an inventory of several pairs of Nikes and Adidas in our closet that we could wear to work.

Computers are perceived (rightly, I think) as being something fundamentally different from shoes. First of all, the computer industry is large enough to be reckoned with. As we will see in Chapter 24, it represented 8 percent of the GNP of the United States in 1985, and it will grow to about 15 percent by the end of the decade. It is already twice as large as the steel industry, and roughly equal to the Big Three automobile manufacturers of whom we hear so much every day. Clearly, the computer industry can form an effective lobby.

More important is the threat of being cut off from the supply of computers and the stream of ongoing technological developments. Since our economy depends on computers, and since the military depends even more on computers, having our supply of computers and "chips" cut off is just as serious as having our supply of oil cut off. Industry would come to a screeching halt, and the military would find that it could not fight a war. Even if the existing computers kept running faultlessly, they would rapidly become obsolete compared to newer, faster, cheaper foreign computers.

It is because of the economic value of the computer industry, and the strategic importance of computers to industry and the military, that many of the government activities described in Chapters 12 and 13 have escalated so much during the past few years. And that involvement will continue, as we will see in the next few chapters.

12

CURRENT GOVERNMENT INVOLVEMENT

> The Federal Government has been a leader in the innovative use of information technology since the 1940's, and is heavily dependent on automated data processing (ADP) for carrying out its programs and performing administrative activities. The President's budget for 1986 requests in excess of $14 billion to acquire and support general purpose information processing technology. More than 120,000 Federal employees will be responsible for programming and maintaining more than 20,000 mainframe computers leased and owned by the Government. As a result, the U.S. Government is the single largest user of information technology (computers and communications) in the world.
>
> *Management for Fiscal Year 1986,*
> Office of Management and Budget

In most countries around the world, the single largest user—or customer—for computers is the national government. State and local governments probably rank a close second in many countries, but they do not have as much influence on R&D activities, nor do they have any significant impact on the activities of the computer industry in terms of imports, exports, etc.

In Chapter 13, we will examine the efforts of national governments to affect the external trade policies of computer companies—e.g., quotas, tariffs, restrictions on foreign computer companies operating within national borders, etc. In this chapter, though, we will examine the activities of federal governments inside their own borders. What role do they play? How do they foster

153

research and development? What kinds of research are they interested in? We will examine the activities of Japan, the United States, England, China, the Soviet Union, and various Third World countries.[1]

JAPAN

Of all the countries outside of our borders, the one that is causing the most concern for the American computer industry at the present time is Japan. Largely because of its success, during the past twenty years, in such diverse areas as automobiles, cameras, textiles, steel, motorcycles, and televisions—as well as its recent dominance in the semiconductor chips that are the basic building blocks for computers and other electronic products—there is great concern that Japan will soon take over the entire computer industry.

Unfortunately, some discussion ascribes almost superhuman powers to the Japanese people, not to mention Japanese companies and Japanese industries. Some authors, like physicist Gerard K. O'Neill, are fond of pointing out statistics such as the following:

- The IQ of the average Japanese is ten points higher than that of the average American.

- Forty million Americans have an IQ of 85 or less; only one million Japanese have such a low IQ.

- Fifteen percent of Americans are functionally illiterate; only 1 percent of the Japanese are illiterate.

- Japan has three times as many engineers per capita as the United States.[1]

No doubt these are important statistics to consider, and they do point to a determined, well-educated work force that is capable of

---

[1] No doubt I will be criticized for the countries I have left out—particularly France, and the joint-venture "Esprit" program taking place within the European community. But I feel that the list that I have included is representative of the major parts of the world, and that it includes the countries most likely to have a major impact on the future of the computer industry in the next ten years. Time will tell.

accomplishing a number of major economic objectives. But whether it means that the Japanese will dominate the worldwide computer industry is still an open question; many experts remain unconvinced in the mid-1980s—and it will be the mid-1990s before we know for sure.

Japan does have a significant share of the world market for computers: it was estimated to be 6 percent at the end of 1981, and 10 percent in 1983.[2] However, it is important to emphasize that 80 percent of Japan's computer-related exports in 1983 were for "peripheral devices"[3]—floppy disks, printers, keyboards, display terminals, etc. This part of the computer industry is very similar to the commodity market for radios, televisions, and other electronic products that Japan has been exporting for years. Japan very definitely knows how to combine (a) high-quality production, (b) low unit-cost production, (c) efficient distribution channels, and (d) good marketing relationships in foreign markets. This combination is currently providing Japan with the same kind of success in the computer hardware peripherals industry that it provided with other products. However, the winning formula that Japan has used is not a secret anymore. American and European electronics companies, having been badly burned in the 1970s, are gradually copying the Japanese success formula with good results. While the Japanese culture of quality circles and consensus management may be unique—or sufficiently different from American and European management styles—it is also true that highly automated production lines can eventually be tuned to achieve very high-quality products. Of all basic industries, the computer industry is probably best able to take advantage of this fact; hence it is debatable whether the Japanese will retain this advantage for very much longer.

However, there is more to the story. One additional reason for Japanese success has to do with the demand for profitability. American companies are measured by top management, the board of directors, and Wall Street (representing millions of investors) every quarter; some Japanese companies, on the other hand, have 200-year plans that they are following. In addition, the Ministry of Industry, Trade and Information (MITI), together with the Japanese Ministry of Finance, plays an active role in the computer industry by providing low-interest loans, tax concessions, and preference to local companies for computer procurements.

In this kind of environment, there is much more emphasis on worldwide market share than there is on short-term profitability. Ulric Weil points out that the profitability of the six major Japanese computer companies is approximately four times lower than that of IBM Japan, and approximately twice as low as that of American computer companies.[4] In July 1984, Mitsubishi reported record revenues and profits for the year; its income before taxes was only 2.2 percent of revenues.[5] IBM, meanwhile, regularly reports pre-tax profits of 20 to 22 percent, some ten times higher than Mitsubishi's.

The short-term future for Japan is fairly clear: its presence in the world market will continue to grow. In 1980, Japan exported 10 percent of its production to the world market; by 1985, it expects to export 15 to 20 percent to the United States alone. Japan currently has 2 to 5 percent of the European and North American computer market, but it expects to capture roughly 20 percent of those lucrative markets by the early 1990s.[6] And, as we will see later in this chapter, Japan is aggressively pursuing new markets in China, Russia, and other parts of the world.

However, in the long term, this is largely irrelevant. The computer industry will come to be dominated more and more by computer software. We will discuss this in much more detail in Chapter 23, and the reasons behind much of the software costs will be discussed in Chapters 27 to 33. But two statistics will help emphasize the importance of this point. First, the organizations that use computers are already spending more than 50 percent of the computer budget on software and on the people who produce software. Second, it is estimated that by 1992, IBM will derive more than 50 percent of its revenues from nonhardware items.[7] Those two statistics alone should be enough to convince many that the future profits of the computer industry will not be derived from manufacturing semiconductors!

Software, as we currently use the term, will probably be a major industry for only another ten years—but it is one that the Japanese intend to participate in with a vengeance. Their quality circle techniques, and their cultural appreciation for high-quality products, have already put them in a position where they can produce normal computer software with ten times fewer errors than comparable software developed in North America and Europe. (We will discuss the reasons for this in Chapter 27.) However, there is an interesting paradox: the most novel forms of computer software (the kinds that are likely to make the most money in the marketplace) now require an understanding of the needs and wants of the "end user," who is typically a business person or white-collar office worker or sophisticated user of home computers. That kind of software is being developed by American programmers who have a better sense of the market (or who are more willing, culturally, to take a gamble) and who can communicate more easily with American business customers and understand the milieu in which the software must be used. Their initial software products are often months late and riddled with bugs; but by the time the Japanese could catch up with their high-reliability copies, the Americans have "shaken down" their products, achieved a certain amount of brand-name loyalty, and moved on to new products. Only when the "applications software" market stabilizes can the Japanese really hope to compete effectively.

Meanwhile, the truly exciting long-term software market is up for grabs. The Japanese announced loudly and publicly in 1981 that they were going after that market, and that is what caused the period of mass hysteria in American, British, and European computer companies. The long-term market is not conventional hardware, and is not conventional software: it is "Fifth-Generation" computer hardware, coupled with artificial intelligence and expert systems. By the mid-1990s, the Japanese hope to be in a position to export encapsulated knowledge, based on machines that are 1,000 to 10,000 times more powerful than today's computers—and based on software that will "reason," make inferences, and gradually become smarter in an applications area, just as a human becomes smarter after a certain amount of on-the-job training.

Whether the Japanese will succeed at this remains to be seen; it is an area of great debate among professional Japan-watchers. After an initial period during which the American computer industry seemed ready to throw in the towel, there is now more of a wait-and-see attitude, coupled with deprecatory articles indicating that

"Japan No Big Threat to U.S. Vendors,"[8] "Speaker Points to Weaknesses in Japanese Plan,"[9] and "Fifth-Generation Threat by Japanese Overrated, Industry Expert Warns."[10] However, it is generally agreed that even if Japan is only partially successful in its research goals, it will have changed the nature of the computer industry permanently.

Indeed, Japan already has changed the nature of the computer industry permanently. National attention has been focused on computer hardware development, artificial intelligence, expert systems, parallel processing, and a number of specialized areas that had never seen the light of day. The level of government spending and research has increased dramatically in the United States, England, and the European Economic Community in response to the Japanese effort.[11]

The Japanese effort is overseen by MITI and is coordinated by an Institute for Generation of New Computer Technology known as ICOT. The ICOT staff in 1984 consisted of fifty-two people (all men) who were mostly under thirty years of age; by request of the director of the group, none is over thirty-five years of age.[2] It has two major projects: the Fifth-Generation Computer Project, which is planned to run for ten years at a total cost of $500 million; and the National Superspeed Computer Project, which is expected to last eight years at a total cost of $100 million. By 1984, three years into the Fifth-Generation project, the Japanese had produced a new computer processor known as SIM (for "sequential inference machine") and a relational database machine known as Delta.[12] While these early developments are impressive, they do not yet indicate whether the Japanese will be able to achieve their overall ten-year goals.

Probably the most beneficial result of the Japanese effort is that it has forced the American computer industry, as well as American academia, to seriously reevaluate the position of preeminence it has long since taken for granted. While some American observers continue to insist that America has a dominant position,[13] most are taking a much more realistic—and balanced—view, as evidenced

---

[2] This raises an interesting question: what happens to valuable staff members when they reach the age of thirty-five? Are they allowed to stay? Are they shot? Are they put into retirement homes?

by a U.S. Department of Commerce panel that concluded in 1984 that the United States is ahead of Japan in basic computer research, equal to Japan in advanced product development, and behind Japan in product engineering or products closest to final application.[14]

The most likely result of Japan's efforts will be that America will eventually lose its near monopoly on the worldwide computer market, but will be forced by healthy competition to offer higher quality, more competitive products at a better price. To the extent that we believe in a free enterprise system, we really can't ask for much more.

THE UNITED STATES

Within the private sector of the United States—the banks, insurance companies, manufacturing companies, and service-oriented companies—data processing activities typically account for 1 to 2 percent of overall revenues.[3] Consequently, a company whose data processing staff numbers 100 to 200 people is considered respectably large; a company whose data processing staff is over 1,000 people is considered enormous. In my twenty years of traveling around the world as a consultant, I have seen only a handful of private industry companies with staffs of more than 2,000 people; the associated annual budget for computers and staff may be in the tens of millions of dollars (that's respectably large), and rarely exceeds $100 million.

Thus, an organization like the U.S. government—with 120,000 people involved in data processing, an inventory of 20,000 mainframe computers (and God only knows how many minicomputers,

---

[3] This might appear to contradict earlier statements that data processing already accounts for 8 percent of the GNP of the United States. However, remember that the computer manufacturing industry, the software industry, and various other peripheral industries contribute all of their revenues toward the overall GNP figure. The figure of 1 to 2 percent is the figure for a General Motors or U.S. Steel, whose primary products have nothing to do with computers; if one examines their profit-and-loss statements, a small amount can usually be found for explicit expenditures on computer hardware and the related software and personnel expenditures. As we will see in Chapter 23, a closer examination of any of these companies would probably find that 60 to 80 percent of their expenditures could be associated with information processing of one kind or another—e.g., the accounting department, most of the marketing department, etc.

microcomputers, and personal computers—the U.S. government surely doesn't!), and an annual budget of $14 billion—is far and away the largest user of data processing on earth. It is interesting to note, by the way, that the computer industry's own estimates of government expenditures on computers are far higher than the government's budget figures. The research firm International Development Corporation estimates that the federal government spent $25 billion on information technology in 1983, and that its expenditure for information technology grew at a compounded rate of 20 percent over the next three years.[15]

General Government Usage

Computers are used throughout the U.S. government, in virtually every agency, including the House of Representatives and the U.S. Senate; current estimates are that there are 3,000 to 4,000 personal computers on Capitol Hill.[16] It is probably fair to say in the mid-1980s that the Congress is indicative of the widespread usage of computers throughout American industry; in this sense, the United States is probably far ahead of most other countries in the world.

Aside from the Defense Department, much of the government's usage of computers is overseen, administratively, by the General Services Administration (GSA) and General Accounting Office (GAO). Orders of up to $300,000 for computer equipment must go through GSA,[17] while larger orders can be conducted by independent competitive bidding procedures.

While the overall usage of computers in the federal government is well organized and efficient, there are major trouble spots caused (more than anything else) by the fact that the government was one of the very earliest users of computer systems and is thus saddled with old, archaic systems that are almost impossible to keep up to date. The IRS, Veteran's Administration, and Social Security Administration (SSA) are among the more troubled agencies. Of these, the IRS came under intense public scrutiny in the spring of 1985 because of problems with converting to a new hardware system, and the Social Security Administration has attracted the most attention because of its ongoing problems.

Indeed, the SSA problems are not unique, and are no reflection on the energy, talent, or dedication of its staff—but rather the accumulation of old hardware, old software, and a general lack of understanding on the part of Congress of the difficulties of dealing with massive volumes of data. For the SSA, massive means 446 billion characters of disk storage to service 650,000 inquiries each day. It means 113 tons of computer printouts per month; 380 million wage reports per year, and 40 million checks per month.[18] As former commissioner John A. Svahn says, only a "daily miracle" gets the monthly checks out on time. Having worked with the SSA computer people, I can personally testify to their enormous energy and professionalism,[4] and I firmly believe that the $478 million, five-year modernization program approved by Congress in 1982 will eventually (though not in five years) get the organization back in control.

The reason for mentioning these statistics is that the SSA is just one of dozens, if not hundreds, of U.S. government agencies struggling with a legacy of twenty-five years of decrepit information systems.

Defense Department Usage

The driving force in American computer research in the 1980s is undoubtedly the Department of Defense (DOD). This should be no surprise. It was the Defense Department (then known as the War Department) that sponsored the research during World War II that led to the first modern computer in 1945. It was the Defense Department that organized the collaborative effort that led to the first widely used high-level programming language now universally used in business organizations, COBOL. It is the Defense Department that is now making a concerted, multibillion-dollar effort to introduce a new programming language called Ada;[19] and it is an agency of the Defense Department, DARPA (discussed below),

---

[4] I was not present, however, during the incident reported by *The Wall Street Journal* in 1983, when one of the SSA maintenance programmers allegedly urinated on one of the computer disk drives to vent (among other things) his frustration. It could have occurred; but it could also occur in any of several hundred maintenance shops in private industry. We will examine the horrible problem of computer software maintenance in Chapter 30.

that has been responsible for most of the major American research efforts for the past twenty-five years.

The mission and objectives of DOD may be unclear to many, and outrageous to some; they are overwhelming and unrealistic to others. It is beyond the scope of this book (and beyond my personal expertise) to comment on the overall American defense posture or the strategic plans of the U.S. military. While I definitely have opinions and feelings on the matter, I leave it to others, far more qualified than I, to comment in writing. However, it is no secret that the success of the American defense policy will become more and more inextricably linked to computer technology, and that, therefore, DOD's interests will be more and more actively involved with the direction and success of the American computer industry. Thus, regardless of whether one is an activist or pacifist, Republican or Democrat, it is becoming virtually impossible to ignore the presence of DOD in the everyday happenings of the American computer establishment.

As mentioned in Chapter 11, military organizations bear a striking resemblance to business organizations and other nonmilitary government organizations. They must manage men and material, inventory and raw materials; they must deal with receivables and payables; they, in their own way, must produce a balance sheet periodically to see where they stand. They must have strategic plans, they must eventually have "enterprise models" that provide nontechnical managers (or generals) with an overall view of the organization. The American defense organization differs from General Motors, Exxon, and IBM only in size: it deals with an annual budget equal to the combined sum of the top ten industrial organizations in the United States. Hence, its information processing needs are that much greater, and its problems are that much greater. And—to its credit—its sense of urgency about solving its information processing needs is that much greater.

Logistics systems and weapons systems are the two broad categories of information systems being built in the Defense Department today. But, through its research efforts, it is involved in everything from A to Z (actually, only through "V"): artificial intelligence, algorithm development, architecture of computers, database management, digital signal processing, fault tolerance, flight control, flight guidance, knowledge-based systems, modeling, navigation, and very high-level languages.[20]

One of the major initiatives of the U.S. Defense Department is the "Star Wars" program (also known as the Strategic Defense Initiative), introduced by President Reagan as a defensive program for shooting down enemy missiles while they are still in space. The cost of this program is astronomical, the politics are mind-boggling, and the interdisciplinary scientific effort required to implement the project makes the American space program of the 1960s look like a kindergarten project. There is considerable debate over the desirability of such a project; there is also debate over the technical feasibility of the project.[21] But whether it succeeds or fails, whether it is implemented or eventually vetoed by Congress, there is no doubt that the Strategic Defense Initiative will advance the state of the art in American computer science simply by focusing attention on difficult issues that have not been dealt with before.[22]

Meanwhile, the DOD continues to sponsor a wide range of computer research activities, ranging from advanced "biochip" computer hardware research[23] to investments in private industry research in artificial intelligence.[24] And it is devoting billions of dollars and major research programs to fundamental research into aspects of computer science, such as the "STARS" program ("Software Technology for Adaptable Reliable Systems" for those unfamiliar with DOD acronyms)[25] that will undoubtedly benefit the entire computer science profession and all of private industry.

DARPA and Other U.S. Government Activities

Historically, the primary patron of computer science research in the U.S. government since 1958 has been the Defense Advanced Research Projects Agency (DARPA). As its name implies, it is an agency within the Department of Defense; its charter is to fund research that will provide useful products and ideas for American defense systems. During its long tenure, it has invested over $500 million in such diverse areas as supercomputers, time-sharing, artificial intelligence, packet-switched networks, and computer graphics. Whether by accident or design, much of this research has eventually trickled into the private sector: many commercial products and services in the computer field can be traced back to funding originally provided by DARPA. Recently, DARPA has stepped up its efforts to counter what it perceives as a "Japanese threat": during the next five years, it plans to invest twice as much as in its entire twenty-seven-year history. The "buzzword" for this newly-launched DARPA effort is Strategic Computing.[26]

Other patrons of U.S. government-sponsored computer research include the National Science Foundation (with a budget of approximately $50 million); NASA (which has an annual budget of approximately $20 million for computer-aided aeronautical design research); and the Department of Energy (formerly known as the Atomic Energy Commission), which owns more than half of the government's supercomputers. These and other government organizations, ranging from the National Institutes of Health to the National Bureau of Standards, maintain a constant series of seminars and research programs to stay abreast of current computer technology.

MCC

Not all American computer research is sponsored by the U.S. government; indeed, it may turn out in the long run that the most important, most innovative computer research takes place outside the U.S. government. For many, that would be a welcome development indeed; even for skeptics and conservatives, there must be some joy and optimism that our eggs are not all in one research basket.

The primary alternative to the U.S. DOD-sponsored research is MCC, a consortium of fourteen American companies who were brought together by one of the pioneers of the computer industry, Control Data Corporation chairman William Norris. Founded in 1982, it now has a staff of approximately 300 people and a budget of approximately $75 million. It is headed by Retired Admiral Bobby Inman, former director of the National Security Agency and a veteran of Washington politics. It is based in Austin, Texas, where it draws upon the resources of the University of Texas, the state capital bureaucrats, and the synergy of private industry plants manned by IBM, Texas Instruments, Intel, and others.

The charter of MCC is similar to that of the DOD research programs: research into computer hardware, software engineering, artificial intelligence, etc. But instead of answering to the Defense Department or Washington bureaucrats, MCC answers only to its fourteen stockholders. Based on a personal visit in July 1985, I can vouch for MCC's professionalism, energy, and foresight. Based on its physical distance from Washington and its relative independence, I have high hopes for its future.

ENGLAND

Though England is still an important member of the Western economic and military alliance, its role in the burgeoning computer industry is much less impressive. It can rightly claim some of the best researchers and theoreticians in the world;[5] its universities are top-notch and actively engaged in leading-edge research in various aspects of computers. But overall, the British economy, and the declining role of England as a world power, have combined to keep the country from playing an active role in the industry. For a time, England's indigenous computer company, ICL, was a noticeable factor in the world market; but since the mid-1970s, it has been largely ignored. Entrepreneur Clive Sinclair attracted considerable attention when he introduced a home computer for less than $100 (a price which eventually dropped even further), but his efforts were overshadowed by the larger success of Apple, IBM, and others.

However, the British government has responded vigorously to the Fifth-Generation project in Japan; its own long-term program is known as the "Alvey program," and is directed by Brian Oakley. Though perhaps somewhat smaller than the Japanese and American programs, it is noteworthy because of its efforts to bring about a full-scale collaboration between universities, industry, and government agencies. Funded projects involve artificial intelligence, computer-aided design (CAD), computer vision and image processing, and computerized speech recognition. Examples of these pro-

---

[5] Much of the theoretical basis for computer programming is based on the brilliant work of British mathematician Alan Turing, who articulated his ideas of a "Turing machine" in the 1940s.

jects include a 3.75 million pound-sterling grant to work on expert systems in flight simulation trainers and engine monitoring. The grant will apply intelligent knowledge-based systems techniques to help pilots, military strategists, and power plant operators being trained for high-stress conditions.[27]

The Alvey program is notable because of its effort to coordinate these disparate groups (universities, industry, and government)—in contrast to the United States, where an enormous range of unrelated research programs are going on, with nobody really in a position to tell what the state of affairs is at any given moment. In England, anyone can subscribe to the *Alvey News*[28] to get an up-to-date picture on the status of British research into future computer technology.

Initial organizational efforts and project funding of the Alvey program have now been finished; a review is underway to see what additional, second-stage research projects should be funded.[29] However, it is interesting to note that the British government, having invested 300 million pounds in the initial Alvey projects, is currently indicating that it expects private industry to pay for all of the second round of research. Sir Robin Nicholson, the chief scientific adviser to the British cabinet, says that,

> In future, the Government will still have a permanent role to play as an umpire to the research 'clubs' formed under Alvey. However, it is up to the companies to continue when Alvey funds dry up in two years time.
>
> If companies see this sort of programme as a permanent source of government subsidy or as a way of getting something from nothing from competitors, then they will have failed.[30]

Whether the British computer industry is able to fund its own continued research remains to be seen. In the meantime, it is going through a period of (it is hoped) temporary paranoia about its ability to be tempted by the American Star Wars computer research efforts. Article headlines like "US Control Could Kill UK Industry," and "General Promises Star Wars Riches," illustrate the nervousness of the British computer "club." Very few are completely confident that they can withstand the offer of American money for research if (a) they lack financial resources of their own; and (b) the

British government stands firm in its determination not to fund Fifth-Generation research any further.

No doubt the argument about Britain's participation in this program will rage back and forth for the rest of this decade. In the final analysis, it is not very relevant: the British can hardly hope that their research efforts, commendable though they may be, will lead to a completely revitalized computer industry. There is too much lacking; the Empire is too old, too tired, too emasculated at this point. It is hard enough for the Americans, with all of their vitality and strength, to realize that at this point, nobody can completely dominate the world computer market; one can hardly fault the headstrong American computer industry for trying. But the British should know better. The best they can hope for is to be participants—"almost equal" partners—in a vast, worldwide research program being led by the Americans and Japanese. In that role, they can profit, as we all can.

CHINA

China is an enigma to most Americans, but one that we can't afford to ignore much longer. Not only does it contain approximately 25 percent of the world's population, but it seems to be embarking on a slow but steady path toward modern industrialization.

For years, China has had primitive, but adequate, computer capacity for its nuclear research and some of its military needs. A few of the computers for this work were built within the country, but most were obtained from outside—either from the Russians, or other Eastern bloc countries, or from the West. During the long years of noncommunication between China and the United States, American computers could not be sold directly to China; however, a few did manage to get into the country through various gray-market and black-market channels.

Today, China is beginning to concentrate on its basic computer industry: the manufacturing of semiconductor chips that form the building blocks of computers. It manufactured its first semiconductor in 1969 and has gradually constructed modern plants to produce semiconductors for other industries, notably for color televisions.

Though it currently produces 15 million semiconductors a year, most of them are used for televisions, radios, and electronic watches.[31] And the technology of the semiconductors is generally considered much less efficient than that used in the West; the cost to make comparable chips is approximately twenty times what it would cost in the United States and Japan.

Recently, China has begun looking toward the United States and Japan for help in improving its semiconductor technology. Because of the export regulations discussed in Chapter 13, trade with the United States is still cumbersome and limited; hence, China buys most of its technology from Japan. However, China has recently signed a $12 to $14 million contract with Intel, a leading American semiconductor manufacturer, to produce modern chips of the kind used in the IBM PC personal computers. And under the "Four Modernization Drives," the People's Republic has been importing more and more computers. By early 1984, the country had installed over 500 foreign mainframes and minicomputers, and during 1983 alone, it imported over $200 million worth of computers.[32] Large-size minicomputers such as DEC's PDP-11/70, as well as mainframes like IBM's 370/158 computer, are gradually being imported into the country.

The real question is when China will be ready to move beyond semiconductors and chips into large-scale manufacturing of real computers. As early as 1984, China produced a computer called the Great Wall 100, which is a 16-bit computer compatible with the ubiquitous IBM PC.[33] Only 1,000 units of the machine were shipped initially, and the cost was approximately $15,000—almost ten times what a similar machine would cost in the United States. Other locally produced computers are similar in form and function to Digital Equipment's PDP-8 and PDP-11 computers, and IBM's System 360 computer.[34] Since the technology of personal computers and minicomputers can be easily copied, even if it can't be directly imported, the Chinese face mainly a manufacturing problem. That problem, given the foundation work that it has already begun with semiconductors, will probably be solved within five to ten years.

Of even more concern is China's ability to deal with software. Since the Chinese use their own character set, much American software cannot be used in its native form; consequently, the most popular American software programs—for database management, word processing, statistics, finance, and accounting—must first be translated into Chinese. It remains to be seen whether the continuing explosive growth in American application programs will eventually motivate countries like China to adopt English as a universal language for computer work.

In the meantime, China is very much aware of the shortage of trained computer programmers that the Western countries are complaining about. There are some interesting efforts to develop a Chinese programming industry, based on the plentiful supply of trained, experienced Chinese programmers who can speak English. The economics are impressive. An acquaintance in Hong Kong told me in 1980 that a programmer in the People's Republic of China, with a college engineering degree and two years of experience, would earn a salary of U.S. $40 per month;[6] government subsidies and allowances would provide the programmer with another $40 per month. At $80 per month, a Chinese programmer costs approximately twenty-five times less than a typical American programmer!

This amazing cost differential has not gone entirely unnoticed. In the fall of 1984, a group of Chinese-ancestry American professors formed a company called the Shanghai Software Consortium to represent some thirty Chinese professors and computer-science professors who can deliver computer programs at one-third the ordinary U.S. cost.[36] Though it is obviously a small-scale operation, and does not presently have government backing, it is indicative of the kind of Third World software activity that we will discuss elsewhere in this chapter and in Chapter 25.

But there still remains considerable debate as to whether China can overcome its "peasant" image and begin to play a significant role in the high-tech computer world of the 1980s and 1990s. On the one hand, most American visitors find that the Chinese are decades behind our hardware and software technology—as expressed by one American visitor reporting on a one-month tour of Chinese computer facilities:

---

[6] By comparison, a university professor earns $60 per month.[35]

We found an underdeveloped software industry which we would estimate at from 10 to 20 years behind the U.S. We also found a naiveté about software that reminded us of our own misunderstandings of the nature of software 10 or 20 years ago. For example, in Beijing on the first day of the tour, one man asked, "We have the IMS data base at the Census Bureau, but we have heard of System R, a relational data base. Which one is better? Which one should we use?"

Even if we could have spoken without an interpreter, it would have been difficult to explain how dozens of factors affect the choice of a database management system (DBMS) and how it would be unprofessional to recommend one over the other categorically.[37]

On the other hand, many would argue that it is exactly this "backwards" situation that creates enormous opportunities for the Chinese, just as it does for several other Third World countries. One businessman interested in the telecommunications industry, Daniel Burstein, has pointed out that the Chinese have less than one telephone per thousand in the population; while that might seem to pose an enormous problem, Mr. Burstein went on to point out that "China has little investment in its existing telecommunications structure, and therefore little to rebuild if a new system is adopted." [38] The situation is exactly the same with computers: since they don't have an enormous capital investment in twenty-five years of old computer hardware, nor an overwhelming investment in old computer software,[7] they have little to rebuild if they begin using new technology.

SOVIET UNION

The situation in the Soviet Union is similar in many respects to that in China: a technological base of computer equipment that is fifteen to twenty years behind the United States, and an industrial infrastructure that has been cut off from much of the rapidly developing technology in the Western countries. The Soviet Union is estimated to have between fifteen and twenty times fewer mainframe computers than the United States; and while the Western

---

[7] In contrast to the United States, which has an installed base of applications programs that cost between $300 billion and $1 trillion to develop.

countries have a combined base of approximately 15 to 20 million terminals, word processors, and microcomputers, the Soviet bloc countries have approximately 150 to 200,000—a factor of 100 to 1 in favor of the Western countries. Admittedly, this comparison may be somewhat misleading. There's no guarantee that all those computers in Western bloc countries are actually being used productively . . . but still, by anyone's reasonable calculations, the Soviet Union is dramatically behind the United States in the computer field.

This does not mean that the Soviets are entirely ignorant in the field of computing. They know how to build computer hardware (though they generally do so by copying the design of Western computers), and they know how to write computer software. In the area of pure computer science, their theoreticians are on a par with American, English, and Japanese computer scientists. It's just that there aren't as many of them.

The real dilemma in the Soviet Union is not technology *per se* —even though it would appear that the Russian computer industry has a long way to go to compare with Western industry. No, the fundamental problem has to do with the Soviet government and the Soviet ideology. By its very nature, it is opposed to the use of computers as a vehicle for rapid dissemination of real information. As British columnist Rex Malik has pointed out,

> The problem with the Soviet bloc's information flow is quite simple. The system uses for its version of reality only those flows it claims exist, and these are built into the structure. Broadly speaking, what passes for information resources is the data that enterprises create as a result of their activities. This data may or may not be real in that it represents what the system wants and needs to know rather than representing behavior. It is then filtered and massed by the party, mostly centrally, which puts its own glosses on the result and then makes it public—or not.[39]

This problem is more than one of abstract political philosophies. As an example, consider the dilemma faced by the typical Russian factory manager. On the one hand, he would love to have modern computer systems for inventory control, production control, process control, etc. But, on the other hand, he is measured—and ultimately rewarded or punished—based on centrally determined quotas, schedules, budgets, and manpower allotments. It is in his interest to show production increases and various other forms of improvement which may have nothing at all to do with the reality of his factory. Since many of his production problems may be the result of failures beyond his control—e.g., raw materials not arriving at the factory when they were supposed to, factory machinery breaking down more often than it was supposed to, etc.—there is an enormous temptation for him to inflate certain figures, deflate others, and generally paint the kind of information picture that he knows the central authorities are looking for. A computer system is anathema to the factory manager. Because it collects data from the source and passes it directly to some higher authority, it eliminates the manager's ability to filter the numbers. Hence, many Western observers think that it will be a long time before true information systems enter the Russian industrial scene—and that it will be a real revolution when and if it happens.

On a social level, computers pose a similar problem. On the one hand, the Russian government has decreed that by 1990, there will be a computer in every school.[8] On the other hand, putting computers directly into the hands of children—and, ultimately, allowing all those computers to communicate with one another—is just the opposite of the centralized, controlled information society that the Russians are trying to perpetuate. Consider, for example, the comments about computers made by academician Velikhov, vice-president of the department of information science at the USSR Academy of Sciences, in a Moscow Radio address in the summer of 1983:

> Today, there are practically no reasons why every inhabitant of the Soviet Union should not have his own computer, one with a good memory and on which one can plan and calculate . . . Forecasts indicate that by the 1990's, computers will be just as common as a television or a car.
>
> It is another question whether they will be in personal use, for on the whole, different countries go different ways. France, for instance,

---

[8] By contrast, England had an average of one computer in every school by 1984. The United States had an average of three computers in every school by 1983.

is basically taking the path of public use. I think that we are to a considerable degree taking the path of the public use of computers. They will, however, be at the disposal of all . . . There will be computers in shops, collective farms, factories, in the transport system and at the disposal of economists.

As to going into every flat, this must be given some thought. After all, it is very important that there should be a need for one in every flat. In a flat, I think it should be something on the lines of a telephone, and it basically should be a system through which one can get information, information you need like booking tickets, weather forecasts, inquiries and so forth.

Data from libraries and inquiry centers is a very important aspect. Such a system should be set up. As to whether it will be needed in every home, well, it must be understood that not many people work at home, but of course such a system will be needed by people who do work at home . . . One could also say that the situation in our country is by no means as good as it might seem.

And now a revolution, the transition to mass service, is taking place in it, to mass introduction [sic]. Technology makes it possible to do it. We have on the one hand to prepare society, to understand its needs and to forecast them somehow, and on the other hand, we have a different situation. It is not the market that is in control; we have planned control.[40]

With this kind of attitude, it is doubtful that the Soviet population will ever be allowed to make effective use of information technology. In the meantime, their practical plans for introducing computers into the schools and factories will prove remarkably difficult. Russian observer Harley Balzer summarizes the situation by saying,

Enormous practical problems will also restrict computer use in the Soviet Union. Few Soviet students know how to type. The telephone system does not have the capability for data transmission. The Soviet economy is notoriously insensitive to the consumer, but computer manufacturers must provide services to the user in order to ensure product acceptance. Repair facilities for even the most basic household appliances are scarce.

The Soviet leadership may be spared the necessity of dealing with some of these problems for quite some time by a simple lack of computers. While education officials talk about 50,000 to 70,000 special classrooms and one million personal computers in the schools as an eventual goal, they are also designing two curricula for courses in computer science: one for schools with computers, and a second for schools without computers. The 1986-90 Five Year Plan foresees modest progress with networks of 15 to 20 personal computers in some 200 secondary schools. There are continuing difficulties in domestic production of personal computers. While some machines may be purchased abroad, it is unlikely the Soviets will spend scarce hard currency for personal computers for their schools. American manufacturers' dreams of a vast Soviet market for Western products are very likely to be disappointed once again.

Computers epitomize the difficulties facing the Soviets in the age of high technology: they must run faster, up an ever steeper slope, just to maintain their position relative to the United States and other nations.[41]

It is probably dangerous to make any definitive statements about the rapidly changing world of computers—but perhaps the safest definitive statement of all at this point is that the Soviet Union is not going to play any role whatsoever in the computer industry unless it radically changes its philosophical stance toward free dissemination of information. Not only that, the lack of information technology within Russian industry, education, and the entire social infrastructure will almost certainly make that country a member of the lower-class Third World by the end of the century.

THIRD WORLD COUNTRIES

Aside from Japan (which is hardly a Third World country) and China, the most significant Third World centers of computer activity are India, Hong Kong, Singapore, Manila, and Brazil. While there is some computer activity in Korea, Taiwan, Pakistan, and Australia, none of these countries is likely to play a major role in the computer industry during the next ten to twenty years.

Indeed, Hong Kong can be effectively ruled out at this point, too. Its role for the past hundred years has been primarily that of a trading "island nation" that brought the Western world together with the world of the Pacific basin; more recently, it served as a convenient way for the People's Republic of China to trade goods with the United States. The intense business activity in Hong Kong has certainly brought computers onto the island, and has spawned innumerable import-export companies that traded personal computers (including illegal copies of the Apple II computer known as the Banana), software, services, and peripheral computer products. For a time, it even seemed that Hong Kong could serve as the marketing agent for the immense labor pool in the People's Republic—a labor pool which, as we noted above, includes a supply of inexpensive computer programmers. But now two things have happened: (a) the People's Republic has seen that it can deal directly with Japanese and American companies in the computer field, and (b) the People's Republic has announced that when England's ninety-nine-year lease on Hong Kong expires in 1997, the British colony will gradually come under Chinese rule. And that, as they say, is the end of that.

Of all the Third World countries, India has the best chance of becoming the leading force in the software industry. Nobody expects to see any significant developments from the Indians in the area of computer hardware.[9] But the necessary ingredients are there for software development: an excellent educational system, proficiency in English, and an ample supply of experienced programmers and systems analysts whose salaries are only a fraction of those in the United States. And there is an awareness of their situation. As a government official, Vikram Sarabhi, said in an opening address at the National Conference on Computers in Education and Training in New Delhi in March 1983:

> Our initial backwardness, our late arrival on the scene, and the small investments we made in the past need not remain as our handicaps, but can be turned into our most valuable advantages if we make the right decisions now, order judicious investments and march forward with determination.

[9] Nor will any other Third World country play a major role in the computer hardware industry, except perhaps as a supplier of basic chips and semiconductors. Even that will gradually disappear as production lines become fully automated, and robot labor replaces even the cheapest Third World human labor.

Several Indian entrepreneurs foresee the possibility of establishing local software houses with large numbers of Indian programmers and systems analysts available to tackle programming projects that cannot be done in Western countries because of the shortage of trained people. The Indian government is making plans to assist in this effort by providing financial and technical assistance for satellite stations that would be used to transmit technical requirements from America (or England, or anywhere else) to India, and finished computer programs from India back to the end-user.

References for Chapter 12

1. O'Neill, Gerard K., *The Technology Edge*, New York: Simon & Schuster, 1984.

2. Weil, Ulric, *Information Systems in the Eighties*, Englewood Cliffs, N.J.: Prentice-Hall, 1982.

3. "Can Japan Ever Be More Than an Also-Ran?", *Business Week*, July 16, 1984.

4. Weil, *op. cit.*

5. "Mitsubishi Net Up 11% in Year," *New York Times*, July 4, 1984.

6. Weil, *op. cit.*

7. McClellan, Stephen, *The Coming Computer Industry Shakeout*, New York: John Wiley & Sons, 1984.

8. Kirchner, Jake, "Japan No Big Threat to U.S. Vendors, DARPA Chief Says," *Computerworld*, March 5, 1984.

9. "Speaker Points to Weaknesses in Japanese Plan," *Computerworld*, August 22, 1983.

10. Batt, Robert, "Fifth-Generation Threat by Japanese Overrated, Industry Expert Warns," *Computerworld*, September 19, 1983.

11. Henkel, Tom, "U.S. Government Aid Asked to Stunt Japan's Tech Strides," *Computerworld*, August 22, 1983.

12. "Japan Reveals Development of Fifth Generation Machines," *Computerworld*, July 16, 1984.

13. Fruin, Mark, "Japan Lags Behind U.S in Software Development," *Infoworld*, August 23, 1983.

14. "U.S. Seen Ahead of Japan in Computer Technology, Behind in Development," *Computerworld*, July 1, 1984.

15. "U.S. Government DP Spending to Top $25 Billion in 1983," *Computerworld*, September 19, 1983.

16. Richman, Sheldon, "Rose Earns Tech Reputation," *Government Computer News*, June 7, 1985.

17. "Micros Invade Government," *High Technology*, January 1984.

18.   *Ibid*.

19.   Wilkins, Bryan, "DOD Asks Defense Contractors to Speed Ada Applications," *Computerworld*, June 11, 1984.

20.   "Pentagon Push for Software Development Tools," *High Technology*, October 1983.

21.   Lin, Herbert, "The Software for Star Wars: An Achilles Heel?" *MIT Technology Review*, July 1985.

22.   "Abrahamson Outlines U.S. Plan for Missile Defense," *The Institute* (News Supplement to *IEEE Spectrum*), August 1985.

23.   Ollmos, David, "DOD Finances Case Western Biochip Research Center," *Computerworld*, September 3, 1984.

24.   "DOD: $1 Million to Intellicorp," *ICS Applied Artificial Intelligence Reporter*, April 1985.

25.   "The DOD Stars Program," *IEEE Computer*, special issue, November 1983.

26.   "New Generation Computing Technology: A Strategic Plan for its Development and Application to Critical Problems in Defense," *Strategic Computing: First Annual Report*, U.S. Government Printing Office: DARPA, February 1985.

27.   Arthur, Charles, "Six Get Alvey Nod," *Computer Weekly*, May 23, 1985.

28.   Cooper, John, British Computer Society; *Alvey News*, P.O. Box 8, Southgate House, Stevenage, Herts, England SG1 1HQ.

29.   McCarten, "Alvey Assessment Could Lead to Follow-up Project," *Computing the Newspaper*, May 16, 1985.

30.   McCrone, John, "Alvey 2 to Lose DTI Cash," *Computing*, July 18, 1985.

31.   Ehrlich, Paul Charles, "China Chips Face Hurdles Ahead," *Management Information Systems Week*, January 23, 1985.

32.   Besher, Alexander, "Portable Computing in China," *Infoworld*, February 20, 1984.

33.   _____, "China Unwraps Micro Compatible with IBM PC," *Infoworld*, January 23, 1984.

34.   D'Auria, Thomas J., "ACM's Visit to The People's Republic of China," *Communications of the ACM*, March 1984.

35.   Mantor, Vaughn J., "Can the People's Republic Catch Up?", *Computerworld*, November 14, 1983.

36.   "Overseas Software Enters U.S.," *The Wall Street Journal*, September 7, 1984.

37.   Mantor, *op. cit.*

38.   Burstein, Daniel, "Don't Ignore the China Market," *CityBusiness*, July 6, 1984.

39.   Malik, Rex, "Communism vs. the Computer: Can the USSR Survive the Information Age?", *Computerworld*, July 9, 1984.

40.   *Ibid*.

41.   Balzer, Harley D., "Is Less More? Soviet Science in the Gorbachev Era," *Issues in Science and Technology*, Summer 1985.

13

GOVERNMENTAL REGULATION

> Sometimes it is said that man cannot be trusted with the government of himself. Can he, then, be trusted with the government of others? Or have we found angels in the forms of kings to govern him? Let history answer this question.
>
> Still one thing more, fellow citizens—a wise and frugal government, which shall restrain men from injuring one another, which shall leave them otherwise free to regulate their own pursuit of industry and improvement, and shall not take from the mouth of labor the bread it has earned. This is the sum of good government, and this is necessary to close the circle of our felicities.
>
> Thomas Jefferson
> *First Inaugural Address*, March 4, 1801

Whether or not Mr. Jefferson would have approved, it is an indisputable fact that government does "regulate [our] pursuit of industry and improvement." To the long list of regulations, proclamations, declarations, restrictions, subsidies, quarantines, tariffs, taxes, duties, licenses, and acts that the government imposes on other aspects of our industrial life, we must now add a variety of restrictions concerning the computer industry.

These restrictions will almost certainly change from day to day; and as one can imagine, they differ widely from country to country, and from one political regime to another. Hence, I cannot make any serious attempt to indicate the precise nature of government regulations that will exist over the next five to ten years. On the other hand, all of the government regulations fall into one of the following five patterns:

- Subsidies or grants to foster local research efforts.

- Import tariffs, duties, or quotas on foreign computer equipment.

- Restrictions on exports of computer equipment to "unfriendly" nations.

- Preferential treatment of local computer companies for government contracts.

- Restrictions on foreign computer companies that wish to start a local manufacturing process, or any other form of local "presence."

I will provide illustrations and examples of each of these categories. While we are naturally interested in seeing what the American government is doing to us and for us, it is also instructive to see what other governments are doing to us, and to their own citizens. You may, of course, form your own opinion as to the goodness, badness, relevance, and value of these actions; the important thing is for you to be aware of them. As John Selden said nearly 300 years ago, "They that govern the most make the least noise."[1]

SUBSIDIES AND GRANTS FOR
LOCAL R&D ACTIVITY

Any country that views computers as an important industry for the next century is likely to consider investing in the industry in one form or another. The investment may come from a government agency interested in long-term, unrestricted pure research, or it may come from an arm of the government concerned with practical research. Typical examples might include:

- Research grants to prestigious universities—either on an unrestricted basis, or as directed research in a specific engineering/scientific discipline.

- Grants to individual professors who wish to pursue research topics of interest to the government.

- Scholarships and grants to students pursuing graduate degrees, or postdoctoral research work in a computer-related area deemed to be in the country's interest.

- Grants of a similar nature to think tanks, consulting firms, laboratories, and normal high-tech computer companies.

- Establishment of government-operated research facilities in specialized areas of computer science, computer hardware development, etc.

- Encouragement of, or tolerance of, research partnerships and joint ventures within private industry.

- Tax concessions or credits for research work in the computer field.

Current examples of these activities in America, France, England, Japan, Singapore, India, and a number of other countries around the world were presented in Chapter 12. As we saw, the major sources of such grants in the United States are DARPA and DOD.

IMPORT DUTIES ON FOREIGN EQUIPMENT

Most countries impose some kind of duty or tariff on almost everything they allow to cross their borders, whether the item is a camera, a computer, or a can of beans. I am not concerned with this kind of normal tariff; rather, I am concerned with the tariff that effectively excludes a foreign computer manufacturer from entering the domestic market—or, equivalently, a tariff that effectively precludes the local population from purchasing foreign computer equipment.

Such punitive tariffs might be levied as a way of expressing disapproval of some other aspect of a country's foreign policy or trade policy—e.g., if the United States felt that Japan were dumping steel into the United States at below-cost prices, it could retaliate by slapping a 100 percent tariff on all Japanese semiconductors and finished computer equipment. More often, though, the tariff is imposed in an effort to protect a country's local industry; and most often, it is imposed in an effort to help a fledgling industry that might not otherwise survive its first few years.

One of the best examples of this policy is Brazil. During the tumultuous 1970s, the military leaders of Brazil decided that Brazil would become a superpower, if not *the* superpower, early in the 21st century. To accomplish this, of course, it would have to become self-sufficient in a number of basic industries, including computers. Thus, in 1978, the government began passing decrees limiting foreign computer imports and encouraging the formation of a local Brazilian computer industry. The earliest Brazilian computers were used by the Brazilian navy for its frigates and destroyers, and the military/defense overtones continued. The fledgling industry was governed by decrees issued by the military government, and the Special Informatics Secretariat formed part of the National Security Council.

This has culminated in a recent bill, passed overwhelmingly by the Brazilian Congress, which excludes foreign computer companies from participating in much of the country's computer and data processing industry.[2] This is no longer justified on the basis of Brazil's desire to become a superpower; now it is justified on the basis of the 18,000 employees of Brazil's computer industry and on the desperate shortage of hard currency in the cash-poor country. Times are no longer as good as they were in the boom days of the late 1970s.

If that were the end of the story, I would have saved it for one of the sections later in this chapter. But there is more: the Brazilians can indeed manufacture their own microcomputers and minicomputers (though at prices often as much as six times higher than an American would pay for the same equipment), but they can't manufacture mainframe computers and a number of other peripheral devices (tape drives, disk drives, high-speed laser printers, etc.) that are attached to computers. These devices can be imported, but only at great cost: the duties often exceed the cost of the equipment. Sometimes the situation is even more bizarre. A local manufacturer of a Type X computer display terminal is told that he can import one Type Y display terminal[1] for every two

---

[1] I've avoided mentioning the specific make and model of computer display terminal, in order to avoid embarrassing some friends in Brazil.

Type X display terminals that he exports. But since the price of their locally manufactured terminals is at least twice what the world market is willing to pay, there aren't many exports.

RESTRICTIONS ON COMPUTER EXPORTS

In the United States, the situation is just the opposite of that found in Brazil: while they are worried about imports, we are worried about exports. Specifically, the American government is concerned about the export of computer equipment to "unfriendly" nations that might use that equipment for military purposes. From time to time, the government also decides to ban the export of computer equipment to countries whose domestic policies are out of favor; the country most out of favor as this book was being written was South Africa.[3] Both computer hardware and computer software are controlled by the Export Administration Act (EAA). The EAA prohibits the export of technical data and certain commodities on the Controlled Commodity List (CCL) without prior authorization from the Department of Commerce's Office of Export Administration. The three reasons cited by the government for these controls are (a) national security, (b) foreign policy, and (c) domestic short supply.

In addition, the Department of Defense is involved in preventing important computer hardware and software supplies or technical data from getting into unfriendly hands. To further confuse matters, even the General Accounting Office has gotten involved in a twenty-six-country study of the impact and effectiveness of U.S. export controls. The result is that, in many cases, potential foreign customers are not sure who controls what.[4] Nor is the CIA happy about this: in a speech made to an audience of Silicon Valley executives, CIA Director William Casey complained that some 300 companies operating in thirty countries were engaged in schemes to divert militarily critical high-technology products to Communist countries.[5]

Not that any of this is new . . . since the early 1960s, the Soviet Union and various other Eastern bloc countries have done their best to get their hands on computer hardware, computer software, and various other forms of computer technology. The Ryad-series computers used by the Soviet bloc throughout the 1970s, and even today, are based on the old System-360 architecture introduced by IBM in 1964. The only thing that is different today is that (a) there is more technology, and thus more to control; (b) it is more widespread, and thus more difficult to control; (c) the hardware technology is smaller, and the software technology can be transmitted by telephone and satellite, making it more difficult still to control; and (d) there are more black-market and gray-market individuals and companies hoping to make a profit from all of this. It's one thing to protect a supercomputer that costs $10 million and fills a large warehouse; it's quite another thing to protect the technology of a personal computer when it costs less than $1,000 and fits into a briefcase.

But the government is still trying. A twenty-one-member "blue ribbon" panel was convened recently by the Committee on Science, Engineering and Public Policy (affiliated with the National Academy of Sciences and various other scholarly groups) to study the effect of international technology transfer on national security,[6] and Department of Defense officials recently met with officials of the IEEE professional engineering society to discuss technology transfer regulations.[7] The export regulations of the EAA still stand; those in the business of manufacturing computer hardware or software (or products in which critical hardware/software components are embedded) are strongly advised to obtain copies of the regulations from the Government Printing Office or the local field office of the Department of Commerce.

Because of the prominent position of the American computer industry, and because of the dominant role that the United States plays in such international groups as NATO, several other European computer manufacturers are also restricted from trading computer equipment with the Eastern bloc countries. But as computer hardware becomes more and more of a multinational commodity business—like potatoes or oil or soybeans—it will become increasingly difficult to effectively exert any control. Even if the government can control the physical export of computer hardware, it is virtually impossible to prevent the export of the underlying technology. Thus, we will continue to find countries like Brazil and Russia, which may be unable or unwilling to buy made-in-America products, manufacturing their own "rip-off" of American computer technology. It may cost them twice as much, but they will get the technology.

PREFERENTIAL TREATMENT FOR LOCAL COMPUTER COMPANIES

This is a phenomenon we see very little of in the United States because of a long-standing political environment that tries to prevent monopolies, or any form of domination of the marketplace. Indeed, many mediocre American computer companies owe their existence to the U.S. government, whose policy requires it, in some cases, to buy a brand X computer even though an IBM computer would have been cheaper and easier to acquire.

But in countries trying to support their own fledgling computer industries, preferential treatment is extremely important. And since the government is typically the largest user of computers in most countries, preferential treatment in government contracts can provide a local manufacturer with a lion's share of the entire market. If the government can extend this by insisting that its defense contractors and other suppliers also use locally manufacturered computers in performance of government contracts for goods and services, even more of the market can be captured.

We can expect to see this kind of preferential treatment in such Third World countries as India, Singapore, Brazil, and Malaysia, and in such industrialized countries as Japan, England, France, and Germany. The real question all of these countries must face is how to deal with the quasi-local multinational companies like IBM, Honeywell, Burroughs, and Univac. That issue is usually determined, sooner or later, based on the percentage of foreign ownership of the local firm, as we will see below.

RESTRICTIONS ON LOCAL PRESENCE OF FOREIGN COMPUTER COMPANIES

We have already discussed one example of this phenomenon: in Brazil, foreign computer companies are finding it harder and harder to establish a local presence. This is frustrating for the large worldwide computer companies, for Brazil is the 8th largest computer market in the world.[8] The normal approach for a multinational computer company in this situation would be to establish a local manufacturing facility in Brazil, but the Brazilians want local control, meaning ownership, as well as local manufacturing.

And so it is in many other countries as well. IBM has been particularly hard hit by this kind of phenomenon, for it traditionally wants 100 percent ownership of its foreign subsidiaries, even though it is very careful to place local nationals in all of the top management positions. Mexico turned down an IBM request to build a manufacturing facility for personal computers in 1984, because of IBM's insistence on 100 percent ownership. And in England, a proposed 50/50 joint venture between IBM and British Telecom was turned down by the British government; one can imagine how flustered IBM must have been when they didn't even ask for their normal 100 percent!

In some cases, the dispute is not concerned with the manufacturing of computer hardware, but rather the distribution of computer software. In the summer of 1984, for example, IBM announced its decision to stop publishing the "source code" for its mainframe operating systems—a decision which could set the Japanese hardware industry back by five to ten years.[2] In response, the Japanese Ministry of Industry, Trade and Information (MITI) announced that it would seek to change Japanese copyright law to force a foreign company to license its software to Japanese competitors. In March 1985, the Japanese yielded to intense lobbying efforts from the United States: it announced that the government would soon submit legislation specifying that computer software would qualify for fifty years of software protection under Japanese copyright law.[9] But no doubt there will be more efforts of this kind in the

---

[2] The "operating system" is the central computer program that keeps track of all the other programs that are running in a computer, and orchestrates their behavior so that they can share such common resources as printers, disk drives, and other devices. "Source code" refers to the program instructions which make up the operating system, written in a near-English form that other programmers can read easily. All of this is important to the Japanese in their efforts to build "plug-compatible" computer hardware that will run all of IBM's computer programs, as well as the tens of thousands of application programs like payroll and inventory that require the IBM operating system. It is roughly as if the Japanese wanted to manufacture plug-compatible automobiles, but suddenly found that they were being denied access to the engineering drawings for the American engines.

future. Indeed, as foreign countries eventually begin to show some creativity and superiority in the field of computer software (as I believe they will), we will see our own government engage in similar stunts.

All's fair in love and war and computers. . . .

References for Chapter 13

1.   Selden, John, "Power," *Table Talk*, 1689.

2.   Riding, Alan, "Brazil Curbs Computer Competition," *New York Times*, October 7, 1984.

3.   Sullivan, Judith A., "Bill Would Ban South African Computer Sales," *Government Computer News*, June 7, 1985.

4.   Schatz, Willie, "A Noisy Turf Battle," *Datamation*, May 1, 1984.

5.   Wilkins, Bryan, "CIA Chief Says 300 Firms Diverting Military High Tech to Eastern Bloc," *Computerworld*, June 25, 1984.

6.   "High-tech Panel to Study Effect of Export Controls," *Computerworld*, June 24, 1985.

7.   "IEEE and DOD Officials Meet to Discuss Technology Transfer," *The Institute* (News Supplement to *IEEE Spectrum*), July 1985.

8.   Riding, *op. cit.*

9.   Burgess, John, "Japanese Yield in Software Dispute with U.S.," *International Herald Tribune*, March 19, 1985.

14

PRIVACY AND COMPUTERS

An American has no sense of privacy. He does not know what it means. There is no such thing in the country.

George Bernard Shaw
Speech, April 11, 1933

American citizens are finally acquiring a sense of privacy—perhaps only recently, fifty years after George Bernard Shaw told us that we didn't have any. And perhaps it is only because we are learning that computers represent a powerful tool that can take away our privacy.

If Shaw were still with us, he might disagree. He might point to all of the Americans who, even today, will tell a perfect stranger over the phone how much they earn, how much they drink, how much money they have in the bank, and how often they have sexual intercourse—all in the name of market research. We willingly fill out forms asking us the most intimate of questions when we open bank accounts, apply for credit cards, subscribe to magazines, join the armed forces, or interview for a job. We are still a very open and trusting people—but, like the Europeans, we are slowly learning to be cautious and reserved.

Given the pervasive presence of computers in the land, there are two things that citizens should worry about: the ability of other citizens to pry into their private affairs, and the ability of their government itself to pry. I will not concern myself very much with the first of these issues, though it is worth pointing out the irony involved: many of us would like the government—that protozoic mass that seeks to crawl into every nook and cranny of our lives —to protect us from the hackers and the criminals who are prodding and poking, looking for the weak spots in our technological armor. If ever there was a case of asking the fox to stand guard over the chicken coop, this is it. Wake up, fellow citizens! Look after your own privacy, and let the government take care of its own affairs.

There is a more practical reason for ignoring the issue of privacy attacks by other individuals (and banks, and insurance companies, etc.). If we can develop the policies, the legislation, the technology, and the cultural "mind set" (the last of which is what George Bernard Shaw says we lack) to keep the government at bay, it follows that the very same mechanisms will keep every teenager and every corporate computer sleuth at bay, too. If the combined forces of the National Security Agency, FBI, CIA, and IRS are unable to uncover aspects of my moral, financial, intellectual, sexual, and political behavior that I legitimately consider private, what possible hope can a teenage computer programmer have? What possible chance does my bank or my insurance company or my employer have? Answer: none.

So my concern is, quite simply, with the government, and, by default, all of the individuals and corporations that get away with some subset of the privacy invasion that the government is capable of. My concerns—which should be your concerns, too—are three-fold:

- Accuracy of existing data in current databases.

- Dangerous use of existing data.

- Possible further encroachment on information that is currently private.

Some Americans were concerned about these issues even in 1933 when Mr. Shaw came to New York City to insult us. However, Mr. Shaw and his audience lived in a different era then: there were no computers, and it was difficult at best for the government or anyone else to really acquire much information about anyone who wanted to maintain his privacy.

Today, billions of juicy tidbits of personal trivia float through telecommunication lines, flash upon CRT screens, and are stored for later review on massive computer disks. The average American currently resides on 240 separate computer databases. Every American's name pops out of a database, on average, thirty-five times a day, and is passed from one computer system to another computer system five times a day.[1]

Think about these numbers for a few minutes before you dismiss them as absurd. If you are married, you probably have at least two checking accounts; you may have even more if you switched to a new bank, but left your old checking account open but dormant. And then there's the savings account in that old savings and loan (if it hasn't gone bankrupt), and the NOW account and the Money Market account; you might be on ten different databases right there! Don't forget your American Express, Diner's Club, Carte Blanche, and your MasterCard and your Visa accounts—those are computerized, too. Your telephone—oh, yes, and the separate phone you have for your teenage son who spends all night talking to God-only-knows-who—are computerized, and you'd better believe that the telephone company can provide details of every call you've ever made to anyone who flashes the proper authorization in front of them. Then there are your tax records at the IRS, and whoever the IRS has loaned them to;[1] your service record if you were in the armed forces, and maybe even if you weren't (who knows what ever happened to the old Selective Service files). The Social Security Administration has been keeping a record of your FICA contributions since your first job; the police department has a computerized record of every traffic violation and parking ticket you've ever had. Your insurance company knows more about you than your mother does. Your stockbroker has always known about your crazy "hot tips" for buying and selling stock, but now his computer sends dividend information directly to the IRS at the end of the year. Don't forget about the department store credit cards, as well as the payroll data that your company keeps . . . and so on and so on. If you really think about it seriously, 240 may be a conservative number for middle-class white-collar Americans. It's not clear to me whether the people on welfare assistance are on more databases than upper-middle-class Republicans, or whether they escape some of those databases by virtue of their distrust for banks and their inability to open quite as many charge accounts.

---

[1] More about this later. As we will see, there is a good chance that the IRS has loaned your tax records to lots of people, both within the federal government and various places outside the federal government.

I will examine in detail the three major concerns with computerized databases that I outlined above. Following that, I will offer some suggestions for citizens who wish to maintain some semblance of privacy in an increasingly computerized world.

THE INACCURACY OF EXISTING COMPUTER DATABASES

Many countries around the world have passed laws concerning the use of, and accuracy of, computerized data concerning private citizens. The federal government, various state governments, and a variety of well-meaning private organizations have attempted to legislate the problem away. But we are faced with three fundamental problems concerning existing computerized databases:

- Much data that currently exist on computer systems was converted from some previous noncomputerized form, with little or no regard for the accuracy of the original data, or the accuracy of the conversion process.

- Much current data that enter a computer system are produced by someone manually typing information on a keyboard. Even in the best of circumstances, human typists make mistakes; in the normal case, they make lots of mistakes. When the volume of such data grows to enormous proportions, it becomes more and more statistically likely that someone's data are inaccurate.

- Many of today's computer systems have no mechanism for checking the accuracy of the data that have been entered. Nor does the average citizen ever see the data. Nor is there any penalty for inaccurate data, other than an occasional requirement for rectifying it.[2]

---

[2] Think how different it would be if there were a penalty of $50,000 for every substantive error in a government-maintained database, and another $50,000 for each instance where that erroneous record was given to another government agency—and if the penalties were paid directly, tax-free, to the injured citizen. A lot of citizens would suddenly pay a lot more attention to the accuracy of the data being maintained about them, and the government might pay a little more attention, too!

These are very real problems, and they are not going to disappear overnight. They are not technological problems, they are technology-transfer problems—i.e., problems associated with the transfer of a new technology into a culture (society) that doesn't quite understand it, and isn't sure what to do with it. Unfortunately, technology transfer is often a long, slow process. It took the military fifty years to go from the technology of muskets to the technology of rifles,[2] and it could take just as long for society to go from manual (incorrect) databases to computerized (less incorrect) databases.

A great deal of information about this problem can be found in the landmark book *The Rise of the Computer State*, written by David Burnham in 1984.[3] Mr. Burnham points out that the volume of data is just as large in corporate databases as it is in government databases. The five largest credit card companies in the United States have a total of 150 million records;[4] two out of every three Americans have life insurance, and those records are certainly computerized; and virtually all telephone calls, bank checks, and other business transactions end up in a computer (or multiple computers).

Consider one specific corporate example. The aerospace firm, TRW, maintains a credit-checking service for corporate clients—i.e., department stores, banks, and any other organizations who need to know whether you pay your bills on time. Here are the statistics on TRW's credit bureau:

- 24,000 customers (e.g., grocery stores) subscribe to the service.

- Data are kept on 90 million individuals.

- TRW issues 35 million credit reports each year to its 24,000 customers.

- 350,000 complaints are filed each year by individuals who feel that the credit data are incomplete, inaccurate, or downright wrong. Assuming that an individual doesn't complain about his record more than once a year, this means that only 1/3 of 1 percent of all individuals complain about their records. But can one therefore conclude that 99.67 percent of the records in the database are accurate?

- 100,000 corrections are made in the database each year.

TRW is known as a reputable, high-technology firm, and it is probably far better than average when it comes to maintaining accurate databases. But even high-tech firms need a little humility sometimes: TRW's telephone access numbers were somehow picked up by a computer hacker and posted on an electronic bulletin board in 1984 for a period of several months before anyone found out. How many data were accessed by unauthorized individuals? How much sensitive personal financial information was distributed to places where it never should have gone?

As I indicated before, my concern is not so much with individual hackers and corporate databases, but rather with the government's databases. If we can create sufficient safeguards in this area, they can be carried across to the private sector easily. To illustrate the dangers in the government arena, consider the interesting statistic that one out of every five living Americans has an arrest record.[5] Many of these arrests are for minor peccadilloes (disorderly conduct, making obscene gestures at an officer of the law, etc.), and 30 to 40 percent of the arrests are cleared or vacated before trial; however, in the age-old tradition of governmental record-keeping, the arrest records may not be thrown away.

This would be bad enough if all of the data were accurate when first entered, for it would leave many citizens vulnerable to various forms of blackmail about "criminal records" that should not legally exist. In the state of Florida, for example, any private company can access arrest records.[3]

The worst part of it is that many of the criminal arrest data are inaccurate. In 1980, the Office of Technology Assessment (OTA) conducted an audit of computerized criminal data in several states. In North Carolina, only 12.2 percent of the criminal records were accurate; in California, only 18.9 percent of the records were accurate; and even in Minnesota, one had less than a 50/50 chance—49.5 percent, to be precise—of having an accurate criminal record. The

---

[3] In many cases, an employer has a legitimate need to know if a job applicant has a criminal record; indeed, some employers and government agencies are legally prohibited from hiring candidates with such records. On the other hand, the information can also be misused if it is available to any company.

same survey found that 80 percent of the states had never conducted quality audits of their criminal justice records.

If the criminal records are inaccurate, it stands to reason that a great deal of other data maintained by the government may also be inaccurate, especially if (a) the data are entered by low-paid, uneducated, disinterested clerical workers who, frankly, don't give a damn if the data are inaccurate, or (b) it is received from another computer database whose accuracy and reliability are unknown, and (c) there are no audits or error-checking mechanisms to ensure accuracy of the data.

Keep in mind also that even if data are accurate when they first enter a database, they can become inaccurate over time. In some cases—admittedly rare, but important nonetheless—this can result from a slow accumulation of computer hardware and software errors. A subtle software error might, under certain bizarre circumstances, cause Mr. Fribble's credit record to be inadvertently deleted when Mr. Frabble's record is updated,[4] or a stray electrical power surge might cause a single digit to be dropped or added to the computer record showing Mr. Grumble's outstanding home mortgage; thus, his home mortgage might be shown as $495,000 instead of $49,500. The chances of this are very slim indeed, but if it happens once out of 10 million times, then there could be ten very unhappy individuals in a database containing 100 million individuals. Furthermore, these errors tend to be cumulative: the ten individuals whose records got "zapped" may not know why they are being denied credit or turned down for new jobs, and it may never occur to them that some mysterious computer system is reporting incorrect information about them; hence, they may never ask to see their data, and the organization (private or governmental) that collected it may never become aware that it has committed the error. This being the case, another ten people may have their records zapped next year; and ten more the year after. . . .

In other cases, the error is more subtle: the data may be correct when entered, but they may become obsolete over a period of time

---

[4] More about errors of this kind in Chapter 27. But for now, suffice it to say that the person who wrote the original computer program may have overlooked certain unlikely combinations of events (maybe Mr. Fribble is Mr. Frabble's father-in-law, and his sister married his mother's uncle, who was also related to his cousin's third wife) that—should they ever occur—will lead the program to behave in an unpredictable way.

precisely because they are not updated. If my own credit record has not been updated since 1965, it will still show my starting salary of $7,500 per year as a computer programmer at Digital Equipment Corporation. Since each of my three children currently has a school tuition of almost that much, someone considering me for a credit card application might come to the conclusion that I was supplementing my income with various illegal, nefarious activities.

DANGEROUS USE OF EXISTING COMPUTER DATABASES

From the discussion thus far, we can see that there is reason for concern about computerized databases. However, the problem is worse than just inaccurate data: there is growing concern that the data—accurate or not—will be misused. Sometimes this concern is caused by an individual political figure, such as Joseph McCarthy or Richard Nixon; sometimes it is aimed at a political party; more often, it is aimed at such government agencies as the IRS, FBI, or local police department.

For those who argue that "those with nothing to hide have nothing to be concerned about," a small lesson in American history might be appropriate. When President Roosevelt decided on February 19, 1942,[5] to detain 112,000 Japanese-ancestry American citizens in internment camps, his Executive Order 9066 was carried out with great efficiency. How was this done? By using "national origin" data requested in the 1940 census.[6] While the Census Bureau did not give out specific, individualized data, it provided everything the government needed by giving out aggregate data: it knew, and

---

[5] The internment was made legal by the Second War Powers Act, which was introduced on January 22, 1942, passed by Congress on March 19th, and signed by Roosevelt on March 27, 1942. But the Census Bureau was providing information on Japanese-ancestry citizens as early as December 17, 1941. Meanwhile, the issue came before the Supreme Court of the United States during World War II, and the Court ruled, six to three, that the mass incarceration of the people of Japanese ancestry was constitutional. Perhaps T.S. Eliot was in a prescient mood when he wrote in 1920:

After such knowledge, what forgiveness? Think now
History has many cunning passages, contrived corridors
And issues, deceives with whispering ambitions,
Guides us by vanities.

Gerontion

thus the Justice Department knew, from the 1940 census that within certain geographical regions, there were, say, 966 citizens of Japanese ancestry. This was done despite the fact that the legal charter of the Census Bureau says that,

> . . . in no case shall information furnished under the authority of this Act be used to the detriment of the person or persons to whom such information related.

If I had been a Japanese-ancestry person in 1942, I would feel that I had been royally screwed by the Census Bureau, over and above whatever other feelings I might have had about the idea of being locked up in an internment camp for the remainder of the war. And as a citizen of any national origin, any religious persuasion, or any political belief, it would be with a slightly queasy feeling that I would answer the questions on the 1990 census.

We can divide our concerns into two separate categories here. There are the cases where confidential, or private, data are obviously misused by an individual or an organization that has access to them—i.e., the cases that will be happily and enthusiastically prosecuted by government attorneys if they ever come to light. Then there is the case where private data are accessed "for a good cause" that was not legal when the data were captured. This is the case of our Japanese-ancestry compatriots, and it may well be the case for more Americans in the future.

Until better use is made of existing technology, and existing laws get tougher (meaning that the penalties get much more severe), and the attitude of the public changes noticeably, we will continue to have cases of blatantly illegal access to confidential data. One of the more dramatic recent cases involved the San Francisco Police Department, which allegedly gained access to confidential computer files maintained by the city public defender's office; as many as 1,500 cases may be in jeopardy (meaning that a mistrial may be ruled) as a result.[7] This kind of unauthorized, illegal access to confidential data is typically detected today only by accident, or because of a clumsy mistake on the part of the perpetrator. For each case that you read about in the newspapers, you should assume that there are 10 cases that the authorities have discovered but have quietly buried to avoid embarrassment, and another 100 cases that the authorities don't even know about.

The use of existing confidential data for good causes raises even more concern; in effect, it is an *ex post facto* use of data. Had the Japanese-ancestry American citizens known, for example, that their census data were going to be used against them two years later (despite the fact that the census charter was not changed), they might have had a very different attitude toward the census questionnaire. And many of us today would feel very differently about the many forms and questionnaires that we so obligingly fill out if we had an idea how the government intended to use them in the future.

In case you're not aware of it, this has been going on for quite some time. On November 9, 1977, Joseph Califano, Secretary of the Department of Health, Education and Welfare (HEW), announced what he thought was a bold initiative to curb welfare abuse: Project Match. Califano's plan called for matching the files of federal employees against the computerized files of state welfare rolls—the idea being to eliminate those who were simultaneously receiving state welfare (much of which was subsidized by the federal government) while employed by the federal government. Despite the outcry Califano's plan raised, it was only the beginning: the New York Civil Liberties Union estimated in 1984 that more than 10,000 computer "matches" have been carried out by agencies of the federal government, state governments, and by the private sector.[8]

One of the more celebrated cases of government infringement on privacy began in 1974, when Congress passed a law requiring every state receiving ADC funds (Aid to Families with Dependent Children) to have an investigative facility search for delinquent parents; the federal government was to pay 75 percent of the cost of the investigative facility. This was based largely on the premise (supported by numerous surveys) that the typical case of a welfare family with dependent children was one where the father had abandoned the family, leaving behind a mother and one or more children; the father was generally not heard from "officially" thereafter, and provided no financial support. (Whether the father was unofficially present or not is a subject of debate among social workers.)

At this point, many law-abiding, God-fearing, tax-paying citizens would not be upset: after all, single mothers (or fathers) have a tough life, and if our tax money has to be used to help provide them with subsistence living, perhaps it's not unreasonable to provide a facility for tracking down the income-earning spouse who is shirking his (or her) responsibility. So far, so good; however (as with many government programs) it didn't stop there. A later amendment to federal tax law (still in effect in 1985) authorized the IRS to withhold tax refunds from parents who are delinquent on child care payments. This turns out to be more than an abstract matter: in 1981, $168 million was witheld from 275,479 parents.[9] And during the past two fiscal years (1984-85), the IRS has provided information on 2.8 million tax returns for child support reasons.[10] Assuming that the basic principle is sound (which I won't argue), do we really want the IRS to play this large a role in tax collection matters stemming from private marital disputes?

For those of you who say "Yes!" with an emphatic pounding of the fist on a nearby table, let me cite one last statistic: the tax law requires that states and counties assist a "woman searching for the father" (sic)[6] even if she is not applying for government assistance. And in 1981, 60 percent of the withheld tax refunds were for persons not receiving government assistance.[11] At this point, a great many citizens would probably say, "Enough!" If there is a private marital dispute, and one spouse has left another in a financially desperate situation, we all feel a great deal of sympathy. But if the dependent spouse is not energetic enough, or poor enough, or desperate enough, to seek financial assistance, why should we be placing the IRS in the position of policeman and divorce court?

The IRS is at the center of a storm that transcends the issue of aid to welfare families: it seems that everyone wants to get his hands on your tax returns. The dangers of this situation became clear after the Watergate scandal, during which it was recognized that the president's authority to release tax data to any federal agency could be easily abused. In 1976, the Tax Reform Act (not to be confused with the Deficit Reduction Act or the Debt Collection Act or any of

---

[6] One assumes that the law is equally generous in helping fathers look for runaway mothers, though I will happily admit that this is not a common situation.

the other funny euphemisms that Congress thinks up in its ongoing efforts to muddy the financial waters of the land) decreed that tax returns would henceforth be entirely confidential . . . except to chairmen of congressional tax committees and the chief of staff of the Joint Committee on Taxation.[7] However, the Office of Technology Assessment (which reports to Congress) reports that since 1976, lawmakers have passed twenty-nine exceptions to the privacy revisions.[12] In effect, almost anyone in the federal government or many of the state governments can get his hands on your tax returns if he exercises a little ingenuity. Here are some examples:

- If you owe taxes in one state, but live in another state, the federal government will let the state tax officials in both states see your federal tax return.

- The Debt Collection Act of 1982 allows federal lending authorities and loan-guaranteeing agencies to screen credit applications against IRS files to check for tax delinquency. (But the IRS has no obligation to tell the applicant that it has released the information.)

- Once a federal loan has been granted, the IRS can help a federal agency find the borrower by disclosing his current address. It can even give the address to private contractors handling debt collection for the government.

- Starting January 1, 1986, the IRS will deduct tax refunds from the outstanding, overdue balance of individuals running behind on paying a federal loan.

- The IRS will provide copies of income tax returns to colleges and universities, as well as state and local scholarship agencies, of the parents applying for student scholarships, loans, and grants for their children. During the 1984-85 fiscal years, it provided such information for 4.7 million scholarship applicants.

---

[7] These lucky individuals could see anyone's tax return by simply sending a written request to the IRS. No questions asked.

- The Deficit Reduction Act of 1984 requires the IRS to disclose wages, dividends, and interest earnings to any federal, state, or local agency administering such programs as Medicaid, food stamps, unemployment compensation, supplementary Social Security payments, and the aforementioned Aid to Dependent Children program.

- The U.S. State Department is, as of June 1985, insisting on certified copies of income tax returns to show that sponsors of immigrants have the financial means to support them. Approximately half a million legal immigrants come into this country each year.

This should be enough to give the general drift of the government's attitude toward confidential data. Many of the items in the above list can probably be justified on an individual basis—but the cumulative effect is enough to make even George Orwell twitch in his grave. The real insult is that the average citizen doesn't even know that it's going on. The landmark Privacy Act of 1974 (which grew out of earlier concerns about privacy, as well as the Watergate fiasco) mandated that the government obtain the consent of a citizen if private, confidential data was to be used for any reason other than that for which it was originally obtained. But, as with the Japanese-ancestry victims of 1942, it hasn't worked out that way: consent isn't required for law enforcement or for "routine use."

Caveat emptor!

FURTHER ENCROACHMENTS ON PRIVACY

As you can see, there is already good reason to be concerned about the accuracy and confidentiality of vast amounts of personal information about your finances, your taxes, your medical history, and various other things that companies and government agencies want to know about you. Among other things, you don't know for sure:

- What information exists about you, and on whose database.

- Whether or not the data are correct, and when they were last updated to reflect the current "truth" about your life.

- Exactly what the information is used for by the person, company, or organization that collected it.

- Under what circumstances it can be given (or transmitted by computer) to other individuals, companies, or government agencies.

This should be enough to frighten you half to death. If not, you've either led a very dull life, or you're an exhibitionist. The rest of us would prefer to keep our private lives more or less private—or at least know when and where and to whom the intimate details of our lives are being displayed.

Unfortunately, that's not the end of it: the government wants more. Most likely, it will always want more; in any case, we already know some of the things that it would like to know more about. Many of these things have to do with tax data: the Internal Revenue Service is most displeased by the fact that some 3.1 million people fail to file tax returns;[13] it estimates that the lost tax revenues from such nonfilers was $3 billion in 1981, and that the lost revenue from underpayment of taxes on legal income earned by individuals and corporations was $81.5 billion.[14] To deal with this problem, the IRS has begun a number of experiments to make official use of data that are private in the sense of existing outside the government, but public in the sense that they can be purchased or rented by anyone—including the government.

One of the first experiments was intriguingly simple: the IRS bought a commercially available list of 300,000 truck owners. It matched that list to its own computerized taxpayer rolls, ordered 10,769 taxpayer investigations, and collected $3.7 million from 10,680 taxpayers.[15] It has also purchased a list of subscribers to a medical journal, in order to determine whether any doctors have forgotten to file.

The IRS also plans to use commercially available market research data that provide such information as the neighborhoods in which families live, how long they have lived there, and the model and year of cars they own.[16] This can be used to provide a "profile" of the family, which can then be compared against the reported income, deductions, and exemptions claimed on the taxpayer's return. Anomalies, of course, would be spit out by the IRS computer.

Is any of this illegal? Not at all. Section 7601(a) of the Internal Revenue Code permits IRS agents to "inquire after and concerning all persons . . . who may be liable to pay any Internal Revenue tax, and all persons owning or having the care and management of any objects with respect to which any tax is imposed." No doubt the Congressmen and Senators who enacted that charming piece of legislation had visions of revenue agents marching up and down the streets, scowling at taxpayers and looking under every rock for deadbeats. One wonders if they had any idea that Section 7601(a) could be enforced so easily with modern computers.

One final example to show that it's not just the Internal Revenue Service that we should be worried about: the U.S. Department of the Treasury recently requested permission to monitor the details of foreign financial transactions, down to the level of charges on individual credit cards in other countries.[17] The motivation for this request is apparently an attempt to combat drug trafficking more effectively; the requirement to prevent imports of narcotics and other controlled substances, said the Treasury Department, "demands the development of new regulatory techniques— techniques that provide necessary information without unduly burdening commerce." The proposal, which was presented on April 5, 1984, would require banks to provide the Treasury with such information as the name, address, and account number of "credit card charges received or shipped by respondent financial institutions," the date and amount of each charge, and the name and address of the merchant submitting the charge.

So much for the privacy of your next vacation to Switzerland!

References for Chapter 14

1.   Rochester, Jack, and John Gantz, *The Naked Computer*, New York: William Morrow and Company, 1983.

2.   Jones, T. Capers, unpublished speech for Wang Computer Laboratory, Boston, Mass., May 6, 1985.

3.   Burnham, David, *The Rise of the Computer State*, New York: Random House, 1984.

4.   Marx, Gary T., "The New Surveillance," *Technology Review*, May/June 1985.

5.   Burnham, *op. cit.*

6.   Burnham, *op. cit.*

7.   "Police Face Allegations of Accessing Confidential Files," *Computerworld*, February 25, 1985.

8.   "Computer Matching: Should It Be Banned?" *Communications of the ACM*, June 1984.

9.   Burnham, *op. cit.*

10.   Hobbs Shirley, Schleibla, "Open Secret? More and More People Have Access to Your Tax Returns," *Barron's*, June 24, 1985.

11.   Burnham, *op. cit.*

12.   Schleibla, *op. cit.*

13.   Kirchner, J., "IRS Plan to Identify Tax Cheats Draws Fire," *Computerworld*, September 15, 1983.

14.   Frank, Allan Dodds, "No More Mr. Nice Guy," *Forbes*, September 26, 1983.

15.   *Ibid.*

16.   Burnham, David, "U.S. May Set New Computer Trap for Tax Evaders," *International Herald Tribune*, August 30, 1983.

17.   _____, "Treasury Wants More Foreign Data From Banks," *New York Times*, July 3, 1984.

15

PREDICTIONS II

The role of government and its relationship to the individual has been changed so radically that today government is involved in almost every aspect of our lives.

Political, economic and racial forces have developed which we have not yet learned to understand or control. If we are ever to master these forces, make certain that government will belong to the people, not the people to the government, and provide for the future better than the past, we must somehow learn from the experiences of the past.

Bernard Baruch
Speech, May 11, 1964

We must indeed learn from the past—for without that guidance, we have no way of knowing what may lie in store for us in the future. Will there be further encroachments on our privacy? Will the government impose further restrictions on exports and imports of computer equipment? Will there eventually be an effort to regulate the computer industry as strictly as, say, the nuclear power industry?

To answer these questions, we can look at two things: current technological trends, and the broad sweep of history. What have governments done in the past when presented with the power of a new technology—whether it be gunpowder, the steam engine, or nuclear power? And how have governments reacted in times of perceived threats—economic or military—from foreign powers? We all have our history books; we can all read. We must therefore draw our own conclusions and take whatever actions we feel appropriate for our individual well-being and our sense of duty toward our family, our nation, and . . . and, yes, our sense of duty toward our government. This I must leave in your hands, for I am writing a book about computers, not civic duty.

I can, however, make some comments about technological trends and the possibilities that technology will offer to government organizations. Much of this has been done in the previous several chapters; here I will summarize those trends and offer some predictions on likely scenarios for the future.

TRENDS IN GOVERNMENTAL USE OF COMPUTERS

As we will see throughout this book, computer hardware and software will become increasingly powerful over the next five to ten years. This is an important point, because it offers increased opportunities for the basic government activities outlined in Chapter 11: information capture, information transformation, information analysis, and information retrieval. After seeing in Chapter 14 what the government is already doing to our privacy, we have good cause to worry about what it would do with computers 1,000 times more powerful and 1,000 times cheaper.

Indeed, even if computer hardware never got any more powerful than it is today, the government's record-keeping activities would continue to improve over the next five to ten years. This is because much of the existing data, as well as the existing computer software that is involved in the process of data capture, was developed ten or twenty years ago, and is not yet making effective use of current computer technology. For example, many government agencies still maintain all of their files and records on magnetic tapes (which movie directors persist in showing us in current movies about large-scale computers), a technology that has been obsolete for more than ten years. If the government agency wants to find a selected record about Taxpayer McGurkle, it may have to read through the entire tape (which may contain tens of thousands of individual records), record by record, looking for McGurkle. Indeed, it may have a database that consists of 500 tapes—and McGurkle's record might not be found until 249 tapes had been scanned from beginning to end.[1]

Not only that, but each government agency has its own set of files and records, and there are currently great incompatibilities among them. Thus, one agency might record your birthdate in a YY-MM-DD format (e.g., 56-01-04 for "January 4th, 1956") while another might record it in a MM-DD-YY format, still another might record it in a MM-DD-YYYY format, and still another might not record your birthdate at all.[2]

So we are saved from further involvement and intrusions by the government's own bureaucracy. But that is changing slowly. There are more and more efforts to standardize data formats and record-keeping conventions, so that information may be traded more easily from one computer to another, from one agency to another. When this is coupled with the ongoing technological improvements provided by the computer industry, it means that the degree of governmental activity can be expected to increase drastically over the next ten years.

Here are some of the things we should expect:

- **Consolidation of law enforcement files.** The National Crime Information Center (NCIC) maintained by the FBI is already accessible to most state police agencies, and there are already mechanisms in place to feed some state police records to the federal government. But the integration is far from complete. There are still thousands of local police agencies in cities, counties, and small rural villages; and there are still many federal-level law enforcement databases that are not thoroughly inte-

[1] The situation is roughly comparable to the annoying wait that you experience when looking for your favorite song on an audio tape cassette, or when you are looking for a particular spot on a TV show that you have recorded on your VCR unit: you have to scan sequentially until you find what you want. Compare this to the speed of a random-access unit like your old phonograph player or your brand-new audio disk player, which lets you select a track instantly.

[2] For those who are familiar with computer technology, I should point out that there is another dimension (if not several dimensions) of incompatibility: one agency might use a "packed decimal" format to record the birthdate, while another might use an "unpacked decimal," while still another might use a "floating point" notation, and yet another might record the birthdate as an "offset" against the year 1945, which some programmer might have decided was the Beginning Of All Time.

grated. To the extent that these databases represent political power, they may never be completely integrated. It is hard to imagine, for example, the CIA and FBI sharing all of their information with the Secret Service, the Drug Enforcement Agency, the Immigration Service, and the police chief in Moose Junction, North Dakota.

- **Integration and cross-checking of other government databases will continue.** As indicated in Chapter 14, there is considerable pressure for the IRS to provide "useful" information to other agencies; and there will be ongoing pressure for other social service agencies to provide data to one another. In many cases, the motivation for such integration will be laudable; indeed, it is even conceivable that it might be helpful for the citizen whose records are being cross-fertilized. But in the aggregate, the result is the same: the government will have the power to know more about everyone—the innocent as well as the guilty.

- **Increasingly automated access to private-industry records.** As we know, most large organizations already have their day-to-day business operations computerized. In many cases, the government already has the authority to subpoena those computer records in the pursuit of a crime. In some cases—such as the requirement for banks to notify the government of all financial transactions over $10,000—the government is being provided data even when there is no evidence whatsoever that anything illegal, immoral, or unethical is going on. The natural thing to expect in the future is the government's request to "hook in" directly to corporate databases, so that it can retrieve records and analyze patterns of records without anyone in the corporation (not to mention the individual customers the corporation serves) knowing what's going on.

- **Requirement for businesses to computerize all financial transactions.** What about the small business that has not computerized its day-to-day operations? Indeed, a small business today might decide that it doesn't want to computerize! The government, in turn, might decide that every business should computerize its records, in order to simplify the tax-collection process, the tax-auditing process, and the never-ending job of looking for "bad guys," wherever they may be. The government of Italy has given us one such example: in the spring of 1985, it decreed that all shopowners would be required to use a new government-installed cash register. The cash register keeps a record of all transactions on a small tape cassette which cannot be accessed (or removed) by the shopowner; at the end of each day (or week) a government representative would remove the tape, thereby gaining access to financial records that would eventually help determine whether the shopowner was paying his taxes. Italians are a very creative people; no doubt they found some way to circumvent this act. Nevertheless, the trend is an ominous one.

- **A requirement for individuals to computerize their financial transactions.** At the present time, we are not legally required to maintain a bank account, and our employer (in most states) is legally required to pay our salary in cash, if we so insist. Thus, it is technically possible to function in today's society without any computerized record of most of our financial transactions. This freedom, I predict, will come under more and more attack. The government will find it more and more difficult to tolerate the possibility of someone conducting his financial affairs without any records. Though it may be true that the majority of people desiring to live this kind of life-style are drug smugglers, pederasts, or Communists, there may be a few decent eccentrics who feel that it's nobody's business how they spend their money. Life will become increasingly difficult for such eccentrics.

PREDICTIONS

Of course, the government is concerned with more than just the private details of the lives of its citizens. In a broader sense, we can look forward to the following general trends for the rest of this century:

- **Continued "protectionist" involvement in the computer industry.** In the mid-1980s, the U.S. government still believes that the

American computer industry is smarter and faster and better than that of other countries; hence, it is not concerned with foreign imports except for the raw materials from which computer hardware is made: semiconductor chips. But as time goes on, our industry will become more mature, and we will face greater threats from foreign countries in the areas of computer software, artificial intelligence, database machines, and a variety of other sophisticated products. To protect American industry, the federal government will come under more and more pressure to impose quotas on foreign imports, just as it does now with automobiles, steel, and textiles.

This is very sad because computer hardware is already a commodity (you can buy an IBM computer, or something that functions like an IBM computer, anywhere in the world), and computer software is rapidly becoming a commodity. Within ten years, the only truly valuable asset associated with computers will be knowledge: the intelligence that can be gleaned from computer databases. If the government establishes import quotas on knowledge, it will be dooming us to eternal mediocrity among the nations of the world.

- **The government will dramatically increase its subsidy of U.S. computer research efforts.** Current research efforts were discussed in Chapter 12; while they are impressive, they come nowhere near matching, for example, the $75 billion expended to put an American on the moon. Nor will the government ever devote that much money to the American computer effort (it's not as sexy as sending an astronaut to an alien planet, and, besides, we don't have anyone as charismatic as John Kennedy to sell the idea to the public). But it will easily spend ten times as much as it is spending now—and that will have a dramatic effect on our national research programs.

- **There will eventually be a serious effort to limit citizens' uses of or access to computers.** It should be noted that by 1984, there was more raw computing power in the hands of individuals than there was in the hands of the government. By itself, that is not very impressive: there are also more automobiles in the hands of citizens than there are jeeps and trucks in the military.

But computers, as we have seen, are powerful because of (among other things) their ability to digest and analyze data. To the extent that the government is not able to protect the data it has so carefully gathered (as well as corporate data that it wants to access, too), it becomes accessible to private citizens—hackers operating their personal computers at home, corporate programmers maliciously modifying corporate data to confuse the government, innocent-looking government clerks deciding to broadcast government databases to the world in the style of the famous "Pentagon Papers" case, etc. Sooner or later, this will concern the American government, just as it concerns the Soviet government today. Indeed, the right to own a computer may become the rallying cry for conservatives of the 21st century, just as the right to own firearms was the tradition of all citizens through the 19th century and the demand of conservative crackpots in the mid-20th century.

- **The government will impose a national identification smart card upon the population before the end of the century.** Smart cards were discussed in Chapter 7 as a way of facilitating electronic banking and paperless business transactions. But the military is also interested in smart cards for identification purposes; so are the government agencies responsible for food stamps, Medicaid, Social Security, and a host of other government benefits. These agencies currently generate enormous mountains of paper that eventually (but only after painful manual processing) find their way into the maw of large computer systems. Smart cards are easier, faster, cheaper, and more convenient. It will be only a small step to ask all citizens to carry the cards with them for identification purposes.

Even George Orwell never thought things would get so bad.

COMPUTERS AND BUSINESS

16

THE ROLE OF COMPUTERS IN BUSINESS

. . . the convergence of computers and telecommunications doesn't resolve any of the ancient puzzles about human rights and responsibilities, man and nature, liberty and authority, productivity and fairness, pursuit of the common good in a world full of individuals, and protection of the global commons in a world full of nation-states.

But the informatization of society does change the *context* in which these durable dilemmas present themselves in the 1980s and 1990s. Out there in the marketplace of ideas, this expandable, compressible, substitutable, transportable, leaky, shareable resource is creating a lot of confusion as it undermines our inherited knowledge and wisdom. . .

The information environment created by the fusion of computers and telecommunications is full of examples of Canutish behavior. The trouble seems to be that we have adopted uncritically for the management of *information* concepts that have proven useful during the centuries when *things* were the dominant resources and the prime objects of commerce, politics, power and prestige. When we do this, our inherited wisdom is somehow transmuted into folly. Nowhere is this truer than in the exercise of power in management, administration and politics.

Harlan Cleveland
The Knowledge Executive[1]

If you work in a large corporation or in a government organization, you are well aware of the presence of computers. For the past twenty-five years, business organizations and government agencies have been the primary users of computers and information processing systems. Unfortunately, most of these organizations—including, most likely, the one you work for—are not paragons of creativity and sophistication. Many never have been and never will be; some may have been leaders and innovators in the Industrial Revolution of steel and railroads, but have not yet grasped the fact that we are living in an Information Age. Some made a valiant effort to enter the computer age in the 1950s and 1960s, but have not progressed since. A few realize that the "window of opportunity" for transforming themselves into a full-scale information-based organization is rapidly closing, but they are not yet able to do anything about it. And a very, very few are actually reorganizing their computer systems, and their manual procedures, and their organization charts, and their product/service offerings, to take advantage of modern computer power.

Let me state this more bluntly, and in more direct terms. Your organization is probably still using the computer as a glorified abacus, and the work that you do, whatever it is, is becoming increasingly inefficient, ineffective, and even irrelevant as a result. It is important for you to understand why this is so, and what you must do about it. You can ignore the situation, of course, or you can shrug your shoulders and say that it's out of your control. But abdication won't make the problem go away; it will only make things worse.

This chapter and the six that follow are about the many uses that modern businesses could make, should make, and do make of computers. As we will see, these uses go far beyond the mundane applications of accounting and inventory control that consume the computer resources of most organizations. The discussion is not limited to the private sector; after all, most government organizations have the same kind of information processing needs as private companies. The discussion is not about computer hardware or software *per se*, though business organizations do use hardware and software to organize much of their information. (Specific hardware and software issues are discussed in the next two sections of this book.)

Before we discuss the information-processing phenomena of modern business—the personal-computing revolution, office automation, expert systems, etc.—I want to establish a baseline. Where is Big Business today with respect to computers and information processing?

THE CURRENT SITUATION

I begin with an obvious observation: virtually all medium-sized and large-sized American businesses have installed computer systems to carry out their day-to-day operations. The Fortune 100 began some twenty-five to thirty years ago; the Fortune 300 began fifteen years ago; and virtually every organization on the Fortune 500 list has had computer systems for at least ten years (except those newcomers on the list that are less than ten years old).

But this doesn't mean very much. As we will see in Chapters 27 and 30, many of the computer systems that these companies have installed are in serious trouble: the software doesn't work, isn't documented, and can't be maintained. More important, though, the individual systems are not integrated. The manufacturing system doesn't talk to the inventory system; the sales forecasting system doesn't talk to the cash forecasting system. Even if (by some miracle) the systems do talk to each other, it is highly likely that much of the information is duplicated—e.g., customer information, product information, vendor information, etc. Also, it is highly likely that many manual systems have evolved in the organization since the development of the automated systems (in addition to the old ones that have been there all along) and chances are that the manual systems don't talk to other manual systems, and they don't talk to the automated systems.

Some of the ramifications of this lack of integration are obvious: duplicated decision making, redundant data, contradictory decisions made in different parts of the same organization because of different versions of the same information, etc. But there is another problem, too: the unintegrated systems virtually guarantee that the organization is using computers only for day-to-day operational processing. Payroll, inventory, accounting, production scheduling, manufacturing control, etc.—these are the things that computers are doing in companies across the land. As we will see in

Chapter 18, there is a much more vital role that computers could play: strategic planning. Spreadsheet programs are used in many companies today for financial modeling and decision support, but this usually represents only tactical planning rather than strategic planning.

Another characteristic of most medium-sized and large-sized organizations today is the almost complete lack of communication between the office automation computer systems and their business data processing computer systems. Office automation is typically interpreted to mean word processing activities: a significant percentage of American companies have "smart typewriters," or word processssors, or general-purpose personal computers that are dedicated to word processing. There may also be systems in place for electronic filing of documents, or for microfiche retrieval, or production of presentation-quality 35mm slides and graphics, or other related office automation needs. But it is rare indeed to find the company where a manager can access his company's mainframe computer to retrieve some production data, download it into his word processing system, and produce a report. And it's equally rare to see a company in which the vast treasure-house of information on the office automation systems ever gets uploaded onto the mainframe and merged into other databases.

Many companies feel that their office automation systems are reasonably sophisticated, often much more so than their mainframe-based data processing systems. In some respects, American business has a right to be proud of its office automation: letters and reports today are neatly typed, neatly printed, checked for spelling errors, and conveniently filed for later reference. (See? A file of all letters written by Manager Jones, or a file of all letters written to Vendor X, is a database! It ought to be accessible to the organization's mainframe computer.) On the other hand, there are many other office automation technologies that are hardly used at all—electronic mail, voice mail, text-oriented teleconferencing, video teleconferencing, etc.—even though they offer as profound an improvement in communications as the telephone did a century ago. We will discuss these facilities in more detail in Chapter 19.

Meanwhile, the overwhelming majority of small businesses in the United States remain uncomputerized. Recent surveys have indicated that as of 1984, only 2 percent of small businesses in the country had computerized their operation.[1] By 1990, approximately 10 percent of them will be computerized, but that is still clearly only a tiny minority. Perhaps it is too much to expect that the small three-person company, with annual revenues of $100,000 to $200,000, should worry about automated payroll, inventory control, etc. But it is obviously not an issue of money or technology: the same small businessperson who runs his grocery store or delicatessen without a computer probably has a home computer for his son or daughter to play Pac-Man. The primary reason that he doesn't have a business computer is that he doesn't see a need, or an opportunity; secondarily, he is still terrified of computers and would rather leave them to his children. Unfortunately, his children will learn computers, and will use them to start their own small businesses, at which point they will be in a position to put their father's and mother's small business out of business.

There is one last problem that big business must worry about: it is investing its energies and resources in building the wrong kind of computer systems. As we will see in Chapter 20, two decades of experience in computer organizations have led to a consistent pattern of hiring a certain kind of programmer and systems analyst who knows how to build a certain kind of system. These are the operational systems, the day-to-day operational systems like payroll. But the user community, meanwhile, has moved on. The army of accountants and engineers and marketing people who run the company are desperately looking for systems that will help them in *ad hoc* retrieval of information, in decision support, and ultimately in expert advice on specialized areas of their business. We will discuss the need for a major shift in the priorities of MIS departments in Chapter 20; the subject of expert systems will be discussed in Chapter 21.

CONCLUSION

The fact that we are living in an Information Age should not come as news. People like Daniel Bell,[2] Peter Drucker,[3] John Naisbitt,[4]

---

[1] As we will see in Chapter 17, approximately 24 percent of the small companies with fewer than twenty people have a personal computer. However, in most cases, it is used for a very limited purpose—e.g., maintaining a mailing list.

Kenneth Boulding,[5] and others[6-10] have been telling us that for years. So why haven't we done anything about it? I suspect that a large part of the answer is that the many public statements about the importance of information have sounded too global and too abstract to be meaningful on a personal level. When someone tells us that the economy of steel mills and coal mines is dying, and that it has led to large-scale unemployment in some parts of the world, it's difficult to translate that into a personal imperative to manage our businesses more efficiently. Nobody tells us very much about how to do that—at least not in terms that a businessperson can understand and act on.

Actually, many of the books listed in the references for this chapter do a very good job of telling managers how to change their mind set for the Information Age; I urge you to read them all. Meanwhile, we will forge ahead with a somewhat narrower, more specific, slightly more technological view of the Information Age in the following chapters.

References for Chapter 16

1.   Cleveland, Harlan, *The Knowledge Executive: Leadership in an Information Society*, New York: Dutton, Truman Talley Books, 1985.

2.   Bell, Daniel, *The Coming of Post-Industrial Society*, New York: Basic Books, 1976.

3.   Drucker, Peter, *The Age of Discontinuity*, New York: Harper and Row, 1968.

4.   Naisbitt, John, *Megatrends*, New York: Warner Books, 1983.

5.   Boulding, Kenneth, "The Economics of Knowledge and the Knowledge of Economics," *American Economics Review*, May 1966.

6.   Branscomb, Lewis, "Information: The Ultimate Frontier," *Science*, January 12, 1979.

7.   Boettinger, Henry M., "Information Industry Challenges to Management and Economics," *New Jersey Bell Journal*, Spring 1984.

8.   Simon, Nora, and Alain Minc, *The Computerization of Society*, Cambridge, Mass.: MIT Press, 1981.

9.   McHale, John, *The Changing Information Environment*, Boulder, Colo.: Westview Press, 1975.

10.   Martin, James, *An Information Systems Manifesto*, Englewood Cliffs, N.J.: Prentice-Hall, 1984.

17

PERSONAL COMPUTING

There are seasons, in human affairs, of inward and outward revolution, when new depths seem to be broken up in the soul, when new wants are unfolded in multitudes, and a new and undefined good is thirsted for. There are periods when the principles of experience need to be modified, when hope and trust and instinct claim a share with prudence in the guidance of affairs, when, in truth, to dare, is the highest wisdom.

William Ellery Channing
The Union (1829)

The most exciting development in the business world in the past ten years is the introduction of the personal computer. Between 1981 and 1984, the number of professional workers with personal computers went from zero to nearly ten percent; by 1990, nearly half of all workers will have on their desks a computer more powerful than any corporation had at its disposal twenty years ago.

It is not yet clear what all of these people—"users," as they are known by computer professionals, vaguely suggesting an addiction worse than heroin—are doing with their personal computers. Many do nothing more than keep their personal calendars; some don't use them at all, except to demonstrate to peers and subordinates that they rank high enough in the corporate pecking order to have one. But a growing number of accountants, engineers, salespeople, and executives are beginning to use their own powerful computing devices to build databases, forecast trends, produce newsletters, and even maintain accounting records for their department.

To understand the personal computing revolution, we need to look at several things:

- Who is using personal computers?

- What are they using them for?

- Who controls the acquisition and use of personal computers?

- Who are these mysterious people called users?

- What are the dangers of the personal computing revolution?

- What are the solutions?

WHO IS USING PERSONAL COMPUTERS?

Obviously, not all businesses are using personal computers (PCs) yet, nor are all white-collar professional knowledge workers using personal computers even in the larger organizations. There are approximately seven million computers in American homes as of 1985, and another 12 million in offices. While it seems evident that eventually every home and every office will have several computers, there will be a period of another five to ten years where it will be easy to distinguish between the "haves" and the "have-nots." Those workers and those companies with extensive PC support will probably be in a stronger competitive position than those without, but this is not always true. Many companies are finding that the hundreds of Apple or IBM computers that they bought last year are sitting in the corner of managers' offices, not being used at all.

One interesting way of looking at the PC revolution is to observe the percentage of companies using a PC (or, in the case of a large company, multiple PCs and mainframe computers) as a function of company size. A recent survey by Dun and Bradstreet found this breakdown:[1]

Company Size	Percentage Using PCs
1–19 people	23.9%
20–99 people	36.3%

100–499 people   47.2%
500–999 people   71.8%
1,000 plus people   85.4%

The reason this information is so significant is that the small businesses are the source of most of the economic growth in this country, and they are the ones that are generally uncomputerized. Conversely, the larger organizations are more heavily computerized, but they are stagnant in at least two dimensions: their revenues (and contribution to the GNP, job creation, increased productivity, etc.) are stagnant, and their computer systems are stagnant. As we will see in Chapter 30, most of the large Fortune 500 companies developed their foundation computer systems ten or twenty years ago; 50 to 80 percent of their data processing budget is now devoted to maintaining those systems. The old systems are so complex and cumbersome that hardly anyone understands them, and it is extraordinarily difficult to modify them to take advantage of such new technologies as personal computers and fourth-generation programming languages.[1]

Small businesses supplied 28 percent of the jobs in the United States in 1984; more importantly, small businesses are creating most of the new jobs in the country. As John Naisbitt points out:[2]

> The entrepreneurs who are creating new businesses are also creating jobs for the rest of us. During a seven-year period ending in 1976, we added 9 million new workers to the labor force—a lot of people! How many of those were jobs in the Fortune 1,000 largest industrial concerns? Zero. But 6 million were jobs in small businesses, most of which had been in existence for four years or less. (The remaining 3 million went to work for state and local, but not federal, government. . . .)

So it is the small businesses that have the vitality and the growth and the opportunities, it seems. And it is also the small businesses that can take advantage of the tremendous productivity gains

---

[1] Fourth-generation programming languages, or 4GLs, are discussed in Chapter 29. Typical exampes of 4GLs for personal computers are dBASE-III, R-Base 4000, and Knowledge-Man. The classical programming languages that you have probably heard about—COBOL, FORTRAN, BASIC, etc.—are considered less sophisticated, and are referred to as third-generation languages.

offered by computers, together with the tremendous technology improvements that weren't available to large companies when they began to computerize twenty years ago, and which they can't take advantage of now because of their maintenance problems.

Another way to look at PC usage is by class of user. I will talk more about categories of users later, but we can begin by distinguishing between clerical people, professional people (engineers, economists, marketing people, etc.), and managers. About the only thing that is clear now is that the fantasy of computers on every manager's desk is just that: a fantasy. As a *Business Week* article[3] pointed out,

> The office of the future had long been talked about as an environment where everyone, from the clerks to the chief executive, would be linked in a centralized electronic network with all the intelligence and memory located in the hub of the system, a large mainframe computer. These networks would quickly move corporate data to a display screen on an executive's desk, whiz correspondence throughout the company, and even keep track of such individual data as appointment calendars and telephone messages. . . .But despite all the hoopla, few office systems of any size have been put into operation. Most corporations have automated only the clerical worker, not the manager.

Further confirming this observation, a survey conducted by *Fortune* found that 56 percent of the MIS managers in American organizations used personal computers themselves, and 37 percent of top management used personal computers. For top managers, of course, there is somewhat of a *Catch-22* situation: part of the motivation of using a PC is that your peers use a PC. As a president or chairman of a company, though, you might argue that most of your job is people-related—i.e., that most of your time is spent in board meetings, dealing with the personalities of people who don't know about computers and don't care about computers. On the other hand, it is indisputable that top management deals with information as well as people. If a top executive can get his own information—unfiltered, unbiased, uncompromised, and even unknown to his subordinates— he can hardly be any worse off than he was before.

Though this is obviously true, we must face an equally obvious reality: the top managers in most of the Fortune 500 (I just typed "Fortunate" on my Apple Macintosh computer while I was writing this, and erased it almost before I saw what I had typed . . . what a laugh! The Fortune 500 are hardly "fortunate" these days) are in their fifties or sixties and are thus entirely oblivious to the computer revolution. They may think that it is a good thing for their organization, and they may issue edicts to their junior managers about PCs and workstations. But do they have a personal computer on their own desk? If they are over fifty years old, the most likely answer is "No!"

WHAT ARE PCS USED FOR?

Merely having a PC on one's desk means very little. It can be very impressive as a showpiece, as exemplified by the frequent TV shots of J. R. Ewing typing meaningless input on the personal computer on his "Dallas" set.[2] A survey conducted by Dun and Bradstreet showed the following use of personal computers in the typical office:

Application	Percentage Using
Accounting	72.5
Financial analysis	65.2
Word processing	56.8
Database management	38.3
Inventory control	31.5
Purchasing	22.8
Customer credit analysis	14.2
Other	78.0

[2] Note that nobody in the "Dallas" show ever mentions the existence of the PC, though great care appears to have been taken to ensure that it is "Texas-oriented": it is a Texas Instruments workstation of some sort. If "Dallas" were truly to portray the real world, either J. R. or Bobby or someone on the show would mention the existence of computers—e.g., "Did you get the electronic mail I sent you on the computer last night?" or, "I didn't agree with the financial model that the controller developed on his PC—did you try running it with different parameters?"

It is interesting to see how these patterns relate to the wishes of office workers who generally have little or nothing to say about the way technology (or anything else) is implemented in their office. A recent survey by Public Attitudes[4] showed the reaction of office workers to the question: "If your company said you could spend up to ten thousand dollars to increase your productivity, what would you do?"

Action	Percentage
Buy computer/micro/PC	41
Buy software	13
Buy a word processor	11
Upgrade/update equipment	7
Buy equipment (all others)	7
Buy database	2
Buy electronic mail	1
Add a staff member	13
Education/training for staff members	10
Increase salaries/benefits	3
Improvement to workspace	2

I do not yet know of any surveys of the amount of time that PC users use their PCs each day. I would guess that it is less than an hour per day for most users today. This is irrelevant for most users. After all, how many of them are asked about the utilization of their company car, or their company typewriter?

WHO CONTROLS PC ACQUISITION?

Until 1981 or 1982, almost all corporate purchases (or rentals, or leases, or any other financial arrangements) involving computers were made by a central group within an organization, usually named the "MIS group," or the "central data processing group," or some other similarly named organization. But by the late 1970s, and certainly by the early 1980s, two things had become abundantly clear: (a) while the MIS organization might argue that every computer system should come from IBM, some user organizations disagreed violently, and (b) while many MIS organizations felt that they should make final decisions about what computer hardware and what computer software should be allowed within the organization, there was a growing feeling—and support from the user community—that the issues of database design and software engineering would come to dominate the petty issues of which computers and which software packages the user uses.

THE NATURE OF USERS

Throughout this book, there have been many, many references to a kind of human being known as a user. Computer people like me use the term user rather casually, as if to suggest that there are two classes of people in the world: all of us smart people who really know how computers work and all of those other dummies (users) who have no idea how computers work but who need them to get their job done. The disrespect suggested by this classification is rarely conscious in the minds of a computer professional, and it is certainly not deserved, but it inevitably creeps into discussions between computer people and noncomputer people.

Perhaps more dangerous than the assumption that computer people are smart and noncomputer users are dumb is the assumption that all users are the same. Computer professionals are almost universally guilty of the assumption that users represent a perfectly homogeneous class of human beings when, in fact, nothing could be further from the truth. Unfortunately, you can't avoid computer professionals. In a large company, it is very likely that you will find yourself communicating with a systems analyst, a programmer, or a database designer from your company's EDP or MIS organization and, as indicated above, that programmer/analyst will probably assume that you are exactly the same as every other person in the organization with a personal computer.

In every discussion that I have had with some other person about some aspect of personal computers, it has been important to learn as quickly as possible what his or her perspective is. As a teacher, or as a consultant, or simply as a friend trying to help another friend overcome some problem with his personal computer, it has been important for me to know such things as: is this person afraid of personal computers? Has he ever used a computer before? Does he have a basic sense of what the computer can and can't do, or is it all black magic to him? The answers to these questions are very, very different for each person.

It's important for you to be aware of these differences for two reasons. First, you will probably begin your own experience with personal computers as a bumbling, fumbling novice, which means that you will be turning to your friends, or to the experts in your company, for help. It's important for you to know how they perceive you. And it's important for you to do whatever is necessary to avoid false perceptions on the part of the people who will be helping you so that they don't underestimate or overestimate your talents, background, and level of interest in the lore of personal computers. The second reason is that you will soon become an expert, passing on advice to others in your organization. As soon as the word gets out that you've successfully mastered your IBM PC, and that you're turning out wonderful charts, graphs, and spreadsheets, people will begin flocking to you for help. If these people are familiar to you, you'll know how to communicate with them; but if they are people from other departments of your company, or if they are people entirely outside your company—e.g., your next-door neighbor, your minister, or your mother-in-law- —then it will be extremely important for you to understand what category they fit into, so that you can effectively communicate with them.

We will take a brief look at the wide spectrum of users from several different perspectives: their experience, their position or job function, and how they got access to personal computing.

Classification by Nature of
Personal Computer Acquisition

To most people, the term personal computer conjures up a specific image—usually that of a person sitting in front of a single, stand-alone microcomputer manufactured by Apple or IBM. But that's only one of several common scenarios:

- **Small businesspeople who buy their own computers.** If you operate a small business, or if you're a self-employed professional, you fall into this category. The money for the computer—probably between $2,000 and $5,000—came from your own checking or savings account. If you have problems, you have no experts to turn to (other than the salesman in the computer store who sold you the machine); if the computer breaks down, you're on your own. This is a small (but rapidly growing) category. One recent survey indicated that only about 2 percent of American small businesses presently have a personal computer.

- **Businesspeople in large companies who buy their own computers.** Almost all large businesses have computers, of course, but the computer is typically a mainframe IBM, Burroughs, or Honeywell machine that cannot be accessed by the fellow in marketing who needs to do a sales projection now, or the administrative assistant who desperately needs word processing facilities to help produce a report. If the company does not provide personal computers to its professional staff and if it is perceived by the staff that the company has no policy or plans for acquiring computers in the future, then the professional may buy one himself.[3] This attitude is prevalent among engineers, scientists, stockbrokers, etc., and is not that different from the attitude of a carpenter who will buy his own tools if he feels his employer's are not adequate. It should be pointed out that this phenomenon was much more common a few years ago when many companies were cautious about furnishing computers to their staff. By the end of the decade, IBM estimates that 50 percent of the American white-collar work force will have personal computers or some form of direct access to a computer

---

[3] This creates an interesting problem in large organizations: even though the professional is entitled to look upon the personal computer as his own (e.g., he presumably feels that he has the right to take the machine with him if he leaves the job), he should not feel that he has the right to do whatever he wants with the data being manipulated or computed by his personal computer. The data (which may have been extracted from a corporate database on the centralized mainframe computer) are a corporate asset.

system, and it is highly likely that the employers will provide that access.

- **Businesspeople with access to "user-friendly" software on the corporate mainframe.** As indicated above, large companies are rapidly beginning to provide some form of direct access to a computer system. While personal computers are the most obvious example, time-shared access to a large centralized computer may be an equivalent, and sometimes far better, alternative. In this environment, the businessperson usually has access to such software packages as FOCUS, RAMIS, MARK V, or NOMAD; or, for complex calculations, the engineer or scientist may have access to FORTRAN or APL or some other algorithmic programming language.

- **Information centers.** The concept of an information center has become quite popular at many of the larger companies and government agencies during the past five years. The businessperson, engineer, or scientist is usually provided with the kinds of tools described above—e.g., personal computers or access to a corporate mainframe computing environment—but in addition, these are combined with training, consulting, troubleshooting, and other forms of support from a team of trained data processing professionals. This is, of course, an attractive option to the person who is unfamiliar with computers and who finds the available textbooks and manuals overwhelming and/or incomprehensible. If your company has an information center, you should definitely take advantage of it; if not, you should suggest that your data processing organization (or MIS organization) consider forming one.

- **User-MIS development teams.** Many large computer systems development projects are beginning to take place outside the MIS empire and inside the user organization—e.g., within the sales department or the accounting department or the engineering department. The project team may have a number of computer specialists, but it also has a number of people from the user organization, including users who are involved in systems analysis, design, testing, quality assurance, and even programming. In most of these situations, the project manager is a person from the user organization.

One thing should be emphasized about all of the scenarios described above: it is becoming more and more common for the user—the engineer, the scientist, the account executive in the sales department—to make his or her own decision about the kind (or kinds) of personal computing that he or she needs in order to get the job done.

Classification by Level of Computer Experience

At the beginning of this chapter, I pointed out that computer professionals have a tendency to think of users as a lesser form of life. When a computer programmer or systems analyst talks to you, he will usually assume that you are an ignorant dolt when it comes to computers, and that he should approach you as if you know nothing at all. Aside from the fact that this condescending attitude may be difficult to tolerate, it may be downright wrong. While it is still realistic to assume that some users are utter neophytes when it comes to computers, it is also true that some users know as much about computer programming as professional computer programmers.

Keep in mind another point that I mentioned at the beginning of this chapter. After you have used a personal computer for a month or two, you will be regarded as a computer professional, and you will be approached by a motley crew of co-workers, friends, relatives, and absolute strangers for advice about computers. If you assume that such people know as much as you do—or that they have learned the same hard lessons that you have—you may give very bad advice indeed.

For simplicity, I divide the universe of users into three categories:

1. **The rank amateur.** If you are in this category, there is no reason to be ashamed. After all, roughly 99 percent of the world's population exists in a similar state of ignorance, and they get along just fine. What is important is to admit your ignorance (at least to yourself) in order to avoid getting

trapped by technology that you can't control. Don't be afraid of asking stupid questions; it could help avoid unnecessary disasters.[4] You should also keep in mind that, as a rank amateur, you are blissfully ignorant of a number of technical details that you will never need to know. Many of today's computer experts acquired their expertise because as recently as two or three years ago it was absolutely necessary in order to make the computer accomplish anything. By analogy, someone who wanted to drive an automobile at the turn of the century was forced (if he could not afford the luxury of a chauffeur) to learn a great many technical details about internal combustion engines; today's driver is, by comparison, a rank amateur on the subject of internal combustion engines, and he has no interest in becoming an expert.

2.   **The cocky novice.** As a result of the recent personal computer revolution, there is a new breed of user: the person who has learned just enough to be dangerous. This is the person who has (a) attended a one-hour free seminar on computers at his local computer store; or (b) taken a four-hour course on BASIC programming at his local YMCA adult education program; or (c) successfully used Lotus 1-2-3 to construct a small spreadsheet with ten rows and four columns; or (d) successfully used PFS-File to build a name-and-address list with fifty entries; or (e) successfully used WordStar to compose a three-page memo. In case you fall into this category

---

[4] An example will help illustrate this point. Not long ago, I loaned an Apple III personal computer to my children's school so that the administrative staff could use it for various word processing and database applications (keeping a file of student health records, etc.). After a few months, I asked the administrators whether they were finding the computer useful. "Oh," replied one of them, "the computer doesn't work. So we never used it." When I investigated to find out why the computer "didn't work," I found that they had been unable to turn on the power to the computer—it had a very visible power switch on the front of the display screen, but the computer also had a power switch at the rear of the main "system unit," and another power switch at the rear of the Winchester disk unit. (All of this had been demonstrated when I delivered the machine to the school, and it was documented in the technical manuals, but it was lost among the overwhelming barrage of new and unfamiliar technical material.) The users' reaction to this situation was understandable: we turned on the power switch and nothing happened. *Ergo*, the computer doesn't work. These users made the mistake of not asking a stupid question earlier; I made the far worse mistake of assuming that the power-on procedure was so straightforward that it didn't need to be emphasized.

and feel that you are being insulted, let me explain: there is a world of difference between the small projects described above and the larger projects you're likely to tackle next. If, for example, you do something grievously wrong while editing your 50-record address file, it takes very little work to recreate it. If the same thing happens to a file of 5,000 records or 50,000 records, your data may be lost forever and you may be out of business. It is deceptively easy to move from a trivial computer application to a large one, and the initial feeling of confidence from having mastered a simple computer application can lead to fatal errors.

3.   **The expert.** There is, today, a small but growing class of users who can truly be considered experienced—i.e., users who know as much about computer hardware and software as the professionals. A small illustration: there are now roughly half a dozen former programmers and systems analysts who are members of Congress. Consider the consequences of a programmer/analyst someday being elected president—he or she might even have the wit to rename the presidential office that of "Prime User"! Of course, not every expert user acquired his expertise by virtue of previous employment as a programmer or systems analyst. Many are experts simply because they have used an Apple or a Wang or a Hewlett-Packard computer in their business every day for the past five years and have come to know every quirk and idiosyncrasy of the hardware and the software.

Classification by Age

At the risk of offending some readers, I want to comment on the different reactions that young people and old people have toward personal computers. I intend no bias or prejudice. A classification by age is likely to cause controversy, but I feel that some generalizations are appropriate, as long as one remembers that they are only generalizations, and that any one of us might prove the exception to the rule. For convenience, I have divided the universe of users into three age groups: older adults, younger adults, and children.

Older adults.   The term "older" means different things to differ-ent people, largely depending on which side of the magic age of thirty or forty you happen to be on. For this discussion, I have arbitrarily decided that older means older than forty. Such a person most likely finished high school or college in the early or mid-1960s or before and thus probably had no exposure to computers in school (and probably didn't even have the pleasure of using a hand-held calculator!). We have all heard the generalization that older people find it more difficult to change their ways and adapt to new ideas, and it probably does explain why many people in their forties and fifties and sixties feel awkward and intimidated by computers. We should also remember that many older adults in the business world don't have to change their way of doing things if they are successful at what they do; they have reached an age and a position in life where they can tell their subordinates to do things for them. They don't word process, or even type; they don't calculate rows and columns of numbers; they don't keep lists and files. They supervise others who do these mundane things. It is probably for just this reason that the older people who do become adept at handling personal computers are viewed with such awe and admi-ration.

Younger adults.   For the purposes of this discussion, "younger" means someone between eighteen and forty. Such a person is likely to have finished high school or college more recently, and may have had some exposure to computers in school. The twenty-five- or thirty-year-old is more likely than an older person to surround himself with electronic gadgets of all sorts—digital stereo systems, VCR systems, etc. And in the business environment, he or she is likely to be in a professional role or a junior executive position, the sort of position where a computer can be a significant aid when it comes to drafting reports, creating spreadsheets, or overseeing a number of other operational aspects of an organization. To put it quite simply, the younger adult is more likely to be in a position where the computer can help him succeed in his career and he is thus more likely to use it as a tool. (The same thing could be said about the older, more senior executive's ability to use the computer and the corporate database as a strategic weapon to make his company more competitive. But this is an issue that is only beginning to be realized in companies today, and it has much less to do with the age of the executive than with the overall lack of sophistication of the MIS department in the company.)

Children.   For the purposes of this discussion, "children" means anyone not yet in the work force. A businessperson reading this book is likely to be more interested in children who will be entering the work force in the next two to three years, but we should be interested in children of all ages, for as we saw in Chapter 2, they will be gradually entering the work force over the next twenty years, and will be quietly causing fundamental changes in the way American companies do business.

While many of us might object to the generalization that older adults are awkward and uncomfortable with computers, virtually everyone agrees with the generalization that children are fearless and facile with computers. And yet it is only a generalization: as I pointed out in Chapter 2, there are children who are uninterested in and unexcited about computers, and others who become nervous and tense when they see that they are expected to keep up with their peers at the computer terminal. The peer pressure is intense in American schools today. For an excellent discussion of the potential psychological problems caused by computers, I recommend Craig Brod's book, *Technostress*,[5] or Sherry Turkle's *The Second Self.* [6]

In any case, it is obvious that American schoolchildren are being bombarded with computer literacy training in the schools, and one might easily assume that the next generation of users in the business community will be as comfortable operating a personal computer as they are operating a television or telephone.

Classification by Job Category

The most obvious classification of all has to do with the kind of job the user is trying to perform. In this chapter, we have already mentioned engineers, scientists, managers, and salespeople, but these obviously represent only a small subset of the many thousands of job descriptions in the United States. If we try to combine all of these job descriptions into a few major categories, we are likely to end up with the following:

Clerical and administrative workers.   In large companies, secretaries, bookkeepers, production clerks, and assistants of all sorts are obvious users of personal computers. Indeed, many of these people have been typing transactions into some form of computer system for years. In smaller companies, though, all of these functions may be performed by one or two people, and the recent advent of the personal computer may have provided the first alternative to adding machines, ledger cards, and other relics from what are rapidly becoming the Dark Ages.

Two common preconceptions are that: (a) the marketplace for clerical-oriented computing has already been heavily penetrated, which ignores the fact that small businesses, which employ more people than the Fortune 500, have not yet computerized their operation; and (b) clerical people carry out one or two narrow-minded tasks, which can be most economically performed by allowing them to communicate, via dumb terminals, with the corporate mainframe computer when, in fact, many clerical users could carry out a variety of sophisticated and creative tasks for their bosses if they had the computing power and a convenient man-machine interface for using that computer power. The traditional corporate mainframe computer environment, with its narrow-purpose, single-function interface, does not usually provide such an environment; the personal computer does. To put it bluntly, the young, junior clerical people to whom we relegate our mindless data entry activities today could easily perform a variety of sophisticated analytical activities with a personal computer. It's likely that smaller companies will stumble on this fact of life more quickly than large bureaucracies.

Professional workers.   This is the category of workers whom we can most easily imagine taking advantage of personal computers. Engineers, scientists, programmers, sales executives, and an overwhelming number of job categories fall into the general classification of knowledge workers. These people will take full advantage of the capabilities of a typical personal computer—word processing, spreadsheets, graphics, statistical analysis, and telecommunications. And this group of users will find it more and more necessary to use such facilities while communicating with other knowledge workers. The professional worker in the mid-1980s may be content to have a Hewlett-Packard or DEC personal computer on his desk in order to carry out some of the functions that he used to do by hand, but by the end of this decade (if not tomorrow!) he will reject such a computer as being useless unless it can communicate with other personal computers being used by other professionals.

Executives.   Middle-level and high-level executives are not heavy users of personal computer systems at present, despite the impressions that one might get from watching J. R. Ewing pecking away at his terminal on the popular TV show "Dallas."

This is partly because the senior executives tend to be older men and women and, as discussed earlier, may be less inclined to use computers because they were not exposed to them during their education and early professional lives. Also, senior executives are typically not involved in the day-to-day operational issues of a company that can be attacked so successfully with a computer. Instead, they are concerned with more global, political, and often speculative issues such as mergers, labor negotiations, boardroom squabbles, etc. There is a growing feeling that senior management will eventually use computers (and the corporatewide data that such computers can access) to help plot strategic directions for their companies, but this is still years away for most companies.

To help put this in perspective: Steven McClellan, a Wall Street investment analyst, interviewed the chief executives of some forty-one computer companies while preparing the material for a book on the computer industry.[7] Of these forty-one, only three had a terminal or personal computer in his or her office. If one makes the normal assumption that the chief executive officers (CEOs) of computer companies are more comfortable with computer technology than the rest of corporate America's CEOs, then we should not expect to see many personal computers in the top executive offices of the Fortune 500 companies during the next few years.

THE DANGERS OF PERSONAL COMPUTING

Now that we have discussed the benefits and advantages of personal computers, it is time to move on to the primary theme of this chapter: the dangers of personal computing. (This material is excerpted from an earlier book of mine, *The Perils of Personal Computing*.[8] You may wish to consult it for a more detailed discussion than is possible here.)

Perhaps the most serious problem with personal computers is that they become an end unto themselves, rather than a tool to help you carry out a job more effectively. Sometimes this happens because the hardware and software manuals are so obtuse that it takes hours to figure out how to accomplish something; sometimes it happens because you suddenly discover that personal computers are fun—perhaps far more fun than the rest of your job!

The most common manifestation of this problem is the sudden urge to learn how to program in such languages as BASIC or PASCAL. If you are prey to such an urge, resist it. You should never have to learn BASIC or FORTRAN or COBOL or PASCAL. Virtually anything that you want to do can probably be accomplished ten times faster, cheaper, and more effectively by (a) buying a software package that does what you want to do, or (b) using a spreadsheet or database package to solve your problem without writing conventional programming statements. Why spend a day or more writing a program in BASIC (which may contain subtle errors that you don't discover for months) when you can probably buy a software package for $100 that does the same job better (and with a greater chance of working correctly, since it was probably tested more thoroughly than you can test your programs)? Regardless of whether you use an existing software package (e.g., a package that will help you estimate your income taxes), or whether you build your own program using a spreadsheet or database program, or whether you use BASIC or PASCAL to write a program from scratch, there are several common pitfalls and problems that you can expect to encounter. The primary dangers that I have experienced—and that I have watched other, more innocent first-time users experience—are summarized below.

Lack of Testing

One of the great benefits of personal computers is the ease and speed with which one can produce reports with spreadsheet programs and file management programs. But things done too quickly and easily are sometimes done sloppily. There is a significant danger that the reports produced by dBASE III or Lotus 1-2-3 are wrong.

We can be reasonably certain that a spreadsheet program will add rows and columns of numbers correctly. But how do we know that the user entered the right numbers and the right formulas in the first place? Most accountants instinctively understand this, and carry out some fairly careful testing before they "trust" the spreadsheet results. But a large number of other users—engineers, sales managers, etc.—never think of testing. The results, of course, can be disastrous.

The same problem can happen with reports that are generated from a large database, using any of the popular file management and database management software packages—PFS File, dBASE III, R:Base 4000, etc. The most common difficulty (aside from entering the wrong data into the database in the first place) occurs when the user has to formulate a complex Boolean expression to select certain records from the database. Suppose the user mumbles to himself, "I need a report of all sales made to customers who are not in Arkansas and not in Alaska." He may try to accomplish this by typing commands like:

```
PRINT SALES FOR .NOT.(STATE = ALASKA .AND. STATE = ARKANSAS)
```

or

```
PRINT SALES FOR .NOT.(STATE = ALASKA .OR. STATE = ARKANSAS)
```

or

```
PRINT SALES FOR STATE .NEQ. ALASKA .AND. STATE .NEQ. ARKANSAS
```

The first version shown above almost certainly will not accomplish what the user wanted. The second version probably will. The third might or might not, depending on the syntax of the database language (a fussy way of saying "the rules by which the database package interprets the commands given to it"). In general, Boolean expressions involving combinations of "AND," "OR," and "NOT" can be very troublesome. If you are working on problems like this, it would be a good idea to review some of the basics of Boolean algebra that you probably first learned in high school. In any case, you should study some of the literature on testing; I personally recommend Glen Myers' classic book on software testing.[9]

Local Databases

Virtually all large businesses, government agencies, and other organizations have created a large number of computerized files and databases over the past twenty years—customer files, vendor files, inventory files, accounts receivable files, etc. One of the greatest worries within the EDP or MIS organization of a typical large company is that of nonintegrated data bases. The same information—e.g., a customer's address—may appear in a dozen different files, which can lead to very serious problems of redundancy, synchronization of updates, backup, and security.

The professional data processing community has been working very hard on this problem for a decade or more, and the problem still hasn't been solved in most large organizations. Before one can eliminate the mechanical duplication of information on magnetic tape files or disk files, it is necessary to develop an overall information model so that everyone will understand the basic entities (real world objects like a customer, about which we know things) and relationships in the organization. This model can then be used to create the corporate database, which can be the foundation of the company's day-to-day operation and its long-term strategic decision making.

In the midst of this long-term effort to create an integrated, corporatewide database, the personal computer has suddenly arrived with its ability to create "local" files, which reside on floppy disks or Winchester disks. In some cases, these local files have been downloaded from the corporate mainframe. In other cases, the files have been created by the personal computer user (perhaps as a replacement for paper files that he kept in his desk) without any thought for how the files might relate to the corporate database.

Once created, these local files are subject to all of the problems that the MIS or EDP department has been trying to deal with on its mainframe computers for the past decade: duplication of data, inconsistent updating of data, etc.

If you are creating files on your personal computer with more than a few dozen records (e.g., something larger and more complex than the names and addresss in your address book), then I urge you to read some books on computer database design or ask your MIS organization for some training. Some of the better (and more readable) books are listed at the end of the chapter.

Problems of Backup and Security

If your personal computer catches on fire and stops working, you can always replace it (though perhaps not right away). If you lose your Lotus 1-2-3 program diskette, you can always buy another. But if you lose the data that you have created on your personal computer, you can be in serious trouble.

Similarly, if the floppy diskettes in your office are subject to unauthorized access or modification, you may wish that you had never acquired a personal computer. Sensitive documents of all kinds—personnel data, financial forecasts, confidential memos, valuable customer lists, etc.—are now being stored on floppy disks that can be stolen, duplicated, or modified effortlessly during the few minutes that you've wandered out of your office to get a cup of coffee.

If you have a personal computer, you must make backups of your important data files on a regular basis. If you have a hard disk, you should not let another day pass without acquiring some convenient form of backup storage—e.g., a tape cartridge system that will allow you to back up the disk in a matter of minutes. Equally important, you should ensure that your backup files are stored someplace away from your computer. If your computer catches on fire or gets drenched by a flood, you should at least have the comfort of knowing that your backups are safe.

The Problem of Documentation

Professional computer programmers and systems analysts have learned over the past twenty years that documentation is a critical part of developing computer systems. Documentation that describes what the computer system is supposed to do; documentation that describes how the system has been organized to carry out its purpose; documentation that explains how the computer programs (e.g., the COBOL statements or BASIC statements) work; and operational documentation that describes how to run the computer programs—all of these are necessary if the oranization is to be able to use a computer system effectively over a period of years.

There is a common tendency among computer programmers not to document the work they do. They understand it because it is their own work, and because it never occurs to them that someone else might eventually have to take over their work. Bitter experience has proved to most programming managers that it is absolutely essential to invest a substantial amount of time and energy, typically 5 to 10 percent of the resources of a computer systems development project, in documentation.

Personal computer users don't have any bitter experiences (not yet, anyway) to motivate them to invest any of their own time and energy in documentation. And yet they face the same problems as the professional programmer. Six months after, say, a Lotus 1-2-3 spreadsheet has been developed, it is likely that (a) the person who developed the spreadsheet will have moved to a different organization; (b) nobody will be able to remember what assumptions went into the development of the spreadsheet; and (c) nobody will be able to find the floppy diskette where the spreadsheet data was stored.

Professional programmers and systems analysts have learned to be extremely wary of the notion of a one-shot program, the proverbial program that is going to be used once and then thrown away and is scarcer than hen's teeth. In fact, most computer programs have a useful lifetime of several years—often as long as ten to fifteen years before they are thrown away—and they are maintained by as many as ten generations of maintenance programmers, each trying with increasing difficulty to understand what his or her predecessor did.

Personal computer users haven't learned this yet. After all, most of them have only been using a computer for six months or a year. And they're now busily writing one-shot programs that they will be living with for the next twenty years.

Personal computer hardware and software manufacturers would love to convince you that you can develop self-documenting programs for typical business applications. Hogwash!! The code (or whatever passes for code) may be fairly readable. One software company, for example, claims that you can formulate your question to the computer in the following sort of language: "Which warehouses shipped more red and green argyle socks than planned?" While this is obviously more readable than something like

"PRINT ALL WAREHOUSES FOR ((SOCKTYPE = GREEN) + (SOCKTYPE = RED)) > PLAN,"

it does not make the program self-documenting and therefore self-maintaining.

In order to maintain a computer program, one has to know what underlying assumptions, schemes, plans, and rationales (or whatever passes for intelligence) went into developing it in the first place. Of course, this leads once again to the need for documentation, and not just documentation to make the program usable today, but documentation that will make it possible for someone else to modify the program five years from now.

Your MIS department can easily give you examples of the documentation they provide for their systems.

The Difference between Programs and Systems

This is, in the long run, the most serious of all the problems that a personal computer user is likely to encounter.

I begin with the observation that anyone can write a program. My son Jamie was taught at age six, in his first grade class, how to write a program; it thus follows that even the most Neanderthal of adult users of personal computers can manage to write some kind of program to accomplish something useful. Maybe it will work, maybe it will make him happy, and if things went no further, I wouldn't complain.

But inevitably (in my experience), that new program opens up a new world of opportunities. The user suddenly realizes that if he could get his hands on type-X transactions from Harry, in addition to the type-Y transactions that he's always gotten from Evelyn, he would then be able to generate an extra type-Z report for Susan to read, in addition to the type-W report that he always sent to George. These extra inputs and outputs—the "data-flow" connections between one user and another, between one department and another—are the essence of a system. And the poor user, who is still rejoicing in the success of his first VisiCalc program or dBASE-2 program, doesn't have the slightest idea of the chaos he is about to create by perturbing a system that is already in place. That same user instinctively knows that he can't change administrative policies (e.g., the number of sick days that he allows a type-A employee to take) without studying the systemwide consequences (e.g., what impact will it have on type-B employees? Will additional temporary people have to be brought in?), but he has been beguiled by smooth-talking personal computer salespeople into thinking that he can blissfully develop computer applications without studying the systemwide consequences.

SUMMARY

The introduction of personal computers into a typical business environment is causing enormous changes in the way people work and in the way they relate to one another. These changes are more fundamental than those caused by the introduction of mainframe computers twenty years ago because now workers interact directly with personal computers and have direct control over the operation of personal computers, which they never had with the mainframe machine.

The benefits of the personal computing revolution will almost certainly outweigh the problems and disadvantages, but the purpose of this chapter has been to point out some disadvantages of which the innocent reader may have been entirely unaware.

There are a number of potential problems which have not been discussed in this chapter, problems which are somewhat more subtle and long-term in their effects. The effect of computers on lifestyles, on modes of communication, and on the level of stress and tension within organizations is just beginning to be studied. Craig Brod's excellent book *Technostress*[10] provides an excellent survey of this area. The following excerpt is an example of the kind of problem Brod explores:

> The wife of a director of computer services for a large bank reports that when she first met her husband, he was a warm and sensitive man. Today he has no close friends, and his only recreation is television. One night she asked him to slow down as they walked home.
> "Walk faster," he replied.
> "I can't walk faster. My legs are shorter than yours."
> "That's no excuse. You have to learn to walk more efficiently."

References for Chapter 17

1. Hillkirk, John, "Little Guy Grows With Computer," *USA Today*, June 10, 1985.

2. Naisbitt, John, *Megatrends*, New York: Warner Books, 1982.

3. "Computer Shock Hits the Office," *Business Week*, August 8, 1983.

4. Derevlany, John, "I'd Rather Have a Computer in the Office," *Computer Living/NY*, February/March, 1985.

5. Brod, Craig, *Technostress*, Reading, Mass.: Addison-Wesley, 1984.

6. Turkle, Sherry, *The Second Self*, New York: Simon & Schuster, 1984.

7. McClellan, Stephen, *The Coming Computer Industry Shakeout*, New York: John Wiley & Sons, 1984.

8. Yourdon, Edward, *The Perils of Personal Computing*, New York: YOURDON Press, 1985.

9. Myers, Glen, *The Art of Software Testing*, New York: John Wiley & Sons, 1979.

10. Brod, *op. cit.*

18

THE DATABASE DILEMMA

The difference is one of order of complexity. Information is horizontal, knowledge is structured and hierarchical, wisdom is organismic and flexible. Any diligent student can, with the help of a computerized system, acquire vast amounts of information; for instance, the population of every township in the United States. But the data are pretty useless because they are stretched out at one level. (Information is horizontal.) For the data to be useful—come to life, as it were—they have to be linked to another rung or category of data. The result is knowledge. (Knowledge is structured and hierarchical.) Every teacher of information knows how difficult it is to pass knowledge, as distinct from information, to students; hence, we give objective tests to determine how much information, rather than knowledge, they have acquired. As for imparting wisdom, it . . . has to do with personal chemistry and slow osmosis.

Yi-fu Tuan
University of Minnesota

As I pointed out in Chapter 16, control over computerized information is a major problem for many American organizations today. Sometimes the problem is manifested in other ways, such as a software problem. The manager of a user department—the accounting department, or the marketing department, or the engineering department—will ask the company's MIS department to synthesize information from several different parts of the company and produce an analysis of marketplace trends. The data processing department, after complaining about being overworked and underpaid, will eventually admit that it simply cannot produce such a synthesized view of the data, even though all of the data is on the computer and has been for years. There may be vague statements like, "We never knew that you would want to look at the data that way," or "Those dummies who wrote the accounting system ten years ago used a nonstandard file format, and we can't interface it with anything else," or "If only we had the new model of the Blatzo mainframe computer and the System X relational database system, this would be no problem."

These statements may or may not be legitimate. My purpose here is not to cast blame or find out who hasn't been doing his job for the past ten years. It's more important to deal with the reality and to recognize it for what it is. When the user finds that he cannot get his hands on data, or that he is having some data-related problem, he is not dealing with a software problem. (There are enough software problems to worry about, as we will see in Chapters 27 through 33.) He is not dealing with a computer hardware problem, though hardware limitations ten years ago may have led the MIS organization to focus on the wrong priorities. The real problem is that the organization has never gotten control of its data; it has not yet recognized that data, or information, is an asset.

This shortsighted approach is perfectly understandable. At the operational level, most managers have spent hundreds of years working in an information vacuum, trying to make intelligent decisions without access to the information they need. So one can hardly blame them for not being farsighted enough to invest some capital assets ten years ago to begin planning an integrated corporate database that could be used today.

Unfortunately, that shortsighted approach continues today in a great many American companies. Managers at a high level in the organization still do not regard information to be a key asset. Oh, they may say they do—after all, it's a popular buzzword, and most managers like to give the impression that they know what's going on. But are they investing time, energy, money and valuable corporate assets as part of a ten-year plan to produce an enterprise model of the system and to translate that model onto a computer system? Probably not: if it can't be funded in this year's budget, it probably won't be done at all.

One of the reasons for this is that the balance sheet of American companies does not show information as an asset, nor does it show software as an asset, unless the software was purchased from an outside vendor (even then, it is usually "expensed" rather than depreciated—giving the impression that the software will wear out during the company's fiscal year). If it is any consolation, the same situation is true in Canada, Europe, Australia, and South America. The moral of the story is: in the boardroom and the stockholders' annual meeting, information doesn't count. If it doesn't count, it doesn't have any value. If it doesn't have any value, it's not worth investing in. If the technicians perceive that the company doesn't value its data and isn't willing to invest in the data, then they certainly aren't going to go out of their way to worry about the problem. Why bother?

Why is it that top management doesn't regard its information as a resource—indeed, as *the* resource to be treasured and protected? Part of the problem, as mentioned above, is that management simply doesn't understand the value of an asset that it never had control over before, an asset that for all practical purposes didn't exist. If you had never heard of gold before, you probably wouldn't be impressed if someone told you that you had a gold mine in your back yard and that there were gold nuggets lying all over the ground. Chances are that you wouldn't build a fence around your yard to protect your assets.

There is something else to keep in mind. The balance sheets and profit/loss statements that corporate managers produce every quarter have a standard format that everyone can understand. That format is set and controlled by a number of professional societies and regulatory agencies that want to make sure that the organization is reporting its business activities in a way that won't mislead the investing public and the tax man. These agencies include the SEC, the IRS, the local tax authorities, and the Financial Accounting Standards Board (FASB), which pass their advice on to accounting firms and corporate controllers across the land. FASB produces a series of documents known as the Generally Accepted Accounting Principles (GAAP), which guide corporate financial officers in deciding what can be shown as an asset on the corporate balance sheet, and how the value of the asset should be determined.

And here is the point of all this: the GAAP policies do not allow information to be shown as an asset on the balance sheet. Nor is software shown as an asset. That's the rule.[1] Information is regarded as an intangible asset; only tangible assets are shown on the balance sheet.

As a consequence, most organizations are dealing with fragmented databases. Some of their information is computerized, some of it isn't. Some of it is protected and locked up every night; some of it is disclosed to the public on a regular basis. Some of it is carefully documented, and its content and meaning are passed on to key people through the organization; but some of it exists only in the mind of the person who captures the data (the data entry clerk) or in the mind of a knowledge worker who analyzes masses of data to produce information and, far more important, knowledge.

CONSEQUENCES OF FRAGMENTED DATABASES

What happens to an organization when its databases are fragmented? Basically, there are four problems:

- Redundancy.

- Inconsistency.

- Security.

- Incompatibility with new hardware/software.

Redundancy problems occur because multiple copies of the same information exist in various parts of the organization. Customer information (name, address, etc.), for example, may be known to the salesperson, the order entry department, the accounts receivable department, and the department that rents mailing lists. (See? The information does have a value—it can be sold, licensed, or

---

[1] The exception, as noted above, is information or software purchased from an external source. Part of the problem is that nobody is quite sure how to place a value on information.

rented.) Often, each group will have its own copy of the customer information, and will set its own procedures for storing it, etc. This means that if the customer moves to a different address, the change must be reflected not just once but multiple times. The same problem exists with product data, vendor data, inventory data, marketing data, competitive data, etc.

Inconsistency problems occur because it is difficult to ensure that all of these copies of data are recorded in exactly the same way. Product names are spelled slightly differently in the marketing department than they are in the accounting department; meanwhile, the inventory control department uses product "codes," which may be cryptic abbreviations that only they understand. Thus, if any of the departments have to talk with one another, they have a difficult time understanding whether or not they are talking about the same product, and if they have to communicate the information to a customer, they run the risk of hopelessly confusing him.

The problem becomes much worse when the information has to be changed. Because of the redundancy, changes have to be made in several different departments to several different copies of the data. In the best of all cases, everyone's copy of the data is on the computer, but each department has its own programs for updating the data, so it is a foregone conclusion that there will be some period of time when one department has updated its data and the other departments have not. Even if this period of inconsistency is only a few seconds, there are possibilities for errors, incorrect business decisions, and customer confusion. This is more and more true today, because each department's computer system is on-line at all times, providing up-to-the-minute information to thousands of people within the organization, and possibly to thousands of suppliers, vendors, and customers outside the organization.

In many cases, the period of inconsistent data is far more than a few seconds; it can range from hours to day to weeks. Department A may decide to batch its changes together and update all of its records every week; department B may decide to do it every month. Department C may not even be aware that the data has changed because nobody remembered to tell anyone in the department, so it could be six months before they catch up. This is often true of accounting departments, which are simultaneously trying to close the books on last month's business and also pay the vendor invoices that were received two months ago, while collecting receivables from a company that is both a vendor and a client. . . .

In addition to the problem of timing, redundancy introduces the problem of errors when changes and updates occur. If customer Jones moves from Main Street to Gane Street, there is no telling how the various departments will reflect that in their individual databases. There is a good chance that one department will ignore the change, thinking that it was a typographical error; others will record it as Mane Street, or Gain Street, or Main Gane Street. It can take quite a while for the departments and the customer to realize the existence of the errors and to eventually correct them.

Security is another problem made worse by the lack of a coherent, integrated corporate data model. If there are several copies of sensitive data, it is all the harder to protect them and prevent them from leaking into the hands of customers, clients, and competitors. Indeed, this problem is worse in today's world of widespread personal computers. As we discussed in Chapter 17, many end-users have local copies of sensitive data on floppy disks that they leave on their desk at the end of the day. Until a few years ago, prospective data thieves had to deal with the clumsiness of hand-copying paper files; now they can duplicate a floppy disk within minutes and walk out of the office with 20,000 customer records in their briefcase or pocketbook.

This is not to suggest that a single master copy of sensitive data is intrinsically secure; such data can still be stolen or compromised. But if security is an issue, virtually everyone will agree that it's easier to protect 1 copy in a well-guarded facility than it is to protect 117 copies, the precise location of which nobody is ever sure of at any given time.

Incompatibility with modern hardware/software is the final problem to keep in mind. It is a "given" in the computer industry that next year's hardware will be faster and cheaper and also that next year's database software will be faster, cheaper, and more powerful. It is the latter part that is really the most important: the software companies that make PC-based database packages like dBase-III, as well as the companies that make mainframe-based database packages like ADABAS and IMS, are constantly working to produce new versions of their software package that will make it easier to organize, store, and retrieve data. And equally important, these companies work hard to provide a "migration path," i.e., a convenient way of uploading data in an older file format to the new format, and mechanically converting older programs so that they can take advantage of the features of the new software. But there is a limit to what the database companies can do: they cannot provide migration paths for everyone, especially the people who have stored their information in a completely nonstandard form that is intrinsically incompatible with everything else in the world. And as we find more and more copies of the same information spread around the organization, there is more and more of a chance that someone will have found a bizarre way of recording the data that cannot be converted into a standard format.

INFORMATION AS A STRATEGIC WEAPON

All of the problems described above are very real problems, and they hamper the organization's ability to operate effectively on a day-to-day basis. But an organization has to do more than just worry about day-to-day concerns: it has to think about how it intends to operate six months from now, six years from now, and six decades from now. To do this effectively, it needs to marshal its data resources much more effectively than is now done.

One of the more obvious areas where information can be used as a strategic weapon is the detailed analysis of customer and marketplace trends and preferences. This information is not needed to run the day-to-day business, so many companies have never organized the customer data they capture so that it can be analyzed in this way; even worse, in some cases, they throw the data away. Some rudimentary financial data may be kept for the obligatory seven years required by the IRS, but all of the detailed information about when the customer bought the product, and why he bought it, and whether all of his family members were with him when the purchase decision was made, and a dozen other nuances . . . these are all lost.

In an industry that has recently been deregulated, this kind of information can be crucial in determining whether the organization should enter new markets or introduce new products; it provides critical information in the life-and-death issue of pricing and discount schedules. The airline industry is finding this to be the case, as are the trucking industry, the banking industry, and a number of other stodgy old industries.

Obviously, strategic information can be important even if the government regulations haven't changed; the marketplace can change on its own accord. Banks, for example, need to have a more and more sophisticated view of the banking relationships of their clients. How many different accounts does corporate customer X have? How many of the accounts are in the branch office in Godzillaville, which has just had a military coup and frozen all dollar-based assets? How is the retail consumer's checking account related to his MasterCard and Visa accounts—are they all overdrawn? Etc.

Not all of the information that is useful to an organization is necessarily in its own possession. There is a vast amount of marketing data, demographic data, consumer profile data, stock market data, and other information gathered by government agencies, public relations firms, and market research companies in the business of producing information for a profit. Most of this information is very generic—e.g., "25 percent of all left-handed adults spend more than $1,000 per year on vacations." By itself, such information may not be very useful for an organization. Similarly, the data in the corporate databases may not be adequate for providing long-range forecasts and strategies. But the combination of the two databases could prove extraordinarily valuable.

If organized properly, a company's data can also provide valuable assistance to its customers and vendors. The obvious case is that of renting or licensing customer-related information and product information to organizations that need it. Renting of mailing lists is already a big business in the United States. There are thousands of list brokers in the United States who generate several million dollars in revenue each year by renting names and addresses (of individuals, business organizations, professional societies, etc.) to businesses around the country.

A less obvious, but increasingly important, form of allowing customers some access to the corporate database is that of customer-controlled order entry. Large companies are already beginning to provide such service; for example, they make it possible for their customers to dial their computer to place orders. Soon we will see companies providing this kind of service to retail customers, too. Indeed, it already exists through such information utilities as Compuserve and The Source.

The same service that a company provides to its customers can also be provided to its vendors. When an organization needs to order raw materials, it could have its computer automatically communicate with the computers of its regular vendors, seeking quotations on price, delivery terms, and other details. The organization could then place its order with the vendor with the most attractive quotation.

Perhaps the most valuable information that a company has is the knowledge that its veteran workers have acquired, over a period of years, about their work. "Knowledge," in this context, is more than just information (which, in turn, is more than raw data); it is the interpretation of information, the judgments that can be based on information, and the rules/guidelines that the veteran uses to guide his day-to-day actions. Some of this knowledge is taught in schools; some of it is written in textbooks; some of it is documented in company manuals. But much of it is acquired through on-the-job training, in the most literal sense of that phrase. In most organizations, it is acquired slowly, over a period of years, over a lifetime career. In some cases, it disappears from the organization when the employee retires or leaves—and that is an asset that a company can ill afford to lose.

Of course, almost all organizations have a variety of formal and informal mechanisms for passing on the knowledge from veteran to novice. But the process is slow and imperfect. Those who are less than enamored with computers may argue that it will always be this way, that judgment is a delicate human skill that is learned slowly as part of a maturing process.

I do not dispute this, but I do argue that part of the process of acquiring knowledge involves learning how to filter the massive amount of data that bombard us every day, and learning how to interpret and understand the small portion that is important. Some of that could be learned at a fairly early age if the rules of judgment were documented. It would be easier still if it were captured in a computer system. Indeed, this is the major thrust of expert systems, and we will examine the subject in more detail in Chapter 21.

The most important strategic use of better organized, more integrated data is that of rethinking the mission of the organization. What is the company's business? Part of the answer to this fundamental question comes from a better understanding of what the market is, who the customers are, and how they interact with the organization. As I pointed out in Chapter 7, for example, my feeling is that banks are really in the financial information business, and that the service of providing bank vaults, safe deposit boxes, and checking accounts are anachronisms that will soon disappear.

Many other organizations must urgently rethink the business they are in because the hard goods and tangible products they provided in the past are becoming a smaller and smaller part of the overall economy. Even if a tangible product is the mainstay of the business, it is still crucially important to use all available data to see how the product can be packaged and distributed to differentiate it from other look-alike products and services offered by competitors.

Consider, for example, a grocery store. It is obviously in the business of selling food to its customers. Every grocery store does that, and it is extremely difficult to differentiate one store's can of beans from another's. The successful grocery store of the 1990s will be the one that uses all available data from its own customers, from its competitor's customers, and from every bit of available market research data to optimize the service it provides to its customers. It may turn out, for example, that carrots are a low-profit item and the store might consider dropping them. However, various market surveys might help indicate that (a) an overwhelming percentage of customers buy carrots on every trip to the grocery store; and (b) the overwhelming percentage of customers strongly prefer to be able to get all of their groceries at one store. Conclusion: better keep carrots in the store. Similarly, market surveys might point out that one of the most important criteria for choosing a grocery store is the friendliness and demeanor of the cashiers and checkout clerks. This information, combined with psychological profiles and an analysis of employee turnover, might provide some interesting clues. Maybe the store hasn't been doing well for the past year because its cashiers are sullen, surly, and argumentative—not because the store's prices are higher.

Even this is a somewhat short-term view of grocery stores. Ultimately, all grocery stores can carry out such an analysis, and all grocery stores that want to stay in business will carry carrots, if that is what the marketplace wants. Ultimately, all will find friendly, helpful cashiers. Food is, as we would all agree, a commodity. While there may be slight competitive differences between one grocer and another in the production, shipping, packaging, and distribution of food, those differences are likely to get smaller and smaller. Ultimately, the only thing that one grocery store can guarantee will be unique is its knowledge: knowledge about the preferences of individual customers (Mrs. Jones always orders her fish on Friday, Mr. Smith always needs two quarts of milk on Tuesdays and Thursdays), and knowledge about food (its economics, nutritional contents, etc.). The successful grocery store of the 1990s, in my opinion, will be the one that can provide value-added information along with its supply of carrots, milk, and bread, such as how to optimize each customer's grocery budget within the constraints of nutritional requirements, personal taste preferences, available supplies, customer storage facilities (e.g., if the customer has enough closet space, maybe he should buy a year's worth of canned beans), and size of the budget.

Many business managers will argue that they "know" their product and their marketplace and their competition. It is hard to imagine that this could be true in a large organization, where top management is by definition far removed from the real product and customer. Even in a small business, there is a very real danger that the owner or proprietor may fail to recognize how rapidly conditions change. Prices and products and policies that may have been enormously successful in 1985 could be disastrous in 1986. The organization is likely to find that it is dealing with new customers, new competitors, new fashions, new trends, and new economic conditions, the significance of which it may not recognize until it is too late.

In ancient times, success went to the hunter who was fleet of foot. Today success often goes to the person or organization who can make fast decisions, but those decisions are often based on incomplete or faulty information. Tomorrow, it will go to the business that can most rapidly assimilate, analyze, and act on the information at its disposal.

CONCLUSION

Having read this far, there is a good chance that your mood is one of general discouragement. Can things really be as bad as I've suggested? Yes! Do top executives really, truly understand the situation they're in? No! Or, if they do understand it, are they taking the necessary steps to restructure their organization? No! Is there any hope? Yes!!

The first thing you should do—assuming that you are gainfully employed in a large corporation or government agency, as so many of us are—is make your own survey of the situation. Ask the highest level manager you can get your hands on if he can provide you with any of the following:

- An enterprise model showing the overall functions, interfaces, subject databases, and data relationships in the organization. You can find a good description of enterprise models in several of the books by James Martin.[1]

- An information model for the organization. Information models are a variant of enterprise models; they provide high-level pictures of the major information "objects" that the organization deals with, and the relationships between those objects. Information models are described by Ward,[2] Flavin,[3] and others.

- An organization chart that shows what kind of information moves back and forth between different departments or divisions.

- Any kind of document that describes the organization's plan to develop the models described above. This plan should indicate how the models will eventually be implemented on a computer, and how the organization's current unintegrated databases will be brought together in some harmonious fashion.

- Any kind of document that affirms the organization's commitment to create a Chief Information Officer, or some similarly titled high-level manager—at the same level as the Chief Financial Officer, or even the Chief Operating Officer—who will oversee the creation of models and plans for an information-based organization.

If you are a high-level executive in the organization, then you should ask as many of your subordinates as possible for this kind of information. The head of your MIS organization is a good place to start; the head of your planning department may have been quietly working on this without telling you. If neither of these managers has anything intelligent to tell you, try the data administration group within your MIS department. (If you don't have such a group, then you're really in trouble.)

Based on the answers you get in response to these questions, you can decide what to do next. If appropriate models and plans are already in effect, then you can relax and gloat over the misery that your competitors will be feeling a few years from now. (At the same time, you might wonder why it was that you didn't know such plans had been developed: it suggests that there are some information blockades in the organization caused either by technological weaknesses or by vestiges of old hierarchical-style managerial policies that tell only a limited few what the corporate policies really are.)

Chances are that you'll find very little written material concerning the specific plans for a corporatewide database. You may find lots of people who can talk about the subject, and you can probably find some research reports, staff memos, and maybe even some urgent recommendations from low-level technicians in your MIS department. But if it hasn't been written down as official corporate policy, it doesn't exist. If the corporate policy hasn't been seen, reviewed, understood, digested, supported, and signed by the top executive in the organization—and perhaps even the board of directors—then it's just empty rhetoric. For all practical purposes, it doesn't exist.

If there are no plans, you must decide what your responsibilities and opportunities are. If you are a top executive in the organization, you have both the opportunity and the responsibility to initiate such a planning process. You can't do it yourself, of course, and you can't get the whole job done within the current fiscal year.[2] But you can gather the experts within your organization, as well as consultants familiar with the relationship between information systems and strategic planning. You can read the books listed at the end of this chapter, as well as the references at the end of other chapters in this section. You can become the champion of this important cause, and you can lead the battle against the many obstacles that will stand in the way: pressure for short-term financial results, the inertia of a large group of people accustomed to business as usual, and all of the other problems that have occurred whenever you have tried to make major changes in your organization.

If you are a middle-level executive, or a junior manager, or one of the workers "down in the trenches," it's more difficult to plan a proper course of action. You can try to be a prophet within your organization and single-handedly convince your peers, your subordinates, and several layers of managers above you that an investment in corporatewide data planning is essential; realistically, you have only one chance in a thousand of pulling off such a revolutionary stunt. If you are less daring, you can make your own realistic assessment of the likelihood that your organization will eventually come to its senses. After all, there's no point in changing jobs if your new employer is just as oblivious to these issues as your current employer.

There is another option to consider, too, one that I feel is the most practical and exciting of all: start your own company. The true litmus test for your current employer is whether it will help you

---

[2] In fact, the process can take one to two years, and cost well over $100,000 in a large organization.

get started. In many organizations today, the concept of intra-preneurship has become popular: the organization acts as a venture capitalist to allow creative, ambitious young (and old) people turn their ideas into profitable businesses. If your employer will not or cannot help, then leave. The corporate ship will sink eventually, and there is no reason for you to go down with it.

It doesn't matter to me what your new business is, manufactur-ing widgets or providing advice to the lovelorn. Whatever it is, if it's new, it can begin with an integrated corporate database. Because it is small at the beginning, it should be easy to develop a paper model of all of the information objects and relationships. Because the new organization generally transacts very little busi-ness for its first few weeks or months, that data model can be implemented on a computer system using current computer hard-ware and software technology (probably even on a personal com-puter). And from that stable foundation, the organization can grow to virtually any size, knowing all along that it has control over its most precious and vital asset: information.

References for Chapter 18

1.   Martin, James, *An Information Systems Manifesto*, Englewood Cliffs, N.J.: Prentice-Hall, 1984.

2.   Ward, Paul, *Systems Development Without Pain*, New York: YOURDON Press, 1984.

3.   Flavin, Matt, *Fundamental Concepts of Information Modeling*, New York: YOURDON Press, 1981.

19

OFFICE AUTOMATION

The first three commandments of the "How to succeed in OA" Bible:

1. Saying no to a user seeking OA tools is a crime against the organization's success.
2. Action with risk of incoherence is better than coherence without action.
3. Your primary OA objective should be to install one workstation for each telephone, as quickly as possible. Five years is the maximum length of time to do it.

Louis Nauges
Office Automation Alibis[1]

The first typewriter was built in the 1700s and demonstrated to the queen of England. However, it was more than a century later, in 1868, that C. L. Sholes patented the device in the United States. Two businessmen bought the patent rights and demonstrated the typewriter at the Chicago Exposition in 1870. Business organizations were slow to adopt this new technology, though, feeling that correspondence demanded the personal touch of a handwritten document. It was not until World War I that the demand for rapid, voluminous output overcame this reluctance. And though the electric typewriter was first demonstrated before 1920, it was another twenty years before it caught on. Even now, we are left with a vestige of century-old office automation technology. The standard "QWERTY" keyboard, which was designed to slow down typists and thus prevent the keys from jamming, is about 30 percent slower than the seldom-used Dvorak keyboard.

The business office, for a variety of reasons, is slow to change and slow to adopt new technology. A century ago, we could afford this: most of the resources of an organization were invested in its factories, its raw materials, and its machinery. But today, a century after the invention of the typewriter, we can no longer afford to move slowly. The office is at the center of the information-based competition for economic supremacy. A company can compete successfully only if its most important assets—the information workers in the office—are properly equipped, properly supported, and properly trained to use the best available technology to help them do their job.

To do this will be difficult: American corporations currently invest only $2,000 to $3,000 per office worker for equipment, and the figure will have to climb to $10,000 to $15,000 within the next five to ten years to provide proper support.[1] A very, very few organizations have done this already; many others (especially the larger ones) have begun the process, and expect that it will take as much as ten years to finish. Somewhere in the 1990-95 time frame, the process will be complete within industry. Those with the "office of the future" will have survived, and those still wedded to the technology of telephone and typewriter will be filing for bankruptcy. For any company of a moderate size—with annual revenues of, say, $100 million or more—the window of opportunity is rapidly slamming shut. It will be far too late to start the office automation process by 1990; it will probably be too late by 1988, and it could be too late tomorrow.

ARGUMENTS IN FAVOR OF
OFFICE AUTOMATION

There are several major arguments in favor of office automation, all involving different aspects of productivity. For example, we know that office expenses currently account for approximately 25 percent of the cost of doing business in most companies; by the end

---

[1] To put this in perspective, the average farm worker is supported by $55,000 of capital investment; the average industrial worker is backed by $30,000 of capital investment.

of the decade, the figure will rise to approximately 45 percent. Increasing salaries, a decreasing work ethic, and the continuing shift toward a service-oriented, information-based economy make it more and more important to improve the effectiveness and efficiency of office activities. While industrial productivity increased by 90 percent in the 1970s, office productivity increased only 4 percent while costs doubled.[2] Clearly, there is a need for improved productivity.

Many organizations are also finding it increasingly difficult to hire competent clerical and administrative people, thus making it necessary for the few competent administrators to be more and more productive, and for managers to do more and more activities for themselves. There once was a time when a manager could dictate a letter, give it to a secretary to type, and expect the secretary to spell the words correctly. Now it is more common for the manager to correct the secretary's spelling; indeed, the manager often finds that it is faster if he types the letter himself. I came to this conclusion several years ago when my secretary asked me if I knew the zip code for New Zealand. When I explained, as patiently as I could, that New Zealand was not a state like New Mexico, she looked at me blankly and asked if I knew the area code so that she could call information and get the zip code. She has, thankfully, moved on to greener pastures. I have been typing my own letters ever since.

Letters, unfortunately, suffer another indignity after being mistyped by the modern secretary: the (shudder) post office. There once was a time when the post office was a relevant, useful, important part of society; that time ended, by my reckoning, around 1963. How American business has managed to survive the post office for the past twenty years is a mystery to me. Why anyone would willingly use the post office today is an even greater mystery. Electronic mail, high-speed communicating printers, intelligent copiers, facsimile copiers, and a variety of other telecommunication products make the post office a more and more irrelevant artifact of society. This is especially true for communications between business organizations (as opposed to communication between business organizations and the retail consumer). Approximately 75 percent of business-to-business correspondence consists of documents generated by the sender's computer, and processed by the receiver's computer. It is an act of madness to put the post office between those two computers.[2]

Business organizations are also finding that transporting workers from home to office is costing more and more money; in addition, the commuter transportation infrastructure is getting more overcrowded and closer to collapse in many cities. If it costs an employee $200 a month for a commuter train ticket, his employer pays for it, usually in the form of a salary high enough to make the job attractive. And if the train is delayed for an hour every day during the winter season, the employer pays for it, usually in the form of decreased productivity, sometimes in the form of increased absenteeism. An attractive alternative, as I discussed at length in Chapter 3, is telecommuting: let the employee work at home. To do this requires not only a personal computer in the home, but also a companywide infrastructure of electronic mail, telecommunications, and other office automation technology.

Office automation will eventually cause a major decline, if not the ultimate demise, of a time-honored tradition: the business trip. Long-distance travel is becoming more and more expensive; more importantly, it is regarded more and more as a time-waster. A business person often finds that he spends a full day traveling to a meeting and a full day traveling back; this overhead for a one-hour meeting is extremely costly. Though video teleconferencing technology still has not been accepted by American business, it looms on the horizon as the replacement for the business trip.

There are also some important secondary benefits that come with office automation. They include the following:

- **Reducing "media transformations"**—e.g., extraneous dictation, converting a rough handwritten document into a typewritten document, etc.

- **Reducing "shadow" functions**—time-wasters that accompany communication-related tasks but contribute nothing to productivity. The information content of a typical intraoffice business

---

[2] If it's any consolation, businesspeople in most other countries I have visited have the same low opinion of their postal facilities.

telephone conversation, for example, is about thirty seconds, but it is accompanied by about five minutes of social pleasantries that both parties would often happily dispense with.

- **Eliminating some functions altogether**—e.g., the mail room.

- **Reducing "information float"**—rather than waiting three days for a report to be mailed from a branch office to Galactic headquarters, electronic mail can move the report in a fraction of a second.

MAJOR COMPONENTS OF OFFICE AUTOMATION

Melody Johnson, an observer of the office automation movement and an analyst at Kidder Peabody, has remarked that "the office of the future will always be in the future."[3] Indeed, our vision of the automated office in 1985 is likely to be very different from our vision in 1990. Much of our 1990 vision will depend on just how much the technology of telecommunications, computer hardware, and computer software (especially such things as artificial intelligence) has managed to advance.

Today, office automation generally means four computer-based technologies in addition to the standard collection of typewriters, dictation machines, duplicating machines, etc.: word processing, electronic mail, electronic filing, and video teleconferencing. Exactly which one is most important depends on the nature of the business and the activities of the professional workers. Walter Ulrich points out that the average professional worker spends his time in the following ways:[4]

15-20%   On the telephone (this could be improved with electronic mail).

40-45%   Face-to-face meetings (these could be more efficient through video teleconferencing and computer-based teleconferencing).

1-5%   Document creation (an obvious candidate for word processing).

25%   Distributing, filing, and retrieving documents (electronic mail and electronic filing could help here).

5-8%   Thinking, planning, analyzing. ("Outline processor" capabilities of some word processing systems can help, as can spreadsheet programs and other software packages found on personal computers. Doing this work at home, away from the office, can vastly increase the effectiveness of the planning work; electronic mail and home-based personal computing facilities make this feasible.)

In general, information retrieval seems to be the most common use of office automation technology at the present time. A recent survey by Honeywell's found that knowledge workers use office automation (OA) technology to communicate with other computer users (43 percent), for word processing (50 percent), to analyze numbers or financial information (73 percent), or to retrieve information from databases (82 percent).[5]

Word Processing

Word processing is the one part of office automation that is widely accepted and reasonably well understood. It is also the OA technology with the least leverage, because it is used by clerical workers more than managers and other highly paid professional workers (the so-called knowledge workers). A study by Booz Allen concluded that knowledge workers in the United States were paid $400 billion in 1979; clerical workers received only $125 billion.[6] It doesn't take a financial genius to understand that a 15 percent improvement in productivity on the part of managers would save a lot more money than a 15 percent improvement on the part of secretaries.[3]

[3] The Booz-Allen study estimated that managerial productivity in the United States could be increased by 15 percent over the next five years, saving approximately $270 billion by 1990.

Nevertheless, it is the secretaries who have received most of the OA technology so far. The market for simple, clerical word processing systems is 60 percent saturated already; the market for OA technology for managers and professionals is only 20 percent saturated. According to Honeywell's survey of office automation trends, 75 percent of the knowledge worker community has access to word processing, and 95 percent of those who have access use their word processors. On the other hand, the same survey showed that nearly eight out of ten knowledge workers with access to word processing equipment still delegated word processing work to secretaries or assistants.[7]

Electronic Mail

Electronic mail is a simple concept, but it represents as important and powerful a form of communication as the telephone. The familiar old telegraph system and its newer cousin, the telex, could be regarded as forms of electronic mail, but these relics are not as important as the "computer-mailbox" form of electronic mail. The latter form requires a dumb terminal, or personal computer, on the sender's desk and receiver's desk; telephone lines link the terminals to a central computer, which can store and forward messages.

Actually, electronic mail (of the computer mailbox variety) has existed since the mid-1960s, when time-sharing and on-line computer systems first began to appear. However, they were generally available to only a small community of end-users who had other reasons for using the computer. For example, airline reservation clerks who accessed the terminal all day long found that, in addition to their normal transactions, they could send electronic messages to other airline reservation clerks. And programmers in an organization's MIS department often had the ability to communicate through terminals, in addition to their normal software development activities.

But now the concept is spreading beyond these special-interest groups. We are beginning to see organizations—including, for example, my own company, YOURDON inc.—where everyone has access to a computer terminal for sending and receiving messages. Indeed, to really make the concept work properly, a large number of the employees need a terminal at home as well as in the office, and there should even be portable terminals for the employees who need to travel away from the office.

Conceptually, there is nothing complicated about electronic mail. The sender simply indicates the name(s) of the person or persons to whom he wants to send a message, and then proceeds to type the message itself. There are many elaborations upon this basic theme, of course: the sender can create different mailing lists so that messages of one kind will automatically be sent to everyone in the marketing department, etc. Some electronic mail systems have a return-receipt-requested feature, so that the sender can tell exactly when the receiver got the message. And the receiver generally has the option of responding immediately to his electronic mail, or printing it on paper, or rerouting it to someone else, or filing it for later retrieval, etc.

Though simple in concept, electronic mail is a fundamentally different kind of communications medium than the telephone. It is, for example, a "cold" medium: the receiver cannot judge whether the sender was in a good mood or a bad mood when he composed his message. And the message does not carry the nuances, the facial expressions, or the intonations that a verbal, face-to-face conversation carries. Electronic mail sent from the boss to a subordinate at 2:00 A.M., on the other hand, does carry with it an unspoken message: if the boss is working at 2:00 A.M., thinks the subordinate, then maybe I should be, too.

Within a single organization, the electronic mail facilities are usually provided by the MIS organization, or by an office automation group; the computer may be the same one that runs the accounting programs, but it is often a separate machine dedicated to communications. For business-to-business communication, it is more common to use a commercial E-mail service: General Electric, ITT, GTE, and MCI Mail are the better known commercial providers at the present time.

Electronic mail, as described here, is not yet a big business. In comparison to the 500,000 telex machines that generate $700 million in annual revenues for Western Union and the 470,000 facsimile transmission machines that generate $650 million in revenues for the telephone companies, there are only 225,000 subscribers, generating less than $150 million in revenues for the commercial E-mail services. And the U.S. Post Office still dwarfs all of these services, with revenues of $24.4 billion in 1983.[8]

However, the future for electronic mail looks bright, and it is obviously a bandwagon that progressive companies are jumping on. One consulting firm, International Resource Development, estimates that the $150 million E-mail business could grow to $5 billion in annual revenues by 1992. Another firm, International Data Corporation, estimates that the number of electronic mailboxes is growing at a rate of 68 percent annually, and that the base of 225,000 mailboxes will increase to more than 3 million by 1987. And Walter Ulrich, a communications consultant, believes that the E-mail market is doubling every year, and will reach the level of 9 billion messages per year by the end of the decade. Yet another firm, the Eastern Management Group, estimated that by the end of 1983, 18 percent of American businesses had some form of computer-based electronic communication, and another 20 percent were actively planning for its implementation.[9]

One reason for the rapid growth of electronic mail is simple economics. Five years ago, it cost as much as $4 per message to send electronic mail; by 1984, the cost had dropped to 86 cents per message, and to as little as five to seven cents for in-house systems.[10] The second important reason is the widespread and continuing proliferation of personal computers. By 1987, more than 16 million personal computers will be installed in offices, and 11 million of those will have communication facilities.[11] Electronic mail is similar to the telephone in one important respect: until both sender and receiver are subscribers on the same network, they can't communicate.

In fact, we can carry this concept one step further. Unless everyone in the organization has immediate access to a personal computer, or a terminal connected to an E-mail facility, electronic mail will remain a relatively unimportant fad. This was its fate during the 1960s and 1970s, when only the programmers in the MIS department could use it. But when there is a terminal on the president's desk, and on the janitor's desk, and on the desk of everyone in between, then it becomes a powerful new "dimension" of communication. The janitor can send a message to the president, even though he might never have the opportunity to meet him in person, and the president can send a message to the janitor. The horizontal communications concept that I discussed in Chapter 4 is an immediate consequence of electronic mail. Some will find this rather frightening, but it is like a breath of fresh air in most companies.

This universal access to E-mail exists only in a handful of small companies today. Even the computer manufacturing companies, with access to computer hardware at cost, have not yet established a 1:1 ratio of terminals to employees. Digital Equipment Corporation, for example, has 25,000 employees generating an estimated 100,000 messages per day on an in-house electronic mail system; another 20,000 are waiting for the chance to join the system.[12] IBM, certainly one of the most efficient organizations in the world, expects to have a ratio of 2.2 employees per computer terminal by 1986.[13] Most other technologically progressive companies—the leading banks, for example—have only a few thousand employees on their E-mail systems.

Steve Caswell, editor of the newsletter *Electronic Mail and Message Systems*, summarizes the possibilities and the future of electronic mail quite well by saying that it

> . . . will open up a whole new world. I don't know how fast it will catch on . . . habits change slowly. But over a 10 to 20 year time frame, it may rival the telephone.[14]

For anyone whose business requires the communication of words, data, concepts, ideas, proposals, and contracts—which is just about all of us—these are important words to consider. The concept of running a business today without a telephone boggles the mind; ten years from now, the concept of running a business without electronic mail will appear equally insane.

Electronic Filing

Electronic filing is an obvious adjunct to personal computers, word processing, and electronic mail. One needs the facility to store, retrieve, duplicate, and transmit documents from one workstation to another. Ten years ago, this was a rather novel concept: if one had any form of office automation, it consisted of a dumb terminal connected to a computer that never had enough storage capacity. Today, the situation is fundamentally different: mainframe computers now have, in the typical case, between 10 times and 100 times as much storage as before; more importantly, personal computers offer the user his own storage space, under his own control. Nobody likes to keep copies of a confidential document on a mainframe computer whose security is suspect. Floppy disks and Winchester disks offer the combination of security and convenience: a single floppy disk can store several hundred pages of information and can be easily locked away in a desk drawer.

The need for electronic filing can be understood by looking at one statistic: American business now deals with 400 billion paper documents; that number is growing by 70 billion documents a year.[15] We are in danger of drowning ourselves in paper.

Today, most organizations have not connected the filing capabilities of personal computers to the microfilm and microfiche equipment used to store massive quantities of documents (documents which were generally not created by the organization's computers).

Teleconferencing

Teleconferencing is the only OA technology that I have my doubts about. The reason is quite simple: it violates what John Naisbitt calls the "high-tech/high-touch" principle.[16] Putting everyone in a conference room surrounded by bright lights and cameras makes them feel uncomfortable. Projecting their image onto a TV screen invites the inevitable comparison with TV actors and news reporters; most of us don't do very well in that kind of comparison. It requires simultaneous participation of all parties, which is a terrific nuisance when the participants are in different time zones. The equipment is expensive, which means that the teleconferencing facilities have to be reserved in advance. Et cetera, et cetera, et cetera.

Figures compiled by Honeywell in its survey of some 700 knowledge workers in September 1984 provide an interesting commentary . . . while 53 percent of the respondents had teleconferencing facilities available in their organization, only 30 percent rated the technology "very useful." By contrast, 75 percent of the group had access to word processing, and 77 percent rated it "very useful." Similarly, electronic mail was judged "very useful" in the same proportion that it was made available: 40 percent had such facilities available and 41 percent said it was very useful.[17] It would appear that teleconferencing has been oversold at the present time.

The time will come in about five years when our computers and our telephones are married together so intimately that we will no longer view them as separate objects. The low-resolution, primitive computer display screens that we use now will have been replaced by high-resolution color graphics screens substantially better than current TV screens. And the "bandwidth" of our telephone lines will have improved to the point that we can transmit voice, data, and graphics images in "real time." And we will all have such a device on our desk, and another at home, and another in our car (or whatever we use for transportation). Then we will have the technology base for videoconferencing; it will be another five to ten years after that before the business culture learns how to use that technology.

In the meantime, the only form of teleconferencing that is technically feasible and attractive is text-based teleconferencing, using electronic mail facilities. The only difference between this form of teleconferencing and standard electronic mail is one of sophistication. Teleconferencing facilities allow a participant to join a conference at any point and see a record of previous communications on the conference topic between other participants. Some of the commercially available teleconferencing facilities, such as the ones offered by Compuserve and The Source, allow participants to use pseudonyms (on the theory that anonymity encourages open, candid discussions) and private exchanges between participants, in addition to the broadcast form of communication.

PROBLEMS WITH OFFICE AUTOMATION

Why has office automation caught on so slowly in the business world? Probably the biggest single reason is that, as Steve Caswell says, "Habits die hard." Consultant Louis Nauges has compiled a list of typical arguments—or, in his opinion, alibis—for not using office automation technology.[18] They include the following:

- Automation is for blue-collar workers, not for white-collar workers.
- It's not for me, it's for the others.
- Nobody else is doing it.
- We don't know who to put in charge of OA.
- Our managers will bicker over control.
- Let's first define an OA plan.
- Our managers will do the work of secretaries.
- Managers will waste their time with OA tools.
- What will our managers do with the time they saved by using OA tools?
- We have always worked this way.
- It's not the right time.
- Our people are not ready for OA.
- We're waiting for the ideal tool.
- The next generation of OA tools will be better.
- OA is too expensive.
- Tomorrow, OA will be less expensive.
- I don't know how to justify my OA investment.

There are, of course, individual cases where these reasons are valid; you must be the judge of that within your own organization. However, the important thing to remember is this: sooner or later, office automation will be an essential ingredient in every business. That much we can all agree on, just as a consensus gradually developed that every office worker should have a telephone. The only question is whether your company will begin installing OA technology today, or whether it will wait for another few years until some magical revelation indicates that the time has arrived.

Today, nobody bothers to cost-justify a telephone; it's accepted as a universal standard. No white-collar worker in his right mind would work for a company whose corporate policy forbade telephones for its workers. Within five years, the same will be true for electronic mail, electronic filing, word processing, and personal OA workstations. So the important question is not whether your organization has OA today; the question is whether it is making plans and commitments to ensure that it will be there within five years.

THE ECONOMICS OF OFFICE AUTOMATION

In many organizations today, office automation is still regarded as too expensive. But the economics are as follows:

- The average well-equipped office automation workstation costs $10,000. (You can buy a dumb terminal for about $300 if you already have a time-sharing system or mainframe to connect it to; you can also spend $30,000 to $40,000 for a high-powered scientific/engineering workstation with high-resolution graphic capabilities and 100 megabytes of disk storage. But will $10,000 buy enough computing power to keep the typical office worker happy?)

- A manager/professional with a salary of $40,000 costs his organization $40/hour (assuming an overhead of 100 percent).

- Accounting practices in most organizations will allow the workstation to be amortized over three years.

With these economic assumptions, the bottom line is this: if the workstation saves the manager/professional one and a half hours per week of work (or about 3.75 percent of the working week), it has paid for itself. Circumstances are obviously different in every organization, but it's hard to imagine that the combination of word processing, electronic filing, and electronic mail couldn't save at least that much.

However, office automation for managers and professionals is really practical only if virtually the entire office has it. Word processing can be used by an individual manager/professional with his own solitary workstation—but such a scenario is almost the same as for a manager who has the only telephone in the office.

References for Chapter 19

1.   Nauges, Louis, "Office Automation Alibis," *Datamation*, November 1983.

2.   Ulrich, Walter, *Information Systems in the Eighties*, Englewood Cliffs, N.J.: Prentice-Hall, 1982.

3.   Brancatelli, Joe, "In Search of the Office of the Future," *Science and Technology*, September 1983.

4.   Ulrich, *op. cit.*

5.   Burger, Shelly Potter, "Knowledge Workers Cite Office Automation as the Key to Personal Productivity," Honeywell Technalysis, January 1985.

6.   Poppel, Harvey, "Who Needs the Office of the Future?" *Harvard Business Review*, November–December, 1982.

7.   Burger, Shelly Potter, "Trends in Office Automation," Honeywell Technalysis, January 1985.

8.   Louis, Arthur M., "The Great Electronic Mail Shootout," *Fortune*, August 20, 1984.

9.   Rifkin, Glenn, "Electronic Mail," *Computerworld OA*, September 1984.

10.   *Ibid.*

11.   "Electronic Mail Business Booms," *Computer Decisions Marketing News*, January 1985.

12.   Rifkin, *op. cit.*

13.   Ulrich, *op. cit.*

14.   Rifkin, *op. cit.*

15.   Brancatelli, *op. cit.*

16.   Naisbitt, John, *Megatrends*, New York: Warner Books, 1983.

17.   Burger, *op. cit.*

18.   Nauges, *op. cit.*

20

THE SHIFT IN BUSINESS
INFORMATION SYSTEMS

[Formulation of strategy] is the task of thinking through the mission of the business, that is, of asking the question, "What is our business and what should it be?" This leads to the setting of objectives, the development of strategies and plans, and the making of today's decisions for tomorrow's results. This clearly can be done only by an organ of the business that can see the entire business; that can make decisions that affect the entire business; that can balance objectives and the needs of today against the needs of tomorrow; and that can allocate resources of men (sic) and money to key results.

Peter F. Drucker
Management: Tasks, Responsibilities, Practices

Business organizations have been using computers for twenty to thirty years. However, in the past two or three years, some fundamental changes have begun to take place in the type of computer systems being developed and used. Some organizations are making these changes consciously and deliberately; others are unaware of the change because they are being "driven" by various end-users in different parts of the organization.

This is important because most organizations depend on a centralized MIS department to develop, operate, and maintain their computer systems; since computers are becoming a more and more essential factor in the success of the enterprise, the MIS department

274

is playing a more and more vital role. Its successes and failures become the successes and failures of the entire organization, and its potential future failures should be of concern to the entire organization. It is the future failures that I am concerned about in this chapter. (Present failures and problems are discussed in several other chapters of this book.)

The failure that I am concerned about is one of priorities. As we will see in this chapter, MIS organizations have traditionally concentrated their attention on a certain class of computer systems. However, the end-user community served by the MIS department has shifted its focus, and is now asking for a very different kind of computer system. Unfortunately, the traditions of twenty years are hard to break, and the training and background of a large MIS staff (often numbering in the hundreds) are hard to change overnight; hence we often find organizations are still investing millions of dollars developing computer systems that the user community stopped asking for two years ago. As one can imagine, this puts the entire organization at risk; as the user community begins to understand the nature of its frustration, it will put the existing MIS staff at great risk, too!

MAJOR TYPES OF BUSINESS SYSTEMS

To understand the nature of this problem, we must distinguish between several different types of computer systems in a typical business organization. Though they may run on different kinds of hardware, and though they may be programmed in a dozen different programming languages, virtually all systems can be divided into three categories. These are shown pictorially in Figure 20.1, on the next page.

Operational Systems

The bottom layer, or foundation, is the great mass of operational systems without which the business cannot function; many MIS departments refer to them as transaction-processing systems. Included in this category are the payroll systems, order entry systems, accounting systems, and manufacturing systems. Typ-

Figure 20.1: **The Three Types of Business Computer Systems**

ically, these systems operate on a regular basis: daily, weekly, or monthly. In many organizations today, they operate twenty-four hours a day, communicating with operational personnel inside the organization (accounting clerks, salespeople, manufacturing personnel, etc.) as well as customers and vendors outside the organization.

The operational computer systems in most organizations have been developed slowly, painfully, and at enormous cost over the past twenty to thirty years; almost all of them are programmed in conventional third-generation languages like COBOL and FORTRAN.[1] Almost all of them suffer from severe software maintenance problems; indeed, as we will see in Chapter 30, 50 to 70 percent of the resources in a typical MIS department are devoted to the maintenance of these operational systems. Almost all of them update (i.e., add new information to, or modify existing information in) computer files or databases that suffer the problems discussed in Chapter 18.

---

[1] COBOL, FORTRAN, and the concept of third-generation programming languages are discussed in Chapter 29.

It is sometimes useful to divide the operational systems into two subcategories: the "normal" systems and the "exception" systems. Normal systems are the ones described above—e.g., payroll, accounts receivable, etc. But in addition to these, virtually all organizations have computer systems that produce output (ranging from printed reports to the ringing of an alarm bell) if something gets out of line. Thus, an order entry system might produce a report of all customers whose orders have exceeded a certain credit threshold; or a banking system might produce a report of all customers whose accounts are overdrawn. An inventory control system performs the normal functions of registering the receipt of goods into the warehouse and the shipment of goods from the warehouse to customers, but more importantly, it contains an exception subsystem that produces a report of items that need to be reordered so that the business will not find itself out of stock.

Decision Support Systems

The second category of MIS system is the "decision support" or managerial support system. As the term implies, these computer systems do not make decisions on their own, but they help managers throughout the organization make better, more intelligent, more informed decisions about various aspects of the business. Often, these decision-support systems are passive: they do not operate on a regular basis like a weekly payroll system. They are used on an *ad hoc* basis, whenever the manager decides that he needs assistance in a decision-making activity.

There are a wide variety of computer systems that can be thought of as decision-support systems: spreadsheet programs (such as VisiCalc, Multiplan, and Lotus 1-2-3), statistical analysis programs, marketing forecast programs, portfolio analysis programs, etc. Another form of managerial support system is the database-oriented *ad hoc* inquiry system that allows a user to browse through a database looking for individual items of information, collections of information, patterns, etc. Many of the fourth-generation programming languages discussed in Chapter 29 provide such an inquiry capability.

A new kind of decision-support system is beginning to appear in some organizations: a decision-support generator that can be used to articulate and mechanize the rules that are used to make a business decision. One of the more interesting systems of this sort is a PC-based package called "Lightyear."[2] It lets the user or multiple users describe the details of a decision-oriented problem; an example might be the problem of deciding where to locate a new office facility. First, the user identifies the criteria that will be used to make the decision. For the problem of locating an office facility, this might include such things as "Must be accessible by public transport," and "Must not be in an earthquake zone," etc. Some of the criteria are binary, in the sense that failure to satisfy them will eliminate a candidate or cause the automatic selection of a candidate. Some of the criteria may be rankable on a numeric scale—e.g., one of the criteria might be corporate income tax rate, which will take on different numerical values depending on the city and state where the new office is located. And the criteria themselves can be ranked in relationship to one another: perhaps tax rate has a value of 5, on a 10-point scale, while convenient nearby shopping facilities has a value of 3.

Having thus defined the criteria for making a decision, various candidates can be evaluated and analyzed; the best candidate will automatically be chosen by the package. There is nothing magic about this, of course; the package is merely applying, in a mechanistic way, the evaluation rules provided by the manager. But the power of the system is more than just the mechanical calculation, it forces the user to articulate his criteria, which is often not done. It also provides a neutral facility for gathering the opinions of many users in situations where it is important to achieve a consensus. On an emotionally sensitive issue like choosing a new office location (which might require relocating the families of those making the decision), it can be very useful to articulate the decision criteria and also to articulate each decision-maker's ranking of the criteria. If two members of the office location committee are going to disagree, it should at least be clear to them what the basis of disagreement is.

---

[2] Lightyear is produced by a company called Lightyear, Inc. Unlike most other companies I know, Lightyear, Inc. is so modest and humble that they do not list their corporate address or phone number on their user manual or the floppy disk for their program. However, you should be able to find it at your local computer store.

Strategic Systems

The third category of system shown in Figure 20.1 is the strategic system. These are the systems used by top management to evaluate, reevaluate, and analyze the mission and direction of the firm. Rather than providing advice or information about an isolated business decision, these systems provide broader, more general advice about the nature of the marketplace, the preferences of the customers, the behavior of competition, etc. All of this is usually within the province of the Strategic Planning Department, or the Long Range Planning Department, though it may be a more informal activity carried out by one or more top managers in the organization.

Strategic planning is a concept that became popular during the Second World War (though some organizations were obviously doing it long before that), and it is the subject of many books[1, 2, 3] and conferences. Strategic planning systems are not computer programs *per se*; they are a complex combination of activities and procedures, much of it carried out by humans using information gleaned from outside sources (market surveys, etc.) and internal data from the two lower layers of systems shown in Figure 20.1. George Steiner points out that there can be many types of strategic planning systems, depending on the size and nature of the organization. He portrays two typical models in Figures 20.2 and 20.3:[4]

THE SHIFT IN INFORMATION SYSTEMS

Recent surveys have indicated that middle management and top management in many organizations are beginning to look for increasing computer support for the decision support and strategic planning systems shown in Figure 20.1. One of the most interesting surveys of this kind was conducted by Robert Alloway and Judith Quillard of the MIT Sloan School[5]; many of the statistics in this section are taken from their survey. The survey covered a number of business-oriented computer systems used by 944 managers in thirteen large companies in the industrial sector of the United States; the resulting patterns might be slightly different for other

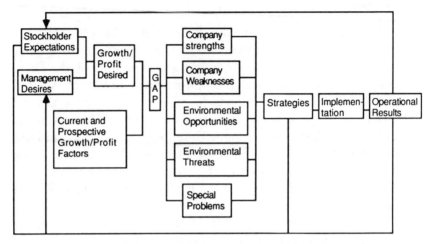

Figure 20.2: **A Strategic Planning Model Centered on Gap Analysis**

parts of the economy (or for government agencies), but I personally believe that they are indicative of trends in virtually all large organizations today.

Alloway and Quillard found, not surprisingly, that the majority of the computer systems installed today are operational systems: 63 percent of them were normal operational systems; 16 percent were exception systems; 12 percent were *ad hoc* inquiry systems; and 9 percent were decision-support systems. Figures like this have to be taken with a grain of salt: They do not necessarily help us understand the cost or complexity of the systems, nor the effort required to maintain them, nor the value that the user places on the system. In this survey, and others like it, a system is a system is a system—they are all counted alike.

However, we can get some idea of the value that the organization places on the system by finding out how it is used, and by whom. Alloway and Quillard found that 65 percent of the computer systems used by managers were normal operational systems; 14 percent were exception systems; 11 percent were inquiry systems; and 10 percent were decision support systems. This is almost identical to the distribution of installed systems, as shown in Figure 20.4; it gives us the impression that user-managers are not showing a preference for any special type of system. However, an additional

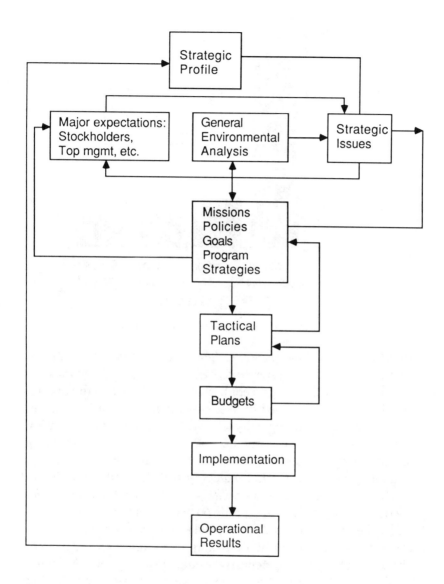

Figure 20.3: **A Strategic Planning Model Based on Market Strength**

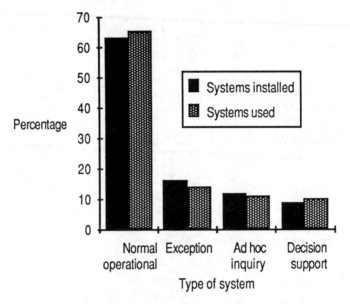

Figure 20.4: **Systems Installed versus Systems Used**

statistic begins to show us some signs of user discontent: only 44 percent of the installed systems were actually used by the managers. Presumably the other 56 percent had some relevance to the organization—e.g., they are used by clerical and administrative personnel—but since they are typically labeled "Management Information Systems," it should be recognized that they are not providing information to management if management isn't using them at all.

Pursuing this theme further, Alloway and Quillard found that of the systems that were used by managers, 70 percent (overall) were judged appropriate. However, only 66 percent of the normal operational systems were judged appropriate, whereas 60 percent of the exception systems, 81 percent of the inquiry systems, and 97 percent of the decision-support systems were judged appropriate. As Figure 20.5 illustrates, the decision-support systems represent only a tiny part of the portfolio of computer systems in a typical organization, but they are highly popular.

Two additional statistics highlight the frustration experienced by user-managers. The managers were asked to list their most important tasks and/or decisions that already were supported, or that

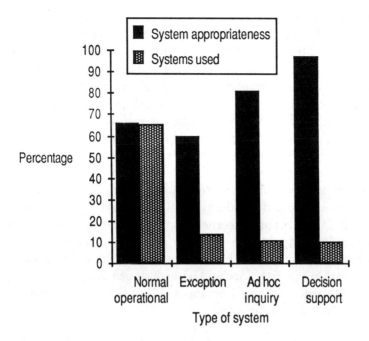

Figure 20.5: **System Usage versus System Appropriateness**

could be supported, by a computer system. It was found that 24 percent of these important activities had no computer support at all. Also, a comparison was made between those systems that were frequently used by managers and those that were relevant to their most important decision-making activities. Alloway and Quillard found that 29 percent of the systems used by the managers were not relevant to their most important needs.

THE DEMAND FOR NEW SYSTEMS

All of this focuses attention on the user-manager's need for new and different computer systems than the predominantly operational systems currently in place. Alloway and Quillard found that most of the organizations they surveyed had a backlog of projects waiting for the MIS organization to work on. Part of this backlog was "visible." It consisted of system development projects that had been funded and approved; these projects were simply waiting in a queue until the MIS department found the time and resources to begin work. In addition, virtually all organizations have an "invisible" backlog of projects that the user community needs—and knows that it needs, and complains vociferously that it needs—but for which it has not bothered obtaining formal approval because of the lengthy queue of visible projects already waiting to be done.[3]

In general, the backlog for operational systems is fairly static because it reflects the organization's intention to continue doing business in a particular way for the next several years. By contrast, the backlog for inquiry systems and decision-support systems is more dynamic and dependent on an individual user. The typical user-manager is often concerned that by the time his request for a new system is approved—not to mention the time required to implement the system!—the business opportunity that prompted the request in the first place will have disappeared.

The statistics on the backlog are impressive. Alloway and Quillard found the following:

- The visible backlog consists of 41 percent normal operational systems, 18 percent exception systems, 19 percent decision-support systems, and 22 percent inquiry systems.

- The invisible backlog was, overall, 5.35 times as large as the visible backlog.

- The ratio of invisible backlog to visible backlog was 2.93:1 for normal operational systems; 5.58:1 for exception systems; 7.39:1 for inquiry systems; and 7.84:1 for decision-support systems.

Clearly, the emphasis in many organizations is shifting toward the inquiry and decision-support systems. However, it appears that MIS organizations have not seen the handwriting on the wall. Alloway and Quillard found the following sharp contrast between

---

[3] Many will argue that there is a third backlog: the "unknown" backlog of projects that the user community doesn't even know it wants yet, but which it will discover as soon as it receives any of the "known" or "invisible" systems.

demand for new systems, and supply of new systems (systems in the process of being developed by the MIS department):

Type of System	Supply	Demand	Ratio
Normal operational	199	385	1.93
Exception	124	263	2.12
Inquiry	158	478	3.03
Decision-support	76	398	5.24

These numbers lead to an obvious conclusion: the MIS department is overwhelmed in general and, from the perspective of the user community, is short-changing the inquiry and decision-support systems that user-managers are increasingly desperate to have.

The political consequences of this backlog, coupled with the extreme backlog of inquiry and decision-support systems, should be obvious. MIS managers are in an increasingly vulnerable position as long as the lopsided statistics shown above continue to be true; users are more and more likely to take matters into their own hands. The personal computing revolution discussed in Chapter 17 is at least partially the result of this imbalance between supply and demand. This is obviously a political solution more than a technical solution. Users are not developing their own PC-based applications because of any newfound technical expertise, but rather because of their frustrations. Within many MIS departments, the most common technical solution to the problem is an enormous emphasis on fourth-generation programming languages (which we will discuss in Chapter 29). These languages often provide a tenfold increase in productivity, and are particularly well-suited to inquiry and decision-support applications.

SOME FINAL CAVEATS

Much of the problem presented in this chapter could be regarded as a priority problem: if the user community strongly prefers a certain kind of system, then the MIS department ought not to be spending all of its resources on something else. The user community should obviously be involved in setting the priorities, and many would argue (quite reasonably) that they should unilaterally set the priorities for the systems they are paying for. Indeed, this is done in many organizations through some form of steering committee, attended by one thoroughly cowed MIS representative and a dozen vociferous user-managers, that sets the priorities and grants the approval for new projects to be carried out by the MIS department.

However, an MIS department can only work on projects for which it has the expertise and resources. Many veteran computer programmers and systems analysts who have spent their careers building operational systems do not have the background, the training, nor the disposition to build inquiry systems and decision-support systems for an increasingly impatient user community, nor do many veteran MIS managers. Indeed, the entire MIS department may be an obstacle: it may insist on continuing to work on those systems it knows how to build. This is not a case of an irresistible force meeting an immovable object. The object, the MIS department, will very definitely be crushed if it persists in such an attitude. Or, more commonly, it will simply be ignored.

In fairness to the MIS organization, things are not as simple as the statistics in this chapter make them seem. As I noted earlier in this chapter, all of the statistics involve a simple count of individual computer-based information systems; a small, simple system counts just as much as a large, complex system. Keep in mind also that all of these figures are concerned with the development of new systems ; they do not reflect maintenance costs. Many MIS departments would love to devote their resources to building new decision-support systems for their users, but 80 percent of their personnel resources are devoted to maintaining and enhancing the underlying foundation of operational systems.

This point must be stressed: decision support systems, strategic planning systems, and inquiry systems all depend on the data produced by the operational systems. If those systems collapse, nobody will bother to develop any of the esoteric analysis and inquiry systems. It is convenient for the user community to shift its attention to the new types of systems. They can easily say, "Oh, we've already built our payroll and accounting systems." But someone has to keep them running. We will see more about this problem in Chapter 30.

Indeed, the problem is even worse than it seems. Not only must these old systems be kept running, they must be rebuilt. The sad truth is that most of the operational systems in large organizations were developed ten or twenty years ago; some were developed twenty-five or even thirty years ago. They have been patched and modified, enhanced and optimized, revised and upgraded, recoded and emulated on new computer hardware . . . and, in general, they have deteriorated to the point where they barely work at all. Even if the software programs work, the files and databases created (and updated) by those programs are generally incompatible with the requirements of fourth-generation programming languages that can facilitate high-productivity creation of new decision-support systems.

The somber conclusion is that most, if not all, of the foundation-level operational systems in American companies today will have to be completely redone before the strategic planning systems at the top of Figure 20.1 can be implemented. Some of the middle-level decision support systems can be built in a "stand-alone" fashion, but there are two problems with this. Such systems are being built by amateur programmers today (i.e., users with their own PCs), and these stand-alone systems must be integrated with one another if they are going to provide a proper foundation for the top-level strategic planning systems.

References for Chapter 20

1.   Steiner, George, *Strategic Planning*, New York: Free Press, 1979.

2.   Drucker, Peter, *Management: Tasks, Responsibilities, Practices*, New York: Harper & Row, 1974.

3.   Ackoff, Russell L., *A Concept of Corporate Planning*, New York: John Wiley & Sons, 1970.

4.   Steiner, *op. cit.*

5.   Alloway, Robert, and Judith Quillard, "User Managers' Systems Needs," CISR Working Paper 86, Cambridge, Mass.: MIT Sloan School Center for Information Systems Research, April 1982.

21

ARTIFICIAL INTELLIGENCE

> As knowledge [becomes] more and more specialized, the fewer
> are the persons who know enough . . . about everything to be
> wholly in charge . . . One of the paradoxical consequences is
> therefore the dependencies of a larger number of human beings
> upon a collection of ill-coordinated experts, each of whom sooner
> or later becomes oppressed and irritated by being unable to step
> out of his box and survey the relationship of his particular activity
> to the whole. The experts cannot know enough. The coordinators
> always move in the dark, but now they are aware of it. And the
> more honest and intelligent ones are rightly frightened by the fact
> that their responsibility increases in direct ratio to their ignorance
> of an ever-expanding field.
>
> Sir Isaiah Berlin
> *Conversations with Henry Brandon*

During the three years that I have spent researching and writing this
book, I have collected, borrowed, stolen, read, and clipped everything I could find on the subject of computers. Given the pervasive
presence of computers, this became almost a full-time job. A casual
reference over the loudspeaker by a Delta Airlines pilot about the
207 computers onboard our Boeing 757 led to a scribbled note on a
cocktail napkin already soaked with my neighboring passenger's
martini. A commentary on computers in jogging shoes that I
noticed in a barbershop running magazine was shamelessly torn out
and stuffed into a pocket, from which it emerged several weeks
later, crumpled and barely legible. Even *Mad* magazine did its part,
contributing computer cartoons to alleviate the tedium of writing
so many pages of dry, technical material.

Gradually, thirty-nine little piles of material began to accumulate on the floor of my den, one for each chapter that I could see taking form. Some of the piles were sparse indeed, but most consisted of a dozen or more interesting books, magazine articles, or newspaper reports. A few of the piles grew enormous by comparison, usually reflecting my predilection for material on software-related issues and children-related issues. But one pile grew larger than all the rest: the material on artificial intelligence. Magazines from *Business Week* and *Forbes* to *Omni* and *Ladies Home Journal* have articles on artificial intelligence. Books like Feigenbaum and McCorduck's *The Fifth Generation* appear in bookstore windows along with the latest Gothic romances. Even the layman can tell that Something Is Happening. That "something" is artificial intelligence, or AI for the sake of brevity. We will concentrate most of our attention in this chapter on a subset of AI known as "knowledge-based expert systems." The references at the end of this chapter provide a much wider, broader survey of AI for those who are interested in pursuing the subject.

WHAT IS ARTIFICIAL INTELLIGENCE?

A definition of AI is somewhat difficult because it is used so widely and with such enthusiasm—indeed, almost approaching hysteria—in the computer field today. However, a conventional definition is something along the lines of that offered by Elaine Rich:

> The goal of computer scientists working in the field of artificial intelligence is to produce programs that imitate human performance in a wide variety of "intelligent" tasks. For some expert systems, that goal is close to being attained; for others, although we do not yet know how to construct programs that perform well on their own, we can begin to build programs that significantly assist people in their performance of a task.[1]

Because artificial intelligence has become so popular, there is a tendency to use it as a marketing buzzword to make almost any other computer-related system appear sexier and more exotic. This has led to an understandable degree of cynicism, particularly within the computer profession itself. There are some who snidely remark that an artificial intelligence application is "anything programmed in LISP."[1] And there are some who will argue, quite sincerely, that none of the examples, applications, or products discussed in this chapter or commercially available in the marketplace today deserve to be called AI applications.

Everyone must judge for himself on this issue; perhaps that is why the Turing Test[2] has remained such a durable litmus test, despite the efforts to dismiss it over the past several decades. In any case, it is fair to characterize artificial intelligence applications in the following way:

- **An enormous number of potential "solutions" that must be examined**. The game of chess is the classical example of this point. While it is easy to write a computer program to evaluate all potential moves in a chess game, the combinations of moves and countermoves are overwhelming: there are 10^{120} unique chess games, each with its own special sequence of move, countermove, counter-countermove, etc. Even if each possible game could be evaluated at the rate of one per microsecond, it would take 10^{104} centuries, or 10^{96} times the current age of the universe, to finish the job.

- **A willingness to accept less than perfect, near-optimal solutions**. In most of the deterministic business computer systems, there is a right answer; the computer is expected to produce it in all

---

[1] LISP is an ancient and esoteric programming language discussed in Chapter 29. It was developed in the early 1960s and is primarily used for AI applications. Business programmers find LISP to be incomprehensible. The other popular programming language for artificial intelligence applications is PROLOG.

[2] The Turing Test is named after Alan Turing, the British mathematician credited with much of the fundamental theory of computing. Turing suggested that one could determine whether a computer was intelligent by seeing if it could mimic human behavior sufficiently well that an observer would not be able to tell whether it was communicating with a computer or a human. Imagine, for example, that you are in a room, with a typewriter keyboard (or CRT display terminal) connected to someone or something in another room; you cannot see the occupant of that room, and must decide entirely on the conversation it/he carries on with you whether it is a human or a computer. (Today, we can make this more lifelike with digitized voice output, so a computer in the other room could be made to sound like Marilyn Monroe or Richard Nixon). If at the end of an arbitrarily long period of time you could not tell that you were communicating with a computer, then (argued Turing) it is only fair to say that the computer is exhibiting as much intelligence as a human.

cases. Employees in most companies would be moderately upset if their payroll system calculated paychecks that were only accurate to within $20, yet users of a chess-playing program, or users of an AI program that diagnoses the nature of software bugs, are generally satisfied with a "good" answer even though they want the "best" answer.

- **A willingness to occasionally accept wrong solutions.** This is somewhat more controversial, and some will argue that it does not apply. To use the chess-playing analogy, though, even Bobby Fischer makes mistakes sometimes. Why shouldn't we allow the same behavior from an intelligent chess-playing program? As we will see later in this chapter, there are mundane applications like diagnosing diseases in houseplants and household pets where a computer program can afford to be wrong occasionally—even if the error leads to the untimely demise of the object being diagnosed!

- **An ability to find potential solutions by means other than straightforward "number-crunching" and exhaustive evaluation of all possible solutions.** Many people argue that it is this characteristic that distinguishes AI applications from normal computer applications, and that people who specialize in AI are nothing more than people who specialize in clever "search algorithms." This is, of course, an oversimplification at best, but the importance of clever searching techniques cannot be overemphasized. If there are 10^{120} different chess games for a computer program to evaluate, and only two minutes before it must make its next move, it needs several good heuristics to help pick a probable good move.[3] This is fundamentally different from most business computer systems, in which a simple, straightforward calculation—e.g., "Hours Worked times Hourly Pay Rate equals Gross Pay"—will produce the answer desired. Even if the calculation is enormously complex, normal

[3] A heuristic is a clever rule of thumb that doesn't always work. In the game of chess, a reasonable heuristic is "don't sacrifice your queen"; another is "if you must sacrifice a piece, it's better to sacrifice a pawn than a bishop." Many other heuristics provide guidelines for the beginning of the game, the middle game, and the end game. None is guaranteed to work; indeed, many of the most brilliant games in chess history have been associated with violations of the heuristics that the opponent didn't expect.

business-oriented and scientific computer programs are deterministic: a known, orderly sequence of steps is guaranteed to ultimately lead to the right answer.

- **An ability to learn from past experience, and thus perform more intelligently in the future.** This is also an area of some debate. If a chess-playing program plays well against human opponents, but never gets any better, should it be called intelligent? Purists would argue that the program is not truly intelligent, meaning that it does not mimic the behavior of most of us amateur chess players who do get better, ever so slowly. A pragmatist would argue that even intelligent humans eventually reach a plateau of performance and never learn anything further about their area of expertise. In any case, an ability to learn and synthesize new rules of behavior from past experiences is certainly a desirable feature for an AI program. For many problem areas where we don't yet understand how humans learn from their experiences, it is entirely beyond our ability to build such programs today.

RELATED AREAS OF INTEREST

The term "artificial intelligence" means more than just computer programs that play chess, but how much more is a subject that is open to some debate. The following areas are either part of artificial intelligence, or subsets of it, or closely related to it, depending on whom you talk to:

- **Robotics.** Technically, the field of robotics does not have to be related to artificial intelligence, but people (and companies) are increasingly unwilling to deal with "dumb" robots that crash into walls and do nothing more than follow rigid sequences of actions. A few of today's second-generation robots, and virtually all of tomorrow's third-generation robots, will use rules of judgment to determine how to cope with unplanned events.[4]

---

[4] I got my first introduction to this concept when I was offered a job at MIT's Artificial Intelligence Laboratory in 1966. The research project underway was to build an intelligent robot that could survive alone on the surface of Mars; because it would be so far from Earth,

Such second-generation robots will demonstrate intelligence of their own, and will probably have some or all of the additional AI technologies of voice recognition, touch, smell, etc. discussed below. A microchip "nose" recently developed at Sandia National Labs, for example, can help a robot smell the difference between ethanol and methanol.[2] Third-generation robots will be capable of supervising subordinate robots; fourth-generation robots will be capable of manufacturing robots; robots in the late 1990s, according to Center for Futures Research at the University of Minnesota, will be adequate sex partners. And that's all I have to say about that.

- **Voice recognition.** Voice output systems already exist, and are adequate for many applications; voice input systems are still relatively primitive and can only deal with limited vocabularies. The technology of voice recognition is like an onion: it is really layer upon layer upon layer of technology. First one has to deal with the mathematics and the physics: the human larynx when producing the noise "Supercalifragilisticexpialidocious!!" makes sound waves that have a specific pattern, or wave form.

---

scientists felt that they would not be able to control its actions by direct radio signals. The prototype for this intelligent robot (which, to my knowledge, has not yet been built) was a TV camera and a multijointed mechanical arm, connected to a DEC PDP-6 computer. The demonstration of intelligent action, pattern recognition, strategic problem-solving, etc., etc., was to be the game of Ping-Pong. If the computer could play Ping-Pong, then it would be easy to use the same principles to recognize that a dark shadow crossing over its shoulder on the surface of Mars was probably an incipient and very hungry Martian, for which the appropriate strategy would be to run away very fast. Though the project sounded fascinating, I was concerned that it had nothing to do with the real world and that I would be disinherited by my parents for frittering away my college education. I decided instead to get a respectable job as a systems programmer at General Electric, working on a massive, ambitious, but poorly conceived medical information system that suffered from all of the problems to be described in Chapter 27. I've often wondered whether I should have taken the artificial intelligence job instead, and whether I would have been any good at it, after having blundered through only one senior-level course on artificial intelligence at MIT. It was only later that I read and understood Robert Frost's durable commentary on such choices:

I shall be telling this with a sigh
Somewhere ages and ages hence:
Two roads diverged in a road, and I—
I took the one less traveled by,
And that has made all the difference.
                    Robert Frost,
          The Road Not Taken (1916)

Thus, in a very primitive way, a computer can recognize a sound, but it has to be trained to recognize different dialects and tonal qualities; each of us, after all, speaks differently. And then there is the problem of homonyms: "two," "to," and "too" all sound alike, and if the human speaker mumbles, the computer might mistake "too" for "tune," etc. This is where the artificial intelligence comes in: there is some chance of determining whether the human said "too" or "tune" from the context of the sentence in which the word appears. This is, after all, how humans understand one another when mumbling over a noisy telephone line.

- **Vision**. Computer vision is a subset of the more general problem of pattern recognition. It is an important area of study now, for many robotics applications and military applications require a computer to scan a two-dimensional area or a three-dimensional surface and "see" what it contains. Scanning a surface is, for a computer, a process of registering the presence or absence of light (or heat, radar reflections, etc.) on thousands of small sections (or "pixels") of the subject area. You can appreciate the problem if you think for a moment about the process of looking at a picture in a typical newspaper: seen by the human eye at a distance of half an inch or so, it is a jumble of black, white, and gray dots; only from a distance of a few inches does it form recognizable patterns. But how does the human eye recognize that certain grouping of black and white dots represent a picture of an airplane or a building? And how should a computer attempt to mimic that form of intelligence? To the extent that the object being seen is well known, recent advances in laser technology offer the possibility of substantially improved vision systems. Digital Optronics recently announced a laser radar 3D vision system so fast and accurate that it could be used to provide visual information fast enough for robot vehicles to steer and avoid obstacles even at speeds of 60 mph.[3]

- **Tactile sensor processing**. For second-generation robots and above, tactile sensor processing is a must: robots must be able to touch, smell, and hear the world around them. This, too, can be regarded as a form of pattern recognition. On an assembly line, a robot must be able to tell the difference between a hammer and a screwdriver; it must know when a part is out of alignment or flawed; it must be able to delicately move and manipulate objects without dropping them or crushing them.

BACKGROUND AND HISTORY

A great deal of work has taken place in AI since the 1950s, particularly at such prestigious universities as Stanford, Carnegie-Mellon, and MIT in the United States, as well as a number of research labs and other universities around the world. Much of the early work was concerned with issues of general intelligence and problem-solving abilities. Some of it was—and still is—concerned with the use of computers as a vehicle for modeling the functioning of the human brain as well as the reverse: using whatever we know about the functioning of the human brain as a model for developing more powerful computer systems.

Games such as chess and checkers were chosen as appropriate problems in the early days of AI development, for they have several useful properties: (a) there are known human experts, so the problem is demonstrably "solvable"; (b) the rules for actually playing the game are well defined and simple to represent in a computer; (c) aside from tic-tac-toe and other degenerate examples, most games have a sufficiently large "solution space" to pose an interesting challenge for AI; and (d) many of the heuristics used by humans have been articulated and can be programmed easily.

Another early area of AI interest was language translation. This was partly assisted by developments in the field of linguistics (which often took place in the same universities as the AI research) and was heavily funded in the 1960s by Department of Defense interests. The prospect of automatic translation of Russian and Chinese documents into English was, and still is, of enormous interest to such organizations as the National Security Agency. The translation of American helicopter repair manuals into Vietnamese was the object of much interest in the late 1960s and early 1970s for obvious reasons.

By the 1970s, a major conclusion was gradually forming: while the search for general intelligence was intriguing and beguiling, the prospect for developing an intelligent general-purpose computer was, and still is, beyond our reach. In the restricted area of game playing, a few impressive results were achieved, but no computer program has yet beaten a human Grand Master chess player. In the relatively limited domain of language translation, the results have ranged from mediocre to dismal. One of the more humorous results of computerized translation was taken from Shakespeare's "The spirit was willing, but the flesh was weak." The computer decided that this pithy statement meant, "The wine was good, but the meat was rancid."

The search for general intelligence continues today and may well produce awesome results by the end of this century. In the meantime, much of the energy and focus in the AI field has shifted to the solution of more narrowly defined problems, where a well-defined expertise can be articulated and translated into computer terms. Thus, instead of general-purpose Russian-to-English language translation systems, we are now concentrating on Russian-to-English translation within a narrowly defined technical field such as banking or software engineering. Instead of a world-class chess-playing program that can beat everyone in the world, we are now concentrating on programs that have a moderate degree of expertise, yet play well enough to have commercial interest.

EXPERT SYSTEMS

This popular new form of artificial intelligence is known by such terms as "expert systems," or "knowledge-based systems," or "knowledge-based expert systems," or "intelligent assistant," or "rule-based systems," or "inference systems." In addition to the general AI characteristics described above, these systems have rules of judgment that allow them to produce an appropriate output—a diagnosis, a solution, a prescription, a move in the game of chess—for a given situation. Feigenbaum and McCorduck define the terms as follows:

Knowledge-based systems, to labor the obvious, contain large amounts of varied knowledge which they bring to bear on a given task. Expert systems are a species of knowledge-based system, though the two terms are often used interchangeably.

Just what is an expert system? It is a computer program that has built into it the knowledge and capability that will allow it to operate at the expert's level. Expert performance means, for example, the level of performance of M.D.'s doing diagnosis and therapeutics, or Ph.D.'s or very experienced people doing engineering, scientific, or managerial tasks. The expert system is a high-level intellectual support for the human expert, which explains its other name, intelligent assistant.

Expert systems are usually built to be able to explain the lines of reasoning that led to their decisions. Some of them can even explain why they rejected certain paths of reasoning and chose others. This transparency is a major feature of expert systems. Designers work hard to achieve it because they understand that the ultimate use of an expert system will depend on its credibility to the users, and the credibility will arise because the behavior is transparent, explainable.[4]

Feigenbaum and McCorduck's point about explainable behavior is crucial; without it, people are unlikely to put their faith in the recommendations of a computer. Consistent behavior is also important; indeed, the possibility of such behavior from a computer is a distinct advantage over the sometimes erratic, unpredictable, inconsistent behavior of human experts (especially those who depend on intuition and "gut" feelings). The other major benefit of expert systems is that the expertise, once captured, can be replicated at will—thus magnifying the efforts of a limited supply of human experts.

There are roughly half a dozen classic examples of expert systems that have been developed over the past decade; they include the following:

- **MYCIN, EMYCIN, PUFF, and INTERNIST/CADUCEUS.** These programs, and other derivatives of them, were begun in the early 1970s and continue to be refined today. Their subject matter is medicine, and their expertise is medical diagnosis and prescription. Given information about the patient's symptoms, they will diagnose a likely disease; given a series of rules about the interaction of medicines with the human body, they will give appropriate prescriptions for the disease.

- **Prospector**. Schlumberger and other oil service and oil exploration companies are constantly faced with the problem of interpreting and analyzing the data from test drillings quickly to see whether it represents a dry hole or a productive well. The analyses have been performed traditionally by highly trained and experienced geologists who are in short supply; an expert system now performs much of the routine analysis, leaving the human experts to deal with only the most difficult and subtle readings.

- **DENDRAL**. Organic chemists, physical chemists, and biologists are often faced with the problem of determining the molecular structure of unknown compounds. DENDRAL was begun in 1965 at Stanford under the leadership of Edward Feigenbaum and Joshua Lederberg, and gradually developed into a program that could infer molecular structure from data available to physical chemists—e.g., gas chromatograph and mass spectrograph data. It has been in use in universities and laboratories around the world for several years, and its coauthors claim that it is "so knowledgeable and effective that its ability to explicate the details of molecular structure from chemical data *now exceeds human capability, including that of its designers.*"[5]

- **HASP/SIAP and other sensor-based detection systems**. The U.S. Navy has developed a passive, computer-based expert sonar system that can distinguish between the sonar signals of dolphins, submarines, freighters, and other typical objects in the ocean. This could conceivably be done using conventional computational methods, but it would require a supercomputer (requiring between 100 and 1,000 times more computing power than the AI approach required) not readily available in current submarines. And it is not even clear whether the conventional methods would work. The HASP/SIAP system does work, and it works at levels equal to and sometimes better than humans.

- **R1/XCON-XSEL**. In a somewhat different kind of application, Carnegie-Mellon University developed a "hardware configuration" system for Digital Equipment Corporation. It helps a salesman or systems engineer create a customized hardware configuration of disks, printers, central processing units (CPUs), and memory for a customer without violating any of the rules. Buying a large, complex computer is somewhat like buying a car: certain options preclude other options; some options require the presence of other options. The rules governing legal and illegal hardware configurations are relatively straightforward, but a deterministic, exhaustive evaluation of those rules would require enormous computation.

POTENTIAL FUTURE APPLICATIONS

The applications for expert systems technology are almost endless. They are limited today by computer hardware not yet powerful enough to produce results as quickly as desired,[5] but far more by the lack of experience in building expert systems. Most of the humans who possess the subject matter expertise are not accustomed, and sometimes not willing, to discuss that expertise with a computer technician.[6] And the computer technician —typically with the title of systems analyst—is not accustomed to interviewing high-level experts about rule-based inference systems. It will take at least five years, and probably more like ten years, before the technology is widely enough understood that expert systems can be built as easily as the common business-oriented MIS systems of today.

[5] This is one of the motivations for dramatically improved computer hardware, as we will see in Chapter 36.

[6] The same was true ten or twenty years ago when companies began computerizing their clerical functions. Veteran clerks who saw computers taking their job away were not overjoyed by the thought of describing their procedures to a systems analyst who was responsible for translating their work into COBOL. But there is at least one significant difference with expert systems: a clerk could generally be commanded to describe his or her procedures to someone else, but a high-level expert is not always cowed by commands from management. A verteran scientist or engineer or diagnostician who has spent a lifetime building his mental library of expert system rules may feel that his first loyalty is to his profession or his career and not his employer.

As this begins to happen, we will see a number of applications implemented on more powerful AI-oriented computer hardware. Today, a clerical or administrative judgment-oriented job that takes three to six months to master, and that involves no more than a couple hundred rules of judgment, is a good candidate for an expert system. Within five years, we will be able to build expert systems with a few thousand rules; toward the middle or end of the next decade, we will almost certainly have a few expert systems with tens of thousands of rules of judgment.

Wall Street analysts and venture capitalists (none of whom know very much about computers, let alone artificial intelligence) are extraordinarily bullish on the possibilities of AI products and services. Recent estimates of the market for natural language systems (an area of artificial intelligence related to, but distinct from, expert systems) suggest that it could grow to $1.8 billion by 1993; the market for general expert systems, and the software needed to develop them, is expected to grow from $20 million in 1984 to $2.5 billion in 1993.[6] Other estimates put the AI market at $75 to $125 million as early as 1983, suggesting that it could easily grow to a multibillion market by the 1990s.[7]

The expert systems we could build today include the following:

- **Medical diagnosis**. This application is one of the earliest that has been investigated, and one of the best known because of such systems as MYCIN and EMYCIN at Stanford and INTER-NIST/CADUCEUS at the University of Pittsburgh. Many people in the United States would probably be reluctant to trust their lives to a computer at this point; some, on the other hand, would be perfectly happy to stop dealing with human doctors that they find overpriced, arrogant, ignorant of current medical developments,[7] and generally uncommunicative. Doctors have

---

[7] The problem of keeping up with rapidly developing technology in any scientific field is a problem that all experts have to worry about. By the year 2030, for example, a fifty-year-old person will have a knowledge base of which 97 percent will have been developed in his lifetime; in a technical field, approximately half of that knowledge will have been developed during the past ten years. This raises some concerns about the kindly, white-haired sixty-five-year-old family doctor. As H.L. Mencken once said, "It's a sin to think evil of your neighbor, but it's rarely a mistake." The advantage of a computerized expert system for medical diagnosis (and many other related applications) is that massive resources can be

their own reasons for resisting the introduction of computer-based diagnosis systems, some legitimate, some not so legitimate. But in the meantime, what about all those parts of the world that don't have doctors? For that matter, what about all those parts of the United States—the backwater rural areas and ghetto slums—that don't have doctors? What about all the anxious parents who can't find a doctor at 3:00 A.M. when their baby is throwing up and running a high temperature? As I mentioned earlier in the chapter, there are situations when the user is willing to accept an approximate answer to his problem; there are even times when he is willing to run the risk of receiving a wrong answer. In economically depressed areas, it's likely to be a small risk. INTERNIST/CADUCEUS covers more than 80 percent of all internal medicine; its knowledge base includes more than 500 diseases and more than 3,500 manifestations of disease.[8]

- **Houseplant, pet diagnosis**. If you are morally opposed to the idea of a computer-based expert medical system prescribing a lethally incorrect dosage of medicine to a human, perhaps you would be willing to take the chance with your tropical fish, or your parakeet, or your potted begonias. Most of us are amateur doctors when it comes to the health of our pets and our plants; indeed, many of us have absolutely no idea of the causes and cures of the many things that ail them. While nobody in his right mind would spend $1,000 or $10,000 for a computerized expert plant/pet diagnosis system, we might spend $100. We would certainly spend $10. The software for such an expert system would probably run on most top-of-the-line home computers today (e.g., a fully equipped IBM PC, or perhaps an Apple Macintosh) but probably would not fit on a Commodore 64 or Atari 800 or many of the other toy computers used in the home for Space Invaders and other intellectual pursuits. The future, though, will not consist of plant diagnosis software on a gen-

---

brought to bear once on the development of diagnostic rules of judgment; it can then be duplicated on a floppy disk (or, considering the sheer volume, perhaps an optical disk; see Chapters 37 and 38) and distributed to millions of doctors around the world.

eral-purpose personal computer. It will consist of a customized "black box" that includes an appropriate sensor to read such things as the temperature and humidity of the houseplant as well as the chemical composition of the soil. If it is manufactured in quantities of several million, the price will certainly be under $100 by the end of the decade.

- **Equipment maintenance.** One of the areas of most interest to large organizations today is the speedy diagnosis and repair of expensive mechanical equipment. The oil industry is especially interested: "downtime" for an offshore oil drilling rig is often measured in the millions of dollars. IBM's field engineering division is currently investigating expert systems technology for the diagnosis and repair of computer hardware. (Imagine the cost of downtime for, say, an airline reservation system or a nationwide on-line banking system with 10,000 terminals.) General Electric is pursuing expert systems technology for locomotive diagnosis and repair.

- **Evaluation of insurance claims, loan applications, expense accounts.** Many administrative and junior managerial people spend the better part of their day analyzing the reasonableness of financial documents submitted by employees or customers; insurance claims, loan applications, and expense accounts are only three of the many possible examples. In all cases, there are some simple deterministic rules that must be applied. If certain information is missing or if certain numbers are not within prescribed limits, the document is automatically rejected. But there is more: the evaluator almost always has his personal hunches and guidelines that he uses to determine whether the document is reasonable. Indeed, these hunches and guidelines often suggest to the evaluator that the standard rules be broken. Company policy might indicate, for example, that the maximum amount allowed for dinner on an expense account is $20, but if the accounting manager in charge of approving expense accounts knows that the employee just returned from several weeks of business travel in a war zone, that his spouse divorced him in his absence, and that his house burned down, he might be willing to allow an additional martini or two on the expense account.

- **Shipping and mailing decisions**. Gone are the days when the only way to ship a package from New York to Los Angeles was to take it to the post office. Now there are several types of service from the post office, as well as UPS, Federal Express, Emery Air Freight, Purolator, and numerous other shippers. Each has its own fees and delivery schedules, and one could argue that the selection of one shipper or another should be a very simple, deterministic process. And it might be, if the shippers actually lived up to their promises. But, in fact, they don't always get the package to its destination by 10:00 A.M. the next morning as they claim on TV; it depends on which city you're shipping to, whether the destination is within the city limits or in the suburbs, and a variety of other factors. Thus, we find shipping clerks in many organizations mumbling to themselves, "Hmmm . . . if I use Federal Express, it will cost more . . . but the last three times I used Express Mail from the post office, it got sent to the wrong country . . . hmmm . . . " An expert system is needed.

- **Software debugger**. If you are familiar with computer software and the concept of debugging, then you can immediately see the virtue of this application. Within any large programming group there are expert debuggers and amateur debuggers. The expert can see clues that the amateur misses entirely—the behavior of the program just before it crashed, the contents of certain registers and variables, etc. More importantly, he knows how to interpret the clues; his experience tells him where the bug is likely to be, so that he doesn't have to go through the tedious line-by-line "breakpoint" approach that the amateur uses to trap the bug. Computer vendors (the people who usually develop programming languages to be used on their own hardware) could do the programming world an enormous service by providing an expert debugger with, say, the COBOL compiler database management system and the telecommunications package that they provide.

- **On-line user consultant.** As personal computers and on-line systems become more and more widespread, we find that many novice users begin communicating with a computer before they have read the appropriate manual. In fact, many users never read a manual; for some, it is a matter of principle. How do we cope with this? The non-AI approach is to provide an on-line help facility, so that the user can always push the help key and get an appropriate tutorial message on his screen. Even this simple concept, though, can escalate into AI technology, for the help system should provide appropriate information in the context of what the user was doing at the time he requested help. A full-blown AI approach allows for a much more sophisticated form of communication than simply pushing a button: the user can ask questions in natural English. Consider, for example, the following dialogue between a user and a computerized help system; the computer's responses are shown as UC:[9]

> USER: How do I delete (or remove) a file?
>
> UC: Typing 'rm filename' will remove the file with name filename from your current directory.
>
> USER: A directory?
>
> UC: Typing 'rm -r directoryname' will recursively delete the directoryname and all the files and directories contained in the directory.
>
> USER: How should one edit (or change) a file?
>
> UC: Typing 'ex filename' will get you into the ex editor; typing 'emacs filename' will get you into the emacs editor.
>
> USER: What is the best way to create (or make) a file?
>
> UC: The best way to create a new file is to use the editor, i.e., - 'ex filename.'
>
> USER: A directory?
>
> UC: Typing 'mkdir directoryname' will create a directory with name directoryname in your current directory.
>
> USER: Do you know how to read (or list) a file?
>
> UC: Typing 'pr filename' will print the file with name filename on your terminal.
>
> USER: How can I find out how full the disk is?

UC: Typing 'df' will tell you how full the disk is.

USER: How can I find out who is on the system or on Unix or using Unix?

UC: Typing 'who' will tell you who is on Unix.

- **Beginner's helper for entry-level personnel in high-turnover jobs.** The same concept described above can be extended to that of entry-level personnel in high-turnover jobs; the only difference is that such a system might have to play a more active role. The user consultant is passive, and only provides information when the user asks for it. A beginner's helper might, conceptually, constantly be looking over the user's shoulder, offering its own unsolicited suggestions if it notices a sequence of activities that are inefficient, clumsy, or against normal company policy.

RAMIFICATIONS OF AI/EXPERT SYSTEMS

Because the very concept of artificial intelligence has overtones of pure magic, it has attracted extraordinary interest on the part of people who are ordinarily very skeptical about new gadgets in the world of science. Japan has made artificial intelligence the major focus of its Fifth-Generation computer effort. The Alvey Directorate in England has responded with a 300-million-pound investment in fifth-generation technology, much of which is aimed at artificial intelligence. In this country, DARPA and various elements of the Department of Defense are investing billions of dollars in AI-based weapons systems and AI research. In the private sector, individual computer companies (IBM, Texas Instruments, DEC, Hewlett-Packard, and others), as well as the research consortium MCC, are also aggressively pursuing AI research.[8] A few large organizations, ranging from insurance companies to banks, from

[8] See Chapter 12 for more details on governmental involvement in computer research in various countries.

General Electric to General Motors, are also investigating AI-based applications.

With all the fanfare surrounding artificial intelligence and expert systems, it is important to keep in mind the possibility that AI has succumbed to Madison Avenue advertising. As AI specialist Gary Martins points out,

> . . . if one listens very closely, a rather different kind of story is being quietly told by users, developers and investors who've had firsthand experience with the expert systems miracle.
>
> Expert systems software development costs are high, development times seem unusually long, and the resulting programs put a heavy burden on computing resources. [10]

Martins also points out that the half-dozen classic examples described earlier in this chapter (and described in most other books and articles on expert systems) had the enormous benefit of brilliant programmers,[9] relatively well-defined problems, generous funding, lots of time, and a favorable environment. Not everyone can expect such a fortuitous combination of events.

It must also be remembered that there is a world of difference between the expert system discussed at length in this chapter and true general intelligence. It is possible that computers will never be endowed with the full range and scope of human intelligence. As Marvin Minsky (one of the fathers of the AI movement) says, " A computer would never be able to build a bird's nest; it wouldn't know where to begin." Others who have written eloquently and passionately about the limitations of computers are Joseph Weizenbaum[10] and Tom Alexander. [12]

Nevertheless, the field of expert systems is certainly one of the

---

[9] The developer of DENDRAL, for example, is Joshua Lederberg, the Nobel prize-winning chemist and current president of New York's Rockefeller University.

[10] Weizenbaum is probably best known as the creator of the "Eliza" program that mimics a therapist; it comes very close to passing the Turing Test! Versions of the Eliza program are available on most personal computers today. If you haven't seen it, you should experience for yourself the spine-tingling effect of communicating with a program that is on the borderline of human. And then you should read Weizenbaum's impassioned arguments[11] against putting too much faith in computer programs—especially his own.

most exciting and tantalizing aspects of computers. If pursued carefully, it could offer benefits to industry, government, and commerce far more significant than anything we have yet seen in the short history of the computer. It may require Nobel scientists to build such truly awesome expert systems as DENDRAL and MYCIN, but once they have built such a system, that computerized expertise—an expertise often bordering on genius—is available for all the world to use, over and over and over. Just as the Industrial Revolution replaced human muscle power with mechanical power, so the AI revolution will eventually replace human brain power with computerized expert reasoning power. The AI revolution may not happen this year or in this decade. It may come more slowly and more painfully than its proponents are willing to admit. But it is coming; of that there is no doubt in my mind.

Artificial intelligence is no longer an area you can afford to ignore, regardless of whether you are a COBOL programmer, a stock market investor, a grocery store manager, or a college student. At the very least, you (or someone whose judgment you can trust) should acquire a reading knowledge of the field; the textbooks listed below[13-18] are a good starting point. If you are a programmer or a businessperson involved in the use and development of information systems, you should consider a pilot project before making any decisions on further investment in this exciting new technology.

If you are a businessperson, or an investor, or just an ordinary citizen, you should investigate some of the commercially available expert systems that run on ordinary personal computers. Several, such as EXSYS[19] and EXPERT-EASE, cost only a few hundred dollars and can be used for a wide variety of real-world knowledge-based applications. The April 16, 1985 issue of *PC World* and the April 1985 issue of *Byte* provide excellent surveys of several of these PC-based packages.

References for Chapter 21

1. Rich, Elaine, "The Gradual Expansion of Artificial Intelligence," *IEEE Computer*, May 1984.

2. *John Naisbitt's Trend Letter*, July 11, 1985, page 1.

3.   "Robot Vision Breakthrough," *Breakthrough Reports*, September 1, 1985.

4.   Feigenbaum, Edward A., and Pamela McCorduck, *The Fifth Generation*, Reading, Mass.: Addison-Wesley, 1983.

5.   *Ibid.*

6.   "Artificial Intelligence Is Here," *Business Week*, July 9, 1984.

7.   Wilkins, Bryan, "AI Expert Systems Making the Grade in Commercial Mart," *Computerworld*, October 1, 1984.

8.   Feigenbaum, McCorduck, *op. cit.*

9.   Wilensky, Arens, and Chin, "Talking to UNIX in English: An Overview of UC," *Communications of the ACM*, June 1984.

10.   Martins, Gary R., "The Overselling of Expert Systems," *Datamation*, April 1985.

11.   Wiezenbaum, Joseph, *Computer Power and Human Reason*, San Francisco: W. H. Freeman, 1976.

12.   Alexander, Tom, "Why Computers Can't Outthink the Experts," *Fortune*, August 20, 1984.

13.   Schank, Roger C., *The Cognitive Computer*, Reading, Mass: Addison-Wesley, 1985.

14.   Rose, Frank, *Into the Heart of the Mind*, New York: Harper & Row, 1985.

15.   Feigenbaum, McCorduck, *op. cit.*

16.   Weizenbaum, *op. cit.*

17.   Negoita, Constantin Virgil, *Expert Systems and Fuzzy Systems*, Menlo Park, Calif.: Benjamin/Cummings Publishing Company, 1985.

18.   McCorduck, Pamela, *Machines Who Think*, San Francisco: W. H. Freeman, 1979.

19.   Derfler, Frank J., Jr., "Expert-Ease Makes Its Own Rules," *PC Magazine*, April 16, 1985.

Additional References

Anderson, John R., and Brian J. Reiser, "The LISP Tutor," *Byte*, April 1985.

"The Brains Behind Artificial Intelligence," *Fortune*, June 10, 1985.

Cornish, Edward, "The Race for Artificial Intelligence," *The Futurist*, June 1985.

Davis, Bob, "More Films Try to Put Skills of Key Staffers in Computer Programs," *The Wall Street Journal*, June 10, 1985.

Deering, Michael F., "Architectures for AI," *Byte*, April 1985.

"Defense Sets AI Goals," *ICS Applied Artificial Intelligence Reporter*, January 1984.

Derfler, Frank J., Jr., "An Affordable Advisor," *PC Magazine*, April 16, 1985.

Dutta, Amitiva, and Amit Basu, "An Artificial Intelligence Approach to Model Management in Decision Support Systems, " *IEEE Computer*, September 1984.

Eisenberg, Jane and Jeffrey Hill, "Using Natural-Language Systems on Personal' Computers," *Byte*, January 1984.

"Expert Systems: Limited but Powerful," *IEEE Spectrum*, August 1983.

Feldman, Jerome A., "Connections," *Byte*, April 1985.

Gallant, John, "AI Future Threatened," *Computerworld*, August 17, 1984.

Hayes-Roth, Frederick, "The Knowledge-Based Expert System: A Tutorial," *IEEE Computer*, September 1984.

_____, "Knowledge-Based Expert Systems," *IEEE Computer*, October 1984.

Hertz, David B., "Artificial Intelligence and the Business Manager," *Computerworld*, October 24, 1983.

Hewitt, Carl, "The Challenge of Open Systems," *Byte*, April 1985.

Hinton, Geoffrey E., "Learning in Parallel Networks," *Byte*, April 1985.

Kinnucan, Paul, "Computers That Think Like Experts," *High Technology*, January 1984.

"Knowledge Representation," *IEEE Computer*, October 1983 (Special Issue).

Kowalski, Robert, "AI and Software Engineering," *Datamation*, November 1, 1984.

Lemley, Brad, "Artificial Expertise: Intelligent Software for Problem Solving," *PC Magazine*, April 16, 1985.

McEnaney, Maura, "Small Tasks Reap AI Gains More Quickly, Report Finds," *Computerworld*, April 8, 1985.

Michaelson, Robert, and Donald Michie, "Expert Systems in Business," *Datamation*, October 1984.

_____, _____, and Albert Boulanger, "The Technology of Expert Systems," *Byte*, April 1985.

Mittal, Sanjay, "Patrec: A Knowledge-Directed Database for a Diagnostic Expert System," *IEEE Computer*, September 1984.

"Newspapers Try Expert Systems," *ICS Applied Artificial Intelligence Reporter*, June 1985.

Roberts, Steven K., "Networking's New Frontier: Artificial Intelligence," *Online Today*, February 1984.

"Robotics Shifts Its Sights," *ICS Artificial Intelligence Reporter*, June 1984.

"Robots in the Workplace," *ICS Applied Artificial Intelligence Reporter*, December-January, 1985.

Schank, Roger, and Larry Hunter, "The Quest to Understand Thinking," *Byte*, April 1985.

Seering, Warren P., "Who Said Robots Should Work Like People?", *Technology Review*, April 1985.

Smith, Emily T., "When Will a Computer Be Able to Communicate like a 6-Year-Old?", *Business Week*, April 1, 1985.

"Speaker: Develop Strategic Plan for Adopting AI," *Computerworld*, November 26, 1984.

Stevens, John K., "Reverse Engineering the Brain," *Byte*, April 1985.

"Study Finds NY Strong in AI Jobs," *Computer Living/NY*, February/March, 1985.

Taylor, Jared, "Lightyear's Ahead of Paper," *PC Magazine*, April 16, 1985.

Tello, Ernie, "The Languages of AI Research, " *PC Magazine*, April 16, 1985.

_____, "Marching to a Different Drummer," *PC Magazine*, April 16 1985.

_____, "Raw Power for Problem Solving," *PC Magazine*, April 16, 1985.

Thompson, Beverly, and William A. Thompson, "Inside an Expert System," *Byte*, April 1985.

Webster, Robin, "M.1 Makes A Direct Hit," *PC Magazine*, April 16, 1985.

_____, "Revealing Business Solutions," *PC Magazine*, April 16, 1985.

White, George M., "Speech Recognition: An Idea Whose Time is Coming," *Byte*, January 1984.

Winston, Patrick H., "The LISP Revolution," *Byte*, April 1985.

Woolf, Beverly, and David D. McDonald, "Building a Computer Tutor," *IEEE Computer*, September 1984.

22

PREDICTIONS III

The voice of the intellect is a soft one, but it does not rest until it has gained a hearing. Ultimately, after endlessly repeated rebuffs, it succeeds. This is one of the few points in which one may be optimistic about the future of mankind, but in itself it signifies not a little.

Sigmund Freud
Future of an Illusion (1928)

Several themes have been evident in the past six chapters of this book. Perhaps the most important one is that the ability of today's large business organizations to compete successfully in the 1990s will depend substantially on their ability to organize, integrate, and consolidate the information with which they work. To accomplish this will require an enormous capital investment over the next ten years. But this is the easiest part of the job. The most difficult task will be to convince a generation of top management, most of whom learned their business lessons in the 1950s and 1960s, that information and expert knowledge is the single most important asset in the organization, and that it must be managed differently than are tangible assets.

It seems evident to me that many large organizations will not survive this transition. Some will never know what hit them; they will continue manufacturing widgets until they discover that (a) nobody wants widgets any more; or (b) a new competitor has suddenly appeared with higher-quality widgets at a substantially lower price; or (c) nobody wants to work for them anymore. New, small, start-up companies will have a tremendous opportunity during the next decade. With a modest amount of capital and a good understanding of information management, they can out-produce older companies several times their size. Because of the growing importance of information, large companies no longer have the advantage of "economies of scale"; indeed, they now suffer from "diseconomies of scale."

PREDICTIONS

For a company to survive and prosper in the middle of the next decade, the following must be true:

- There must be a corporatewide integrated database of all relevant information needed to run the business. Equally important, there must be a visible, understandable, maintainable model of the organization's information resource. It must be possible for everyone from the chief executive to the lowliest clerk to understand the relationships between different pieces of information with which they come in contact.

- Office automation technology must be fully installed and universally available to all members of the organization. This must include word processing, electronic mail, and appropriate electronic filing facilities. Managers and knowledge workers alike must be familiar with this technology and must be able to use it as productively as they use the telephone today.

- The primary emphasis of the organization's MIS department must shift from transaction-processing systems to decision-support systems. However, to do this, MIS will first need to rewrite virtually all of the transaction-processing systems that were in place in the mid-1980s.

- The end-user departments and the MIS department must also lay the groundwork for full-scale development of expert systems throughout the organization. Expert systems technology will make it possible to build systems with knowledge bases of 10,000 to 100,000 rules and to generate new rules at the rate of 10 per hour. Such systems, if they can be built, will exceed the intellectual ability of any individual human expert and will represent a new threshold for business, society, and the human race.

CONCLUSION

The most important implication for you is to start now making plans for this new business world of the 1990s; you cannot afford to wait until New Year's Eve in 1989. The nature of your plans will depend, of course, on whether you are a manager or a worker, whether you are an investor or a citizen who is somehow uninvolved in the business world.

If you do work in the business world, as most of us do, then it is essential that your organization have a strategic plan developed soon to implement the technologies discussed in Chapters 17 through 21. If you are a high-level manager in the organization, it is your responsibility to see that such a plan is developed, and that it is then put into action. This is far, far more important than worrying about the profits for this quarter or next quarter. If you are a middle manager or junior manager, you must bring these issues to the attention of your senior executives. It is very possible that they are blissfully unaware of the drastic changes that lie ahead of them.

If you are a knowledge worker with no clout in the organization, then—as I have said several times in the past six chapters—you owe it to yourself and your family to abandon your organization if it does not appear willing or able to implement computer-based information technology over the next five years. Top management will not appreciate my saying this, but it is part of a *quid pro quo*: the very same management has no hesitation about laying off its workers in poor economic times.

There is an important implication for investors. The balance sheet and financial statements that are used today to describe a company's state of health will become increasingly irrelevant over the next few years. Meanwhile, the IRS, SEC, FASB, and other regulatory agencies may or may not revise their reporting standards. Thus, it is highly likely that some organizations will be grossly overvalued within the next few years, while others may be grossly undervalued. Similar opportunities have occurred in the past—e.g., in cases where organizations showed real estate or other assets on the balance sheet at their original cost, instead of at current market value. For the investor who has the time, energy, and ability to research an organization's information assets, the next five to ten years will be a period of enormous profits.

PART

IV

THE COMPUTER INDUSTRY

23

COMPUTERS: BIG BUSINESS

> The world is entering a new period. The wealth of nations, which depended on land, labor and capital during the agricultural and industrial phases—depended on natural resources, the accumulation of money, even upon weaponry—will come in the future to depend on information, knowledge, and intelligence.
>
> Edward Feigenbaum and Pamela McCorduck
> *The Fifth Generation*

The computer industry is a phenomenon that deserves attention on its own behalf, independent of the attention that I will give to the technology of computer hardware and computer software in Chapters 27 through 38. As an industry, computers currently have as great an impact upon modern society as the telephone, steel, automobile and railroad industries had 50 to 100 years ago.

To compare the computer industry to these other basic industries is appropriate in many ways: as in the early days of the steel, automobile, telephone, and railroad industries, the computer industry is growing remarkably quickly.[1] And as with many of the earlier basic industries (particularly the telephone industry), early predictions grossly underestimated the rate of growth of the computer industry. Computer experts in the late 1940s predicted that all of mankind's computing needs forevermore would be satisfied by

---

[1] This is true despite what you may have read about slumps in the semiconductor industry, losses and layoffs in certain computer companies, or problems in the home computer sector. I will discuss these anomalies, as well as the shakeouts in the computer industry, in Chapter 25.

twelve computers—but now there are more computers on earth than people!²

In one important respect, the computer industry is now different from the basic industries: it is larger. By 1984, the computer industry in the United States had grown larger than the steel industry and roughly equal to the Big Three automobile manufacturers. By the early 1990s, computers will surpass the moribund oil industry and reign supreme as the largest industry on earth.[4] The consequence of this development is obvious: computers now have a major impact on the national economy of the United States, of the other major industrialized nations, and of many of the more ambitious Third World countries.

This is true despite the intense fragmentation of the computer industry. It is convenient to think of the American computer industry as IBM alone—a company that is indeed large enough to suggest a new phrase, "What's good for IBM is good for the country." But in fact, IBM represents only a small part of the overall computer industry. (In 1984, IBM had 39.6 percent of the worldwide market for computers, according to International Data Corporation.[5]) As I write this book in 1985, there are approximately 500 computer hardware manufacturing companies in the United States; approximately 4,000 service companies; and approximately 8,000 software companies vigorously competing for a share of the market.[6] Various parts of the industry are growing at rates of 10 percent annually (which many other basic industries would be deliriously happy to achieve), while other parts are growing at rates of 50 percent per year, compounded (a growth rate normally associated only with cancer cells).

What does all of this mean? For most of us, the meaning is: it is critical to know which parts of the computer industry will continue

---

² Similar estimating errors have been made by leaders in the computer industry throughout the 1950s, 1960s and 1970s. Ken Olsen (president of Digital Equipment Corporation) remarked at the Convention of the World Future Society in 1977, "There is no reason for any individual to have a computer in their home."[1] Thomas J. Watson, chairman of the board of IBM, remarked in 1943: "I think there is a world market for about five computers."[2] And the editor in charge of business books at Prentice-Hall responded to a proposal for a book on data processing in 1957, "I have travelled the length and breadth of this country, and have talked with the best people in business administration. I can assure you on the highest authority that data processing is a fad and won't last out the year." [3]

growing rapidly (so we can ride the tidal wave), and which parts of the computer industry are already stagnating. No one wants to make the mistake of investing in, say, a company that manufactures punched cards for computers when they aren't being used any more. This is important regardless of whether one is a user, a producer, an investor, or a citizen. A user of computers needs to know which computer companies are going to succeed and which are going to fail—and also which computer products he may soon be unable to purchase because of the kind of government restrictions discussed in Chapter 13. Producers of computer systems need to know this information for the same reason. Investors have an even more immediate and obvious reason for wanting to know which computer companies are likely to do well, and which are not: fortunes are made and lost each day on Wall Street based on investors' guesses about the future of the computer industry.[3] And even the ordinary citizen, muddling along from one day to the next, ought to be interested. If nothing else, it gives him some clues about possible involvement, or meddling, by his government.

The phrase "government meddling" sounds intrinsically bad; for many, it is a reminder of George Orwell's *1984*. Governmental involvement in our private and personal life is, of course, a source of concern, as we saw in Chapter 14. However, we also need to examine the possibility of government meddling in the computer industry, which is the subject of Chapters 25 and 26. Over the past several decades, we have witnessed a variety of efforts—both on the part of the American government and the governments of most other countries around the world—to protect what they regard as important (or strategically important, in the eyes of military leaders) national industries.

Consider the kinds of industries that have received this sort of attention from governments in the past: the steel industry, the aerospace industry, the automobile industry, the agricultural industry, the shoe industry, and the fishing industry, to name only a few. The computer industry has begun to receive the same kind of

---

[3] Many of the statistics presented in this chapter, and the industry trends discussed in Chapters 24, 25, and 26, have been compiled by computer industry analysts who work for major Wall Street investment firms. Two of the respected analysts in the field are Stephen McClellan[7] and Ulric Weil.[8]

attention. It will intensify over the next ten to twenty years as computers continue to play a more and more important role in every aspect of society. This is something that clearly affects all of us as citizens.

THE SIZE OF THE COMPUTER INDUSTRY

A few statistics will illustrate the size of the computer industry:

- In 1981, worldwide information processing revenues were approximately $500 billion.[9] Given the industry's current growth rate, we can expect a trillion-dollar industry sometime in the latter part of this decade. Indeed, TRW Executive Director Simon Ramo predicts that the U.S. information processing industry could grow to $2 trillion.[10]

- In 1983, the revenues of the computer industry in the United States alone were approximately $110 billion[11]—twice the size of the steel industry, and the same size as the Big Three automobile companies. IBM President John Akers estimates that 1984 worldwide computer industry revenues were $250 billion.[12] By the early part of the next decade, the computer industry will surpass the oil industry.

- Information processing represented 5 percent of the GNP of the United States in 1980; in 1985, it will represent approximately 8 percent, and by 1990 it will represent 12 to 15 percent.[13]

Note that I have used the term "computer industry" and "information processing industry" almost interchangeably in the comments above. That's because computers are part of a larger phenomenon described by many people as the "information economy." A classic study by Marc Porat[14] showed that as early as 1967, approximately 25 percent of the United States GNP was involved in primary information production: computer manufacturing, telecommunications, printing, advertising, etc. Another 21 percent of the GNP was involved in secondary information production: production, dissemination, and consumption of information within goods-producing and manufacturing companies.

Estimates of the size of today's information economy vary; Mr. Porat does not provide specific figures, but is content to say that the 1967 figures have grown by "leaps and bounds." John Naisbitt estimates in *Megatrends*[15] that the information economy accounts for 60 percent of the GNP. Whatever the figures, the shift away from a manufacturing economy toward a service-oriented, information-based economy is well documented; Alvin Toffler's *The Third Wave*[16] is one of the more eloquent commentaries on this shift. This is important to remember, for there are many who feel that only IBM employees are directly involved in the information economy. From the comments above, it should be evident that today computers are involved in a much broader portion of our society.

Keep in mind also that the term computer industry is a loose term that includes a large number of specific industries: computer hardware manufacturing; computer software; telecommunications; office automation equipment; companies that manufacture paper, printer ribbons, floppy diskettes and other supplies for the industry; service bureaus and consulting firms; etc. In Chapter 24, I will describe in more detail the various categories of the computer industry.

It should be no surprise to learn that the computer industry is large and that it is growing rapidly. Almost any newspaper or popular magazine will tell you that, though some are preoccupied by the downfall or short-term problems experienced by a few computer companies. But let's look further ahead than the short-term future. What are the consequences of continued growth in the computer/information-processing industry? Various commentators have predicted annual growth rates of 15 percent, 20 percent, or even 50 percent (particularly in such areas as personal computer or software). Since the computer industry represented 5 percent of the GNP in 1980, 8 percent in 1985, and an estimated 12 to 15 percent in 1990, we can extrapolate the growth of the computer industry as shown in the graph in Figure 23.1.

With a 50 percent growth rate, it appears that more than 90 percent of the GNP will be associated with the computer industry by the year 1995. Note that I am using the narrower term computer

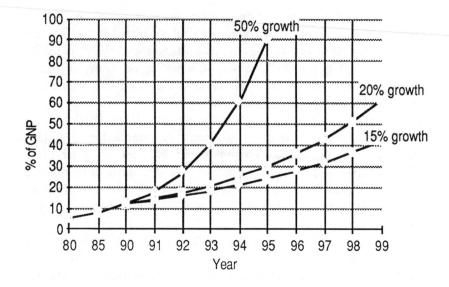

Figure 23.1: **Growth of the Computer Industry**

industry here, and not the broader term information processing, which already accounts for roughly 60 percent of the working population. However, it's unlikely that the computer industry will continue growing unabated for another thirty years; that's a lesson we can learn from watching other geometrical explosions that take place in nature.

There are three important things to remember when looking at projections like the one shown in Figure 23.1. First, the computer industry as a whole is not growing at 50 percent per year, and probably never will. Some portions of the industry are growing at that rate, but other parts are stagnating. I will examine this in more detail in Chapter 24 and 25.

Second, a variety of forces will almost certainly lead to shake-outs and stagnation in all parts of the computer industry as it continues to mature, including those that are growing most rapidly now. I will examine the phenomenon of shakeouts in more detail in Chapter 25.

Third, remember that the computer industry can't grow unless people buy computers and use them.[4] Just as the growth of other basic industries—especially the automobile and the telephone (and the telegraph before it)—was eventually limited by the infrastructure required to support the technology, so we will find that our homes, our businesses, and our governments will eventually be unable to continue absorbing new computer technology at the rate the industry is able to produce it.

I conclude this chapter with one last observation of the predictions shown in Figure 23.1: they bear a striking resemblance to the predictions made about the demand for telephone operators in the 1920s and 1930s.[17] Several studies indicated that if the demand for telephones continued, within fifty years every man, woman, and child in the United States would be a telephone operator. Such a statement appeared foolish at the time. But it has come true! Perhaps there is a similar future for computers.

---

[4] I am ignoring the possibility of people buying computers and throwing them away. Many would argue that this is what the military establishment is all about.

References for Chapter 23

1. Cerf, Christopher and Victor Navasky, *The Experts Speak: The Definitive Compendium of Misinformation*, New York: Pantheon Books, 1984.
2. *Ibid.*
3. *Ibid.*
4. McClellan, Stephen, *The Coming Computer Industry Shakeout*, New York: John Wiley & Sons, 1984.
5. *Market Data: 1985 IDC Briefing Session*, International Data Corporation.
6. McClellan, *op cit.*
7. McClellan, *op cit.*
8. Weil, Ulric, *Information Systems in the Eighties*, Englewood Cliffs, N.J.: Prentice-Hall, 1982.
9. *Ibid.*
10. "$2 Trillion Potential Forecast in U.S. MIS Industry," *MIS Week*, November 21, 1984, page 43.
11. McClellan, *op cit.*
12. "John Akers," (interview), *Computerworld*, July 2, 1984.
13. Weil, *op cit.*
14. *Information Economy: Definition and Measurement*, Washington, D.C.: U.S. Government Printing Office, U.S. Department of Commerce/Office of Telecommunications, OT Special Publication 77-12(1), May 1977.

15.   Naisbitt, John, *Megatrends*, New York: Warner Books, 1982.

16.   Toffler, Alvin, *The Third Wave*, New York: William Morrow and Company, 1980; Bantam, 1981.

17.   Pool, Ithiel de Sola (a genius and a prince), ed., *The Social Impact of the Telephone*, Cambridge, Mass.: MIT Press, 1977.

24

WINNERS AND LOSERS

Any coward can fight a battle when he's sure of winning; but give me the man who has pluck to fight when he's sure of losing. That's my way, sir; and there are many victories worse than a defeat.

George Eliot
Janet's Repentance, Chapter 6 (1857)

The computer industry is enormous, but it is by no means monolithic. There are dozens of different segments of the industry, and literally thousands of companies competing for a share of the market—or for a new market niche. To explore all aspects of the computer industry would require an entire book. Such books have been written, and I recommend Weil's *Information Systems in the Eighties*[1] and McClellan's *The Coming Computer Industry Shakeout*[2] if you are interested in a thorough discussion of the various segments of the computer industry.

Weil points out that the computer industry can be studied from several different viewpoints:

- **By market and application:** Office automation, personal computing, electronic funds transfer, packaged software, etc.

- **By vendor and product:** Mainframe manufacturers, minicomputers, microcomputers, office equipment, etc.

- **By class of user:** Individuals, very small businesses, small businesses, major corporations, etc., or scientific users, engineering users, commercial users, military users, etc.

- **By type of hardware technology:** MOS, TTL, ECL, bubble memory, Josephson junction technology, organic computers, parallel (non-von Neumann) technology, etc.

While all of these are interesting, I will focus primarily on a vendor viewpoint—i.e., which companies have the largest piece of the computer market(s)? I will also focus on the technology issue, but in a different way from Weil. I find it interesting to distinguish between the hardware industry and the software industry.

THE VENDORS' SHARE OF THE MARKET

With so many vendors in the computer industry, it's obviously difficult to tell exactly who has how much of the market at any given moment. But as everyone knows, the marketplace is dominated by a few big players: IBM, AT&T, and "Japan Inc." In the large-scale, or mainframe computer marketplace, IBM had 74 percent of the U.S. marketplace in 1983,[3] and 72 percent of the worldwide marketplace in 1984.[4] By definition, everyone else is far behind, though such giants as AT&T and the entire nation of Japan are trying mightily to catch up. But they have a long way to go: Japan's share of the world market was 6 percent in 1981, and 10 percent in 1983,[4] an admirable growth but nevertheless puny compared to IBM.

The market research firm International Data Corporation provides annual estimates of market share for large-scale systems, small-scale systems and personal computers. The data for 1984 are summarized in Figures 24.1, 24.2, and 24.3. Note that Japan appears only as a minor player in the mainframe marketplace, with its NAS subsidiary (National Advanced Systems) holding less than 1 percent of the market. And AT&T appears only as a minor player in the personal computer marketplace, with less than 1 percent of the market. Japan's role is more important than the figures below would suggest because it supplies many of the peripheral devices (printers, floppy disks, etc.) used by American companies, and because it supplies many of the "chips" that are the heart of the computer. Similarly, AT&T is more important than the figures below would suggest, because of the marriage of computers and telecommunications; however, as a supplier of computer systems *per se*, they were not a significant factor in 1984. As we will see in Chapter 25, it is likely that AT&T will be a much more significant force in the market in the coming years.

THE AWESOME POWER OF IBM

I doubt that anyone really understands IBM completely, not even the people who run the company. But an enormous number of people certainly try! Virtually every Wall Street brokerage company has one or more people who spend full time watching IBM's every move; every business magazine and newspaper reports on IBM developments on a regular basis. So many books have been written about IBM, IBM hardware, and IBM software that it's hard to know where to begin. When I consulted Bowker's *Books In Print*

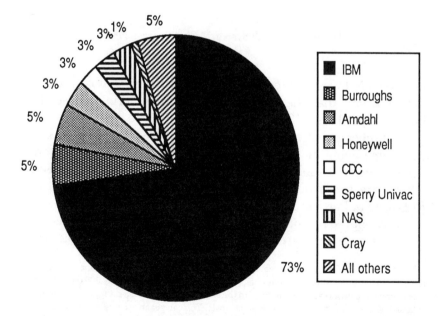

Figure 24.1: **Mainframe Market Share in 1984**

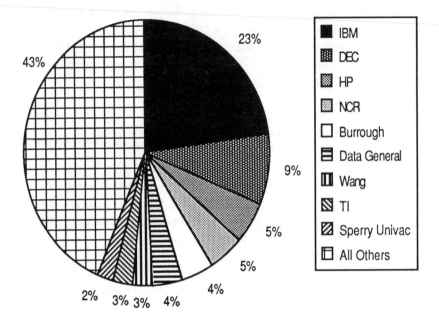

Figure 24.2: **Small System Market Share in 1984**

in July 1985, I was told (courtesy of the Lockheed Dialog Information System[1]) that there were 3,572 books in print whose title included the phrase "IBM"!

A number of consultants and market research firms make a handsome living by providing advice, predictions, seminars, and newsletters on the subject of IBM. Some of the better-known newsletters are the Yankee Group's *Impact:IBM*, Esther Dyson's *RELease 1.0*, Patricia Seybold's *The Seybold Report*, and the newsletters produced by Future Computing, Inc.[5] These sources, as well as the endless stream of new books and magazine articles, will

---

[1] The Lockheed Dialog system is an invaluable research tool for anyone conducting research on anything. It is an on-line computer system consisting of nearly 500 databases on everything from Bowker's *Books in Print* to the *U.S. Public School Directory* to biographical data on 130,000 American and Canadian scientists. You can get an account on this system by calling the Dialog folks at 415-858-3749. Better yet: get the "front-end" system called In-Search that runs on an IBM PC; it's available at any computer software store, or direct from the Menlo Corporation, 4633 Old Ironsides Drive, #400, Santa Clara, CA 95050, phone 408-986-1200.

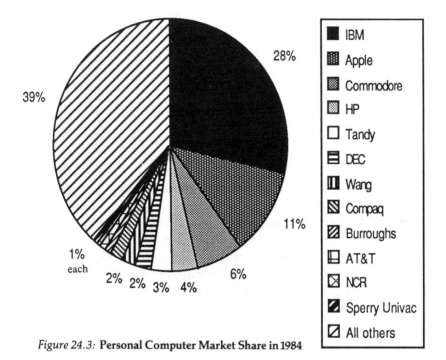

Figure 24.3: **Personal Computer Market Share in 1984**

provide you with as much information about IBM as you care to digest.

There are some key facts about IBM that you should remember even if you don't read anything else:

- **IBM's size is awesome.** Its growth from 1983 to 1984 was larger than the total revenues of the second largest computer company, Digital Equipment Corporation. Its R&D expenditures were larger than DEC's revenues.[6] Its 1984 revenues of $46 billion were approximately ten times as large as DEC's.

- **IBM intends to continue growing.** The new president of IBM, John Akers, expects to maintain a growth rate of 14 to 15 percent per year. *Business Week*, among others, predicts that IBM will achieve revenues of $100 billion by 1990, and $185 billion by 1995.[7]

- **IBM doesn't dominate the entire marketplace.** As I pointed out in Chapter 23, IBM held only 39.6 percent of the worldwide market for computer hardware in 1984. IBM's John Akers is even more conservative, estimating that "It [the computer industry] is five to six times the size of the IBM company."[8] Though IBM does dominate the mainframe marketplace, it captured only 30 percent of the medium-scale computer marketplace, 23 percent of the small-scale computer marketplace, and 28 percent of the personal computer marketplace in 1984.[9] Significantly, these three segments of the marketplace are also growing much more quickly than the mainframe marketplace: the mainframe market grew only 8.1 percent in 1984, while the personal computer market grew 66.2 percent![2] Though there are ongoing concerns about IBM's ability to monopolize the industry,[10] the marketplace clearly demonstrates that it is possible to compete.[11] And IBM's problems with the PC/AT personal computer[12] and its difficulty formulating an acceptable office automation offering[13] demonstrate that the company is not omnipotent.

The "BUNCH"

After IBM, every other company in the computer industry seems like "small potatoes." But as we will see in Chapters 25 and 26, they can't be ignored—at least, not all of them can be ignored. But there are five computer companies that are rapidly approaching anonymity: the five mainframe companies collectively known as the "BUNCH" because of the first letter of their respective corporate names: Burroughs, Univac, NCR, Control Data, and Honeywell. Collectively, they accounted for 14 percent of the mainframe market, and 9 percent of the total worldwide computer market in 1984.[14] Years ago, these companies were important contenders in the marketplace; today, they are held in such low esteem that when two of them—Burroughs and Sperry Univac—discussed the possibility of a merger in the summer of 1985, *Megatrends* author John Naisbitt dismissed the event as "the mating of dinosaurs."[3]

The BUNCH companies are important to us not because they

---

[2] I will discuss these growth rates in much more detail in Chapter 25.

[3] The merger fell through; presumably nobody blames Mr. Naisbitt.

represent a major force in the market, but simply because they exist. If they should disappear from the industry, then we—as users, producers, investors, and citizens—will be left with one American choice for mainframe computers: IBM. Even IBM wouldn't like that scenario because it raises the specter of government regulation. However, the dismal performance and lack of momentum of the BUNCH almost certainly means that one or more of them will disappear in the next ten years.

MINICOMPUTERS AND MICROCOMPUTERS

In the 1950s, the entire computer industry consisted of large, centralized mainframe computers. The marketplace consisted of major corporations and government agencies that could afford million-dollar machines with the attendant air-conditioned computer rooms and trained staff of computer operators.

In the 1960s and 1970s, a number of new computer companies found a niche overlooked by IBM: the small minicomputer with a price tag of less than $100,000 and no requirement for air conditioning or computer operators. Companies like DEC, Wang, Hewlett-Packard, and Data General created the market, exploited it, and grew to an enormous size before the mainframe companies like IBM and the BUNCH realized the opportunity they were missing. DEC is now the second largest computer company in the United States; Hewlett-Packard ranks 5th; Data General ranks 9th; and Wang ranks 10th.

And in the late 1970s, personal computers arrived. The premiere personal computer company, Apple, did not even exist in 1975. Ten years later, it has grown to the fourth largest computer company in the country, and though beleaguered by its problems with the Macintosh computer,[15,16] it is well entrenched on the Fortune 500 list. Commodore, manufacturer of the ubiquitous Commodore-64 computer, ranks 6th.

Mainframe computer companies have realized that personal computers and medium/small computer systems represent a significant portion of the overall market—and they have gone after these new markets with a vengeance. IBM, for example, has a somewhat dubious track record in the home computer market (as witnessed by the demise of the IBM PCjr[17,18]) and has yet to overtake Apple in the educational market, but it has clearly conquered the business market for personal computers.[19] Indeed, IDC estimates that IBM captured 29 percent of the worldwide market for personal computers in 1984,[20] more than twice as much as Apple.

SOFTWARE

All of the statistics thus far are associated with computer hardware. But perhaps the most significant aspect of the computer industry today is that hardware doesn't matter. Computer software is now the driving force in the industry, and virtually all of the major companies are aware of it.

Organizations that use computers have known this for some time. Approximately 50 percent of the computer-related budget of the average company is spent on computer hardware, and the remainder is spent on computer software and other nonhardware expenses.[21] In some organizations, the situation is far more dramatic: a recent article in the *Atlantic Monthly*[22] estimated that the U.S. Defense Department (DOD) spends 80 percent of its computer budget on software today. Unless software technology improves dramatically (which will almost certainly happen: see Chapters 31 and 32), software costs will represent as much as 10 percent of the entire defense budget by 1990.

Even though this phenomenon has existed for more than a decade, computer manufacturing companies could afford to ignore it because most organizations developed their own customized software with their own in-house staff of programmers and systems analysts. The federal government—clearly the largest user of computers in the world—estimates that in 1985, 90 percent of its software was customized.[23] But the situation is changing. More and more organizations are buying packaged software to handle their payroll, their accounting, their inventory control, and all other standard applications. And because there is currently a dearth of experienced computer programmers and systems analysts,[4] many

---

[4] I will discuss this phenomenon in much more detail in Chapter 28. But in case you don't get that far, let me warn you now: the shortage is real, but will only last for another few

companies are "farming out" their software work to outside contractors.

Smart computer companies have seen this trend developing, and
are doing their best to take advantage of it. Consider the case of
IBM: hardware sales accounted for 59 percent of IBM's revenues in
1983, according to Stephen McClellan[24]; McClellan predicts that
by 1992, IBM's nonhardware revenues will exceed its hardware
revenues.[5]

At the present time, 63 percent of software sales go to computer
manufacturers, according to Ulric Weil.[26] 75 percent of the
applications software market (e.g., payroll systems, accounting
systems, etc.—distinct from compilers, operating systems,
database management packages, etc.) is held by 1,200 vendors, but
IBM has 10 percent of that market and the next largest independent
software company has only 5 percent.

The most exciting segment of the software industry is personal
computer software. McClellan[27] estimates that in 1985, PC software revenues will exceed mainframe software revenues, thus
creating enormous opportunities for small companies like Microsoft,[28,29] Lotus Development Corporation,[30,31] Borland Software,[32] and other newcomers.[33] Large companies like IBM are
keenly aware of the importance of PC software, too; however, it
remains to be seen whether the large companies can develop new
software products as innovative and elegant as those of the new
start-up companies. Almost all of the truly elegant and innovative
software for personal computers—with the exception of the software produced by Apple Computer for their remarkable Macintosh
computer—has been produced by individuals or by small (meaning
fewer than 100 people) software companies. IBM may be big,
profitable, and successful but thus far, it gets no kudos for exciting
software products.

---

years. Don't be misled by statistics you may see in tomorrow's newspapers about the
shortage of programmers. And for God's sake, don't encourage any child under the age of
twelve to train for a career as a computer programmer! To do so is to doom the child to life on
the unemployment line. Now maybe you'll read Chapter 28. . . .

[5] I have to be careful here, lest you jump to the conclusion that IBM will be a software
company by 1992. Nonhardware revenue includes a number of things besides software
revenues: typewriter ribbon sales, consulting services, interest earned from its investments,
etc. But IBM itself expects that software could account for a third of its revenues by the early
1990s.[25]

CONCLUSION

All of the statistics in this chapter are intended to give you a sense of where the computer industry is now, as I write this book. By the time you read it, things will have changed. IBM will undoubtedly be the Number One computer company long after you finish reading this book, but a number of other trends that are in motion already will have drastically changed the fortunes of some of today's thriving computer companies. This is the subject of Chapters 25 and 26.

References for Chapter 24

1.   Weil, Ulric, *Information Systems in the Eighties*, Englewood Cliffs, N.J.: Prentice-Hall, 1982.

2.   McClellan, Stephen, *The Coming Computer Industry Shakeout*, New York: John Wiley & Sons, 1984.

3.   "The Daunting Power of IBM," *New York Times*, January 20, 1985.

4.   *Market Data: 1985 IDC Briefing Session*, Framingham, Mass.: International Data Corporation.

5.   "Watching IBM for a Living," *PC Magazine*, May 15, 1984.

6.   "For the Sake of IBM and Science," *Computerworld*, April 8, 1985.

7.   "IBM: More Worlds to Conquer," *Business Week*, February 18, 1985, pages 84-98.

8.   "John Akers," (interview), *Computerworld*, July 2, 1984.

9.   Market Data, *op cit.*

10.   Uttal, Bro, "Is IBM Playing Too Tough?", *Fortune*, December 10, 1984.

11.   Magnet, Myron, "How to Compete With IBM," *Fortune*, February 6, 1984.

12.   Kneal, Dennis, "IBM's AT Computer Puts Pressure on Rivals and Rest of its PC Line," *The Wall Street Journal*, October 17, 1984.

13.   O'Keefe, Linda, "IBM's OA Puzzle," *Datamation*, February 1, 1985.

14.   Market Data, *op. cit.*

15.   Morrison, Ann M., "Apple Bites Back," *Fortune*, February 20, 1984.

16.   Wise, Deborah and Catherine Harris, "Apple's New Crusade," *Business Week*, November 26, 1984.

17.   Fisher, Anne B., "Winners (And Losers) From IBM's PCjr," *Fortune*, November 28, 1983.

18.   "IBM's PCjr Manual Reveals Computer's Strengths, Flaws," *The Wall Street Journal*, January 10, 1984, page 25.

19.   "Personal Computers: And the Winner Is IBM," *Business Week*, October 1, 1983.

20.   Market Data, *op. cit.*

21.   Lientz, Bennet P., and Swanson E. Burton, *Software Maintenance Management*, Reading, Mass.: Addison - Wesley, 1980.

22.   "Star Wars Won't Compute," *Atlantic Monthly*, June 1985.

23.   Special Analysis, Budget of the United States Government, FY 1986, Washington, D.C.: U.S. Government Printing Office.

24.   McClellan, *op. cit.*

25.   "IBM: More Worlds to Conquer," *op cit.*

26.   Weil, *op. cit.*

27.   McClellan, *op. cit.*

28.   Sherman, Stafford P., "Microsoft's Drive to Dominate Software," *Fortune*, January 23, 1984, pages 82-90.

29.   "The Met Grill," *Metropolitan Home*, July 1985.

30.   Petre, Peter, "The Man Who Keeps The Bloom on Lotus," *Fortune*, June 6, 1985.

31.   "Early Returns: Lotus' Jazz is Splashy and Easy, but Is It Powerful Enough?," *The Wall Street Journal*, June 7, 1985.

32.   "In the Silicon Valley, L'Enfant Terrible Is Also L'Enfant Riche," *The Wall Street Journal*, June 4, 1985.

33.   "Why It's More Important to Build a Company Identity Than to Sell a Hot Product," *Magazine Age*, October 1983.

25

COMPUTER INDUSTRY TRENDS

The best of prophets of the future is the past.

Lord Byron
Journal, January 28, 1821

Chapters 23 and 24 provided an overview of the American computer industry in the mid-1980s. This chapter addresses the question: where will the industry be in the mid-1990s and beyond? I will explore four aspects of the future development of the computer industry:

- **Growth curves in the industry**: Which parts are growing rapidly and which are stagnating?

- **Shakeouts in the industry**: What segments of the computer industry are overcrowded? Where can we expect to see bankruptcies or other apparent contractions in the industry?

- **Major marketplace shifts**: In what ways is the computer marketplace changing fundamentally, and how will this affect the industry?

- **Governmental influences**: How are government regulations, subsidies, etc., affecting the activities and economic fortunes of American computer companies?

GROWTH CURVES IN
THE COMPUTER INDUSTRY

Observers of the computer industry have somewhat different expectations of the growth of the computer industry over the next five to ten years. However, the following estimates of annual growth are within the general range of most published forecasts, including those of Weil,[1] McClellan[2] and IDC[3]:

Computer-aided Design(CAD/CAM)	45-50%
Software revenues	28-30%
Personal computer hardware	40-45%
Personal computer software	45-50%
Mainframe computer hardware	10-12%
Computer services industry	21-24%
Office automation	30-35%
Terminals, modems, peripherals	16-19%
IBM's revenue growth	14-15%

These numbers speak for themselves: they say that the era of the centralized mainframe computer is over, and that the future belongs to personal computing, software, and office automation. However, there are some caveats:

- Beware of projections that call for ongoing, 50 percent compounded annual growth rates. That kind of growth means that in the space of four short years, the market will grow by a factor of five. As I indicated in Chapter 23, a 50 percent compounded growth rate for any of the market segments shown above would put us in the position where 90 percent of all American citizens were working in the CAD/CAM industry or the personal computer software industry by 1995. More likely, the rapid growth will continue for another two to four years and then level off sharply.

- When trying to estimate how long a segment of the computer industry will continue growing rapidly, we must also ask whether computer products are gradually saturating a stable industry, or if new (and presumably faster, cheaper, and more powerful) computers are continuing to open up brand new applications. In the area of office automation, for example, the market for simple clerical word processing systems is estimated to be 60 percent saturated—hence we should not realistically expect continued explosive growth in that area of the industry.[1] On the other hand, continued technological developments in the personal computer hardware/software segments could continue to open up new applications and could, for several more years, make computers attractive as a business tool to small businesses and self-employed professionals who could not afford them before.

- The fortunes of the computer industry and the state of the overall economy are now deeply intertwined. If the country is in a deep recession (for whatever reason), the computer industry will be affected and vice versa. There are still a few situations where a recession will motivate business managers to develop new computer systems to achieve immediate savings (e.g., by achieving better control of inventory or receivables; or by automating clerical functions, thus allowing staff reductions), but most of these computer systems have already been built. The 1982-83 recession taught us that computer programmers and systems analysts could be laid off just like everyone else. Hence, all of the rosy industry projections above should be tempered by the realization that we may have (a) an oil crisis, (b) a war in the Mideast, (c) a plague of locusts, (d) a real earthquake at the San Andreas fault, or (e) a madman as president.

[1] The experience of Wang Computer Labs in the summer of 1985 is a good example of this. Wang has grown for the past several years at a compounded rate of approximately 40 percent; this year it showed a loss and laid off 1,600 people. The company is still healthy and will probably prosper in the future, but not by selling simple word processing systems to secretaries.

You should also keep in mind that not everyone agrees with the industry projections outlined above. For example, not everyone agrees that the mainframe hardware industry is dead. Jack Kuehler, IBM's senior vice-president in charge of large-computer systems development, argues that the proliferation of personal computers and workstations will actually create more demand for mainframe computing, because it is the mainframe that will act as the repository for an organization's centralized database. Consequently, Kuehler predicts "a continuing and explosive growth of high-end mainframes," equal to or greater than the 10 to 12 percent growth rate forecast above.[4]

PROSPECTS FOR IBM

As I indicated in Chapter 24, IBM is already the largest computer company on earth, and is well on its way toward becoming the largest company of any kind (with the possible exception of certain religious organizations). IBM itself plans to quadruple in size between now and the mid-1990s, and observers ranging from *Business Week*[5] and the Gartner Group[6] agree that it will happen. As I also indicated in Chapter 24, IBM is not omnipotent. It is not an altogether unstoppable force. It will have to overcome a number of obstacles in order to grow to $185 billion annual revenues. Among the consequences of such growth are:

- IBM's success will depend significantly on its ability to become the most efficient manufacturing organization on earth. Its success over the years has often been associated with superior marketing and service, which are crucial for high-cost mainframe computers but perhaps less significant for mass-merchandised, low-cost personal computers. To succeed, IBM must couple its ability to use every conceivable distribution channel with manufacturing technology that makes it a low-cost producer on a par with Japan.

- If IBM succeeds in growing to its projected $185 billion revenue level in the mid-1990s, it will account for approximately 2 percent of the GNP in the United States.[7] This alone raises the possibility of increased federal government supervision and regulation, which could in turn hamper IBM's ability to grow. In any case, it keeps alive the constant debate about IBM's ability to stifle competition.[8]

- Growth from $46 billion to $185 billion will almost certainly mean a continuation of acquisitions, joint ventures, or minority stakes in other high-tech companies over the next several years.[9] Thus, IBM's recent acquisition of ROLM, its investment in Intel and its joint venture with MCI Telecommunications should be seen as a phenomenon that will continue. Keep in mind that IBM will be competing in this area with other giants like General Motors and AT&T.

- If IBM is to grow from $46 billion in revenues in 1984 to, say, $186 billion in 1994, then it must generate a grand total of approximately $1.4 trillion in revenues over the next ten years, assuming that it maintains fairly steady growth. This is a truly mind-boggling number, and I believe that IBM will only be able to achieve it if (a) industry and government continue to depreciate its hardware investment and continue to see the need for replacing its depreciated computers; (b) IBM is able to take away some of the market share from its competitors in the area of personal computers, office automation, and other non-mainframe segments of the market; and (c) IBM is able to find new markets, new customers, and new applications requiring computers.

THE EMERGENCE OF AT&T

One of the newer players in the computer industry is AT&T. While it has been involved with computers since the 1940s,[2] government regulations forbade it from marketing general purpose computer products. However, with the government-ordered split-up of the nation's telephone utility, it became possible for AT&T to enter the

[2] The transistor, which was the technological heart of early computers, was invented at Bell Telephone Laboratories.

computer industry. In March 1984, it introduced a series of mini-computers (the 3B series) and a "clone" of the IBM PC known as the PC 6300. Both the minicomputers and the personal computers were a marketplace flop, as indicated in the market statistics presented in Chapter 24. One market research firm estimated that AT&T sold only $205 million of 3B minicomputers to outside companies in 1984, while selling almost four times that amount to in-house and local Bell companies.

However, AT&T is not a company to be ignored; its revenues of $33 billion make it almost as large as IBM.[10] In March 1985, it unveiled a new personal computer that uses its own operating system, UNIX.[3] And it reorganized its Information Systems subsidiary by product line to coordinate product development and marketing more efficiently. But most observers—including me—still feel that AT&T lacks momentum, breadth of product offering, and a fundamental understanding of the marketplace. It's tough making the transition from a regulated monopoly to an unregulated competitor in a fast-paced, high-technology marketplace.

At this time, nobody is really sure what will happen to AT&T. Its enormous financial strength and basic technological R&D resources, together with its apparent determination to stay in the market, make it almost impossible to count AT&T out. And it does know how to make telephones and telecommunication equipment, which computers need in order to communicate with one another. So the safest prediction, as articulated by McClellan,[11] is that AT&T will be one of the top ten computer companies by the mid-1990s, but not very high on the Top Ten list. As IBM President John Aker said of AT&T, " . . . they're going to have to learn to take [their] capabilities and learn to merchandise them and persuade the marketplace that their products are good and that their support and service is good. I think the marketplace is prepared to listen very carefully. . . "[12]

---

[3] UNIX will be discussed in more detail in Chapter 31. For now, consider an operating system to be the software "brains" that coordinate the work performed on a computer. IBM's PC and many of the other compatible personal computers use an operating system known as MS-DOS, developed by Microsoft. UNIX is considered technologically more advanced, but more difficult for computer novices to learn.

SHAKEOUTS IN THE COMPUTER INDUSTRY

The rosy predictions of future growth in the computer industry are at odds with reports of computer company bankruptcies that began appearing in the newspapers and financial magazines in the mid-1980s. Cover stories like "America's High-Tech Crisis"[13] and "The Computer Slump"[14] in *Business Week* certainly create the impression that all is not well in the land of computers. Articles like "The Shakeout in Software: It's Already Here"[15] and "As Software Products and Firms Proliferate, A Shakeout Is Forecast"[16] focus attention on problems that many people didn't even know existed.

Actually, nothing new is happening: computer companies have been getting into trouble and occasionally going bankrupt since the very beginning of the computer age. Veteran observers of the computer industry have watched RCA, GE, and hundreds of smaller companies fall by the wayside. And they will continue going bankrupt until the industry matures and the technology settles down. Just as large agri-business companies are steadily replacing small individually owned farms around the country, so we will see large IBM-like computer companies slowly replacing small ten-person computer companies currently operating in garages. But this won't happen for a while: as long as there are new developments in computer hardware and software technology, and as long as there is a market for such developments, small companies will thrive. In this kind of environment, the only business failures will be due to cash flow problems, poor management, and other universal problems.

Compare the computer industry—now in its heyday—to the thriving automobile industry of the 1920s. In 1929, there were 108 American automobile manufacturing companies, in addition to several thousand smaller suppliers of automobile components (tires, gaskets, spark plugs, etc.). By the beginning of World War II, the number had dropped to 44; by 1950, the number was down to 5. And in the computer industry, there are some 500 hardware manufacturers and 8,000 software companies. Will they suffer the same fate?

The most likely answer is, "Yes." The reason for the precipitous decline in the automobile industry was hysterical optimism on the part of 108 marketing managers: they projected combined sales of 8 million cars in 1929, a level that was not actually achieved until the 1950s. Similarly, the personal computer industry forecast sales of 6 to 9 million units in 1983, a level of sales that we will probably not see until the mid-1990s. That kind of optimism generally leads to overproduction, which leads to price-cutting, which leads to bankruptcy for the weaker players in the game.

There are four areas where we will see major shakeouts over the next ten years:

- Personal computers—primarily the home computer area, but also the clones of IBM PCs in the business marketplace.

- Non-IBM mainframe computer manufacturers.

- Minicomputers.

- Small software companies.

Shakeouts in the PC Industry

The primary problem in the personal computer industry has been overestimates of sales. In the home computer area, computer manufacturers have not yet managed to convince the American public that the applications described in Chapters 2 through 10 are worth spending $2,000 for. And the public has learned that the $200 "toy" computers are inadequate for anything other than video games. Coleco and Sinclair have learned this the hard way. Indeed, even IBM is not immune: in early 1985, the company announced the discontinuation of manufacturing of its IBM PCjr (which is a very elegant way of announcing that it didn't want to be in that segment of the business anymore).

A second major problem for personal computer companies is the rapid, brutal price cuts that generally accompany improved hardware technology, or that may be made possible by efficient, high-volume production. Texas Instruments learned this the hard way: it introduced the TI-99/4 computer at a price of approximately $1,000. Two years later, when TI decided to get out of the home computer business (they still sell personal computers to the business marketplace), they had been forced to drop the price to approximately

$100. It's hard to make a profit when you have to cut the price of your product by a factor of ten in such a short period of time.

On the positive side, consider IBM's experience: in 1984, it sold approximately two million PCs, mostly to the business market. With that kind of volume, there are lots of opportunities for high-efficiency economies of scale. Unfortunately, it makes life more difficult for the clone manufacturers like Corona, Columbia, ITT, Compaq, Kaypro, Zenith, Olivetti, Canon, Panasonic, Eagle, and others; several of these, along with Osborne Computer Corporation, have filed for bankruptcy.

Software—or the lack of it—has been a third factor in the success (or lack of it) in the personal computer industry. One of the major reasons for the success of the Apple II and IBM PC is the enormous number of available software packages: both computers have approximately 10,000 different programs. Conversely, one of the major factors hampering sales of the Apple Macintosh (and the Apple III before it) is the lack of software: as of July 1985, there were only 400 to 500 programs available for the Macintosh. Paradoxically, this is a Catch-22 phenomenon: when a machine is first announced, the enormous industry of software companies (most of whom have relatively little capital to invest in new product development) try to assess the future market success of the machine. If they think it is going to be a winner—as they did with the IBM PC—then they write lots of software for it, in the hope that they'll make lots of money. If they think the machine will not do well (or that it won't be available when the manufacturer says it will be available), then they won't write any software. But if they don't write any software, then nobody will want to buy the machine—which will reinforce the software industry's collective decision not to write any software. It's a vicious circle.

Prospects for the non-IBM Mainframe Companies

Life is even more grim for the non-IBM mainframe companies. The likely prospects for the BUNCH companies are as follows:

- **Selective merging with each other.** This would have the advantage of creating economies of scale: many duplicated operations could, in theory, be consolidated. On the other hand, it is difficult to accomplish because of incompatible hardware: Burroughs hardware, for example, is utterly unlike Control Data hardware, and NCR hardware is incompatible with Honeywell hardware. I see this as an unlikely option.

- **Focusing on selective submarkets.** This has been a major strategy of many of the BUNCH companies all along: CDC has concentrated primarily on supercomputers and scientific computing, while NCR has focused on point-of-sale systems, banking systems, etc. While this is a safe strategy, it does not allow participation in the burgeoning new markets of office automation, small business computing, home computing, etc. Thus, while some of the BUNCH companies will certainly opt for this strategy, it will almost certainly lead to stagnation in the 1990s.

- **Offer an IBM-compatible line of products.** Some of the BUNCH companies already do this for computer peripherals—e.g., tape drives, disk drives, etc. Some, like Amdahl, offer a plug-compatible mainframe computer; at this point, almost all of the BUNCH computers offer plug-compatible clones of the IBM PC. The major problem with this approach is that it exposes the customer base to direct competition from IBM: some customers will buy the BUNCH computers if they are 30 percent faster and 30 percent cheaper, but many will forgo the savings to have the psychological comfort of knowing that they are dealing with IBM. And IBM, with its larger, more efficient manufacturing facilities, can always take the initiative with new product announcements and sudden price reductions.

- **Evolve toward being a "systems house."** Many of the BUNCH companies would be better off if they marketed Japanese hardware and perhaps even Japanese software. The value-added service that the BUNCH companies could offer is knowledge of the needs of specific market segments, and the ability to integrate, install, customize, and service the systems. Unfortunately, I think that most of the BUNCH companies will view this as a humiliating retreat from their former position of strength; it is a viable option that they will pass by.

None of these options offers the BUNCH companies an optimistic view of the future. Just as the American automobile industry gradually shrank to three companies, so I think that the mainframe computer industry will shrink to two or three.

Shakeouts Among Software Companies

The vast majority of software companies today are tiny—ten to fifty people. However, the industry is already beginning to evolve and mature as larger, more stable companies use the cash raised by public stock offerings to acquire smaller firms.

Though software businesses require virtually no capital to get started, they now require more and more capital for marketing and distribution to an increasingly sophisticated and savvy marketplace. Thus, the smaller, undercapitalized software companies are likely to find themselves gradually forced out of the marketplace. The simplest solution for them will be to merge with the larger, more successful companies, such as CSC, EDS, Microsoft, Lotus Development Corp., and Ashton-Tate.

There is one other alternative that may continue for another few years: treating software as something to be published. Several of the large American publishing companies, having made enormous profits from the sale of computer books in the 1979-83 period, decided that they could make even more money by treating software developers as "authors," and publishing their software products in return for royalty payments. Unfortunately, book publishers don't know much about software products or the software marketplace; in fact, the experiences of 1983-85 showed that most of them didn't even understand the marketplace for computer books. Most publishers are now abandoning or curtailing their computer efforts; I expect them to abandon the field entirely within the next few years.

GOVERNMENTAL INFLUENCES

As we saw in Chapters 12 and 13, national governments are beginning to play an active role in the computer industry of many countries around the world. I mention this point here only for the sake of completeness: one cannot hope to predict the future of the computer industry in this country or any other country without simultaneously predicting what policies the government will set.

Thus far, the American government has played a relatively modest role in the commercial portion of the computer industry; most of its involvement has consisted of investment in R&D projects for defense systems. But as the computer industry occupies a larger and larger part of our economy, we can expect the federal government to take a more active interest in protecting the local industry against foreign incursions or foreign restrictions on American computer companies. We have recently heard much complaining from the semiconductor chip manufacturing companies about unfair trade practices in Japan; and President Reagan has officially complained about Brazil's restrictions on American computer imports. We will eventually hear such clamorings from the personal computer industry and even the software industry.

SOFTWARE: THE NEXT MAJOR TREND

Throughout this chapter—and indeed, throughout this book—I have been stressing the importance of software. It is a major factor in the successful use of computers; and from that perspective, we are not doing a very good job, as we will see in Chapters 27 through 33.

Software is a major factor in the computer industry, and will thus eventually become a major factor in the government's involvement in the computer industry. By the end of this decade, software revenues and expenditures will greatly exceed hardware revenues and expenditures; computer companies will be devoting a major part of their resources to developing software, as will the companies who purchase computers.

But software is currently perceived, in this country, as an expensive, error-prone, labor-intensive, unmanageable "black art," developed by unsociable magicians who are in increasingly short supply.[4]

---

[4] Statistics documenting the messy, error-prone nature of software development are presented in Chapter 27. The shortage of programmers in the United States is discussed in Chapter 28.

This suggests a major potential market for Third World countries who may not have the capital to build competitive manufacturing facilities, but who do have an ample supply of cheap, well-educated, well-disciplined workers. At the present time, those Third World workers are being used extensively on the assembly lines of computer hardware manufacturing companies whose headquarters are in America, England, Germany, and Japan; by the end of the decade, a majority of the workers will have shifted to software development (and the assembly lines for computer hardware manufacturing will be manned by robots).

For a Third World software industry to thrive, three criteria must be met:

- **A plentiful supply of cheap labor.** Because of the disadvantages of the Third World software industry (which I will elaborate upon below), a cost differential of 20 to 30 percent is not enough to make such an industry viable. But if the programmers are four times cheaper, or six times cheaper, then it is attractive. Programmers in Singapore and Manila presently earn about six times less than Americans; Chinese earn roughly twenty-five times less. Because of the strength of the dollar, even the Canadian, Irish, and British programmers are 50 to 100 percent cheaper.

- **A well-educated supply of programmers and systems analysts who are familiar with current hardware and software technology.** There are lots of inexpensive, illiterate farmers and laborers in Third World countries; they wouldn't have the faintest idea of what to do with computers. And there are many countries that are still using hand-me-down computers from the 1960s; they would not be competitive with programmers using state-of-the-art hardware. However, many Third World countries have an excellent educational system—often inherited from the British, French, or other former rulers. And many have access to modern computer hardware; indeed, assembly lines in those same countries are manufacturing the very same state-of-the-art machines that are being used in banks, insurance companies, and aerospace companies in the United States. As for software technology, many of the Third World countries are at a distinct advantage: they don't have twenty years of obsolete software to maintain, nor do they have twenty years of bad software practices to unlearn. Many Chinese, Japanese, Malaysian, and Indian programmers (to mention only a few examples) are diligent, disciplined, well-educated, and thoroughly familiar with the latest software development techniques from America, England, and Europe.

- **Proficiency in English.** English is the universal language of computing, if only because of the combined dominance of American and British computer companies. To work effectively in the computer industry, one must be able to read computer manuals written in English; one must be able to read American computer magazines and technical journals to keep up with the field. And one must be able to talk to English-speaking customers (who make up a large part of the available marketplace for Third World countries) and write coherent user manuals in English. Former colonies of the British Empire generally fulfill this requirement easily: English is either the official language, or a strong second language. Countries like Brazil, on the other hand, have a problem: there is not much demand for Portugese-speaking programmers.

Several countries meet all three of these criteria: India, Singapore, Japan, Korea, Malaysia, and China are the most obvious. Other countries, such as Brazil, will have to decide soon whether they want to get on the bandwagon.

Some American industry observers argue that the Third World software industry will never flourish: after all, they argue, even if a Chinese or Japanese programmer can write better software, he does not know the customs, regulations, and milieu of American business well enough to understand its needs. And several of the Third World countries are better characterized as followers than leaders—so they might not have the foresight and initiative to think of exciting new software products.[5]

---

[5] One could make a similar argument within the United States: most of the exciting new software products during the past decade have come from small software companies, and even single individuals. Look at what VisiCalc and Lotus 1-2-3 have done to the software industry and to the hardware industry.

While these observations may be true, they certainly do not preclude the Third World countries from participating actively in the burgeoning software industry. The most likely scenarios are these two:

- **Partnerships between Third World software companies and American/British software companies.** It is easy to imagine a partnership where the American software companies do the "front-end" work of systems analysis—i.e., determining what the users want the computer system to do, and documenting those requirements. The Third World partners could then be responsible for the "back-end" work of systems design, programming, and testing. This would give the Americans about one-third of the work, and the Third World partners about two-thirds of the work.

- **Concentration on maintenance and conversion projects.** As we will see in Chapter 30, software maintenance consumes 50 to 80 percent of the resources of most American software organizations; if these resources could be freed up, (a) many American programmers would be overjoyed, and (b) those resources could be applied to the five to seven year backlog of new systems that users are desperate to acquire. Maintenance work is considered boring, demeaning, and downright unpleasant; many American programmers consider it to be "dirty work," and will change jobs to avoid it. Third World programmers, on the other hand, are happy to take on such work—and generally do a much better job of it than their American counterparts. The same is true for conversion projects—translating computer programs from an old vintage 1965 computer to a new 1985 computer.

References for Chapter 25

1.   Weil, Ulric, *Information Systems in the Eighties*, Englewood Cliffs, N.J.: Prentice-Hall, 1982.

2.   McClellan, Stephen, *The Coming Computer Industry Shakeout*, New York: John Wiley & Sons, 1984.

3.   International Data Corporation, *Market Data: 1985 IDC Briefing*, Framingham, Mass.

4. "IBM: More Worlds to Conquer," *Business Week*, February 18, 1985, pages 84-98.

5. *Ibid.*

6. Batt, Robert, "IBM Predicted to Grow Fourfold in 10 Years," *Computerworld*, October 10, 1983.

7. *Ibid.*

8. Harris, Catherine, "Does Big Blue Spur—or Stifle—The Competition?," *Business Week*, July 16, 1984.

9. "What's Next in IBM's Product Strategy?," *Computerworld*, January 2, 1984.

10. Lewis, Geoffrey, and Mark Maremont, "AT&T Makes a Second Stab at the Computer Market, *Business Week*, April 1, 1985.

11. McClellan, *op. cit.*

12. "John Akers," (interview), *Computerworld*, July 2, 1984.

13. Wilson, John, "America's High-Tech Crisis," *Business Week*, March 11, 1985.

14. Wise, Deborah, and Geoffrey Lewis, "The Computer Slump," *Business Week*, June 24, 1985.

15. "The Shakeout in Software: It's Already Here," *Business Week*, August 20, 1984.

16. Kneale, Dennis, "As Software Products and Firms Proliferate, A Shakeout is Forecast," *The Wall Street Journal*, February 23, 1984.

26

PREDICTIONS IV

Our hour is marked, and no one can claim a moment of life beyond what fate has predestined.

Napoleon Bonaparte
Letter to Dr. Arnott, April, 1821

What conclusions should you draw from the mass of statistics presented in the past three chapters? If you learn nothing else from this book, I hope you will remember this: none of the statistics in Chapters 23, 24, or 25 really matters. It doesn't matter whether IBM's revenues reach $185 billion in 1994, as so many smart people are currently predicting. It could be 1995 or 1996, or it may turn out that IBM is never able to exceed $175 billion in revenues. What does matter is the trend. We want to see the general direction of the road to the future, not the various bumps, squiggles, and small detours around obstacles. As the noted science fiction writer Arthur C. Clarke points out,

> Any attempt to predict the future in any detail will appear ludicrous within a few years. If we regard the ages that stretch ahead of us as an unmapped and unexplored territory, what I am trying to do is to survey its frontiers and to get some idea of its extent. The detailed geography of the interior must remain unknown—until we reach it. [1]

The overwhelmingly clear pattern that we have seen in the past three chapters is that the computer industry is enormous and getting more enormous each day. The industry is virtually certain to continue growing for the remainder of this decade, and probably well into the 1990s. In more specific terms, I have several predictions.

A DRASTIC REDUCTION IN THE NUMBER
OF COMPUTER COMPANIES

By the mid-1990s, I foresee the number of computer manufacturing companies shrinking to three to four mainframe manufacturers, and two to three mini/micro manufacturers in the United States.[1] The same reduction should take place in Europe and the rest of the world, but national politics may interfere: the government of, say, Brazil, may decide to subsidize eighteen local hardware manufacturers even though it makes no market sense.[2]

The reasons for this drastic reduction were presented in Chapter 25. It is a phenomenon that we have seen in several previous technology-oriented industries: the railroad industry, the telephone industry, the automobile industry, and the aerospace industry. If the technology and/or the marketplace matures (as I expect it will by the 1990s), then the same will happen to the computer industry.

Remember that all of this could happen even if the technology of computers is capable of continued improvement. If nobody wants to buy a computer—even a computer ten times faster, cheaper, and smaller—then eventually companies will stop building them.[3]

The only thing that will permit the current industry fragmenta-

---

[1] I am not prepared to say which three or four mainframe companies will survive, other than IBM. I think that all of the BUNCH companies are in trouble; which ones survive is likely to be as much a matter of luck as anything else.

[2] This is already happening in Brazil. There are more than a dozen Brazilian hardware manufacturers producing clones of the IBM PC. As I pointed out in Chapter 13, the price of these locally produced machines is roughly six times the price of the American IBM PC. Brazilians are not stupid people: they come to the United States on vacation and take American machines home in their suitcases. If they find next year that even cheaper machines can be purchased in Singapore or Taiwan or Ireland, then they will change their vacation plans accordingly.

[3] Once again, I am ignoring the influence of the military establishment, which will continue to want faster, cheaper, smaller computers *ad infinitum*. But even here there are limits: somebody has to provide the money for the military to buy the computers, and those somebodies (assuming that we haven't enslaved the world and forced the entire human race to pay a computer tithe) are the citizens of the country. Defense spending in the proposed federal budget for the 1986 fiscal year represents 29 percent of the federal budget, which in turn represents 22 percent of the GNP of the country.[2] Even if DOD got 100 percent of the federal budget, and even if the federal budget consumed 100 percent of the GNP, we would still reach a point in the mid-1990s where it would be impossible to "consume" larger quantities of computers.

tion to continue is the combination of two criteria: (a) continued dramatic improvements in the technology and economics of computer hardware and software; and (b) the continued willingness and ability of individuals and companies and government agencies to acquire the new hardware and software. The first criterion will almost certainly be met; the second is more doubtful.

By the early part of the next century (if any of us are still alive), I believe that there will be only two to three computer companies in the United States, one to two in Japan, one to two in Europe, and one to two in the Third World countries. The reasons are the same as presented above; the only change is that the European and Third World countries will eventually have to bow to the same market pressures that the United States will experience in the 1990s.

COMPUTER COMPANIES
WILL BE NATIONALIZED

Readers outside the United States will be neither surprised nor impressed by such a prediction. But Americans suffer the illusion that the free enterprise system is alive and healthy, and that it will continue well into the next century. This will not be the case with the computer industry.

We already have examples in this country; only a clever choice of words and a fervent belief in capitalism prevents us from recognizing them. Consider for a moment whether any of the following is truly a free enterprise industry, allowed to pursue the market wherever and however it wants: banking, food, ethical drugs (medicines), first-class mail delivery, telephone, television, nuclear power, air travel, construction (e.g., of homes and office buildings), electrical power generation, etc. Some of these industries are merely regulated, and the degree of regulation changes ever so slightly depending on whether the government is controlled by Republicans or Democrats. Some (like the electric companies) are known as "utilities."[4] Some, like nuclear power and banking, are

---

[4] You may think all of this is irrelevant, but consider the notion of generating your own electric power for your company or your home. Chances are you could do it much more cheaply than the local power company can. Chances are that you could also provide more

widely perceived as "public menaces" that should be controlled by the government. And some, like mail and air travel, are considered services to which every citizen should have equal access.

I don't wish to argue the merits of these forms of regulation. All I ask is that you recognize the reality. There is no way on earth that you could consider these major segments of the economy as "free enterprise." Having recognized this, you should understand why I think that the computer industry will eventually fall into the same category. One or more of the following arguments will be made by the federal government within the next ten years:

- The computer industry is vital to the nation's defense, and we can't afford the possibility that our American computer companies may be driven out of business by those rascals in Japan.[5] So the federal government has decided to (a) buy all of the stock in IBM, and (b) put all computer companies under the control of the newly appointed Secretary of Information Systems, and (c) set up a Federal Agency for Regulation of Computer Enterprises (FARCE) to ensure that all computer companies are operating in the best interests of the nation.

- The computer industry is vital to the country's economic well-being, and we can't afford the possibility that those rascals in Japan will put all of our hard-working computer employees out of work. So the federal government has decided to . . .

- Equal access to computers is a God-given right that every American citizen should enjoy. But there are children, and senior citizens, and minorities throughout the land who don't have the money to buy their own computers, and who don't know how to use computers. So the federal government has decided to . . .

---

reliable power, without the brownouts and voltage surges that the local power company produces. But can you do this? Perhaps so, if you live on a farm: nobody will object if you use a windmill or solar reflectors to generate electricity. Unfortunately, most of us live in major urban centers. Check the local regulations in your city; there's about a 97 percent chance that the answer is, "No way!"

[5] . . . or Brazil, or Singapore, or the People's Republic of China. Japan is a popular scapegoat in the mid-1980s, but this may change during the next ten years.

- Privacy is a God-given right that every American demands. But a few unscrupulous hackers are threatening to take away that right by tapping into computer databases and exposing sensitive personal, corporate, and governmental data. This cannot be allowed to continue. So, to protect our citizens, the federal government has decided to . . .

Some of this regulation is already happening, as we saw in Chapter 13. But the regulations are not as far-reaching and complete as they are in several of the other industries mentioned above.

Additional regulations and nationalization will probably take place gradually over the next ten years. It may happen so slowly and quietly that we will not recognize it. But it is also possible that some national crisis will lead to an outcry in Congress, in which case the arguments presented above will be the opening paragraphs of speeches made by outraged politicians. Legislation will then be proposed and passed, and it may even show up on the front page of the nation's newspapers.

SOFTWARE COMPANIES WILL ACQUIRE HARDWARE COMPANIES

This has already begun. In 1985, Lotus Development Corporation acquired Dataspeed, a small manufacturer of hand-held terminals used to monitor the stock market. Presumably, Lotus intends to put their spreadsheet software and various expert systems into the terminals.

I won't predict that Lotus will acquire IBM in the near future, but I would not be surprised to see a software company like Microsoft acquire a hardware company like Apple, even though Apple's revenues in 1985 are approximately twenty times larger than Microsoft's.

A more likely scenario is that the software divisions in many of the major computer companies will begin to dominate the hardware divisions. Recall from Chapter 25 my prediction that by the mid-1990s, more than 50 percent of the revenues generated by the computer industry will be from software sales and services. It thus follows that today's smart computer hardware companies will begin devoting more of their resources to software, with the result that 50 percent or more of their revenues will come from software within ten years. At that point, the software folks will take charge. Some of them will decide that they don't want to be in the hardware manufacturing business at all; they will sell that part of the business or shut it down.

THE THIRD WORLD WILL BECOME A DOMINANT FORCE

Computer hardware manufacturing is already shifting to a number of Third World countries where an abundant supply of cheap labor can be found. This will continue to be important for the next five to ten years but will eventually become less important as hardware manufacturing becomes increasingly automated. At that point (which will occur sometime during the mid-1990s), the major factor in determining where to manufacture computer hardware will probably be government policies. Some governments may encourage foreign computer companies to establish manufacturing facilities, using tax concessions and other economic incentives as a bribe; others may forbid foreign-owned computer hardware companies (as is already happening in such countries as Mexico and Brazil).

But as I have said already, hardware doesn't really matter very much. And it won't matter at all by the mid-1990s: computer hardware will be a commodity like cameras and digital watches, readily available around the world. The name of the game will be software, and it is in the software arena that I expect to see major activity in the Third World. The reasons for this were discussed in Chapter 25: the current shortage of competent programmers and systems analysts; the enormous backlog of software projects waiting to be done; and the abundant supply of experienced, inexpensive, English-speaking people in the former colonies of the British Empire.

STRATEGIC IMPLICATIONS

What should you do to prepare for the future that I have outlined above? One thing that you should not do is ignore the future, or look for a way of escaping the computerized world of the 1990s. Attempts to escape will be as futile as trying to escape the threat of nuclear war by moving to an uninhabited island in the Pacific.[6]

If you are a user of computer systems, you should be increasingly wary of depending on foreign computer systems. This is sometimes difficult to do: if you bought an Olivetti PC in 1984 (as I did), you would discover that it was actually manufactured by Corona Data Systems, an American company. But if you bought an AT&T 6300 personal computer in 1984, you would find (if you looked carefully) that it was manufactured by Olivetti. If you bought an IBM PC, you would discover that the printer was manufactured in Japan, and that many of the other components were manufactured overseas.

You might also argue that such companies as IBM, Apple, and Burroughs are really multinational companies, with manufacturing facilities and marketing organizations around the world. John Akers, president of IBM, points out,

---

[6] Friends of mine described a classic example recently. Some friends of theirs had decided in 1982 to search for a place to live free of the dangers of war, pestilence, pollution, and all of the other problems of modern society. They searched in vain for such a place in the United States and Canada; they scoured maps of the world and rejected Europe, South America, and even Australia and New Zealand. Finally, they found the place of their dreams and moved their family quietly, without telling anyone where they were going. At Christmas time in 1982, they sent a postcard to my friends, saying "We have found Heaven. We have settled in the Falkland Islands." It was only six months later that Britain and Argentina came to blows over this small chain of islands they had been arguing about for nearly a century. I suspect that our unlucky escapists have since memorized all of the words of John Donne's immortal sermon:

> No man is an island, entire of itself; every man is a piece of the continent, a part of the main; if a clod be washed away by the sea, Europe is the less, as well as if a promontory were, as well as if a manor of thy friends or of thine own were; any man's death diminishes me, because I am involved in mankind; and therefore never send to know for whom the bell tolls; it tolls for thee.
>
> John Donne,
> *Devotions*, 1623

IBM is really a business that does its development and manufacturing and research activities all around the world, and the marketing and service operations are remarkably similar. You go to Germany, they're all Germans; you go to Japan, they're all Japanese; you go to South Africa, they're all South African; and here they're all U.S., but they look and act and conduct themselves about the same way.[3]

The issue here is whether the multinational corporation is stronger than the State: specifically, is IBM stronger than the United States? If you think IBM is stronger, or that it will eventually become stronger, than the U.S. government, you can ignore the advice given here and buy a computer from your favorite foreign/multinational manufacturer. I won't argue with you. Your crystal ball may be better than mine.

Even though IBM and many other large computer companies are multinationals, the fact remains that they are headquartered in the United States and are regarded by our government and foreign governments as American companies. It's exceedingly unlikely that you will ever be prevented from buying an IBM or Apple computer; it's much more likely that someday you will be prevented from buying a computer manufactured by ICL, Olivetti, Siemens, Fujitsu, Philips, or Hitachi.

Assuming you stick with an American company (or a British company, if you happen to be a British reader, etc.), which one should you pick? If my crystal ball is accurate, the 500 computer companies in existence today will shrink to three to four within the next ten years. It's a safe bet that IBM will be one of the survivors. I have my own personal guess about the identity of the other two or three survivors, but I have little or no factual evidence to support the guess—and I don't want to run the risk of a libel suit. So you'll have to make your own guess.

If you are a producer of computer systems, you should conclude from the material in these last few chapters that hardware is becoming a stagnant industry; you should begin shifting your resources to software. You should take advantage of software development resources in the Third World by (a) importing Third

World programmers through any possible legal means,[7] (b) moving the software development activity into a cooperative, friendly Third World country; or (c) forming joint ventures or partnerships with existing Third World countries. This advice is valid regardless of whether you work in (a) a computer hardware company, (b) a computer software company, or (c) the MIS organization of any other kind of company. It probably isn't valid if you work in the MIS (or ADP) department of a government agency, but that's only because the government is generally pigheaded; maybe you can find a way around the problem (e.g., describing such Third World software activities as "economic assistance").

If you are an investor, you should look for companies that appear to be following the advice given above. This may take some research, for a company may not wish to advertise its strategic moves in the area of software or Third World partnerships. But you can probably rule out investments in a number of companies whose actions identify them as dinosaurs.

If you are nothing but a lowly citizen, you should consider the impact that the computer industry will have on your life and the lives of your children during the next ten years. As I will discuss in Chapter 28, developments in the software industry will have major ramifications in the job market within the next five to ten years: the current shortage of programmers will disappear, and there will be a period (which has already begun) of oversupply of programmers.

The most important thing that all of us must do as citizens is watch the activities of our government *vis-a-vis* the computer industry. The regulatory actions described above will be unstoppable unless there is an effective lobby that begins pressuring congressional committees and other governmental bodies as early as possible.

Note that I have carefully avoided saying what kind of lobbying

---

[7] A trick that worked well in the early 1970s with British programmers (whose salaries qualified them as Third World programmers) was to bring them into the United States on a cultural exchange visa. The poor Liverpuddlian "savages" obviously had to be immersed in American culture, and the State Department allowed them to stay for a year. Lots of people made lots of money (but not the British programmers!) until the State Department wised up. That loophole is closed, but enterprising entrepreneurs will presumably find others.

should be done. I personally prefer a free enterprise system. I prefer the freedom to purchase computer hardware and software from any country I want. Since I work in the computer industry, I also prefer the freedom to sell my company's products and services to any country willing to pay for them. You may disagree; a number of intelligent, conscientious people feel that the computer industry should be regulated, and that the federal government should control the import and export of computer hardware and software.

God only knows what Congress and the Senate and the president think of all this. My guess is that they understand very little of the major industry trends discussed in Chapter 25, and that they react (if at all) only to short-term, emotional issues. Thus, our job as citizens is to educate our leaders, and present them with cogent evidence to convince them to develop a sensible long-range policy. This is almost certain to be a self-defeating effort, since politicians rarely act on long-term issues (long-term meaning anything longer than the period for which they are elected), but it is an effort that must be made nonetheless. To their credit, politicians are beginning to grapple with such difficult issues as pollution, arms control, and world hunger; we must convince them to add computers to their list of Important Issues.

References for Chapter 26

1. Clarke, Arthur C., *Profiles of the Future*, 2nd edition, New York: Holt, Rinehart & Winston, 1984.

2. *Budget of the United States Government, Fiscal Year 1986*, Executive Office of the President, Office of Management and Budget, Washington, D.C.: U.S. Government Printing Office, February 4, 1985.

3. "John Akers," (interview), *Computerworld*, July 2, 1984.

PART

V

COMPUTER
SOFTWARE

27

THE SOFTWARE CRISIS

Computers are to computing as instruments are to music. Software is the score, whose interpretation amplifies our reach and lifts our spirit. Leonardo da Vinci called music "the shaping of the invisible," and his phrase is even more apt as a description of software. As in the case of music, the invisibility of software is no more mysterious than where your lap goes when you stand up. The true mystery . . . is how so much can be accomplished with the simplest of materials, given the right architecture.

Alan Kay
Chief Scientist, Atari Computers[1]

Software threatens to wreck American industry today. More accurately, the lack of abundant, high-quality, reliable software threatens to asphyxiate companies, large and small, all across the land. It is a very real threat. And it is very immediate. Whether we can meet this threat successfully remains to be seen; the outcome is not at all clear. The problem, as I have suggested in several previous chapters, is not primarily one of technology, but of technology transfer. Unfortunately, the technology transfer problems associated with software are incredibly complex. In the case of software maintenance, as we will see in Chapter 30, the problem is roughly comparable to changing a tire on a car while the car is moving at 60 miles per hour.

Software is defined in *Webster's New World Dictionary* as "the programs, data, routines, etc., for a digital computer."[2] Programs and data that can be changed at will—even while the programs are being executed—are considered "soft," in contrast to the "hard-wired" instructions that are built by the computers that control your dishwasher and coffee maker. A "program," according to Webster's, is "a logical sequence of operations to be performed by a digital computer in solving a problem or in processing data." The cookbook recipe whose steps you follow when making a blueberry pie could be considered a program also. But it is a "finished" program in the sense that the cookbook author tried it, tested it, corrected as many errors as he could find, and then published it for the world to see.

Much the same happens in the software industry. Presented with a problem—whether it is the problem of computerizing payroll, or the problem of guiding a space shuttle into proper trajectory—the programmer tries to devise the proper sequence of instructions[1] that will make the computer accomplish the stated objective.

Sometimes this can be done easily; for example, a computer program whose purpose is to guess your age, starting with a blind guess and being told whether each subsequent guess was high or low, could be written in a dozen or so program statements. (Figure 27.1 shows an age-guess program.) Most serious computer programs are much larger. A computer program developed for typical business applications (payroll, inventory, etc.) would typically require between 10,000 and 100,000 program statements. Complex programs that carry out a wide range of related activities, such as an airline reservation system, often require between 100,000 and one million statements. And a few enormous projects—mostly military in nature—require vast armies of programmers who will

---

[1] Throughout this chapter and the next several chapters concerning software, I will interchangeably use the terms "computer instruction," "program statement," and "line of code." They are all the cookbook equivalent of "add two eggs to the batter." In very simple-minded terms, you can think of computer instructions in terms of the operations that you can perform on a hand-held calculator: multiply the number in the working register by seventy-nine, or store the number in the working register into the calculator's memory storage for later recall. What you accomplish by manually pressing a button on the calculator is accomplished by the computer programmer with an "instruction" that is fed into the computer and then carried out. The instructions are written in a language that may look vaguely like English, or that may look very mathematical and obscure. I will discuss programming languages in Chapter 29.

eventually produce between one million and ten million program statements.

Any program larger than a few thousand statements is typically referred to as a "system" by software people; this reflects the fact that such a large body of work is typically broken into smaller components (which may be referred to as modules, or subroutines, or programs, or subsystems); the smaller components, working together, carry out the overall objectives specified by the end-user.

To put all of these numbers into proper perspective, keep in mind that an average computer programmer can develop about ten to fifteen working program statements per day.[2] Thus, a project requiring 100,000 program statements involves approximately thirty to forty-five person-years of work. And a project involving one million program statements is a massive project involving several hundred person-years of work. In a recent study of some 200 American MIS organizations, consultant Capers Jones found that projects involving more than 500,000 lines of code typically lasted for four to five years; projects involving less than 64,000 lines of code typically lasted fifteen to thirty-six months; and projects involving less than 2,000 lines of code typically lasted five to fifteen months.[3] These numbers are especially significant in light of the dynamic nature of American business today, as well as the fickle nature of American programmers.[3]

One of the major problems with software, as we saw in Chapters 16 through 22, is that there isn't enough of it. The backlog of unimplemented systems and unwritten software in most large organizations is between five and seven years long. This is a crisis—a crisis of productivity. If we had more programmers, or if we could make our existing computer programmers ten times more productive, perhaps this crisis would disappear.

[2] He can, in a single day, write an almost infinite number of program statements that don't yet work. This is a source of great confusion for programmers and end-users alike. Programmers tend to remember the burst of creative genius that inspired them to write 2,000 program statements during forty-eight sleepless hours; they would prefer to forget the period of three to four months that it took to get all of those statements working properly.

[3] As we will see in Chapter 28, roughly one-third of American programmers expect to change jobs within the following year. The average time spent before changing jobs is 1.4 years.

This has led to what is often described as the "software crisis."[4,5] It takes the following forms:

- The crisis of productivity.

- The crisis of predictability.

- The crisis of quality.

- The crisis of maintainability.

- The crisis of professionalism.

These crises have put a great deal of pressure on the community of half a million programmers and systems analysts in the United States. They are unprepared for it: for the past twenty-five years (since they first became conscious of themselves as members of an elite class, separate from the rest of the human race), software people thought they were safe. There has always been a desperate shortage of trained computer programmers and systems analysts—and there is now, as we will see in Chapter 28. So even if a programmer's employer went bankrupt, there was always some other company that would offer a salary increase and a larger computer to work on. And if the employer didn't go bankrupt, a programmer would probably quit after a year or two anyway, just to get a bigger salary or the chance to work on a more interesting project.

Of course, there were some anomalies. Programmers in some of the automobile companies in Detroit found that because they belonged to a union (which is a silly thing for a professional programmer or systems analyst to do), they were laid off during recessions according to their seniority. And since seniority generally has little or nothing to do with a project manager's real needs, it turned out that the software consulting industry generally flourished in places like Detroit during recessions. Rather than bringing the most senior employee back onto the payroll, the project manager would hire a short-term consultant with the requisite skills. Many a junior programmer found that it was more profitable to quit the company and the union and become a consultant.

By the mid-1980s, things began to get rough for the software industry; the hardware-oriented part of the computer industry had already begun to suffer, during the 1982-83 recession, and then again during a slump in mid-1985. Banks and insurance companies, and even software consulting firms, began laying off their program-mers as they found there wasn't enough work to keep them occupied. In many companies, it turned out that the recession-inspired decision not to buy additional computer hardware also meant that the end-users wouldn't buy additional computer soft-ware; thus, all of the people employed by software companies and by the software divisions of computer manufacturing companies to build software products found that their jobs were vulnerable.

Something else began to happen in the mid-1980s: American industry began to lose respect for its computer programmers and systems analysts. For twenty-five years, they had been looked upon as an elite breed of magicians, people who could make inert machines sing and dance and occasionally even produce useful output. Though their projects were often (indeed, almost always) over budget and behind schedule, a meek user community put up with it. This complacent acceptance of expensive, shoddy work was due to a very simple fact: business had struggled for thousands of years without computers and without real time, on-line informa-tion systems—so anything that the programmers provided was considered a luxury that the user community had never had before.

For various reasons, this has begun to change: computers are rapidly becoming an essential part of a business operation. More accurately, information systems and decision support systems and knowledge-based systems are becoming essential to the success, and even the survival, of many large enterprises. It is no longer sufficient to use one's computer as a glorified abacus for payroll and accounts receivable and inventory control applications; now the computer is, as we saw in Chapters 16 through 22, a strategic weapon.

There are many reasons for this change. Part of it has to do with the steady acceleration in the pace of business: decisions that a businessperson in the past could contemplate for several days or weeks must now be made in a matter of hours or minutes. Part of it has to do with the gradual shift away from national economies and national markets to a global economy. We now find that our markets and our competitors are all around the world, and that at any given moment in a twenty-four-hour day, someone is awake and working hard to take away our market share. And part of it, in the United States, is associated with the gradual trend toward deregulation of major industries so that major companies in such industries as transportation, communications, and banking can now compete vigorously with each other and with new start-up companies.

All of this has made information systems and computer software essential to the well-being of American enterprise. And this drastically changes the view that top managers have of the software profession. When their corporate careers depend, quite literally, on the ability of a bunch of scruffy-looking programmers to get their project done on time, businesspeople tend to be much less tolerant of "artistic" behavior and much less willing to listen to explanations that "the software just can't be changed to accommodate what you want."

Before we look at what's wrong with the software industry, we first need to have an idea of its size and impact upon American business. This, I feel, is very important because it helps explain why we got into such a mess, and why it is now perceived as a mess by people outside the software profession. Quite simply, the situation is this: for thirty years, people thought that software didn't matter and/or that it could be ignored. Now, as we will see in the discussion below, it is evident that software is big business, and that it dominates all other aspects of computers. More significantly, it is beginning to play a dominant factor in the ability of an organization to compete in the marketplace, regardless of what product or service the organization is trying to provide.

THE STATE OF THE SOFTWARE INDUSTRY

As we saw in Chapters 23 and 25, software is a major part of the computer industry. The revenues of software companies—the companies whose only business is software development and the sale of software products—is expected to reach $8.4 billion in 1985.[6] And revenues of software companies are expected to grow at annual rates of 28 to 30 percent for the remainder of the decade.[7]

More important, the organizations that use computers—which means just about every organization with more than one or two people—are finding that they spend at least 50 percent of their computer budget on software. And the portion devoted to software is steadily increasing, while the portion devoted to hardware is steadily decreasing. By the end of this decade, most large organizations will be spending 80 percent of their computer budget on software; some large organizations are approaching that level already. The U.S. Air Force estimated that it reached the 80 percent level in 1985, and the Defense Department as a whole estimates that it will spend 80 percent of its computer budget on software by 1990.[8] Indeed, unless things change, the DOD estimates that as much as 10 percent of the U.S. defense budget in 1990 could be devoted to computer software.

There is an important aspect of the software industry that is often overlooked: a lot of software has already been written. Estimates of the installed base of application programs (payroll, accounting, etc.) in the United States range from $300 billion to $1 trillion;[9] and one industry consultant, Capers Jones, has estimated that the Defense Department has between 200 million and 300 million lines of installed code.[10] The significant thing about this is not how much money has already been spent, but rather the fact that all that old code won't go away overnight.

Much of this old code was written five, or ten, or even twenty years ago; much of it was written in obsolete programming languages that are not used any longer. Much of it was written by people who are no longer with the organization. (Or, even worse, people who have been promoted to management positions, and who are still defending the code they wrote ten years ago.) Much of it is not documented; or, as we will discuss in Chapter 31, the original requirements for these ancient systems have been lost. All of this contributes to an enormous maintenance problem, which I will discuss in Chapter 30.

The software component of the computer industry is enormous;

the software component of the MIS organization within a company is also enormous. Both are growing; within many MIS organizations, software costs have been rising at 10 percent per year[11] and often more. And all of this is taking place in an environment that end-users and MIS managers are increasingly unwilling to accept: low productivity, shoddy quality, unpredictable schedules, and a lazy, sloppy, unprofessional work force.

THE CRISIS OF PRODUCTIVITY

In defense of programmers and systems analysts, some of the criticisms levied at them about poor productivity are not fair. For the past ten or twenty years, many top-level managers have been spirited away to executive briefings on computers, conducted by their computer hardware vendor or by the company that would like to be their hardware vendor. In addition to hearing the latest marvels from their research laboratories, the executives are usually treated to a small session on programming: they are given the opportunity to write five or ten BASIC statements on a time-sharing terminal or personal computer. Inevitably, when they return home, they call up their MIS manager and say, "Hey! This software stuff is easy! Why, I wrote twenty lines of code in five minutes! There's nothing to it! How come that motley crew of programmers of ours takes forever to get anything done?"

Ah, if only it were that simple! As the executive briefings so amply demonstrate, any dolt can write ten lines of BASIC. Even a manager. Even an end-user. Even my five-year-old son. The problems, which nobody wants to point out in most of the executive briefings, with this simplistic view are the following:

- Describing the work as ten lines of code can be very misleading. And nobody can seem to remember whether it was ten lines or twenty lines of code—or whether the time required was ten minutes or twenty minutes or two days.

- "Scaling up" from ten lines of code to a million lines of code is not a linear exercise. In fact, Fred Brooks[4] has argued that productivity often goes down as project size goes up. So much for economies of scale.

- Writing a program and making it work are two different things.

- Writing a program so that someone else can understand it is not the same, nor is it as easy, as just writing it for one-time use.

- Unfortunately, two programmers won't solve the same programming problem in the same way, nor will they take the same amount of time to do the job. Nor will their finished programs use the same amount of computer time or computer memory. Nor will their programs have the same number of errors.

- Writing a formal statement of the requirements of the program, in addition to writing the program itself, takes considerable work.

Unfortunately, even veteran programmers, systems analysts, and MIS managers are sometimes guilty of the oversimplification that nontechnical managers fall prey to so often.

Identifying the Unit of Work

It is a disastrous comment on the state of the software industry that after thirty years we haven't identified the basic unit of work in a software project. It makes virtually all discussions about productivity subjective and highly political. For decades, most MIS organizations have used the easiest and most common measure available: the line of code. In simple terms, a "line of code" is a BASIC statement, or a FORTRAN statement, or a COBOL statement, or a "low-level" assembly language statement, or a "high-level" fourth-

---

[4] Everyone likes to quote Fred Brooks: he was the person in charge of much of the early work on IBM's OS/360 operating system, which was one of the largest softwares conceived by the mind of man in the early 1960s. His book, *The Mythical Man-Month*, is one of those classics that veterans in the computer field try to reread at least once a year. MIS managers who have not read it should be shot.

generation language statement.[5] For example, the program shown in Figure 27.1 contains five statements. But a line of code is a dangerous measure; here are some of the difficulties you'll see within an individual organization:

- Usually only the executable lines of code are counted—i.e., those program statements that the computer actually performs. But some organizations include comments as well, on the theory that it will motivate the programmer to document his code more thoroughly. If we measure things in this fashion, then the program in Figure 27.1 contains six statements.

- Some organizations include the job control language (JCL) statements as well as the program statements; others do not. The JCL statements are instructions to the computer's operating system that describe the external data files that will be required, the amount of memory that will be needed to execute the program, and various other environmental factors. Some organizations feel that the JCL statements are as difficult and time consuming as the COBOL and BASIC statements, and thus should be counted toward the productivity measure.

- Some organizations will include, in the productivity measure, lines of code that were originally written for a different project and then copied (or reused) again for this project; others will count reused code only if it has to be modified; others won't count it at all.

- Some organizations compute a productivity measure (lines of code per day) based only on the period that the project team spent writing code; testing, systems design, documentation, and various other project activities are not included. Other organizations include the time spent for systems design, but not for the definition of user requirements (the project phase normally called systems analysis); and there are a dozen other variations. Also, some organizations include in their productiv-

[5] When we discuss programming languages in Chapter 29, we will see examples of BASIC, COBOL, FORTRAN, and other programming languages. If you're puzzled or confused at this point, you might want to interrupt your reading and scan quickly through Chapter 29.

ity measure only those people who actually write code; other organizations include the systems analysts and systems designers who are involved in the front-end work of the project; still other organizations include everyone whose time is charged to the project, including technical writers, quality assurance personnel, supervisors and project managers, clerical people, etc.

```
* THIS ROUTINE PRINTS THE FIRST 100 SQUARES

I = 1

DO WHILE I < 101

@ PROW() + 1,1 SAY "THE SQUARE OF" + STR(I) + "IS" + STR(I*I)

I = I+1

ENDDO
```

Figure 27.1: **A Typical Computer Program**

Most project managers recognize that measuring an individual line of code written by an individual person on an individual day creates a version of the "Hawthorne Effect"[12]—i.e., if a programmer thinks he is being measured (and rewarded) by the number of lines of code that he writes, then he will automatically write more lines of code. "More code" doesn't necessarily mean "better code"; indeed, it can often mean "less efficient" code, or extraneous lines of comments in the code if the programmer thinks they are being counted. In a more general sense, programmers (being somewhat human animals) will attempt to optimize those characteristics of a program that they perceive as important. A classic study by Gerald Weinberg[13] showed that a programmer would try to maximize an individual technical characteristic of a program such as "memory utilization" or "CPU efficiency" or "maintainability" or "length of time to get the job done"—usually at the expense of other characteristics—if he was told that characteristic was important.

Some organizations attempt to measure something less microscopic and more meaningful than an individual line of code—e.g., measuring "KLOEC" (Kilo Lines Of Executable Code), or "modules," or "function points." The rationale behind measuring an aggregate of a thousand lines of code is that it tends to smooth the differences between one day's performance and another—i.e., it focuses attention on how much work the programmer is able to carry out over a period of several weeks or months. However, it still suffers from the weakness of measuring quantity versus quality. Measuring modules or subroutines or procedures may be more meaningful, except that there are so many different definitions of these three technical terms.

Note that none of these measures means anything to the person (or people) paying for the information system of which the software is such a key component. That is, a typical end-user wants to know how much it will cost for something like a payroll system; he doesn't care how many lines of code it took to make the payroll system carry out its function(s). The functionality of payroll is something the user can talk about—he can tell us whether the system has to account for part-time employees as well as full-time employees; whether it has to handle overtime as well as normal pay; etc. He cares, or he should care, how much it costs to buy a working, finished, documented implementation of that functionality. He should also care how much it costs to operate the system (can he run it on a PC, or does it require a mainframe?). And he should care how much it costs to maintain, modify, and revise the functionality of that system.

With this end-user perspective, there has been some interest in measuring the productivity of programmers—as well as the many other key players on a project team—in terms of function points, or some other measure of delivered end-user functionality. Several measures of productivity are offered by Boehm[14] and DeMarco;[15] I will discuss them further in Chapter 31.

Before I leave this aspect of our discussion on software productivity, I want to emphasize the bottom-line problem in many organizations: there is little agreement on the proper thing to measure. There is little or no consistency between the productivity measures of one project and another project in the same organization; there is virtually no consistency among organizations. And, even worse, in many organizations—probably 50 percent—there are no measurements of productivity at all!

Individual Productivity Differences

Further compounding the productivity problem is the fact that some programmers are an order-of-magnitude better at writing programs than others. This has long been recognized in the software industry. One of the first published examples was a classic paper published in 1968 by Sackman, Erickson and Grant[16] that demonstrated a 26:1 ratio in coding time for veteran programmers working on the same problem. In this same programming experiment, some programmers produced working programs that ran ten times faster than the programs produced by others; some produced programs that required eight times more computer memory than the programs produced by others. Most discouraging was the fact that there was no correlation between years of experience and programming performance; nor was there any correlation between scores on programming aptitude tests[6] and programming performance.

Since that time, there have been dozens, if not hundreds, of similar experiments involving small groups of experienced programmers, all working on the same programming problem to compare programming performance. Most of these experiments take place in a university environment or an industry training environment—which is funadamentally different from a normal industry environment, where every programmer is working on a different task. But time and again, the experiments have shown an order-of-magnitude difference between good programmers and bad programmers.[7] And Boehm's software cost models[17] indicate that

---

[6] Perhaps this is an indictment of programming aptitude tests. The students in the Sackman experiment took the Basic Programming Knowledge Test, used at the time by the U.S. Navy.

[7] The differences are not just restricted to productivity; they extend to quality, too. Some programmers have an order-of-magnitude fewer errors in their programs than other programmers.

individual programmer skills are a larger factor than any other factor in predicting overall project productivity. More important than the choice of programming languages. More important than the availability of automated tools.

The Effect of Testing on Productivity

Many MIS organizations perceive that the reason their productivity is so low is because of the amount of time spent testing the systems being developed. On a typical systems development project, approximately 35 percent of the project schedule and resources are spent on systems analysis and design (determining what the system should do, and getting a rough idea of how it will be implemented); 15 percent is spent on programming (writing the COBOL or FORTRAN statements); and fully 50 percent of the project is spent testing.

Spending 50 percent of the project to see if the right statements were written to solve the right problem is awfully discouraging. What makes it worse is that testing occurs at the end of most systems development projects; thus, if time runs short (as it inevitably does), there is a tendency to hurry the testing and turn things over to the user as close to the deadline as possible. Some organizations have independent testing groups and quality assurance groups, but the pressure from the user and the development team to put the system into operation will often overwhelm the best efforts of the QA team.[8]

---

[8] There is also a problem with the way that the testing is done in many projects: components of the system are assembled in a bottom-up fashion, as if they were components of an assembly-line product. Thus, individual modules or subroutines are tested for correctness; those modules are then combined into larger programs, which are tested; then the programs are assembled into subsystems, which are finally collected together into an entire system. While this is an admirable way to test the components of an automobile on the assembly line, it is only done after the prototype has been fully tested. Most MIS systems are one-of-a-kind prototypes; the bottom-up testing approach has the disadvantage that nothing works (from the user's perspective) until the whole system works. An increasingly popular alternative is top-down testing, in which a skeleton of a system is built quickly and then fleshed out with additional program statements. This concept is discussed in more detail in a number of computer textbooks.[18,19]

Associated with this problem is the frustration that many MIS managers and end-users have with the early stages of a systems development project, the 35 percent spent on systems analysis and systems design. Many managers and users seem to view this suspiciously as a form of resting up, a prelude to the real work of the project: programming. Programming is tangible, in the sense that one can observe lines of code. If it is the official measure of productivity, then it is (by definition) the thing that people care about. Everything that precedes it (like systems analysis and design), and everything that gets in the way (like testing) tends to get short shrift. Unfortunately, this usually turns out to be a misguided view: extra work invested in systems analysis and design will usually reduce the amount of time spent testing a program. Studies by software engineers have found that 50 percent of the errors that are eventually found in a computer program are errors of analysis—i.e., misunderstandings between the systems analyst and the customer who asked to have the program developed.

THE CRISIS OF PREDICTABILITY

I observe that few (if any) software projects, somewhat independent of the issue of productivity, have an accurate budget or schedule. If the end-user and the MIS manager knew in advance how much it would cost to develop a new system—together with such related information as duration (timetable) and manpower requirements—then they might be prepared to accept it, even if the cost seemed extravagantly high. However, one of the most frustrating aspects of many MIS projects is that the initial estimates of cost, schedule, and manpower requirements turn out to be wrong by as much as a factor of ten. Indeed, even the estimates in the middle of the project (or the estimates provided on the day before the deadline!) turn out to be wrong.

I do not understand how a project manager can rationally develop a budget and a schedule for his project if he doesn't know how productive his people are. But, in fact, many efforts to estimate a project schedule are really thinly disguised exercises in negotiating the project schedule. The end-user and/or top management knows, at a fairly early date, when they will need the system in order for it to be at all useful; similarly, the project manager has a "ballpark" estimate of when he thinks it can be done. Somehow, the two dates (which may be radically different) are put together, and a compromise deadline, schedule, budget, and resource staffing schedule emerge.

By whatever form of science or magic this is performed in most organizations, the result is the same: it doesn't work. The vast majority of software projects are substantially over budget and behind schedule. This has been true since the late 1950s, and it continues to be true in the mid-1980s. The survey by Capers Jones showed that the average project was one year late and one hundred percent over schedule.[20] It is also worth noting that, throughout the industry, approximately 25 percent of all large software projects never finish; they quietly die away and are cancelled, buried, and forgotten.[21]

THE CRISIS OF QUALITY

The enormous amount of time spent on testing, and the enormously low productivity (which many feel is related to the time spent on testing), might be acceptable if the result were highly reliable, easily maintainable systems. The evidence of the past twenty-five years is just the opposite: the software produced by American programmers is riddled with errors, and is almost impossible to change.

"Riddled with errors" means different things to different people. On average, software developed in North America has between three and five errors for every hundred program statements, after the software has been tested and delivered to the customer.[22,23] A few exemplary systems development projects have reported as few as three to five errors for every 10,000 program statements;[24] and there have been recent pessimistic reports suggesting that American software may have as many as three to five errors for every ten lines of code.[25]

Software errors range from trivial to the sublime. A "trivial" error might consist of output (results) that are correct, but not printed or formatted quite as neatly and tidily as the user desires. A "moderately serious" software error might include a case where the program refuses to acknowledge certain kinds of inputs, but the end-user can find some way to circumvent the problem. "Serious errors" are those that cause the entire program to stop working, with an associated major loss of money or human life. Examples of some serious software-related errors that have been documented over the years include the following assortment:

- In 1979, the SAC/NORAD (Strategic Air Command/North American Air Defense) system recorded fifty false alerts, including a simulated attack whose outputs accidentally triggered a live "scramble."

- An error in the F16 fighter simulation program caused the plane to flip upside down whenever it crossed the equator.

- An F18 missile thrust while it was clamped to the plane, causing the plane to lose 20,000 feet.

- The train doors on the computer-controlled San Francisco BART system sometimes open on long legs between stations.

- A NORAD alert from the Ballistic Missile Early Warning System (BMEWS) detected the moon as an incoming missile.

- The Vancouver Stock Index lost 574 points over a twenty-two-month period because of roundoff errors—e.g., rounding off 3.14159 to 3.1416.

- On November 28, 1979, an Air New Zealand flight crashed into a mountain; later investigation showed that an error in computer course data had been observed and fixed, but the pilot had not been informed.

The list, sad to say, goes on and on;[26] many others are never reported because the "guilty" individual or organization would rather not make a public admission. There is now widespread concern that software errors of this sort could lead to grievous consequences with the Defense Department's "Star Wars" program, or with some of the other major, complex software-controlled air defense systems.[27]

In many cases, nobody is quite sure how many errors a system has because (a) some errors are never found before the system expires of old age; and (b) the process of documenting and recording the errors is so slipshod (as we will see in Chapter 30) that half the errors that are found are not reported, even within the MIS organization. In any case, the typical phenomenon of "error discovery," over the period of several years of useful life of a software system, usually takes the form shown in Figure 27.2.

The shape of this curve is influenced by a number of factors. For example, when the software is first released to the end-user, he is often unable to put it into full-scale production; it takes him a while to convert his old system (which may have been manual), and to train his clerical staff, etc. Also, he's a little wary of the computer, and doesn't want to push it too hard, so not many errors are discovered. As he converts his old operation over to the computer, and as his clerical staff is better trained, and as he loses his feeling of intimidation, he begins to push the software much harder, and many more bugs are found. Of course, if this continued indefi-

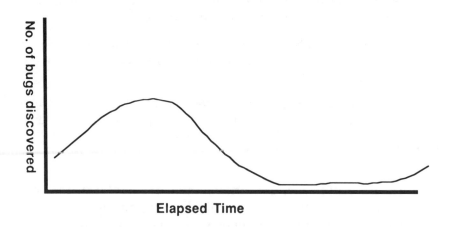

Figure 27.2: Errors Discovered as a Function of Time

nitely—more and more and more bugs found each day—the user would eventually stop using the software and throw it away. In most cases, the programmers are frantically fixing new bugs as users discover them. In most cases, there comes a time when the system begins to stabilize and the users find fewer and fewer bugs.

Unfortunately, there are three depressing aspects of Figure 27.2. First, the curve never returns to zero; that is, we almost never find a situation where time goes by without any new errors being discovered. Second, the area underneath the curve—which represents the total number of errors discovered over time—is atrociously high; as I pointed out above, it averages three to five errors for every hundred program statements. And third, the curve eventually, usually after several years but sometimes after only a few months, begins rising once again. Eventually, all software systems reach such a state of crazyquilt patchwork that any effort to fix one error will introduce two new errors, and the changes required to fix those two errors will introduce three new errors, etc.

There is one last crisis to point out about software errors: they aren't easy to fix. When someone—either the programmer or the end-user or some other intermediary—discovers that the software is not working properly, two things must happen: (a) the programmer must identify the source and nature of the error; and (b) he must find a way of correcting the error (either by changing some existing program statements, or removing some statements, or adding some new statements) without affecting any other aspect of the software's operation. This is not easy to do; in fact, the programmer has less than a 50 percent chance of success. Studies have shown that the chance that a programmer will successfully fix an error on the first attempt are an interesting mathematical function of the number of program statements that have to be modified.[28] This is shown in Figure 27.3.

As you can see, the programmer has about a 50 percent chance of success if he only has to modify five to ten program statements. If he changes only one or two statements, he suffers from overconfidence; his haste and sloppiness get the best of him. On the other hand, if he has to change forty or fifty statements, there are so many possibilities for errors (and also for insidious side effects and so-

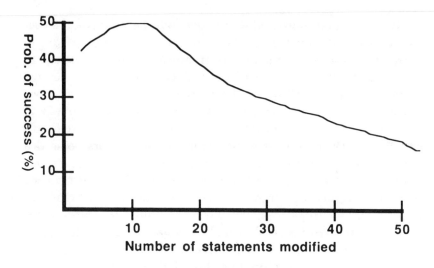

Figure 27.3: **Correcting Program Errors**

called ripple effects elsewhere in the program) that the chances of success drop to about 20 percent.

THE CRISIS OF MAINTAINABILITY

As we will see in Chapter 30, the correction of ongoing errors in a system is just one aspect of software maintenance. Maintenance also entails modification of a system to reflect changes in the hardware; or modifications to speed up certain operational aspects of the system; or modifications to reflect a change in the end-user's requirements of the system.

Software maintenance is a crisis in itself: it is too slow, too tedious, too errorprone, too boring, and too expensive. And it occupies too many of our software people: between 50 percent and 80 percent of the software people in the average software organization are involved in maintenance.[29] The result, in more and more MIS organizations, is that existing systems which were built ten or twenty years ago simply cannot be modified to meet the new demands of the government, or the economy, or the weather, or the fickle mood of the user. As our companies and our society become increasingly dependent on computers, we will find an interesting parallel: to the extent that software stagnates, the company or society served by the software will stagnate.

The problem is even worse than this. If it were simply a case of the software being bad, we could consider throwing it away and replacing it. But most organizations have never capitalized their software (the costs are expensed each year), and their accounting and business policies make it prohibitively expensive to replace ancient systems. And there is an even more fundamental problem: in most organizations, there is no coherent description of what the major software systems are doing. Whatever documentation exists is almost always obsolete and confusing. In any case, it provides—at best—some idea of how the software works, but not what its underlying purpose is, or what business policy the software is supposed to implement.

Consider the following analogy. All of the local town ordinances and local judicial codes that we live by in the United States represent a specific "how to" interpretation of the fundamental judicial philosophies laid down in the Constitution and the Bill of Rights. But suppose the Constitution were written in ancient Syrian, for which there are no living interpreters and no current dictionaries. Since the authors of the Constitution are no longer alive to advise us, it would make the job of modifying local town ordinances exceedingly difficult: nobody would know whether the new ordinances violated the Constitution. We would be tempted to throw out the old Constitution, organize a new Constitutional Convention, and begin anew. But the political uproar and the economic cost of throwing out two centuries of legal code would make it almost impossible.

THE CRISIS OF PROFESSIONALISM

All of the problems discussed in this chapter are compounded by the fact that many of the people working in the software profession have little sense of professionalism. The software industry is a community of amateurs, charlatans, fools, and rogues—and a very small number of people who work hard, who try hard, who care about the quality of their work, and who refuse to participate in organizations that encourage or tolerate slipshod software development techniques. Even these people are often in danger. The entire computer industry changes so rapidly that the true professional of the 1970s is totally obsolete today, unless he has invested considerable energy in studying ongoing advances in technology. The professional of 1985 will be obsolete in 1990. And so forth.

There are a number of professional societies that promote higher standards, better methods, and more effective communication between computer people and the rest of society; among them are the IEEE, ACM, DPMA, ASM, and ICCP.[9] These organizations also do an excellent job of keeping their members aware of important technological developments. They sponsor seminars, workshops, conferences, and colloquia to educate their members and debate important, controversial issues. Unfortunately, only a small percentage of the computer community belongs to those societies. Two researchers conducting a survey of software professionals observed that,

> Industry and academic studies of software specialists have been based on convenience samples that are not representative of the general software work force. For example, membership in professional societies is confined almost exclusively to academics and managers.[30]

Sadly, there is a general lack of interest in reading and education among those who spend their lives working with software. In 1980, Prentice-Hall editor Karl Karlstrom made the dismal observation that "if you took all of the copies of all of the books that have ever been published on computer science, you would have less than the

---

[9] For those not familiar with the acronyms: IEEE stands for Institute for Electrical and Electronic Engineers; ACM means Association for Computing Machinery; DPMA is the Data Processing Management Association; ASM is the Association of Systems Management; and ICCP is the Institute for Certification of Computer Programmers. Almost all of these societies have numerous special interest groups that concentrate on various issues.

number of computer programmers in the United States." The situation may have changed marginally since then,[10] but it is still true that the average programmer and systems analyst has less than a handful of computer books on his bookshelf, and he rarely subscribes to computer journals. Indeed, in many large MIS organizations that I have visited throughout North America, there is a circulation list even for free computer journals. I am not sure whether it is laziness or sloppiness that prevents each individual from placing his own subscription.

On a deeper level, the lack of standard terminology and metrics is dramatic evidence of a science that does not yet deserve to be called a science. As John Riganati and Paul Schneck, two researchers in the field of computer hardware, point out:

> The absence of complete and consistent taxonomies is one characteristic of an immature science. Computers and computer science must mature much more before a complete and consistent taxonomy emerges . . . .[31]

It is terrifying to think that so much of the human race is in the hands of a group of amateurs and alchemists. But take heart: it has happened before. In medicine and biology, in aeronautics and nuclear physics, in chemistry and economics, we have put our trust in people who basically didn't understand what they were doing. Serious, dedicated people in each of these sciences made it a science; there are a few dedicated people who think the same miracle can be repeated in the field of computer software.

---

[10] Keep in mind that an estimate like this eliminates the computer books sold to the general public, books sold to business people fumbling with their PCs, and university students. There was an unconfirmed statistic floating through the publishing industry in 1983 that the average first-time purchaser of a personal computer bought eight computer books along with his computer. With hindsight, this can be seen as an indictment of the terrible computer manuals that accompanied the computer, as well as an indication of the level of terror on the part of the consumer. Since then, personal computer manuals have gotten significantly better, and consumers have gotten marginally less terrified. And they have discovered that the computer books didn't answer many of their questions. The publishers and the bookstores learned this the hard way: their revenues from sales of computer books declined by some 20 percent from 1984 to 1985.

THE CHALLENGE FOR THE NEXT DECADE

Somehow, we must find a way to change the state of affairs in the software industry. We must change it drastically, and we must change it as quickly as the culture will allow. We need more than just a 10 percent improvement or a 15 percent improvement: we need between a factor of 100 and a factor of 1,000 improvement over the next ten years. This will be difficult to accomplish. It will be painful for many veteran programmers and systems analysts who are perfectly content with the methods they have been using to develop software for the past twenty years. It will be difficult for end-users who have grown accustomed to shoddy software and five-year backlogs. But we must bring about this improvement of two to three orders-of-magnitude. We must. If we don't, we will be replaced by the Japanese, or the Malaysians, or the Chinese, or the Irish, or some other group of people who have the willpower and the stamina to accomplish the change.

What we need, as should be evident from the discussion in this chapter, is:

- **More software**—so we can build more systems and reduce the enormous backlog in end-user organizations.

- **More quickly**—we need to be able to develop certain kinds of systems overnight, or even within ten minutes. We especially need to make simple maintenance changes—revisions and modifications that do not involve major functional changes—within a matter of minutes, instead of the current pattern of six months.

- **More economically**—computer hardware is now so cheap that it can almost be ignored as a factor in building many information systems; if it is not cheap enough, we know that we need only wait for a year for the price to come down. We need the same degree of economy with software. We should be able to focus all of our energies on deciding what problems we want to solve, and be able to almost ignore the cost of converting the problem definition into a working program.

- **With more reliability**— as we will see in Chapter 37, current computer hardware architecture was influenced by John von

Neuman's distrust of unreliable hardware components in the late 1940s; vacuum tubes and electromechanical components simply broke down and wore out too often. Now computer hardware is incredibly reliable; it's the software that is almost always the weak link in the system. We must change that. We need to build systems that have no more than one error for every million lines of code. Right now, the state of the art is one error for every 10,000 lines of code; the average is three to five errors for every 100 lines of code.

- **With more maintainability**— as we will see in Chapter 30, 50 to 75 percent of the software budget in most MIS organizations is devoted to maintenance. Software maintenance covers many sins: fixing errors that should never have been put into the software; making changes in the software because the hardware has changed; and making changes because the end-user has changed his requirements. By drastically reducing the number of errors, the cost of maintenance goes down. By drastically improving our methods for designing the architecture of software, we can reduce by at least a factor of ten the cost of incorporating new functional features in a program. By using more modern programming languages, we can also reduce by a factor of ten the cost of making trivial changes in a program.

- **With more predictable schedules and budgets**— if someone asks a professional, experienced contractor to build a house, the contractor can usually estimate the cost of the house within 5 to 10 percent, and he can determine, within 5 to 10 percent, how long it will take to build. We should be able to do that with software. Right now, our estimates are only accurate to within 50 to 100 percent at best, and often only to within 500 to 1,000 percent of the actual figures.

POTENTIAL SOLUTIONS TO THE CRISIS

Almost everyone agrees that there is a challenge before us. This is important, because until recently only a small group of fanatics within the software community (as well as a small group of truly professional MIS managers) were crusading for major improvements in productivity, quality, reliability, and maintainability of systems. Now end-users and top-level managers are joining the crusade. Who knows, maybe even politicians and Hollywood actors will get on the bandwagon.

The real question at this point is one of strategy: How on earth can we accomplish a thousandfold improvement in software? Or even a tenfold improvement? This is much more difficult to accomplish politically than it is in the hardware industry, because we have no track record of success. The hardware industry has already demonstrated its ability to build machines that are 1,000 times faster, cheaper, smaller, and more reliable than the machines of the 1940s; software people haven't done that yet.

This doesn't mean that we should believe every promise that a hardware designer makes; nor does it imply that hardware designers have unanimously agreed on a master plan for achieving yet another thousandfold improvement in hardware performance.[11] But there doesn't appear to be quite the same degree of anarchy and chaos in the hardware industry that we see in the software industry — perhaps only because the development of software in end-user organizations makes it so much more visible than hardware being developed in laboratories and research divisions of computer manufacturers.

Throughout the software profession, there are many ideas on how best to accomplish the thousandfold improvement that is demanded of us. The most popular approaches are these:

- More programmers.

- Better programming languages.

- Drastic improvements in software maintenance techniques.

- Software engineering methods.

- Automated development tools for programmer/analysts.

- Increased use of commercial packages.

[11] But they have publicly committed themselves to achieve this kind of improvement, as we will see in Chapter 37.

We will discuss each of these solutions to the software crisis in the following chapters. All of them should be explored by an MIS department that expects to help its end-user clientele survive in the 1990s.

References for Chapter 27

1. Kay, Alan, "Computer Software," *Scientific American*, September 1984.

2. *Webster's New World College Dictionary*, 2nd College Edition, New York: Simon & Schuster, 1980.

3. Jones, T. Capers, "A Software Productivity Survey," speech at First National Conference on Software Quality and Productivity, Williamsburg, Virginia, March 1985.

4. Orr, Ken, "Managing the Software Crisis," *Computerworld*, July 15-22, 1985.

5. "Software: The New Driving Force," *Business Week*, February 27, 1984.

6. Weil, Ulric, *Information Systems in the Eighties*, Englewood Cliffs, N.J.: Prentice-Hall, 1982.

7. International Data Corporation, *Market Data: 1985 IDC Briefing Session*, Framingham, Mass., 1985.

8. Jacky, Jonathan, "The Star Wars Defense Won't Compute," *Atlantic Monthly*, June 1985.

9. McClellan, *The Coming Computer Industry Shakeout*, New York: John Wiley & Sons, 1984.

10. Jones, T. Capers, unpublished talk, Boston, Mass.: Wang Computer Company, May 6, 1985.

11. Weil, *op. cit.*

12. Peters, Tom, and Nancy Austin, *A Passion for Excellence*, New York: Random House, 1985, page 242.

13. Weinberg, Gerald, *Understanding the Professional Programmer*, Boston: Little-Brown, 1980.

14. Boehm, Barry, *Software Engineering Economics*, Englewood Cliffs, N.J.: Prentice-Hall, 1982.

15. DeMarco, Tom, *Controlling Software Projects*, YOURDON Press, 1982.

16. Sackman, H., W.J. Ericson, and E.E. Grant, "exploratory, etc." *Communications of the ACM*, January 1968.

17. Boehm, *op. cit.*

18. Yourdon, Edward, *Managing the Structured Techniques*, 3rd ed., New York: YOURDON Press, 1985.

19. _____, *Techniques of Program Structure and Design*, Englewood Cliffs, N.J.: Prentice-Hall, 1976.

20. Jones, I., *op. cit.*

21. Jones, I., *op. cit.*

22.   Jones, I., *op. cit.*

23.   Yourdon, II, *op. cit.*

24.   Baker, F. T., "The Chief Programmer Team Project," *IBM Systems Journal*, January 1972. (Reprinted in *Classics in Software Engineering*, Edward Yourdon, ed., YOURDON Press, 1979.)

25.   Sanger, David, "Software Fears on Star Wars," *New York Times*, July 4, 1985.

26.   Neumann, Peter G., "Some Computer-Related Disasters and Other Egregious Horrors," *ACM SIGSOFT Software Engineering Notes*, January 1985.

27.   Jacky, *op. cit.*

28.   Yourdon, I., *op. cit.*

29.   Lientz, Bennet P., and E. Burton Swanson, *Software Maintenance Management*, Reading, Mass.: Addison-Wesley, 1980.

30.   Boehm, *op. cit.*

31.   Riganati, John P., and Paul B. Schneck, "Supercomputing," *IEEE Computer*, October 1984.

28

THE PROGRAMMER SHORTAGE

> Between the amateur and the professional . . . there is a difference not only in degree but in kind. The skillful man is, within the function of his skill, a different integration, a different nervous and muscular and psychological organization. . . A tennis player or a watchmaker or an airplane pilot is an automatism but he is also criticism and wisdom.
>
> Bernard de Voto
> *Across the Wide Missouri*, 1947

One of the interesting consequences of the current software crisis is a widespread perception that there is a severe shortage of programmers and systems analysts in the United States. Along with this perception, there is a widespread belief that career opportunities for computer programmers and systems analysts will be rosy through the rest of this decade and well into the 1990s.

While there is some basis for this perception, it is dangerously naive. As we will see below, there is a shortage, but a very special kind of shortage. And while there is a shortage this year, it is not at all clear that the shortage will persist through the end of the decade. Nature abhors a vacuum.

STATISTICS ON THE PROGRAMMER SHORTAGE

Widespread concern about the shortage of programmers first arose when the U.S. Bureau of Labor Statistics (BLS) began publishing

393

the results of 1980 employment statistics. The BLS estimated that there were 228,000 computer programmers and 205,000 systems analysts in the United States in 1980;[1] it estimated that the number of programmer jobs would grow by 49 percent between 1980 and 1990, while the number of jobs for systems analysts would grow by 68 percent. In less glamorous jobs, the BLS estimated that jobs for computer service technicians would grow by 93 percent, jobs for business machine repair technicians would grow by 60 percent, and jobs for computer operators would grow by 66 percent.

Of more concern to many in business and government is the possibility that there won't be enough programmers and systems analysts to fill those jobs. The BLS estimated, for example, that there would be a shortfall of 25,000 programmers and systems analysts each year from 1980 through 1990. A separate study by the National Science Foundation estimates that the United States "could be faced with a shortage of systems analysts and programmers, amounting to 115,000 to 140,000 workers in 1987."[2] The report went on to say that the projections for 1987 indicated that it would take a 25 percent to 30 percent increase in the number of computer programmers and anlaysts to meet the demand.¹ In summary, it said,

> Combining the projected requirements for systems analysts and programmers in 1987, 578,000 to 604,000 computer specialists will be needed. However, supply projections showed that only 462,000 to 466,000 qualified computer specialists will be forthcoming from schools and from immigration.[3]

To keep this in perspective, note that a number of other industries are also looking forward to tremendous growth over the next five to ten years. A recent job survey conducted by Stanford University, for example, estimated that there will be a demand for 200,000 new systems analysts by 1990—but it also estimated that there would be a demand for 600,000 new janitors. And while there will be a demand for 150,000 new computer programmers, accord-

---

¹ It is interesting to note that the NSF projections were based on an econometric model carried out by Data Resources, Inc. I will have more to say about such models in Chapter 37; however, given the frequent inaccuracies of many other econometric models, I am suspicious of this one.

ing to the Stanford survey, there will be a demand for 800,000 new jobs for kitchen helpers and workers in fast-food companies. Similarly, a report in *Time* magazine predicted that the two categories with greatest job growth in the 1980-90 timeframe will be secretaries and nurse's aides. So if you are a parent offering career advice to your child, keep in mind that the computer field is not the only one with optimistic growth projections.

Do these projections reflect the opinions and attitudes of data processing managers in the real world? That depends. It depends on the company, on the industry, and on the geographical location, among other things. There is a strong demand for computer programmers and systems analysts in such urban centers as New York, Washington, San Francisco, and Chicago; there is not so much demand in the rural areas of South Dakota and Indiana. There is often an urgent demand for additional computer programmers and systems analysts in fast-growing companies. For example, the recent merger of General Motors and EDS has led to an overwhelming demand for new computer technicians in that company. There is often a very strong demand in the leading-edge high-technology companies—e.g., the computer manufacturing companies, the new start-up companies in Silicon Valley, the personal computer software companies, etc. On the other hand, there is considerably less demand in stagnant industries, or in state government agencies whose budgets have been cut.

What is the significance of these statistics? As we saw in Chapters 16 through 22, and again in Chapter 27, there is currently an enormous backlog of new systems and applications waiting to be developed in most organizations (even the stagnant ones). From this, one naturally concludes that the backlog must indicate a shortage of programmers and systems analysts. And while most MIS managers will tell you that the long-term solution to the backlog is not adding hundreds of new programmers to the staff, they will only do so when they are calm and rational. Because of the pressure they are under, most MIS managers are never calm and rarely rational.

An MIS manager is not that different from other kinds of managers, or from politicians. When talking about vague generalities and the philosophies of life, he espouses very reasonable policies. But when someone is yelling at him—directly at him, while staring into his face—about a project that he is responsible for, things are very different; he begins to contemplate, for example, the personal consequences of a project failure. And, being human, he looks for explanations (sometimes known as excuses), and he looks for solutions (sometimes known as quick fixes). An obvious quick fix for the project that's behind schedule—or for the MIS department with a major backlog—is more programmers and more systems analysts.

"If only I had ten more programmers," the project manager will lament, "I could have this project finished on schedule." In the extreme case, this leads to something known as the "mythical man-month," after Fred Brooks's classic book by the same name.[4] That is, a project manager often falls prey to the illusion that people and time are interchangeable resources: by doubling the size of the project team, he hopes to cut the project time in half. It doesn't work that way in the computer field, nor does it work that way in most other industries. More than one project manager has learned that, in general, adding more people to a late software project just makes it later. But even if the project manager knows this, it's hard to resist the temptation. And it's hard to explain to higher levels of management, especially those who have no idea of what software is all about in the first place, why the project can't be speeded up by adding ten more people.

All of these factors contribute to the popular notion that there is a programmer shortage, and that it will get worse over the next five years. But as we will see below, the shortage is not what it seems.

THE NATURE OF THE SHORTAGE

The nature of the programmer shortage is very simple: it is a shortage of experienced people. There is no shortage of trainees; if anything, there is a glut. Not only that, experienced means, to most MIS organizations, more than just having survived in the industry for five years. The typical MIS organization wants someone with five years of experience in some specialty—e.g., banking experience, or insurance experience, or aerospace experience, or experience with military/DOD systems, or experience in the apparel industry. And it usually wants someone with several years of experience on the specific combination of computer hardware and software that it uses. While it is possible for someone with five years of experience on a DEC minicomputer to make the switch into a company with an IBM mainframe, the employer would much rather find someone who is already familiar with the IBM hardware and software combination that it has.

Thus, the job ads that you'll see in most newspapers will specify such specialties as the UNIX operating system, or the C programming language, or it will ask for veterans of the IMS database package, or the CICS telecommunications package. It will require experience on a specific model of Burroughs equipment, or DEC VAX computers. It will ask for an MS in chemical engineering in addition to five years of scientific programming experience in FOR-TRAN; or it will insist on an MBA, combined with five years of banking experience with COBOL. Only if such people can't be found will the employer begin to consider veterans with other specialties. In many cases, those veterans will be turned down, or will be offered a lower salary than they might have expected.

In any case, one thing is clear: the MIS organization has a relatively limited use for trainees fresh out of school. Some are necessary, of course; after all, old programmers eventually have to be put out to pasture, and a certain amount of fresh blood is needed. But many companies find that they have greater success converting other professionals (bankers, engineers, scientists, even secretaries and clerks) into the MIS profession than they do with newly graduated computer scientists.

In some cases, this is because the university training has little or nothing to do with real world requirements. The graduate with a BS degree in computer science has probably spent a considerable amount of time learning about theoretical issues; he has learned how to develop such systems programs as compilers and operating systems; he has learned how to write computer programs in half a dozen formal programming languages. But there is a good chance that he has gained only superficial knowledge of COBOL, the universally used business programming language. There is also a good chance that he has done little or no programming on an IBM computer, using IBM business-oriented software packages. And he knows little or nothing of the world of maintenance programming, which we will explore in Chapter 30. Thus, the typical MIS organization finds that three to six months of training are required before the new graduate can be turned loose; and one to two years of on-the-job training may be necessary before practical results are seen.

In other cases, the preference of the MIS organization for its own in-house people is not so much an indictment of university training as it is a recognition that business savvy is far more important than computer programming skills. After all, we have already seen, especially in Chapter 2, that nearly every high school graduate and every college graduate, regardless of his major field of study, has had some exposure to computers and computer programming. And the organization is already faced with the massive problem of making its white-collar workers comfortable with terminals, personal computers, fourth-generation programming languages, and a number of other tools that get the end-user directly involved in the systems development process. So, given that this is all going on anyway, it is easy for the average MIS organization to conclude that someone with five years of experience in the accounting department is going to be much more useful, with much less training, than a bright young college graduate who has never heard of double-entry accounting or general ledger systems.

The bottom line is rather grim: in 1983, American industry had job openings for 25,000 trainee graduates, i.e., people with a formal degree in computer science but no practical experience. But the American educational system turned out 50,000 graduates. Simple arithmetic will tell you that there are a lot of disappointed young men and women out there, wondering what happened to their dream career. You won't hear about this very often because the better graduates will continue to get jobs. Graduates of the Ivy League schools, and the top engineering schools, and the universities well known for turning out practical graduates (like Northern Illinois University, which has a reputation for turning out graduates who are better than most five-year veterans) will have no trouble getting jobs. But someone with an Associate degree from an unknown two-year school in an outlying rural area will find that it's a tough world out there.

There is one other area where the United States is facing a serious shortage: PhDs in computer science. These people are desperately needed for two reasons—one important, and one disastrous. The disastrous reason has already been discussed: because of the widespread perception of a programmer shortage, most university computer science programs are overwhelmed with applicants, so there is a cry for more PhDs to staff the faculty.[2]

The important need for PhD computer scientists is in research, both in industry, and in the universities. Because of the current popularity of such fields as artificial intelligence, advanced hardware design, and software engineering, many PhD graduates are being lured into industry at salaries of $75,000 to $100,000 per year, especially if they have acquired some practical experience during their undergraduate and graduate studies. This compares with teaching salaries of $20,000 to $30,000 in the universities. For the past ten years, the United States has produced an average of approximately 250 PhD graduates per year; in 1984, the figure was 268.[6] It is even more interesting to observe that approximately half of the PhD computer science candidates are foreign nationals—bright young men and women from Japan, India, Korea, China, Israel, Germany, England, Pakistan, and a dozen other countries. I leave it to the reader to contemplate the potential consequences of this phenomenon.

CONSEQUENCES OF THE SHORTAGE

As I pointed out at the beginning of this chapter, nature abhors a vacuum. Shortages don't last long in a supply-and-demand economy; there may be some violent short-term consequences of a shortage, but a variety of market forces eventually conspire to make the shortage go away.

[2] One survey reported that 10 percent of the 1984 high school graduating class in the United States expressed a strong desire to enter the computer profession, presumably as a computer programmer or systems analyst. There were 2,680,000 high school graduates in the United States in 1984;[5] it appears that more than a quarter-million children look forward to careers in the computer field, and the universities simply can't handle that load at the present time. Fortunately, as one of my professor friends has observed, 75 percent of them drop out along the way as they discover that a computer science degree represents real work. Even so, that translates into roughly 67,000 computer science graduates each year by the end of the decade, if the trend continues.

In the case of the programmer shortage—to the extent that it exists at all—there will definitely be some short-term consequences. Indeed, there already are such consequences, and they have been a part of the industry since I wrote my first computer program in 1962. How much longer the short-term consequences continue is anyone's guess, but it is evident that there are some major forces at work to change things.

Meanwhile, here is what we can expect:

- Artificially high salaries, and high turnover in the programming industry.

- Continued frustration in user organizations; continued large backlogs of unfinished systems.

- Enormous short-term opportunities for Third World countries.

- Growing interest in user-friendly programming languages.

- Increased emphasis on methods for making professional programmers more productive.

I will examine each of these below.

High Salaries and Turnover

American programmers and systems analysts are notorious job-hoppers; they change jobs, on average, every 1.4 years. As a recent survey of software workers pointed out,

> On the surface, job satisfaction is high. Ninety-two percent of our respondents said they were somewhat or very satisfied with their jobs. There was no overall difference in job satisfaction between men and women.
>
> Although the 92 percent satisfaction level appears high, American workers in virtually all occupations consistently report high levels of job satisfaction. . .
>
> A better indicator of job satisfaction is whether employees intend to change jobs in the near future. Thirty-six percent of the software specialists said they were somewhat or very likely to look for another job in the next year. Most of those who said they were expecting to

look for another job indicated they would look for a different job in the same field, indicating dissatisfaction more with their current job than with the software field in general.[7]

Another survey of 624 computer specialists found that 27 percent expected to look for a new job within the next year.[8] This kind of turnover is almost unheard of in Europe and Japan. True, some of this is due to basic cultural differences—but it's a lot easier to change jobs in the United States when programmers know there are others across the street who are probably willing to pay 10 to 20 percent more money, or provide a more challenging project, etc. Similarly, the annual employee turnover in the Australian software industry reached levels of 40 to 50 percent in 1985, largely because of the enormous demand caused by the sudden influx of sixteen new international banks.

It is this same supply-and-demand phenomenon that has made the cottage industry movement, discussed in Chapter 3, so important. In many professions, a worker feels locked in to the company he works for, or at least to the employment standards of typical companies in his industry. This is much less true for experienced programmers and systems analysts, especially those who have a "hot" area of expertise. Constant reminders in the "help wanted" section of their newspaper make them reconsider the possibility of becoming self-employed consultants. And the desire of progressive MIS organizations to keep their best people—especially in high-tech areas like Boston and Silicon Valley—makes it easier for a programmer to continue working as a normal employee without having the burden of having to drive to the office each day.

Frustration in User Organizations

As we saw in Chapters 16 and 20, the backlog in many user organizations is several years long. Though the shortage of programmers has kept the backlog from growing,[3] it certainly hasn't gotten any smaller. Thus, we are faced with grumpy, frustrated, impatient

---

[3] At least, it has kept the official backlog from growing. The unofficial and invisible backlogs may continue to grow as the users see new business opportunities, and new applications for personal computer systems.

users and equally grumpy managers of user departments. To the extent that they gradually realize that the competitive position of their entire company depends on their ability to implement coherent, integrated information systems quickly, the grumpiness will escalate into higher and higher levels of the organization.

This means that we can expect more turnover among higher-level MIS management positions either because top management got fed up with what they regarded as excuses, or because the MIS manager got fed up with his inability to get the capital-investment perspective supported by top management. Turnover among top-level MIS managers is no better and no worse than in any other key department of an organization: sometimes it is enormously healthy, and other times it is a disaster. Many organizations will churn and thrash for the next several years as they try to find top-level MIS managers who can bring order out of chaos.

Opportunities for Third World Countries

We have already discussed the opportunities for Third World programming enterprises in Chapters 25 and 27. Many countries are already working diligently to take advantage of this window of opportunity that the American software industry has so generously provided.

There will continue to be an opportunity for Third World countries as long as the software industry in the United States is regarded as a sloppy, error-prone, labor-intensive "art," one whose "artisans" can pack up their tools and work for the company across the street whenever they get bored with their present employer.

Most serious MIS managers agree that the current state of affairs cannot continue much longer. The American software industry, I hope, will become enormously more productive and quality conscious, largely through the adoption of software engineering techniques and automated tools discussed in Chapters 31 and 32. If not, one or more other countries will have developed a strong software industry by the early 1990s that will use software engineering methods and automated tools to provide high-quality products and a competitive price.

In any case, the days of "wetback labor" in the software industry are numbered. Today it is possible for any country to provide a boatful of programmers just outside the limits of American jurisdiction; desperate users can row out to the boat with their specifications, and row out again the next day to pick up their finished systems.[4] But within a few years, there will be high-quality, low-cost software factories all over the world, ready and able to provide finished systems at an attractive price.

Interest in User-Friendly Programming Languages

In 1928, Mercedes Benz commissioned a market survey and was told by experts that the total world demand for its automobiles would never exceed 10,000. The reason: the limited number of available chauffeurs. Similarly, some organizations are either being told explicitly or implicitly by their MIS organizations that that there is an upper limit to the number of developed systems they may have because of the lack of available programmers and systems analysts.

In the automobile industry, there was an alternative to the Mercedes paradigm well before 1928: Henry Ford. Mr. Ford made it possible—and temptingly attractive—to become one's own chauffeur. Even today, many of the radio and television commercials concentrate on how much fun it is to drive a car; the ads spend much less time describing the functional advantages of the automobile as a method of moving from point A to point B.

Similarly, many software vendors are busily convincing endusers that they can be their own computer chauffeurs, and that it is fun to write computer programs. I really doubt that most users would willingly choose this way to have fun—sex, alcohol, fishing, and pizza come to mind as preferable alternatives. But if the user must have an information system, and if the MIS organization cannot or will not build it for him, then he must build it for himself, and he might as well think that he is having fun in the process.

Whether or not you respect this somewhat cynical point of view, you must admit that it has some validity. In any case, it is making a

---

[4] This is not just a wild metaphor. A Japanese software house recently approached a major bank in San Francisco and offered to provide just that: a boatful of Japanese programmers just outside San Francisco harbor.

lot of money for some software companies, and it is lowering the threshold of pain in some organizations. Some systems are being built that would never otherwise be built.

I will discuss the issue of user-friendly programming languages in more detail in Chapters 29. As I already pointed out in Chapter 17, there are many situations where a user can get himself into terrible trouble by writing his own computer program on a personal computer, just as there are many times when an untrained driver can wreak havoc upon himself and several innocent bystanders. User-friendly programming languages are not the solution to all of the MIS backlog, but they will enjoy a certain amount of popularity as long as that backlog exists.

Efforts to Increase Programmer Productivity

This, in my opinion, is the long-term solution to the perceived shortage of programmers. All of the other solutions discussed above have merit. And some of the solutions may offer long-term relief for certain classes of problems—e.g., Third World programmers for the maintenance programming that will continue to burden us for the next twenty years, and fourth-generation languages (4GLs) for the class of simple problems that users can solve on their own. But the best solution for the important class of complex information systems, in the long run, is to make our existing professional computer programmers and systems analysts substantially more productive than they are today.

There are several ways to accomplish this. One is to give them better programming languages; this I will discuss in Chapter 29. Another approach is to find some way of relieving the burden of maintaining old computer systems—a job which consumes 50 to 70 percent of the people resources in many MIS organizations; I will discuss this in Chapter 30. Still another approach is a collection of methods and techniques known as software engineering; this will be discussed in Chapter 31. And finally, a number of automated system development tools have become feasible now that the cost of hardware has dropped to the point where we can realistically consider putting a powerful workstation on every programmer's desk; this subject will be discussed in Chapter 32.

But all of this will only work if it can lead to a massive increase in the productivity of today's computer programmer and systems analyst. A factor of ten is the minimum we can accept. Actually, it would be more appropriate to say that it is the minimum that the user community will accept before they begin to turn away from the other solutions discussed above. A factor of 100 improvement will eventually be necessary if we intend to continue developing computer software as an industry in the United States; for if we do not, surely other, more ambitious nations will.

References for Chapter 28

1.   Wallace, John, "Where to Find Jobs," *Family Computing*, October 1984.

2.   Betts, Mitch, "NSF Predicts 1987 Shortage of Analysts, Programmers," *Computerworld*, August 13, 1984.

3.   *Ibid*.

4.   Brooks, Fred, *The Mythical Man-Month*, Reading, Mass.: Addison-Wesley, 1975.

5.   *Reader's Digest 1985 Almanac*, page 198.

6.   Informal discussion with the dean of the department of computer science at Northern Illinois University, April 1985.

7.   Kraft, Philip, and Steve Dubnoff, "Software Workers Survey," *Computerworld*, November 14, 1983.

8.   "Computer People: Yes, They Really Are Different," *Business Week*, February 20, 1984.

29

PROGRAMMING LANGUAGES

It is impossible to dissociate language from science or science from language, because every natural science always involves three things: the sequence of phenomena on which the science is based; the abstract concepts which call these phenomena to mind; and the words in which the concepts are expressed. To call forth a concept a word is needed; to portray a phenomenon, a concept is needed. All three mirror one and the same reality.

Antoine Laurent Lavoisier
Traite Elementaire de Chimie, 1789

Computers are called upon to do many things, and getting a computer to do something requires that the underlying process be described, on some level, with enough precision to be carried out by the machine. Thus, computer scientists have devoted much of their talent and energy to developing powerful descriptive formalisms. One might even say that computer science is wrongly so called: Most of it is not the science of computers, but the science of descriptions and descriptive languages. Some of the descriptive formalisms produced by computer science are exactly what are needed to get a handle on the process of learning a physical skill.

Seymour Papert
Mindstorms[1]

A programming language is more than a notation for giving instructions to a computer. A language and the software that "understands" it can totally remake the computer, transforming it into a machine with an entirely different character. The hardware components of a typical computer are registers, memory cells, adders and so on, and when a programmer writes in the computer's native language, these are the facilities he must keep in mind. A new language brings with it a new model of the machine. Although the hardware is unchanged, the programmer can think in terms of variables rather than memory, of files of data rather than input and output channels, and of algebraic formulas rather than registers and adders. A few languages even give the computer a split personality: it becomes a collection of independent agencies that do their own calculations and send messages to one another.

Lawrence G. Tesler
"Programming Languages,"
Scientific American, September 1984

There are over 400 known programming languages in use in North America and Europe, and probably many others in Eastern Europe and Asia that we never see. New programming languages are born every day; old ones gradually fade away into oblivion, leaving behind the detritus of old code whose meaning becomes more and more vague to disinterested maintenance programmers.

Programming languages are a source of great joy, and also of great frustration, for professional programmers. In this context, programmers are like professional writers, struggling to achieve clarity and elegance, passion and humor, wit and charm—while using verbs and nouns and a grammar over which they have no control. If they are lucky, they can put all of these building blocks into an elegant computer program, which nobody outside of their professional ranks will appreciate properly. To the rest of the human race, all the programmer has done is to write a program—"only a program." Jane Austen must have been a programmer at heart; she expressed similar feelings about the solitary, bittersweet experience of writing a novel,

"Only a novel" . . . in short, only some work in which the greatest powers of the mind are displayed, in which the most thorough knowledge of human nature, the happiest delineation of its varieties, the liveliest effusions of wit and humor are conveyed to the world in the best chosen language.

Jane Austen
Northanger Abbey (1818)

Programming languages are also a source of intense debate among the computer scientists who invent them.[1]

Inventors of one language are notorious critics of other languages and passionate champions of their own. University professors are fond of making statements like those of Edsger Dijkstra, "If FORTRAN can be considered an infantile disorder, then PL/I must be classed as a fatal disease." Similar rude remarks have been made about COBOL, Ada, BASIC, and most other popular programming languages just as the English, French, Americans, and Spanish insult one another about their native tongues.

But I can safely assume that you, the reader, are not in the business of inventing new programming languages. It is more likely that you are in the business of using a programming language to earn your living or to solve some problem on your personal computer. Or perhaps you are trying, as an MIS manager or a businessperson, to gain some understanding of why programming languages matter so much, and what is likely to happen to them over the next ten years. Or perhaps you're not interested in the computer field at all (in which case I congratulate you for having suffered through twenty-nine chapters of this material) but your fourth-grade son or daughter has told you that it is absolutely imperative that you learn BASIC or Logo.

With this in mind, I begin by summarizing the reasons why programming languages are important to us, and how the nature of

---

[1] In this respect, programming languages are fundamentally different from spoken languages like English or French. We can invent new programming languages on a daily basis to suit our whim, without consulting anyone or asking anyone's permission. But we humans could also invent new spoken languages if it suited us; it might turn out that nobody else understood us, but we might find new verbs, new nouns, and a new grammar to be very useful in forming certain ideas. For most of us, though—programmer and nonprogrammer alike—languages are inherited, passed down to us from an older generation. We modify them ever so slightly to deal with new situations, but we rarely question the foundation on which the language was built.

the programming languages influences our ability to solve programs and develop useful software. I will then review several of the popular programming languages and offer some predictions about their likely future.

THE IMPORTANCE OF
PROGRAMMING LANGUAGES

The details of a computer programming language, and the decision to use this language or that, are indeed important. As Lavoisier and Papert point out so eloquently, language is inextricably linked to the underlying scientific concept or physical process we are trying to manipulate on a computer; and, as Tesler observes, the programming language allows the programmer to form a mental model of the machine—the computer—that he is working with.

If we work with a primitive, weak programming language, we tend to build primitive models in our minds; we then translate those models into primitive, unsophisticated computer programs. If we work with a powerful programming language—one that allows us to create abstractions that usefully highlight certain aspects of the problem we are grappling with—then we can create models that are spare but elegant. If we have a programming language that allows us to hide the ugly, mechanical details of the computer that we use, then we have some hope of modeling the problem in such a way that the model can be executed directly on the computer. We want a programming language that allows us to model accounting problems in a form as close to the reality of accounting as possible, and a programming language that allows us to model the intricacies of nuclear physics in the same words and terms that nuclear physicists use when communicating with one another.

There is more: we want a programming language that encourages clear thinking, and which discourages sloppy, muddleheaded thinking. In spoken languages, we sometimes favor the fuzzy, the ambiguous; it is sometimes pleasing to realize that the same word or phrase might be interpreted a dozen different ways.[2] When developing software, or when trying to articulate some subtle, complex scientific phenomenon, this won't do.

Before we examine specific programming languages, keep one thing in mind: a good programming language does not guarantee that someone will write good programs. Conversely, a bad programming language does not make it impossible to write good programs. Some of the most elegant algorithms and brilliant programs were written in primitive second-generation "assembly language," and some of the most stomach-turning programs have been written in sophisticated, high-level programming languages.

The issue is one of influence: a primitive, weak, informal programming language encourages sloppy thinking and poor programming habits; we will see examples of this in FORTRAN, BASIC, and COBOL below. A formal, rigorous programming language with well chosen "constructs" encourages the programmer to think in algorithmically precise ways. If, for example, the programmer wants the computer to repeat a set of instructions, a language like Pascal will encourage him to precisely formulate the actions that should be carried out before the repetition begins, the actions that should be carried out at the end of each repetitive iteration, and the conditions that determine when the repetitive process should terminate. Sloppy languages like COBOL, BASIC, and FORTRAN blur these issues, and, even worse, provide no encouragement for the programmer to think about the issues at all.

THE FOUR GENERATIONS
OF PROGRAMMING LANGUAGES

Just as there are epochs and eras in the history of major civilizations, there are epochs and eras associated with the computer field. We refer to generations of computer hardware to distinguish between computers built from vacuum tubes, transistors, integrated circuits, etc. And we also refer to generations of program-

---

[2] *New York Times* columnist Russell Baker once casually reversed a common phrase and observed that, at times, "A word is worth a thousand pictures."

ming languages. Two of the generations are dead, and can be forgotten by almost everyone (except a few unlucky maintenance programmers); two of the generations are very much alive; one generation is on the horizon, but not yet available to us.

First-generation programming languages were the machine languages used in the 1950s; programmers wishing to make a computer do something useful would code their instructions in binary ones and zeros.[3] There are still times today when a faulty computer system disgorges pages of mind-numbing digits; and there are a few misguided youths who think that machine language is the best way of playing with personal computers. But the rest of the world stopped thinking about machine language some twenty-five years ago.

Second-generation languages are, as one might guess, the successor to machine language; they are generally known as assembly languages, or assembler or BAL (for Basic Assembly Language). Second-generation languages are low-level languages in the sense that the programmer has to write one statement for each machine instruction. Thus, while he might conceptually think in terms of the statement $X = Y + Z$, he would have to write the following statements in assembly language:

CLEAR ACCUMULATOR

LOAD X INTO ACCUMULATOR

ADD Z TO CONTENTS OF ACCUMULATOR

STORE ACCUMULATOR IN X

Even this tiny example demonstrates the major disadvantage of assembly language. Rather than being able to think in terms of the problem that he wants to solve, the programmer must think in terms of the machine. Starting around 1960 more powerful lan-

---

[3] Sometimes programmers used "octal" notation or "hexadecimal" notation to compress the information into more convenient units. The octal digit 7 is equivalent to the binary number 111, etc. Since a typical computer instruction on early computers required 12, 24, or 36 binary digits, it was much more convenient to deal with 4, 8, or 12 octal digits. But it is even more convenient not to have to deal with numbers at all!

guages began to be introduced; most sane programmers have long since abandoned assembly language. Unfortunately, there are still a few situations where such languages are needed. Most of them involve very small, low-power computers (which can be manufactured very cheaply, and which are small enough to fit, say, into a digital watch) that do not have the capacity to tolerate the "overhead" associated with higher-level languages. Thus, the computers that control fuel mixture and emissions on your car are probably programmed in assembly language; the software for your home banking system, on the other hand, was probably programmed in a higher-level language, because it runs on an adequate-sized personal computer, which is connected to an enormous mainframe computer.

Third-generation languages are the norm today; they include BASIC, COBOL, FORTRAN, Logo, Pascal, and many others. They are high-level in the sense that a single statement (such as "MOVE A TO B" in COBOL) usually represents five to ten assembly language statements; they are high-level in the more important sense that they allow the programmer to express his thoughts in a form that is somewhat more compatible with the problem area in which he is working. However, they are low-level in some important respects. They require the programmer to become intimately involved in the tedious business of formatting the layout of computer reports, editing and validating input to the program, and organizing the data with which the program works. Often the programmer will think to himself, "This report should have the standard heading at the top of each page, with a page number on the right and the date on the left," but he may have to write twenty or thirty program statements to accomplish it.

Third-generation languages are also characterized as procedural languages. They require the programmer to think carefully about the sequence of computations—or the procedure—necessary to accomplish some action. In a scientific application, for example, the progammer may know that he wants to add array A to array B; however, he may be forced to write the procedural steps to add each element of the two arrays, rather than simply saying, "Add these two arrays" without having to worry about the procedural steps.

Fourth-generation languages are the current rage and are considered by some computer consultants to be the most important development in the software field in the past twenty years. Some of them have been in existence for nearly a decade, but they have only become popular in the past few years. Examples of fourth-generation languages are FOCUS, IDEAL, MARK IV, RAMIS, MANTIS, MAPPER, and dBASE-III. Most are associated with database management software packages that make it extremely easy to create complex files, retrieve selected records from the file, and produce reports quickly and easily. The advantages of fourth-generation languages, or 4GLs, are easier to understand after we have learned more about the more common third-generation languages.

A SURVEY OF THE POPULAR
THIRD-GENERATION LANGUAGES

A thorough review of all of the third-generation programming languages would fill several volumes. It would also put reader and author into a coma from which neither would ever recover. Most of the programming languages that are available today are too obscure to bother discussing. In fact, approximately 80 percent of all of the business-oriented programs ever written for computers were written in COBOL; about 80 percent of all the engineering and scientific programs were written in FORTRAN. Clearly, we need to look at these two languages. And there are about half a dozen other languages that everyone, amateur and professional programmer alike, should be aware of.

FORTRAN

FORTRAN is one of the oldest of the third-generation languages, having been developed at IBM in the late 1950s. It is used primarily for engineering and scientific applications—the acronym FORTRAN stands for FORmula TRANslation—though fanatics have occasionally used it to write payroll systems and other business applications. It has some strong advantages:

- It is widely taught in universities to engineering students, science students, economics students, and others who have to use a computer for their coursework. Hence there are literally millions of professional engineers and scientists around the world who may not know very much about serious programming but who can read and write FORTRAN.

- There is a version of FORTRAN on virtually every mainframe and minicomputer in the world. The vast majority of microcomputers and personal computers also have FORTRAN available, though not all.

- There is an enormous library of scientific programs that have been developed in FORTRAN over the past twenty-five to thirty years. In many cases, it is not necessary to know anything about the FORTRAN language in order to be able to use the programs—one just has to supply the appropriate parameters in order to get results.

- Many FORTRAN compilers,[4] and some of the mainframe supercomputers have been developed to make FORTRAN programs run as efficiently as possible. This is very important for scientific applications that carry out millions upon millions of arithmetic calculations.[5]

Unfortunately, FORTRAN has a number of weaknesses, too. Among the more important ones are these:

- The language does not permit meaningful names for program elements or data elements. Most versions of FORTRAN restrict programmer-chosen names to six characters; hence there is a tendency to see lots of names like GRP46Q and FLMPH7.

- The older versions of FORTRAN (which many people still use, and in which much of the libraries of scientific subroutines are

[4] A FORTRAN compiler is a program (usually provided by the computer hardware vendor) that will translate any FORTRAN program into the machine language for a specific computer. There are, in a like manner, COBOL compilers, PASCAL compilers, etc.

[5] See Chapter 36 for a discussion of computer applications that require more powerful hardware than that which is currently available.

written) do not provide convenient facilities for describing IF-THEN-ELSE decision sequences, nor do they provide adequate facilities for describing a repetitive sequence of instructions; in short, the structured programming constructs are lacking.[6] Consequently, many FORTRAN programmers organize their programs without thinking about these fundamental logic sequences in an orderly way; their program logic is built with GOTO statements, and is usually extremely hard to follow.

- Most versions of FORTRAN provide very primitive data types: integers, floating-point numbers, and characters. This is adequate for conventional numerical calculations, but not for general-purpose programming, where we need the ability to form complex data objects: lists, arrays, records, etc.

- The language is not strongly typed. That is, the programmer is not required to declare the type of data that he manipulates in his program; indeed, he is not even required to formally declare his variables. Thus, the FORTRAN programmer can write the statement

$$K = A + J$$

without ever indicating what kind of information variable A and J contain, nor how the resulting sum should be represented in variable K. If the information is not specified (and FORTRAN programmers quickly get used to the fact that they don't have to bother specifying such tedious details), then the FORTRAN compiler will automatically assume that variable J contains integer data (i.e., whole numbers like 14 or 789), variable A contains floating-point data (e.g., 3.14159) and that the resulting sum should be stored as an integer in variable K.[7] This may be fine most of the time, but these unspoken defaults have been the cause of many subtle programming errors over the decade.

[6] Structured programming is discussed in Chapter 31.

[7] By default, variables whose names begin with the letters I, J, K, L, M, or N are assumed to be integers. This can lead to confusing situations: the statement I = 3.14 will cause the integer 3 to be stored in variable I.

- Local variables are provided in a very primitive fashion. FOR-
TRAN programmers have a tendency to make widespread use
of variable names like A, B, X, Y, I, and J. This may be because
the programs they write often mirror the mathematical equations they used to solve the underlying scientific problem.
Unfortunately, the same A, B, X, and Y are used in several
different parts of the program for different purposes; this can be
a source of great confusion and many subtle errors. It is roughly
the same as if everyone in your family used the same hand-held
calculator and left it on all the time. If you picked up the
calculator, you wouldn't know for sure whether some other
family member was in the middle of a long calculation when he
got called away to the phone. Maybe the number showing in the
display panel of the calculator is the result of hours of hard
work, which you're about to destroy when you press the "clear"
button. For an extra dollar or two, you can give every family
member his or her own calculator; and in FORTRAN, it should
be possible for every chunk or block of program logic to have its
own A, B, X, and Y variables, even if each block uses the same
name. It can be done in FORTRAN, but only in a limited,
clumsy way.[8] Other languages provide far more powerful, far
more convenient facilities for this important aspect of programming.

BASIC

As a form of entertainment or social intercourse between consent-
ing adults in the privacy of their own homes, I have no criticism of
BASIC. But as a public form of social intercourse, or as a vehicle for
teaching computer literacy to innocent children, I think it is a
disaster. Teaching children BASIC is like showing them X-rated
movies. They aren't ready for it. They can't handle it. BASIC
should be abolished from the schools and banished from the land.[9]
    Why do I dislike BASIC so much? Is it really that bad? Is it a

[8] The way to do it is to make each block of FORTRAN code a separate subroutine. Aside
from the verbosity and general clumsiness of this approach, it also takes much more CPU
time and memory: a subroutine call must be made to invoke the block of code.
    [9] A student of mine in an Amsterdam seminar reported to me in March 1985 that Norway
had recently abolished BASIC from their educational system. I have not been able to confirm
this yet; if it is true, it may be the Norwegians who win the software wars of the 1990s!

Communist threat? Well, no, of course not. I have written BASIC programs with productive results, and the experience has not caused blindness or syphilis. But I knew what I was doing at the time (at least I think I did); I knew what to watch out for in BASIC; and I used it only when I had no alternative. Unfortunately, BASIC is not presented in that perspective to most children or owners of personal computers.

From a technical point of view, BASIC has many of the same weaknesses and limitations as FORTRAN. Indeed, some versions of BASIC are even more limited: they require the programmer to use no more than two characters (the first of which must be a letter) to name his variables—e.g., A7, QQ, or B9. Heavy emphasis is put on "line numbers" (although a line can have more than one BASIC statement, and a BASIC statement can extend past the end of one line onto another—very confusing!) rather than "labels" or "names." This is an enormous perversion; it virtually destroys any interest the programmer might have had in top-down design. With a top-down approach, the programmer breaks the original problem into subproblems, which are further decomposed into sub-sub-problems, etc. Thus, if the programmer were developing a payroll system, he might write the following code:

```
WHILE MORE-EMPLOYEES = 'YES'
    BEGIN
    CALL GROSS-PAY-CALC-ROUTINE
    CALL TAX-CALC-ROUTINE
    CALL OTHER-DEDUCTIONS-ROUTINE
    CALL NET-PAY-ROUTINE
    CALL PRINT-CHECK-ROUTINE
    END [10]
```

Unfortunately, BASIC does not provide a facility for calling subroutines by name. The programmer would have to write a

---

[10] This is not a real payroll system, nor is it written in a real programming language. I have presented it here only for illustrative purposes.

statement like GOSUB 4380, where 4380 is the line number where the subroutine begins.

A great many useful programs have been written in primitive languages like FORTRAN, and virtually every mainframe computer is equipped with FORTRAN; however, FORTRAN has the advantage of being so unfriendly that children don't learn it. BASIC has a syntax, a vocabulary, that is somewhat less alien, and thus has the disadvantage of being learned easily. It is widely touted as an easy language, and unfair pedagogical comparisons are made between BASIC and other elegant languages like Pascal. Worse, it is usually implemented as an interpretive language, rather than a compiled language.[11] This means that as soon as the innocent user types a BASIC statement, it will be executed right in front of him, thus providing instant gratification. Worst of all, BASIC is provided as a built-in, hard-wired language on virtually every available personal computer in North America, Europe, and most other civilized parts of the world. When you turn on a bare-bones personal computer (one that has no floppy disk and no other peripheral input/output devices), BASIC starts running. Thus, for a school that has a limited budget for computer literacy, BASIC becomes the language of choice. Yechh!!!

COBOL

Most, but not all, of the bad things that I can think of to say about FORTRAN are also true of COBOL. This is not surprising, because COBOL was invented at about the same time as FORTRAN. One must admire Commander Grace Hopper and her colleagues at the U.S. Navy for having done such an admirable job nearly thirty years ago—but times have changed, and we now expect much more from our programming languages.

In some ways, COBOL is superior to FORTRAN. It allows long, meaningful data names so that one can refer to a piece of information in the computer as STATE-TAX-RATE. It has a complete IF-

[11] An "interpretive" version of a programming language runs about ten times more slowly than a compiled version, for reasons that you either know already or that you can learn by asking a programmer. Hence you won't see many interpretive versions of "serious" languages like COBOL and FORTRAN. For "serious" BASIC programmers, there are BASIC compilers for almost all available computers.

THEN-ELSE statement, and it has a slightly more powerful facility for constructing a sequence of instructions to be executed repetitively (the PERFORM-UNTIL statement). It requires the programmer to declare the nature and size of all his variables, and is thus more "strongly typed" than FORTRAN.

On the other hand, the problem of local variables is present with COBOL, just as it is with FORTRAN. And while the PERFORM statement facilitates the top-down decomposition of a complex problem into smaller pieces, it does so clumsily. It allows the programmer to invoke a subroutine (in COBOL terms, a paragraph or SECTION) without explicitly specifying what data will be provided to the subroutine to do its job, or what data the subroutine will furnish to its caller when it finishes. Since the language doesn't require it, the programmer is not encouraged to think very carefully about the issue . . . especially because all of the data used anywhere in the program can be accessed by any COBOL statements anywhere in the program.

Probably the worst thing about COBOL is its verbosity. Instead of being able to write $X = Y + Z$, one must say COMPUTE $X = Y + Z$. And while almost all programming languages provide five different ways of doing some task, COBOL probably provides fifty. This is important, because it means that "dialects" of the COBOL language can develop; the programmers in Des Moines may be using a subset of COBOL entirely unknown to the programmers in Albuquerque. Indeed, with "rich" languages like COBOL and PL/I, surveys show that programmers use less than 10 percent of the verbs and constructs that the language offers—very much the same way that people use only a tiny subset of the English language to communicate. With English, though, we have an advantage: we all watch the evening national news program, so we all see examples of a neutral, accentless pattern of speech that we know will be understood in every city across the land. With COBOL, this doesn't apply. You may never see the Des Moines dialect until you get transferred there by your boss and set to work in the maintenance department.

Whatever its faults, though, COBOL is a major force in the software industry. Approximately 80 percent of all the business-oriented programs ever written have been written in COBOL. This means, somewhat superficially, that approximately 80 percent of all the business-oriented programmers who have ever existed speak COBOL. The language itself is slowly evolving: a new standard (which remedied some of the shortcomings listed above) was introduced in 1974, and is still being debated in 1985. Because of the enormous problem of modifying old programs and retraining old programmers, many MIS organizations are doing their best to delay the introduction of the new version of COBOL.

Logo

Logo is one of the more exciting languages to appear on the scene. It is not entirely new: it is based on a research project that has been going on since the early 1970s at MIT. However, it has only been widely distributed and discussed outside the university environment for the past three to five years. Versions of Logo now run on almost all popular personal computers; dozens of books and educational programs have been developed, though Papert's *Mindstorms* is clearly the genesis of everything that has appeared in the past few years. Use of the language is widespread in many American, European, Canadian, and Australian schools, though it is restricted primarily to the lower grades, with BASIC making its ugly appearance around the fifth or sixth grade.

Logo is an apparently simple language, one that succeeds far better than BASIC at enticing a novice into using the computer without being frightened. It has many of the features of the languages already discussed, and it can be used to write serious programs. However, its primary emphasis is on graphics, and its primary use is education. Most of the Logo commands involve a small (usually triangular) object known as a "turtle," shown in Figure 29.1; at the beginning of a Logo program, the turtle is displayed in the center of the CRT screen.

The turtle can be instructed to move forward a specified number of "turtle steps," drawing a line as it goes; for example, "FORWARD 10" makes the turtle draw a line roughly one inch long. There are commands to make the turtle go backwards, turn left or right (e.g., "LEFT 90" makes the turtle turn 90 degrees to the left), erase a line that has already been drawn, or pick up its imaginary pen (and thus move about the screen without leaving a trace). With

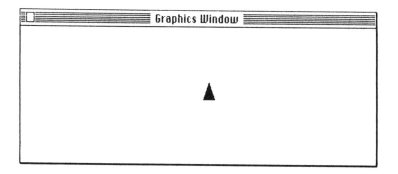

Figure 29.1: **The Logo Turtle**

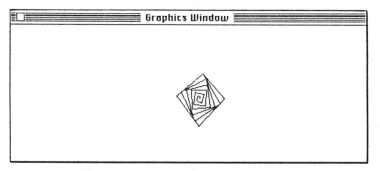

Figure 29.2: **A Typical Logo Diagram**

these very simple building blocks, young children can begin draw-ing boxes and triangles within a matter of minutes; within a few days, they can create drawings like the one in Figure 29.2.

Logo has the wonderful virtue of being very friendly. If the programmer makes a mistake, the Logo interpreter typically says something like, "I don't know how to X," where X is the unintelligi-ble command that the programmer has typed. This is far less threatening than a message that says, "SYNTAX ERROR 143; CORE DUMPED." At the same time, it is a very powerful program-ming language: it has subroutines (procedures), structured pro-gramming facilities,[12] and even recursion (subroutines which can

[12] Structured programming is discussed in Chapter 31.

invoke themselves). In fact, the diagram in Figure 29.2 was created by a program that invoked itself recursively. Here is the Logo program.

```
to spiral :size :angle
   if :size > 1
      [forward :size  right :angle
         spiral :size-2 :angle]
end
spiral 50 93
```

Figure 29.3: **A Logo Program**

So, children (and adults) who learn Logo have an opportunity to learn the best programming habits available (assuming that the teacher has some idea of what to emphasize). Even without being consciously tutored, many children instinctively practice some of the concepts of top-down program design. At the same time, the nonthreatening, friendly nature of the language encourages children to try things that they might not understand completely and that they might do incorrectly the first time. In most cases, the manifestation of their error is a drawing that did not turn out as they wanted; the remedy is to undo the mistaken activity and try again. By contrast, an error in a program written in a typical third-generation language will cause the entire program to stop, and will usually produce one or more cryptic, nasty messages that will make the novice programmer think he has caused irrevocable damage.

Pascal

Pascal was developed in the early 1970s by one of the fathers of software engineering, Niklaus Wirth. It was originally designed as a pedagogical tool, a language for teaching university computer science students about programming and software engineering. But it has grown to be a very practical language in industry. It is a widely taught programming language in colleges, and it is taught at the

12th-grade level in some high schools; students can take an advanced placement test in Pascal on their College Board exams.

The language itself is very similar to a language called ALGOL that was developed around 1960 and used widely in Europe (and on Burroughs computers in the United States). Pascal addresses virtually all of the problems mentioned in the earlier discussion of COBOL, FORTRAN, and BASIC (ugh); indeed, the language makes one embarrassed to write a sloppy, poorly designed program.

However, the Pascal language was obviously not designed with the real world in mind. The official language does not have any facilities for dealing with real-time issues of interrupts, signals, and timing. Thus, the engineering/scientific community is somewhat reluctant to use Pascal for developing aerospace, command-and-control, and process control systems. And the language has little or no facility for producing business-oriented reports, nor does it provide any assistance to the programmer who wants to develop an on-line transaction-oriented system (e.g., an order-entry system, or a billing system); hence business programmers are not enamored of the language.

The most unfortunate aspect of Pascal is its reputation as a language that is difficult to learn—in contrast to BASIC, which is regarded as an easy language to learn. In fact, both languages are either easy or difficult, depending on how they are presented and whether the student is required to learn almost everything about the language before he can do anything useful. Many Pascal textbooks are very serious in tone, and intimidate the casual reader; BASIC textbooks, on the other hand, often imply that one can begin writing useful programs after reading one page of the first chapter. Both extremes are unrealistic: one can learn a subset of Pascal quickly and gradually absorb some of the more sophisticated features of the language; and one can eventually find a way to write serious programs in BASIC, even though the language is aimed at amateurs and idiots.

C

C was developed in the early 1970s by Dennis Ritchie at Bell Laboratories; it is inextricably linked to the UNIX operating system, which is discussed in Chapter 31. For a long time, the C language was only available on machines that ran the UNIX operating system, but now it is much more widespread. Virtually all personal computers and minicomputers have some version of the C language available; and most mainframe computers have C also, though it tends to be used mostly on the smaller computers.[13]

In some respects, C is like Pascal; it has many of the structured programming features that BASIC, COBOL, and FORTRAN lack. On the other hand, it has been described as "Pascal that is not afraid to get its hands dirty"—that is, it lets the programmer get away with "dirty tricks" that would not be possible in Pascal. Pascal is a pedagogical language primarily concerned with enforcing good programming habits; C is a language that encourages good programming habits but which allows the programmer to violate all the rules if necessary. This is particularly attractive to people working on projects of the sort normally associated with assembly language, as discussed earlier—programmers who want to ensure that their programs are efficient and make maximum use of the available hardware resources.

Ada

Ada is a programming language created by the U.S. Department of Defense (DOD) as the "language of the 80s" to replace the myriad programming languages used in the 200 to 300 million lines of code already written. Over the years, DOD has developed, championed, sustained, or tolerated innumerable programming languages (which in many cases the rest of the civilized world has not had to endure—JOVIAL and CMS-2 are just two examples); the most notable example is COBOL, which DOD sponsored in the late 1950s.

Ada is named after the Countess Ada of Lovelace, a companion of Charles Babbage (father of the "analytical engine," the forerunner of the modern computer). It was developed in the late 1970s through a series of competitive design contests sponsored by DOD,

---

[13] C is a great language for "Trivia" fans: it is an improvement on an earlier language, B, which was a subset of an even earlier language called BCPL (Basic Control Programming Language).

and it became an official language in 1982. DOD has mandated that all systems developed after January 1, 1984, be developed in Ada; however, there are enough exceptions and loopholes that it will probably not become the official language of the DOD until the end of the decade. Even if all new DOD systems were programmed in Ada, the maintenance and enhancement work on old systems would keep the old languages alive for several more years.

As a programming language, Ada has many of the features of Pascal. It strongly encourages the programmer to write a formal, well-defined, well-engineered program. It has features that Pascal lacks: real-time features that allow the programmer to deal with signals and interrupts, as well as packaging features that allow the programmer to encapsulate programs and data into separable units that can be reused elsewhere. On the other hand, purists argue that Ada has the primary disadvantage of PL/I, a third-generation language foisted upon the industry by IBM in the late 1960s: a language so rich, so verbose, that several hundred distinct dialects are possible. Just as a citizen of Hunan province might not easily understand a resident of Kowloon—even though both are, to the casual observer, Chinese—so an Ada program written by a Hunan programmer might not be understandable to a Chinese programmer in any other part of the world.

It remains to be seen whether the might and the pocketbook of the American Defense Department can truly establish Ada as a significant language. At the present time, Ada is important within the DOD community, and among the aerospace companies and the government contractors who service DOD; to the rest of the computer software community, Ada is about as significant a language as Esperanto.

LISP

LISP is the granddaddy of programming languages for artificial intelligence applications. It was developed by Joseph McCarthy and Marvin Minsky in the early 1960s at MIT and Stanford. FORTRAN provides a number of facilities for dealing with arithmetic and scientific manipulations; COBOL concentrates on the manipulation of business-oriented data items; but LISP concentrates on data items as "items of knowledge" that are linked to other items, which are linked to other items, and so forth. In FORTRAN, the object of interest might be a scientific formula in which the primary components are real numbers that are related to one another through some mathematical relationship; in COBOL, the object of interest is a customer record (or patient record, or employee record, etc.) in which the components are elements of information about that object; but in LISP, the object of information might be some abstract entity like an English sentence, in which the components are nouns and verbs.

LISP is not used by the vast majority of professional programmers in the United States; in fact, it is safe to say that 95 percent of the programmers in the United States have never seen a LISP program. However, 99.9 percent of all programmers involved in AI are familiar with LISP (though more and more are beginning to favor a more modern variant known as Prolog). To the extent that AI eventually becomes a popular concept within the business world (the premise of Chapter 21), LISP will become a more widely understood language.

COMMENTS ON THE FOURTH-GENERATION LANGUAGES

The vast majority of computer programs written today—indeed, the programs that are being written now, even as we communicate through the pages of this book—are being written in a third-generation language. If you work in a business organization, the programs being written in your MIS organization are almost certainly being written in COBOL; if you work in an engineering organization, then FORTRAN is the language being used. If you work in an educational institution, then you might see Pascal, Ada, Logo, or some of the other languages discussed in this chapter.

However, the fourth-generation languages are rapidly coming to play a major role in business organizations. They would play a major role in scientific organizations, too, but scientists and engineers tend to be strongly opinionated (at least insofar as their dealings with computers are concerned): they think they know everything, and they think that computer hardware resources are so precious that they should be preserved at all costs. Hence what we will see over the next ten years is the continuation of FORTRAN programs by engineers and other scientific programmers, and the gradual shift toward fourth-generation languages by business programmers.

Many people will argue that the shift should take place sooner, and that scientific programmers who defend FORTRAN (and business programmers who defend COBOL) should be shot or sent to work at the (shudder) U.S. Post Office. But there is one sad fact to keep in mind: in most organizations 50 to 80 percent of the work involves fixing, enhancing, improving, and upgrading old programs written in an old programming language. The only solution is to rewrite the entire program in a more modern language.

The fourth-generation languages have a number of advantages over the older languages:

- Most of them contain the "structured programming" features that FORTRAN, COBOL, and BASIC lack.

- Many of the tedious programming details associated with getting data into the computer (via the keyboard) are hidden from the programmer. With one simple command, the programmer can specify that the computer should accept a specified kind of data from the keyboard, validate it (i.e., check to make sure it is of the proper type and/or within the proper numerical range), and store it in a designated area of memory. The same job might require 10 to 20 statements in a third-generation language, and 100 statements in a second-generation language.

- Similarly, many of the tedious programming details associated with producing an "output report"—e.g., an inventory listing, or paychecks, or invoices, or a summary of the day's orders —are handled automatically by the fourth-generation language. If the precise placement of information on the computer printout is relatively unimportant (as is often the case), the programmer does not even have to specify it; otherwise (as in the case of a computer-produced paycheck, where dollar amounts must be printed in a precise position), the details are easily specified in a few programming instructions.

CONCLUSION: WHAT LANGUAGES SHOULD YOU LEARN?

If you have been patient enough to read through this entire chapter, you may still be wondering what it means to you. If you are a professional programmer, of course, you probably have strong opinions already about programming languages—and you probably either agreed strongly or disagreed strongly with my views. But if you are an end-user, or an MIS manager, or someone uninvolved with computers, what conclusions should you draw from this lengthy discussion of programming languages?

Let's deal with the professional software community first—the computer programmers and their managers. My strong feeling is that anyone programming in assembly language today should be given a lobotomy; and any MIS manager who forces his programmers to work in assembly language should be shot. Immediately.

Assuming that you and your cohorts are using a conventional third-generation language like COBOL or FORTRAN, you must begin developing a strategic plan for moving to a more productive environment over the next five to ten years. You won't be able to do it overnight; there are too many old programs that must continue to be maintained in COBOL and FORTRAN (more about this in Chapter 30), and there are so many programmers to retrain that it can't be accomplished in one fell swoop. But unless you and your organization begin planning for something better—e.g., code generators, fourth-generation languages, software packages like Meta-COBOL, etc.—now, you'll still be plodding along in COBOL in 1992.[14] As part of this strategic plan, you should periodically monitor the U.S. Defense Department's success (or lack of success) with Ada; the language itself may turn out to be irrelevant in the long run, but the Ada support environment could eventually make it well worthwhile to gradually drop COBOL (or FORTRAN, etc.) and move into the Ada world.

---

[14] If you show this to your boss, and he jumps on top of his desk and shouts, "We'll never abandon COBOL! Never!!" then you should take it as a sign. God is speaking to you. God is telling you to update your resume and move on to some other organization that is not quite so determined to remain in the Dark Ages.

If you are an end-user of software, you may feel that you can ignore all of this. You can. But remember that you are paying for software, even if you don't write it yourself. There is no such thing as a free lunch. If your MIS department is still programming in assembly language, or if it is determined to stick with COBOL into the 21st century, it's costing you a lot of money. Ask your MIS people what they think about all of this, and listen carefully to their answers. Don't accept a lot of mumbo-jumbo. Don't let them tell you that it's none of your business. Don't let them tell you that it's too technical, and that you wouldn't understand. If you've understood most of what you've read in this chapter, then you understand the issues. If your MIS people don't understand—or if, as is more likely the case, they don't want to deal with the difficult problem of retraining their people—then you should fire them. If you can't fire them, ignore them. Let them wallow in their own mess. Meanwhile, find someone else who will develop software for you in modern programming languages.

If you are simply an ordinary citizen, you may be even more tempted to ignore all of this discussion about programming languages. But as you've probably noticed, it isn't easy: everyone is telling you that you need to learn how to program in BASIC in order to be computer literate. Balderdash! If you've learned enough about electronics to repair your TV set, and if you've learned enough about auto mechanics to repair your automatic transmission, then maybe you should consider learning to program. Otherwise, stick to programs that someone else has written. Whatever it is that you want to do on a computer, someone has already written a $99 program that will do it better, faster, and more accurately than you could.

If you really must learn about programming, I hope you will do me the courtesy of staying away from BASIC. The country already has enough brain-dead people; don't join their numbers. (Keep your kids away from BASIC, too; put them in a different school if you have to.) I recommend Logo as an easy, low-stress, educational, fun programming language. I strongly recommend that you first read Seymour Papert's *Mindstorms* before you learn Logo. It will give you a feeling for the decade of work and love and inspiration that went into that language, and it will give you an appreciation of the awesome pedagogical power of such an apparently simple language.

With Logo, you must realize that you probably won't accomplish anything practical. Purists will bristle at this apparent insult. Okay, I give up: if you insist, you can probably even write the software for the space shuttle control program using Logo. But if you really want to write a payroll program or an inventory control program, or even a game program (e.g., a better version of Pac-Man), I think you would be far better off learning a language like Pascal. There are many books that will teach you the elements of the Pascal language, while also teaching you the elements of good programming style, all without overwhelming you with intricacies of computer science that you don't want to know. One of the better books, in my opinion, is written by Tim Wells.[2]

References for Chapter 29

1. Papert, Seymour, *Mindstorms*, New York: Basic Books, 1980.
2. Wells, Tim, *A Structured Approach to Building Programs: Pascal*, New York: YOURDON Press, 1986.

30

THE MAINTENANCE ICEBERG

Up to now, the key computer professional was someone who could learn enough about the needs of organizations to express them in computer language. In the future, as our society becomes irrevocably computerized, the key professional [will be] someone who can learn enough about computerized systems to express them in human language. Without that someone, we [will] have lost control of our society. That someone is the reverse engineer. Software maintainers are the reverse engineers of society.

Nicholas Zvegintzov, publisher,
Software Maintenance News

Maintaining a computer program is one of life's dreariest jobs. For most American programmers, it is a fate worse than death. They dread it . . . no, that is not quite right. It is not that programmers are afraid of maintenance, but rather that they look upon it as demeaning work. To be called a maintenance programmer is to be called a second-class citizen. A junior programmer must put up with this, because that is all he is offered; but as soon as he has enough experience and/or seniority, he looks for ways to remove himself from this form of indentured servitude. If his employer won't help him, he quits.

Yet software maintenance is one of the most common jobs in the software world. Between 50 percent and 80 percent of the software work done in most organizations is associated with the revision, modification, conversion, enhancement, or debugging of a computer program that someone else wrote long ago. It is expensive work: in the early 1970s, the Defense Department reported that the cost of developing computer programs on one project averaged $75 per computer instruction (or line of code); the cost of maintaining the system ran as high as $4,000 per instruction.

To put this into even more vivid terms, consider the following examples from the U.S. Social Security Administration:

- Calculating the cost-of-living increase for 50 million recipients of Social Security benefits takes 20,000 hours of computer time on older computer systems within the Social Security Administration.[1]

- When the Social Security Administration upgraded its computer systems in 1981 from five-digit checks to six-digit checks, it required 20,000 man-hours of work and 2,500 hours of computer time to modify 600 separate computer programs.[1]

- The morale in the Social Security Administration maintenance group was so bad at one point that one of the programmers was caught urinating on a disk pack. Disks don't function very well in that kind of environment.

Before you laugh too loudly at this, remember that the Social Security Administration has one of the better MIS organizations in the country. They deal with gargantuan volumes of data, and they work in a political environment that defies imagination—but they get the job done, and they get the checks out each month. I don't think I could say this about the maintenance departments in most of the banks, insurance companies, automobile manufacturers, and government agencies I visit in the United States.

The thesis of this chapter is very simple: software maintenance is a troublesome activity that is largely ignored by MIS managers; worse, it is largely unknown to the people above the MIS organization. Most of the problems associated with maintenance are management problems. And if the problems are left unmanaged, then maintenance will gradually grow to consume all of the resources, all of the energy, and all of the people in an MIS organization.[1]

---

[1] This is based on a principle of General Systems Theory: the larger a system becomes, the more of its energy must be devoted to maintenance.

There will be no people left to develop new systems. And then, gradually, the people involved in the maintenance effort will leave, not only because it is boring, but because the very existence of the work is evidence that management doesn't care about quality work. The maintenance programmers will go somewhere else, hoping to find a company that will not damn them to eternal maintenance work, and the organization they leave runs the serious risk of having its computer systems come to a screeching halt. Or, more realistically, it will find that it simply cannot make any further changes in its computer programs, so it will be unable to respond to government regulations, new computer hardware, or new market conditions.

The purpose of this chapter is to explain the nature of software maintenance, and to suggest some ways of reducing the burden that it places on most organizations. Almost everything in this chapter is very simple and straightforward: one of the features of software maintenance is that it does not (yet) have much of the "razzle dazzle" flavor of high technology associated with it.

THE NATURE OF SOFTWARE MAINTENANCE

One of the major problems with software maintenance—as with many other aspects of the software crisis—is that every MIS organization seems to think that its problems are unique. Another problem is that many organizations keep few or no records on their maintenance work; they don't know how much time and money they spend, or what kind of work the maintenance effort entails.

For this reason, it is extremely useful to see large-scale surveys of MIS organizations. One of the best such surveys in the field of software maintenance was conducted by two UCLA professors in 1980. The results were published in a slender volume that has unfortunately not attracted much attention in the industry: *Software Maintenance Management*.[2] If you are a maintenance programmer or a manager of maintenance programmers, you should get this book. If you are an end-user whose information systems are being maintained by those scruffy rascals in the MIS department, you should buy the book for them and force them to read it. You might even read it yourself, to get an interesting picture of the maintenance effort in 487 U.S. computer installations.[2]

Overall, the survey found that the average organization spends 50 percent of its software budget on maintenance-related activities; some organizations spend as much as 70 to 80 percent of their budgets on maintenance. There is usually a strong correlation between the percentage of the budget spent on maintenance and the number of years the company has been using computers. A company that just began using computers two or three years ago typically spends most of its money developing new systems, while the companies that began computerizing in the early 1960s now spend almost all of their money on maintenance.[3]

One of the most interesting statistics provided by the survey was a breakdown of the maintenance dollar in the average MIS organization. Figure 30.1 shows the major maintenance categories. Note that a total of 21.7 percent of the maintenance budget was spent correcting errors, either in emergency mode or as part of the 9:00 to 5:00 humdrum of everyday work. We can translate this into dollar figures in the following way: the computer industry accounted for approximately 8 percent of the GNP in 1985; of that, roughly half was spent on software.[4] In turn, Lientz and Swanson report that roughly half of the software expenditure was for maintenance, and 21.7 percent of the maintenance was spent fixing errors. Since the 1985 GNP is estimated to be $3,948 billion[4] it means that we are spending roughly $17.13 billion each year fixing software errors.[5] This is about $72.89 per year for every man, woman, and child in the United States.

The other maintenance categories in Figure 30.1 are fairly straightforward. At first glance, it is encouraging to see that nearly

---

[2] For another, more detailed view of the economics of software maintenance (as well as additional comments on the Lientz & Swanson work), see Barry Boehm's classic tome, *Software Engineering Economics*.[3]

[3] There are exceptions to this. Some new organizations have enormous systems that they have inherited from other divisions, or from outside software vendors. In such cases, there may be little or no development work; everything consists of modifying inherited or purchased packages.

[4] These statistics were presented in Chapter 23.

[5] This is only a rough approximation of the cost of software errors. By using the figure of 8 percent of the GNP to estimate software expenditures, we ignore the software written internally within end-user companies.

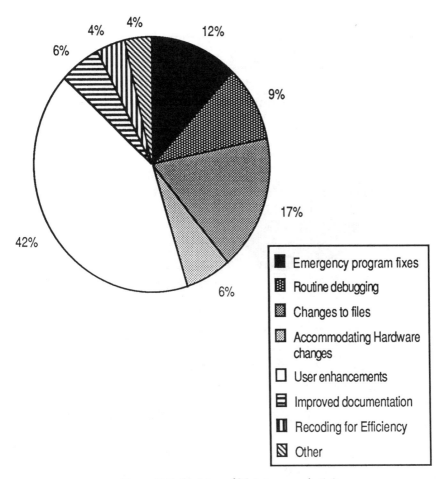

Figure 30.1: **Division of Maintenance Activity**

half of the maintenance budget was spent on user-requested improvements. However, it is not clear from the survey (nor could one hope to obtain the information in any straightforward way) how many of the improvements were legitimate. Many of the so-called improvements were probably made because the systems analyst (or the programmer) and the end-user didn't understand one another when the system's requirements were first specified.

Let us assume for the moment, though, that all of the user-requested improvements were legitimate. Figure 30.2 shows a fur-

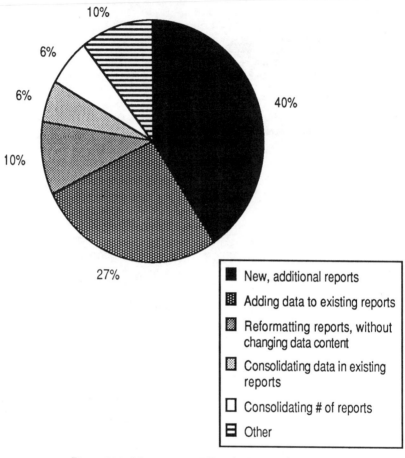

Figure 30.2: **Maintenance Effort for User Enhancement**

ther breakdown of just a portion of the maintenance dollar. Note that almost 90 percent of the user-requested improvements are concerned with the nature of the output reports produced by the computer system. Only 10 percent of the improvements involved "functional" changes—e.g., additional computations, additional forms of input, etc.

Some additional statistics from Lientz and Swanson provide an interesting view of the world of maintenance:

- The amount of code in a system grows by approximately 10 percent each year; the database grows by roughly 5 percent.

Software systems are not static; they grow steadily. One can almost imagine COBOL statements copulating with each other in the middle of the night and producing new little baby COBOL statements.

- One-third of all systems are maintained by a single person; another one-third are maintained by two people. This is more significant than it might seem at first glance. It often turns out that that solitary individual is the only person in the organization with intimate knowledge of the workings of the system. There is little or no written documentation, and often very little control over the physical safety of the programs themselves. Stories abound of grumpy maintenance programmers who, after asking for a promotion and a transfer for years, only to find that they are doomed by management to remain on the same maintenance project forever, quit abruptly, leaving behind no copies of the computer program or any other documentation.

- Slightly under 50 percent of the people involved in the maintenance of a computer program were involved in its original development. At the other extreme: a study conducted by the British computer manufacturer, ICL, indicated that some programs are maintained by ten generations of programmers before they (the programs and the programmers) collapse.[5] The tenth maintenance programmer is engaged more in archaeology than computer programming.

Lientz and Swanson also reported some fascinating statistics on the manner in which software maintenance is managed. The numbers below show the percentage of organizations that could say "Yes" to the associated statement of policy.

78.9%   All user requests for changes to an application system must be logged and documented.

32.9%   All user requests for changes to the application system must be cost-justified.

51.3%   All troubles enountered in the operational processing of an application system must be logged and documented.

77.0%   All changes to the application programs must be logged and documented.

58.5%   All changes to the application program must undergo a formal retest procedure.

28.1%   Except for emergency fixes, all changes to application programs are batched for periodic implementation according to a predetermined schedule.

32.1%   A formal audit of the application program is made periodically.

33.5%   Equipment costs for operating and maintaining the application system are charged back (in whole or in part) to the end-user.

30.8%   Personnel costs for operating and maintaining the system are charged back (in whole or in part) to the end-user.

These figures basically document a state of utter anarchy that exists in the majority of maintenance departments within MIS organizations. In general, people don't keep track of errors and bugs; they don't test their programs after modifications; they don't make the users financially responsible for the operation or maintenance of the software they use; they don't use their outside auditing firm (e.g., the accounting firm that prepares their annual statement) to ensure that things are under control. Given this chaotic state of affairs, it's a wonder that anything is successful in the world of software maintenance.

STRATEGIES FOR IMPROVING
SOFTWARE MAINTENANCE

What can be done to alleviate the maintenance mess? In a word: lots! But improvement can only come if the situation is recognized as a real problem, and if everyone—the programmers, the MIS managers, and the end-users—understand that real money must be invested, and that real care and concern have to be invested in the maintenance of computer software. Everyone knows that machinery needs constant lubrication and overhaul; most people are willing to invest in preventive maintenance for machinery and computer hardware. But software is somehow perceived differently: once the computer instructions are written, they are not supposed to wear out. And indeed they don't; a COBOL or FORTRAN statement can continue executing indefinitely. But the circumstances and assumptions that led to the writing of that COBOL or FORTRAN statement do change, and that, in turn, necessitates the changing of the program statements.

Here are some of the things that can be done to improve the maintenance situation in a typical MIS organization:

- **Develop a strategic plan for maintenance improvement.** The situation won't improve overnight, no matter how much money is thrown at the problem. But a five-year, or ten-year plan can be developed to gradually attack the worst systems, gradually introduce tools and techniques of the sort described below, and gradually change personnel policies to make the job more attractive. Such a plan can be developed by any MIS group with common sense and dedication; the plan can be audited or evaluated by an outside consulting firm, or even the company's auditors. But without a plan, and a commitment for change, nothing much will happen. The plan—like all strategic plans—should include a situational audit to let everyone know how bad (or good) things are. It should establish long-term goals, objectives, and priorities. It should include a return-on-investment so everyone knows what the effort will be worth. It should include plans for a survey and study of available tools and technology, as well as a survey of personnel policies and management procedures for improving maintenance. And it should include a timetable and list of assignments that will ensure that someone gets the job done.

- **Let the user make his own maintenance changes.** As we saw earlier, approximately 90 percent of the user-requested improvements to a program are relatively trivial data-oriented changes that do not involve the functionality of a program. When the user asks for such a change in a typical company, he is told by the MIS department that it cannot be done for six months (or longer), and that it will cost $50,000 (or more). This strikes the user as patently absurd, and it is, given today's software technology. If the original version of the program is developed using any of the fourth-generation programming languages discussed in Chapter 29, it should be possible for anyone—either the programmers in the MIS organization, or the end-user himself—to make the change in a matter of minutes. In this kind of environment, the user can make the change himself with less effort than it takes to describe the change to the programmers. As we saw in Chapter 17, this requires a certain amount of training, but it is easy and straightforward.

- **Use documented evidence to discover "high-risk" modules.** Software maintenance is an excellent example of the Pareto Principle: 80 percent of the work is usually associated with 20 percent of the code in a computer program. Indeed, for many large systems, 90 percent of the work is often associated with 5 percent of the code. If the manager in charge of the maintenance effort can find out which 5 percent is causing all of the work, he can choose among several intelligent options: he can assign his best people to work on that critical 5 percent; he can scrap the code and rewrite it; etc. But as we saw earlier, many maintenance organizations keep no records of operational problems with their systems and thus they have no way of knowing where to focus their efforts.

- **Use complexity theory to identify high-risk modules in advance.** The suggestion above is an after-the-fact, reactive solution to a common maintenance phenomenon. A far more rewarding approach is to find out in advance where the problems are going to be. If the MIS manager can see at the end of the design phase of a project that the proposed design of the program will lead to serious maintenance problems later on, he can at a relatively modest cost ask his technical people to look for a simpler design. Numerous studies have shown that it is much cheaper to make changes early; one such study[6] demonstrated that a correction made before formal testing was eighty times cheaper than after formal testing, and twenty times cheaper than the same change made during the formal testing phase. A number of mathematical models of program complexity have been developed over the past decade; these can be used to determine whether the program will be difficult for the average human brain to comprehend. If so, the development programmer will have trouble getting the program to work in the first place, and the maintenance programmer will have trouble modifying it. Several complexity models are discussed in detail by Boehm[7] and DeMarco;[8] we will discuss the subject again in Chapter 31.

- **Use economic models to determine when old code should be replaced.** There is always a tradeoff between replacing an old software system and continuing to make "just one more change." The tradeoff is conceptually the same for software systems as for any other kind of system. We make these tradeoffs every day in our personal life (should we replace the transmission in the old car, or trade it in for a new one?) and in our business career. The problem with software is that the "hard numbers" have not been readily available. How much will it cost to replace an old system? What will the maintenance characteristics of the new system be? And how much will it cost to continue maintaining the old system this year, and next year, and the year after? But statistics and mathematical models are beginning to appear;[9] a responsible MIS manager is obligated to study them and apply the models to his own systems. He is obligated even more to present the economic tradeoffs to higher levels of management. Replacing an old, large, complex system is a multimillion dollar exercise for many organizations—but the return on investment is probably staggeringly higher than any other investment that top management is contemplating. It certainly beats investing the company's liquid assets in T-bills.

- **Use automatic restructuring tools to improve bad code.** One of the biggest headaches for many maintenance programmers is that they simply don't understand the "flow of control" in a program they've inherited: the program logic jumps from one page to another in such a disorganized fashion that anyone trying to follow it quickly gets lost or goes stark raving mad.

"Structured" code, on the other hand, has the desirable property of being readable in a linear, top-to-bottom fashion.[6] Any program can be translated into an equivalent structured program; mechanical algorithms for accomplishing this have been known for at least ten years.[10,11] There are now several companies in the United States that will automatically translate existing unstructured code into equivalent structured code. Some will even allow the MIS organization to transmit its "dirty" code over a telecommunications link; "laundered" code is sent back within a day or two. The cost for this service ranges from 50 cents to $2 dollars per line of code.[12]

- **Make use of software tools for better documentation and organization.** Sometimes the maintenance problem is even more severe than unstructured code: there may be no documentation available to help the maintenance programmer. One of my first programming jobs, while I was still a student at MIT, was that of maintaining the PDP-5 assembler program for Digital Equipment Corporation. The original program had been written by one of DEC's salesmen (that's a story in itself, but I'll spare you . . .) who left the company shortly thereafter. One of his last official acts was to give the program listing to his secretary, requesting that it be typed as a memorandum. Goodness only knows what the secretary thought of this mindless work; in any case, subsequent investigations confirmed that the memo was at best a rough approximation of the real program. This was more difficult to ascertain than you might think: the salesman either lost or destroyed the program listing and the source program containing intelligible program instructions. I had only the object program consisting of the binary ones and zeros that the computer actually executes. I would have given anything for a disassembler that can turn object programs back into source programs. I would have given almost anything for a program that could analyze the program and produce a flowchart. These and many other related documentation programs have been available in the industry for a decade or more. A maintenance

---

[6] Structured programming is discussed in more detail in Chapter 31. A detailed example of a computer program that does not flow in a linear fashion is also given.

programmer who does not have these tools available is being forced to work in a substandard, subhuman environment. He should immediately demand such tools; if they are not forthcoming, he should quit. Pronto.

- **Look forward to AI technology to improve maintenance.** In Chapter 21, we discussed a number of business applications for the emerging field of expert systems. One of the more promising applications for expert systems is in software maintenance; after all, it is a form of medical diagnosis that is not very different from the conventional medical applications addressed by such programs as MYCIN. A veteran maintenance programmer realizes that he is dealing with a situation involving uncertainties and fuzzy reasoning. He develops rules of judgment that help him decide whether or not to attempt a certain kind of modification to an existing program. These rules of judgment could be incorporated into an expert system—an AI program that could also incorporate the complexity models discussed earlier. Such a program could effectively say to its owner, "I think we can implement the new feature that the user wants by making the following change to subroutine XYZ. However, there is only an 87 percent chance that it will work successfully, and there is a 13 percent chance that the change will cause some problems elsewhere."

PEOPLE-ORIENTED SOLUTIONS

If you read the beginning of this chapter carefully, you may have concluded that the battle to improve software maintenance was already lost. As is true in so many aspects of the computer revolution, the key is not technology, but technology transfer. The solution to many of our problems is not to buy more computers or invent new forms of computer science, but rather to change the attitudes and thought processes of the people doing the work.

This is particularly important in the field of software maintenance. If a programmer thinks that he is a second-class citizen, he is likely to do second-class work. If he sees that his managers ignore his work and refuse to make a capital investment in software maintenance, then he concludes that it is not very important work. He begins doing only enough work to get by, and meanwhile begins to update his resume so that he can find work in an area that does have the respect of management: development of new systems.

A few MIS organizations have managed to change this perception of software maintenance. In some cases, the term maintenance programmer has been replaced by production specialist. More importantly, though, the entire culture of the MIS organization reflects the importance of the software maintenance job. A key factor in making this work is personnel assignment. Rather than always assigning the junior people to perform maintenance work, and always allowing the senior people to work on new projects, the work is divided more evenly: some of the more senior computer programmers are assigned to maintenance projects, and some of the more junior people are assigned to new development projects. As one manager at Shell Oil in Melbourne, Australia, remarked to me, "We want to make it clear to everyone that the 'production systems' are the most important systems around here. If they stop running, we're in deep trouble. So we put our best people on those projects."

If software maintenance is regarded as an important, respectable job, and if the programmers see tangible evidence that management really believes this, then it can be managed in much the same way that any other kind of work is managed. Quality and productivity can be stressed; appropriate rewards and recognition can be given to the people (or groups of people) doing the best work. And at the same time, management must recognize that, for most people, no job is interesting for more than a few years. Assigning someone to maintain the same software for nine years is not a bad idea because the work involves maintenance—it's just a bad idea in general.[7]

In many cases, software maintenance is unpleasant because the

---

[7] Obviously, there are exceptions to this. Some people prefer the security of knowing what project they will be working on year after year. Some people take great pride in the fact that they become more and more expert in the idiosyncrasies of a large, complex software system. And some people recognize, like the MIS manager at Shell Oil in Australia, that maintenance work involves the front-line systems that keep the organization running every day; it can be exciting, demanding, challenging, and hair-raising. Just ask any of the programmers working on the space shuttle at NASA, or the maintenance programmers at the Social Security Administration. They may get frustrated, they make get ulcers, but they don't get bored.

programs being maintained were written twenty years ago, or were acquired from some external source (another division of the same company, or perhaps an independent software vendor). Sometimes the programs were poorly written to begin with; sometimes the programs were well written, but have suffered from years and years of sloppy, undocumented changes. In situations like this, the temptation to throw the program away and rewrite it is almost unbearable. Telling a programmer that he can't throw the program away and rewrite it is truly sentencing him to eternal suffering.

Virtually every programmer and every MIS manager has had a conversation like this:

PROGRAMMER: "This program is disgusting! It takes days to make the simplest modification, and then I have no idea whether it will work. If you would just give me a week, I could rewrite it completely."

MANAGER: "I'm sorry. It's not in our budget."

PROGRAMMER: "To hell with the budget. You'll save so much money with a new version of the program that you'll look like a hero. Why, I could write the program so that it would run three times faster and take seven times less memory."

MANAGER: "The last time someone told me that, it took six months to rewrite the program, and the new version ran three times slower and took seven times more memory."

PROGRAMMER: "Yeah, but this is different . . ."

MANAGER: "That's what they all say. I just can't take the risk."

PROGRAMMER: "Look, I'll do it on weekends, and at night; I'll do it on my own time. I'll give up my vacation. I'll do anything to get rid of this disgusting program!"

MANAGER: "Sorry. I just can't authorize it. Look, the program isn't really that bad. I should know: I was the lead programmer on the development project back in '68. Now if you have any questions about how it works, you just come ask me . . . ."

PROGRAMMER: "(Censored)"

The practical aspects of rewriting the old software are not at issue here. What is important is the impression that the programmer has at the end of the conversation: he concludes that the manager will never authorize any major overhaul of the program, and that he simply doesn't want to hear about the problems.[8]

If there are legitimate reasons for turning down the programmer's request to rewrite the program, and his offer to contribute his own time and energy gratis, then the manager should seriously consider turning the maintenance effort over to someone else, or finding some other way to make the work attractive. If he doesn't, he will soon lose the programmer with whom he has had the above conversation. One option is to use free-lance programmers for maintenance. As we discussed in Chapter 3, free-lance programmers have the benefits of a more comfortable life-style—working at home, using their own personal computers or terminals, as well as earning more money—and that may compensate for the otherwise degrading work that they are being asked to do. Or, as a variation on this theme: turn the maintenance work over to an outside software house, and let them deal with the problem of morale.

Even if the software is in reasonably good shape, it may still be difficult to motivate the average programmer. After all, the computer industry has, for twenty-five years or more, cultivated the belief that maintenance work is uninteresting "slave labor." In some cases, bonuses or additional pay might compensate for the bad reputation that is associated with maintenance. In other cases, it is even simpler: give the maintenance programmers terminals and personal computers at home. Since some of their work takes place in the middle of the night (when the software "crashes" in the middle of a six-hour production run), the home terminal will allow the maintenance programmer to work in his pajamas, without having to drive for an hour to get to the office.

Another approach is to organize maintenance programmers into teams of three or four, then assign several systems to the team. This approach has several benefits. It reduces the boredom and loneliness that an individual maintenance programmer usually feels. It provides an insurance factor if one of the members of the group leaves: the others can fill in for him. This is in contrast to the usual

---

[8] Note that there isn't anything terribly unique about software in this context. One could imagine the same discussion taking place between a technician and a manager regarding the replacement of any major system—an automobile, a plumbing system, a building, a refrigerator, etc.

case, where nobody else in the organization has any understanding of the program that the individual was maintaining. It also provides the opportunity to double-check sensitive program changes. Since most of the programs being maintained were written ten years ago by persons unknown and long forgotten, nobody is quite sure what will happen when a modification is made to the program.

References for Chapter 30

1. Rochester, Jack, and Gantz, John, *The Naked Computer*, New York: William Morrow, 1983.

2. Lientz, Bennet P. and E. Burton Swanson, *Software Maintenance Management*, Reading, Mass.: Addison-Wesley, 1980.

3. Boehm, Barry, *Software Engineering Economics*, Englewood Cliffs, N.J.: Prentice-Hall, 1982.

4. *Budget of the United States Government, Fiscal Year 1986*, Washington, D.C.: U.S. Government Printing Office, February 4, 1985.

5. "The Maintenance Iceberg," *EDP Analyzer*, April, 1972.

6. Remus, H., "Planning and Measuring Program Implementation," *Proceedings of the Symposium on Software Engineering Environments*, 1980.

7. Boehm, *op. cit.*

8. DeMarco, Tom, *Controlling Software Projects*, New York: YOURDON Press, 1982.

9. Wiener-Ehrlich, Willa-Kay, and Hamrick, James R., "Modeling Software Behavior in Terms of a Formal Life Cycle Curve: Implications for Software Maintenance," *IEEE Transactions on Software Engineering*, 1980.

10. "Effective Manpower Utilization through Automatic Restructuring," *Proceedings of the 1975 National Computer Conference*.

11. Baker, Brenda, restructuring paper, *Journal of the ACM*, March 1977.

12. Gillin, Paul, "'Spaghetti Code' Glut Spawns Program Restructuring Services," *Computerworld*, January 28, 1985.

31

SOFTWARE ENGINEERING

The whole of science is nothing more than a refinement of every-day thinking.

Albert Einstein
Physics and Reality (1936)

As long as we restrain our ambitions and agree to write only small, simple computer programs, we need not refine our everyday thinking as Einstein did so brilliantly. We need not impose the discipline of science upon ourselves. We can use any number of techniques, including brute force, to create computer programs that might eventually perform the task that we have set out to perform. We can ask almost anyone to write computer programs: children, adults, businesspeople, artists, poets, engineers, nuclear physicists, idiots, drunkards, and fools. And there is no doubt that, in this fashion, we can write a lot of computer programs, accomplish a great deal, and make a number of people very happy.

Unfortunately, there are some problems that will not lend themelves to this approach. There are problems whose solution requires a correct computer program—problems for which an erroneous or incomplete solution can be measured in millions of dollars or dozens of lives. There are problems so large and so complex that a ragtag army of artists, poets, children, and other amateurs cannot even attempt a solution. Even an army of normal professional programmers cannot successfully solve these problems; the software industry has learned the hard way that there are problems which cannot be solved by the "Mongolian horde" approach. Most of these problems, or applications, lie at the very heart of our society. They are the air defense systems, the international airline reservation systems, the nuclear reactor process control systems, and the interbank electronic funds transfer systems that move billions and billions of dollars every day at electronic speed.

I do not wish to insult amateurs. After all, we are all amateurs in some ways, and at some times. Even those of us who make a living writing software, and who try to be as professional as possible most of the time, find that there are myriad small programming problems for which we just can't muster the energy required for a formal, disciplined, rigorous solution. But though I don't wish to insult the amateur instincts within us all, I do mean to distinguish between those programming problems that demand an engineering approach and those that will tolerate something less formal. This is especially important today, because many people, both in the software community and outside in the real world, have been perilously tempted by the siren song of fourth-generation programming languages.

As I discussed in Chapter 17 and then again in Chapter 29, such languages make it easy for an amateur to produce results from a computer. But they do not—they cannot—guarantee correct results. Even if the programming language understands English, French, and Serbo-Croatian, there is no way for it to know whether your command to "print a report of all the left-handed customers in Montana and Idaho" was meant to be "print a report of all the left-handed customers in Montana, and also print a report of all the left-handed customers in Idaho," or instead, "print a report of all the left-handed customers in Montana, and also print a report of all the customers in Idaho." The fact that an amateur can attempt this at all is cause for great celebration. As recently as two or three years ago, such a command would have required two weeks of full-time programming in COBOL; now it takes five minutes. Fourth-generation languages have brought problems formerly considered difficult down to the ranks of the amateurs, but they haven't eliminated the possibility of errors.

So, for simple programming jobs where you can afford to be wrong, bring on the amateurs, bring on the fourth-generation languages. But for the problems that are intrinsically complex, we need something else. We need, more than anything else, professional software developers and professional end-users. The need for a professional end-user may not be obvious, but it is as important in the field of software as it is in any other field. An end-user who thinks he can get something for nothing may end up driving a hard bargain, and he may get his software developed at a cheap price. But it will be a shoddy, unreliable, unmaintainable product, and he will pay more in the long run. It is more and more clear to us every day that we cannot tolerate this for large, complex software applications.

In addition to professional programmers and professional users, we need a disciplined, orderly way of approaching the task of developing complex computer programs; we need software engineering. Software engineering is a term that has been used since 1968, when it was introduced as the theme for a conference sponsored by NATO (yes, the North Atlantic Treaty Organization) in Garmisch, Germany.[1] Since then, it has been used as the title for countless textbooks, seminars, conferences, papers, magazine articles, videotapes, university courses, and even software companies. All that is missing is a Hollywood movie and a paperback novel to make software engineering truly popular.

Though the phrase software engineering has been used many thousands of times, it does not have a universally accepted meaning; different people interpret the phrase in different ways. To some, it means a collection of rules that determine what a programmer is allowed to do when writing a program and what he is not allowed to do. To others, it means a picture-oriented notation for representing various aspects of programs and software systems. To still others, it is a well-defined series of activities or tasks that must be carried out when developing a computer program. It is all of these things, and it is more: software engineering is a state of mind.

A large part of the mind set of software engineering is derived from—indeed, stolen from—other engineering disciplines. For example, engineers of all kinds are used to building large complex things (buildings, bridges, computer hardware, etc.) from error-prone, or potentially faulty, components. In the case of software engineering, the faulty component that we worry most about is the human: the human end-user who describes the problem he wants computerized, the human systems analyst who records his understanding of that problem, and the human programmer who translates those requirements into a programming language for execution on a considerably more reliable machine. If we are to be engineers, our system for building systems must take into account the fallible nature of the human participants.

Engineers also have a tendency to build large, complex systems from small, standardized components. They spend little of their time reinventing the wheel by redesigning the basic building blocks, or components, of their trade; they spend their time instead thinking of new combinations and permutations of those building blocks that will provide a novel solution for the problem they are trying to solve. Software engineers try to do the same thing: they try to avoid programming everything from scratch, and instead rely heavily on libraries of standardized modules from which almost any complex system can be built. Though this seems an obvious concept, it runs counter to the artistic instincts of many programmers, who would prefer to approach each programming problem as if it had never been seen before.

There is more to software engineering, but (as with most sciences and engineering disciplines) these philosophies form the foundation. Much of what you will see in the textbooks and conferences are trappings laid on top of the foundation. Several of the more important philosophies of software engineering are outlined below; some of the specific techniques of software engineering are then discussed.

THE AXIOMS OF SOFTWARE ENGINEERING

There are three unspoken axioms that software developers take for granted when they use software engineering methods or tools on a project. Perhaps they should be called something other than axioms, for they are not prerequisites, or necessary conditions, for the use of software engineering; however, they represent assumptions that nobody bothers to prove:

Axiom #1: Software engineering is used on "critical" projects.

"Critical" is not defined here in a universal sense, but it usually has a well-understood meaning within the context of a specific project: it means, "We can't afford to fail." Critical projects are typically very large and very complex—e.g., the "Star Wars" program being contemplated by the U.S. Department of Defense, or a nationwide banking system involving thousands of terminals. One could also imagine, though, critical systems that represent only one or two person-years of work: a computerized communications sytem for a military agency, or the computerized emission control system for an automobile.

Axiom #2:   The requirements are sufficiently well known that they can be documented before the program is designed and coded. I do not suggest that it is easy to formulate the requirements, nor do I suggest that the requirements must be "frozen" once they are articulated. But software engineering does not tend to be used on projects where the user has no idea what he wants—i.e., where the act of writing the program becomes part of the creative thinking process of solving the underlying business or scientific problem. Many small, simple business applications fall into this latter category: by writing a program quickly and seeing the results (which may or not be correct), the end-user gets a better idea of what he would like to do. The software engineering approach, on the other hand, assumes that the end-user is willing and able to begin the software development process with a careful, thorough, and fairly formal statement of his requirements.

Axiom #3:   The project is large enough, and expensive enough, that everyone agrees to follow some kind of project life cycle. Small, non-critical projects are often carried out in an informal seat-of-the pants method. There is often only one person involved, and he is often doing everything at once. If you ask such a software person whether he is doing systems analysis, or systems design, or programming, or testing, he will look at you blankly and say, "Yes." By which he means that he is doing all of those things simultaneously, and that all of the activities are deeply inter-twined. On most software engineering projects, there are so many people involved, and there is such a demand for visibility and tangible results, that everyone agrees to follow some form of game

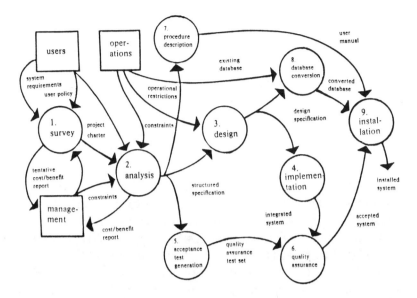

Figure 31.1: **A Typical Project Life Cycle**

plan for the major steps of the project. One such "game plan" is shown pictorially in Figure 31.1; the details are outside the scope of this book but are discussed in a number of computer textbooks.[2-4]

ONE FORM OF SOFTWARE ENGINEERING: STRUCTURED TECHNIQUES

Among the more popular forms of software engineering is a collection of tools, techniques, and philosophies known as "structured techniques." Structured techniques have been widely taught to professional programmers and systems analysts around the world. My consulting firm, for example, has distributed nearly half a million textbooks on the subject, and has trained nearly 150,000 people in industry. Between 50 percent and 80 percent of the programmers and systems analysts in American MIS organizations are using some form of structured techniques, though it must be admitted that not all of them are using the techniques diligently, conscientiously, or even regularly.

There are individual structured techniques associated with each of the major activities of systems analysis, systems design, and programming, as we will see below. However, structured techniques, as the term is generally used in the software industry, also include some concepts that affect all of the major activities of software development. One such concept is a peer-group review of any technical product produced by systems analysts, designers, and programmers; this review process is known as a "structured walkthrough."[5]

Another concept related to the structured techniques is known as "top-down implementation." While it tends to focus attention on the testing and implementation stages of a programming project, it is actually a strategy for performing several of the activities shown in Figure 31.1 in parallel. This is in sharp contrast to the conventional approach to software development, in which the activities are performed in a serial fashion: programming is not allowed to begin until design is finished, and design is not allowed to begin until systems analysis is finished. Carrying out several of the activities in parallel can make better use of people resources. More importantly, it provides feedback to earlier activities—e.g., the person working on design can point out to the person working on systems analysis that the specification that he is developing cannot be implemented within the constraints of hardware capacity, budget, etc., imposed on the project. The top-down approach also provides the opportunity to demonstrate a partially-finished skeleton version of the final system to the end-user at an early stage, in contrast to the conventional approach, in which nothing of any significance can be shown to the end-user until the entire system has been specified, designed, coded, and tested. There are a number of other benefits to the top-down approach;[6] however, it should be emphasized that it is difficult, if not impossible, to conduct a top-down software development project unless some form of structured programming, structured design and structured analysis is also used.

Structured Programming

The first of the structured techniques to be widely used in the software profession was structured programming. There is still some debate about who invented the concept, who first used it, who proved that it would work, etc. However, it is generally agreed that the phrase was coined by Professor Edsger Dijskstra in 1965,[7,8] that it is based on mathematical principles described by Bohm and Jacopini in 1966,[9] and that it was popularized and legitimized by IBM in 1972.[10]

The premise of structured programming is very simple: any program logic can be composed from combinations of the three constructs shown in Figure 31.2.

In programming terms, this means that all program logic can be constructed from sequences of simple instructions (e.g., X = Y + Z), binary IF-THEN-ELSE decision constructs, and DO-WHILE loops that have a single entry and a single exit. Indeed, all three of the structured programming constructs have a single entry and a single exit, and can be considered a "black box." Thus, each of the constructs can be substituted in place of the elementary black-box operations (the rectangular boxes) in Figure 31.2. We might find a structured program whose program logic looks like Figure 31.3.

The reason for organizing program logic in this fashion is to ensure that it flows in an orderly way, from the top of a program listing to the bottom. The alternative style of programming, which was more common until the late 1970s, and which is still common for high school programming students being taught by amateur teachers, is something like that shown in Figure 31.4.

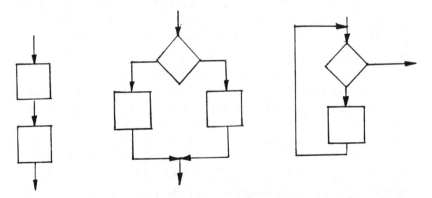

Figure 31.2: **The Structured Programming Constructs**

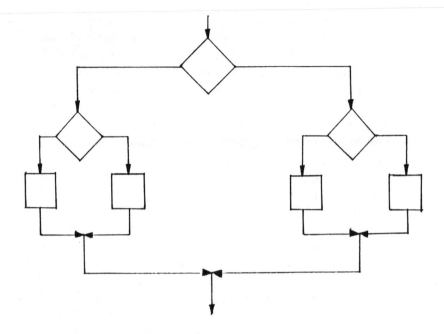

Figure 31.3: **A More Complex Structured Program**

It is easy to see that the program logic in Figure 31.4 is more complicated and difficult to comprehend than the logic shown in Figure 31.3. When the flowchart is eventually implemented as a computer program in a typical third-generation programming language, the branching arrows become GOTO statements. Hence, structured programming is often described as "GOTO-less" programming, or an effort to write programs in which the control logic is carried out by nested sequences of simple statements, IF-THEN-ELSE constructs, and DO-WHILE constructs. This was quite difficult—indeed, impossible—in the versions of FORTRAN, COBOL, and BASIC used by most programmers in the 1960s and 1970s (FORTRAN, for example, did not have an IF-THEN-ELSE statement, but only the more limited IF-THEN). Programmers using more sophisticated languages like ALGOL, PL/I, Pascal, and C had no difficulty and wondered what the fuss was all about.

Today, most programming languages (e.g., enhanced versions of BASIC and FORTRAN) support the structured programming

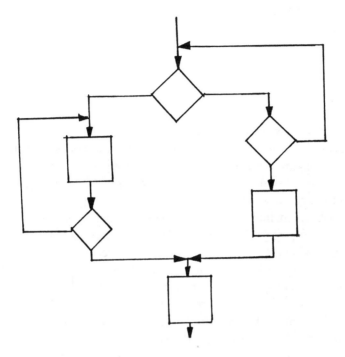

Figure 31.4: **An Unstructured Program**

concept reasonably well; GOTO statements might be necessary for a few unusual programming situations, but most of the logic can be organized in the manner shown in Figures 31.2 and 31.3. And the structured programming movement is no longer a "religion" in which the GOTO statement is considered evil incarnate: instead of GOTO-less programming, most programmers are content with less-GOTO programming. Structured programming is now used in 75 to 80 percent of the programming projects in American business organizations. It is taught as a standard approach in virtually all university computer sciences. And it is recognized as an important concept in a few high school and elementary school programming projects.

To see why structured programming is such an important concept, imagine for a moment that you are a maintenance programmer responsible for the upkeep of your company's payroll system, which was written ten years ago by someone you've never met. As we saw in Chapter 30, this kind of job can be very time-consuming and unpleasant. To see why, let's imagine that you are awakened from a deep sleep one night at 2:30 A.M. by the computer operator. He informs you that the payroll system has just "aborted" in the middle of its three-hour weekly run, and that you should come to the computer center right away so that you can find the problem and rerun the system in time to produce the paychecks for the vice president of finance at 8:00 A.M.. If the vice president doesn't have the paychecks by 8:00, he will be very unhappy, as will everyone else in the organization.

In a situation like this, philosophical issues of structured programming are of little interest. All you want to do is find the problem, correct it, restart the program and return to bed. If you're lucky, you might be able to accomplish this work from a terminal or a personal computer in your living room. If not, you'll have to put on some clothes and drive to work. Let's imagine that you are able to determine the general area where your program "blew up"—perhaps from something the computer operator has told you or from various other clues. In fact, let's assume that you've narrowed the problem down to one page of program coding on, say, page 345 of a 600-page program listing. Turning to that page (which you have probably never looked at in the years you've been maintaining this program), you see the following sequence of program statements:

```
MOVE STANDARD_HOURS TO HOURS_WORKED.
ADD OVERTIME_HOURS TO HOURS_WORKED.
CALL GROSS_PAY ROUTINE USING HOURS_WORKED.
GOTO AFGHANISTAN.
MULTIPLY EXEMPTIONS_CLAIMED BY EX_AMT.
   .
   .
   .
```

The first two statements are relatively straightforward even if you've never seen a COBOL statement. You might wonder whether STANDARD_HOURS is thirty-five hours or forty hours. You might wonder why all of this is taking place on page 345 of the program listing. You might have a number of other detailed questions. However, there are two things of which you can be reasonably certain: (a) the MOVE statement works correctly; and (b) when the MOVE statement has finished moving the information in STANDARD_HOURS into the HOURS_WORKED memory area, the computer will go on to the next instruction. If you were feeling slightly paranoid, you might wonder whether the COBOL compiler generated correct machine instructions for the MOVE statement. If you were feeling exceptionally paranoid, you might wonder whether the computer hardware was functioning correctly and whether control really did proceed from the MOVE statement to the subsequent ADD statement. But pursuing such questions is hardly a sensible way of spending your time at 2:30 in the morning!

Thus, you would treat the MOVE statement as a black box whose details are of no interest to you, and whose correct implementation can be taken for granted. The only question that you should concentrate on is whether it is, in fact, appropriate for the program to be carrying out this MOVE of this information (STANDARD_HOURS into HOURS_WORKED) at this particular part of the program. If so, you would move on to the next statement in search of the bug; you would treat the ADD statement in the same way.

In fact, you would treat the subsequent subroutine call—the CALL statement—in the same way. The legitimate questions to ask at this point are: (a) why are we calculating GROSS_PAY here? (b) is GROSS_PAY really supposed to be computed based on HOURS_WORKED; and (c) where are the results of the GROSS_PAY calculation left? It is unproductive to ask whether the gross pay calculation itself is working correctly (unless there is obvious, incontrovertible evidence to that effect). Only later, if we exhaust all of our debugging efforts on page 345, should we drop down to the next lower level of detail.

All of this careful, orderly debugging is shot to hell when you stumble upon the next statement, GOTO AFGHANISTAN. There are a number of detailed questions that you must ask and that you cannot ignore at this point. They include: (a) "Where is AFGHANISTAN?" (b) "Why am I going there?" (c) "What's going to happen when I get there?" and—most important—(d) "Will I ever come back to page 345?" It would be nice to know that AFGHANISTAN is just a cleverly named subroutine for calculating federal income taxes, and that the program will eventually return, in some mysterious way, to the statement immediately after the GOTO. But you can't tell. So at this point you must do two things: (a) put a finger, or ruler, or pencil in the listing on page 345 just in case the program logic does return there; and (b) memorize everything that was going on and what information was in which memory variables, on the assumption that you're not ever going to return to page 345.

Things are bad enough already, but in typical maintenance situations things get worse. Let's imagine that you finally found AFGHANISTAN on page 101 of the program listing. Here is the sequence of program statements.

```
AFGHANISTAN.
  COMPUTE FEDERAL__TAX = GROSS__PAY * TAX__RATE.
  CALL STATE__TAX USING GROSS__PAY.
  GOTO ISTANBUL.
  CALL MISC__DEDUCTIONS.
    .
    .
    .
```

Once again, you can carry out an orderly, top-down approach to debugging—until you hit the GOTO statement. Where is ISTANBUL? Why are you going there? Will you ever return? Another finger goes into the program listing, and you turn to page 566 to find yet another sequence of program statements . . .

It usually requires only three or four of these jumps for you to completely forget what the program is doing, where you started from, or why you even bothered getting out of bed at 2:30 in the morning. Let the vice president make up the paychecks himself; spend the rest of the night updating your resume, and start looking for a new job tomorrow morning.

Structured Design

When structured programming first became popular in the late 1960s and early 1970s, it was seen by many as the salvation for the software problems described in the last several chapters. After all, programming appeared to be the problem; while systems analysis and systems design are important, the program statements written by the programmer are, as my colleague Scott Guthrie likes to say, "where the tire meets the road." If things don't work the way they're supposed to, it's the programmer who has to fix it; the systems analyst and many other members of the original project team have moved on to new projects. It is the programmer who often appears so alien to the user, the businessperson or scientist or engineer who asked for the software in the first place. The programmer has long hair (or no hair, or hair dyed purple, or some other form of hair that is socially unacceptable to the user). He wears strange clothes. He speaks a strange language. He refuses to work a normal 9:00 to 5:00 schedule, and he seems generally out of touch with civilization.[1]

But after several years of experience with structured programming, it gradually became clear that "good code" does not necessarily mean "good systems." Most of the information systems built by large organizations consist of dozens, even hundreds, of separate computer programs, each of which may contain thousands of program statements. All of the programs interact, or interface, with one another, often through one or more common data files. Even if all of the code is written in a top to bottom, structured fashion without any GOTO statements, there can still be serious maintenance problems if the programs (or modules, as I prefer to call them) are strongly coupled to one another—i.e., if a change in one module necessitates a change in one or more other modules. Consider what would happen, for example, if the Social Security system suddenly decreed that henceforth American Social Security numbers will have eleven digits instead of nine, and that one of those digits will be used as a check digit for error checking? Not only

[1] Curiously, many programmers say the same thing about users! To such programmers, the highest accolade is to be called a hacker—e.g., someone capable of creating such dazzling programs as MacPaint on the Apple Macintosh, or (if he's in a bad mood) breaking the security system at the local bank's computer center.

would every business oriented database in the country have to be changed, but every module that deals with Social Security numbers would probably have to be changed.[2]

This architectural view of large software systems is the subject of structured design. Most of the concepts of structured design were developed during the mid 1970s[11-15] and gradually refined over the years by practitioners.[16,17] Rather than using flowcharts to model procedural logic within a module, structured design uses a graphical modeling tool called a structure chart, in which the basic building blocks are entire modules. A typical structure chart is shown in Figure 31.5.

Just the act of modeling the design of a large software system has improved the state of the art considerably. Diagrams like Figure 31.5 make it easier for the system designers to see the major components of a system and the interfaces between the components. In addition, structured design includes several guidelines to minimize the possibility of a bad design. One of these, as we saw earlier, is the concept of coupling. The objective is to design systems whose modules are loosely coupled to one another, so that a change to one module has a minimum chance of impacting another module. A related concept is cohesion. Structured design encourages designers to build systems from small, single purpose, narrow minded, highly cohesive modules. Modules which carry out only a fragment of a task are to be avoided, as are modules that carry out several unrelated tasks.[3]

---

[2] This is not such a crazy example. We will eventually run out of nine-digit Social Security numbers. As another example, imagine the grief and gnashing of teeth that took place in computer departments around the country when the post office announced a change from five-digit zip codes to nine-digit codes? (Did you ever wonder why the Post Office didn't make it mandatory?) Think for a moment about the system-wide consequences that will occur when December 31, 1999, rolls over into January 1, 2000. Or, for the scientists and engineers who feel they can ignore such mundane problems, consider the apocryphal story of the state legislature in Indiana that once passed a law (which, fortunately, nobody pays any attention to) decreeing that henceforth the value of pi would be adequately approximated by 3.14.

[3] Several years ago I witnessed an amazing example of poor cohesion in one of the telephone operating companies in the Midwest. For traditional reasons, most of the software systems in this organization were divided into two major subsystems: "intrastate processing" and "interstate processing." In the system I examined, those two subsystems (or very large modules) probably had reasonably strong cohesion. But there was a third subsystem called "miscellaneous functions" that was much more dubious. And there was a fourth subsystem called "nonmiscellaneous functions" whose purpose I could never determine. On a ten-point cohesion scale, it would rank somewhere below zero.

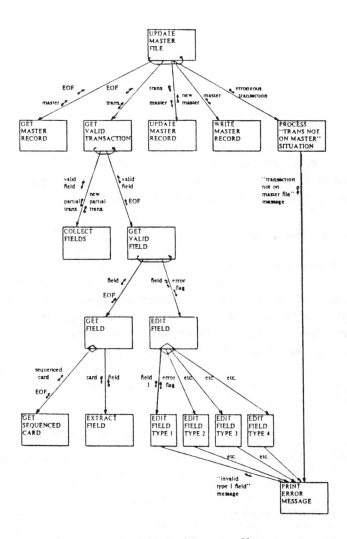

Figure 31.5: **A Typical Structure Chart**

Structured design does not attempt, in any deterministic fashion, to produce the best design for a system. There are many design issues that must be determined by the personal judgment of the designer. However, structured design does try to avoid bad designs—i.e., designs that will lead to systems that are difficult to debug and difficult to maintain. This approach was borrowed from Professor Christopher Alexander, who expressed it in the context of architectural design in a book generally unknown to software people, *Notes on the Synthesis of Form*.[18] For any given problem, there are potentially an infinite number of possible designs that will work. Most of these designs are very bad; many are mediocre; and a very small number are good. As Alexander points out, designers will argue interminably over the merits of the good designs, often without reaching any consensus; but they will all unanimously agree on the dangers of the bad designs. So if we can highlight the features of a proposed software design that would be universally recognized as bad,[4] we have a good chance of eliminating all of those potential designs from further consideration.

Structured Analysis

Just as structured programming was thought to be the salvation of the software industry, so many people thought that structured design would solve all of the problems discussed in the last several chapters. And, indeed, structured programming and structured design brought about notable improvements in productivity, maintainability and reliability of software systems—often a 50 to 100 percent improvement in productivity, and as much as a factor of ten improvement in maintainability and reliability (absence of errors).[5]

---

[4] One example of a bad design feature is a pathological connection between two modules. The worst form of pathological connection is the modification of program statements inside one module by the program logic in another module—i.e., module A changes the code inside module B. Obviously, nobody in his right mind would consider rewriting module B without carefully studying module A, thus making the maintenance job doubly difficult.

[5] This improvement has to be understood in the proper context. For the economy as a whole, productivity has been increasing at the rate of only 1 percent per year in the mid-1980s, and approximately 3 percent per year for the decade before that. Over the long term, this can be extremely important. One of the major reasons for the worldwide dominance of the American economy by the middle of the 20th century was a productivity rate increase about 1 percent higher than England's, compounded each year for almost a century. Unfortunately, things move much faster in the computer field, and we have much higher expectations. Dramatic improvements in computer hardware technology—e.g., computers 100,000 times more powerful than they were forty years ago—have drastically shifted the balance of costs into the software arena, and have led to demands for similar improvements in software productivity.

Ironically, though, this sometimes made matters worse. Some MIS organizations found that structured programming and structured design allowed them to arrive at a disaster faster than ever before. That is, they found that they were developing brilliant solutions to the wrong problem. When building information systems, the ultimate problem is determining what the user wants the system to do; then there is the problem of deciding how the system will be implemented.

Structured analysis is concerned with the issue of "what" rather than "how." It is a collection of techniques and graphical diagramming tools that provide a formal, rigorous—and yet easy to understand—model of the requirements of a system that the user is contemplating. It replaces the conventional "Victorian novel" specification that is based almost entirely on narrative text. The narrative text specifications, which are still popular in some organizations, suffer from a number of weaknesses: they are verbose, boring, ambiguous, monolithic, redundant, and therefore usually obsolete. Because they are verbose and boring, it is difficult for the reader to concentrate on the document. Because they are ambiguous, it is difficult for the reader to have a precise understanding of what he is reading. Because they are monolithic, the narrative descriptions have to be read in their entirety; conversely, if one doesn't read the entire document, one doesn't understand any of it. And because the document is monolithic and redundant (the same information is repeated several times, usually to impress the reader), it is almost impossible to update as requirements change. So the document is not updated (it's easier to change the programs than the specification, which says a lot about computer programs and a lot about specifications). The result is that most of the major computerized information systems in the United States—indeed, probably as many as 80 percent of such systems—do not have an up-to-date, accurate statement of requirements. To compound the problem, the original users and the original software development team have usually left the organization by the time everyone begins to realize that the only statement of requirements is the code itself. This is why Nicholas Zvegintzov describes maintenance programmers as the "reverse engineers of society."[19]

Structured analysis was developed in the mid- and late-1970s and

was popularized in a number of textbooks.[20-22] After several years
of use, the techniques have been extended to include information
modeling[23] and to deal with the timing issues of real-time systems.[24] Recent books have also dealt with the practical issues of
using structured analysis on real-world projects, and the issue of
making users proficient in the techniques.[25]

The major tools of structured analysis are the data-flow diagram
(often referred to by software engineers as a DFD), the state-
transition diagram (also known as an STD), and the entity-relationship diagram (referred to by software engineers and database

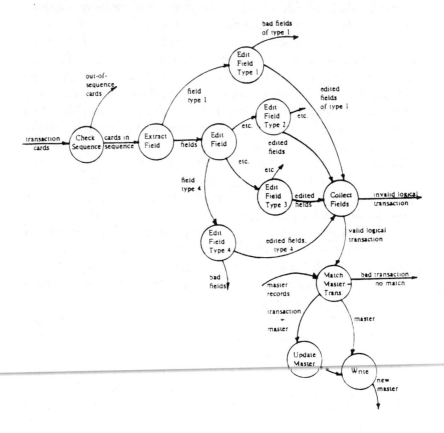

Figure 31.6: **A Data-Flow Diagram**

specialists as an E-R diagram). The purpose of a DFD is to show, graphically, the major components of a system and the interfaces between those components. A state-transition diagram, on the other hand, helps illustrate the time-dependent behavior of a system—i.e., what states are meaningful and how the system can change from one state to another. And E-R diagrams focus on yet another key aspect of a typical system: the objects of stored data that the system must remember, and the relationship among those objects. Typical DFD, STD, and E-R diagrams are shown below.

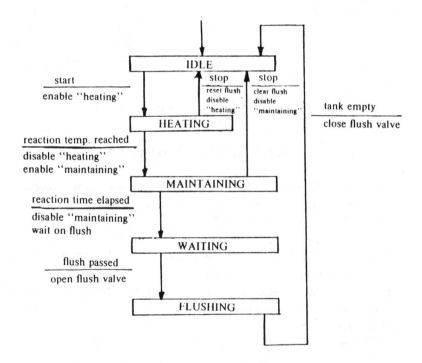

Figure 31.7: A State-Transistion Diagram

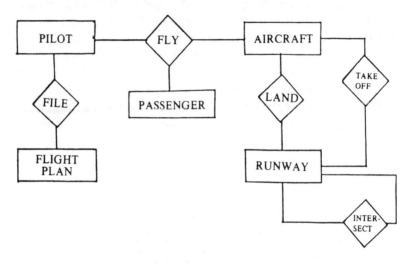

Figure 31.8: **An Entity-Relationship Diagram**

SOFTWARE METRICS

As we have seen in previous chapters, many software projects are prone to outrageous errors of estimating, sometimes errors of a factor of ten. As T. Capers Jones found in a recent survey, the average project is one year late and 100 percent over budget.[26] Better software development methods (such as the structured techniques discussed above) can improve the situation. But there is no guarantee that diligent use of structured programming, structured design, and structured analysis will enable a software project to be completed on time.

One of the major reasons for this is that much of the estimating that takes place in software development projects is really negotiating. Before the project even begins, the user has a strong opinion about the deadline for the project. Sometimes a new system must be finished in time for the beginning of a fiscal year, or in time to conform to new government regulations; sometimes the deadline is based on a whim. Similarly, the project manager often has a good idea of what will be acceptable and what will not. He reasons (sometimes subconsciously) that if he told the user what it would really cost to develop the proposed system, the user would scrap the project. This may seem like an overly cynical view of the discussions between user and project manager, but it is extremely unusual for such discussions to take place without some form of negotiation.

USER: "So, how long is it going to take you to build this new reporting system the government wants?"

PROJECT MANAGER: "Oh, I would guess that it would take about a year. And we'll have to hire two new people, because everyone else is tied up on other projects."

USER: "That's no good. It's got to be finished in six months."

PROJECT MANAGER: "Well, I don't know . . . I suppose that if I had three new people instead of two, and made them work lots of overtime, we could get it done in nine months."

USER: "*Three* new people? Haven't you heard about the corporate hiring freeze? Listen, I can hire one person to replace the accountant who committed suicide last week. We'll hire a programmer instead of a new accountant. But that's the best we can do."

PROJECT MANAGER: "Well, there's no way we can get it done in nine months then . . ."

USER: "Who said anything about nine months? Listen, the best I can do is make it in seven months. We'll file a request for a time extension for the report the government wants from us. But it's got to be finished by then."

The project manager might be in a stronger position if there were a database of similar projects that had been developed in the organization over the past several years, and if the estimating were done by someone other than the project manager. This would not eliminate the political negotiations entirely, but it might make the discussions more rational if the project manager could say, "You know, the last thirteen times we built a system like this, it took an average of fourteen months of elapsed time, and it required a project team of 2.5 people, on average."

It would be even better if the project manager did not have to say this himself. The response is likely to be, "Well, Fred, I'm sure you can do much better than average. Top management will really be watching this project, and it could do a lot for your career." In such a situation, it is only human for the project manager to be affected by the perceived career impact. It is only normal for him to volunteer lots of overtime work for himself and his subordinates in order to get the job done. And, in general, it is almost certain that he will overestimate his ability to perform the job.

A much better solution is to have a separate, independent, objective estimating group that develops estimates for all of the important metrics for a software project: cost, manpower, duration, size of the finished system, resources required, etc. Such an estimating group would have the benefit of carrying out several such estimates over a period of years. The individual project manager often has only two or three such experiences before being transferred to an entirely different environment, or being promoted. An excellent discussion of the advantages of a separate metrics group can be found in Tom DeMarco's *Controlling Software Projects*.[27]

Assuming that the project manager or the software metrics group is allowed to develop an objective estimate of project size, cost, duration, etc., one major problem remains: the abilities of the people working on the project. As I pointed out in Chapter 27, there is a 25:1 difference in the productivity of programmers and in the quality (number of errors) in the code they write. This was observed in the late 1960s,[28] and has been confirmed several times since. The differences in abilities cannot be easily correlated to years of experience; a project manager cannot be sure that a ten-year veteran will outperform a junior programmer with two years of experience.

A 25:1 difference in abilities swamps most other productivity issues and makes discussions about a six-month deadline versus a seven-month deadline irrelevant. It makes an independent metrics group even more valuable. If the group can gather information about the productivity of individual programmers on previous projects, their estimates for future projects will be considerably more accurate. In organizations where the programmers think of themselves as artists, this kind of calibration will not be very

popular. Even in organizations where programmers act in a professional way, there is a tendency to say, "You can't compare my work
to Susan's work—after all, my program was harder!"

This brings up one of the remaining problems in the software
metrics field: What is the unit of work that we are measuring? In
other industries we can count tangible units of output: so many cars
produced, so many bricks laid, so many tons of steel produced, etc.
As we discussed in Chapter 27, the obvious temptation in the
software field is to count lines of code—e.g., COBOL statements or
FORTRAN statements. Aside from the trivial problems (Do we
count comment statements? Do we count additional statements
that tell the computer operator how to run the job?), there is the
fundamental problem that a programmer can inflate his productivity by writing many more lines of code than necessary. Consider
this trivial example:

```
         DO 333 I = 1 TO 10
   333   TABLE(I) = I**2
```

versus this code:

```
   TABLE(1) = 1
   TABLE(2) = 4
   TABLE(3) = 9
        .
        .
        .
   TABLE(10) = 100
```

Both of these sequences of code produce a table of the first ten
squares, but the second version involves five times as many program statements. Should we consider the programmer who wrote
that version five times more productive than the one who wrote the
first version? I hope not!

For the past few years, software metrics specialists have been
concentrating on a more meaningful unit of work known as a
"function point"; in some organizations, it is referred to as "functionality delivered to the user." For example, it might turn out that

the coding shown above was written because part of the visible functionality that the user required in his system was the computation of the first ten squares; both sequences of code accomplish that same delivered functionality. But presumably the first programmer could finish his version much more quickly, so he would be considered the more productive.[6]

THE UNIX PARADIGM

As I pointed out at the beginning of this chapter, software engineers try to borrow many of the concepts familiar in other engineering disciplines. One of those common concepts is that of reusability. Most large systems are built from small components (the job of structured design is to figure out how to break down the enormous totality of the system into appropriate small components). If those small components have already been built, then the implementation job is reduced to that of "plumbing"—i.e., fitting together the pieces and making certain that data "flows" in the right direction, at the right time, between those preconstructed pieces.

This is a terrific concept, and it has been discussed for many years in the software industry. My boss gave me a lecture on the subject when I got my first real programming job at Digital Equipment Corporation in 1964. But somehow it has never worked. Part of the reason for the failure was the size of the components: enormous programs of 10,000 lines of code were thrown into a general-purpose library from which nobody ever retrieved anything. A program that attempted to do all things for all people usually succeeded only in disappointing everyone.

One of the best examples of how software reusability can be

---

[6] The difference in time may not be as obvious as it looks. While it clearly takes much less time to write two statements than ten, the two-statement FORTRAN DO-loop might be the cause of errors and problems that the straight-line coding sequence would not encounter. For example, if the programmer had previously worked with a different programming language, he might be unsure whether the DO loop terminates when I is equal to 10, or when it is greater than 10; and is the termination test performed after the body of the loop has been carried out or before? Problems like this often lead to off-by-one bugs that might take more time to resolve than simply coding ten statements in a row. While I am certainly not arguing against the use of loops, I think it is dangerous to assume that the increase in productivity is a linear function.

accomplished in a practical, realistic fashion is the UNIX operating system.[7] Though it was developed in the early 1970s in the research labs of Bell Laboratories, UNIX did not achieve real prominence until the early 1980s, when it began to appear on several microcomputers and personal computers. Now it is the subject of much debate between hobbyists, programmers, and venture capitalists. However, my interest in UNIX in this chapter has little or nothing to do with the concerns of hobbyists.

In contrast to the 10,000-line "monster" program components that we attempted to reuse in the 1960s, UNIX has a library of seventy or eighty tiny components, each of which does one single, narrow-minded, well-defined job. Also, the UNIX library routines obey a very important guideline. They make no assumptions about the source of their inputs or the destination of their outputs. This allows the UNIX modules to be connected, and reconnected, and reused in a variety of environments unanticipated by the original UNIX inventors. The connections are made as part of the "job control language" when the user tells the operating system what programs to run.[8] A trivial example of such a connection is the command:

who | wc

The first command produces a list of "who" is using the computer. It is a simple list showing user-names, terminal-IDs, and the time the user logged in. For example:

ed	ttyaa	8:07
herb	ttyab	8:13
andrei	ttydf	7:44
trice	ttyde	9:02

[7] As an operating system, UNIX is usually compared with MS-DOS or CP/M on personal computers. It also runs on a variety of minicomputers, as well as a few mainframe computers. Its primary function is to coordinate the processing, input/output, file management, and terminal activities of one or more users; however, it is important also because of the features it offers software developers for building systems from reusable components.

[8] These instructions can be put into a text file, known as a "shell file" or "shell script," and invoked by name. Thus, they are roughly equivalent to cataloged procedures on IBM mainframe computers, or the batch files on CP/M and MS-DOS personal computer systems.

and so forth. The second command is the "word count" command that counts words and lines of text. It is normally used to count words of text in a manuscript, but it can be used in other situations as well. In fact, running the two programs together with the "|" pipeline (which connects the output of the "who" program to the input of the "wc" program) produces the output:

12 4

This tells us that the "who" command produced twelve words of output, and four lines of output. Since each user logged on our computer system generates one such line of information, we have thus learned that there are four users on the computer. All of this could have been accomplished, of course, by having someone write a special-purpose "how many people are on the computer" program. But it is interesting to see that it can be done by connecting two existing programs that were not originally intended to have anything to do with one another.

To see a counterexample of this concept consider the text editors used on most personal computers and most large mainframe computers. Invariably, they spew forth friendly messages when you start running them. "Hi! Today is Wednesday, and it's cloudy outside," the word processing program will say. "By the way, do you want to edit a new file, or an old file?" And so the friendly, chatty dialogue continues, throughout the session—because the text editor assumes that it is communicating with a human. While this friendliness is commendable (and perhaps vitally important for the novice user), it means that the text editor cannot be used in the UNIX pipeline approach shown above. It sends too much garbage down the pipeline. By contrast, some of the text editors available with the UNIX operating system make no such assumption: they speak only when spoken to. Consequently they can be used, conceptually as a subroutine, to accomplish pattern-matching and string-searching functions that are useful in a number of other contexts.

As I said earlier, there is much debate about UNIX today. Will it take over MS-DOS? Will it appear on more mainframes? Will there eventually be more application software? All of these are important questions, of course. But from a software engineering perspective, UNIX has already succeeded. It has become a paradigm—a shining example that stands above most other ugly operating systems—that will serve as a baseline for operating systems of the future.

PROVING PROGRAM CORRECTNESS

One could argue that all of software engineering, as I have presented it in this chapter, is doomed to failure for it relies on testing to determine whether the software has been built correctly. Testing, in the software business, means: think of a test case that the software should be able to handle, determine what the correct result should be, and then see whether the software actually produces that result.

Unfortunately, one never has the opportunity to try all possible test cases. This unreachable objective is known as exhaustive testing, and many programmers labor today under the illusion that they are actually achieving it. But it is a myth. Even the simplest of programs has billions and billions of different test cases that would have to be explored, one by one, if we were to be absolutely certain that the program was operating correctly.

Part of the problem is that the correct result often has to be determined manually; then it has to be put into a computer database so that anticipated result and actual result can be compared by the computer, rather than trusting the human eyeball to make the comparison. Indeed, even when the correct result can be computed mechanically, there is still room for error. Consider, for example, one of my early programming assignments at Digital Equipment Corporation: I was told to write the math library for the PDP-6 computer. This included sine, cosine, logarithm, exponential, etc. Most of us vaguely recall from high school trigonometry that the sine of 0° is zero, the sine of 90° is 1, and the sine of 45° is .7071 (square root of 2, divided by 2). But how could I tell whether my subroutine was generating the proper sine of 36.772°? And did I have to test 36.773° and 36.774°, too?

My solution was to develop some automated tests. I remembered, for example, the old high school formula

sin2(x) + cos2(x) = 1

and I also remembered that the sine function could be computed using a simpler, more cumbersome formula than the one I had chosen.[9] So it was easy to write a program that would generate millions of values of "x," and then test to see whether the "$\sin^2$ + $\cos^2$" formula worked, and whether my algorithm matched the results of a different algorithm. The test program that I thus concocted used all computer resources on our test computer over an entire weekend. My boss was horrified, but impressed with the sheer volume of testing that I was carrying out.[10]

Does this prove I was doing a good job of testing? Not really. Consider the following potential problems:

- The testing sequence that I used might have had errors in it. It is certainly true for example that $\sin^2(x) + \cos^2(x) = 1$, but there is no guarantee that my testing program correctly computed that formula.

- Testing the sine subroutine required the existence of other subroutines—e.g., the cosine subroutine, or the alternative-algorithm version of the sine. What if those subroutines had compensating errors that offset the errors in my sine routine?

- My testing program tried the various formulas and alternative calculations for sin(x) for an enormously large range of values. But what if I neglected to test carefully the boundary values, or if there were a bug in the part of my program that generated new test cases? In fact, the latter situation turned out to be true. I spent forty-seven hours of computer time repeatedly testing to

[9] My subroutine used a continued-fraction algorithm because it was faster. The alternative approach (which I used for testing) was the Taylor series expansion

$$\sin(x) = x - x^3/3! + x^5/5! - x^7/7! + \ldots$$

[10] All this just to test a miserable sine routine? That was what my boss wanted to know. The answer was "No." I was also carrying out similar tests for exp(x), log(x), sqrt(x), atan(x), cos(x), etc.

ensure that my sin(x), cos(x), log(x), exp(x), atan(x) and sqrt(x) subroutines produced correct results for $x = 0$. I didn't have the courage to tell my boss.

An alternative to all of this massive testing is the concept of proof of correctness. As software guru Edsger Dijkstra pointed out nearly two decades ago, "testing exposes the presence of errors, not the absence." We can increase our level of confidence in a program by testing the normal cases, the exceptional cases, the boundary cases, and so forth—and we can draw some comfort from a program that has run for ten years without any apparent sign of defect.[11] But we can't be sure. Consequently, some computer scientists argue that we should create a formal, mathematical proof of correctness similar to the geometry proofs that we constructed in high school.

Very, very few people working in the software industry today would be capable of creating such a formal, mathematical proof of correctness of any program they were working on. Fewer still would be willing to spend the time. And there is a more fundamental problem: a proof of correctness is possible only if the requirements definition for the program is equally formal and rigorous. For mathematical subroutines like sin(x) and sqrt(x), this is easy;[12] for a payroll system, or air defense system, the requirements are often too "fuzzy" for a formal mathematical proof of correctness to be seriously considered.

For the past two decades, computer scientists have labored with the concept of formal proofs of correctness. Small computer programs—e.g., 50 to 100 lines of code—have successfully undergone such proofs. But, of course, almost all computer systems of any

[11] "Apparent" is the operative word here. There are many, many programs that have bugs which are never seen. In a seminar I conducted in San Francisco in 1983, a participant told me of an audit that had just been finished of several hospital billing systems in state hospitals in California: every bill was wrong. Nobody died as a result of that error; nobody noticed the error; nobody cared about the extra money (or the insufficient money) billed by the computer.

[12] At least one would think that the requirements are easy. After all, the mathematical definition of the sine of an angle is about as well-defined and rigorous as one could hope to find. But in the real world of 1966 at DEC, I was told that the "correct" definition of sin(x) for any value of x was, "Whatever answer the IBM 7090 math library generates." Competitive accuracy, in this case, was more important than mathematical accuracy—though I doubt that anyone ever compared the results.

interest are several thousand times larger than this. There has not been, and probably will not be (before the end of this century) a formal proof of correctness of a software system involving more than a million lines of code. However, several universities and government agencies are working on computer-assisted proofs of correctness for software systems involving 5,000 to 10,000 lines of code. Systems of this size are not truly complex, but they are clearly not toy systems either.

In the long run, we will see a combination of top-down proof of correctness (computer-assisted, of course) and bottom-up certification of basic modules from which complex systems are built. In a software development environment like the UNIX system described in the previous section, it is conceivable that the bottom-level primitives could be subjected to rigorous, human-oriented, computer-assisted, proofs of correctness. Larger systems, built from combinations and permutations of these components, might not be error-free, but at least they would be working with higher-level components whose correct behavior had been certified.

References for Chapter 31

1. Naur, P., and Randell, B., eds., *Software Engineering*, Brussels 39, Belgium: NATO, Scientific Affairs Division, January 1969.

2. Yourdon, Edward, *Managing the System Life Cycle*, New York: YOURDON Press, 1982.

3. Dickinson, Brian, *Developing Structured Systems*, New York: YOURDON Press, 1980.

4. Metzger, Philip, *Managing a Programming Project*, Englewood Cliffs, N.J.: Prentice-Hall, 1981.

5. Yourdon, Edward, *Structured Walkthroughs*, 3rd ed., New York: YOURDON Press, 1985.

6. _____, *Managing the Structured Techniques*, 3rd ed., New York: YOURDON Press, 1985.

7. Dijkstra, Edsger, "Goto Considered Harmful," in *Classics in Software Engineering*, Edward Yourdon, ed., New York: YOURDON Press, 1979.

8. _____, "Programming Considered as a Human Activity," in *Classics in Software Engineering*, Edward Yourdon, ed., New York: YOURDON Press, 1979.

9. Bohm. G., and Jacopini, C., "Flow Diagrams, Turing Machines and Languages with Only Two Formulation Roles," in *Classics in Software Engineering*, Edward Yourdon, ed., New York: YOURDON Press, 1979.

10. Baker, Terry F., "The Chief Programmer Team Project," in *Classics in Software Engineering*, Edward Yourdon, ed., New York: YOURDON Press, 1979.

11.   Stevens Wayne, Myers Glen, and Constantine, Larry, "Structured Design," *IBM Systems Journal*, April 1974.

12.   Myers, Glen, *Composite Design*, Princeton, N.J.: Petrocelli Books, 1975.

13.   Yourdon, Edward, and Constantine, Larry, *Structured Design*, New York: YOURDON Press, 1975.

14.   Jackson, Michael, *Principles of Program Design*, New York: Academic Press, 1975.

15.   Warnier, Jean-Dominique, *The Logical Construction of Programs*, New York: Van Nostrand, 1976.

16.   Stevens, Wayne, *Using Composite Design*, New York: John Wiley & Sons, 1979.

17.   Page-Jones, Meilir, *The Practical Guide to Structured Systems Design*, New York: YOURDON Press, 1980.

18.   Alexander, Christopher, *Notes on the Synthesis of Form*, 2nd ed., Cambridge, Mass.: Harvard University Press, 1971.

19.   Zvegintzov, Nicholas, *Software Maintenance News*.

20.   DeMarco, Tom, *Structured Analysis and System Specification*, New York: YOURDON Press, 1978.

21.   Weinberg, Victor, *Structured Analysis*, New York: YOURDON Press, 1978.

22.   Gane, Chris, and Sarson, Trish, *Structured Analysis and Systems Design*, Improved Systems Technologies, New York: YOURDON Press, 1977.

23.   Flavin, Matt, *Fundamental Concepts of Information Modeling*, New York: YOURDON Press, 1979.

24.   Ward, Paul, and Mellor, Steve, *Developing Real-Time Systems*, Vol. 1-3, New York: YOURDON Press, 1985.

25.   Keller, Bob, *The Practice of Structured Analysis*, New York: YOURDON Press, 1983.

26.   Jones, T. Capers, "A Software Productivity Survey," Williamsburg, Va., March 12-14, 1985.

27.   DeMarco, Tom, *Controlling Software Projects*, New York: YOURDON Press, 1982.

28.   Sackman, H., W. J. Ericson, and E. E. Grant, "Exploratory Experimental Studies Comparing OnLine and OffLine Programming Performance," in *Classics in Software Engineering*, Edward Yourdon, ed., New York: YOURDON Press, 1979.

32

AUTOMATED TOOLS

Man is a tool-using animal . . . Without tools he is nothing, with tools he is all.

Thomas Carlyle
Sartor Resartus, Book I, Chapter 4

In the past several chapters, I have painted a rather gloomy picture of the American software community as an overpaid, labor-intensive, sloppy, error-prone, ragtag band of anarchists. Whether or not you agree with this completely, you must by now understand my feeling that the software industry won't show dramatic improvements unless we can change the attitude and mind set of the half-million people who write COBOL and FORTRAN statements for a living.

Unfortunately, even if we do this, it may not be enough to save the American software industry. Even if every programmer decided to reform tomorrow morning by taking a bath, wearing clean clothes, and approaching his or her work in a thoroughly professional manner, we would probably find that the entire software industry had gravitated to one or more Third World countries within ten years. Even if every MIS manager took a solemn vow that he would no longer sacrifice quality for expediency when managing a programming project, and even if every top manager suddenly became enlightened and began treating his company's software as a capital asset, we would still be in trouble.

We are hamstrung by two major disadvantages: our high salaries, and our enormous mountain of twenty-five years of bad code that won't go away. American programmers earn salaries between six and ten times higher than those of Malaysian, or Indian, or Chinese programmers. And at the present time, the American programmer is a disorganized, unprofessional amateur; the Chinese, Japanese, Malaysian, and Indian programmers are careful, disciplined, organized, and thoroughly professional about their work. So even if we clean up our act and approach the level of professionalism that they already have, we will still be dealing with an enormous salary differential. The only thing that American programmers have working for them is their knowledge of the local idiosyncrasies of business practice, as well as their local, physical presence. The Third World countries will be working very hard over the next ten years to overcome these two obstacles, by forming joint ventures, partnerships, and marketing relationships with American firms. Thus, by the early to mid-1990s, the issue of who is chosen to do the software development work may be decided on salaries alone.

Our other problem is the millions and millions of lines of old code written in COBOL, FORTRAN, PL/I, JOVIAL, ALGOL, LISP, assembler, MAD, AUTOCODER, SLIP, FORTH, Pascal, Logo, (ugh) BASIC, SMALLTALK, MUMPS, CMS/2, and dozens of other arcane programming languages. This code won't go away: American business can't afford to let it go away. So it stays—all $300 billion of it—festering, growing in size by 10 percent each year, consuming more and more of our available programming resources. It would be a supreme irony if we found ten years from now that all of our American programmers had been relegated to the second-class citizen work of maintaining old programs, while all of the new, exciting, challenging development work was being given to Third World programmers. It could happen; indeed, I believe it will happen unless major changes take place within the American software business during the next five years.

The solution, in my opinion, is the combination of a radical transformation of the mind set of the American software community, coupled with radically improved technology for building software systems. Even this may not be enough, for the kind of technology I have in mind is widely discussed in technical journals, and well known around the world. There is nothing at all to prevent Third World countries, or enterprising European software organizations, from taking advantage of this technology more rapidly than we can. The primary bottleneck that will limit the dissemination of the technology is the availability of capital. As we will see in this chapter, I feel that organizations that produce information systems should invest $25,000 to $50,000 per programmer for automated workstations that will increase each programmer's productivity by a factor of ten or more.

Improved programming languages, as we discussed in Chapter 29, are another approach to increased productivity. I am very much in favor of this approach, but I caution that for most large software projects, it improves only the programming phase of the project. The systems analysis phase and the design phase are more time consuming and more important; similarly, the testing, documentation, and configuration management functions are crucial and currently being short-changed and performed sloppily. We need automated tools to help improve the productivity of these functions.

THE BACKGROUND OF AUTOMATED TOOLS

An automated tool can be defined as anything that replaces manual work on the part of the computer programmer, the systems analyst, or even the end-user who must somehow communicate his requirements to the computer professionals. Thus, there are many things that could be regarded as tools:

- **High-level programming languages**, ranging from COBOL and Pascal, to the current fourth-generation languages that allow the programmer to use high-level, Englishlike statements that are automatically translated into the low-level, primitive instructions that the computer understands.

- **Cross-reference listings, "pretty-print" programs**, and other utility programs that provide the programmer with ancillary static information about his program.

- **Testing tools, debugging tools, simulators, etc.**, that provide the programmer with information about the dynamic behavior of his program as it is running. Testing tools help the programmer create a wide variety of test cases to ensure that his program is well-tested. Debugging tools help the programmer track down errors once he knows that something has gone wrong. Simulators provide the programmer with a more visual, graphic representation of the execution of the program—e.g., by showing the program as a flowchart on a CRT screen, and simulating the behavior of the program as it executes by showing the flow of control through the flowchart.

- **Time-sharing terminals** that replace "batch" development environments. This battle was fought and won ten years ago in most software organizations, but it is important to realize that the time-sharing terminal is a tool. In the 1960s and early 1970s, programmers had to write their programs, manually, on large coding pads; the program statements were then keypunched on cards (remember punched cards?) and then fed into the computer in the middle of the night. If something was wrong (because the programmer wrote a syntactically incorrect statement, or because the keypunch operator mispunched something), an error report would be waiting for the programmer the next morning. And the cycle would begin anew. . . . That all disappeared by the mid-1970s in most organizations: a programmer now types his program directly into a time-sharing terminal, shared with hundreds of other programmers and/or end-users. His program can be checked for syntactic correctness on the spot, and he can test and debug his program on the spot. Today, it is hard to imagine any other environment. But that is partly because dumb terminals can be acquired for less than $500. Ten years ago, the cost was typically $3,000 or more, and nobody was quite sure whether a programmer merited that much of a capital investment.

- **Personal computers that allow off-line program development**. Today, the $3,000 investment is a personal computer. Dumb terminals are OK, but only if the mainframe computer to which they are connected can provide sufficiently consistent, fast response time to allow the programmers to work productively. Many of them simply cannot; they often provide a five-second response to the most trivial input, and a ten-second response to significant inputs. An attractive alternative is a dedicated personal computer that the programmer can use to compose his computer program, and make appropriate corrections and revisions by using a standard word processing program; compile his program to see if there are any syntax errors that the mainframe computer would reject; and carry out some limited off-line testing.

- **Source code control packages** that prevent the programmer from making unauthorized changes to official versions of a program in the middle of the night. In a large programming project, one of the difficulties is configuration management: making sure that there is a firm control over the various pieces of the final system. Each programmer works on his own piece, and may need dozens of revisions to that piece before it is finished. But his piece interacts with similar pieces being worked on by a dozen other programmers. Unless everyone knows which version of which piece is to be considered the official version, anarchy prevails. A source code control package is like an automated librarian: it prevents unauthorized withdrawal of or tampering with official documents.

- **Systems analysis and design workbenches**. The tools described above are concerned primarily with the job of writing programs—i.e., deciding what COBOL statements or FORTRAN statements are required to solve a well-defined problem. But that is not where we have the major difficulty in building a software system. The real problem is in the early stages of systems analysis (figuring out what the system should do) and design (figuring out what the overall architecture of the system should be). Now we are beginning to see tools that provide assistance to the systems analysts and systems designers.

Most of the tools described above have been available for the past ten to fifteen years, and many are widely used in MIS organizations. The "workbenches," on the other hand, are very new and have not even begun to permeate the software industry as of 1985. It is these tools, in my opinion, that have the potential of saving the American software industry.

As we saw in Chapter 31, software engineering relies heavily on models of a system that is to be computerized. The "analyst workbench" and "designer workbench" tools are primarily concerned with the effective development of those models—e.g., they help the systems analyst construct graphical diagrams that enable the end-user to understand what the system will do for him. The workbenches also help the analyst and designer ensure that the model is complete, accurate, and consistent, so the errors discovered downstream in the programming phase will be only programming errors, and not a reflection of an ongoing misunderstanding between the end-user and the systems analyst.[1] And, finally, the workbenches may assist the programmer in translating the model into a working program. In the future, we may expect the workbenches to completely automate this process.

The software industry has been talking about tools like this for five years or more; however, nothing much was done about it. This was partly because the technology of software engineering had not yet permeated the industry, but it was more a question of economics. As I indicated earlier, it was not until the mid-1970s that most MIS organizations accepted the notion that every programmer should have a dumb terminal on his desk, and it took another five years for many organizations to actually purchase the terminals and provide a separate mainframe computer for the systems development staff. (In the interim, two or three programmers often had to share one terminal—much like two or three people having to share the same phone in an office[2]—and the entire systems development staff had to share the mainframe computer with hundreds of end-users trying to accomplish useful work on their terminals.)

Meanwhile, personal computers and workstations were gradually beginning to appear in the consumer marketplace. In the late 1970s and early 1980s, most programmers ignored the machines, for they were not very powerful—not by the mainframe standards by which they judged computer power. A sufficiently high-power

---

[1] This is important, because we know that 50 percent of the errors in a typical systems development project today are due to misunderstandings between the end-user and the systems analyst; 75 percent of the cost of error removal in an operational system is associated with errors that originated in the systems analysis phase.

[2] In the opinion of most programmers, it's more like two or three people sharing the same toothbrush.

workstation capable of helping the analyst/designer with his software engineering models would have cost $50,000 to $100,000 in the 1980-81 timeframe, and that was simply out of the question for most MIS organizations. Only a very few organizations, with enormous projects and enormous budgets, could even consider such a expenditure; and then, the most one could hope for was one workstation for an entire department of hundreds of people. Some early workstations were developed for aerospace companies, defense contractors, and manufacturers of sophisticated computer graphics workstations, but the mainstream MIS community studiously ignored the concept.

By 1983, things had begun to change. Powerful personal computers, with high-resolution graphics and adequate storage capacity, had dropped below a magical price barrier of $10,000.[3] Some of these were engineering-oriented workstations, made by aggressive new computer companies like Apollo Computer and Sun Computer; some turned out to be a "flash in a pan," like Apple's Lisa computer. Most, though, turned out to be customized configurations of IBM's immensely popular personal computer. By providing an open architecture, IBM made it possible for anyone to build a special-purpose configuration to suit his own needs. Thus, the software tool industry could construct a powerful workstation consisting of an IBM PC chassis, a graphics board from vendor A, additional memory from vendor B, and a high-resolution display screen from vendor C.

This ability to construct a powerful workstation that says IBM on the front is crucially important in the marketplace. The political reality is that in business organizations—banks, insurance agencies, and the nonmilitary government agencies—the personal com-

[3] The number $10,000 is "magical" because it is the level at which higher levels of authorization are required before spending corporate funds. A project manager can often see the practical benefits of a software engineering workstation and can often provide realistic cost-benefit figures. But if the decision involves $20,000, it will escalate up to the level of an assistant vice president who has spent weeks trying to stay awake long enough to do something useful in the organization. Now he can organize a committee, develop standards, survey the industry and write memos to dozens of other equally sleepy assistant vice presidents. While all of this high-level decision making is taking place, the project manager shrugs his shoulders, tries to forget that he ever submitted the requisition in the first place, and goes back to using his tried-and-true Stone Age techniques for building systems. As you can tell, I am entirely objective and have absolutely no emotional feelings about this subject.

puter must say IBM on the front panel; this is, unfortunately, more important than technological superiority of the hardware. Engineering and scientific organizations don't care as much whose computer they use (though many of them would prefer that any personal computer they buy look like a DEC VAX computer), and defense contractors don't care what kind of computer they use, as long as its cost can be included in the government contract.

There are now several dozen companies in the United States building software products and hardware workstations to assist the systems analyst and designer. Among them are McDonnell Douglas Automation Company (McAuto), Tektronix, Index Systems, Nastec, the YOURDON Software Engineering Company, ISDOS Inc., and Boeing. One of the driving forces behind this cadre of companies is the belief that within the next five to ten years, virtually every white-collar worker in the United States—and especially every programmer, systems analyst, systems designer, and end-user of computer systems—will have a powerful personal computer on his desk. The hardware power will be there; now all we need to do is augment that power with a few additional hardware gadgets, and some very powerful software.

IMPORTANT FEATURES
IN AUTOMATED TOOLS

It is easy to think of automated workbenches for systems analysts and designers as nothing more than "electronic etch-a-sketch" products. It is certainly true that the graphics capability of these products is the most visible and the most "sexy," but it is only one of the important features. The workbenches must provide the following features to be of significant use in the development of a complex system:

- Graphics support for multiple types of models.

- Error-checking features to ensure model accuracy.

- Cross-checking of different models.

- Additional software engineering support.

Graphics Support

Software engineering models rely on various forms of information: text, data dictionaries, and graphical diagrams. Text and data dictionaries can be automated using word processing systems and conventional mainframe computers; it is the graphics support that has always been lacking. The systems analyst needs a workstation that will allow him to compose, revise, and store the following kinds of diagrams:

- Data flow diagrams (DFD).

- Structure charts (SC).

- Flowcharts (FC).

- Entity-relationship diagrams (ERD).

- State-transition diagrams (STD).

Thus, an analyst workbench might allow the systems analyst to compose the DFD shown in Figure 32.1.

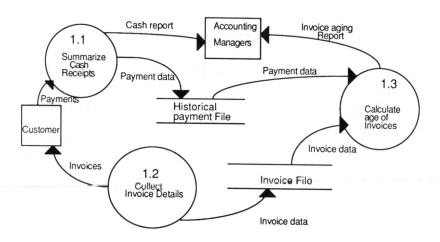

Figure 32.1: **A Typical DFD**

I should point out that I composed this diagram using a simple etch-a-sketch facility on the Apple Macintosh computer that I am using to write this book. It is called MacDraw.[4] It took me fifteen minutes to compose the diagram, and another five minutes to copy it directly into the text of this chapter. I could have drawn the diagram by hand in three minutes, and I could have pasted it into the chapter, using scissors and tape, in about thirty seconds. The benefit of graphics support clearly does not come from the initial drawing of the diagram—it comes instead from the ease of modification.

In a typical systems development project, a diagram like Figure 32.1 might be modified a dozen times. Indeed, one systems analyst at Tektronix told me that he and the end-user had modified a DFD like Figure 32.1 over a hundred times before they finally agreed that it was an accurate model of the user's requirements.[5] Nobody in his right mind would consider redrawing a diagram manually a hundred times; however, making a small change in a diagram on the computer display screen usually takes only a minute or so. Some early results from the Hartford Insurance Group, which has over 250 workstations installed in its information systems division, indicate as much as a 40 percent improvement in productivity just because of the automated graphics support.[1]

I should also emphasize that general-purpose graphics programs like MacDraw or MacPaint (on the Macintosh), or LisaDraw (on the ill-fated Apple Lisa), or PC Draw (on the IBM PC) are not really adequate for the software engineer. To build formal software engineering models, we must first decide what icons, or graphical symbols, will be allowed. We must then devise rules that define the

[4] I would have preferred using the Analyst Toolkit developed by my firm, the YOURDON Software Engineering Company. But then I would have been accused of being biased. And I would have had to figure out how to merge the diagram generated by our IBM PC-based software package into the text file for this chapter, which I am writing on the Macintosh; that would have taken all night, and I want to finish this chapter tonight. Anyway, I'll be happy to tell you more about the YOURDON Analyst Toolkit, which is the greatest thing since sliced bread. Write to me at YOURDON Software Engineering Company, 1501 Broadway, New York, NY 10036.

[5] It was obviously a more complicated diagram than the one shown in Figure 32.1. Indeed, most real-world data flow diagrams are: they have seven or eight "bubbles," three or four data stores, a dozen or more data flows, and several external sources or "sinks."

properties of the icons and the legal connections between icons. Figure 32.1, for example, uses the four icons associated with a standard DFD: a circle, a rectangle, a notation for a data store, and a line showing the flow of data from one place to another. Mac-Draw, however, would have happily allowed me to include triangles, hexagons, and any other graphic representation on the diagram. And it doesn't know that once a data flow has been connected to a bubble, the two objects should thereafter be treated as a group or composite object. On a simpler level, I had a difficult time creating bubbles (circles) that were the same size, and it took forever to put arrowheads at the end of the lines.

Error-Checking Features

Though graphics support is clearly necessary, it is by no means enough to justify the expense of a $10,000 computer workstation. An analyst workbench must examine the model created by the systems analyst or designer to ensure that it is complete and internally consistent. Figure 32.1, for example, could be analyzed in the following way:

- Are all of the icons connected? Are there any free-standing data stores or process bubbles floating around on the diagram, with no inputs and no outputs?

- Does each process bubble have at least one output? If not, it is a suspicious "black hole" that gobbles up data but never produces any output.

- Are all of the data flows (the named lines connecting the boxes and bubbles) named? Do all of the names exist in a data dictionary?

- Do all of the processes (the bubbles) have unique names?

Similar error-checking can be done on SCs, FCs, ERDs, and STDs. And the error-checking can be extended to different levels of modeling. Figure 32.1, for example, might be a low-level subsystem represented by a single bubble (bubble number 1) in a higher-level accounting system modeled in Figure 32.2.

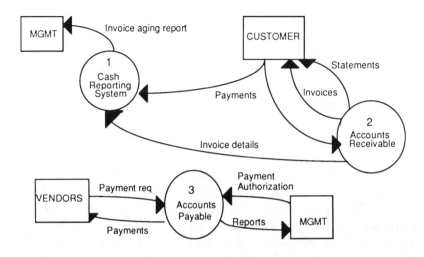

Figure 32.2: **A Higher-Level DFD**

The analyst workbench should ensure that the inputs and outputs shown in Figure 32.1 match those shown for "bubble 1" in Figure 32.2. If they do not match, the model is inconsistent, and there will be hell to pay weeks later (or months later) when someone tries to translate the graphical model into COBOL. The same kind of balancing can be applied to several other graphical models that provide a top-down view of a system.

Cross-Checking of Different Models

The most important feature of an analyst/designer workbench is its ability to cross-check the consistency of several different types of models of a system. There are two aspects to this: cross-checking different models in one phase of a project, and cross-checking different models at different phases of a project.

In the systems analysis phase of a project, for example, the primary objective is to determine what the user wants from the system—with little or no reference to the particular computer technology that will be used to implement those requirements. To do this, we need DFDs to highlight the division of those requirements into separate functions, and the interface between the functions. We need ERDs to highlight the objects of stored data in the system, and the relationship between the objects. And we need STDs to highlight the states in which the system may find itself, and the time-dependent behavior of the system. In addition, we use a data dictionary to maintain a formal definition of all the data elements in the system, and some form of textual description to define the formal business policy for each bottom-level function in the system.

The key point is that all of these models must be consistent with one another. If the DFD refers to a data element that is not in the data dictionary, something is wrong; if the data dictionary defines data elements that do not appear in any other model, something is wrong. If the DFD shows data stores that are not defined in the ERD, there is an inconsistency; and if the ERD shows objects that are not defined in the data dictionary and not shown in a DFD, there is an inconsistency. All of this cross-checking could be done manually, but it is a tedious, error-prone process at best. My several years of experience with software engineering in typical MIS environments allows me to say with some confidence (unfortunately) that it will not be done manually, despite the exhortations of project managers and the best intentions of the technicians.

In addition to consistency checking between models in one phase of a project, it is important to compare the models developed during different phases. For example, the models developed during the analysis phase should be compared with the models developed during the design phase. This comparison should demonstrate a one-to-one correspondence between the two: every requirement described in the analysis model (i.e., the DFDs, ERDs, etc.) should be represented somewhere in the design model (i.e., the SCs, etc.), and every feature described in the design model should correspond to a requirement described somewhere in the analysis model. The most common problem, of course, is that a requirement in the analysis model gets dropped and doesn't show up anywhere in the design model.

This is particularly common when the systems analysis model is developed by one group of people, and the design model (and subsequent coding and testing) is developed by a separate group. In the extreme case (which often occurs on government projects), the two groups may work for different companies. In any case, the two groups often represent different interests and perspectives, and they may not communicate well with each other on any level. Hence, a requirement that the analysis team thought was perfectly clear may not be understandable to the design team.

Sometimes the problem is just the opposite of the above: the design team decides to introduce features (or functions) that were never requested by the user and never documented in the analysis model. This may happen innocently, but it usually occurs when someone on the design team says, "Even though they didn't ask for it, I'll bet the users will really love this feature." Or the veteran, slightly cynical, designer says, "Even though the users didn't request feature X today, I know from past experience that they'll want it next week. It's easier to put it in now than to wait for them to ask for it." Whether or not this is reasonable is beside the point. The important thing is to get this discussion out in the open, rather than letting the designer make a unilateral decision.

In the same way, the design model should be compared against the actual code. Again, there should be a one-to-one relationship between components of the code (the actual implementation of the analysis and design models) and components of the design model.

FUTURE TECHNOLOGY OF AUTOMATED TOOLS

Many of the features described above exist in the analyst/designer workbenches in the market today. Some of the features are implemented in a somewhat crude and primitive form, but the products are being improved on an almost daily basis. Nevertheless, all of the products must be regarded as first-generation tools; they represent just the beginning of a long series of developments that will take place over the next five to ten years.

The timetable for second-generation and third-generation automated development tools is somewhat unclear. Some of it is dependent on the resources of the companies building the tools; some of it is dependent on the continued development of hardware technology that will provide more and more power in the personal workstations. And much of it is dependent on the technology transfer issue. Large organizations are just beginning to experiment with one or two workstations in the mid-1980s, and it will take several years for even the first-generation technology to permeate the software development industry.

However, I am confident that if you visit a large, professional MIS organization in 1995, you will find that every programmer (if there are any programmers left by then) and every systems analyst and every end-user and every project manager will have a workstation on his desk that is between 10 and 100 times more powerful than today's workstation. It will provide the following features:

- Networks for project-wide use.

- Customized software engineering methodology support.

- Document control.

- Project management facilities.

- Productivity statistics and software metrics.

- Early checking for excessive complexity.

- Automated testing and simulation.

- Computer-assisted proof of correctness.

- Code generation.

- AI support of reusable code.

- Project team "blackboards."

Networks for Project-Wide Use

Automated tools are useful even on small, one-person projects; so is software engineering. But a small project has the advantage that the work can be done over and over again until it is right, so that the use of formal models and formal tools does not have much sense of urgency.

Automated tools will be of most use on the large, multiperson, multiyear, multimillion dollar software development project. In projects of this kind, there are several systems analysts (often a dozen or more), several end-users (often in different geographical locations), and several designers and programmers. In this kind of environment, it is important not only that the work of each systems analyst be internally consistent, but also that the work of Analyst A and Analyst B be consistent with one another.

This means that there has to be a level of intelligence above that of the individual systems analyst or programmer. Though there are many ways of implementing this, one of the more attractive architectures is shown in Figure 32.3.

The project-level minicomputer should have enough storage capacity and enough processing power to carry out project-wide consistency checking. It should also have enough power to perform additional functions. It should allow the programmers to connect directly to the organization's mainframe for testing and other normal duties. And it is the obvious place to put the intelligence associated with many of the functions described below.

The addition of such a minicomputer—together with associated disk storage, communication channels, etc.—obviously increases the cost of automated support. In 1985 dollars, the cost of an appropriately configured stand-alone workstation is between

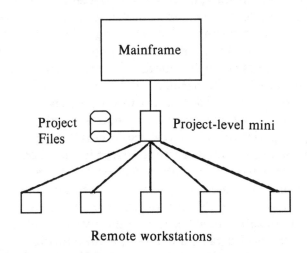

Remote workstations

Figure 32.3: **A Project-Level Analyst/Designer Workbench**

$8,000 and $15,000; with the hardware and software for the project-level minicomputer, the price could easily double. It is a price well worth paying, but it probably cannot be funded out of a single year's operating budget for a large MIS staff—it would cost millions of dollars for an organization with a few hundred system developers. It must be recognized as part of a capital investment in the effort to make the staff more productive and more professional.

Customized Software Engineering Methodology Support

The automated tool usually supports a specific form of software engineering notation and procedures. The diagrams in this chapter, for example, as well as the ones in Chapter 31, use the notation described in several YOURDON incorporated textbooks and training classes.[2-11] Surprise! But the YOURDON Analyst Toolkit also supports other popular software engineering methodologies, such as the Gane/Sarson notation,[12] as well as the Warnier/Orr notation.[13] Some of the other automated support tools currently available also support more than one brand of software engineering methodology.

But there is something much more important than just supporting the methodology of vendor A or vendor B: the automated tool should allow for a customized methodology. An MIS organization will almost always find that any of the popular software engineering methodologies fail to provide an adequate notation or adequate set of guidelines for the peculiar kind of system it is developing. Perhaps, for example, the MIS organization feels strongly that it wants to use triangles to emphasize inputs and outputs from Martians and Captain Kirk's Star Trek explorers (most of us don't have to worry about such inputs and outputs, so it's never occurred to us to ask for triangles on our automated tool). And maybe the MIS organization has decided to pass an edict that no data flow diagram will have more than thirteen (a baker's dozen) bubbles on it; another organization may decide that no system should have more than three levels of data flow diagram. And so forth.

Clearly, this kind of customization should be allowed. It must be allowed, or the tool will gradually fall into disuse as systems developers find that it does not meet their needs. Most of the currently available automated tools do not have this facility; virtually all second-generation products will have such a feature, or they will disappear from the marketplace.

Document Control

As we have seen, software engineering relies on a number of formal graphical models, supported by such textual materials as data dictionaries and process specifications; the workstations automate the development and maintenance of these documents. However, they permit something else: the control of the documents. While this may seem straightforward, it is a radical concept for most MIS organizations. Many of them have only recently begun to control the source code that is produced in the programming phase of the project.

But just as it is disastrous to allow a programmer to make a teeny-weeny change in an operational computer program in the middle of the night, so it is equally disastrous to allow a systems analyst to make a teeny-weeny change in a DFD or ERD in the middle of the systems analysis phase of a project, unless that change has been authorized and approved.

To make this work, we must distinguish between the private libraries that each project member maintains on his stand-alone workstation and the project file maintained on the project-level minicomputer shown in Figure 32.3. It is the project file that we want to control. Once a systems analyst or designer has indicated that he has finished a model (or diagram) and is ready to submit it to the project file, he is no longer the unilateral owner of the material.

Project Management

Document control is one aspect of another feature that can be provided by a project-level minicomputer: project management. The project manager can have his own workstation and can use the facilities of the minicomputer to coordinate and supervise the activities of his project team. With appropriate software support, he can make sure that he knows when analyst A finishes the DFD he was working on; he can instruct the minicomputer to send that DFD to analyst B for review and comments; he can then assign another piece of work to analyst A. He can use all of this material to update his project schedule and budget; and since the mini-computer keeps its own neutral record of when analyst A began and finished his DFD, he is likely to get much more accurate, unbiased input for his project scheduling activities. The project manager can use the electronic mail capabilities that will almost certainly be provided by the architecture of Figure 32.3 to communicate with his staff. It may be difficult to provide a "hard" estimate of the value of such a facility, but most project teams will find that it is a feature that they cannot live without once it is given to them.

Productivity Statistics and Software Metrics

As mentioned above, the project minicomputer can keep its own record of the starting date and ending date of each piece of work—the development of a DFD, the revision of the DFD, the walk-through of the DFD, etc.—that a systems analyst or designer or programmer carries out. Thus, productivity measures can be generated almost invisibly, which will, it is hoped, lessen the impact of the Heisenberg Uncertainty Principle.[6] Compare this to the typical software development project today, where programmers and systems analysts spend an hour or so each week recording information about how they spent their time. There is a barely disguised tendency to fill out the form to make it look the way the boss wants it to (programmers may be rascals and charlatans, but they are not entirely out of touch with reality). Also, if the recording process takes an hour, then it is interfering with the work itself; this is a form of what nuclear physicists call the Heisenberg Uncertainty Principle.

In addition, almost any other software metrics that the project team decides to keep track of can be carried out by the project-level

---

[6] Though the Heisenberg Uncertainty Principle is usually associated with the field of nuclear physics, it applies here as well: very simply, the principle says that you can't measure a phenomenon without changing the phenomenon. If a worker has to spend 10 percent of his time measuring his own work, then his productivity goes down by at least 10 percent—and the fact that he knows that he is being measured (by virtue of measurements that he captures himself) is likely to alter his behavior.

minicomputer. Thus, the project team may decide that it is important to know how many DFDs are required for the system, or how many data elements, or how many "functional primitives," or how many revisions were required of a DFD before it was finally accepted by the user, etc. This information may be useful for future projects; it may also be useful for estimates of project size and cost.

Early Checking for Excessive Complexity

One of the most useful metrics, in the long term, is that of complexity. As indicated in Chapters 30 and 31, there are mathematical models of program complexity that can be used to predict the difficulty of testing and maintaining a computer program. If the mathematical models are applied automatically to every module or program in the system being developed, then the developers and the project manager will have an early warning of potentially dangerous portions of the system; alternative designs can then be explored.

Computer-Assisted Testing and Simulation

As mentioned earlier in this chapter, there are already computer-assisted testing packages and animators that provide the programmer with a graphical representation of the execution of his program. There is no reason why that intelligence could not be put into the remote workstation or the project-level minicomputer.

Indeed, almost all of the conventional program-support tools listed at the beginning of this chapter could be incorporated into the automated workbench. As personal workstations become more powerful, it should be possible for the programmer to follow up the modeling process with actual writing of code (if it can't be generated automatically), as well as compilation and testing. Only when his program is finished should he need to upload it to the project-level minicomputer.

Computer-Assisted Proof of Correctness

As we discussed in Chapter 31, the field of computer-assisted proofs of correctness is still not developed to the point where average programmers and systems analysts can make use of it. But there is a wide spectrum between informal consistency checking and formal proofs of correctness. With automated support tools, we will gradually find that we move farther and farther away from informal consistency-checking and closer and closer to complete, formal proofs of correctness. To accomplish this will require a higher level of training and sophistication on the part of the programmer than can be expected today. Hence, we should not expect to see this feature in most business-oriented workstations for another five years.

Code Generation

A major goal of many tool builders is the automated generation of COBOL or FORTRAN code by the workbenches. Thus, nobody would ever have to look at the code, just as today hardly anyone looks at the binary ones and zeros that the computer hardware actually understands. In this context, we would be dealing with computable specifications, developed by the end-user and the systems analyst.

We may never be able to achieve this for all systems, nor will we be able to insist on the necessary level of formal, rigorous specification from all end-users. But by putting more and more emphasis on the analysis and design activities, we can easily reduce programming to a simple clerical activity. Even if we can't completely automate it, we can arrange for it to be carried out by junior clerks, rather than computer science graduates earning $40,000 per year.

AI Support of Reusable Code

Far more appealing than the concept of automated code generation is the concept of reusable code. In the vast majority of projects—business-oriented and scientific/engineering-oriented—most of the software we intend to develop has already been done before. This year's brand new system is, in fact, almost like last year's system, and not too different from the one before that. And most of the bottom-level functional primitives have been programmed before hundreds of times, and exist free as library routines supplied as part of the vendor's operating system. The only thing that distinguishes this year's brand new system as unique is the particular combination of those previously implemented functions, or some parameters that can be fed into the program when it begins running. For example, this year's payroll system is basically the same as last year's, but the FICA tax rate has changed.

This suggests that the systems analyst—and, even more, the systems designer—should not look upon each new project as a grand experiment in scientific exploration, but rather as a "scavenger hunt" to see which existing library modules, subroutines, and programs can be connected together to satisfy the user's needs.

This is where artificial intelligence could come in handy. By matching the characteristics of a function identified by the systems analyst—e.g., number of inputs, nature of outputs, and transformation specifications (the rules that describe how inputs are turned into outputs), etc.—with an existing library of implemented functions, an expert system could suggest to the designer a number of potential candidates to be used to implement the system. And it could interact with the systems analyst to show him that by making a small change in the requirements (i.e., by compromising the user's original requirements a little bit), an existing library function could be used *in situ*.

Project Team "Blackboards"

Some of the leading researchers in the country—e.g., at research labs like MCC in Austin, Texas[7]—feel that the real productivity improvements in the 1990s will come from the synergistic effects of a project team rather than the individual. Most of the concepts described thus far concern the improved productivity of an individual worker, but the intelligence of the project-level minicomputer could be used to provide a convenient project-level view of an entire system as it gradually takes shape and grows.

This concept of a project blackboard is being implemented at MCC as part of the Leonardo project; it should provide fascinating

[7] MCC is a sterling example of why we should not look to the government to provide research funding or directions for computer software research. As you will see in Chapter 33, I feel that the only useful role for the government is to provide industry-wide information on the current state of the art in software development in other countries. For more information on MCC, see Chapter 12.

results by the end of the decade The research group is experimenting with the notion of a communal blackboard in the form of a wall-sized CRT. They are also investigating the idea of using the sense of smell and sound, as well as color, to add new dimensions to the graphical models described in this chapter and Chapter 31. If it is successful, the Leonardo project will be the third-generation or fourth-generation automated workbench for software developers in the mid-1990s.

CONCLUSION

My bias for, and excitement about, this aspect of software development is obvious; I cannot hide it. I do not apologize for it. I truly feel that it represents the only mechanism that can help us catch up and keep up with the hordes of programmers in countries around the world who would take away the magical industry we have created in the United States over the past twenty-five years.

Some will say that this technology is too expensive, that no programmer is worth an investment of $25,000. Perhaps not—but since hardware is getting cheaper all the time, today's $25,000 is tomorrow's $10,000 and next year's $5,000. It strikes me as highly ironic that a country that invests $50,000 to $75,000 in capital equipment for its farm workers and factory workers should begrudge a few thousand dollars for its information workers. This reluctance, this grudging acceptance that investments may be necessary, is the last gasp of the Industrial Revolution, the last gasp of what Alvin Toffler calls the "second wave."

I will admit that a software profession dominated by automated workstations does raise some serious questions: Does it make programmers obsolete? Will it destroy our creativity? Can we afford the cost? And does it guarantee that we will make dramatic improvements in our ability to produce high-quality software more productively?

There is nothing magical about automated software tools; anyone with common sense can answer these questions. Automated tools will certainly not make programmers obsolete in the short term, and will not make maintenance programmers obsolete for another twenty years or more. In the meantime, it should help deemphasize the business of programming, which will continue a trend that has been in motion since the first high-level language was invented in the late 1950s. It does not threaten the job of any programmer: remember that backlog of seven years in most organizations!

Will an automated workstation destroy the creativity of software developers? Bah! Humbug! Do CAD/CAM (computer-aided design) systems destroy the ability of a designer to design an aesthetically beautiful automobile or airplane? No! Quite the contrary. The availability of automated support tools helps the programmer and systems analyst concentrate on the truly creative part of the job and spend less time worrying about the mundane parts of the job. Since an analyst workbench allows the systems analyst to spend more time inventing more models of the user's requirements, it makes him more creative.

Can we afford the cost of these workstations? The simple answer is this: we cannot afford the cost of not using these workstations. With these workstations, we have some chance of saving the American software industry; without them, there is virtually no hope. For those who want something more practical, keep in mind that the cost of a workstation, assuming that we include the project-level minicomputer support, is about $25,000. That is about equal to the annual salary, in 1985, of a typical computer programmer with one to two years of experience. If one includes the overhead cost (insurance, pension benefits of 100 percent), it represents about six months of the cost of a programmer. Since we can easily justify amortizing the cost of the hardware and associated software over three years, the cost is roughly equal to 15 percent of a programmer's annual cost. In other words, if it increases the programmer's productivity by 15 percent each year, it pays for itself.

But does an automated software development workbench guarantee to improve productivity by a factor of ten? Anyone who can seriously ask such a question must still believe in the Tooth Fairy and the Easter Bunny. Does going to church every Sunday guarantee that you will go to heaven? Stupidity, arrogance, laziness, and other related human frailties will always make it possible to fail despite the best of tools and support; there is no way that we can preclude this possibility. But if we believe in the power of information systems and automated support for society and for business, we should believe in it for the profession that builds systems for the rest of the human race. It should not always be true that the cobbler's children are the last to wear shoes.

References for Chapter 32

1.   Crawford, Jack, "Productivity Tools at Hartford Insurance Group," speech at Wang Computer Company, Boston, Mass., May 6, 1985.

2.   Ward, Paul, and Steve Mellor, *Structured Systems Development for Real-Time Systems*, Volumes 1-3, New York: YOURDON Press, 1985.

3.   Page-Jones, Meilir, *The Practical Guide to Structured Systems Design*, New York: YOURDON Press, 1980.

4.   McMenamin, Steve, and John Palmer, *Essential Systems Analysis*, New York: YOURDON Press, 1984.

5.   Ward, Paul, *Systems Development Without Pain*, New York: YOURDON Press, 1984.

6.   Dickinson, Brian, *Developing Structured Systems*, New York: YOURDON Press, 1980.

7.   Yourdon, Edward, *Managing the System Life Cycle*, New York: YOURDON Press, 1982.

8.   _____, and Larry Constantine, *Structured Design*, Englewood Cliffs, N.J.: Prentice-Hall, 1979.

9.   King, David, *Current Practices in Software Engineering*, New York: YOURDON Press, 1983.

10.   DeMarco, Tom, *Structured Analysis and System Specification*, New York: YOURDON Press, 1978.

11.   _____, *Concise Notes on Software Engineering*, New York: YOURDON Press, 1979.

12.   Gane, Chris, and Trish Sarson, *Structured Systems Analysis and Design*, Englewood Cliffs, N.J.: Prentice-Hall, 1977.

13.   Orr, Ken, *Structured Systems Development*, New York: YOURDON Press, 1977.

33

PREDICTIONS V

New terms such as techno-stress and techno-shock have been coined to define the psychological manifestations of a public overwhelmed by everything from microwave ovens to home Pac-Man games. Unfortunately, these terms do not accurately describe progress within the data processing industry as it pertains to software development. For many data processing professionals, techno-stress is better defined as frustration with the slow pace of change in software development methods, in the face of ever-increasing demand for dp services.

While there is no question that some progess toward better systems development methods has been made during the last 30 years, there is equally no question that, overall, any process of change is relatively slow and discontinuous. Speaking from an historical perspective, it seems that for true progress to be realized, there must be a periodic, collective rethinking of basic ideas. The periods between each great leap forward can be tens of years to hundreds of years.

F.J. Grant
"Twenty-First Century Software," *Datamation*, April 1, 1985

By now, I hope you have gotten the impression that software is the key issue that will determine whether we can successfully integrate computers into our lives. If you work in the software field, you knew this already. If you are an end-user who has dealt with software people, you probably suspected it. If you are a top manager or government official or an ordinary citizen who has managed to remain isolated from computer systems, you may not have been aware of the state of chaos in the software field. Now you know.

I finish this discussion of software by making some specific predictions about developments over the next ten years. I also have some recommendations on what you should do about it, depending on whether you are a software producer, an end-user, someone concerned about the government's role, an investor, or just an ordinary citizen.

SPECIFIC PREDICTIONS

With so much attention on software development today, it is hard to predict what will change, and when the change will take place. As F. J. Grant observes, the next great leap forward could take place in the space of a few decades, or it could take centuries. Some optimists (including me) feel that the worldwide software industry is poised to make a great leap forward between now and the middle of the next decade; some pessimists (including me) worry that the inertia, laziness, and smugness of American programmers may prevent them from advancing as rapidly as other countries. Whether you are an optimist or a pessimist, the future of software is something you should think about. As Charles Franklin Kettering once said, "We should all be concerned about the future because we will have to spend the rest of our lives there."[1]

With this in mind, I predict that the following will happen within the next ten years.

Software Will Be Publicly Recognized as the Dominant Segment of the Computer Industry

As I have pointed out, software consumes approximately 50 percent of the MIS budget in most organizations. In a few large government organizations (including the U.S. Air Force), the figure is closer to 80 percent. For the U.S. government as a whole, software costs rose from 20 percent of overall computer expenditures in 1965 to 60 percent in 1985.[2] By the mid-1990s, software will consume 80 to 90 percent of everyone's budget and will thus become universally recognized as the dominant factor in computer systems. This will happen because the technology of computer hardware is almost guaranteed to improve by a factor of 10 to 100 during this period.[1] So even if software development techniques improve by a factor of 10 to 100 (which is much less certain), it will still be as expensive, compared to the cost of hardware, as it is today.

Because of the dominant role of software, many of today's major companies will have drastically changed their role in the marketplace. As I pointed out in Chapters 24 and 25, companies like IBM will find that more than 50 percent of their revenues are derived from nonhardware products and services by the mid-1990s. Such companies, if they want to be successful, will gradually stop promoting their role as a hardware company, and will begin promoting their role as a full-service information company.

Customized Software Development Will Virtually Disappear

Most large MIS organizations develop customized software today. While externally developed application packages are becoming more popular, they still represent a minor part of a company's software portfolio. This will change drastically in the next ten years. As the Office of Management and Budget observes of the federal government,

> The Federal Government continues to custom develop software for more than 90 percent of its software. Customized software offers the potential benefit of initially performing exactly what the user wants. It is, however, quite expensive. Initial development is laborious, and difficult to modify. Transition to more modern, efficient hardware is often inhibited by large volumes of customized software that require conversion.
>
> The private sector also is investing more in off-the-shelf software packages than in custom developing new software. Such packages have the advantage of being maintained by the vendor, and do not require substantial in-house technical staff.
>
> The software management initiative is intended to ensure that Federal agencies reduce the annual cost of maintaining computer

[1] As we will see in Chapter 37, current research and development efforts in the hardware field could produce improvements of a factor of 100 to 1,000 in this period. I have chosen a much more conservative figure here.

software by moving away from custom development toward use of commercial software packages and the sharing of operational software.[3]

This statement accurately reflects the feelings of many government agencies, as well as that of many MIS managers in the private sector. But it is based on some interesting assumptions; in fact, I think that many organizations will be making the right decision about customized software, but for the wrong reason. Note the emphasis in the above statement on current inferior software development techniques: "Initial development is laborious, and difficult to modify . . . " and "Transition to more modern, efficient hardware is often inhibited . . . " This implies that if the software development staff could improve their productivity by a factor of ten, and if their systems could be modified ten times more easily, there might not be such a sense of urgency to use off-the-shelf software.

But such an argument ignores economies of scale. If the developer of a single, customized software package can improve his productivity by a factor of ten, so can the developer of an off-the-shelf package. And since he can amortize the cost of development over a thousand copies—or, in some cases, a million copies—he always has the ability to provide a more cost-effective solution than the person developing a customized approach. Off-the-shelf software in 1985 is typically ten times cheaper than customized software. I expect this cost differential to increase in favor of off-the-shelf software as time goes on.

But there is one factor that is ignored in this discussion: the ability and willingness of the end-user to adapt his business policies and procedures to accommodate the idiosyncrasies of the off-the-shelf package. Customized software is a legitimate, necessary choice if the user cannot or will not compromise his requirements. In some cases, particularly in bureaucratic government organizations, he simply cannot make procedural changes without an Act of Congress. The situation is often the same in large, old, tradition-bound private industry companies. Two centuries of "this is how we do things around here" are almost certainly at odds with the operating procedures required to use a $49.95 accounting package.

There are two trends that will eventually militate against this problem. One trend is the gradual death of large, old, dinosaurlike companies and their replacement by small, new companies that can easily adapt their business procedures (since they have no history and no traditions to maintain) to accommodate the off-the-shelf packages. The other trend is the continued increase in flexibility of the off-the-shelf packages: they are more and more parameter-driven and menu-driven. And they take more and more advantage of powerful computer hardware in an attempt to provide moderate customization facilities to all customers. It's hard to build a completely flexible package when it all has to fit into 64,000 bytes of computer memory, but it's a lot easier when one has 256,000 bytes available.

No Programming Language Will Dominate; Everyone Will Become Multilingual

COBOL will not disappear, but it certainly won't dominate the industry in ten years the way it does today. FORTRAN will (please, God!) no longer be taught in any respectable university, but the immense libraries of scientific FORTRAN programs will not have vanished from the earth. Pascal will still be taught in high schools and universities, but it may have been overshadowed by newer languages like Modula-2. LISP and Prolog will still be competing as the official language of artificial intelligence. Ada will have become an important programming language, thanks to the billions of dollars invested by the Defense Department (more on this below). Logo will have been extended and improved and revised and reformed to the point where it resembles (shudder) PL/I. There will still be a few fanatics, buried deep in underground mountain bomb shelters, who will write assembly language programs and will curse all of the microseconds of computer time being wasted by those who use high-level languages. Indeed, such high-level languages as FOCUS, RAMIS, DBASE-III, MANTIS, and IDEAL will overshadow COBOL in the business community.

And, God help us all, BASIC will still be warping the minds of innocent young children across the land. We can only hope that they never have any need to use the language, and that they will look upon the educational experience the same way that schoolchildren in centuries past looked upon their Latin and Greek lessons—deadly boring and generally irrelevant.

There are three important things to keep in mind about the issue of programming languages. First, no matter what anyone tells you, improved programming languages are not going to make the software crisis disappear quickly. Second, a professional programmer in the mid-1990s will have to be fluent in at least three languages, and probably more like half a dozen. And third, everyone will know how to program, because everyone will have been exposed to it in school. It's possible that educators will have discovered by the mid-1990s that learning to program in BASIC is irrelevant for most children, but we will have an entire generation of amateur programmers entering the workforce by then.

Ada Will Finally Become an Important Factor Outside the DOD Community

Within the next five years, Ada will probably be the dominant language within the Defense Department of the United States. However, the nonmilitary government agencies and the private sector can safely ignore Ada for another five years. Starting around 1990, I feel that the private sector and nonmilitary government agencies should begin looking for opportunities to take advantage of the investment in Ada.

The issue here is not the language itself. Purists can debate the merits of the Ada language forever, just as they can debate that advantages and disadvantages of Pascal, MODULA-2, and COBOL. A much more important short-term issue is whether there are available Ada compilers and available Ada programmers; the answer to both questions in the mid-1980s is "No!" Engineering companies with defense contracts must begin to learn about Ada now. Engineering companies building process control systems and other forms of embedded real-time systems may want to consider gradually switching over to Ada and educating their programming staff. But the overwhelming number of non-real-time engineering applications and all of the business applications will ignore Ada for the rest of the decade.

The important long-term issue is the support software and software tools accompanying the language. Are there telecommunications packages and database management packages? Are there user-friendly "query languages" that can be used in conjunction with Ada? Are there programmer workstations of the kind discussed in Chapter 32? Does the Ada environment allow the systems analyst and the end-user to concentrate almost all of their efforts on developing computable specifications, with the language itself almost completely hidden in the background? If the Defense Department is successful, the answer to all of these questions will be "Yes!" within five or ten years. At that point, Ada should become the language of choice for all professional software development organizations, though it will never be the right language for all applications under all circumstances. The time of the single-language MIS organization should have disappeared two or three years ago; such organizations will look foolish by the end of the decade.

Maintenance Problems Will Cause Bankruptcies in Several Fortune 500 Companies

In Chapter 30, I discussed the maintenance iceberg that is threatening to sink many unwary MIS organizations. None of the information in that chapter is new or surprising to any maintenance programmer, nor should it be surprising to any MIS manager. The question is whether anyone will do anything about it, and whether the solutions will be applied quickly enough.

For several of America's largest organizations, I think the answer will be "No." I think that several dozen of the current Fortune 500 companies will find themselves increasingly unable to deal with the fast-changing pace of global business. That inability is due to a number of factors, one of which is the lack of the right information in the right place at the right time. Part of this is a human, organizational problem: it is more and more difficult to maintain an effective, centralized, vertically organized chain-of-command company. Today, for example, most military organizations are an anachronism best left to history books. Yet neither they nor most other billion-dollar companies will be able or willing to change their basic organizational structure.

The other major problem facing large organizations is the inability to provide the proper computerized information to the right people at the right time—the generalists, who must analyze and synthesize information. This will be coupled with an inability to change existing software to provide new information or a different organization of the same information. I am not worried that the nation's banking systems are going to stop functioning one morning, or that all of the computerized telephone systems will refuse to provide a dial tone—though such things might be possible if all of the country's maintenance programmers went on a nationwide strike. No, it is more likely that companies will stagnate or suffocate because of their inability to change their software to respond to new conditions.

What will happen to the nation's software, for example, on December 31, 1999? How many programs will function correctly on January 1, 2000? What will happen when more and more customers live past the age of 100? What will happen if interest rates ever go above 10 percent per month (thus requiring an extra digit), or if Congress passes a law one morning dictating that employees have to be paid every fifteen minutes for their work? The combination of government regulations (or deregulations), market conditions, economic changes, hardware changes, and personnel changes will be more than some maintenance departments will be able to bear.

Many MIS organizations are on the brink of disaster today. Their systems are fifteen years old, and they can barely keep up with today's information requirements. In another five years, they will no longer be capable of further enhancement, modification, revision, upgrading . . . or anything other than continuing to do what they are then doing. And it will be too late, at that point, to begin thinking about how to solve the problem.

Software Engineering Technologies Will Be Fully Implemented On Programmer/Analyst Workstations

The automated tools for software development, which we discussed in Chapter 32, will be in widespread use by the mid-1990s. The tools may not be used properly or intelligently—after all, anyone can misuse a tool—but they will be available.

The reason I am so confident about this is that the technology transfer has been going on for nearly ten years already. The underlying concepts of software engineering, which we discussed in Chapter 31, have been published in technical books and journals since the late 1960s, and have been widely promoted by consulting and training organizations since the mid-1970s. Several hundred thousand programmers, systems analysts, project managers, and students around the world have been exposed to the graphical modeling techniques of structured analysis and structured design; however, they have been frustrated by the lack of automated tools.

Now that such tools are becoming available, and now that there is a trend toward placing powerful workstation hardware on everyone's desk, I believe that they will gradually become a universal fixture in every programmer's repertoire.

Techniques of Artificial Intelligence Will Be Widely Used in Systems Analysis and Maintenance

As I pointed out in Chapters 30 and 31, artificial intelligence technology offers some exciting possibilities in the field of systems analysis and software maintenance. Both could be thought of as diagnostic activities; both have sick patients; both areas are populated by experts and amateurs.

In the mid-1980s, there is such an enormous demand for AI and expert systems, and such a shortage of trained practitioners, that the initial applications will be the most exotic, or the ones for which the most money is available. Thus, the research departments in banks, insurance companies, oil companies, and military organizations are likely to keep the artificial intelligence community quite busy for the remainder of this decade.

I expect the initial developments in this area will be modest, and will be more properly described as decision support than artificial intelligence. Consider, for example, the case of the executive who has just formed a new business operation; it currently has no employees, but the executive wants to acquire a computerized payroll system in time for the first payroll a month from now. He certainly doesn't want to write his own payroll system, and his question is, "Which payroll system should I buy?" Since it is a new operation with no history, no traditions, no employees, and no political infighting (we hope), it should be possible for a decision-support program to ask a number of simple questions (e.g., "How many employees will you eventually hire? Will they be paid over-time? What states will the employees be residents of?" etc.) and recommend one of the dozens of commercially available payroll packages, based on the answers provided to the questions.

From decision support, I think we will find expert systems gradually making their appearance. As I suggested in Chapter 32, they might take the form of expert advice in the applicability of existing library modules to implement individual primitive functions that a systems analyst uncovers when asking the end-user for the requirements of his system.

Similarly, expert systems could provide an educated guess in maintenance situations. What is the probable effect of making a modification to module X? If I can accomplish a user-requested improvement by modifying module A or module B, which one is safer? And so forth.

The State of the Art in Software Development in 1995 Will Be 100 Times Higher Than in 1985—But Not in the United States

There are several different, but complementary, ways of accomplishing order-of-magnitude improvements in software development. Among the more important ones are:

- Fourth-generation languages, which can improve productivity by a factor of ten in situations where little or no systems analysis has to be done—e.g., simple maintenance activities, or small one-shot programs.

- Better trained, better-motivated professional programmers who are provided with cottage industry facilities and other appropriate support. We already know that some programmers are twenty-five times more productive than others—and this is without any conscious cultivating on the part of management.

- Diligent use of current software engineering technologies, supported by automated tools that can help spot errors when they are cheap to fix.

- Advanced software engineering technologies—e.g., software metrics and computer-assisted proofs of correctness.

- Systems development environments that encourage and facilitate large-scale reuse of existing software components.

Any one of these solutions would improve the productivity of an MIS organization by a factor of ten, and would improve the quality of the delivered products by a factor of ten. Almost all of them were developed in the United States; in any case, they have been widely publicized, debated, and discussed in American journals and computer conferences. There is no mystery about how to put them to use.

Nevertheless, I do not believe that the United States will take the lead in software development in the 1990s. We are not scared enough of the competition. And I do not believe we are hungry enough. We do not want badly enough to be the best programmers and systems analysts on earth.

STRATEGIC IMPLICATIONS

Given this rather gloomy forecast, what should you do? That depends, of course, on whether you agree with my view of the future. It also depends on your perspective: as an end-user, for example, you may not care whether your software is developed in Teaneck, New Jersey, or Taiwan, or Timbuktu.

If you are in the software business—either as a programmer, a systems analyst, a manager, or a marketing person—I suggest that you take the warnings in this chapter (and the previous six chapters) to heart. Set your own goals for productivity, quality, and professionalism. Don't base those goals on the mediocre performance you see all around you, but rather on the world standard that you will be seeing during the next five years. If your employer won't make the necessary contribution to improve your productivity and professionalism, invest your own money; it will be the best investment you've ever made. Buy some of the books listed at the end of each chapter of this book. Invest in some professional training courses.

And start looking for another, more professional employer. It

516   NATIONS AT RISK

may be necessary at some point in the near future to be like the wandering minstrels of medieval times, looking for a kingdom where your professionalism will be respected. One thing is for certain: if you stay where you are—fat, happy, and complacent, while you continue to maintain COBOL programs written twenty years ago by the man or woman who is now your fat, happy, complacent boss—you'll be on the unemployment line in ten years.

If you are an end-user, you should be less and less willing to put up with mediocre software. If your MIS organization continues to tell you that it will be five years before they can produce a system for you, look elsewhere. Look for packaged software that will suit your needs. At the same time, recognize that the key issue for any software developer is his ability to understand what you want; that burden must be shared equally by you and by him. Thus, it is important that you learn the fundamentals of the software engineering modeling techniques discussed in Chapter 32; books like *Systems Development Without Pain*,[4] for example, are intended to be read by nontechnical businesspeople.

What should the government do about all of this? Of course, the government operates, on a day-to-day basis, like any other big business except that government is the biggest business of all. Thus, if the federal government has any serious intention of remaining in control of events over the next decade, it should be even more concerned than General Motors, General Electric, and General Foods about the software situation.[2] Alternatively, the government could acknowledge that there is no way to control the effort required to develop appropriate software, and spend the next years instead delegating its functions downward to state and local governmental agencies.

The government is already investing large sums of money, as we have seen, in defense-oriented applications of better software. I see no other useful role for the government in improving the state of the art other than serving as an information agency to make it clear to everyone in the software industry how much of an economic/

[2] Clearly, the Department of Defense is concerned, and is spending billions of dollars trying to improve the productivity and quality of its software organization. But many other moribund agencies are utterly unaware of these issues.

industrial threat various other countries represent. Various government agencies regularly publish statistics on wages, productivity, and other employment statistics for a number of basic industries. They could do the American software industry a great service by publishing similar statistics on software.

If you are neither an end-user nor a producer of software, then you must be an investor, or just an ordinary citizen. To investors, the message should be fairly clear: American software companies are likely to be a less-rewarding investment over the next ten years than the software companies in Asia and parts of Europe. Thus far, it seems to me that investors and venture capitalists have been overly enamored with razzle-dazzle technology, especially in the area of decision support systems and expert systems. Some of the investment blunders in the mid-1980s have been simple-minded "me-too" mistakes. While the marketplace clearly wants a choice between two to three word processing packages and two to three spreadsheet packages, it does not need 200 to 300 different word processing packages, nor does it need 200 to 300 different spreadsheet packages.

At the same time, the investment community seems to have an instinctive caution about software, probably because investors don't understand software, can't see it, and can't touch it. In any case, the caution is healthy. Maybe some of the venture capitalists I have met were expressing more wisdom than I gave them credit for when they said, "We don't like to invest in software because we never know if it's going to be delivered when the entrepreneur says it will be."[3]

Ordinary citizens can afford to sit on the sidelines and watch the great software battles of the 1980s and 1990s without caring too much who wins and who loses, as long as they don't have friends or relatives employed by the software industry, and as long as they are not personally dependent on the quality or productivity of American software. Unfortunately, consumers and citizens are dependent on the quality and productivity of software: it controls the behav-

[3] The same is true of entrepreneurs in the computer hardware area, too: they, like software developers, are trying to attract investors before they have even built a prototype, let alone a full-scale production model.

ior of every computerized device and every computerized service in the country. There was a time when Americans had to put up with shoddily built cars, until the Japanese appeared on the scene with high-quality, inexpensive automobiles. The same will happen, I predict, with software, but it may not happen until the end of this decade or the early part of the next decade.

In the meantime, the most important thing that you can do as a citizen is to begin complaining about the quality of software. When a clerk in the bank tells you that your bank balance is wrong "because the computer messed up," you should yell at the top of your voice, "It's not the computer! It's those mediocre, unprofessional dolts that you have programming your computer!" And then you should close your bank account (if you can) and move it to another bank. You may go through a lot of banks this way,[4] but if enough people do it, the message may start to sink in.

Within the next five years, citizens will begin to see more and more computer-controlled (and thus software-controlled) products and services offered by other countries whose software technology is superior to ours; at that point, they can express their opinion on the matter by using the power of the pocketbook. During the past ten years, most American citizens have ignored political exhortations about patriotism and local jobs when they have had the opportunity to make a choice between locally produced shoddy products and foreign-produced high-quality products. I see no reason why they will act any differently when the product is software.

[4] Try one of the Japanese banks, or one of the Chinese banks. Maybe they'll be better, unless they are depending on American software written by American programmers.

References for Chapter 33

1. Kettering, Charles Franklin, *Seed for Thought*, 1931.

2. *Management of the U.S. Government*, Fiscal Year 1986. Washington, D.C.: Office of Management and Budget, U.S. Government Printing Office, February, 1985.

3. *Ibid.*

4. Ward, Paul, *Systems Development Without Pain*, New York: YOURDON Press, 1984.

PART
VI

COMPUTER HARDWARE

34

DOES HARDWARE MATTER?

For centuries, because of the ships, journeys were longer and
more tragic than they are today. A voyage covered its distance in
a natural span of time. People were used to those slow human
speeds on both land and sea, to those delays, those waitings on
the wind or fair weather, to those expectations of shipwrecks,
sun, and death. The liners the little white girl knew were among
the last mailboats in the world. It was while she was young that
the first airlines were started, which were gradually to deprive
mankind of journeys across the sea.

Marguerite Duras
The Lover

I have made several comments throughout this book suggesting
that you could afford to ignore the entire field of computer hardware. I do believe that computer hardware is overshadowed by the
growing importance of computer software . . . but I must also
admit that there are some important reasons for paying attention to
computer hardware technology.

One reason we ignore the ongoing miracle of computer hardware
technology is that the annual improvements are not very
impressive. Typically, we can expect computers to improve at a
rate of 10 to 15 percent each year. Improvements consist of increases
in speed or capacity, decreases in cost, decreases in physical size, or
combinations of these factors. Then, from time to time, we witness
sudden quantum jumps in the technology: someone invents a new
chip or a new storage device that is ten times as fast, or eight times
cheaper.

Even if we never did better than a 15 percent improvement each year, the cumulative effect would be staggering. We all know about the miracle of compound interest; in the case of compound technological improvement, a 15 percent annual growth means that the technology doubles after five years, quadruples after ten years, and increases by an order-of-magnitude (10.761261, to be somewhat more precise) after seventeen years.

Seventeen years sounds like a long time. And an order-of-magnitude sounds like a scientific phrase that should be banished from polite conversations. But order-of-magnitude (factor of ten) improvements are important here. They are important to you, to the way you live your life. They were important to our parents and our grandparents when they experienced similar order-of-magnitude improvements in other technological disciplines. But they had a lifetime (often several lifetimes) to adjust; we have, at best, seventeen years.

Consider the technology of transportation as an example. For several millennia, the human animal transported itself around the earth on its own hind legs, or on the back of some other larger, more stupid, animal. For short bursts of a mile or so, a horse could be whipped to a speed of thirty miles per hour, but the average speed of this technology was about four miles per hour. At an incredible cost, we used the technology to build a telecommunication system known as the Pony Express (yes, telecommunication system—it was the precursor of the telegraph and the telephone).

But then came the technology of internal combustion engines. Within a few short years after the turn of the 20th century, it suddenly became possible for mankind to move about the dry surfaces of the earth at average speeds of forty miles per hour—an order-of-magnitude improvement. And more recently, the technology of aeronautics has made it economically feasible to move over land and water at average speeds of 400 miles per hour, with occasional short periods (on the Concorde) at 1,200 miles per hour.

I chose this example deliberately because it illustrates an important aspect of the "order-of-magnitude" phenomenon. When a technology improves by a factor of ten, it is not just a quantitative change, it is a qualitative change. Society functions in a fundamentally different way today, because of current transportation technology, than it did 100 years ago. Our businesses are different, our cities are different, our governments are different, and our personal lives are fundamentally different from those of our great-grand-fathers and -grandmothers.

The few great-grandfathers and -grandmothers who are alive today understand this perfectly well. But most of us don't under-stand it, because we were born in the midst of the aerospace revolution. Many of us made our first visit to a distant city (more than 200 miles away) in an airplane, and that airplane was probably a jet. So it's very, very difficult to imagine what it must have been like to go through the revolutionary change from horse-drawn carriage to automobile to airplane.

To help you imagine this revolution, consider a possible future development in transportation technology. Scientists at MIT have developed a plan for a transcontinental tunnel that would permit supersonic subterranean travel. In plain English: an underground tunnel from, say, New York to San Francisco, that would allow travel at speeds of approximately 4,000 miles per hour. There you have another order-of-magnitude.

What would you do if this transportation technology were made available to you at an economically attractive price? Would your business be different if you could travel from New York to San Francisco in an hour for $50? Would your personal life be different if you lived in San Francisco but could make a date to attend an opening night Broadway play in New York? Of course it would, but the change would take place a little differently than you might think. . . .

Before I get to that point, let me bring the analogy back to computers. Since the 1940s, we have witnessed five order-of-magni-tude improvements in computer hardware. Computers today are approximately 100,000 times faster, cheaper, and more powerful than the famous Eniac computer constructed in 1945 at the Moore School of Engineering. Once again, I have to assume that you're not impressed for the simple reason that you weren't there to observe the improvement (nor was I—my intellectual skills in 1945 were concentrated on the task of learning how to walk). Most people working in the computer business today have personally experi-enced one order-of-magnitude improvement; veterans like me have suffered through two orders-of-magnitude; and the ancients (peo-ple like Commander Grace Hopper of the U.S. Navy) have played important roles in three order-of-magnitude improvements.

But chances are that you didn't have any personal, hands-on experience with a computer until someone put an IBM PC on your desk, or until your child harassed you into buying an Apple Macintosh for his or her schoolwork. You probably have no concept of the power of that machine: it is more powerful than the most powerful computer in all of New York City in 1965, and both would have cost over a million dollars in the 1950s.

So what? I tell you this only because of one virtually certain fact about the future: we will experience between three and four orders-of-magnitude of continued improvement in computer hardware over the next ten to twenty years. The national governments of Japan, America, and England (among others) have publicly committed themselves to this task. (How they accomplish it is the subject of Chapter 37, but it is of no significance at this point.) Thus, the computer you buy today will be between 1,000 and 10,000 times cheaper, faster, and more powerful by the end of the century.

How will our lives and our businesses and our governments change as a result of this improved technology? To understand this, we can look at past history. What happened when radically improved communications technology (e.g., the telephone) was introduced? What happened when the automobile was introduced, and then the airplane? This will give us a clue, but only a rough clue: those changes took place over a relatively long period of time, and the cumulative improvement was only two or three orders-of-magnitude. With computers, we will witness approximately six orders-of-magnitude (a factor of one million) over, roughly, a fifty-year period. And each order of magnitude improvement occurs over the space of five to ten years. It would require, as I pointed out above, seventeen years if the improvements took place at the steady rate of 15 percent per year, but it doesn't work that way. The small, incremental improvements are interspersed with occasional quantum leaps in technology.

FUBINI'S LAW

An Australian colleague, Rob Thomsett, once described to me a principle that he called "Fubini's Law." I still haven't found out who Fubini is (there was a mathematician named Guido Fubini who invented the Fubini Theorem, but I think that must have been someone else), but the principle makes a lot of sense anyway.

Basically, Fubini's Law (as described by Rob) says that people initially use advanced technology to do the same things they are already doing—just a little faster or cheaper. Only over a period of time do people gradually begin using advanced technology to do brand new things. These brand new things eventually change life-styles and work-styles; the new life-styles gradually cause soci-etywide changes . . . which eventually change technology (by pos-ing new problems or creating new opportunities for scientists and engineers to work on). And the new technology starts the cycle over again.

Two examples will help illustrate the concept. When Alexander Graham Bell traveled around the country trying to popularize the telephone (after having failed in his effort to sell all of the patents to Western Union for $10,000), he told his audiences that the telephone would make it possible to stay at home listening to live concerts that were taking place at a remote site. Aside from the fact that the idea sounds foolish today, notice what Bell was doing. He—the inventor!—was assuming that the telephone would make one-way remote communication more convenient than ever before. That was the only kind of remote communication people were used to (e.g., letters, telegrams, smoke signals, etc.), and it never occurred to him that the telephone might be used as a two-way interactive communications device. As we saw in Chapter 5, E. J. Hall, a vice president of AT&T, was still promoting this one-way use of tele-phones as late as 1890.

Similarly, when the motion-picture camera was developed, it was first used to make movies of live plays. This made it possible for people to watch a live play more conveniently than ever before, but it wasn't giving them anything truly new. Only later did people gradually begin using the camera to film things that could not be seen in any other way. It never occurred to anyone then to make a movie like *Star Wars*—or if it did occur to anyone, the idea was dismissed immediately because there was no evidence that movie technology would advance fast enough to keep up with such fan-tasies. Computer people live in a perpetual fantasy world, with the important difference that fantasies are fulfilled.

Historically, computers have been used to automate computations that were previously done by hand; indeed, the motivation for the first modern computer, the Eniac, was to automate the calculation of bomb trajectories for World War II. We have only begun to use computers for things that humans never did before. The most exciting projects of this nature fall into the category of artificial intelligence, which we discussed in Chapter 21.

You may disagree with this conclusion. After all, the speed of modern digital computers makes it possible to carry out calculations which, if performed manually, would take so long that they would never be done. Scientists estimate, for example, that a modern supercomputer has approximately the same computational power as the entire human race, each of whose members is equipped with a modern hand-held calculator. The mind boggles at the prospect of trying to get the human race to collectively cooperate and work in unison on some computational problem—but a supercomputer can and does carry out such computations, for weather prediction, for the design of nuclear weapons, and even to generate the animated graphics for the battle scenes in the 1984 science-fiction movie *The Last Starfighter*. (The graphics required one hour of computer time on a Cray-1 computer, and would have required several generations of mankind, working in unison, if done by manual calculations.)

So in this respect, computers are making it possible for us to do things that were never done before. But it happens slowly. When a businessman first gets a personal computer, he doesn't use it at all (for various reasons that I discussed in Chapter 17). Then he uses it to keep track of his calendar—hardly very innovative. Then he starts using the popular spreadsheet programs to add the rows and columns of numbers required for his annual sales budget. And finally he starts doing something new: he tries three different versions of the budget and begins exploring "what-if" scenarios, which he never had time for before.

Meanwhile, the computer continues to be used, in many cases, to keep on doing the same old things that we've always done with little or no thought of innovation. Consider the task of payroll, which every business has to deal with. A hundred years ago, all of the necessary calculations and records were produced with pencil and paper; people were paid monthly, weekly, or daily, depending on local custom (sailors often didn't get paid until their ship reached home port, on the theory that they wouldn't need the money at sea anyway). Today, we do the same thing, but the computations and recordkeeping are done faster and cheaper on a computer.

If we were innovative, we would pay employees every millisecond and deposit the money directly into their bank accounts. We would make it possible for people to pay their rent on a millisecond-by-millisecond basis. That might not make much sense for apartment rentals (because people generally stay in their apartment for more than a few milliseconds), but it makes great sense for hotel room rentals. If I check into a hotel room at 3:57:42.653 P.M. and check out the next morning at 7:04:44.977 A.M., I should only have to pay for the exact number of milliseconds that the room was mine.

The consequences of such a change are almost beyond comprehension. Our entire society takes advantage of various forms of "float." Banks use our money for a few days while our checks clear (whatever that means); hotels use our money to cover the cost of the few hours when their rooms are vacant. And so on. All of this was probably necessary a hundred years ago because we didn't have the technology to calculate the cost of goods and services on such a microscopic basis. But now we do . . . and yet we continue to pay people once a month. Fubini's Law prevails.

THE CHALLENGE

Now you see why hardware is important to us: because it gives us the possibility of new life-styles and work-styles. The challenge for most of us is to find a way of short-cutting Fubini's Law. A few organizations (mostly military) have a desperate need for supercomputers now, and they know of their desperate need; we will see examples in Chapter 36.

But most individuals, companies, and government agencies have absolutely no idea what they will do with computers 10,000 times faster than the ones they have now. In fact, most of them haven't figured out what to do with the computers they have now. Many vintage 1985 computers are still running computer programs based on the hardware technology of 1962.

This wouldn't matter so much if the technology of computer hardware had stabilized. But it hasn't, and it won't slow down until the end of the century—unless, as I discussed in Chapter 26, everyone stops buying computers, which will put the R&D groups out of work. The Defense Department, however, is almost certain to continue funding supercomputer research through the rest of this decade, and Japan committed itself to a ten-year plan in 1983 to build a fifth-generation computer 1,000 times more powerful than current computers. So hardware technology will continue developing regardless of what the private sector economy thinks of it.

There are new markets, new products, and new services that are not feasible today, but which will be very feasible in five years. We should start working today to prepare for these new markets. If we don't, someone else will—most likely the Japanese, but possibly some other country (or company) that is quietly progressing without the fanfare that Japan has attracted. It's convenient to think of this as a national issue, but it is also an individual issue: my friends Jack Goldberg, Milton Cooper, Ellis Kern, and Larry Saper are running very succesful businesses today, and they are making some use of computers. But they have counterparts whose names and national origin we don't even know, and those counterparts are busy thinking of products and services that they can introduce in 1991, with computer support that is outrageously expensive today but which will be incredibly cheap then.

What are these new products and services? To be honest, I must admit that I am as much a victim of Fubini's Law as anyone else: I, too, have a tendency to use computers to do the same thing I've been doing all along. As a veteran computer programmer, I suffer from an additional weakness: I've been brainwashed in a number of subtle ways by the hardware technology I used during my first few years as a junior computer programmer. This brainwashing problem is common to almost all people who work in the computer field, some 500,000 computer programmers and systems analysts in the United States. We probably won't invent the new markets and products; it is probably a mistake to even ask us, though we won't hesitate to offer suggestions. Chapter 39 will give you a good idea of what happens when scientists make predictions about the impact and continued development of new technology.

Maybe our children can help us, though they are currently being brainwashed, right now, in their schools. They are learning (ugh) BASIC, and they are being introduced to relatively primitive personal computers. The impressions they form will probably be lasting ones. A child of the 1980s who grows up to be a computer programmer will probably write computer programs in the fashion that he was taught in high school, and he will conceive of uses for computers based on the technology of his Apple II or IBM PC. The educational foundation that he receives in elementary and secondary schools is not even adequate for today's hardware technology, as we saw in Chapter 2; in any case, it has nothing to do with the hardware technology that they will inherit in the 1990s. And I have yet to see a teacher below the college level giving any thought at all to the future of computer technology and how we should be helping our children to prepare for it. (This has nothing to do with the issue of whether your children should learn about computers; go back and read Chapter 2 again. All I am saying here is that you probably should not expect your children to be your salvation.)

Chapter 36 provides a short, partial list of some things that could be done with improved computer hardware. We need to disseminate such lists as widely as possible to serve as a starting point for other, nontainted, imaginative people to begin thinking of truly creative uses for computers.

35

HARDWARE TECHNOLOGY

> I submit to the public a small machine by my invention, by means of which you alone may, without any effort, perform all the operations of arithmetic, and may be relieved of the work which has often times fatigued your spirit . . . .
>
> Blaise Pascal
> 1623-62

My job in this chapter is to describe current computer hardware technology to you. This is difficult, because current depends on whether you read my comments within the same year (or month) that I write them, or whether you read them at some point in the future. I must assume the latter.

My choices are (a) to be deliberately vague, or (b) to make it very clear to you what the technology is like today, so that you can extrapolate into the future and see how all of this affects you tomorrow. I've chosen the latter approach, for better or worse. Be aware that I am describing the technology of computer hardware that is readily available in the public marketplace in August 1985. You can extrapolate improvements at the rate of 1 percent per month, unless you read about some earth-shaking new development in your daily newspaper.

I won't describe some of the exotic computer hardware currently used in military agencies, because (a) I don't know about it; (b) I don't want to know about it; (c) even if I did know about it, I wouldn't be allowed to talk about it; and (d) you couldn't get your hands on it anyway, unless you already work in one of those agencies. Similarly, I won't talk in this chapter about one-of-a-kind advanced computers, nor the experimental computers at some of the leading universities; those will be discussed in Chapter 37.

The purpose of this chapter is not to make you an expert on the subject of computer hardware, nor even to explain very much about how computers work. There are lots of good books on that subject, but I can't imagine why most people would want to read them. If you were just beginning to learn about the technology of automobiles—either because you intend to drive one or ride in one—would you begin by reading a book on the theory of internal combustion engines?

To carry the analogy a little further, let me suggest what you would want to know about an automobile if you had never seen one before: how much does it cost? How fast does it go? How many people can it carry? Will next year's model be cheaper? Will it go faster next year? And so forth.

When we look at computer hardware in this chapter, we will ask similar questions. The important characteristics are these three:

- **Speed.** How fast does it go? How many computations (of the $2+2 = 4$ variety) can it carry out per second? How quickly can it move information (a number or an alphabetic character like "a") from one place to another?

- **Size.** How big is it? How much does it weigh? How much electrical power does it consume? How much heat does it generate?

- **Cost.** How much does it cost to purchase? How much less does it cost if I buy a thousand? How much does it cost to operate?

These are the dimensions that are improving each year. Each is important in its own right, as we will see.

THE COMPONENTS OF A TYPICAL COMPUTER

Figure 35.1 shows the components of a typical computer. Not all computers have all of the components shown—just as not all automobiles have four doors and a radio, even though we might show such things as typical components. However, the diagram is fairly representative of all general-purpose computers, including mainframe, mini- and micro-computers.

The Central Processing Unit

The key component of a computer is the Central Processing Unit, or CPU. It is the brain, the workhorse that carries out computations and coordinates the movement of data to and from memory, disk, keyboard, telephone lines, and printers. The CPU is to a computer what an engine is to a car.

When computer people talk about a CPU, they often refer to its manufacturer and its model number. In the world of personal computers, for example, you'll hear people discussing the merits of the Motorola 68000 and the Intel 8088 and 80286. Although it seems a little confusing, there's an important difference here between computer and CPU. The machine we all know as the IBM PC is really a collection of several components (some optional, some required) organized around the Intel 8088 CPU which acts as the

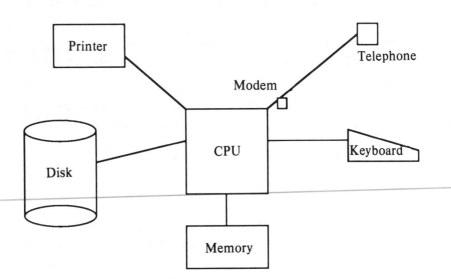

Figure 35.1: **Components of a Typical Computer**

brain of the machine. Similarly, the elegant Apple Macintosh is built around a Motorola 68000 CPU, and the IBM PC/AT is built around the Intel 80286 CPU.

There are many ways of characterizing the features of a CPU, most of which I won't bore you with. But one simple measure is useful as a rough guide to the horsepower of a CPU: the number of instructions that it can carry out per second. An instruction that a computer carries out might be any one of the following:

- "Add the number in memory cell #2336 to the number in memory cell #6654, and leave the result in memory cell #1112."

- "Move the alphabetic character in memory cell #1234 into memory cell #4567."

- "If the number in memory cell #5567 is zero, proceed with the next instruction. Otherwise, skip the next instruction."

- "Instead of carrying out the next instruction, go look in memory cell #2234, where you will find the next instruction to carry out."

Note that these instructions don't look very much like the Logo or Pascal or (ugh) BASIC computer programs your children may be learning. Those are high-level programming languages, whose commands must eventually be translated into dozens, or thousands, of individual machine-level instructions of the sort shown above. In Chapter 29, we characterized these machine instructions as a first-generation language.

There is a special kind of instruction of interest to scientists and engineers: the "floating point instruction." These instructions carry out mathematical operations (adding, subtracting, multiplication, division, etc.) on numbers that are expressed in scientific notation. Examples of floating point instructions are:

- "Add the number 3.14159 times 10 to the 3rd power (which is more easily recognized as 3,141.59) to the number 2.78128 times 10 to the 2nd power."

- "Divide the number 1.944 times 10 to the 3rd power by the number 10."

Depending on the precise model of computer, a floating point operation is typically equivalent to approximately 10 to 100 normal instructions.

Now that you know about these instructions, you're ready to learn some industry jargon:

KIPS   Kilo instructions per second, or thousands of normal instructions per second.

MIPS   Millions of normal instructions per second.

FLOPS   Floating point operations, or instructions, per second.

MFLOPS   Millions of floating point operations per second.

BFLOPS   Billions of floating point operations per second.

LIPS   Logical inferences per second.

The last item on the list is a relatively new buzzword, and it is associated with the field of artificial intelligence. An example of an "inference" is, "If a patient has red spots all over his body, and if he also has a temperature of 102 degrees, then there is a high likelihood that he has chicken pox."

Now that we have our list of buzzwords, we can survey the speed of typical vintage 1985 CPUs:

Personal computers	0.5 - 1 MIPS
Minicomputers	2 - 4 MIPS
Normal mainframe computers	3 - 25 MIPS
IBM M3081KX mainframe	16.3 MIPS
IBM 3090 Model 200 "Sierra"	29.3 MIPS
Cray-1 supercomputer	160 MFLOPS
Cray-1XMP supercomputer	420 MFLOPS
Cray-2 supercomputer	1 BFLOPS

As you can see, the Cray-2 supercomputer is approximately 200,000 times faster than a typical personal computer. Only in rare cases does this cause anyone concern. People working on personal computers typically don't have the sort of computational problems that Cray-2 customers (people like the Atomic Energy Commission and NASA) deal with.

A few final words about CPUs: they're small, they're cheap, they consume very little electricity, and they generate very little heat. A typical CPU for a personal computer costs less than a dollar to manufacture (keep in mind that this is largely because of volume: millions are manufactured each year); the CPU for your digital watch costs only a few pennies to manufacture. As you well know, the CPU for your digital watch runs for a year or more on a tiny battery, and its physical dimensions are small enough that we can realistically consider embedding a CPU in almost anything, including the human body (more about that in Chapter 36).

So why do computers look so big? It's because of all of the other things attached to the CPU: the memory, the disks, the printers, the telecommunication modems, etc. Many of these other components are large, and many of them generate substantial amounts of heat, so fans or other cooling mechanisms (ranging from water to Freon-based liquid coolants requiring a 25-ton compressor) are sometimes needed. And the other components require considerably more electrical power, so large, bulky power supply units have to be included. Meanwhile, the CPU sits, tiny and nearly invisible among all of the other electronic gadgets, quietly controlling the show.

Memory

Memory for a computer is like memory for a human: a repository of items of data. Computer memory is measured in simple on-off units called a "bit" (a clever acronym which means "binary information digit"). A group of bits taken together as an integral unit is known as a "byte." Most computers today use 8-bit bytes, though there are machines with 6-bit bytes, and others with 7-bit bytes, and others that don't use bytes but rather "words" (which are 32-bit units, or 36-bit units, or 60-bit units).

An 8-bit byte is capable of representing any (decimal) number between 0 and 255. Standard coding conventions, such as ASCII (yet another acronym: this one stands for American Standard Code for Information Interchange), have been developed so that everyone knows that "a" is represented by 01100001, while "A" is represented by 01000001, etc.

In the 1950s, a typical computer had only a thousand or so bytes of memory; consequently, they weren't able to work with very much information at one time. But this is another area where the order-of-magnitude improvements have been occurring steadily over the years: most current personal computers have between 64,000 and 256,000 bytes of memory, and the large mainframe computers have millions of bytes.

Since we are dealing with relatively large numbers, some abbreviations are handy: computer people use units called "K," which means "kilo." Any reasonable person would expect that this means 1,000, but in the computer field it doesn't. It means 1,024—which is a handy power of 2, namely 2^{10}. Thus, when you buy a personal computer, you will probably find that it has 64K (which really means 65,536) bytes, or 256K (which really means 262,144) bytes. Similarly, the term "megabyte" means, loosely, "one million bytes"—but it really means 2^{20} bytes, which is precisely 1,048,576. A few personal computers have a megabyte of memory; most mainframes today have a minimum of 16 megabytes, and some can handle 64 megabytes or more.

The amount of memory that a computer has typically determines the size of a problem that the computer can work with conveniently, just as the number of telephone numbers that you can memorize determines whether or not you need an auxiliary address book. In some cases, a computer programmer can make a tradeoff between the CPU and memory; that is, he can program the solution to a problem in such a way that it takes a great deal of memory but requires very few computer instructions, or he can choose a different algorithm and solve the same problem in a fashion that requires little memory but takes a long time to compute.

Similarly, the programmer can almost always make a tradeoff, as necessary, between memory and external storage. If the problem won't fit in memory, then the program must be organized so that part of the problem can be brought from the disk, shown in Figure 35.1, into memory, to be solved; the partial solution is then stored on the disk. Then another part of the problem is brought from the disk into memory, and so forth. This is tedious and time consuming. The program may require 10 to 100 times longer to run than if the entire problem could be worked on, at once, in memory.

Even more tedious is the partitioning of the problem (i.e., the computer program itself and the data it is working with) into "chunks" that will fit into the available memory. Fortunately, this problem is now handled automatically by most operating systems supplied by the computer vendor, so that the programmer can work with a "virtual" memory that is large enough to deal with the problem as a whole. The business of chopping the computer program and data into small pieces is thus largely invisible to the programmer, except for the fact that it causes the program to execute so slowly.

There is a Parkinson's Law for computer memory: computer programs have a tendency to grow to fill all available memory. Somehow, people managed to get useful work done twenty years ago, even though their computers had only 4K bytes of memory. When personal computers appeared in the late 1970s, most had only 16K bytes—and early customers were deliriously happy until they realized that there were some problems that didn't fit comfortably in 16K. By 1980, almost all serious personal computers had 64K; by 1982, 256K was the norm; now 512-640K seems to be the norm. Similarly, mainframe computers in the 1960s managed to get by with 64K; then 128K; then 512K. The first megabyte-memory machine was typically a cause of great wonder and amazement in a computer department in the 1970s; now we are blasé when we see 16-megabyte machines. Yet somehow we have always managed to fill all available memory.

Printers

Printers, as one would expect, are the typewriterlike devices that are used to produce printed output. They come in all sizes, shapes, and colors; they range in price from approximately $100 to $50,000 or more.

The cheaper printers, typically in the $300 to $500 range, are known as "dot matrix" printers; they are now familiar to just about everyone who has seen computer output. The dot-matrix printer produces characters by using a matrix of print wires to choose a unique combination of dots from a five by seven combination; alternatively, the five by seven matrix might be used to squirt ink through tiny jets in order to form a unique pattern.

The speed of these printers has been steadily increasing, as has the quality of output. Most dot-matrix printers produce 100 to 200 characters per second in draft mode; at slower speeds of 50 to 100 characters per second, they can produce near-letter-quality output by printing a character, shifting the print head a tiny fraction of an inch, and then printing it again.

This is much faster (and also much quieter, in most cases) than the letter-quality printers once considered mandatory for word processing and any other computer output that might be sent to a customer or someone outside the organization. The most common letter-quality printer is known as a "daisy wheel" printer because of the printing mechanism. Rather than using the "golf ball" technology found in the IBM Selectric, most of these printers have characters attached at the end of long spokes emanating from a central hub. The hub can be spun, under computer control, at fairly high speeds, stopping whenever necessary to print a desired character. However, the overall speed is much slower than dot-matrix printers (typically fifteen to thirty characters per second), and the noise level can be deafening. To make matters worse, the printers are generally more expensive, too: a rugged, high-quality daisy wheel printer is almost always over $1,000 and can sometimes approach $2,000.

None of this is acceptable in the world of mainframe computers where tons of paper may be printed each month. Most mainframe computers use so-called line printers; as the term implies, an entire 80-character or 132-character line of output is produced at once. Such printers generally produce entire lines of output at speeds of 200 to 1,200 lines per minute—and some can go faster than that. The size and cost of such printers is commensurately higher, too.

Most recently, we have begun to see "laser printers" for high-speed, high-volume output. IBM, for example, announced the debut of a laser printer for its new "Sierra" mainframe computer; the printer prints text, graphics, and digitized images (e.g., company logos, letterhead, signatures, etc.) on one or both sides of cut-sheet paper, at speeds of up to twenty pages per minute. Costs for the printer begin at approximately $30,000. For considerably less money, typically $3,000 to $6,000, one can buy a laser printer for a personal computer. These lower-priced machines will generally produce near-typeset quality printing at speeds of five to eight pages per minute, thus opening up the possibility of in-house type-setting and a variety of new publishing applications.

Disks

Disks have become the standard form of external storage for most computer systems, just as magnetic tape was the standard of the 1960s and much of the 1970s. Conceptually, a disk is very much like a phonograph record: it has tracks that the computer can locate quickly, and information can be recorded on each track.

The most common form of storage on a personal computer is the so-called "floppy disk." It gets its name from the thin, flexible sheet of mylar plastic, coated with a metallic oxide upon which data can be magnetically recorded. The mylar sheet is encased in a thin cardboard (or plastic) housing, and the result is a handy "floppy" that can be easily handled. In the 1970s, 8-inch floppy disks were common; today, the 5.25-inch variety is most common, though many newer computers use a smaller, more durable 3-inch micro-floppy.

Though the disks are cheap (the mylar diskettes themselves cost between $1 and $5, depending on quality and quantity desired), they have their limitations: speed and capacity. The typical 5.25-inch floppy diskette can record between 80,000 and 1,200,000 bytes of data. The low end is typical of such computers as the Commodore 64 and Apple II, while the high end is typical of such powerful machines as the HP-150 and IBM PC/AT. While this looks impressive, personal computer owners are amazed by the rapidity with which they find themselves overburdened with floppy disks. They also find that such simple-minded tasks as organizing a mailing list of 10,000 names and sorting it by ZIP code are horrendously cumbersome with floppy disks.

Enter the Winchester disk, or "hard disk." Most personal computers now have, as optional equipment, a storage device that is conceptually like several record platters stacked on top of one another. Instead of one recording device analogous to the familiar phonograph needle, the disk devices have several, one for each platter. The disk platters are kept in constant, high-speed rotation, and each read-write head can move in and out independently, seeking the track that it wants for reading or writing. The result is a storage device that, in 1985, typically has 10 to 20 million bytes of recording capacity for a cost of approximately $1,000 to $2,000.

For mainframe computers, of course, the numbers are substantially different, though the concept is still much the same. The major difference between the typical mainframe disk and the typical personal computer disk is that the mainframe disks are removable; that is, the spindle and platters are encased in an overall unit known as a disk pack. The disk pack can be removed from the disk drive, and a different disk pack can be put in its place. A typical mainframe disk will store 200 to 400 million characters; the mainframe computer will often have five to ten such disk units on-line, bringing the total available on-line storage to one to two billion characters of data. Very large computer systems—such as the ones found in banks, insurance companies, etc.—may have as many as 100 or more large-capacity disk units, thus providing enormous amounts of data to the computer.

Communications

As I have mentioned on several occasions in this book, most computers are far more interesting when they begin communicating with other computers. Thus, the telecommunications link is often an important component of a computer.

In Figure 35.1, I have shown just one communication line emanating from the CPU. On a mainframe computer, there may be hundreds, or even thousands, of such communication lines; indeed, there is often a separate computer—or several computers—that concentrate exclusively on the inputs and outputs from communication lines.

On a personal computer, there is usually just one communication line; if the connection is to another computer in the same building, the line may be a simple copper wire between the two machines. If (as is more common), the computer is connected to a distant, or remote, computer, then standard telephone lines are generally used. An interface unit known as a modem connects the computer to the telephone line.

There are generally two important aspects of telecommunications: the speed at which data can be transmitted, and the number of errors, or "noise," on the line. If a "direct" connection exists between two computers—i.e., a simple cable—then communication speeds of 50,000 bits per second are easily achieved, and speeds up to a million bits per second may be possible; very low error rates are generally expected since a high-quality cable can generally be used.

Using normal telephone lines, together with a modem, is a different matter altogether. Personal computer owners are accustomed to speeds of 300 to 1200 bits per second (which is roughly equivalent to 30 to 120 characters or bytes per second); people communicating with a mainframe computer may be more accustomed to speeds of 19,200 bits per second, and occasionally as many as 50,000 bits per second. The error rates for such remote communications tend to be higher, especially for the lower speeds. This is because the same physical telephone lines that humans use for voice communication are used for computer communications. The same static and noise that you occasionally hear in the background of your everyday phone conversation is enough to garble the communication of data between computers. This happens less often with higher-speed communications for the simple reason that higher-quality conditioned telecommunication lines are used. Depending on the quality of the modem (and often depending on the communications software), any errors that do occur will either (a) not be detected either by the computer or the human observer; or (b) will not be detected by the computer but will appear as garbled characters to the human observer; or (c) will automatically be detected by the computer, which will then request that the data be retransmitted by the sender.

36

APPLICATIONS FOR MORE POWERFUL COMPUTERS

We're losing sight of the fact that we need supercomputing for entirely different objectives than technology. The race we're really in is between countries, not for supercomputers, not for national security. . . We're in a race to control the resources of the world, both natural resources and informational resources. . . We're looking at the supercomputing area as a race . . . That may have totally obscured the real problem. For example, I'm not sure what the finish line is. I'm not sure how to tell when we have won the race or lost the race. It's like high-energy physics: If we're there, it ain't high energy; if we're there in computers, it isn't supercomputers.[1]

Dr. Ruth M. Davis
*former director of
the National Bureau of
Standards' Institute for
Computer Sciences and Technology.*

If you had an automobile that could drive at speeds of 500 miles per hour, an automobile that required only a gallon of gas to drive across the country, what would you do with it? What changes would you make in your social life? What new business enterprises would you create?

That was the perspective of Chapter 34; in this chapter, we

reverse the perspective. What new business enterprise are you desperately trying to start today for which an order-of-magnitude improvement in automotive technology is imperative? What social relationships are you desperately trying to salvage today—family disputes, torrid love affairs, an association of professional colleagues desperately concerned with nuclear disarmament, etc.—that simply cannot be salvaged without order-of-magnitude improvements in the speed and price of transcontinental travel?

And—to return to the obvious theme of this book—what business problems, what social relationships, and what government issues are we desperately trying to deal with today with computers that are ten times or a hundred times slower than what we really need? What are the problems that already require machines a thousand times smaller, a hundred times cheaper, and a thousand times faster?

The list in this chapter is, almost without exception, an evolutionary expansion of needs and desires currently perceived by government leaders, business entrepreneurs, scientists, doctors, children, educators, and parents. The revolutions that might be associated with thousandfold improvements in computer technology are generally dismissed as science fiction because they are so disconnected from the present reality in which we live. Recall the words of Colin Cherry from Chapter 10:

> Inventions themselves are not revolutions; neither are they the cause of revolutions. Their powers for change lie in the hands of those who have the imagination and insight to see that the new invention has offered them new liberties of action, that old constraints have been removed, that their political will, or their sheer greed are no longer frustrated, and that they can act in new ways.

While revolutions are more interesting to talk about, they are also more difficult for us—the "immigrants in time," as Margaret Mead calls us—to imagine. However, even the evolutionary uses of new computer technology will be important. If nothing else, the current perceived need for improved computer power will provide the research monies to actually build the new machines. And once the new machines are built, they will be used to solve those current problems, and then they will be available—sitting there, quietly blinking their lights, waiting for someone to start a revolution.

We, the elder generation, will build the machines that we need to solve our rather mundane problems. Our children will then take those machines into dimensions and galaxies unknown to us. That will be fun to watch; if we're lucky, maybe they'll take us along.[1]

Two last points before we begin to see the details. First, recognize that many of the applications, or new uses, of improved computer technology require improvements in several different dimensions: size, speed, price, etc. For simplicity, I have picked the dimension that seems most important, and will discuss the application in the appropriate section below.

Second, keep in mind that many of the applications are defense-oriented—i.e., applications that the U.S. Department of Defense (and similar departments in every country around the world) desperately wants. As of 1982, Lawrence Livermore Laboratories (which specializes in nuclear weapons and other defense projects) had five of the country's forty-two supercomputers; the Department of Energy's Los Alamos Labs had five; Sandia National Labs had two; NASA had three; and major oil companies had seven.[3]

I know very few of the details of these military applications, and have thus kept the discussion below deliberately vague. If you want to know more about the Defense Department's use of computers, go talk to your senator.

---

[1] There is a major counterargument to this philosophical view: the current generation of children may not be able to do anything creative with supercomputers because they aren't being exposed to any such computers in their current educational environment. A number of educators are desperately concerned about the shortage of Class VI (current state-of-the-art) supercomputers in the universities. As one observer, Gene Dallaire, points out,

> . . . it is hard for supercomputer centers to attract paying research customers, for the fees to use these supercomputers are typically $2,000 per hour or more. Most academic researchers don't have that kind of money in their educational grants. The fact is that the vast majority of American universitives cannot afford to purchase a supercomputer.
> . . . universities are not turning out graduates today who know enough about supercomputers—and that, in turn, leaves industry without human resources to bring about the pending supercomputer revolution. The vast majority of today's science and engineering graduates know little about the possible applications of supercomputers and know little about how to program these machines or how to operate them.[2]

PROBLEMS REQUIRING
FASTER COMPUTERS

The applications requiring faster computers fall into five major categories:

- Defense applications.

- Engineering applications.

- Simulation and forecasting applications.

- Artificial intelligence applications.

- Ordinary business applications.

Defense Applications

One of the "delightful" occupations of the military establishment is the design of nuclear weapons. I am told that this exercise requires vast amounts of computational power for the mathematical modeling of nuclear reactions and for the design of the weapons themselves. I have had the pleasure of visiting the computer installation in Los Alamos, New Mexico, where some of this research is done, as well as one of the facilities at Lawrence Livermore Laboratories in California. All I saw at Lawrence Livermore was a parking lot and an auditorium, but at Los Alamos (where they must be sufficiently bored by their isolation to spend more time entertaining guests), I was given an official tour through the computer room. Red lights flashed from the ceiling, and a loud klaxon voice boomed out, "Unsecure person in the room," which I assume was a signal to anyone with sensitive data to scurry away. But I did see a large Cray computer and several other enormous machines—indeed, more raw computer power in one room than I have ever seen in my life. I assume that the scientists are not using the machines to play chess or tic-tac-toe, so I am willing to take it on faith that the machines are necessary for nuclear research.

Another favorite military application is cryptography. Sooner or later, everyone will be concerned with the protection of his confidential computer communications. The military has been concerned with this problem since army generals began sending messages to one another thousands of years ago. Trusting a courier with the contents of a message is something that politicians and military leaders have long been loath to do; as Benjamin Franklin wisely observed, "Three may keep a secret, if two of them are dead."

But for every man who would send a secret message, there are ten others who would move Heaven and Earth to discover its contents. Thus, the science and art of cryptography have long been supported by military and political organizations. The subject of cryptography is beyond the scope of this book; suffice it to say that computers can be a powerful tool for creating cryptographic codes, and also for for decoding someone else's encrypted message.

Cryptography was, in fact, one of the early driving forces for the development of the modern computer. During the Second World War, the brilliant mathematician Alan Turing oversaw England's efforts to crack the German "Enigma" encoding machine. Though the British effort did not lead to a general-purpose, stored-program computer (which was under development in the United States during that same period), it did lead to a special-purpose electronic decoder known as Colossus. Ten versions of Colossus were built during the war, the first of which was installed as early as 1943. Each could process a phenomenal (for those days) 25,000 characters per second as it attempted to match a German message with known Enigma codes.

Even then, speed was of the essence: there is very little value in decoding a military message six months after it is transmitted. Aside from the fact that the information itself is probably obsolete by then, it is almost certain that the cryptograhic code (or the "key") will have been changed. On the other hand, if the message can be decoded quickly—or, better yet, in real time, as it is being transmitted—its value can be enormous.

In the United States, each of the military organizations has its own concerns with cryptography. But the center of expertise for this technology is the National Security Agency (NSA), located near Baltimore. Its charter is to assist other government agencies (both military and nonmilitary) in the technology needed for secure communications; it is also charged with receiving and decoding communications from other governments and military organizations around the world. It wants, it needs, it literally hungers for larger, faster computers.

In addition to the job of decoding "known" messages, NSA also has the job of scanning messages of all sorts, to see whether they convey information of interest to the U.S. government. One might presume that all messages communicated by certain world leaders would be interesting; even if there were little or no factual content, the messages might reveal the individual's mood, health, and state of mind (or lack thereof). But NSA obviously can't record and analyze every conversation of every minor government clerk in every country around the world. All it can hope to do is monitor as many telephone, telex, and radio communications as possible, looking for key words and phrases. The monitoring part of the job is done by satellites and a variety of high-technology electronic gadgets; the information (either in raw form, or in filtered form, depending on how much computerized intelligence the remote gadgets have) is then transmitted back to NSA headquarters for additional filtering and analysis.[2]

Engineering Applications

The primary engineering need for increased computer power involves the simulation of airflow around automobiles and airplanes. The objective, of course, is to design more aerodynamically efficient vehicles—cars and planes that have less drag, less wind resistance, less trouble moving through the thick, soupy stuff we call air.

Current computer technology, impressive though it may be to most of us, is not up to the job. The business of modeling the airflow around, over, and under a three-dimensional vehicle involves the solution of massive numbers of highly complex mathematical equations. To its credit, the computer is currently able to do what would

---

[2] The ominous side of this is the likelihood that all American conversations will eventually be monitored by computer. Rumors abound that all international telephone calls and telexes are already monitored, and that all conversations emanating from the mouths of "dangerous" people (which can mean almost anything) are similarly monitored. It's not clear whether the jurisdiction for this sort of thing falls under the NSA, the CIA, or the FBI—or all three.

never have been attempted at all by hand; even so, only one portion of the vehicle at a time can be modeled with current computer hardware. Thus, engineers simulate the airflow around an airplane wing, or around the tail section, but not the entire plane at once. Or they make other limitations and simplifications; as Geoffrey Fox, dean of educational computing at Cal Tech says,

> I know of several research groups at Cal Tech who know how to solve much larger problems than they can now solve on their VAX super-minicomputers. But they hold back and restrict their areas of research because of this lack of access to supercomputers. In numerous fields (geophysics, fluid dynamics, etc.), scientists and engineers would like to solve problems in three dimensions but must restrict themselves to solving a problem in two dimensions because of the limited power of computers available to them. To solve some of these problems in three dimensions would require computing speeds 100 to 1,000 times greater than today's state-of-the-art supercomputers (like the Cray-1).[4]

A major goal for the early 1990s—when the next generation of powerful computers is expected to arrive—is to carry out three-dimensional airflow models of an entire airplane in transonic flight, down to the molecular level. The expected improvement in aerodynamic design—coupled with newer, stronger, lighter materials for the plane's construction—will result in major improvements in fuel efficiency. Since the cost of fuel is a major component in an airline's expenses (and since it limits the range of the vehicle in flight), such a savings can have an enormous impact. The Japanese, for example, estimate that their $150 million investment in the National Superspeed Computer project (discussed in Chapter 12) is equal to one year's fuel bill for five wide-bodied airplanes.

Another engineering application is the processing of seismic data to determine the geology of an area thought to contain oil deposits. At least eight American oil companies have now purchased super-computers for this application; all are aware that the savings in the drilling of a single hole can pay for a supercomputer several times over. Supercomputers are also being used to simulate petroleum flows in underground reservoirs, in the hope that "exhausted" wells can be resurrected for secondary oil recovery.

Still another area is the engineering needs of the computer industry itself, primarily in the design of circuit layouts and individual components of electronic chips. The vast majority of designs now being carried out are two-dimensional; that is, the designer worries about the layout of components in terms of length and width. Three-dimensional chips, with components stacked on top of one another, are literally a new dimension of design, but one that cannot be practically carried out until more powerful computers are available for the task.

Simulation and Forecasting Applications

Modeling of airflow is a form of simulation—engineers want to simulate the behavior of the airplane before they build it. Indeed, what they really want to do is simulate the behavior of the airplane without even building plywood models and operating them in a wind tunnel.

There are other types of simulation problems that also demand more computing power. Of these, weather forecasting is probably the most important. Most of us have little or no respect for the weather reporter who attempts, in vain, to convince us that it will rain tomorrow; perhaps we have become cynical after listening to too many weather reporters telling us that it is raining outside when a simple glance out the window confirms that there isn't a cloud in the sky.

I do not mean to insult the efforts of witch doctors and the *Farmer's Almanac*, but weather forecasting is a relatively straightforward problem of thermodynamics. It is the scale of the problem that is so difficult to deal with. Because we lack adequate computer power to provide accurate, up-to-the-second forecasts for each square centimeter of the earth's surface, we are forced to compromise: our models cover broad areas, while simultaneously leaving out broad areas. Thus, a weather forecast might predict weather conditions for the entire eastern half of the United States as if it were one homogeneous region, while simultaneously ignoring the effects on that region caused by an earthquake in the Philippines and a drought in Siberia.

The savings that could be achieved by accurate, timely weather forecasts are so staggering that they boggle the mind. In 1984 alone, there were 2,247 reported deaths from major hurricanes, typhoons, tornadoes, and floods around the world;[5] many of these deaths could have been prevented with better weather forecasting. The cost of weather damage from such storms is not easily ascertained, but even a conservative estimate would be several billions of dollars—much of which could be avoided or minimized with better forecasting techniques.

Other large-scale simulations could have similar savings, but it is not always clear that a larger computer would help. On the other hand, knowing that the computer power was there might motivate scientists to get off their collective rear ends and attack the underlying theoretical problems. Probably the best example of this at the moment is the problem of econometric modeling: what is the effect on the gross national product of an increase of 2 percent in cigarette taxes? If Social Security payments are increased by $1.98 next year, what will that do to the budget deficit? Questions like these are debated by politicians, economists, and all 235 million citizens in the country—and yet none of us knows the answers. Why? Because none of us has an accurate model of the economy; we are all like the proverbial blind men touching different parts of an elephant and coming to very different conclusions about what we are dealing with.

Many econometric models have been developed over the years, some with literally hundreds of parameters whose mathematical relationship to one another should (in theory) help us predict the consequences of certain tax decisions, etc. Indeed, there have even been global models that take into account economic conditions and actions around the entire world. But most of these models have been crude, at best; some, like the one developed by the "Club of Rome" and published as *The Limits to Growth*[6] in 1972, have turned out to be disasters. It is with characteristic honesty that three eminent modelers recently referred to their profession as "groping in the dark."[7]

I intend no disrespect to this community of crystal ball gazers, nor do I wish to insult the economists who try their very best to forecast the consequences of man-made and natural changes in the economic climate. But I think it is important to emphasize that while faster computers could help them do a better job of what they are now doing poorly, they are all—as a professional community—cursed by the lack of a complete, coherent, accurate mathematical model of the reality they are trying to understand.

In an entirely different area, medicine, there is also a desperate need for more powerful computers. As futurist and computer guru Charles Lecht points out,

> . . . now inhibiting discovery of a cure for certain types of cancer is our inability to gather and process the massive volumes of data needed to clarify our view of our biological selves and to create the simulations needed to conduct experiments quickly. Improved CAT scanning via supercomputer image processing, allowing us to see what would otherwise remain unseeable, should speed our development of such cures decisively. The same could be expected in the case of other major diseases for which there now exist no cures.[8]

Note the emphasis on speed in Lecht's words: it would be nice to complete the computer model of a patient's cancer before he dies of it. Unfortunately, I am not yet convinced that we know how to construct the model; nevertheless, without the possibility of faster, more powerful computers, today's young medical students may not be applying enough creativity to the problem.

Artificial Intelligence Applications

In Chapter 21, we discussed the area of artificial intelligence and the special subset of artificial intelligence known as expert systems. It is apparent already that there are dozens, if not hundreds, of business applications and commercial uses of expert systems technology—but to make them practical, we need more powerful computers. In addition to speed (which is the area people focus on most often), AI applications will also require smaller, cheaper, more compact computers (which I will discuss below).

Today, the major stumbling block in the development of more complex expert systems is the difficulty of acquiring the "rules of judgment" by which a human expert makes his decisions. Each one has to be discovered through a tedious process of interviews between the expert (who has often never bothered to articulate his innate skills) and a skilled systems analyst. But once those rules are captured, then it is a matter of simple computer power to evaluate the rules for each problem at hand, whether it be a problem of chess or the diagnosis of a fault on an oil drilling platform.

The game of chess is a good example of the tradeoff between brain and brawn, and the occasional opportunity to combine the best of both. Brilliant strategy—of the type employed instinctively by a Bobby Fischer—is clearly better than a straightforward, exhaustive analysis of every possible move, and countermove, and counter-countermove. But if an expert system could narrow the range of possible moves down to just two or three (using some rules of judgment acquired from an expert chess player), then it might use its exhaustive approach to examine each of the two or three potential good moves to see what the consequences might be, seven or eight or nine plays later on. The strategy decisions require a lot of up-front human analysis once, combined with a moderate amount of computer power; the exhaustive investigation requires relatively little up-front intelligence (the rules of the game of chess can be programmed very easily), but an unlimited amount of computer power. Further investigation into the strategy of chess—which will proceed at its own pace over the next twenty years—will probably lead to order-of-magnitude improvements in chess-playing programs on today's computers; but these can be combined with order-of-magnitude improvements in computer hardware independent of any further developments in chess strategy.

There are other areas of artificial intelligence that require additional computational power. One is voice recognition; another is pattern recognition (or computer vision). All of these require significant amounts of mathematical computation. In the case of voice recognition, the computer must make a mathematical analysis of the "wave forms" of the sounds spoken by the human larynx. This can then be matched against a library of known wave forms in order to make a first guess, or to narrow the possibilities down to a few distinct words.

But as we saw in Chapter 21, there are immense problems of strategy: did the speaker, who was mumbling at the time, say "two," or "to," or "too," or "through," or "threw," or "tune," or something else? Conceptually, the computer can deal with this the same way a human would: by using its knowledge of English grammar (which it presumes the human speaker to know, though grammar differs a little depending on whether one is talking to a Northerner, or Southerner, a Texan, or someone from Maine) and from the context of the sentence or paragraph. There is still much work to do in this field, but enough is known that we could build substantially better voice recognition systems today if we had computers that could carry out their calculations a thousand times faster.[3]

The military is fascinated with the possibilities of artificial intelligence. As Norman Augustine, chairman of the Defense Science Board, observed,

> We have smart weapons now, but only in comparison to the unguided ones of the past. I'd give the laser-guided bomb or shell at best an IQ of 90. But we'll have truly brilliant PGM's starting in the latter half of this decade. With their autonomous seekers, they will have an IQ of 130 to 140, by my way of thinking.[9]

Not everyone is convinced that the military organizations will be successful in using artificial intelligence technology to build smart weapons, or that the technology is even relevant.[10] As consultant Richard Garwin points out, "The struggle for air superiority, contrary to popular conception, is largely a question of which side can destroy the airfields of the other side first."[11] But successful or not, one thing is reasonably certain: the military will continue spending money for AI research for their smart weapons. And they will need faster, more powerful computers.

Ordinary Business Applications

As we have seen throughout this book, more and more medium-sized and large-sized companies are computerizing almost every aspect of their day-to-day operation. For many companies, this means putting a personal computer on the desk of every white-

---

[3] There is an issue here that is common to cryptanalysis and weather prediction: the time element. Voice recognition systems are more useful if they can keep up with the real time speech of the human speaker. At the present time, voice recognition systems available on personal computers can handle only one voice (i.e., they have to be trained to understand the way that one voice pronounces common words), and can handle only a vocabulary of about 200 words . . . and they would probably go crazy trying to keep up with the speech pattern of a Brooklyn taxidriver.

collar worker. For many others (particularly those who began large-scale computerization efforts in the 1960s and early 1970s) it means putting a dumb terminal on every desk, a terminal that is connected, through telephone lines or direct cabling, to a centralized mainframe computer.

To an increasingly large extent, these terminals are being used for almost every kind of business transaction and activity: word processing, data retrieval, inventory control, accounting operations, order entry, etc. This means that everyone in the organization—from the lowliest clerk to the most senior of managers—will, in the future, spend a great deal of time typing something (a command, or a request, or a piece of information) on a terminal, and then waiting for the computer to respond.

It is this last part that is causing the problem. If the computer doesn't respond immediately, what should the worker/manager do? Well, that depends. If the computer isn't going to respond for fifteen minutes, and we are aware of the delay in advance, there are many other useful things that we can do while we're waiting. Indeed, we can even organize our work (or our manager will organize it for us) in such a way that we always have something useful to do while waiting for the computer. Of course, as more and more of our day-to-day work moves from the familiar manual mode (i.e., scraps of paper, Pendaflex files, etc.) into the automated mode, there is less and less useful work to be done while waiting for the computer.

Most of the time, the computer doesn't take fifteen minutes, unless the job is staggeringly complicated, as in the examples discussed earlier in this section. Indeed, most of the time the delay is more on the order of fifteen seconds. Or maybe thirty seconds. Or maybe a minute. That's the problem: we don't know (nor does the computer know) how long the delay will be. It's a complex function of (a) how many other people are using the computer; (b) what kind of work they're doing; and (c) how much of the computer hardware is available for work at the moment.[4]

---

[4] For companies that require their computers to work twenty-four hours per day, a "degraded" level of operation takes place if a portion of the computer hardware malfunctions or has to be taken out of service for maintenance. Thus, there are times when the poor response time is the result of one disk drive being out of service, or one of the CPUs not being available.

If the response time to a computer command is one to two minutes, and if the delay is known in advance, and if we have reached a logical breaking point in our work, then we may decide to get a cup of coffee while waiting or perhaps just stretch and relax. But if we don't know how long the computer will be, we don't know whether to leave the terminal; indeed, for some applications (such as an airline reservations terminal at an airport), the user can't leave the terminal anyway, because a customer is hovering on the other side of the desk, anxiously awaiting some intelligent response from the computer and/or the reservations agent.

In many cases, the unpredictable delay from the computer occurs before we have reached a logical stopping point. Perhaps the application is "order entry," and we have finished typing the customer's name and address, and now we're waiting for the computer to ask us for the description and quantity of products that the customer is ordering. We haven't finished dealing with the customer, obviously; indeed the customer may be standing in front of us, or at the other end of a telephone.

If the customer is present, there is an awkward silence; if the customer is not there, then the most natural thing for the user to do is daydream. Depending on the time of day and a thousand other factors, we might begin thinking about the weekend, or the upcoming lunch break, or the movie we watched on TV last night, etc. And then, when the computer finally indicates its willingness to accept more input (which we might not notice, unless it beeps at us), it takes a moment or two to remember what we were doing.

All of this leads to a very simple conclusion: with more powerful computer hardware, we could ensure consistently fast response times and thus dramatically higher worker productivity.[5] Consistency is just as important as speed. A computer that responds erratically—one second for some transactions, and thirty seconds for others—is one of the most frustrating things that one can encounter in today's business world. It leads to ulcers and high blood pressure; it leads to the physical destruction of computer terminals. The next time you discover that your secretary has

---

[5] Remember: in this context, "worker" means everyone who uses the computer in his or her day-to-day work. That includes clerical and administrative people, of course; but it also includes engineers, marketing people, accountants, scientists, computer programmers, and managers. Especially managers.

poured coffee onto the keyboard of her terminal, you'll know why; the next time you see your manager punch her fist through the display screen, you'll appreciate the reason.

"Fast" means different things to different people: in most cases it means less than one second. Studies conducted at IBM by A. J. Thadhani and Geoffrey Lambert in the early 1980s first focused attention on the dramatic improvement in human productivity that could be achieved with faster response time. This conclusion has since been confirmed by a number of business organizations— including Hallmark Cards, Inc., which conducted its own study of a system serving an average of 450 active users, of whom 200 were systems development staff (programmers and systems analysts)—running on an IBM 3081K mainframe computer with TSO:[6]

> . . . the conclusions we draw from our analysis are:
>
> - The Thadhani curve is realistic; transaction rates do increase dramatically in the subsecond response-time range. Furthermore, the curve can be verified in any TSO environment.
>
> - The diverse TSO usage in a large-shop environment makes it unrealistic to expect subsecond response time for all transactions, but when provided for 85 percent or more of TSO activity (trivial transactions), productivity will increase dramatically.
>
> - Service-level objectives and daily monitoring are essential in justifying and maintaining subsecond on-line development service on a day-to-day basis. [12]

A somewhat different kind of business application requiring more powerful computers is graphics—the manipulation, retrieval, and display of diagrams, charts, and computerized representations of what we like to think of as pictures. Most businesspeople are still getting used to the idea of reasonable-looking graphics on their personal computer; it might not occur to them that there is a bottleneck of any sort. However, we must keep in mind that this sort of graphics borders on the trivial.

---

[6] TSO means "Time Sharing Option." It's a large software system provided by IBM to facilitate on-line access to the computer from remote terminals. I provide the information primarily for computer professionals who will appreciate the significance of attempting to provide subsecond response time with such a pig of an operating system.

To appreciate the nature of a real-world graphic problem, consider the dilemma of an advertising agency that has just spent a considerable sum of money photographing a model for a bathing suit advertisement. The client, in his infinite wisdom, has requested that the model be moved from the left side of the ad to the right side, that he be shown wearing a different color bathing suit, and that his twin be shown somewhere else on the page. How can this be done in time to meet a deadline, especially if the model has no twin? The two obvious answers are (a) rephotograph the entire scene, or (b) send specialists into the darkroom to cut and paste and work miracles with their airbrushes. Both options are time consuming, expensive and unpleasant.

All of this could be done on a computer, but the scale of the problem exceeds what the average ad agency could afford. To store one magazine-quality 8-inch by 10-inch color photograph takes about 30 million bytes of data.[7] New computer systems that can deal with this kind of problem are beginning to appear on the market, but the price of the "image processing systems" starts at $25,000 and escalates quickly to $200,000. Even so, a recent market analysis estimated $7 billion in image processing sales by 1990.[13]

A different form of computer graphics has also begun to attract business attention: high-quality, three-dimensional graphical images that can be animated by a computer to produce lifelike motion. The movie industry has already invested money for supercomputers in this area. The 1984 movie *The Last Starfighter* used more than one hour of computer time on a Cray-1 computer to produce the graphics for the space battle scenes. The advertising industry may follow; the cartoon industry will be close behind, much to the dismay of a generation of animators.

PROBLEMS REQUIRING LARGER, FASTER EXTERNAL STORAGE

Many of the problems described above can benefit from additional memory and external storage as well as additional computing

[7] That's roughly the equivalent of 15,000 typewritten pages. Whoever said that a picture is worth a thousand words was off by a factor of 4,500! On the other hand, keep in mind Russell Baker's brilliant observation that there are times when a word is worth a thousand pictures.

power. Large computational problems generally mean lots of data to compute as well as lots of computing to do on the data.

However, there are some applications that require additional storage capacity independent of their need for additional processing power. We already saw one example in the previous section: image processing systems. If one picture requires 30 million bytes of data of computer storage, then a 300-page art book requires 10 billion bytes of storage, more than almost any organization has in its computer facility at the present time.[8] A library of 10,000 art books would require 100 trillion bytes of data, and so forth.

In addition to the storage needs of large government organizations and business enterprises, there is a need for large-scale storage for consumer-oriented applications. For home computers, storage is measured in ranges of 80,000 to 1.2 million bytes of data for a floppy disk (the low end is characteristic of the Apple II and Commodore 64 computers, while the high end is characteristic of the professional computers like the HP-150 and the IBM PC/AT) or ten to twenty megabytes for hard disks. Many information retrieval applications would become feasible if the average household had 100 billion bytes of storage. A number of novel applications, most of which we can't even imagine, would be possible if every household appliance—the TV, the dishwasher, the toaster, and the VCR—each had 100 billion bytes of storage.

I have deliberately led this discussion astray in the past paragraph to illustrate how easy it is to confuse a limitation in one dimension of computer performance with a limitation in another dimension. It is possible to put 100 billion bytes of data storage in the home today but it would cost more money than anyone other than the Rockefeller family could afford, and it would take up every square inch of space in the household. Also, it's not clear that the architecture of the typical home computer processor could successfully deal with 100 billion bytes of storage: it's roughly

---

[8] When I use the term "storage capacity," I really mean on-line storage capacity. For decades, government organizations and businesses have had tape libraries of thousands of magnetic tapes, each one of which might contain 50 to 100 million bytes of data. But before the computer could access the data, someone would have to retrieve the proper reel of tape and mount it on a tape drive. Most modern computers now use disks, as discussed in Chapter 35. The relevant issue is the amount of disk storage that the computer can have on-line, and therefore immediately accessible, at any instant in time.

analogous to putting a 100,000-gallon gasoline tank on a Volkswagen. So it might be necessary to install a mainframe computer in the household, too.

Clearly, what we want for the household application—and for many small-business applications, too—is a large amount of computer storage at an affordable price, in a physically compact area. And indeed this will happen. Already, a subsidiary of Eastman Kodak has announced its intention to market a 13-megabyte floppy disk by mid-1985; this is roughly 100 times the storage capacity of the current Apple IIe floppy disk, and roughly ten times the capacity of the floppy disk drive on the top-of-the-line IBM PC/AT. By the early 1990s, we should see another several order-of-magnitude improvements.

PROBLEMS REQUIRING SMALLER, CHEAPER COMPUTER SYSTEMS

For many people, the most exciting developments in computer hardware have to do with the dimensions of size, power consumption, weight, and price. More powerful computers are important, as is the issue of more computer memory. But if we could take today's computer power and shrink it to one-tenth, or one-hundredth, of its current size, then we would have some interesting new applications.

Among the more popular applications under consideration today are the "bionic implants": computers embedded in the human body. Probably the most urgent need is for computers that can monitor life-critical processes and sound an appropriate alarm if the patient is in danger. Heart patients, diabetes patients, premature babies, and a host of others come to mind as obvious candidates. The computer technology already exists for monitoring heartbeat, blood pressure, glucose level in the blood, and a vast array of other medical factors; the problem is that the computers are in the hospitals or doctors' offices, and cannot be moved. Nobody wants to strap a 500-pound computer on his back to keep track of his blood pressure; the weight alone would kill the very patient that the computer was trying to save.

If we embed a monitoring computer in the human body, we might also give it the ability to regulate critical body functions, or to regulate the flow of life-saving drugs, enzymes, or food supplies. The same computer that monitors glucose levels in a diabetes patient can also administer microdoses of insulin, thus sparing millions of patients the daily agony of stabbing themselves with a needle (prototypes of such an internal microchip have already been developed[14]). The heart attack victim already has a pacemaker, but it is large, clumsy, and primitive. We need smarter, cheaper, smaller pacemakers.

If we could accomplish even this much, we would affect the lives of millions upon millions of suffering people in all walks of life; the savings in emotional terms, in dollar terms, and in terms of the productive, useful lives it would permit would be staggering. But meanwhile, what about—as the ads for the Apple Macintosh always ask—the rest of us? What about those of us who are reasonably healthy, but who eat too much, drink too much, jog too much, or exercise too little? What about those of us with gradually deteriorating eyesight, and what about those of us who are growing slightly hard of hearing? What about those of us who are never sure if we took enough Vitamin C, or whether our diet provided enough potassium today? What about those of who aren't really sure whether we're allergic to clams? Why can't we have a computer embedded in our body? Why can't we have lots of computers embedded all over our bodies?

The answer, of course, is that we can. And we should, if we want to. We are already beginning to see a few primitive examples. An enterprising dentist has come up with a "chip in a lip" to assist those who wear braces. The tiny computer helps move teeth by stimulating the enamel buildup on one side and helping it recede on the other side. [15]

We know enough about the medical requirements of heart victims and diabetes patients to put microscopic embedded computers to work right away. But there are other medical/physical problems that we don't yet know how to solve. How would we use a computer to restore the sight of a blind person? Experts in the artificial intelligence field are still working at the very, very early stages of pattern recognition and computer vision; but even if we could get a computer to identify a Modigliani by recognizing the characteristic patterns of the art, we would have no way of transmitting that information to the optic nerves and thus into the brain. That problem is probably twenty years away from solution—unless or until our children, or our children's children, come up with revolutionary solutions.

An equally difficult problem is that of restoring ambulatory motion to paralyzed, or nerve-damaged, patients; experimental work is taking place in this field. There has already been a partially successful experiment involving a young child, injured in an automobile accident, strapped to an Apple II computer. The computer, connected to the child with a hideous jumble of wires and cables, sent electrical impulses to leg muscles that could no longer be controlled by the brain. The child walked a few steps, for the first time since her debilitating accident. She and her parents and her doctors wept with joy at their success; every computer technician who watched the report on a recent "Sixty Minutes" TV program wept with frustration at the primitive computer hardware that held her back.

On a more mundane level, we need smaller, cheaper computers for process control, but process control of a kind never before seen. We need a computer embedded in every cow and every pig to tell us whether it is eating properly. We need a computer implanted in every ear of corn, in every pea pod, in every rice plant, on every stalk of wheat. There should be a computer attached to every fish and every chicken, every tomato plant above ground, and every potato plant below ground.[9] We should have computers in the soil and in the water, computers floating like tiny seeds on currents of air, all reporting to Galactic Headquarters to tell us whether the air is pure, whether the water is polluted, whether the ground needs to be fertilized.

Could this happen? Yes! Will it happen? Who knows? If the technology is available, in a form that every citizen on the face of the Earth can have, then some of these applications will be implemented. We don't know which ones will be important, which ones will be frightening, or which ones will turn out to be irrelevant. But

---

[9] And since we generally intend to consume these products, the computer should be digestible, too.

for now, it is all moot: our computers are too big, too bulky, too noisy, too fat, too expensive, too slow, too penurious in their memory capacities—all in all, too limiting for even our limited imaginations. How on earth could they serve our children?

I think we will know that we have developed adequate computer power when we have not only implemented all of the applications described in this chapter (or at least demonstrated our ability to implement them), but also when we have achieved one more miracle: the disposable computer. When we have developed a computer that can be used once and then thrown away, then we will be free, mentally, to think of applications that we dare not dream of today.

This, I argue, cannot be done by today's generation of computer programmers because they are too awed by the fact that a supercomputer costs $2,000 per hour to rent and that a decent home computer costs $5,000. My generation of computer technicians cannot comprehend the notion of a computer that would be considered "dirty" after it had executed a program a single time.

A rough analogy will help illustrate this point. Someone I know recently went into a camera store to buy a roll of film. At the checkout counter, he happened to notice a large basket filled with hand-held calculators and a sign indicating that they were on sale for $1 each. Now, I should point out that this fellow is a veteran of the calculator wars: he bought one of the very first Hewlett-Packard calculators in 1973 when the price was somewhere between $500 and $600; he has dozens of calculators, of all sizes, shapes, and colors, at home. To this collection, he added four of the $1 calculators, thinking that his wife and his children might also need one. When he got home, he casually looked at the bottom of the calculator to see what kind of battery it required. When he could find no opening in the casing, he thought that perhaps it was solar-powered; a quick experiment demonstrated that sunlight was not the source of power. After another ten minutes of puzzled experimenting, he finally concluded that the calculator was battery-powered, but that the battery was not replaceable. It was a real shock: this man has not yet gotten accustomed to the idea of disposable razors. The concept of a disposable calculator was so horrifying to him that he could not bring himself to use it for several weeks—after all, he would be using some of its precious, nonreplaceable energy. He still feels guilty every time he turns on the power switch.

This man works in the computer field. This man is me.

References for Chapter 36

1.   Kirchner, Jake, "Supercomputing Seen Key to Economic Success," *Computerworld*, October 3, 1983.

2.   Dallaire, Gene, "American Universities Need Greater Access to Supercomputers," *Communications of the ACM*, April 1984.

3.   *Ibid.*

4.   *Ibid.*

5.   *Reader's Digest 1985 Almanac and Yearbook*, pages 33-39.

6.   Meadows, Donella, et al., *The Limits to Growth*, New York: Universe Books, 1972.

7.   _____, John Richardson, and Gerhart Bruckman, *Groping in the Dark*, New York: John Wiley & Sons, 1982.

8.   Lecht, Charles, "Supercomputers: More Than Just for Defense," *Computerworld*, October 17, 1983.

9.   Rochester, Jack, and John Gantz, *The Naked Computer*, New York: William Morrow, 1983.

10.   Lind, William S., "A Doubtful Revolution," *Issues in Science and Technology*, Spring 1985.

11.   Garwin, Richard L., "Smart Weapons: But When?" *Issues in Science and Technology*, Spring 1985.

12.   Lundy, Harold, "Justifying Subsecond Response Time," *Computerworld*, November 21, 1983.

13.   "Image Processing—A New Direction for the Computer Revolution," *Breakthrough*, June 1, 1985.

14.   "Internal Microchip Medicine," *Breakthrough*, November 15, 1983.

15.   Rochester, Gantz, *op. cit.*

37

FUTURE TRENDS IN
HARDWARE DEVELOPMENT

Fellow men! I promise to show the means of creating a paradise within ten years, where everything desirable for human life may be had by every man in superabundance, without labor, and without pay; where the whole face of nature shall be changed into the most beautiful of forms, and man may live in the most magnificent palaces, in all imaginable refinements of luxury, and in the most delightful gardens; where he may accomplish, without labor, in one year, more than hitherto could be done in thousands of years.

J.A. Etzler
Comments on the steam engine, 1842

Before the end of this decade, the cost of carrying out a million computations per second, for an entire month, will be less than the cost of an American computer programmer—indeed, less than the cost of any average white-collar professional worker. Whether that will lead to the paradise predicted by Mr. Etzler over a century ago remains to be seen. Technology will be available to create almost any kind of material paradise we can imagine. I leave it to other, wiser, men and women to speculate on the possibility that we will put it to good use.

Research on one form of technology, computer hardware, is

taking place at a feverish pace all over the world. As I pointed out in Chapter 12, much of this research is being funded by national governments—and that, in turn, is motivated largely by defense interests and concern over national security. However, there is also a great deal of research in private industry, as well as the leading universities. And, as always, there are inventors working in their basements and their garages.

To describe all of this research is impossible; much of it is hidden in secrecy. Military organizations don't want the "other side" to take advantage of their research; private corporations don't want their competitors to know what they're up to; and university professors don't want their colleagues to publish research results before they do. Some collaboration, of course, is taking place; some rumors do leak out; and last year's research eventually finds its way into the press. But today's research, and next year's research, is known only to a few.

All of this is a very tedious way of saying that I don't know everything that's going on the field of computer hardware research, nor would I be capable of understanding everything that's going on, even if someone showed all of it to me. But enough has been published, leaked, rumored, and patiently explained to me by cooperative engineers and researchers that some broad patterns are clear. These patterns, or broad trend-lines, are the subject of this chapter.

I will limit the discussion of future hardware trends to two main areas: central processing units and external storage devices. Impressive developments are also taking place in telecommunications, high-speed printers, and other specialized parts of the hardware industry, but they are of less crucial concern to most of us. Also, I feel that much of the improvements in these ancillary, or peripheral, technologies will be the result of improvements in CPU technology, chip technology, and storage technology discussed below. Telecommunications technology will improve considerably, for example, with the widespread introduction of fibre optics; but it will also improve tremendously because of improved computer-controlled switching, error detection, error-correction, and multiplexing of signals.

FUTURE TRENDS IN
CENTRAL PROCESSING UNITS

As I observed in Chapter 36, there is intense interest in the possibility of making computers faster, smaller, and cheaper. But how do we accomplish this? How can we make next year's computer 20 percent faster than this year's model?

Though there may be hundreds of different answers to this question, almost all of the research and development currently underway falls into four broad categories:

- More efficient organization of current hardware technology.

- Multiple CPUs working in tandem with one another.

- "Optical" computers.

- "Organic" computers.

The first two categories are the most promising in terms of results that we can expect over the next two to five years. Optical computers and organic computers are, in many ways, far more exciting, but we will probably not see practical results for another ten years.

More Efficient von Neumann Machines

Current computer architecture, especially the architecture of the central processing unit, is often referred to as "von Neumann" architecture, in deference to John von Neumann's work in the 1940s. It is interesting to note that the use of "parallel" computers had been discussed much earlier,[1] but that von Neumann argued in favor of single-processor machines because of the failure-prone device technology of the times.

Regardless of the technology used to build the computer —whether it was vacuum tubes, transistors, or semiconductors— almost all computers built in the past forty years have been based on the concept of carrying out one command or instruction at a time;

---

[1] As early as 1922, L. Richardson suggested the possible use of up to 64,000 human processors to help predict weather.[1]

when that instruction has been completed, the computer goes on to the next one.

As we will see below, many computer scientists are challenging that paradigm and are beginning to build "non-von Neumann" machines. However, there is still a great deal of efficiency that can be squeezed out of the conventional architecture of today's computers. Indeed, it is highly likely that we will achieve at least two, and possibly three, order-of-magnitude improvements over the next ten to fifteen years simply by building more efficient von Neumann machines.

One of the primary goals of this conventional research is to build more compact electronic circuits so that the electrical signals have less distance to travel. In this conventional world, the speed of light is a major barrier, so cutting the distance that a signal must travel in half can effectively double the speed of the computer. Compare any of the early first-generation computers, whose CPUs filled entire rooms, with a current computer, whose CPU is smaller than a thumbnail, and consider the distances that an electrical signal must travel. It takes approximately 0.00000085 seconds for an electrical signal to travel an inch, which is considerably less than the 0.000002 seconds it takes a signal to travel across an average room.

There are two ways to accomplish this kind of improvement. We can find new, smaller, more efficient materials or methods for carrying out the operations required of a central processor. Or we can find clever ways of cramming more of the components that we already have into smaller physical units. Or we can do both.

The most promising new material on the horizon is gallium arsenide. While it has been heralded by computer experts as the key to the future for almost twenty-five years, we are only now beginning to use it to replace the "stuff" of current computers: silicon. The major problem that has delayed the introduction of gallium arsenide is, quite simply, price. In contrast to silicon, which is the second most abundant element on the earth's surface after oxygen, gallium is a very scarce and precious element. It makes up less than 0.01 percent of the earth's crust. At the present time, a gallium arsenide "wafer" for making chips costs about $200, which does not compare favorably with the $10 cost of a silicon wafer.[2] However, some applications, particularly the military applications, need the improved performance of gallium arsenide and the additional cost can therefore be justified.

The advantages of gallium arsenide over silicon are numerous:

- It uses less power than silicon.

- It has a high degree of "radiation hardness," thus making it relatively impervious to blasts of EMP (Electro-Magnetic Pulses) associated with nuclear explosions. This is obviously important for DOD applications, and also for space satellites and other applications in harsh environments.

- It is three to six times faster than silicon.

- It absorbs sunlight better than silicon, thus making practical the use of solar cells for power.

- It can operate at much higher temperatures than silicon, thus reducing the cooling requirements for the computer.

- It can combine the processing of both light and electronic data on a single chip.

We will not see gallium arsenide computers for another year or two. Cray Research, for example, has set 1987 as its target date for introducing a Cray-3 computer based on gallium arsenide.[3] Ironically, of the top ten silicon chip manufacturers, only three—Texas Instruments, Motorola, and RCA—are involved in gallium arsenide digital chip development, and this is probably due more to government contracts than foresight. Meanwhile, it appears that gallium arsenide chips will be used more to complement the power of silicon-based computers for most applications. Only the most demanding applications will be able to justify all-gallium computers.

Meanwhile, the Silicon Valley companies, as well as IBM and about thirty other companies, are investing much of their energy and research (financed by approximately $1 billion in Defense Department research funds[4]) in techniques of packaging more components on a single chip. In 1985, integrated circuits with more than a million components began to appear on the market. They will be in volume production by the spring of 1986. Integrated circuits with 4 million components are in development labs today, and will probably be in volume production by the end of the decade. Quarter-micron chips with tens of millions of components are considered quite likely by the middle of the 1990s, and scientists like James D. Meindl, co-director of Stanford's Center for Integrated Systems, foresee "gigascale integration"—a billion components to a chip—before the end of the century.[5] Since today's standard technology involves 256,000 components on a chip, it is evident that we will see one to two orders-of-magnitude improvement within the next ten years, and possibly three orders-of-magnitude improvement before the year 2000.[2] This will mean, for example, that a single integrated circuit in the mid-1990s will have more power than a dozen of today's $4 million supercomputers, and it will cost only a few hundred dollars.

There are a variety of associated problems and issues when one tries to build immensely more powerful von Neumann machines, including mundane issues like packaging, which most hardware designers would prefer to ignore. But as Albert Blodgett, Jr. points out,

> Clearly, every computer needs packaging of some kind, but the nature of the packaging would not appear to have much influence on the functioning of the machine. The facts are otherwise. In many high-speed data-processing units packaging technology is the factor that determines or limits performance, cost and reliability.
>
> One reason packaging has become so important is the imperative to make the central elements of a computing system exceedingly compact. Improvements in the design and fabrication of microelectronic devices have greatly increased the number of logic functions that can be put on a chip as well as the speed at which arithmetic operations are performed. As a result a major source of delay in the central processing unit of many computers now is the time needed for a signal to pass from one chip to another.[7]

---

[2] Not everyone agrees with this optimistic view of the future. Some researchers —especially the ones working on the parallel-processing machines—feel that the von Neumann machines are within one factor of ten of their maximum possible speed. Others, like Riganati and Schneck, argue that "silicon is within a factor of five of the maximum achievable limits."[6]

Another survey of the limits of computational power estimated that the limitations in supercomputer cycle times in the following way:

> Causes of limitations in supercomputer cycle times are the switching speed of the devices (30 percent), limitations in the drivers (30 percent), packaging and interconnection delays (25 percent), and compromises in design to account for realistic tolerances of parameters in the timing of individual components (15 percent). While these percentages are dependent on system construction details, even a dramatic improvement in any one, say switching speed, will not be enough to greatly impact overall system performance. For this reason, increased dependence on parallel hardware and software is unavoidable.[8]

Another related issue is switching time—the speed at which a circuit can be switched on and off. Today's best computers, based on gallium arsenide, can switch on and off as often as 100 billion times per second. But scientists at Bell Laboratories are working on a "ballistic transistor" that may have switching speeds of 100 trillion times per second[9]—1,000 times faster than current machines. The research project is based on the notion of making the gap between components so small that an electron will be able to shoot straight through at the speed of light without bumping into any other electrons along the way. Other companies, including IBM, Texas Instruments, and Westinghouse, are working on similar projects, with hopes of introducing a machine with switching speeds of 1 trillion times per second by 1988.[10]

Parallel Processing

The concept of parallel processing is deceptively simple: if one CPU is good, then multiple CPUs must be better. Or to put it another way, if the CPU is the bottleneck in processing speeds, then having multiple CPUs will eliminate the bottleneck.

This concept can take many different forms, and has been in existence for nearly two decades. It is the scale of today's parallel processing systems, and of the ones that are in the laboratories, that is so impressive. Beginning in the 1960s, some computer manufacturers recognized that the execution of an individual computer instruction required several distinct steps, some of which could be done in parallel. Adding two numbers, for example, involves the following steps:

- The instruction must "decoded" so that the computer knows that addition, rather than subtraction or some other operation, is required.

- The operands—the numbers to be added together—must be "fetched" from the memory locations where they reside, and placed in arithmetic registers that can be used for the operation.

- The actual arithmetic operation of adding must be carried out (which in itself might consist of several individual microinstructions).

- The results of the operation must be stored in a specified memory location.

Many early models of computers were built to optimize the simultaneous execution of these parts of a single computer instruction; so-called data flow machines and pipeline machines of the 1960s and 1970s achieved impressive speed improvements using these techniques. By the early 1980s, a number of very different approaches to building such machines had evolved. Indeed, there are now so many different forms of pipelining, connected machines, and parallel machines that battles have erupted over the proper taxonomy of multiple/pipeline/parallel computers.[11]

Much of the research and development today involves the use of several relatively independent CPUs, each working on different parts of an overall problem, such as the solution of a differential equation or linear programming problem. Within each CPU, the pipeline concept discussed above can be used to optimize the exeucution of individual instructions. Various experimental machines involving sixteen, or sixty-four, or even hundreds, of CPUs have been built;[12,13] one experimental machine built by Goodyear Aerospace for NASA has 16,384 processors for processing images transmitted from Earth-surveying satellites. Another interesting experimental parallel machine has been built by NCR. Called GAPP (for Geometric Arithmetic Parallel Processor), it packs seventy-eight tiny CPUs on a single chip; because it is a chip, it can be incorporated as an add-on "board" for existing computers. GAPP chips currently cost approximately $500,[14] but the price is expected to drop in half within the next one to two years, and the technology for 512-CPU chips is now under development.

Only a few of these machines have found their way into the marketplace. Most of the current parallel computers, such as Cray's X-MP and Cray-2, or the top-of-the-line mainframe computers built by IBM, Burroughs, and others, use two or four normal processors to improve speed. The forthcoming Cray-3 supercomputer and Denelcor's HEP-1 will have sixteen processors. As Riganati and Schneck point out,

> Our experience with parallelism has been limited to a small number of processes (<100), but we must soon learn whether algorithms and programming tools will scale up to thousands, perhaps hundreds of thousands, of processes. We see through biological evolution that such parallelism does exist, but because we do not yet understand the principles, we may not succeed in exploiting it. Whether out of respect for the lessons of history or with the belief that Amdahl's Law[3] is valid, all current commercial and planned supercomputers are based on the use of rather modest numbers of parallel processing elements.[15]

A related approach to parallel processing has had much more impact, especially on smaller computers: assign a separate CPU to different input/output tasks so that the central CPU can spend virtually all of its time carrying out calculations. Thus, many current personal computers have one CPU to control the keyboard, another CPU to control the display screen (particularly for the display of graphic images on the screen), and yet another CPU to control input/output from the floppy disk or Winchester disk. Since each CPU costs only a few dollars, the overall cost of the system is

---

[3] Amdahl's Law warns that it is dangerous to rely on a large number of parallel processors if each has a performance considerably below that of a single high-performance sequential machine.

not much greater, but it does mean that "number-crunching" activities can be carried out as efficiently as possible. This same concept is used, obviously on a larger scale, on most mainframe computers.

With this approach to parallel processing, the software problems are relatively straightforward: each CPU is equipped with software (or "firmware," perhaps) that knows how to handle the specialized task of keyboard input/output, etc. However, the generalized approach to parallel computing poses software problems that still confound computer scientists. How do we take an arbitrary computational problem and break it into discrete pieces, so that multiple CPUs can work on different parts at the same time? For certain mathematical problems, the solution is straightforward. Certain mathematical operations upon matrices or vectors can be "factored" trivially so that different CPUs can work on individual "cells" of data. In the general case, though, CPU #N may require the results of computation performed by CPU #N-1 before it can go any further. In the extreme case, known as "deadly embrace," CPU #N-1 is waiting for results from CPU #X, which is waiting for #Y, and so forth until we find that the chain closes by virtue of a machine that is waiting for CPU #N.

Whether the software problems associated with parallel processing will be solved in the near future remains to be seen.[16] Extensive research on the problem is currently taking place at a number of universities throughout the world, as well as defense-related research in the United States, and government-sponsored research in Japan, England, France, and the Soviet Union.[17]

Optical Computers

A completely different approach to new-generation computers is known as optical processing. Based on the concept of using light beams instead of electrons, the optical computer promises a factor of ten improvement over conventional computing devices. Theoretically, optical computers are capable of speeds 100 to 1,000 times faster than conventional computers, but American researchers are currently frustrated by the bottleneck of getting data into and out of the computer fast enough to keep up with its computing abilities.

Research in optical computing is taking place at the Georgia Institute of Technology, Carnegie-Mellon, the Battelle Institute, and within the U.S. Army and Navy; at least two private companies, Aerodyne and Guiltech, are conducting research and building prototype machines.[18] Japan and the Soviet Union, among other countries, are also making a heavy commitment to military uses of optical computers.

Organic Computers

Organic computers, sometimes known as "biochips"[19] or "biosensors,"[20] are based on the concept that individual molecules, or "molecular functional groups," can be made to function as electronic switches so that computers can be constructed, literally, molecule by molecule. The molecules of most interest are enzymes, which already exhibit computerlike capabilities in living organisms. Not only would such molecular computers be considerably faster for some applications, they would be considerably smaller—as much as 1,000 times more compact than today's conventional machines.

At the present time, this concept is based almost entirely on theory, with virtually no prototype machines having been built. Nevertheless, there is intense interest in the concept, if only because, as David Waltz says,

> Molecular technology is possible, We are walking examples of its feasibility. The question is whether we can engineer such technology to be competitive.[21]

Consider, for example, how easy it is for the human eye to track a moving source of light. Doing that same job with conventional computer technology would require massive amounts of computation. If we could capture the intelligence of the enzymes that have been biologically programmed to detect light, we could improve the performance of some specialized computer applications by an enormous amount.

Interest in biochip research seems to be picking up slowly. The Department of Defense recently funded a four-year, $2.4 million research program at Case Western Reserve University,[22] and the

Association for Computing Machinery (ACM) devoted its May 1985 issue of the *Communications of the ACM* to the subject of molecular computing. But there is a general feeling that the area is not receiving the research funding that it requires;[23,24] in any case, it is definitely not receiving the kind of massive financial support that other hardware research areas have now come to expect. Consequently, it is not likely that we will see even a prototype organic computer before the end of this decade; production machines—assuming that the theory can be turned into practice—will not be seen before the mid-1990s, at the earliest.

FUTURE TRENDS IN
EXTERNAL STORAGE DEVICES

The most interesting development in the world of external storage devices is the optical, laser disk. This is basically the same kind of technology that we have begun to see in other home entertainment areas; now it is being married to the computer.

Glowing promises and market predictions for optical disk technology have been seen in computer publications for fifteen years. Consider the following news items:

> Precision Instrument Company, Palo Alto, landed a second order for its trillion-bit laser record/reader storage system last month and said it will market a smaller 10 million-bit version.

> *Datamation*
> July 15, 1970

> Lower component costs are being credited in price cuts for a read-only optical memory system announced only a year ago. A 25% drop, to 3 cents per bit for a 100Kb model in quantities of 100, is due this month from Optical Memory Systems, Santa Ana, Calif. Prices will get down to a penny a bit two years from now.

> *Datamation*
> April 15, 1971

Holographic memory systems with capabilities in the 10 trillion-bit range and with microsecond speeds have long been talked about. They're still in the lab. But next month, first units of a holographic system are scheduled to be shipped by a new firm, Optical Data Systems, Mountain View, Calif., for field testing.

Datamation
February 1972

Unfortunately, none of these plans came to fruition. Optical Memory Systems and Optical Data Systems vanished; Precision Instruments went into Chapter 11, was revived later by Heiser Corp., and then put up for sale without ever having gone into production.

But optical disk technology is still alive. And now, once again, companies are beginning to promise deliveries of computer storage devices with memory capacities that boggle the mind. A single optical disk platter can hold two million pages of information, roughly two billion bytes of data. There are now seventeen or eighteen companies ready to deliver products by the end of 1985, according to recent surveys;[25] the companies include such well-known names as Control Data, Philips, RCA, Shugart Associates, and Storage Technology.

There is one major problem with most optical disk systems: once recorded, the data on an optical disk cannot be erased, and therefore cannot be updated. For some (like banks) this is a tremendous advantage; for most potential users, though, it is an enormous disadvantage. Actually, there are three separate types of optical disk technology under development: the "read-only" disks (ROM), the "write once read memory" (WORM), and the "erasable" disks. ROM disks have been available for the audio market since 1983, and simple disks for the computer market will cost only $15. The WORM disks are scheduled to appear on the market in 1985-86; though they offer more flexibility, they have the disadvantage of costing $500.[26]

At the present time, the primary markets, or applications, for optical disk technology are the database applications. The entire *Encyclopedia Britannica*, the unabridged *Oxford English Diction-*

ary, and a few Agatha Christie novels will fit onto one optical disk. With WORM disks, the end-user could be supplied with baseline data, or reference material, to which he could make a one-time addition, or revision, to customize the material for his own work. Because of this limitation, the optical disk manufacturers are currently assuming that their major clients will be law offices, the patent office, keepers of medical records, publishers of databases, and keepers of pharmaceutical records. And because almost everyone ultimately wants to add some data of his own to the existing mass of reference material, it is likely that optical disks will coexist for the next five years with the hard disks that are already in use.

The hard-disk technology is improving most noticeably in the personal computer field. In 1982, a 5-megabyte hard disk was the most anyone would ask for; by 1983, 10-megabyte disks were standard; by 1984, one could buy a 20-megabyte disk for under $2,000, and the difference between a 10-megabyte and 20-megabyte disk was typically less than $300. In 1985, personal computer users can choose between 20-, 40-, 60- or 70-megabytes of disk storage for their computer; unfortunately, most of them forget to purchase ancillary "tape cartridge" backup devices, so they leave themselves vulnerable to massive data losses if there is a hardware or software failure.[4]

[4] The failure to "back up" large personal computer databases was discussed in Chapter 17; it is only one of the many sins committed by naive end-users of personal computers.

References for Chapter 37

1.   Richardson, L. S., *Weather Prediction by Numerical Process*, London: Cambridge University Press, 1922.

2.   Bylinsky, Gene, "What's Sexier and Speedier Than Silicon," *Fortune*, June 24, 1985.

3.   *Ibid.*

4.   Broad, William J., "The First of the Superchips Arrive," *New York Times*, July 23, 1985.

5.   Wilson, John, and Levine, Jonathan B., "Super Chips," *Business Week*, June 10, 1985.

6.   Riganati, John P., and Paul B. Schneck, "Supercomputing," *IEEE Computer*, October 1984.

7.   Blodgett, Albert J., Jr., "Microelectronic Packaging," *Scientific American*, September 1984.

8.   Riganati and Schneck, *op. cit.*

9.   "Word of New Transistor Leaks out of Bell Labs," *USA Today*, February 11, 1985.

10.   "Another Computer Revolution," *Breakthrough Reports*, June 15, 1985.

11.   Flynn, M. J., "Some Computer Organizations and Their Effectiveness," *IEEE Transactions on Computers*, September 1972.

12.   Douglas, John H., "New Computer Architectures Tackle Bottleneck," *High Technology*, June 1983.

13.   Alexander, Tom, "Reinventing the Computer," *Fortune*, March 5, 1984.

14.   "The Chip That Beat the BEST," *Breakthrough Reports*, February 15, 1985.

15.   Marcom, John, Jr., "Search for a Better Computer Poses Problems for Designers," *The Wall Street Journal*, May 24, 1985.

16.   *Ibid.*

17.   Hwang, Kai, "Multiprocessor Supercomputers for Scientific/Engineering Applications," *IEEE Computer*, June 1985.

18.   Alexander, Tom, "Computing With Light at Lightning Speeds," *Fortune*, July 23, 1984.

19.   Hall, Stephen, "Biochips," *High Technology*, December 1983.

20.   DeYoung, H. Garrett, "Biosensors," *High Technology*, November 1983.

21.   Shrady, Nicholas, "Molecular Computing," *Forbes*, July 29, 1985.

22.   Olmos, David, "DOD Finances Case Western Biochip Research Center," *Computerworld*, September 3, 1984.

23.   Gallant, John, "Bio-Chip Researchers Bemoan Lack of Funding," *Computerworld*, October 31, 1983.

24.   "Key Scientists Say That Molecular Computing Needs More Funding," *IEEE Institute*, January 1984.

25.   Myers, Edith, "Optical Disks Foreseen," *Datamation*, June 1, 1984.

26.   "The Optical Disks Are Coming," *Breakthrough*, April 15, 1985.

38

PREDICTIONS VI

Obviously, a man's judgment cannot be better than the information on which he has based it. Give him the truth and he may still go wrong when he has the chance to be right, but give him no news or present him only with distorted and incomplete data, with ignorant, sloppy or biased reporting, with propaganda and deliberate falsehoods, and you destroy his whole reasoning processes, and make him something less than a man.

Arthur Hays Sulzberger
Address, New York State Publishers Association (1948)

The question before us is this: do we have enough information to make an educated guess about the future? Or have we, to use Mr. Sulzberger's language, received nothing but propaganda and deliberate falsehoods from self-serving computer manufacturers and from reporters looking for an exciting story?

There is certainly some evidence to suggest that the computer field has been the victim of hyperbole, or perhaps just hysterical optimism on the part of marketing directors, industry observers, and excited scientists. Optical disk technology, as we saw in Chapter 37, is finally being used as a computer storage device some fifteen years after products were first announced. Gallium arsenide chips are just now being manufactured, even though the properties of gallium arsenide have been known for twenty years. Parallel processing machines are just being built now—and on a quite modest scale—even though predictions of thousand-CPU machines have appeared in newspapers and magazines for more than a decade.

Nevertheless, we have witnessed steady improvements in almost all aspects of computer hardware technology over the past thirty

580

years. At the Los Alamos National Laboratory, an interesting survey was conducted of the time required for computational processing rates to double, at several points in history:[1,2]

Sample Point	Years to Double
1952	1.45
1962	2.06
1972	2.93
1982	4.50

If we take these figures as a guideline, then it means that (a) the rate of improvement in computer hardware is declining, and (b) it may take until the end of this decade for computer power to double again.

However, it is also important to observe that throughout the 1960s and 1970s, the computer industry did not receive the kind of attention and subsidized research that it has received in the 1980s. A relatively modest investment from the DARPA research arm of the Defense Department was spread over hundreds of projects, and covered a dozen or more different aspects of computer science. Now the research funds from Japan, England, the European community, and the Soviet Union, as well as the United States, run easily into the billions of dollars. And much of it is aimed at improved computer hardware.

It is also important to distinguish between the three major stages of development of new computer hardware (or new technology of almost any kind):

- Basic research.
- Advanced product development.
- Product engineering.

If we listen to predictions about computer hardware in areas where the basic research has not been finished and validated, we run a major risk of disappointment. Two major areas that are still, in my opinion, in the stage of basic research are parallel processing machines and ballistics transistors. It may turn out that we are simply unable to build computers that can effectively use more than, say, sixty-four processors, and it may turn out that the efforts to build chips with "pathways" only one electron wide are to no avail. And, as we saw in Chapter 37, organic computers and optical computers are still in the early stages of research; such machines may never be built outside the laboratory.

However, most of the improvements that were discussed in Chapter 37 have moved well past this stage and into the advanced product development stage. Several versions of superchips are already being worked on in the laboratories, and researchers are confident of their ability to manufacture computers with several million components on a single chip in the early to mid-1990s.

In some areas, computer manufacturers have moved even farther, into the product engineering stage. For example, modest-sized parallel processing machines are being built now, with plans for introduction into the marketplace by 1986-87. Though they may be useful only for specialized applications, the speed improvements will be one to two orders-of-magnitude—for precisely those problems that need the speed improvement. Meanwhile, gallium arsenide is being used now for high-speed, rugged computer applications; while expensive, it works.

PREDICTIONS

Because of the massive research funding, and because of the technology that is already in the advanced product development stage or the product engineering stage, I think it is almost a certainty that the computer industry (working in conjunction with universities and government-sponsored research labs) will achieve at least one order-of-magnitude improvement in computer hardware over the period from 1985 to 1995; indeed, I think that it is safe to predict two orders-of-magnitude during this period. I think we will see these improvements in all of the important dimensions of computer hardware—speed, cost, amount of external storage, and size.

I am also very optimistic that we will see functioning prototypes of optical computers and organic computers by the mid-1990s. If these two areas of basic research fail, I think it is highly likely that they will be replaced by other "revolutionary" approaches to new computer technology.

On the other hand, I believe that the efforts to develop large-scale parallel processing computers will prove to be a massive disappointment, except in the very specialized cases of mathematical number-crunching. This will prove to be an enormous boon for weather forecasting, aerodynamic modeling of airplanes, econometric simulation, nuclear weapons design, and a few other important applications.

But it will not help, for example, in many of the artificial intelligence applications. The reason for this disappointment will have little to do with computer hardware, but rather with the associated software requirements. How can we break down a software programming job in such a way that parts of it can be worked on in parallel? As we saw in Chapters 27 through 33, we have another ten years of work before we finally will have solved the problem of developing conventional software problems; we are nowhere near solving the problem of parallel processing.

Will we solve problems like this by the early 21st century? Will organic computers and optical computers give us an additional one to two orders-of-magnitude improvement? I believe so. I believe that the combination of (a) computers in the 1990s that are 100 times more powerful than today's machines that can themselves be used in the effort to design even faster machines, and (b) the solution of most classical software engineering problems, and (c) the application of artificial intelligence techniques to such problems as parallel processing, and—most important!—(d) the fresh creativity of a whole new generation of scientists will carry the technology to a level between 1,000 and 10,000 times more powerful than today's computers.

STRATEGIC IMPLICATIONS

For those directly involved in the development of new hardware technology, the details are important. The dates are important. The failures and successes of each experiment are important. As in so many other scientific disciplines, there are thousands of brilliant, dedicated men and women who have devoted their careers to the development of newer, faster, more powerful machines. Having achieved one level of improvement, they scarcely have time to catch their breath before moving on to the next level.

But the vast majority of us are not caught up in this whirlpool of frenetic activity. We sit on the sidelines. A few of us wait, impatiently, for the next computer to emerge from the laboratory so that we can put it to work on a problem that has overwhelmed our current computer equipment. But most us spend our time trying to figure out what to do with the awesome computer power we have already been given.

And therein lies an important point, I think. Most computer programmers and systems analysts have not yet thought of any useful application of today's computer hardware, nor have the managers, clerks, administrators, and other white-collar professionals whom these computer programmers serve. In my opinion, it is a top-priority obligation of computer professionals to advise top management in their organizations of the implications of the 1,000-fold improvement in computer hardware that will be available within the next ten years.

It doesn't matter whether this hardware arrives in 1992 or 1994. It doesn't matter whether it ultimately turns out to be 1,500 times more powerful than today's computers or only 873 times more powerful. Whatever the precise number, and whatever the precise date, the results will be awesome. Those who have planned for it—those who begin working toward that day now—will enjoy enormous advantages over the individuals, or the companies, or the nations with whom they compete. Those who do nothing will find themselves drifting into the category of second-class citizen, bankrupt company, or Third World nation. It is as simple as that.

And yet, as we have seen, it is more complicated. As I have pointed out over and over again, the real problem is not technology but technology transfer. Because of this, it is all the more important not to dwell on the details of the technological developments. Who cares how many transistors the computer scientists squeeze onto the head of a pin? Who cares whether the technological improvements result from the Bell Labs ballistic transistor, or IBM's successful use of gallium arsenide chips, or Control Data's superior design of parallel processing machines? As someone investing in the stock of these organizations, it might be terribly important but as end-users of the technology, it is largely irrelevant.

Meanwhile, we will have our hands quite full simply trying to distribute the new technology through our companies, our government organizations, and our families. This means that, in addition to convincing our corporate comrades to start looking now for new products and services, we must convince them to start planning for the redevelopment (or redesign) of existing application systems and existing products that are based on vintage-1968 hardware. This means convincing people to make a capital investment before it has become an emergency. It means convincing people to plan for the euthanasia of systems that they are quite comfortable with now.

It will not be easy. But there are some on this earth who will do it. There are some—not brighter than you and me, but simply more determined—who understand that truly awesome computer power is on the horizon, and that it will give us very nearly the power of the gods. Though Winston Churchill knew little or nothing about computers, he may have had the next generation of computer hardware in mind when he remarked at the Lord Mayor's Day luncheon in November 1942:

> No, this is not the end. It is not even the beginning of the end. But it is, perhaps, the end of the beginning.

References for Chapter 38

1. Lincoln, Neil, "Great Gigaflops and Giddy Guarantees," *Proceedings of the Spring Compcon*, February 1984.

2. Henderson, D. B., "Computer Performance," *Conference on Frontiers of Supercomputing*, August 1983.

PART VII

CONCLUSION

39

LOOKING AHEAD

What, then, has happened in the last twenty years? In some ways, remarkably little. The streets are still full of automobiles, a little smaller and more expensive than they were. Airports are busier than ever. Skyscrapers are still going up. People all over the world are still busy shopping. The Portugese empire, on which I was a little hard, has disbanded, with some rather tragic results in some of the old colonies, like Timor. The Soviet Union has really changed very little, apart from the disastrous excursion into Afghanistan. China has changed a good deal, though like the Soviet Union it remains one of the last of the 19th-century empires. There is a sense of incipient crisis, or at least a malaise, pretty much the world over, although it takes different forms in the different systems. The crisis of Communism is felt certainly in China, Poland, Romania, and Hungary, but there is also a crisis of capitalism, perhaps too drawn out to deserve the name of crisis, but, again, a very serious malaise, with rising unemployment, higher rates of inflation, and a very worrying international debt situation.

Kenneth Boulding
*"The Meaning of the Twenty-First Century:
Reexamining the Great Transition"*[1]

In the midst of all the exciting developments taking place in the computer field, it is sometimes difficult to remember that there are other major forces shaping the remaining fifteen years of this millennium. I thought it appropriate to end this book by briefly discussing some of those major forces so that we can put the computer revolution in its proper perspective.

589

Statesmen and philosophers tend to agree on very little, but there is almost unanimous agreement that the most important issues of our day—the issues that may well determine whether our children can make any sensible plans on this planet for their children —include these major components:

- The threat of nuclear war.

- The population explosion.

- Pollution.

- Depletion of our natural resources.

George Gallup also argues in a recent book[2] that we will have to face a national crisis of health, especially reflected in drug and alchohol abuse, as well as a major challenge caused by national economic weakness. Others, like John Naisbitt[3] and Alvin Toffler, [4] do not discount the threat of nuclear war, but concentrate instead on major shifts taking place within society: the shift from a national economy to a world economy, the shift from a representative democracy to a participatory democracy, etc. Others, ranging from occult writers like Rene Noorbergen[5] to politicians like Ronald Reagan,[1] seem overwhelmed by many of these issues, and suggest that God has scheduled Armageddon for some fine summer morning in the next few years.

Each of these could be considered far more important and far more powerful than the computer revolution discussed in this book. After all, if a nuclear war breaks out, most of the future developments in the computer field will be moot. However, computers play an increasingly important role in each of these issues. Hence it is interesting to consider the impact of computers on such issues as pollution and the arms race, and the impact of pollution

---

[1] In a private meeting on October 18, 1983, with Thomas Dine, executive director of the American-Israel Public Affairs Committee, President Reagan mentioned that he had talked to the parents of one of the U.S. Marines killed in Beirut the night before. Then he said, "You know, I turn back to your ancient prophets in the Old Testament and the signs foretelling Armageddon, and I find myself wondering if—if we're the generation that is going to see that come about. I don't know if you've noted any of those prophecies lately, but, believe me, they certainly describe the times we are going through."

and the arms race on computers. I do not pretend to be an expert on nuclear disarmament, or acid rain, or renewable energy resources. However, I can offer some comments on the role that computers will play in these issues during the next ten years. That, I feel, is a useful perspective for all of us, regardless of our profession and our specialty. If nuclear war and pollution loom above us, how can we use our training and our experience and our special skills—whether they be in carpentry or computers or dentistry—to help keep the world in one piece? We are, after all, common inhabitants on Spaceship Earth,[6] and our disparate skills are all essential to the maintenance and upkeep of our fragile home.

On the positive side, there are major technologies that promise to advance the human race to new levels of prosperity and happiness. Of these, biotechnology and a wide panoply of space technologies appear the most promising to me. Like the computer field, bio-technology and space technology have their own fundamental scientific principles, but their progress is inextricably linked to the developments in the computer field. Some futurists like the late Herman Kahn[7,8] argue that these new technologies will be respon-sible for a coming boom during the next decade.

Is there anything besides technology, whether computer-related or space-related or gene-related, that offers us any hope for the future? In a 1984 survey of 1,346 national opinion leaders, George Gallup, Jr. found the following answers to the question, "Are there any developing trends in society today that you would regard as encouraging?"[9]

Awareness of nuclear threat	11%
Awareness of world problems/relations	9
Education	9
Individual responsibility	8
Ecology movement	7
Attempts to deal with problems	7
Quality of youth	6
Equality for all	5

Trend toward religion/peace/protesting nuclear arms	5
Greater emphasis on health	4
Reduced government spending	4
Human relations	4
Trend toward less government	4
Less racial tension	4
Reactions to poor government	3
Better communication	3
Morals/values/ethics	3
Technology	3
Awareness of inflation	2
Increased productivity	2
Less materialism	2
Energy conservation	2
Planned parenthood	2
Desegregation	1
None	6
Miscellaneous	6

To the opinion leaders of the country, technology obviously isn't a very important encouraging trend for the future; it ranks slightly above awareness of inflation, but slightly below morals/values/ethics. On the other hand, the opinion leaders paid homage to the presence of, if not the positive influence of, computers and technology when asked, "In what ways do you think life in the United States in the year 2000 will differ from life today?" Their answers were:

Greater use of technology/computer technology	12
More advanced technology	9

More automation/computerization	8
More crowded/overpopulated	8
Lower standard of living	6
More impersonal/regimented	6
Greater threat of war/nuclear war	4
Advanced health care	4
Less energy/natural resources	4
Higher standard of living	4
Higher quality of life	3
Scarcity of necessities, e.g., food, water, clothing, space	3
More economic/governmental international interdependence	3
More pollution	3
More older people	3
Lower quality of life	2
Dependence on alternative energy sources	2
Service economy (U.S. more service-, marketing-oriented)	2
Trend toward socialism	2
Fewer/no people left due to nuclear war	1
Decline of U.S. world power/status	1
Less racial discrimination	1
Less crime	1
Dependence on oil lessened	*

Less than half of one percent

On a more somber note, this same group ranked the threat of nuclear war as the most serious problem facing the United States today, and the most serious problem likely to face the United States in the year 2000.

NUCLEAR WAR

So many people have written so much about the lunacy of nuclear war that I feel powerless to add anything more. So many wiser, stronger, more passionate, and more eloquent men and women have marched and protested and fought and begged and prayed for an end to the arms race that I, like many well-meaning citizens around the world, wonder whether there is any point to my efforts, to my few mumbled, incoherent words of horror and despair. But then I remember: I have three children, safely sleeping in warm beds while I write these words and think these thoughts. It is for them, and for the fate of the earth (to use Jonathan Schell's phrase[10]), that I must add whatever protest I can muster to the growing clamor of voices around the world seeking to make the missiles and the bombs and the endless nightmare of Hiroshima and Nagasaki go away. Even to think about it for this brief paragraph is to render every-thing in the preceding pages of this manuscript dull and lifeless. But if I care about my work and my profession—as I hope you can see that I do—then it must be that it is the arms race that is dull and lifeless and barren. So I must work, in whatever way I can, to banish it from the earth. And so must you.

Is nuclear war any more likely now than it was twenty years ago? From the Gallup survey cited above, it would appear so. In any case, it is clear that the country's opinion leaders think that it is not only the gravest problem facing us today, but that it will continue to be the gravest problem facing us upon the dawn of a new millennium. That is depressing. And it is apparent that many scientists are more worried today about nuclear war than they were before. As Kenneth Boulding says,

> It is now even more clear than it was twenty years ago that nuclear war could easily be an irretrievable disaster, not only on account of the destruction of the ozone layer, but the development of a cloud from the innumerable fires, which could produce what Carl Sagan has called a "nuclear winter," in which nothing would grow for perhaps

four years over most of the earth, including the tropics. Yet the United States still talks about "limited nuclear war" without any apparatus whatever for limiting it once it has begun. Even a limited nuclear war would probably make Europe uninhabitable. It is clear that unilateral national defense has become not only the greatest enemy of national security, but also the greatest enemy of the human race. The world system of unilateral national defense is not intended, of course, to produce the destruction of the human race. Neither are automobiles intended to kill several tens of thousands of people a year; it just happens that they are designed to do so. Similarly, unilateral national defense is designed as a system to bring the evolutionary process on earth to a stop.[11]

It is a sad fact that computers are inextricably connected to the issue of nuclear war—in the design of nuclear weapons, the communication systems for NSA, and for the proposed "Star Wars" program, as well as for AI-based guidance systems for nuclear missiles. To put this in the proper perspective, I must point out that the Hiroshima bomb was built without the benefit of modern computers, but modern bombs and modern nuclear warfare could not exist without modern supercomputers. A large fraction of the country's supercomputers, as I pointed out in Chapter 37, are computing at a feverish pace in computer facilities at Lawrence Livermore Laboratories and Los Alamos Laboratories; similar computers are presumably just as busy in Russian, Chinese, English, and French laboratories . . . and, unhappily, perhaps in a few other countries as well.

One positive thought: some of the issues of complexity that have such obvious life-and-death consequences for nuclear war also apply to other ecosystems. If we can develop defensive systems to detect the outbreak of war, perhaps we can use the same technology to detect the outbreak of acid rain and other systemic breakdowns. Thus far, I have not seen any overt evidence of such a cooperative effort. The money and talent that went into building the NORAD (North American Air Defense) and BMEWS (Ballistic Missile Early Warning System) systems do not seem to have been applied to the problem of detecting worldwide pollution. But we are gradually finding that more and more of our critical issues are deeply interconnected: the problem of detecting worldwide "fallout" of acid rain is not that different from the problem of detecting worldwide fallout of nuclear radiation from covert atomic tests. Maybe there is a chance for cooperation.

THE POPULATION EXPLOSION

Optimists like Buckminster Fuller felt that the population problem would have disappeared by now. Here is what he wrote in 1969:

> The population explosion is a myth. As we industrialize, down goes the industrial birth rate. If we survive, by 1985, the whole world will be industrialized, and, as with the United States, and as with all Europe and Russia and Japan today, the birth rate will be dwindling, and the bulge in population will be recognized as accounted for exclusively by those who are living longer.[12]

Sorry, Bucky. Fertility rates around the world have declined substantially in the past twenty years, but not enough to make the population problem go away. Population in the United States and parts of Europe (and in highly developed countries in general) is actually decreasing. It is being dealt with in China (but only in cities), and is still out of control in most Third World countries.

The Third World countries, as we and they know, have not yet advanced to postindustrial information-based societies. They still operate on the premise that more children can raise more pigs and till more soil. They still deal with the reality that many of their children will die of disease or malnutrition before they reach adulthood. Where this will lead is unclear; most social scientists did not foresee the dramatic drop in the birth rate in the United States in the 1960s, and it is possible that the birth rates in other countries could either rise or fall dramatically for reasons that we do not anticipate today.

Computers offer some hope to the overpopulated Third World countries as an industry that could produce more wealth than soybeans, rice, pigs, gold, and copper. Many Third World countries have become manufacturing centers for computer hardware. As I discussed in Chapter 12, several of the more ambitious Third World countries are devoting significant resources to the formation of software industries that can compete with the United States, Europe, and Japan. Computers can also be used to provide AI-based medical diagnoses, thereby decreasing infant mortality rates. They can be used for agricultural process control systems, thus increasing the productivity of farmers who still till their fields with oxen and wooden plows.

The trend that we are seeing is that of exporting technology needed to make Third World countries more productive and thus less dependent on additional children. However, it may be far more difficult to change the underlying cultures. It could easily take a generation or two before newly affluent Third World parents decide that they no longer need eight children.

Meanwhile, the saddest consequence of the population explosion is widespread poverty and hunger around the world. We cannot easily make poverty go away without solving a number of fundamental problems, of which overpopulation is only one; however, we can make much of the hunger in the world disappear. Computers can help solve this problem in an indirect, but very important, way: by helping people communicate more quickly and effectively with one another, we can focus the energy and the care of a massive number of people at one time on the same problem. As I pointed out in Chapter 4, the "Live Aid" concert focused the attention of nearly half of the human race on the problem of hunger in Africa. In a single day, it raised over $70 million in contributions. Without computers, there would have been no concert or, more accurately, there would have been a concert with only 70,000 in the audience instead of two billion.

POLLUTION

This is a major problem, and one that shows little sign of decreasing. Toxic wastes, acid rain, asbestos, fertilizers in the water supply, chemical poisons in the entire food chain—the list goes on and on. Part of the problem is laziness, sloppiness, and unwillingness on the part of producers and consumers to deal with the problem.

But pollution also occurs because we don't understand the systemwide consequences of new technologies. Proponents of the fertilizer industry, the chemical industry, the nuclear power industry could probably argue very sincerely that for a long time —indeed, until it was too late—they didn't understand the consequences of the products they were introducing. Indeed, we have much to learn in this area, as evidenced by the reaction to a recent study conducted by the Environmental Defense Fund:[13]

> For the first time, changes in the acidity of rainfall have been directly linked to changes in pollution emissions hundreds of miles away, according to a new scientific report.
>
> The existence of such a correlation has been the subject of intense debate, and drafts of the report, which is being published today, have already stirred more controversy.
>
> Government experts questioned its conclusions, while other scientists said the report represented a major advance in acid-rain research. The Reagan Administration has maintained that too little is known about acid rain to justify costly efforts to contain it.
>
> The study was prepared by scientists from the Environmental Defense Fund, which has advocated strong measures against acid rain. Its findings are being published in the journal *Science*, whose managing editor, Patricia A. Morgan, said it passed muster in independent peer review "with high marks."

Another part of the problem is associated with the short-term view of many civic leaders. They introduce new systems or new legislation without understanding the 50-year or 500-year consequences of their decisions. Nor do civic leaders understand the global-system consequences of their decisions.

Computers can help in this area by allowing both industry and government leaders to simulate and model the consequences of new chemicals, fuels, fertilizers, etc. And new supercomputers can help model such phenomena on a larger scale. But if we don't understand the system parameters, it is to no avail. There is an urgent need for more research in the science of global models, which has been characterized by its own proponents as a process of "groping in the dark;"[14] early experiences, such as the 1972 report to the Club of Rome, have shown how misleading our present primitive models can be.

DEPLETION OF NATURAL RESOURCES

When we think of the depletion of mineral resources, we typically think of energy-related resources, and, in particular, oil. However, it became evident in the late 1970s and early 1980s that we could eventually find a number of alternatives to oil—geothermal energy, solar energy, wind power, coal, oil shale, energy from the ocean, etc. While some of these alternatives create problems of their own—e.g., pollution problems and the issue of public vs. private investment in the new technologies—it is apparent that we can address this issue in a creative way. When the last Saudi Arabian oil well is depleted, we will have found alternative ways of powering our cars, or, more likely, we will have found an alternative way of providing the function that cars perform. Meanwhile, there are other mineral resources that may run out sooner than oil: platinum, gallium, and even gold. However, our recent experiences with oil have shown us that humans can be remarkably creative about recycling, conservation, and substitution of resources. If South Africa, Canada, and Russia eventually run out of gold, the "hard money" group may decide to switch to something like 1969 New York Mets baseball cards as a medium of financial exchange.

What do computers have to do with all of this? Unfortunately, computers contribute to the problem whenever they require scarce resources: gallium arsenide chips, as we discussed in Chapter 37, are a good example. But on the positive side, computers are probably the most powerful technology available (aside from political and religious techniques for changing the consumption habits of the general public) for increasing the productive use of scarce resources. Computers have played a major role in the design and development of fuel-efficient cars, planes, and ships, and computers play a major role in the smart use of fuel-hungry vehicles in the transport industry.

On a more philosophical level, computers are a manifestation of the human mind, and the human mind is described by Julian Simon[15] as an "ultimate resource" that is, to put it mildly, a long way from being exhausted. Through more clever conservation techniques, more effective recycling, and more ingenious substitution of plentiful resources for scarce resources, we can probably postpone the depletion of our materials resource for another two or three centuries.

BIOTECHNOLOGY

Bioengineering, biogenetics, etc., offer enormous possibilities for improved food production, and for conquering a wide class of diseases. To the extent that biotechnology can produce pollution-guzzling microbes, it even offers some hope for solving the pollution problem.

Computers are useful in many of the operational aspects of biotechnology research. More importantly, AI-based computer systems like MOLCON can help chemists and biologists better understand the intricate biological and molecular issues involved in gene-splitting.[16]

SPACE TRAVEL

Space travel remains one of the more glamorous frontiers of modern science, despite the fact that most adults have seen so many lift-offs from Cape Kennedy that they hardly bother watching any more. In the mid-1980's, space travel is confined to fairly regular one-week orbital trips of the U.S. space shuttle, as well as occasional space probes conducted by Russia, France, the United States, and other countries—including a U.S. satellite that will rendezvous with Uranus in 1986, as well as another (Project Galileo) that will be launched toward Jupiter in the spring of 1986.

The problem with manned space travel at the present time is that it is so outrageously expensive. Astronomer Carl Sagan says that a manned mission could put a small group on Mars by 2003 at a cost of $40 billion. (Though this is indeed an astronomical expense, Sagan points out that the B1 bomber fleet cost $25 billion and that the Apollo program cost $75 billion.[17])

The short-term advantages of such a move are primarily the possibilities of scientific advances in astronomy, physics, and chemistry, as well as the possibility of manufacturing exotic products in the weightlessness of space; and we cannot ignore the military/defense interests in space stations and space research. There are also communication satellites already in place with important commercial and scientific benefits. Altogether, the commercial development of space is seen as a $100 billion/year enterprise by the end of the century,[18] with products and services ranging from mining to agriculture. At least two companies expect to have permanent space labs in orbit within the next five years, and a permanent space station suitable for human habitation and work is being planned for 1992—the 500th anniversary of Columbus's voyage to the New World.

The long-term advantages, though, are far more profound. We may be able to scatter the seed of humanity upon other planets and life-sustaining stars in the galaxies. It is not at all clear to me how far in the future this is, perhaps a hundred years or more. And I am not sure one can justify the cost of sending forth such an expedition when so many millions—even billions—of people are dying of starvation on Earth. But the same adage that argues, in various aspects of our lives, that we should "not put all of our eggs in one basket" suggests that we should not put all of humanity on one planet. There are too many things that can go wrong, too many opportunities for global disaster caused by a chain of events emanating from one misbegotten deed.

THE FUTURE OF THE HUMAN RACE

One of the largest problems facing us today is that everything is connected to everything else. Everything is deeply intertwined. As Kenneth Boulding puts it,

> Until the Great Transition human society was divided into a large number of relatively isolated cultures; even on the relatively small island of Papua-New Guinea there are some seven hundred different languages. The American Indians had two or three hundred, suggesting that there were a large number of virtually isolated groups, with representatives meeting very rarely for trade or even warfare. The Great Transition, however, is making the world a single social system and in some respects even a single ecosystem, as the human race

transports species, both plant and animal, from their original habitat to different habitats all around the world, often with considerable extinction of older species. The trouble with one world is that if anything goes wrong, everything goes wrong. With many worlds, we could have a catastrophe in one, like the destruction of the Mayan civilization or the extinction of the dinosaurs, or the eruption of Krakatoa, leaving the rest unscathed because of isolation.[19]

On an optimistic note, Buckminster Fuller argues that all will end well:

But we can scientifically assume that by the twenty-first century either humanity will not be living on Spaceship Earth or, if approximately our present numbers as yet remain aboard, that humanity then will have recognized and organized itself to realize effectively the fact that humanity can afford to do anything it needs and wishes to do and that it cannot afford anything else. As a consequence Earth-planet-based humanity will be physically and individually free in the most important sense. While all enjoy total Earth no human will be interfering with the other, and none will be profiting at the expense of the other. Humans will be free in the sense that 99.9 percent of their waking hours will be freely investable at their own discretion. They will be free in the sense that they will not struggle for survival on a "you" or "me" basis, and will therefore be able to trust one another and be free to cooperate in spontaneous and logical ways.[20]

Of course, nobody can be sure whether things will go well or poorly for the human race over the next few hundred years; the arguments of the pessimists are just as convincing as the arguments of the optimists. Our ability to project and predict the future, enhanced immeasurably by the computer, has barely kept up with the increasing complexity of the world around us. For now, we must admit that we are groping in the dark.

CONCLUSION

Now we come to the moment that every author dreads: the end of a book. Now is the time when I can no longer suggest, "Any confusion that I have caused up to this point will be cleared up in the next chapter."

Ah, well, it is as good a time as any to end this treatise. A half moon has risen high above Mecox Bay in the tiny corner of Long Island where I have written most of this material. The geese flew overhead several hours ago, wending their way home for a night's rest on a local pond before setting forth again tomorrow. I promised my wife that I would finish this and come to bed several hours ago. I am late, as usual. My children are thrashing in their beds and need to have their blankets drawn over their shoulders by a father who unfortunately seems to pay more attention to them in the middle of the night than during their waking hours. . . .

What does an author think, at the end of his book, when he has exposed all of his hopes and dreams, his fears and his often naive observations about The Way Things Really Are? Well, I suppose that every author is unique, but I don't mind copying a famous one from the past. My own thoughts, on this late August night, as the mosquitoes dance over my glass of wine, are exactly those of Charles Dickens, who wrote at the end of *American Notes*, in 1842:[21]

> I have now arrived at the close of this book. I have little reason to believe, from certain warnings I have had since returning to England, that it will be tenderly or favorably received by the American people; and, as I have written the Truth in relation to the mass of those who form their judgments and express their opinions, it will be seen that I have no desire to court, by any adventitious means, any popular applause.
>
> It is enough for me to know that what I have set down in these pages cannot cost me a single friend on the other side of the Atlantic, who is, in anything, deserving of the name. For the rest, I put my trust, implicitly, in the spirit in which they have been conceived and penned; and I can bide my time.

Amen. May the Force (of computers) be with you. And may my children continue to sleep safely in their beds. Regardless of whatever computer-controlled robots may serve us or rule us in the future, I will always come to cover them up, wherever they may sleep.

References for Chapter 39

1.   Boulding, Kenneth, "The Meaning of the Twenty-First Century: Reexamining the Great Transition," *World Future Society BULLETIN*, July/August 1984.

2.   Gallup, George Jr., *Forecast 2000*, New York: William Morrow and Company, 1984.

3.   Naisbitt, John, *Megatrends*, Warner Books, 1983.

4.   Toffler, Alvin, *The Third Wave*, New York: William Morrow and Company, 1980, Bantam Books, 1981.

5.   Noorbergen, Rene, *A.D. 2000: A Book About the End of Time*, New York: Bobbs-Merrill, 1984.

6.   Fuller, R. Buckminster, *Operating Manual for Spaceship Earth*, New York: Simon & Schuster, 1969.

7.   Kahn, Herman, William Brown, and Leon Martel, *The Next 2000 Years*, New York: William Morrow and Company, 1976.

8.   _____, *The Coming Boom*, New York: Simon & Schuster, 1982.

9.   Gallup, *op. cit.*, pages 165-166.

10.   Schell, Jonathan, *The Fate of the Earth*, New York: Alfred A. Knopf, 1982.

11.   Boulding, *op. cit.*

12.   Fuller, *op. cit.*

13.   "Distant Pollution Tied to Acid Rain," *New York Times*, August 23, 1985.

14.   Meadows, Donella, John Richardson and Gerhart Bruckmann, *Groping in the Dark: The First Decade of Global Modelling*, New York: John Wiley & Sons, 1982.

15.   Simon, Julian, *The Ultimate Resource*, Princeton, N.J.: Princeton University Press, 1981.

16.   Feigenbaum, Edward, and Pamela McCorduck, *The Fifth Generation*, Reading, Mass.: Addison-Wesley, 1983.

17.   Sagan, Carl, "Instead of SDI, a Joint U.S.-Soviet Mission to Mars," *The Futurist*, October 1985.

18.   "Space Biz—Really Taking Off," *Breakthrough Reports*, September 1, 1985.

19.   Boulding, *op. cit.*

20.   Fuller, *op. cit.*

21.   Dickens, Charles, *American Notes*, New York: Fromm Publishing, 1985.

INDEX